Lovingly Yours, Nellie

LETTERS HOME
&
PUBLISHED ARTICLES

Written by
Nellie R. Campbell

Edited and compiled
by
Sandra Hyslop & Pat Klassen

Note for Librarians: a cataloguing record for this book that includes Dewey Decimal Classification and US Library of Congress numbers is available from the Library and Archives of Canada. The complete cataloguing record can be obtained from their online database at:
www.collectionscanada.ca/amicus/index-e.html
ISBN 1-4120-4371-9
Printed in Victoria, BC, Canada

TRAFFORD

Offices in Canada, USA, Ireland, UK and Spain
This book was published *on-demand* in cooperation with Trafford Publishing. On-demand publishing is a unique process and service of making a book available for retail sale to the public taking advantage of on-demand manufacturing and Internet marketing. On-demand publishing includes promotions, retail sales, manufacturing, order fulfilment, accounting and collecting royalties on behalf of the author.
Book sales for North America and international:
Trafford Publishing, 6E–2333 Government St.,
Victoria, BC v8t 4p4 CANADA
phone 250 383 6864 (toll-free 1 888 232 4444)
fax 250 383 6804; email to orders@trafford.com
Book sales in Europe:
Trafford Publishing (uk) Ltd., Enterprise House, Wistaston Road Business Centre,
Wistaston Road, Crewe, Cheshire cw2 7rp UNITED KINGDOM
phone 01270 251 396 (local rate 0845 230 9601)
facsimile 01270 254 983; orders.uk@trafford.com
Order online at:
www.trafford.com/robots/04-2179.html

10 9 8 7 6 5 4 3

We would like to dedicate this book
to our father Emerson Rudolph Campbell
(son of George & Nellie)

from your ten children

Sandra Hyslop
Shirley Fillion
Terry Campbell
Margaret McMorrow
Peter Campbell
Donald Campbell
Patricia Klassen
Suzanne Campbell
Juanita Dalziel
Caroline Kristensen

who taught us that:

*when the going gets tough
it's just right for you and me...*

Ness Lake, B.C.

Dear Auntie Marie,

I know you have been looking for a letter and I have thought of you often even if I haven't written.

We have had a busy fall - first the harvesting and threshing and then the auction sale. We had a rotten day so things went cheap and we didn't get as much as we hoped for things. It was a job packing and keeping house for this family at the same time. We left Lorenzo, Saskatchewan for Edmonton, Alberta a little after nine and got there in time for breakfast the next morning. We had all day in there. I wanted to do a little Christmas shopping but we had so much baggage that I couldn't carry much. There are no 5 and 10 cent stores here but 10 and 15 cent stores instead. I got some books for Ruth's boys and cloth for three aprons, - that's all besides a few cards.

The train didn't go until 11:30 that night. The berths were already made so we could retire if we wished and Sonny was pretty sleepy so I was glad to get him to bed. We were going through the Rockies when we woke up in the morning and we were in the mountains all day. They were very beautiful. We got to Prince George, British Columbia at 7:30 p.m.

George hired a truck the next day to take us to our homestead at Ness Lake. We had two trunks, a big packing box, roll of bedding and I bought over $50.00 worth of groceries in town. About half way out we came to a ravine. The road first hugged the hill on one side and dropped off straight down for 50 feet or more on the other. The fellows suggested we walk down and I was glad to do so. It rained the night we got to Prince George and the roads had frozen but thawed, so they were just sticky mud. Emerson's rubbers kept coming off and it was some job getting him to the top of the opposite hill without leaving his rubbers behind. We made it and the car got to the bottom of the hill and about half of the way up the opposite hill, and then stopped. The wheels just spun round and they slid all over the road. I was afraid they would go over the edge into the ravine. They had to take everything off the truck and then they couldn't make it. They decided to go back to town but they couldn't get up the hill they had come down. We found a log house a little beyond the top of the hill and then George and the two fellows began carrying our supplies up the hill. George carried 100 lbs. of sugar, 100 lbs. of flour and 100 lbs. of onions upon his back and in some places it was so steep and slippery, he had to crawl. It began to rain so I covered the sugar and flour up with a blanket and then Emerson and I toted what we could from where the men left it, up to this log house. We got lots of the things in the barn, as the house was locked.

Continued …On letter dated November 29, 1929

PREFACE

*Perhaps these letters were not intended for future
generations...but somehow it seems they were.*

*This book was compiled and edited by Nellie (Richner) Campbell's
granddaughters, Sandra Hyslop and Pat Klassen. It took over twenty-five
years to collect these old letters from the recipients and endless hours of
searching for the many articles that you will read about in this amazing book
of Nellie Campbell's memoirs. Together they compile a heart-warming account
of Nellie and George Campbell's life together.*

Follow the lives of Nellie Richner Campbell and her family
through the Saskatchewan Prairies to Central British Columbia
where they homesteaded. This journey began in Maine in 1920
when Nellie travelled by train through Ontario along Lake Superior
to the vast Canadian Prairies to meet and marry George Campbell.
Together they built their lives along with their only child, Emerson,
homesteading on the Prairies until 1929 and then they moved to
Ness Lake, British Columbia. They farmed, trapped, raised mink,
wrote and published numerous articles and Nellie also taught
school.

George and Nellie Campbell had a vision to start a non-
denominational Bible Camp for children. In 1953 they founded the
Ness Lake Bible Camp starting with their gift of seven acres of
lakeshore property.

Throughout this wonderful collection of letters and published
articles you will find a woman who never complained of her hardships
and was grateful for the little she had. Although Nellie missed her
family back home a great deal, you might think she was lonely. You will
find her quote in the article titled "I Never Get Lonesome" where she
says, *"Loneliness is more a matter of the heart. If one has real peace and
contentment within, I doubt if he ever could be lonely."*

ACKNOWLEDGMENTS

Sandra Hyslop lives in Kamloops, British Columbia with her husband Larry and has four grown children, Erich Hilbrecht, Joyce Taylor, Larry Hyslop Jr. and Juanita Hyslop-Cato.

Special thanks to my husband for his never-ending support and encouragement.
Thanks to my son Larry Hyslop Jr. for hours of typing, editing and research.
Special thanks to my granddaughter Jenna Hilbrecht for helping to type.

Pat Klassen lives in Prince George, British Columbia with her husband Bill and has two grown daughters, Lindsay and Jenny.

Thank you to my husband for his patience and understanding.
Special thanks to my daughter Jenny for helping to read the many letters while I typed.
Thank you to my daughter Lindsay for your enthusiasm and support with *Lovingly Yours, Nellie*.

**This book, *Lovingly Yours, Nellie*
was made possible because of the
generous time given by many.**

-A special thank you to our dear mother, Jeannie Campbell for her collection of valuable information and memories. Also for her never-ending encouragement, love and understanding.

-Thank you to our sister Shirley Fillion for her help proofreading, her enthusiasm and fond memories of our grandparents that she shared with us.

-Thank you to our sister Margaret McMorrow for being the "Keeper of the Recipe Box" that held the clues that got us started in our search for the many published articles.

ACKNOWLEDGMENTS
continued

-A special thanks to our good friend Wendy Kineshanko for her amazing insight and endless editing with *Lovingly Yours, Nellie.*

-Thank you to Louisa Vance from Boston, Massachusetts for giving me (Sandra) the first letters in 1978 which, unknowly at that time would be become *Lovingly Yours, Nellie.*

-Thank you to Richard and Lois Allen from Carmel, Maine and their daughter Kathy Heijermans of Luxembourg, for sending copies of Nellie's letters over the past several years.

-Thank you to Paula Ring from North Jay, Maine who much to our delight and at the last minute contributed the final letters that made *Lovingly Yours, Nellie* complete.

-Thank you to the Vancouver Daily Province Newspaper and the Copyright Board of Canada for permission to use the published articles that were written by Nellie R. Campbell.

-Thank you to MENDED MEMORIES® for the illustrations and artwork by *Family History Journal* www.mendedmemories.net

-Thank you to York University in Toronto, Ontario for the use of their Microfilm Department to research old magazines and newspapers.

-Thank you to the Prince George Public Library and the Kamloops Public Library for their assistance in our search for published articles.

CONTENTS

BOOK ONE:
From Portland, Maine to
the Saskatchewan Prairies
1920-1929

BOOK TWO:
From the Saskatchewan Prairies
to Ness Lake, British Columbia
1929-1944

BOOK THREE:
Published Articles

Family Tree

George Herbert Campbell	Nellie's Husband
Emerson Rudolph Campbell	Nellie's Son
Rudolph Richner	Nellie's Father
Florence Richner	Nellie's Mother
Eliza Richner	Nellie's Stepmother
Dana (Rudy) Richner	Nellie's Brother
Marion Richner	Nellie's Sister-in-law
Donald	Nellie's Nephew
Dorothy	Nellie's Niece
Ruth (Reta) Allen	Nellie's Sister
Ray Allen	Nellie's Brother-in-law
Hamblin	Nellie's Nephew
Carlton	Nellie's Nephew
Richard	Nellie's Nephew
Marie Davenport	Nellie's Aunt
Ida Richner	Nellie's Aunt
Louisa Vance	Nellie's Cousin
Flora	Nellie's Cousin
Pinga	Nellie's Cousin
John	Nellie's Cousin
Winfield	Nellie's Cousin

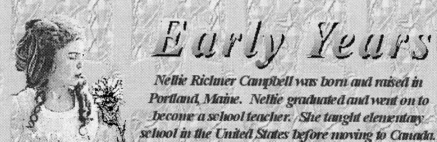

Early Years

Nellie Richter Campbell was born and raised in Portland, Maine. Nellie graduated and went on to become a school teacher. She taught elementary school in the United States before moving to Canada.

Nellie and her sister Ruth

Nellie's Graduation ~ 1905

Nellie's home in Maine.

Book One

From
Portland, Maine
to the
Saskatchewan
Prairies
1920-1929

On the banks of the Saskatchewan River
July 30, 1920

Dear Reta,

Well I don't wonder that you were in doubt whether I was still living or not. We certainly didn't have much time to say farewell in Portland (Maine). My train came in on the track and while I was hunting up mother and my suitcase, you and Dad disappeared. I went through one car but the next was the smokers, so I thought I had better get onto my train. We pulled out just as yours did, but I couldn't see you although I looked.

I had a very pleasant trip out and met some very nice people. A lady sat beside me from Boston to Montreal and she was very interesting. I didn't have any trouble with my baggage and they didn't even look into my trunks. I had the keys and nothing was said about them. They came with me all the way.

When we got to Montreal the porter took my suitcase and disappeared with it and when I got onto the other train my suitcase was there.

There was a nice old lady across from me and a young lady with two small children.

The scenery was wonderful through Ontario along Lake Superior.

Friday morning we had struck the prairies and everything looked barren to me, but I'm getting use to it now so I don't think much about not seeing trees.

I met a Presbyterian Minister on the train who was in charge of a boys" school in Moose Jaw. He was very interesting and then I met a newspaperman from Chico, California, one night at dinner and he came in our car and called on me every day.

He helped me with my suitcases when we reached Moose Jaw and saw me onto the other train.

George got onto the train three stations before we reached Hawarden (Saskatchewan).

When we arrived we went at once to Mrs. Pringle's. Mrs. Pringle was young and looked a great deal as Clara Lufkin did. She took me into the bedroom and I washed up and fixed my hair. George had two of his bachelor friends come into town in their Ford and they stood up with us. We were married between five and five fifteen, which would be eight by your time. We went to the restaurant at the Hotel for supper and then the boys took us home. It was about eight or a little after when we got there.

The night we were married we had a "chivalry." At home we would say we were serenaded. There were twelve that arrived that night and they made quite a noise on their tin pans. Of course they all came in to see the bride and George passed the cigars.

Monday evening a second crowd from another section arrived. George said some of them came a long ways and you should have heard the noise they made. They brought disks off of a harrow and I think the din lasted fully twenty minutes. They got on the roof and pounded the sides of the house until you couldn't even think. They came in and made quite a call.

Almost all of the houses on the prairie are little shacks with just one or two rooms. There are a few larger ones near the towns but nothing like the eastern homes. It's a new country and everyone here "roughs" it. Our house would not be much in the east but it is very good here. We haven't much room so we bought very few things. I bought a few dishes, not a whole set, as all I could get here were plain white and rather cheap looking things. I got just enough to get along with. We sent to Eatons, a big mail order house and ordered the chiffonier and one chair as I had to either sit on George or the trunk. We bought an Oil Perfection Stove with an oven as everyone here uses soft coal and there is so little wood, it means to keep a coal fire all day. I like the stove ever so much and we don't plan to stay through the winter. There isn't much he can do on the place after harvest is over so we probably will go to the city for the winter and he will get work there until spring. You see we have nothing but the horses and there is nothing else here for us.

This has been quite a busy week. On Sunday afternoon George wanted to go down to the grove. At home it wouldn't be but a large clump of bushes. They are young trees about the size of small birches. I suggested taking a lunch so we did and returned home at eight and found two callers. Tuesday the crowd got up a supper for us at the next house. They had cold pressed meat, potato salad, beans, bread and butter, fruit jelly and cake, lemonade and in the middle of the evening opened up the ice cream. It came down on the afternoon train from Moose Jaw. Just think of sending ninety miles for ice cream. It was so rich I couldn't eat very much but you should have seen some of the men. Nearly everyone had two enormous dishes full.

They sang and recited and no one thought of going home until morning. It was about two when we got home.

The next day was the fair at Hawarden. We left home early and drove in. George wanted to put something into the fair but I wanted to see what a fair was like first. We had a very good time. They had a ball game in the afternoon. Baseball is all the rage here. We went to the hotel to supper and then took in the movies.

George has been around the house all day and made me a shelf for the clothes closet, a bookcase and a cover for the box my things came in so we can use it for a table in front of the attic. It sloped a little and he thought a step would be nice for me. He is so delighted to have someone around the house that I can't drive him away very far.

He suggested finishing up the week by taking a trip to the Saskatchewan River. We decided to do it so I did some cooking and yesterday we packed up and started.

It was a nice drive, about twenty-one or twenty-two miles. I wish you could have seen the country. We went for a long way across the prairie and just before we reached the river, we ran into sagebrush. Where we are now is just like the scenery in the movies, especially the pictures where the Indians ride it full speed and suddenly drive over a big bluff and you hold your breath to see how the horse ever gets to the bottom. The Saskatchewan lies between a bluff fifty or sixty feet high.

Occasionally one can find a place not quite so steep and a little path that leads down to the river but in most places it is a steep drop from the edge of these big bluffs.

We found a nice place to camp and then went down by the river and ate our lunch. It tasted very good. We took a walk after supper and then George led the horse down to the river for water. It was so steep. I was afraid she would fall but she made it all right. In the east we never would think of driving over such rough places but the horses here are used to it. About eight thirty we rolled up in our blankets to sleep. I slept very well on the ground, much better than George did. We built a fire and cooked bacon and eggs and warmed up some beans for breakfast. It was lots of fun. After breakfast we went for berries and got a two-quart pail full and then a shower came up so George rolled out the blankets and we crawled in. He has been sleeping peacefully with his head in my lap while I have been writing this lengthy epistle. It has stopped raining and the horse has been calling for her dinner so George has gone to attend to her. It is noon so we will eat and then start for home. This is the end of our honeymoon, as George has got to go to work in earnest on Monday, as there is a lot to do.

Give my love to Ray and Mother Allen and write often.

Letter continued the next day....

I am happy and contented since I came and think I shall grow to love the prairie; there is something fascinating about it. I'm very much in love with George so I suppose the prairies do not matter much.

Write to me often. George sends his love, but he says he'll keep a little here for me, so he can't send it all.   Come out and see us.

Love to all, Nell

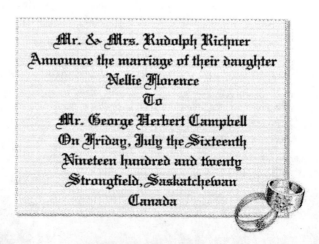

Mr. & Mrs. Rudolph Richner
Announce the marriage of their daughter
Nellie Florence
To
Mr. George Herbert Campbell
On Friday, July the Sixteenth
Nineteen hundred and twenty
Strongfield, Saskatchewan
Canada

Strongfield, Sask.
Saturday Afternoon

Dear Aunty Marie,

I arrived safely (from Portland, Maine) and George got on the train three stations before I reached Hawarden. He had seen to everything so we went right to the ministers. They were both young people and very pleasant. Mrs. Pringle took me into the bedroom and let me wash up and fix my hair. George had two of his bachelor friends come down as witnesses. The ceremony was very short so we were married in about ten minutes. It was between five and five fifteen, which would be eight by your time. After the ceremony we all four went to the hotel to supper. The two fellows with George had a Ford. After supper we came right home.

About nine thirty a crowd came to serenade us. They brought with them tin pans and made all of the noise possible. We had to go out and of course George passed the cigars. The crowd came in and stayed about three-quarters of an hour.

You see it was quite an exciting day for me.

Tell Fay that George is all right so I don't think I shall have to send for him. (He is very considerate and I think I shall be contented here.)

It is very flat and one can see for miles and there aren't any trees at all. Once in a while you may see a little clump of bushes but they are so low I wouldn't call them more than bushes.

There is a man here today tinting all the walls and ceiling. I can't unpack or settle much until he gets through. I think we can make it very cozy when we get a few things that we really need. At present it is more like camping. It has been hot for the last two days. They said yesterday was 108 degrees.

I must go down to the garden to see what I can find for supper. I'll try to write to you again soon.

Love to all, Nell

Strongfield, Sask.
July 25, 1920

Dear Auntie Marie,

Well, I have been married over a week now and it has been a very happy week. George is just as nice as I expected him to be.

I sent you a letter the day after we were married. One of the neighbors took it in and I heard tonight it didn't get mailed until Tuesday, so I suppose you have been wondering if I arrived safely.

I had a very pleasant trip out and met some very nice people. There was a Presbyterian minister who had charge of a boys' school in Moose Jaw who came in and talked with me several times and one night a newspaper man from Chico,

California sat opposite me at dinner. He was in another car but he came in several
times to call on me. When we reached Moose Jaw he took my suitcase and found
the other train for me and saw me onto the other train. We had half an hour there
so he asked a young fellow on the train to look out for my things while I got some
lunch. It was very nice to have him look out for me and as he was old enough to be
my father it was perfectly all right.

George got on before I reached Hawarden and tell Fay that he knew exactly
the proper thing to do.

There was just a notice of the ceremony in this week's paper. If I can get
another copy I'll send you one.

I haven't been lonesome yet. George took a week off and has stayed around
the house most of the time. He cleaned out the well, weeded the garden and put up
some shelves for me. We have had quite a lot of company.

Saturday there was a man here painting the walls and then Shorty came up with
my trunk, so I had two men to dinner. You know we had twelve come Friday night
and Monday evening we had a second "chivalry." There were twenty-four that
evening and you should have heard the noise. They brought disks out of the old
harrow and pounded them together. You should have heard this noise. It was
perfectly awful and they kept it up for nearly twenty minutes and then came in to
call on us.

Tuesday we went to Strongfield for the day. I went to the bank and put in
some money and then we went shopping.

We decided to buy a new Perfection Oil Stove with the money you people gave
us.

You see there is very little wood here so it means keep a coal fire, as we don't
have gas here so we thought our oil stove would be nice for the summer. It has an
oven so I don't have to have a coal fire.

It was very hot the day I got here, in fact it was unusually hot for several days.
The day we went to Strongfield the thermometer in front of the hardware store
registered 118 degrees at three in the afternoon.   It doesn't seem much hotter than
in the States as long as one keeps out of the sun but the sun is scorching.

They had a dry spell here and it hurt the crops a lot but last Thursday and
Friday we got rain and it has been cooler since then. Even when it is so hot during
the day the nights are actually chilly.

Wednesday "Nick", a friend of George's, came up just at noon so he stopped
to dinner.

Saturday the two fellows who stood up with us when we were married came up
to supper and they brought Nick along with them so I had quite a family. I cooked
a big pot of beans and made potato salad and tapioca pudding and cake and coffee.
After supper I left the dishes and we all went to Hawarden in their Ford.

There is a Mrs. Howell about half a mile from here and I have been down
there several times. Yesterday George and I walked down just before dinner and

she insisted on our staying there to dinner. About six o'clock George suggested that we go down to the grove so I packed a picnic lunch and we took an "American Magazine" and went on a picnic.

When we got back we found Mrs. Howell and a friend of George's here waiting for us.

Tomorrow night we are invited out to supper so you can see there is quite a lot of excitement even if the neighbors aren't very near.

It seems queer to me to have so much room out of doors. We haven't any locks on the window and no lock on the door. We went to town the other night and left the house wide open. It seems queer to me to have things like that.

The houses are all small, mostly shacks. We wouldn't think much of them in the east but everybody seems to live that way here. There are a few large houses near the town but they are very plain and none of them have piazzas.

We have a very comfortable house. It is just one large room. I bought some very pretty cretonne and made a curtain for the closet door and one for the front of the dish closet. The walls are a soft blue and the ceiling cream color. It is really very home like since I have put the muslin curtains up and we have hung the pictures.

George has gone down to the Shoetree's this evening on an errand so I have been alone. It is nearly nine so he'll probably be home soon now.

Give my love to all of your big family. I know you are busy but if you have a few minutes sometimes I'll be glad of a letter.

I know you would like George. Every night he takes me on his knee and reads the Bible and then he kneels down beside the bed and says prayers so I don't think you'll have to worry about his not being good to me. I think I shall be very happy here and I have been contented so far.

Just lots of love to you. Nell

Strongfield, Sask.
Oct 4, 1920

Dear Auntie Marie,

I guess it is your turn for a letter. Somehow I have been thinking about you people a lot the last few days and I'd just love to run in for a little chat tonight.

My husband has been away all day on a threshing rig so I have been alone. I manage to keep busy even if I have only one room.

Today I mended and relined a cap for George. It had fur earflaps and he wanted it for winter. All of his clothes needed mending and it seems as if I had sewed everything since I came, trying to get him mended up. Last Friday I relined a blue chinchilla overcoat for him. It was hard work as the lining was worn to shreds so I didn't have anything to cut the new lining by. It came out fine and I am quite proud of the job. There isn't much sense in his putting on anything new as long as he is doing dirty work so I'm patching the old things.

Yesterday we harnessed up and went calling in the afternoon. We planned to go to Hawarden to church but it is such a long drive we couldn't get started early enough. Two weeks ago we went down to Theobalds, friends of George's, for the afternoon and evening. We planned to go in the morning and stay to dinner and then go to church and Sunday school with them. When we got to the barn we found one of the horses sick so I went back to the house and put on the teakettle and got the liniment and George led her to the house. I held her head while he poured in the liniment. By the time we were sure she was all right to leave, it was too late to go to dinner, as it was a twelve-mile drive.

We drove down after church and stayed to supper and came home in the evening. I had a very nice time and liked them a lot. Mrs. Theobald is a year younger than I am and Mr. Theobald a year younger than George.

I have had several people want me to come and cook during threshing but George doesn't want me to go. You see women are very scarce in the country.

I ripped up my summer hat today and covered it with the velvet that I got off of my last winter's hat that was too big. I need a small close fitting hat here, as it is so windy.

Sometimes the wind blows two or three days without stopping and it is some wind too.

George will be late tonight, as he always is when he goes threshing. He probably won't get home until eight or after for supper. I expect the threshing crew will get here sometime this week and then I'll have a busy day, as you have to feed them while they are on your place and there are usually twelve in the crew.

I'm very much in love with my husband and he is with me so we are very happy together. I like teaching but I'm a lot happier with a home of my own. George is a very good man and I know you would like him. I wish you could know him. Are you saving up your pennies to come out?

How is the Dr. feeling? Is B Far just the same as ever? I often think of him.

Is Pinga still working in the Assessor's Office and how is Bill?

I intended to write Flora before this. I was glad to get a card from her while she was on vacation.

I had a very nice letter from Miss Edgecombe and I was pleased to get it.

I suppose you are just as busy as ever and all of your crowd are back once more. I just wish you could all drop in and see my cozy little home. It wouldn't be much back east but it is very good here as things are so different, and it is a new country yet. We are happy in it anyway and I suppose that is all that counts.

Give my love to everybody and keep a good big lot for yourself.

Nell

Strongfield, Sask.
November 12, 1920

Dear Reta,

I was so glad to get your letter as it had been so long since I had heard from you but sorry to hear you had been sick. We're both sorry it had to be that way and know you must be disappointed.

George and I came down to Mr. Swanson's yesterday for the winter. He and another young fellow have a whole section so one side of their land comes right across from ours. The land is all divided in squares called a section. Most people have a 1/4 section or 160 acres. If they can afford it they buy more and some people have a half or even a whole section but one has to keep help to work 640 acres. We thought at first we would go to the city for the winter but so many of the people here go to the cities as soon as it freezes that work is very uncertain. We would have to have someone take care of the horses while we were away so with car fare and their board and our living expenses we thought we had better stay here. Mr. Swanson and his partner are going to Wisconsin to work in a machine factory so they offered to furnish coal (and that is a big item here), kerosene, potatoes, pork and beef and we have two cows so I can make butter. They will also pay us twenty-five dollars a month. Of course that isn't much but George thought it was better than going away. There is always work in the woods but I couldn't go there and we thought we would rather have less and be together. George can look after his own horses and they will get better care than if he left them to someone else.

I wish you could see this country. Of course it is still new and people put up just a shack. The barns are low usually and often the roof is made of poles spread across with a load of straw heaped on top. There are still some sod barns here. They are built with squares of sod piled up and a flat roof of straw. A few of the wealthier have put up big barns and they are invariably painted bright red.

This was a very poor year for crops here. We had a hot dry spell in July and the crops burned up. George cut the oats green because he was afraid of frosts so we are using them for bundle feed for the horses. We save our wheat for seed and bought 100 bushels of oats for seed in the spring. George had only a little flax-- hardly got his seed back and it costs 60 cents a bushel to get it threshed so we won't get much out of that. They say next year will be a good year and we all hope so.

You asked what we did for food. Well, it really is quite a question. There are no fruit trees here but apples are shipped from British Columbia. They are usually two pounds for a quarter or four dollars or more for a square wooden box. You never see berries of any kind in the stores.

Some people have a garden but lots of the bachelors don't bother with one. I don't know what they do as they must have to buy everything and I think things are higher here than in the States. George put in a good garden this year but we had such hot dry weather through July that things stopped growing. Then the 20th of August we had a frost that blackened the beans, squash and cucumbers. The cucumbers had just blossomed and the frost finished them. We had beans and peas just once. You can't buy cucumbers so I haven't seen one since I left the east. I wish we might have had some of your extra ones.

We managed to raise two sacks of potatoes besides what we used all fall, a sack of carrots, beets and a few parsnips, swiss chard, lettuce and parsley. My dill did splendidly but it didn't do me much good, as I couldn't get any cucumbers for pickles.

I did put up a jar of small button onions and made a little carrot marmalade but that was all I could do, as there was nothing to put up. Our garden helped us out a whole lot but I miss fruit and berries. The only kind of bean you can buy here is a little white bean something like a California pea bean but a bit larger. They don't have red kidney beans, lima beans or yellow-eyed beans and act as if they never heard of them. I asked the store man for them and said I didn't want white beans and he showed me peas.

I tried for about two months every time I went to town to get codfish and finally the meat man bought some. George said he never saw it here before. I guess I asked so often he laid in a supply.

I think maybe if I plant some cucumbers in the house and get them pretty well started before I put them out I may be able to get some next year.

We have had two small snowstorms and the ground is white in places but it blows off of the prairie a good deal.

It seems queer to me but just as soon as the work is over in the fall every one turns their horses loose. There is lots of grain left on the ground; the oat stubble comes up quite green so it makes good feed. They run about all winter. Every few days they round them up and if a bad storm or blizzard comes up they put them in for the night otherwise they are out days at a time. Mr. Swanson asked George to look up his horses yesterday and George walked three or four miles north and they were feeding there on the prairie--ours were with them. I should think they would freeze to death as we are having below zero weather now but George says this isn't cold. I see where I stay in this winter.

It might be a good idea for you to send the Nurse's Text Book, as it is eight miles or more to a doctor. There have been some trouble about taxes--I believe the telephone rate goes on the taxes so they cut off everyone from Central who hadn't paid up. All this fall people could talk just on their own line but a week ago they cut the wires so the phone isn't any good. We haven't one in yet but Mr. Swanson has one. His is disconnected so I don't know whether we can use it this winter or not.

Haven't you a book called Taxaloy? There are some things I'd like to know that I don't think are in the Textbook. If you would send that I'll send it back to you.

I must get supper now. Hope you will write often this winter. Give my love to Ray and Mother Allen.

Lovingly, Nell

Strongfield, Sask.
Dec. 9, 1920

Dear Auntie Marie,

It is a long time since I have written and I guess I owe the whole family letters so I'll begin on you.

We have had beautiful weather here. A little over a month ago we had two small snowstorms and a few real cold days and I thought winter had really come but the snow didn't last and it has been pleasant and warm ever since.

Just a month ago today we came down to Mr. Swendson's for the winter. He and a Mr. Holland have a whole section, 640 acres. One corner of their land is just across from ours and their house is a little over a mile from our house.

There are many young fellows, twenty-three, twenty-four and rather jolly. They planned to go away to work for the winter and all wanted us to move down here so George could look after their stock while they were away. We could bring our four horses over with us. There isn't anything a man can do here in the winter but the chores so George felt he had better earn what he could.

The boys have a very comfortable shack --three rooms, and it isn't as lonesome here as it is on the road to Strongfield, as there is much more passing.

Thanksgiving came the 18th of October and I planned to celebrate, but George had to haul flax all day and I went out and helped him load. I can drive the horses and make the load so it saves time and he can get more on the rack than when alone. I didn't get a big dinner that day so we decided we would celebrate the regular Thanksgiving.

We were here but decided we would have a regular celebration. Mr. Swendson was in Elbow and Mr. Holland at Moose Jaw but they both came home and we invited the Brown's, a young married couple and Mrs. Brown's sister. They came from Wisconsin and Mr. Brown looks enough like Archie Prihn to be his twin brother and he talks exactly like him. Mrs. Brown is about twenty-four and her sister about twenty.

We killed a turkey and had cranberry sauce, plum pudding and all of the fixings.

We had our dinner at night and then spent the evening playing Flinch. About eleven Mr. Swendson and Mr. Brown decided they would go to Saskatoon on the four o'clock train from Bladworth the next morning, so we decided not to go to bed.

About one-thirty I got another meal and we ate once more and about two-thirty the boys drove to Bladworth, seventeen miles from here to get the train.

It was just three a.m. when I went to bed. We had quite a celebration.

It is a lazy life here in the winter. There is nothing to do but the chores and no one gets up until eight or nine in the morning.

The boys killed the pig this week so we have been having all kinds of "pig". One of them shot two rabbits today. The rabbits here are big, eight or ten pounds and taste much better than the ones we get in the east. We have had several and I have made rabbit pies and fricasseed them.

I have been busy trying to get my Christmas presents ready to send but it has been rather hard work this year, as there is just a general store at Strongfield and it is quite a trip to Strongfield. I don't enjoy going to town now that it is cold, as my feet get so cold before I get there, that I'm uncomfortable. I had to make nearly everything this year. It isn't as much as I would like to send but maybe I can do better next year. Hope you get the packages in time for Christmas and that you will all have a very nice Christmas day.

I shall think of you all and wish we could be with you. George is just the nicest husband possible. He is so thoughtful about bringing the water and coal and he loves me a whole lot. I wouldn't swap him for anybody I know.

Well, I must stop now as George is waiting for me to read aloud. Give my love to everyone. I was glad to hear from the girls and I'll try to write to them soon.

Lots of love to you, Nell

Strongfield, Sask.
Jan. 2, 1921

Dear Auntie Marie,

Your big box came all right just the night before Christmas and we couldn't imagine what was in it. George was as bad as any small boy. He just couldn't wait until Christmas so we had to open things as fast as they came. The picture was a beauty. I have a fondness for pretty pictures and pretty dishes. One of the teachers at school gave me a picture very similar for a wedding present. It was done by the same man and is just the same size and the frame is the same but the picture is different, however they are both of white birches so they will look well together.

We had a nice Christmas but a very quiet one. We were alone nearly all day. One of the neighbors made a little call in the afternoon. We had three books for Christmas so we read aloud nearly all day. Nick came Christmas Eve to supper and I had part of the Christmas pudding and nuts and candy then. When Nick tasted the gravy he said, "that is just like mine mutter used to make". He always says mine. We played Flinch until nearly twelve.

George is a man after your own heart, auntie; he doesn't play cards and won't have a pack in the house. I don't think he was very anxious to learn to play Flinch but likes it now he has learned. He doesn't approve of dancing so you see it is very fortunate for me that I'm not fond of dancing.

We have had a wonderful winter here. Of course there has been a few cold days but most of the time has been warm and pleasant. We haven't had any storms so far. There is a little snow on the ground but it has come so gradually that it is hard to tell just when it came. Sometimes in the morning I think it is snowing a little but everybody says it is frost falling. People are just getting out their sleighs.

If it is a nice day tomorrow we plan to drive to town but I won't go unless it is warm and pleasant.

George bought me a pair of boots for driving. The bottom part is black leather and the tops are heavy gray felt and they are lined with felt. I wear a pair of his heavy wool socks over my stockings and then put another pair of stockings over them. He also gave me some blue and white cloth for a dress. I want to get it made as soon as I can. I have two neighbors with sewing machines so I can go calling and do my stitching while I'm there.

Tell Flora I was very much pleased with the little apron. It was very dainty. I will try to write to her very soon.

I'm so sleepy I must go to bed. George played a while on the guitar and whistled and then retired about two hours ago. We had callers all afternoon and they stayed to supper so I didn't get any letters written today. I wanted to mail as many letters as I could tomorrow for it may be some time before I get another chance. Bennie came out a week ago and said there was a slip for registered mail in our box but the office was closed so he couldn't get it and no one has been in since. I miss getting the mail regularly.

Give my love to all of your family. I'll surely answer Flora and Pinga's letters soon.

Lots of love for yourself, Nell

Strongfield, Sask.
Jan. 14, 1921

Dear Reta,

My paper seems to be getting very scarce and I'm down to odds and ends. George and I want to thank you very much for our wedding money. We have decided to put it in the bank for the present and buy two little pigs in the spring-- one to kill in the fall and the other to raise. I think I shall have two or three dollars left over and I think we will invest the remainder in eggs for setting.

It is storming for a change. We have had a wonderful winter here. We haven't had a regular stormy day since last fall. Sometimes it will be snowing a little when we awake or it may snow gently by night but we have had no storms. The roads are nearly bare. We used the cutter for the first time about two weeks ago and last week when we went to town the road was bare in lots of places. This may be a regular snowstorm although the sun is trying to come out.

It is light now until five o'clock. I shall be so glad when spring comes and we can work on the land once more. I want to get a good garden started this year but gardens are uncertain things here. I didn't see any cucumbers but once all last summer and they were fifty cents a piece and all withered up. Mrs. Mills has lived here fifteen years and raised one cucumber in that length of time but I think I'll try it just the same. I do want something to can but people do very little of it here. I guess because there is nothing to can.

George has been reading "The Sea Wolf" aloud and just finished it. We have "The Call of the Wild" to read next. He is busy reading "The Farm Journal" just at present. I think we will subscribe again this spring, as we subscribed for only one year. There seems to be a lot of interesting things in it.

I'm sorry Mother Allen has been sick and hope she is feeling all right once more.

George gave me some cloth for a housedress and I have been busy making it by hand. I have several neighbors who have machines but it takes me just as long to get ready and go two or three miles, as it does to do it by hand.

George and I walked down to Mrs. Mills one afternoon this week and stayed to supper. People here usually stop for a meal if they come. There was a dance in the schoolhouse next door a week ago but George doesn't dance or approve of dancing at present so we didn't go. They are all night affairs here and last until from four to six in the morning. I left a good fire and plenty of water and a can of milk out and at midnight two of the fellows came in and made tea. In the morning they came over to breakfast and visited until noon then drove home.

We have had lots of company this winter but when spring comes everyone will be too busy to visit.

It is beginning to get dark so must start supper.

Had a letter from Eunice last week. Han has been sent to Florida for three months and she is with him but finds Florida "punk" and thinks of going home.

Had a card from Maud from Germany. She said she would send me a tablecloth from there for a wedding present. Her address is Lt. W. S. Hamlin, A.P.O. 927, Air Service A.F. in G.

Must get supper.

Love to all. Nell

Strongfield, Sask.
Feb. 12, 1921

Dear Auntie Marie,

I am mailing you a little package for your birthday. We both wish you a very nice one and lots of them and wish we could be there to have some of the ice cream and a piece of birthday cake but we can't this year.

We have had such a nice winter with very little dreadfully cold weather.

I have been busy the last few weeks. We have had lots of company. You see people are too busy to do much visiting in the summer so they do it all during the winter.

Last week I had four bachelors besides a married man and George one night to supper. They just drop in during the afternoon and stay.

Another night there were nine of us and it is sure some stunt to set the table for nine when there are only six of everything. Bennie used a sugar bowl for a cup and George and I had a tin coffee can between us. There are five chairs so we used a trunk at each end of the table and managed nicely. Nobody minds such things here. I suppose good old New England wasn't much, as it is now after it had been settled only ten to fifteen years.

I have a farm all my own. You see crops have been very poor here for the last two years so George had quite a number of bills and not much to pay them with. I thought we ought to save the wheat for seed so I paid some of the bills with my money. It has bothered George a great deal as there was nothing to show it was my money in the place. Last week he had a chance to turn over some land he owned here for a place a hundred and fifty miles north west of here. He sold it and had the transfer of the other land made to me and gave it to me for a wedding present. There are 160 acres with some timber on it, a house with three rooms downstairs and one large room upstairs and a good cellar and also a well right near the back door.

We shall stay on the farm here until he has a good chance to sell it. Maybe if crops are good we will stay here anyway but George said he felt better to know if anything happened to him, I had something of my own.

I haven't told the family as what mother doesn't know won't hurt her and I would rather you didn't mention it to them, but I wanted to tell you, as you seem more like my family anyway.

It is twelve o'clock Saturday morning so I guess I better get some dinner and do the rest of my work. Bennie was going to town so I took time to write to you. Tell Pinga we would love to have the "Youth's Companion." I meant to write to her before this but her turn will come next. George is the nicest husband possible. We have been married 7 months and haven't had a single little scrap yet. Perhaps I ought not to brag to you. I think he grows nicer all the time.

Love to all, Nellie

Strongfield, Sask.
Feb. 18, 1921

Dear Reta,

I really don't know whether I owe you a letter or not but it seems a long time since I have heard from you.

It is quite cold this week but we have had a beautiful winter. Of course we have had a few cold days but it has been pleasant for the most part.

George is shaving and when he gets through we will probably read. The "American Magazine" has just come and there is a good continued story running in it, "Marries?". Do you take the "Woman's Home Companion"? Emma sent me some money Christmas for the "Woman's Home Companion" but I don't know where to send it. No one here has it and I don't know where it is published.

George liked the "Farm Journal" and he was very much amused at the cover on the last one.

We want to put in a big garden this spring. Perhaps if we have a lot of things I can manage to get a few put up before the frost finishes things this year. We sent away for a catalogue and we have been picking out early varieties of everything. It is kind of fun to pick out things you would like to try. I'm going to see if I can manage to raise a few cucumbers. Perhaps if I can start them in the house and put some window frames over them nights I might get a few.

I had a letter last week from the Secretary Treasurer at Hawarden saying he had heard I had been a teacher and asked me to take a school there. The school board has asked me to take the school in this district. It is hard to find a place for the teacher to board and the last one lived over five miles from the school and left as

soon as it got cold. In some places they have a teachers' residence in connection with the school and the teacher lives right at the school. We are only a mile and a half from the school so it wouldn't be very hard for me. I'd rather like to do it. The children are all small, none above the sixth grade and probably about fifteen children in all. School begins in April and lasts until Christmas if the weather is good.

I hope Mother Allen is better than she was at Christmas time. Did she receive the photo I sent her? Give her my love.

Love to you and Ray from us both. Nell

Strongfield, Sask.
Feb. 27, 1921

Dear Reta,

We were so glad to get your letter. I'm sorry you are feeling so mean and hope everything will go all right this time. You rather take my courage away. There aren't any signs of any little Campbell's at present and I'd like a year or two anyway before we have a family.

I guess I wrote you that I was planning to teach this year. School begins the first of April so I shall be a busy lady this summer.

We plan to have a big garden and as we picked out the very earliest varieties of everything I hope we can get something to can this summer before the frost gets everything.

Nick, George and Bennie are looking at the "National Geographical" and studying the map giving the new boundaries in Europe. My Sunday dinner is cooking so I have a few minutes to write. We are having roast beef, baked potatoes, and mashed turnip, prune pie and coffee for dinner. George and I are reading "Desert Gold" by Zane Grey. I read it several years ago but George had never read it so we are reading it aloud.

I washed last Monday and when I hung a few towels out it was a glorious day-- warm and sunshiny. Before I got a few more ready to hang out the wind was blowing so I couldn't get them on the line. I was nearly five minutes hanging out two things. I gave it up as I thought the wind would stop. It increased and blew the snow in clouds and then began to snow and before night the air was so full of flying snow you could hardly see the barn. I had some time trying to dry all the clothes in the house. George managed to rescue the few I had out but they were black and the wind just whipped holes right through them. It became warm and the last three days have been just like spring, --I hope it isn't a false alarm and we are going to have an early spring.

I put up three jars of rabbit this winter and I'm going to can some beef this week.

I must write to Mother Allen this week. We didn't get her letter and I have been wondering if she got the photo I sent. It was nice of her to remember us even if we didn't receive it.

We surely will name our pigs for you and Ray when we get them. Ninnie, the big mare, will have a colt in about two weeks we think and George says he will give me the colt for a birthday present.

I am beginning to get anxious to go home. If this nice weather holds Olie will be coming back before long and then the boys won't need us any longer. There are two fellows on the next place--twins--that look and talk enough like Archie Prihn to be his brothers. They have been gone all winter but one of them is coming back tomorrow. I imagine he will come here until the other brother and his wife get back from the States so I shall have three men next week.

It is now six-thirty and George is doing the chores. I guess I'll get some supper and have it ready when he comes in.

Give my love to Ray and Mother Allen. I'll surely write to her and thank her. I'm sorry we never got her letter. Take care of yourself. I'll enclose a letter I had from Anna Owen recently. She plans to visit you this summer and as you're not feeling well perhaps you would like to change her plans.

Lovingly, Nell

Strongfield, Sask.
April 14, 1921

Dear Auntie Marie,

I guess it is your turn for a letter this time.

This has been a stormy day but I guess it is beginning to clear. I thought at first I wouldn't come to school but I decided some of the children might come so George brought me down. I have three small boys today. I only have nine enrolled and one of them will move this week so it isn't very hard work. George brings me nearly every morning but one day last week I drove. It is only a mile and a half from home. The children are just as good as can be and so still I can hear the clock tick all day. I am to get $125.00 a month so you see it will help out a lot to have that coming in, as George can spend all of his time on the farm.

I got the box Nora sent and was very much pleased with the little candles.

I invited six bachelors up to supper and we had fricasseed chicken, baked potatoes, string beans, ice cream, birthday cake and coffee. I made a round cake with jelly in the middle and thick white frosting on top. The red candles looked very pretty on it and George was much pleased. About twelve I made coffee and we had apple pie and cake. The bachelors here are very fond of strong coffee.

I wondered if you celebrated Louise's birthday Saturday or Sunday? Sometimes perhaps, she and George will be able to celebrate together.

Saturday morning Mr. Clark rode up on horseback and hitched his horse outside the shack. (Tied horse with trunk strap to an old stove). I got him some breakfast and then he went to the barn with George. I went out to empty a pan of ashes and the dust from the ashes frightened the horse so she broke loose. I was afraid she would go off before they came back so I took a pan of oats and went after her. There are hundreds of horses running loose yet, so by the time I got near her I had about a dozen horses all after the oats. I caught her and started to lead her home when one of the other horses jumped and frightened the bunch and they ran. The one I was leading jerked my arm so that it wrenched my shoulder and I couldn't hold her. It made it awfully hard to get ready for the party, as I couldn't lift my right arm. I couldn't move my shoulder or raise my arm. I was afraid if I stopped I couldn't use it at all, as it would get stiff. When George came home he rubbed my shoulder in liniment and swept and did the dishes for me. He was awfully good and helped me all he could so I got along nicely. I'm still lame but can write or do anything, as long as I don't raise my arm.

George was delighted with his necktie and it was nice of you to remember him. It is a very pretty one and looks like one Flora would pick out. Did she get it for you? Thank her so much for the candles. I'm afraid she didn't have quite enough for the postage. I'll enclose a dime to pay for the extra.

I have had my children read over and over and at present they are playing with plastercine. It is mainly time for school to close and I expect George will come for me soon.

He is just as nice as ever. I wish you could know him. When are you and the Dr. coming out? Give my love to all of the family and keep a lot for yourself.

Lovingly, Nell

Strongfield, Sask.
May 8, 1921

Dear Auntie Marie,

Thank you so much for the pretty handkerchiefs and the money. The little birthday card had such a nice verse on it. Bennie and Olie went to town Thursday evening, so I drove in there on my way to school Friday morning and they gave me sixteen letters and cards.

The family sent me a two-pound box of chocolates and a pound of salted peanuts. George gave me the colt for a birthday present. I'm quite delighted with him. We have named him Major. He is as tame as can be. I suppose because we play with him so much. My hens are doing well, we get anywhere from twelve to eighteen eggs per day from twenty-two hens. You see there is much grain lying around and we have the screenings from the grain that had been cleaned so it doesn't cost a cent to keep them. They pick their own living now and can until winter and then we have the screening to feed them. We have all of the fresh eggs that we can use and I have about four-dozen a week to send into the store. I got twenty-two cents a dozen for the last, so you see eggs are cheap here but even that is clear profit.

We are going to have some little pigs. Four I believe, as I have to throw away so much milk. I take a big kettle full to the hens nearly every day and we might just as well be raising some pigs.

I began this after dinner but George wanted to go for a walk, so we wandered over the farm and looked at the land he had plowed. He showed me what he was going to disk and where he was going to plant the wheat and the oats.

Wednesday

Somehow it is hard for me to get a letter written these days.

Mr. Lu drove up Sunday morning before I had done any work and stayed until about four in the afternoon, so I didn't get my usual Sunday letters written.

I have fourteen children now enrolled in school; the most there have ever been here. They are good little youngsters; all Norwegian but one and I guess he is German. They haven't come very regularly in the past so are old for the grade they are in and as lots of them talk Norwegian at home, they are rather slow in reading our language. I have a boy fourteen in the third grade and one eleven in the second grade.

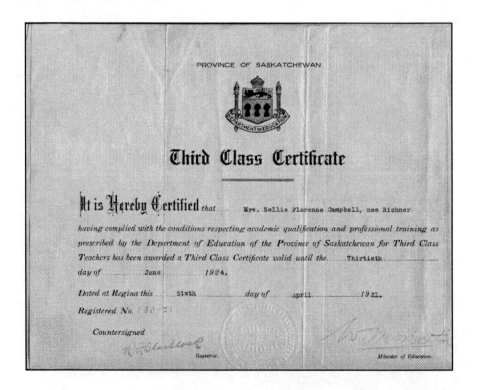

George and I have been making a garden in the evenings. We have onions and radishes and last night some of the peas were showing through the ground. We have planted Swiss chard, beets, carrots, cabbages and turnips and have some cabbages nearly three inches high in the house ready to transplant. I have started tomatoes in the house; they aren't doing well so George said he would get me some better soil.

I had a long letter from Marion and they are at Gatun now, as Rudolph has been transferred. They are expecting a little stranger in September and Ruth and Ray expect about the same time. Reta has not written home about it and doesn't want the family to know until she sends out announcements, so please don't write them, but Marion has broken the news to the family. We aren't expecting any little Campbell's. I would like to teach school this year anyway and possibly next, as the $125.00 a month helps George so much on the place and I want things running smoothly before I undertake a family.

We are hoping for a good year and George will have 80 acres in wheat and oats. Of course that isn't much here in the west but it will help out a lot if we get good crops.

I am going out to supper tonight. One of my children at school has invited me. George was invited but he is busy seeding, so he wouldn't go as he has to leave off work so early and time is precious. This is the first time that I have ever been anywhere alone and left him. We are very happy together and it has been a happy year for us both. He is just the nicest husband possible and awfully good to me.

I suppose Lidi is married now. I want to hear about the wedding.

Was sorry to hear of Mrs. Ripley's death but am glad Dot is married and has a good husband, as she won't be quite so lonesome as she would be otherwise.

Did I write you Benny and Olie came over one day with six horses to move our house? They didn't pull evenly and some of the underpinning gave away so they were afraid this would pull the house off the skids. They got it just a little ways and left it in the field in a hollow. One end of the house is over six inches lower than the other. We have to stay there until George can go to town for lumber and put in new sills. Of course nothing can be done until after seeding, as everyone works early and late without doing any extras. I was awfully disappointed.

We had a dreadful windstorm a week ago Monday. I came to school but went home again as no one came. You people don't know what wind is. It began to blow on Friday night and Saturday I couldn't wash as the wind blows the hems right off the towels and it is almost impossible to hang the clothes out. The next Monday it was dreadful. I didn't mind it so much while I was up as I did in the night. I could feel the shack shake and you bet I just held on to George. The Howel's hen house went with a crash and the lumber blew all over the yard. Nearly everyone lost their little owl houses. The boy's hayrack blew right out into the field and the wind lifted the top off of it and smashed it all to pieces. I don't know why we didn't blow away but our shack is heavy and we have lots of furniture in it. I guess we were pretty well weighted down, even if the shack was just on skids in the field. I tried three times to get into the house and I blew right around the corner. I hate such winds and they last two or three days. The last spell lasted a whole week.

This is quite a lengthy letter so I guess I had better stop for this time. I just wish you all could drop in and see us and know George, as he is so nice. If we have good crops George says we will take a trip east in two or three years. I hope we can.

Give my love to all of your big family. Thank the girls for their birthday cards. I'll try to answer their letters next.

Lots of Love to you, Nell.

Strongfield, Sask.
June 14, 1921

My Dear Louisa and Bill,

I received Flora's note the day you and Bill were married. You may be sure George and I wish you both all of the happiness possible, even if I am a bit slow in writing to you. We hope you may be as happy together as we have been and you won't need to be any happier than that. I shall want to hear all about the wedding and your little trip and your future plans. George and I will send you something as soon as we can get something. Our general store doesn't happen to carry a line of wedding presents. I do most of my shopping, even groceries, from a mail order catalog but we thought we would rather see what we are buying this time. We plan to go up near Battleford to see the farm George gave me and see if everything is all right there, sometime during my vacation which comes in July. We will go to Saskatoon and stay for a day or two there, and as that is quite a city I can get something there.

Our house is still on skids in the field, but seeding is nearly over so I hope to get moved before long. I shall be so glad to have the house anchored even more, as we have had two dreadful storms since we have been here. One was a windstorm that blew down buildings but the old shack stood. Tell the Dr. that when he used to tell me about the wind here I didn't half believe him, but I do now. The other was a thunder and hailstorm that came one night right after supper. George thought we would get a lot of wind so perhaps we had better not stay in the shack. I put on my winter coat and woollen cap and some heavy leather and felt boots and we went out on the prairie when the storm struck. George took me in his arms and crouched down with a heavy quilt tucked in over us. The buggy blew down over the hill, but the shack stayed, although I expected to see it sailing off any minute. The rain came in torrents and the lightening was so constant it was light as day. There wasn't as much wind as we thought there might be, so as soon as the worst was over we ran for the shack. The prairie is uneven and you should have seen the water in the hollows. We had a regular lake around the shack. Of course, as it is all open underneath at present, the water ran under the shack too. Our cat had kittens under the house the day before and of course they got drowned. She was howling and I knew she was frantic and the poor kittens were crying but we couldn't get them out. George sawed a hole through the floor but we couldn't tell where they were and after we got a hole made we couldn't get them. I tried to get her to bring them to the opening, but she was so frightened she didn't know enough. I suppose she was afraid to leave for a minute. The next morning she brought one little, bedraggled kitten in her mouth and put it in the closet, so I made her a bed in a box and she has kept her kitten in ever since. It recovered although we thought the first night it would die as it got so chilled.

Tell Auntie Marie that I bought a rooster with my birthday dollar she sent me. I had one rooster that I had given to me last summer when I had only one hen. He was given to us to kill for Thanksgiving, but we didn't celebrate the Canadian Thanksgiving. The U.S. one we were at Bennie's, so he didn't get killed. I grew very fond of him so he still lives. When the new rooster arrived there was some fight of course. George kept separating them but they kept it up until the new rooster had both eyes closed for two days and lost a spur for good. Poor Theobold, my pet rooster hurt his mouth so he couldn't shut it. I thought he would be all right in a day or two, but he couldn't eat because he couldn't pick up anything with his bill. I brought him up to the house and we discovered his lower bill was broken where it joined his head. He was half starved so I fed him milk out of a silver spoon and made him some thick cornmeal porridge with sour milk. For two days it took me an hour a day to feed him with a spoon, but he was awfully good. He would walk right up to me and let me pour the mush down with a spoon. He can eat now by himself if I mix him up lumps of meal soaked in milk or fried potatoes or anything big enough for him to get a hold of, but he can't eat small things. I think he will recover in time if I keep on fixing his food and soaking his head in disinfectant. The other rooster has recovered and at present rules the roost. I have one hen sitting and one of my children took some eggs home and set two of their hens for me as they had lots of sitting hens and no eggs and my hens didn't want to sit. George said last night there were three wanting to sit so I may get some chickens after all.

I just wish you could come out and see the farm and everything. The colt is awfully cunning. If I don't play with him when I go over to the barn, he will come over to me and stand awhile. If I don't pay any attention he will pull my sleeve with his lips and then if I don't pat him he will nip my arm. We have named him Major.

I guess I have written all the news of the farm. Give my love to all of the family and good big lot for you and Bill, with all of the good wishes possible from us both.

Lovingly, Nell.

Strongfield, Sask.
August 1921

Dear Reta,

I received the basket some time ago and it was awfully nice of you to make it for me. I don't see when you find time for such things. I've been so busy this summer that my husband's clothes don't get mended and I don't iron anything except my outside dresses. The Little Jew [a plant] was pretty badly wilted. George declared there wasn't anything but moss but I found two little pieces and they are really growing. I do hope it will live and I guess it will.

I guess I haven't written you since we took our little trip. I had two weeks vacation and we went to Saskatoon for a few days, starting on the 16th of July, our wedding anniversary-and got home the 21st. We went to the movies and saw "The Sky Pilot". We don't have movies here. From Saskatoon we went up to Hafford. It is about a hundred and fifty miles northwest of here. George bought a hundred and sixty acres there last winter and gave it to me for a wedding present. Of course I was anxious to see the place. It is a beautiful country, much prettier than here, as it is part prairie and part timber. About a hundred acres are prairie and the rest bush and small trees. The big timber begins just north of our place. George thought the land was much better than here. The only trouble is the country is still undeveloped. We are twenty miles from a railroad. You can't realize so much land with no one on it. It will be real pioneering if we go there. It seems too bad to let the land lie idle. Shorty wants to hire this place next year and put in the crop so we may go up there but we are still undecided. I'd like it as there are trees and I could have a pretty place.

Friday

I began this last Sunday and here a week has nearly gone by. I have twenty minutes before it is time to call my little cherubs in so I'll make another beginning. George has been laid up this week with a stiff neck. It took him all of a sudden and one day he couldn't move his head. The next day he complained of a lame shoulder. He has been cooking for Bennie and Olie and they have been cutting for us, as we haven't a binder. It put him back to have to lay off for two days but he went to work yesterday.

It hasn't been nearly as hot here this year, as it was last summer and the crops are better. The last two days have been hot but it is nice and cool at school. We have a school fair in Strongfield the 14th of Sept. so we are busy getting ready for that.

I have been busy canning and have 60 pints of various things put up, string beans, peas, spinach, swiss chard, plums, rhubarb/conserve, and citron preserve. Fruit is expensive as it is expressed from British Columbia. I had to buy all new jars and quart jars are $3.10 a doz. and pints $3.00 so it costs a lot if you have to buy fruit and sugar besides Saturday is the only day I have and I usually have a big washing. One week I washed, had Shorty and Dewey there to dinner and put up sixteen pints of beans but I was so weary I decided not to do so much in a day. Last week I canned so this week I have two weeks washing and I think I'll omit the canning, although we have lots of peas just ready to can.

I'm going to send Sophie something but I shall have to send to "Timothy Eaton" for it as I haven't a machine and it takes me so long to get anything made by hand that Sophie will outgrow it before I ever finish it. It is school time so I'll say farewell for the present.

The Little Jew [a plant] has done wonderfully well this week. Many thanks.

Love to all, Nell

Strongfield, Sask.
August 4, 1921

Dear Aunt Marie,

I'm having two weeks vacation and George and I are off on a little trip. It is nice to go away and see things but I'll be glad to get home for all I've had a nice time.

You know George gave me a farm of 160 acres for a wedding present. We went to Saskatoon last Saturday and stayed there until Monday night. We went to the movies that night, church three times Sunday and visited some stores and saw the town generally on Monday morning. That afternoon we saw the "Sky Pilot". We left about six on Monday night to go to see the farm. It is only a hundred and twenty miles from Saskatoon and we have been from Monday night until Thursday night going that distance and back. We went as far as Denholm and had to stay overnight then as that was the only train we could get into Denholm, and the train to Hafford left there every other day. We went to a country hotel for the night and went to Hafford the next day. It was a mixed train, mostly freight with one or two passenger coaches in the rear. We stopped anywhere from twenty minutes to half of an hour at every station to unload the freight. When we reached Hafford we couldn't leave there until the next day. We hired an auto and went out to the farm. It is a beautiful country, there are a lot of trees so much prettier that the prairie. George thought the land was very good but it is a new country and still undeveloped. Most of the people are Galatians or Russians. It is twenty miles from the railroad to the farm, but they are working on a railroad now that will mean about five miles from our place if they were to get it finished. You wouldn't believe that there would be so much land with no one on it. It is a beautiful country and maybe someday we will go there to live. I don't think I would get lonesome.

I began this on the train but the ink in my pen was poor and it was jiggly so I couldn't write.

We are home once more. I left two bachelors here keeping house and they had a grand cleaning up the day we got back so I found things pretty clean but they were getting hungry.

George and I planned to take an easy Sunday today and go down in our little clump of trees and read, but we have had company all day. Shorty, a bachelor friend of George's came a week ago Wednesday and brought his nephew with him, a young returned soldier from the east. We only have one room but there is an unfinished loft so George put in a window in the end of the house and they have been with us ever since and sleep upstairs.

This morning Olie drove up with the mail and stayed to dinner and just before we sat down Mr. Clark came so I had quite a family to feed.

School begins tomorrow and I don't see where my vacation has gone, as I haven't done half of the things I planned to do.

We have a splendid garden and I have spent a lot of time on it. We have had lettuce, radishes, green peas, swiss chard, beet greens, onions and small beets. Our potatoes are big enough to use but I still have some old ones, which I'll use first. The string beans are ripe but I had so many peas I thought I wouldn't pick the beans until tomorrow.

Our colt is awfully cunning. We put two of the horses and the colt in the pasture before we went away and they are still there. I miss having the colt run around the back yard.

We got the house moved at last and it seems so nice to be near the barn and garden. I can run out and see the pigs and hens and go to the garden now quite often. I have twenty-eight little chickens and they are all doing fine. My rooster is getting better. When we moved the house down to the barn I tied both of the roosters so they couldn't fight. We drove to church that day and while we were gone, Turner broke loose and when we got home he had nearly finished my pet rooster. Of course he was tied and he had the string all tangled up in a barb wire fence and around both feet, so he couldn't move and his bill was just getting better so he didn't have any kind of a show. He certainly was a bloody bird when I rescued him. George killed Turner so Theobold could have peace and I stuffed and roasted him and invited Bob and Jim and Jim's sister up to supper.

I had a letter from Reta today, also one from Ida. They both said Rudy had hired on at a farm. I should think he would have held onto his job if he had one, as I don't think he likes hard work well enough for a farmer. It certainly is hard work and long hours from early spring to late fall but not much to do through the winter.

Well I must stop and study more Canadian history before tomorrow, as I have two girls taking history and I don't know much about it.

George and I have been married over a year and we have been very happy together. I wish you could come out and see this country some time.

Love to all of your family and a whole lot for you.

Nell

Strongfield, Sask.
Oct. 6, 1921

Dear Reta,

It is almost a week since I got the announcement and over a week since your letter came. I am ashamed to think I didn't answer it sooner. I'm quite proud to be auntie and I'm glad it's a boy. I think it's nice to have the oldest a boy.

I have a pair of booties for the baby and will send them as soon as I can get them to town. Everyone is threshing so mail often stays here a week or ten days before I can find anyone going in. I was glad to get Ray's letter and hear about everything.

George went away threshing a week ago. The rig he is working on started about five miles from here and was working the opposite direction from home so it made it too far for George to come back and forth night and morning and ten or twelve extra miles was a lot for the horses after a hard days work. George stayed Friday night and I stayed alone. He put Minnie and the colt in the pasture and took two horses so that left just the horse I drive to school, the cow, pigs and hens to see to. I got along beautifully Friday night. George came home Saturday night for over Sunday but I did the chores before he came.

He left Monday morning to be gone all of the week. Tuesday night I did all the other chores and then went to milk the cow. She was tethered in a patch of green oats. I took the chain off of the stake to lead her to the well and the old cow bolted. She was on one end of a fifty-foot chain and I was on the other. I pulled with all my strength but you never would have known there was a thing on my end of the chain as far as her progress was changed. My hat flew off and my hair came down and I simply let her go. She stopped by an oat stack and I got near enough to get the end of the chain and wind it up. When she thought I was too close she started again but I sat down back of the stack and hung on and I gradually pulled her in until I could get her halter. We yanked each other down to the well and back to the oat field. I thought my troubles were over but they had just begun. When I sat down to milk she deliberately walked off. Of course I picked up the stool and pail and followed. All of a sudden she turned and bolted the other way and the chain hit me right across the knees and pail, stool and I went down rather suddenly. I struck my right shoulder and arm and when I got wind enough to sit up I couldn't move my arm. I sat in the field and wept for George and then I got up and pursued the cow. I finally got her milked with one hand.

My arm hurt so by the time I got in the house I sat and wept awhile and then I bathed in hot water and rubbed on capicreme vaseline and went to bed. About eight I heard George whistle. He missed me so he walked home and thought he would hike back in the morning. You bet I was glad to see him. I haven't been to school since and don't do much but lie down. I don't seem to have any desire to move.

George has been coming home every night but it makes it hard for him to come so far after a long days work and he has to get up at four in order to get back, as they begin at daylight. Mrs. Howell rubbed my arm and shoulders with some liniment she had and wrapped me up in flannel and combed my hair this morning. The swelling has gone down a lot but is various shades of purple, blue and green from my elbow to my shoulder. I can move my wrist and fingers so can write nicely by sitting with my arm close to me and writing in my lap providing I keep moving the paper instead of my arm.

I put up ninety odd jars of things besides two stone crocks full of pickles. I wanted to do more but the jars were so high and with the washing on Saturday, I couldn't can as much as I wanted too. Just the time things were ready to can I had two extra men here so there was a lot of cooking besides my school work.

George has let the place here to Nick for two years and we are going north in the spring. You know George gave me a farm for a wedding present and we are going there next year. It is lovely there, as about sixty acres are trees and bush and a hundred is prairie. There is a little pond in one corner. We will be twenty miles from a railroad but another railroad is being built and when finished will go within five miles of us so eventually we will be nearer town than we are here. The mail is brought out once a week to Lorenzo, a small store two miles from our place so we will get the mail as often as we do here.

Friday Morning

My arm got so tired I gave it up last night; maybe I can get this letter finished today.

I went to town a week ago Friday after school. I had the buggy and one of the heavy workhorses, as the road was bad and I had to get a case of groceries from the station besides a crate of peaches and some fruit jars and go to a teacher's meeting. It was quarter of seven before I left town and getting dark fast. About three miles from town we turn on to the prairie and it is just like driving over a big field for five miles--nothing but a trail. A thunderstorm came up and the sky was as black as ink. I expected it would pour any minute. It sure was some job keeping the trail, as I couldn't see a thing. If I felt the buggy got out of the wheel rut I yanked Clyde back quick. I spotted Mill's light and drove for it and then I located Bennie's light. When I got there I was tempted to drive in and ask one of the boys to drive around the slough with me but I saw a light ahead on the prairie. I thought it might be George so I drove toward that light and I was some glad to see George with a lantern. We got in the yard just as the rain came.

I planned to wash and can peaches Saturday but when we got up Saturday morning a horse Shorty had left here was sick. She had been sick for over a week and he had been doctoring him but she seemed better when he left so he said he'd be back for her in a few days. She seemed so sick George said I'd better go for Shorty. I had to go about six miles across the prairie and back. The road and trails were bad so it was noon before I got back. Then I had to help George give the horse some medicine and get dinner. Shorty and Nick came soon after and Mr. Howell came up. They thought the horse would die so Shorty said he wouldn't stay. We covered her over with lots of blankets and I kept making warm gruel for her and held her head while George poured it in. In the midst of my troubles Nick brought me his Sunday pants to clean and press. These bachelors don't ever own a flat iron and as Mrs. Howell and I are the only women in this neighborhood we have to look out for all the bachelors. You may be sure I didn't get any washing or canning done that day. We were both up a lot through the night with the horse. I went out at five on Sunday morning to see if she was covered up and she was so sick I came in for George. We got her liniment but she died soon after. We were both so weary we slept late and before we finished breakfast Nick came for his trousers. He sat down with us and visited awhile after breakfast and before I got the dishes done Bennie and Olie came to dinner and spent the afternoon and Mrs. Howell came to supper and spent the evening so you see we have company even if our neighbors aren't very near.

I'm so sleepy and my arm is tired so I guess I'll turn over and sleep until noon. I'm dreadfully lazy but it seems nice to do nothing but lie still.

Hope you get along nicely and the baby grows fast and is well.

Love to you and Ray and mother Allen.

Lovingly, Nell

Strongfield, Sask.
Jan. 1, 1922

Dear Reta,

Your package arrived safely sometime this week and one of the neighbors brought it to us yesterday. George was pleased with his tie and I like my dress ever so much. I tried it on immediately and was so busy viewing myself in the glass that I burned the top of the pie I was making for Sunday's dinner.

I dressed up in it yesterday afternoon and Mrs. Howell came up just as we were having our supper and thought I looked quite fine. She wants to cut out one like it. Can you buy the colored bias seam binding or do you have to cut the binding yourself? We can't get anything like that here nothing but white not even colored rick-rack braid. Mother Allen's package came the same day and I was delighted with the bureau scarf. I'll write her soon.

We had a nice Christmas--in fact our Christmas lasted a long time. Mrs. Howell brought up a book Wednesday night and said there were more packages down at her house but she couldn't carry them. As George had sent for the book for me he opened it and gave it to me then. We had a blizzard the next day, but George went down to Mrs. Howell's and came home with a flour sack full of boxes. We put them away as I wanted everything for Christmas but it stormed hard all day and George teased to open them, so at last I decided we might as well have Christmas on Thursday as any other day. I fried some pork for supper, baked potatoes and we opened a can of sour kraut and then after supper we opened our presents.

We had six books between us so we have been having a good time reading. Mabel Windell sent me "Main Street" by Sinclair Lewis. She is teaching in Sauk Center, his hometown this year. Have you read the book yet? George went to town Saturday with Olie and brought home more packages so we had another celebration. Shorty went to town Tuesday and got the "Home Journal" for a year for Emma. She also sent George a tie. George gave me a pair of blue comfy slippers so I'm well supplied. We had three pounds of chocolates. As I hadn't had any since May I ate so much I had a bilious spell [upset stomach] but didn't mind a little thing like that.

Have you heard from Marion? She wrote me the baby had some sort of navel trouble and for some reason she had to stop nursing it and they had quite a time finding some food that agreed with it. Her mother came down for Thanksgiving and the Dr. insisted both she and the baby would be better if her mother took it home with her. When Marion wrote the baby was in Lowell and improving fast. She planned to go home for Christmas and bring the baby back. I had a package from her sent from Lowell so she evidently went home for Christmas.

We have a young dog now--he followed us home from town three weeks ago and has evidently adopted us for keeps. George planned to take him in again and try to leave him but when he went in Jimps refused to follow.

We have a very nice cat. She is very neat and although I insisted she should be a barn cat as soon as zero weather came I didn't have the heart to put her out so she stays in but she never steals or gets on the table or jumps on the bed at night. She really is a very remarkable cat.

One of our horses died this winter. We had planned to shoot her, as she was old and even had the day set--Olie was to do it for us. One morning George went out and found her dead in the manger. It is a mystery how she ever got in. He had to tear down the whole manger to get her out.

The little colt is a dear and so tame. His coat is as thick as wool this winter. You know people here turn the horses loose and they roam over the prairie and pick their own living in the winter. This year there was lots of grain left on the ground but the snow came early and covered it up. You should see the horses paw the snow away and feed. Lots of horses are gone for days or weeks at a time. Last year Fred went with a bunch of Nick's horses and we never saw him all winter. This year George has been feeding them a little in the barn so they come home nearly every night. You should see Major--the colt--paw the snow. He is a great little rustler.

I shall be so glad when we have milk once more. The cow has been dry so long now.

My Little Jew [a plant] was just beginning to grow a little when it got touched by frost. I watered it and maybe it will revive but it looks pretty droopy today.

I suppose we will go north as soon as we can in the spring as George wants to get in a big garden and as much feed for the horses as he can.

It sure will be like pioneering with no house and twenty miles from a railroad. George will have to go in the car with the stock so I shall have to go alone and meet him there.

This is getting to be quite a lengthy epistle and I haven't done my dinner dishes yet. We are having only two meals a day now, as it is so late when we get up. We never have breakfast until nine-thirty or ten so we dine once more between four and five. We certainly lead a lazy life in the winter but enjoy it. Give my love to Ray and Mother Allen and tell her I will write soon.

Lovingly, Nell

Strongfield, Sask.
Feb. 4, 1922

Dear Auntie Marie,

We were so glad to get your nice long letter and hear all the news about all of your family. We hadn't been to town but one of the neighbors brought out the mail and I had eight letters and lots of papers. I was in the midst of washing, but I just sat down and read all of my mail.

We have been having some cold weather, fifty below zero. For a week I didn't venture outside the house. It was much warmer now but still good cold winter weather.

I'm awfully lazy this winter. We don't get up until late and then after George does the chores we read most of the day or rather George reads aloud to me. I have been sewing some. I have Mrs. Howell's sewing machine so I'm having a grand time. Some of the quilts need recovering and I hope to do it if it ever gets warm enough to wash them, but I don't want to cover them while dirty. I have the covering for one already and have made a patchwork top for another. I suppose it sounds queer to you people to be making patchwork but when you are living in a country like this you save all of the little pieces. I thought I'd get the covers made and then if it ever gets warm enough to wash it won't be much work to put them together. I plan to make over my old red dress I had eleven years ago. It has been made over twice but I think there is still enough left to get out a respectable looking gown.

Have I written you since the little calf arrived? It is so nice to have plenty of milk. I wish you could have some of the nice cream we are having. I fill the pitcher full of cream every morning and we use all we want. I have made about three pounds of butter a week besides. The hens are beginning to lay once more so we are getting fresh eggs.

I'm getting anxious to get moved now, but suppose we can't go until the snow goes. It is such a pretty country there and it seems so nice to see trees once more. Nearly all of the houses there are built out of logs that have been squared and the chinks are filled with cement. We plan to put up a log house.

The coyotes have been plentiful here this winter. One has come right into the dooryard several times in the middle of the day. Nick, Bennie, Olie, Mr. Brown and George all went out after coyotes about two weeks ago and then came back to dinner that evening. George and I walked to Howell's and stayed to supper.

There is a lot of snow here now, more than we had all last winter.

I hope Rudy finds something to do soon. I guess work is pretty scarce everywhere. George heard his two youngest brothers have been out of work ever since last August and his oldest brother is giving them enough to live on.

It is fortunate for Rudolph that he has an Aunt Marie. I wish I were wealthy and could help the poor kid out, but we don't have much extra money. We have a good living with plenty to eat, but all of our money has gone into running the farm.

I had a letter from Marion, the next day yours came. Have you seen the baby yet? Mother Allen writes that Hamlin is a dear and her husband says she "acts real silly over him". I guess Ray's toe must be better, as I had a letter from his mother today and she never mentioned him.

Have you had a long letter from Pinga lately? I haven't written her since Christmas but must. Alice McCausland sent me a whole pile of magazines the first of January so we have had quite a picnic reading them.

There doesn't seem to be much news to write about tonight. Give my love to all your family. Is Fay's eczema all right now? You haven't mentioned him lately.

I believe you have a birthday this month. I have a little package all ready to mail to you. I haven't been to town in a long time, so had to make the things for you. Hope you will have a very nice birthday and many of them. I wish I could be there to help you celebrate, but I'll surely think of you on the 18th.

Lovingly, Nell

Strongfield, Sask.
Feb. 24, 1922

Dear Flora,

Bennie, Olie and Nick came up tonight bringing the mail and I was glad to get your letter.

We planned to kill the pig today and they were coming up to help but went to town and it was late when they got home, so nearly five before they reached there. George and I have been melting snow today to scald the animal. I'll be glad when things thaw out enough so we can get some water. We have the water barrel in the house, the washtub on the oil stove and a broiler full on the floor. You can imagine how much room I have in a 12 X 14 foot room with a bed, chiffonier, dish closet, wash stand, oil stove, table, sewing machine, clothes closet that fills up one corner of the room, stove, bookcase, a box that we use for a seat, two chairs, a nail keg that makes another seat and Bennie and Olie have my trunk tipped up on the side for a seat. There also are four men here at present playing Flinch. There were five this afternoon. Ted Butler came for some potatoes. The farmers are queer here. They are so busy growing grain very few ever raises a garden. We had a nice garden last summer so have plenty of vegetables to last all winter and have sold some.

I played two games of Flinch and beat both games so they excused me. When they get through playing cards I shall have to serve refreshments but I find these men prefer something hearty. I have a dish of beef and potato salad all ready; some baked beans to warm up, a pan of baking powder biscuits ready to go in the oven, and will have citron sauce, cake and coffee with real cream in it. Don't you wish you were here? I wish you could all come sometime to see me. You know I'd love to have you.

It has been from 20-50 below zero for a month or six weeks and we have lots of snow. I don't go out very often, as one has to go so far in this country to get anywhere that I'm nearly frozen before I arrive. I drove to town with George two weeks ago and wore a pair of George's heavy wool drawers and his shirt over my union suit, a wool dress, knit jacket, my sweater and my all red plush coat. I relined it this winter and put in an inner lining made from a wool blanket. I have a cap that pulls over my ears and then I tied my head up in a woollen scarf. On my feet were a pair of woollen stockings, a pair of comfy bedroom slippers and a pair of lumberjacks felt boots that came to my knees. I think they were about size ten. I look like Barnum's fat lady when I get ready to start. When I got to town I took off my footgear and put on my boots but they were so cold my feet nearly froze. They were comfortable until I changed, but I couldn't walk around town in that rig. I went to the rest room and warmed my feet and put on my slippers once more and George drove there for me. I didn't care if folks did see my size 10 lumberjack shoes when I got into the sleigh.

Did I tell you about the sleigh? Well, we couldn't afford to buy one this winter but had to have something. George made two runners from heavy planks and built a sort of sled and then we put a big packing box on the top of it and George put a seat in it. It is very comfortable to ride in. People use the worst looking rigs here so our sleigh is perfectly all right for this part of the country.

Did I write you we had a little calf? It is nice to have plenty of cream and you bet I use all I want. I wish you could have some of it.

I've just finished my sixteenth lesson, a story of 3000 words. I've got 96-97-98 and 99 on all of my other lessons. I don't suppose I'll get quite a good mark on this. The course is interesting but there is an awful lot of work to it.

Sometimes I don't think I'll ever be able to write a decent story, but George seems to think I can. I hope I will be able to write a respectable story some day.

This seems to be quite a lengthy letter. The game is ended and we have had our supper and George is reading a book of jokes, so I can't keep my mind on what I'm writing.

I'm sorry Rudy has been such a trial to you. I'm afraid Auntie was too good to him and maybe it would have done him good if you had given him a piece of your mind. I don't know just how much good it would have done. I used to relieve my mind occasionally and I think it did some good for the time being. I do hope he will get something profitable to do soon. It makes it hard for Marion to have him do such crazy things and I think she is an awfully nice girl. I'm glad George and I can get along peacefully and not have any disagreements.

Give my love to all your big family.

Lots of love to you, Nell

Strongfield, Sask.
March 14, 1922

Dear Reta,

I am visiting at the Theobald's who live about twelve miles from us. George has left me for a week so I'm a widow lady. We moved yesterday and Shorty, his hired man, Olie and George all took a load to Bladworth, seventeen miles from home and Shorty stayed and helped him load the car. I went with George on the load as far as Churchill's and we stayed there to dinner and Mr. Theobald came there for me. George called me up today before the train left and said he had quite a time, as the hen crate broke and the hens got out and he spent over an hour trying to catch them. At last he caught the rooster and tied him in the car and he called all of the hens back in.

I have had a lazy day and it seems good after the last few strenuous days. It is certainly a job to move a long distance. Mr. Poty wrote that we could use the buildings on the next quarter to ours so it will be nice to have a place to move into.

George didn't know just how long it would take him to go, as freight is often slow so he thought it best for me to visit until he had time to get there and make at least one trip out to the place with the stove and a few of the most essential things before I came.

We have had a long, cold winter here. It was between forty and fifty below zero for about six weeks. Both of our wells were frozen so we had to use snow water entirely and I spent most of my time melting snow. It certainly was some job to wash. Water is quite a question on the prairie. We will have plenty of water where we are going and I will be glad. I had a nice letter from Mother Allen and I don't think I answered it.

I tried to do some sewing this winter and had Mrs. Howell's sewing machine for a while but it was mostly mending and covers for quilts. I made one patchwork top, as I had a lot of small pieces that I hated to waste. I got that comforter finished but the others I planned to cover were all soiled and it was impossible to wash them without water and so hard to get them dry if I did wash them that I got the covers made and will finish them when I can. I had a long letter from Marion a week or more ago. She was at her mothers and Rudolph had a job as an attendant in the State Asylum at Mattapan. I guess they have had a hard time to get along this winter, as Rudolph hasn't had any work. She wrote that she was planning to go to the country for the summer. I wish I lived near enough so she could visit me, as I'd love to see her and the baby. We will be twenty miles from a doctor anyway and I'm not sure that he has come to Hafford yet. They were expecting a doctor there when we were up last summer but I have never heard whether he arrived and I'm afraid Marion wouldn't care to be so far from a doctor.

Flora writes to me quite often and Louisa writes occasionally. She and Billy are living in Bath and are very happy. Bath is quite near you, isn't it? There doesn't seem to be much news this time. I'll try to write to Mother Allen soon. Give my love to Ray and Hamlin.

When you write, address it to Hafford, Saskatchewan, Lorenzo Post Office.

Lovingly, Nell

Strongfield, Sask.
March 15, 1922

Dear Auntie Marie,

My husband has left me for a week so I am a widow lady. It has been very cold here all winter but began to thaw about ten days ago so we thought it best to move while the snow was still on the ground, as the roads are so bad as soon as they get muddy. We hurried on our packing and George, Shorty, his hired man and Olie all took a load to Bladworth on Monday. It is some job, as we had to haul the things seventeen miles on this end and twenty when we get to Hafford.

George sent me to visit some of his friends for a week. He had to go in the car to take care of the stock and freight is so slow that he thought I had better visit until he had time to reach Hafford and make at least one trip to the place and put up the stove and open up the most essential things.

The Theobalds are very pleasant people and it seems nice to be lazy after the last few strenuous days of packing.

I'm going to Saskatoon tomorrow and plan to stay over Sunday with the Lees and get to Hafford Monday noon. George telephoned me from Bladworth just before the train left Tuesday. He said something happened to the hen crate after he got it in the car and all the hens got out. He spent over an hour trying to get them back and finally caught the rooster and tied him in the car and he called his family back in again.

It has been cold again the last few days and is storming tonight, but I'm hoping it will be pleasant tomorrow so that I can start. I miss my hubby and will be glad to see him once more.

Saskatoon is a city as large or larger than Portland and has been built only ten or twelve years. I want to go to the dentists while there and do a little shopping as George has a birthday on April 1st. I'm afraid we won't know our new neighbors well enough this year to have a party.

There doesn't seem to be much to write about tonight, but I wanted to send you our new address. I have left word here to forward any mail. When you write send it to Hafford, Sask. Lorenzo P.O.

Hope you are well. It is some time since I have heard from you, but I know you are busy. I wish I could see you all. Give my love to all of your big family and write when you can.

Lovingly, Nell

Hafford, Sask.
March 29, 1922

Dear Auntie Marie and family,

I don't know just where to begin to tell you about our moving, so I'll begin way at the beginning before we left Strongfield. We had ten days of lovely spring like weather and the snow was melting fast so we decided we had better move before the snow left, as the roads are so bad through mud time.

George left Monday and I went to Theobalds and stayed until Friday. He telephoned me before the train left Bladworth on Tuesday and wrote to me from Prince Albert. He got to Hafford Thursday but they were having a big snow storm there so he telephoned to Strongfield Friday, that I had better not come for several days. I had already started for Saskatoon when he called up so he sent me a telegram there. It had cleared when he telegraphed and looked like good weather so he told me to come Monday. He thought he could get out to the place with one load and fix things up a little and get back in time to meet me. He left town Saturday with quite a load. The roads were dreadful. They had drifted in so one could hardly see the trail at all. If the horses step a bit out of the road, they went in to the snow up to their stomachs and had to be shovelled out of the drifts. About five miles out from town a Scotchman passed him and about half a mile further stopped until George came up before he turned into his place. He asked George where he was going and then insisted on his coming in for a cup of tea. After that he only went about ten miles and stopped overnight with a young married couple. They had only one room but hung up a blanket in the middle of the shack. They liked my cat and wanted her and finally persuaded George to leave her there until he got settled. He started on Sunday morning and was eight hours going ten miles. The load upset twice and he had to keep shovelling the horses out and sometimes go ahead and shovel before they could get through the drifts. It was dark Sunday night when he got here. He stopped overnight with the man on the next quarter, a Belgium with a French wife. She is nice and speaks English too. He made a trip to the empty buildings where we plan to live and unloaded the things and started back to town to meet me Monday.

I got to Saskatoon Friday night and Mr. Lee met me at the station. Mrs. Lee went downtown with me Saturday afternoon and I went to the dentist, as I didn't know when I should ever have another opportunity. I left Saskatoon Sunday night, as I had to stay overnight in Denholm. The little country hotels in western towns are funny places, although the one at Denholm is better than lots of them. The train was supposed to leave for Hafford at eight o'clock the next morning but couldn't get through until the snowplow came down the line. They said there were drifts twelve feet high on the tracks. The train didn't get to Hafford until nearly two, as we were over four hours late leaving Denholm. You see I had a nice little wait. When I reached Hafford George wasn't at the station so I left my suitcase with the station agent and found out by then that George had unloaded the car and had gone out Saturday so I knew he would be in sometime. I went to the restaurant (they are mostly Chinese ones in these western towns) and had my dinner and then went back to the station and waited two hours before George got to town. There is no hotel in Hafford so we got a room at a Greek's house and spent the night there and left for the farm Tuesday morning.

It was a miserable day, cold and snowing a little. By the time we reached the Scotchman's place I was glad to go in. Mrs. Munro was a big, fat motherly person and she got us a nice hot dinner. I got nice and warm and we started out again. It is cold riding perched up on top of a load when the horses have to walk every step of the way. We came to several bad places where I thought sure the whole load was going over, but the sleigh righted itself each time. Before night it was snowing hard and the road was so bad that George thought we had better stop at the Post Office, twelve miles out of Hafford. A Frenchman who came into this country when his nearest town was sixty miles away ran it. So you see, twenty isn't so bad after all. We got to Mr. Poty's, our nearest neighbors at noon on Wednesday. In the afternoon we drove to the buildings where we plan to stay. It was an old log house and the doors and windows were all missing. There were two good rooms downstairs and one up and I love to have had so much room after living in one room, but it was full of cracks and rather breezy in this cold weather. We decided to move into the one room upstairs, as it would be warmer and besides our stovepipe was too short to use downstairs. Very few of the houses have brick chimneys. They are mostly small shacks and they run the stovepipe through the roof and out the side of the shack near the top. As we had no windows until someone went to town we nailed one of my narrow sheets over the window and it did very well. George made a slough door to lay over the top of the stairway but it was heavy and had to be moved every time anyone wanted to go down or come up.

We had no hen house and the hens get under the horses and they are loose in the barn, so George let them all out downstairs. I had quite a time persuading the hens that they couldn't roost on the stairs.

We moved in Thursday but I unpacked only the essentials. In fact we didn't have much else with us, as we had to bring the hens and pig and they took up so much room that we only brought the bedding, a few boxes, dishes and the trunks. All the rest were still on the loading platform at Hafford. But I unpacked just as little as possible, as there was absolutely no place to put anything.

The next day George and I drove over to the remains of our house and I decided we would be far more comfortable here than in the other old buildings. If we were going to fix a place so it was liveable, we might as well fix up our own place. I want my garden here and we would do so much more fixing the place up if we were here than if we had half to three-quarters of a mile to go.

Mr. Poty went to town Saturday and we sent for a window and Monday morning we packed some of the things and came over to our shack. About two thirds of the front had to be boarded up. George shovelled the snow out of the shack and I swept what ice and frozen mud I could out and then he ripped up the roof of the main building and used the boards to close in the front of our one room. As fast as he got the boards I pulled out all the old nails and got them ready to use again. He got the front boarded up and the window put in and then we set up the stove. While I got dinner George made the door.

The house is this shape made of logs.

The cracks between the logs are filled with mud and grass mixed and the mud has been white washed on the inside of the house so the wall is sort of a striped affair, rough logs and white wash. Nearly everyone here has a log house but I'd like my house plastered on the inside, as the stuff in the chinks keeps falling out. I spent part of an afternoon standing on a box stuffing pieces of an old blanket into the cracks between the logs with a knife and then I nailed tarpaper over the front that we boarded up to keep the little breezes out.

George got me settled and cut some wood and got some hay and then had to go to town, as most of our household goods – chairs, bedstead, etc., were still on the station platform and the cow and calf were in the livery barn at Hafford. He left Wednesday morning and expected to be back Thursday night so I thought I would have to stay alone here only one night. There isn't a house in sight and I guess it must be nearly a mile to Poty's. I kept the dog home for company. George got to town Wednesday night but one of the horses was taken sick and he could hardly get her unharnessed before she lay down. She had weird colic and George had to buy a bottle of liniment and a blanket to cover her up with and it was ten that night before he dared leave her, so he didn't dare start back with her the next morning, as he planned. He tried to hire a horse so Clyde wouldn't have to pull but couldn't, so finally started home about four and stopped at the Scotchman's overnight and got here late Friday afternoon. He couldn't hurry Clyde and besides the cow couldn't walk fast through the snow. So you see I was alone three days and two nights. The other horse, colt, pig and hens were all in the barn at the other place so it made a long trip for me to feed them. I was glad to see my husband back once more.

I have had two schools offered to me since I arrived. I decided I might as well teach this year as long as we had no family or any prospects of any and the hundred a month helps out a lot, especially as we probably can't get anymore than grain enough for the stock this summer and land ready for crops next year. School begins tomorrow so I shall be busy for a while.

The mail is brought out once a week so we have only two miles to go for it. George got his candy and tie yesterday, on his birthday. It is nice of you to remember him. I enjoyed the candy very much. We have had a lazy day today, the first one for sometime. We have spent the day reading and eating candy. George was pleased with the tie; it is a very pretty one.

I got my story back last week and got very good on it. He wrote my work was promising. I shall be so busy teaching and doing housework, gardening and tending to my children that I won't have so much time to spend on my lessons, but I want to keep them up so I will have to squeeze in a little time somewhere.

George has gone out to explore the place. It is such dreadful walking I wouldn't go. We walked up from the barn last night and I went through the snow over my knees and stumbled all over the trail and sat down several times. I told George I walked as if I was drunk but I wasn't. I thought of you with your stiff legs coming home from the entertainment and I don't believe you had any worse time than I did last night.

This is quite a lengthy letter and I must stop. Write whenever you can, as I love to hear from you.

Give my love to everyone and keep a lot for yourself.

Nell

Hafford, Sask., Lorenzo P.O.
April 2, 1922

Dear Reta,

Your letter came yesterday and I think I'll answer it before it gets put away and I start some of the many tasks ahead of me. The last month has been such a strenuous one that you won't wonder I haven't written many letters.

We had a week of lovely spring like weather early in March and the snow around Strongfield was melting fast so we thought we had better move while the snow was still on the ground. It is almost impossible to haul a load over the roads through mud. We wanted time to get settled and the machinery put together again before it was time to work the land.

George had a chance to get rid of the place in Strongfield entirely so there were legal matters to attend to and then he made a trip to Bladworth to see about getting a freight car. It was on Saturday and he found if he didn't go out on the freight Tuesday noon he couldn't go for another week. We spent all day Sunday packing and got up at four Monday morning. Olie, Shorty, Nelson and George each took a load to Bladworth -- seventeen miles away, and George took a load of machinery the Saturday before.

I went to Theobalds on Monday and stayed until Friday. I had a very pleasant little visit with them. Friday Mr. Theobald took me to Bladworth and I went to Saskatoon. Mr. Lee met me at the station and I stayed until Sunday night with them. I had to stop overnight in Denholm, as the train for Hafford left there early Monday morning.

George got to Hafford on Thursday and they were having one of the worst storms of the winter. It took him all day Friday to unload the car and it was Saturday noon before he could start for the farm. It was twenty miles over drifted roads. The trail had drifted in during the snow storm so George could hardly see the old road and if the horses got a little to the side they went into the drifts up to their stomachs and had to be shovelled out. George met a Scotchman on the road who insisted on his coming in for a cup of tea. They got him a regular meal and then he drove on but went only eight or ten miles in all before dark. He stayed overnight with a married couple that had a one room shack but took him in and hung a blanket up in the middle. They fell in love with my cat and wanted her and finally they persuaded George to leave her there until I came and we got settled. She is still there. He started on Sunday morning and was eight hours going ten miles. In several places he had to go ahead and shovel before the horses could get through and the load upset twice.

It was night before he finally reached here. He stopped overnight with the man on the next quarter and Monday morning went to the vacant buildings on the quarter next to ours, as we planned to stay there until we could get our house fixed. He unloaded the things and started right back to town for me. I was supposed to leave Denholm at 8:20 but there was so much snow on the track that the train waited there until twelve for the snowplow to come from Prince Albert and clear the track. We were over four hours late when we reached Hafford and then I had to wait over two hours for George. It was so late that we decided not to start for the farm until the next day. There is no hotel in Hafford so we hired a room at a Greek's house. The next morning was miserable -- cold and sleeting. George didn't take a very big load as the road was so bad but among other things we had the pig. Several times the sleigh would be nearly on its side and I'd hang on for dear life but it always righted itself. It was cold riding perched up on top of the load and I was glad to stop at the Scotchman's. They made George promise he would bring me in. Mrs. Munroe is a big fat motherly person with grey hair. She got us a nice hot dinner and I got nice and warm before we started again. It snowed hard all afternoon and the horses were so tired pulling that we decided to stop at Alberton over night. Alberton is really a small store and post office in a house.

The next day we finished our trip and got to Mr. Poty's at noon. We stayed there to dinner and then George took me up to the buildings we had planned to stay in. The house was made of logs and as no one had lived in it for six years it was minus doors and windows and the stuffing in the chinks between the logs had fallen out in several places. There was so much snow we didn't think we could get over to our place, as we'd have to break a trail and the whole front of our house was gone, so there was just the one room. We decided to move in the one room up stairs, as our stovepipe wouldn't reach the roof from down stairs. Very few of the houses have a brick chimney but people run the stovepipe through the roof or out the side of the shack near the top. It was a dreadful dirty place as there were no doors—and as the horses, rabbits, etc., had wandered about downstairs.

We had no window so nailed a bed sheet over the window and it did very well. George made a rough door to lay over the opening in the stairs but it was heavy and had to be moved every time anyone wanted to go up or down stairs. I didn't unpack anymore than I had to, as there was absolutely no place to put anything. George had to cut wood and got feed for the horses and I bundled up and went with him, as it was warmer than trying to keep warm at home.

The next day we ploughed our way across the field to our place. George had to shovel one place before the horses could get through. They would get in up to their stomachs and struggle awhile -- sometimes they got out themselves and sometimes George would have to get out and shovel them out, as they would lie right down in the snow.

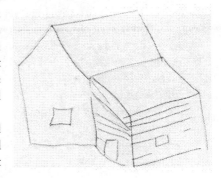

This is the way our house looked originally but someone removed the front wall and the front half of the roof so the rest collapsed in a heap in front of the lean-to. We decided we would be more comfortable in our one little room and we had better fix up our own place, as I don't propose to dig out roots and bush on land we can't use next year. I thought we'd do lots more if we were on our own place than we would if we had to go over half a mile to do it. Our one room is 12 x 12 and so rather crowded but George and I packed up a few things on Monday morning and went to the place. George tore the remaining part of the fallen roof apart for boards and I pulled out the old nails and got them ready to use again. We boarded up the front, as about two thirds of the front where it joined the main house was open. We shovelled out the snow and George put in a window one of our neighbors brought from town for us and I helped George set up the stove. While I got dinner he made a door and we stayed there that night.

The next morning I got down on my knees with a hammer and pounded the ice and frozen mud off of the floor.

George had to go to town, as we left a lot of our things on the station platform and we needed the bed, table, etc. We slept on the floor and ate off an old box and used my trunk for a seat when we found time to sit down.

He left Wednesday morning and planned to be home Thursday night. I thought I should be alone only one night but old Clyde was taken sick with wind colic when she reached town and George could hardly get her unharnessed before she laid down. He bought a bottle of liniment and a blanket to cover her and it was ten that night before she got easy. He didn't leave town until the next afternoon, as he didn't dare have her pull hard. He hated to start then with her but he couldn't hire another horse so divided the trip and stayed over night with the Munroes and got home Friday night as he had to go slow on account of Clyde and the cow. She was following behind. So you see, I had to stay alone for three days and two nights. The pig, hens, one horse and colt were still in the barn on the other quarter so it made quite a walk for me to do the chores while George was gone. You bet I was glad to see him back once more. He plans to get out some logs as soon as he can build a barn, as it is hard to have the animals so far away.

There will be a railroad in here eventually, as the plans for one have already been approved. The land is good and there is still a lot of government lands so we will go in for more cattle and let them run.

Did I write you I had been taking a course in Short Story Writing this winter from the Homes Correspondence School in Springfield, Massachusetts? There sure is a lot of work to it. It would have been lots easier for me if I had taken it while I had access to a library but here I can't look up any of the references given or read any of the suggested reading. The highest they ever rank is 99, which means extraordinarily good. 98 means exceptionally good, 97 - 96 mean very good and 95 is good. Down to 90 is satisfactory work. I have got from 96 to 99 on all of my lessons and the last one, a story of 3000 words, was very good and he wrote at the end that my work was promising and enclosed a list of names and addresses of

Women's magazines. George wants me to send it to one of them but I haven't had time to make the changes he suggested and copy it over.

They offered me teaching positions at two schools here the week we landed so I decided to take the one nearest home, as the money would help us out a lot, as we can't possibly raise more grain than feed for the stock this summer. School began yesterday with six and today is stormy so there are only five so my duties aren't very strenuous yet. But of course I'm gone all day and I have to get up pretty early. I've had a lazy winter so ought not to mind. It is time to begin school again. I began this letter on Sunday and am finishing it during my noon hour.

I guess I've written you all of the news. Let Mother Allen read this, as I don't know when I'll get time to write her. I shall be so glad when this snow goes and we can see the ground once more. It is pretty here and I think I shall like it a lot.

Love to all, Nell.

Lorenzo, Sask.
May 12, 1922

Dear Auntie Marie,

If I don't get a letter to you written today I can't send it for another week so I think I'll make an attempt.

I am at school but none of the children have yet appeared, as the wind is howling and we are having a driving snowstorm. I never should have been here but I stayed at school all night. You see we are over three miles from school. George is plowing and trying to get in enough oats for feed and then wants to get as much land ready for crop next year as he can. We have only three horses this year so George needs them all. I find six miles a day rather a long walk with other work to do. If I didn't have a hearty meal to get when I got home and a lot of dishes to wash, I wouldn't mind the walk. And then I want to work in the garden and clean up the yard so I work until nearly ten every night. George said I had better stay at school part of the week, as it would be easier for me. The last teacher lived at school; they quite often do in this country. There is a new Perfection Oil stove in the school and lunch dishes, dishpan, etc., so I get along nicely and I have time to work on my lessons. I stayed last Monday and the wind howled and the building cracked and you bet I wished I had George. Tuesday morning it was simply pouring. I didn't expect anyone to come to school but five appeared looking like drowned rats and I spent most of the morning drying their clothes. They went barefoot all day while I was drying their shoes and stockings. Wednesday night I walked home. I was some glad to see George and he was equally glad to see me. I don't like to leave him very long at a time for he doesn't cook right and just eats bread and tea or the quickest thing he can get with the fewest dishes.

I want to thank you for the birthday present.

Last Saturday was a beautiful day and I had a big washing to do but I thought as long as it was my birthday I'd celebrate. We agreed to buy a cow and yearling off some people that live seventeen miles from us, so went for her Saturday. We knew she would have to come slowly so took our blankets and I packed bacon and eggs, potatoes, etc. and we planned to come part way with her and camp over night. We met the postmaster going to Alberton and he said if we would stop at Alberton he would give us our mail there. Of course I was anxious to get a birthday present so we went to the office there and got our mail before it was put into the Lorenzo sack. The candy was very nice with our lunch and we jogged along in the buggy and ate candy all afternoon. I was so busy reading my letter aloud that we didn't notice where we were going and made a wrong turn so we didn't come out onto the main road for a long time. We found a nice spot and George built a fire and I cooked bacon and eggs while he made the tea. We had gone so far out of our way that we hated to go back and George said we would come to the main road some time as long as we kept going in the right direction. All of a sudden our road ran into a big slough. It was a regular pond and looked quite deep to me. George drove through but the water came way to the floor of the buggy. I don't like to ride through such places.

We reached Monroe's about four but they decided they wouldn't sell the cow as she had a calf the day before and they thought it wouldn't cost much to keep her through the summer, as they had plenty of good pasture. I was sorry we made the trip for nothing, as George had so much he wanted to do at home, but we had a nice little picnic together.

The sun is trying to come out but it is still snowing. I expect the snow will go fast as soon as the sun shines and it is warm out, even the wind is a warm wind.

You couldn't have sent me anything I needed more than I did a chemise. It is very pretty and most acceptable, but I'm afraid you spent too much on my birthday.

I didn't hear from my family but maybe I will this Saturday. George gave me a pair of white canvas shoes with rubber soles and heels. They are very comfortable and easy to walk in.

We plan to build a new house this summer and fall. We have picked out a nice spot near the road allowance. There isn't any road there now but the road will eventually run along the east line. There are trees on the east and west and big bushes on the north. It is a pretty spot with a nice view. We plan to build a log house- 14 by 16 with a room upstairs and then we can have a regular bedroom and a living room and kitchen downstairs. It will seem so good to have a little more room. Next year we hope to put up another piece and use this for the ell.

Helen Cushing writes she is coming to visit me next summer if she can save up the money enough before then. I'd love to see some of the people from home. I wish you would come out. It's a lovely country and I like the west. You know you have a standing invitation to come anytime. Give my love to all of your family and many thanks for my birthday presents.

Lots of love to you, Nell

Lorenzo, Sask.
July 28, 1922

Dear Reta,

I believe I owe you a letter but am not sure. Somehow my letter writing gets sadly neglected these days.

We are having nice summer weather but it is very dry and we need rain badly.

This had been a busy spring. You know what it is like to go on to a place that has been vacant for several years. We didn't have a barn or much of a house -- only one room 12 x 12, so it has been much like camping out. I haven't been able to unpack much as there is absolutely no place to put anything.

George broke twelve acres and put it into oats but it was slow work as there were so many bushes to cut and burn. He broke a little more after he got the crop in so we would have some land ready for crops next year. He plowed and harrowed the garden and I did all of the rest. The garden looks well but I was very late getting things planted. George needed all of the horses so I had to walk to school. Seven miles a day is quite a walk and then I had a hearty meal to get when I got home and dishes to do. It was usually seven thirty or eight before I could do a thing on the garden so I couldn't get more than two or three rows planted each night. We have had onions, beet greens, turnip greens, lettuce and green peas so far. There was a heavy frost the 12th of July that killed a lot of garden stuff. It touched one end of the potatoes and also the beans but they are growing again. Some people lost nearly all their garden.

We bought a black horse for me to drive to school. He is a good saddle horse but we haven't a saddle and it is hard to ride bare back. George came down to meet me one night while I was walking and I rode the horse home bare back but it makes me so sore I decided I'd walk until the buggy was mended. The wheels had to be re-set and the blacksmith took a whole month at it.

I have had quite a time getting any hens to set this year. One Galatian woman set a hen for me and I got nine chickens and I borrowed three hens from various people. One hen set for three days and left. Another one was so wild she took to the bushes whenever I took her off to feed her and I had quite a time with her for the first ten days. She didn't have a single chicken but sat on even after I took the eggs away. At last I put a board over the barrel and she patiently sat on top of the board for three days so I gave her some new eggs and she sat another three weeks.

She has seven little chickens now. I have just thirty chickens in all but have four hens still setting. I know it is awfully late but I'd like fifty chickens anyway.

Mr. and Mrs. Lee drove up Saturday from Saskatoon and stayed until Monday forenoon. We went for a little drive Sunday to show them the country and picked enough wild strawberries for dinner, supper and breakfast the next morning.

I had a letter from Shorty last Saturday saying that two young fellows there said they were coming up to see us the first of August and look for homesteads here. Shorty said he was coming about that time or sooner if he could get enough money before then and Nick planned to come with him. With one small room, I don't know where I shall ever put all of these men if they all arrive at once.

George is cutting logs for a house and we hope to have a snug log cabin before winter. He planned to begin digging the cellar today. We have picked out a lovely building spot near our east line. The road allowance is along the east side of the place. The remains of the old house are in the middle of the quarter so we have to go across the next farm to get to a road. There is no road on the east yet but there will be eventually, as I would rather have the buildings near the road. I'm anxious to get the house built now. It is quite a task to build a good log house and barn.

I suppose Marion visited you. I haven't heard from her for a long time. Dad wrote that he and Ida had been out to Cumberland to see her and the baby looked much like Rudy did when he was little. Emma and Smithy came the same day and took Dad and Ida back to Portland in the car. Dad wrote Em looked poorly and she wrote me she wasn't at all well and had been to the Doctors several times to get some tonic. I'm afraid she works too hard.

Well, I must begin school and move as my noon hour is up. Give my love to Mother Allen. I guess I owe her a letter too, but she knows I lead a busy life.

If you have any discarded dress patterns I'd like them. There might be something I could use and I haven't any patterns. I want to make over my wool dress and mother wrote she was going to send an old suit I could make into a dress for school.

Nell

Lorenzo, Sask.
Aug. 6, 1922

Dear Reta,

I was very glad to get your letter and the snapshots. The babies are very cunning. I wish I might have dropped in while Marion was at Jay (Maine) and saw you all, however Jay is a long way from here so I'm afraid it will be some time before I get that far. I'm sorry your eyes are troubling you. I don't know what I would do without my glasses.

George has gone to hunt for Clyde and the colt. They broke out of the pasture Friday and haven't come back yet. I was sleepy after dinner so thought I'd lie down. The bushes were wet so I didn't care about a long tramp with him. We have been having our first rain in about six weeks. I wish we might have had a little of the rain you didn't need. We got showers all the spring but it was pretty dry before the rain came. I was afraid my garden would dry up entirely. I was very late getting it planted, as George was using the horses and I had to walk to school and seven miles a day is quite a walk. By the time I got home I hated to get a hearty meal and by the time I got that done and the dishes for the day washed and maybe some cooking for the next day, I wasn't very keen about working the garden. George was busy all the time so left all the planting to me. I'd get a little piece raked and perhaps two or three rows planted before it was dark. You see it was new land that had never been plowed and I had a lot of roots to pull out. I guess it was a good thing I was so slow for lots of these people that had their gardens planted early had them killed by a heavy frost the 12th of July. It just touched the tops of the beans and they look as good as ever now. We have had lots of peas, onions, beet greens, small beets and carrots. The hens have discovered the garden and I'm having a dreadful time trying to keep them out of it. If I was home day times I could do it pretty well but I'm not and they pick the cabbages and shell the peas and eat the whole tops of the turnips. I caught the rooster and tied him out by the barn and some of the hens stayed with him and if I see a hen coming I chase her so they don't dare come very near the house.

They were awfully late setting this year. I borrowed two hens before mine began to set. I have sixty little chickens now and one hen still sitting. They are all Plymouth Rocks. I hate to have so many tiny chickens so late. I have to get up about five in order to get them all fed and watered before I go to school.

George has been cutting logs for a house. We found a pretty building spot near our east line. The old buildings were about in the middle of the quarter and we have to go across the next farm to get to a road. The road allowance is on the east side of our place. Of course there is no road there now but it won't be long to make a trail to the road a half-mile south. I would rather have the buildings near the road. We plan to put up a log cabin 14 x 16 and high enough so we can have a room upstairs. George will get out more logs this winter and we will have some lumber sawed and next year build a larger house and use this for the ell. It will be nice to have an upstairs so I can put some of the trunks and the bed up there. I've felt that I was sort of camping out ever since I came, as we haven't been able to unpack much, as there is no place to put anything.

Mr. and Mrs. Lee came up from Saskatoon in their auto about two weeks ago and stayed over Sunday with us. They have their auto fixed so the back of the front seat falls back and fills up the space between the two seats and makes a very good bed. They go on long trips and camp out on the way, sleeping in the auto. I was very glad they brought their bed with them. Shorty wrote that two young fellows at

Strongfield said they were coming up the first part of August. Shorty said he and Nick planned to come about the same time or sooner if they could get enough money so I'm looking for a crowd of bachelors any night when I get home from school. I'm sure I don't know where I'll ever put them at night.

I went strawberrying several times and got plenty for supper. There are gooseberries here and high bush cranberries, also blueberries, Saskatoon's and a sour cherry. There weren't any berries on the prairie. I planted some currant bushes this spring so next year I'll have currants. I miss fruit, as we never have anything but dried fruits.

George has got home and I must feed my little chickens and then get supper. I owe Mother Allen a letter. You read this to her and tell her I'll really try to write her a letter before long. We had a card from Mrs. Hill yesterday. Do you ever hear from her?

Love to all, Nell

Lorenzo, Sask.
August 1922

Dear Auntie Marie,

I believe I have owed you a letter for a long time and one likes to get mail when one is on a vacation. I don't know just when you will be visiting but this will probably reach you finally if I sent it home.

I had a letter from Reta last week and she said they had just arrived from the photographers and she had sent some pictures on to Marion but there was one extra one so she enclosed it. They planned to have more finished and send them to the relatives. The babies were very cunning and I wish I might have seen them together.

We are having warm weather. It has been very hot and dry but the nights are cool with heavy dews so that helps a lot.

My garden is doing well considering I was so slow getting it planted. It has been very dry and I don't see how anything could grow. Last week was the first rain for six or seven weeks and then we didn't get a real soaker. It was wet and drizzly for several days, but not a lot of rain, however it refreshed things a good bit.

I wanted to go to town and George thought he ought to cut hay last Saturday. Friday he broke the mower knife and Friday afternoon I drove to Alberton with him ten miles from here to get it fixed. The blacksmith was gone so we had over a twenty-mile drive for nothing. It rained Saturday, just a disagreeable drizzle so George couldn't have cut hay anyway if he hadn't broken the knife, as we couldn't drive away to town.

I began this over a week ago and hoped to get it mailed last week but it didn't get finished. Last Saturday we drove to town. We have to leave before six in the morning in order to get to the bank and do our business before noon. I had to get up at 4:30 in order to get my chickens fed and get breakfast before we left. It was a nice day and I didn't mind the drive much. It rained when we got about three miles from home on our way back but we didn't get very wet.

We are to have a school picnic tomorrow. The trustees gave fifteen dollars for it and I am supposed to put up a lunch for the whole school. There are twenty-eight children at school and probably some of them will bring their small sisters and brothers so I plan on thirty-six anyway. I shall have to get up early in the morning to make enough sandwiches for everyone. I made a big  fruitcake night before last and last night I fried enough doughnuts to fill my bread mixer and this morning I made a white cake before I came to school. We are going to have salmon, egg and jam sandwiches, cake and doughnuts, oranges, candy, peanuts and fruit punch. Then there will be $3.00 to be divided among them for prizes in their races. George is going to take the whole bunch in the hayrack up to a lake about three miles from here. I bet I'll be weary by tomorrow night.

I have a big supply of dirty clothes stored up, as I went to town last Saturday and it rained the Saturday before and water has been very scarce. Saturday is my washday but I believe the minister is to call Saturday or rather spend the day.

They have a young college chap in Hafford and this summer he has been holding a service every other Sunday in a school house six or eight miles from us. We have planned to go but George has been using the horses on weekdays. We didn't like to drive them Sunday and then the buggy was out of commission quite a while, as we had to have the wheels all reset and the blacksmith kept it over a month. Last week when I was in town this young chap rushed up to me and seemed quite delighted to see me. He said he was the English Church man and he had heard about me. He was planning to come out a day early this week and come up Saturday morning and spend the day with us, so I guess I won't get washing done this week either.

I have nearly sixty little chickens so they keep me busy. They all were late. I have a hen sitting in the bushes and she just hatched out last night and this morning. I hate to have so many late ones, as we have no hen house yet. I have to keep them in boxes and it is quite a job to keep them dry when it rains.

George has cut logs for the house and dug the cellar and hoped to get Mr. Dyck to help him begin the house today. We will just put up the ell this fall, as we have to build a barn and henhouse and there is a lot of work to get them up and mudded so they will be warm.

I surely thought I have written to Louisa since Christmas. I'll try to write to her soon and send my apologies for my neglect. I want to get this in the mail tonight and must stop now. Hope you have a nice vacation and get rested. I wish you could come out to see me. I'd love to have you.

Love to all the family, Nell

Lorenzo, Sask.
Sept. 12, 1922

Dear Reta and Mother Allen,

I wrote to Mother Allen a week ago and her letter came Sunday so I guess we must have mailed them about the same time so I'll write a joint letter this time. I was very glad to hear from you and pleased with the snapshots. I certainly would like to see my young nephew.

Our summer is about over. We have nice days but it is cool nights and mornings and the ground is white with frost nearly every morning now. I pulled the onions Saturday and we have quite a lot of them. I have some nice little white pickle onions but only a little vinegar at present so I'll have to wait until I can get to town. It is hard to get tomatoes or cucumbers here. I had a few small cucumbers that I picked when the first frost came, so will have a taste of cucumber pickles.

Mrs. Huard, a Galatian woman with a French husband, bought some green tomatoes the other day. She got eleven pounds for a dollar and she sold me half of them. I took my recipe for sliced tomato pickles but it called for half a bushel of tomatoes and she couldn't see how to divide the recipe. I don't believe she can read English anyway, so she asked me to take her tomatoes home and make her pickles with mine. I got hers made last night but didn't start mine, as it was nearly nine when I got her tomatoes and onions sliced and salted and I had dishes to do. I put up two jars of chicken last night. Three of my young roosters met with a peculiar accident. I have kept them in a little pen near the house and they run out in the day time but the hawks are so bad that they aren't safe until there is someone there to watch them so I shut them up in a big box George built to hold grain and only let them out after I get home from school. I can't seem to teach them to go to bed in the big box but they go back in the little pen every night and I have to put them to bed. I removed their box in the hopes they would go where I wanted them to but instead they all jumped into a little barrel in the yard and when I went out to shut them up I found them packed two deep in the barrel. Three of them had smothered. One's heart was still beating and we tried to resurrect him, but couldn't. They were still warm so George cut off their heads and we cleaned them and I canned them last evening. I'll make my pickles when I get home tonight.

I'd like a whole day to do a little canning but by the time I get the washing done and some cooking Saturdays I don't get much canning done.

Two weeks ago Saturday I went haying with George in the afternoon and last Saturday I went logging. Mother Allen thought probably I hadn't done that but I try most everything. George had ten big logs cut to be sawn into rough lumber for roof boards and the lower floor, etc. He dragged them out of the woods but they are hard to load on the wagon alone. He places two skids against the rear and front wheels of the wagon--fastens a fifty-foot chain to the front and one end to the rear on the farther side of the wagon and then brings the chain around the log. I back Kate up close to the wagon, fasten the chain to the single tree and then when everything is ready drive her and she pulls the log up the skids onto the wagon. It is lots easier for George as sometimes he has to leave the horse to tend to the log and she backs and lets the log down again. I have done it several times and it saves a lot of time if I tend to the horse and hitch and unhitch her while George tends to the logs. It isn't hard work as Kate does all the pulling.

I haven't had much milk this summer so couldn't give any to my chickens. We have just one cow and she will come in fresh in November so isn't giving a great deal and George has let the calf run most all summer so she got more milk than I did. We have a dandy calf though and she is as fat as can be. When I have a little milk I give it to the chickens and they like it a lot. I have lots of little chickens, as they were very late hatching out. Over half of them hatched the first of August and one lot the 16th of August so you see I have a lot of small chickens yet. I hate to have them so late especially as I haven't a very good place to put them.

People are threshing here now. Our oats are still some green but we are going to cut it and thresh the ripest and use the rest for green feed. The horses like oat bundles in the winter and the cow does well on them. We had a big stack of bundle feed last year.

I've had several spells writing this. I get most of my letters written during my noon hour or at recess. The trustees buy cocoa and sugar and the children take turns bringing milk so I make cocoa every noon. It takes a big water pail two-thirds full, as nearly every one drinks two cups full and sometime they have three so I plan to make about fifty cups every day.

We have been planning for two weeks to go to town. George thought perhaps we had better postpone our trip a week, as he wasn't quite ready for the lumber. The next week we planned to start Friday and camp out overnight but it rained and was so cold George didn't think it was fit for us to sleep out so we gave it up. I must drive to Alberton for some flour. There is a small store at a house ten miles from here. I lent the Dyck's enough flour for two bakings, as there are eight or nine in the family it makes quite a hole in my bag of flour. They haven't returned it so I have been out for over two weeks. I borrowed a little flour of Mrs. Huard and she had made me two loaves of bread. There aren't many people here to borrow from so I guess if we don't go to town I'll drive to Alberton. George thought he would have to stook the oats Saturday so I'll drive to Alberton after school tomorrow night. Twenty miles is quite a drive but I need flour. I asked the mailman to bring a sack last week but they didn't have any then at the store but probably will be now. I hate to take my Saturday to go, as I want to do some pickling. Thanks for the recipe. I can't use it this year, as I haven't the necessary ingredients but hope to try it next year.

There are lots of prairie chickens and partridges here and they are very tame. George shot several about two weeks ago. I baked three prairie chickens a week ago Saturday and on Sunday fried a partridge in butter, made a bread pudding with raisins in it and also a pan of baking powder biscuits. Then we took a quilt, the bed pillows, a magazine and Eaton's Catalogue and went picnicking in the woods back of our new house. We had a nice day and I enjoy spending my Sundays that way. George says it is the only way he can keep me from working.

I have had several spells at this letter and if I don't mail it on my way home from school I can't for another week. It is Grandma Rand's birthday the 27th of this month and I want to write her a little letter too. I planned to send Hamlin something but it is impossible for me to send anything until I can get to town. They don't have much there so I'll probably have to send to Eatons. You won't mind will you if it is a little late?

Love to all, Nellie

Lorenzo, Sask.
September 29, 1922

Dear Auntie Marie,

I have been thinking about you and suppose you are back home once more and your vacation is only a memory. The summer has just flown and I haven't done half I wanted to.

George is still working on the house but it seems to progress slowly. It is hard to build a good log cabin all alone. He has got it up higher than his head and it looks fine but he has to pull the logs up with a horse and it is hard to tend to the horse and the logs at the same time. I went with him twice to the woods and drove the horse while he was loading logs to be sawn into lumber. Mr. Poty will probably saw sometime this next week and then we can get the roof on and the floors in. I hoped to have a house before this but there are so many things to be done that George could only work on the house at odd times.

A week ago Saturday, I drove to Alberton for a sack of flour. It is about ten or twelve miles from here. There is a post office there and a small store. I wanted to go after school Friday, but it was cold and I knew it would be dark by the time I had driven twenty miles. Mrs. Huard, the postmaster's wife, said she would go with me if I'd go Saturday morning so I went home from school and did my washing and went Saturday. We had to bring back the mail. There wasn't much to take down but I guess everyone had sent to Eaton's for merchandise of some sort and there was an enormous sack full of bundles besides the sack of letters and papers and I had a sack of flour, coal oil, vinegar, besides various other small things and the buggy was just about full. It was two when we got back to Huard's and I went in to have a cup of tea and get my mail. I wanted some butter but everyone came for their mail and Mr. Huard went threshing so I had to wait until three o'clock. I had about two a half miles further to go so it was nearly four by the time I got the horse unharnessed and fed, as George was away threshing. I started some pickles Friday night and just got them on and my fire built when I went to the garden for a cabbage and discovered nine horses in our oats. They were knocking over the stooks and tearing open the bundles, so I started after them. I chased them all over the field and as fast as I'd get part of them off, the rest would come back. I decided the one thing to do was to get on horse back and round them up so I went to the barn and got on Fox. I'm not an expert rider but I got along all right until Fox began to go on a merry gallop. I was riding bareback so there wasn't anything to hold on to and I fell off. I hit the back of my head also the end of my backbone, although I don't see how I could hit both places at once. It hurt for the time being but I have recovered. I decided, if I couldn't ride horseback on a gallop, the buggy was the next best thing but riding up and down on a rough field in a rickety buggy after a bunch of horses isn't much fun. I finally went for Mr. Poty and he happened to be at home so he came to my assistance. It was after nine before George got home and we talked until after ten. The whole bunch of horses were back at eleven, so he had to dress and he chased them several miles east so it was after one before he got home. He sat up and read until two and at four they were back so he went out again and chased them until six. I got up then and we decided that the only thing to do was to haul all of the grain from the lower end of the field up to the upper end and put up a fence. We thought it would be quicker to move the grain than try to fence the whole field, as we hadn't much wire.

It didn't look like a very interesting way to spend Sunday but we had to save what little grain we had. George went to do the chores and the calf caught his chain around George's ankle and then ran. She dragged him a long way before he could get his leg out of the chain. When he got back to the house he was quite lame and his overalls were torn the whole length of one leg and he was decidedly black and blue in spots. Nevertheless we began to haul the oat bundles. I drove the rack and George pitched them off. The horses kept coming back but George was lame. He couldn't run much so I kept chasing them away. I discovered they were very much afraid of an umbrella so I used that and the whip but by night my legs were so weary I could hardly make them go. About six George got on Fox and chased them four or five miles north into the woods and I finished unloading the rack and unharnessed the horses. Monday morning I was so lame from tumbling off Fox, running, and throwing heavy oat bundles from the rack, that I felt quite as old as Methusala. It was an effort for me to move but I got up and went to school and I recovered in a few days.

You see this is open range here and anyone can turn their stock loose. You can't do anything if they get into your grain unless you have it fenced with three wires and the poles just so many feet apart. We have a fence on the north, south and west but 160 acres is quite a space to fence and we haven't the fence on the east yet. I hope we will get it up next spring and then we won't be troubled with other people's animals.

I want to go to town but George is busy and it is such a long trip that he hates to take the time to go. It is hard to do it in a day if one has a load to bring back. The weather is getting chilly now, especially the mornings and evenings.

I have had several spells at this letter. I believe I began it last Friday and it is now Wednesday noon.

It is a question, what I can make for Christmas this year. I looked my things over and found a linen centerpiece and a bureau scarf. I had never embroidered so sent to Eaton's for some embroidery floss and began the centerpiece last night. I guess I'll have to do all my shopping by mail, as the stores in Hafford are very poor and the prices are outrageous.

Some of the people here are very poor and I don't see how they ever manage. A man came to school this week and said when it got a little colder he would have to keep the children at home as they didn't have clothes to wear and he couldn't buy any. Some of them come with just patched overalls and barefooted -- I should think they would freeze. Mabel Windell sent me two packages of discarded clothing but they were mostly things for a very small boy so I divided them between two families and they were very grateful. I have written to the Red Cross to see if I can get some clothes for some of these children. If you have any discarded clothing in your big family it surely would do a lot of good here. I have several boys at school larger than I and two larger girls. Anything in underwear no matter how worn, shoes or outside clothing would be acceptable, as all of the women can mend and make things over, they simply don't have anything to do it with. If you find anything it had better come by freight, as they will take only four pounds by mail. Mail comes to Lorenzo but freight or express has to be sent to Hafford.

I have lots of mending to do but sometimes don't seem to get it done. I have been longing for a good rainy day so I could stay at home and do some of the many things I wanted to, but we don't seem to have any stormy weather. I didn't get nearly as much canning done this summer as I did last.

There is a lot of game here. We have had quite a number of partridges and prairie chickens. They are so tame that they come down and eat with the hens. We had a nice little rabbit fried tonight. The dog often kills a muskrat right in the dooryard. He catches lots of small animals but he won't eat them. He prefers bread and fried potatoes. A hawk killed one of my chickens and George scared him away so he dropped the chicken. George cut it up for Jimps and he wouldn't eat it. Most dogs are crazy for meat.

I began this letter a week ago last Friday and now it is Monday so you see ten days have gone by. I planned to mail it Saturday but left it at the school Wednesday and then was sick Thursday and Friday so I didn't come to school. I don't know whether it was my liver or a spell of indigestion, but I couldn't keep anything on my stomach and I didn't want to do anything but be perfectly still.

We had our first snowstorm Thursday. The ground was white when we woke up. It snowed a good part of the day on Thursday and was cold, wet and cloudy on Friday. I wanted to go to school, as I felt better but George made me stay in, as he was afraid I would get cold. Saturday was a lovely warm sunshiny day and the snow melted fast so it is dry again. The snow was a good thing, as we have been having dreadful forest fires here. There was a big fire near the school two weeks ago and it looked so bad at noon that I sent all of the boys over to help fight it. They came back at recess and Hamilton went away again to get a can of drinking water for the men at the fire. The youngsters said George was there so I did the chores, as I didn't know when he would be home but he got home about eight that night. There was such a big fire east of us that we slept on our haystack one night, as we didn't know just how far away it was. The next day George plowed a fireguard around the stacks.

George is helping Mr. Poty saw lumber today. He took the logs down some time ago but Mr. Poty wanted to get his grain in first. It takes a long time to build a house when you have to go to the woods and cut down the logs and haul them. He has the logs up but it was slow work, as they are so heavy to handle alone— especially when the house begins to get above our heads. As soon as we get some boards and the rafters sawed out Mr. Dyck will help him put on the roof. George thought we might be in it in a couple of weeks but the way things have gone I don't expect to be in it before the last of the month. We have been planning for nearly two months to go to town but it has been busy every week or it has been cold so we haven't gone. I told George yesterday he could go without me someday this week, as it is so cold. I don't enjoy driving forty-five miles on a bouncy wagon. He has to take the wagon to bring back the lumber, doors and windows, etc., as we sent to Saskatoon for them, so it means a slow trip home. He will probably take two days for the trip and I would rather stay at home. I'm glad I'm not afraid to stay alone at night.

Your letter came Saturday and we were glad to hear from you all. It seemed quite awhile since I had heard from you.

I wish you could have some of the dry wood that is just rotting on the ground here. We have twenty miles of wood north of us. Three fires have been through some of the woods and killed lots of the trees and eventually they fall down. We have all the fuel we can use by simply going after it. We surely can keep warm at no expense but the effort of chopping wood and George does that.

I wish you could come out to visit me. You had better give up taking boarders and come and live with us in our little log house. We don't have much money but we have plenty to eat and clothes don't cost much here, as people don't dress as they do in the city. You know I'd love to have you, but I don't suppose you ever will give up your boarding house.

My noon hour is up so I must stop. Give my love to all of your big family.

Lots of love to you, Nellie

Lorenzo, Sask.
November 22, 1922

Dear Auntie Marie,

Your letter came last Saturday and you may be sure we were glad to get your letter and hear about all of the family. A whole week has gone and the mail goes out tomorrow morning, so I must mail this on my way home tonight or I can't send it for a week. We have had a lovely fall and winter so far. We have had five snow flurries but the snow stayed only a day or two each time and we have had lovely sunshiny weather. I guess it is well, for our house isn't finished yet. I'm really quite proud of it, as George did a real good job on it. He had never built a log house before and he hasn't hardly any tools to work with. It is hard to get a log house even, as the logs are big on one end and small on the other. He didn't have a level so put it up by eye and when he got ready for the roof I borrowed a spirit level and he had to raise one corner less than an inch. He said he guessed it was an accident and he never could do it again. He is putting in the windows and doors and I guess tomorrow we will mud it. Lots of people here put up willow poles on the inside and plaster with mud as we plaster on laths but it cracks and drops off and they are always patching up their houses. We are just going to mud the cracks between the logs now, as the mud freezes and it is too late to make a smooth wall. Next summer when it is warm and we get a little more money we hope to put on real laths and have a good plastered wall. I'm not at all crazy over these mud walls. You don't know how nice it seems to have a little more room and know that the house belongs to you.

You don't realize how much there is to do on a place that has no buildings on it and nothing done. George can only work on the house when he has nothing else to do but we are near enough to the woods so we can get plenty lumber for buildings at very little expense by going after it. It costs about $8.00 a thousand to get it sawed. In time we will get some good, comfortable buildings. When I see what people who have been here ten and twelve years have done, I think we have done a lot for the time we have been here.

I think, Auntie, you had better give up your boarding house and come out and live with me.

Everything is so high in the city and your expenses are so large you don't have anything left for yourself and you work hard all of the time. We don't have much money here but we don't have much chance to spend it either. We get a good living from the farm and things will go much better in a year or two as we are getting some stock together. George didn't have any stock when we were married. Now we have four horses and a colt a year and a half old and hope to have two colts and a heifer and three pigs and about forty hens and pullets. We plan to kill a pig soon. There are lots of prairie chickens, partridges, rabbits and some deer and moose here, so we have plenty of meat. With butter, eggs and cream and all the vegetables we need, we get a good living from the farm. I shall probably teach next year, as we have had quite a few expenses this first year and no crop to sell, as we kept all of the oats for the horses. Then there were three years back taxes on the place so we had quite a tax bill to settle and George's insurance, etc. So we find my salary very useful. I want to get cows enough so we can ship a can or two of cream a week and have enough hens and turkeys to make it pay and then just stay home and take care of them.

I think you better sell out and come out with me. You won't need much money here and your company is worth more than your board. I'll feed you cream on your cereal and lots of nice fresh eggs and you needn't get up until eight, or after all winter. You'll have lots of time to read and George reads aloud a lot so you still hear the story. In the summer we could jog over the country behind Kate or Fox and you can even have some chickens of your own and go into the poultry business for pin money. Now doesn't that sound interesting to you? You know we'd love to have you with us.

Thank you so much for the box. I'll send you some money to pay for sending it. The dress Flora sent is worth the cost of sending the box. I really didn't need one this winter but didn't feel I could buy one. I know lots of people who will be very glad of the things and what I can't use I'll give away. I won't get my check until next week and am a little short of money now but will send it next week. If you haven't sent the box you might wait till I send you the money, as I know you have a great many demands on yours.

If you have already sent it, I will refund the charges for sending it.

I must begin school once more. I thought school would close December 1st but we are having such lovely weather there is talk of keeping open until Xmas. Give my love to all of your family and thank everyone for the old clothes they donated. I'll see that they are made good use of.

Lots of love to you, Nell

Lorenzo, Sask.
Jan. 4, 1923

Dear Auntie Marie,

Tomorrow is mail day once more and I must write to you before another week flies by. Thank you so much for the things you sent us. The box arrived all right in time for Xmas and you couldn't send me anything I needed more. In fact, I didn't have anything but summer nighties which are rather chilly this time of year so have been wearing one of George's that was small in the neck for him. He was very much pleased with his ties. We received the box of clothing a few days after Christmas and you may be sure we're pleased. There were quite a few things we could use so kept everything we wanted and have given away part of the other things. I have several bundles ready to give to other families. There was a house about six miles from here burned down just before Xmas and the people lost everything except the clothes they had on so we are going to send them some of the things. It was awfully good of you to send such a big box. I feel I ought to pay the expenses though. There was no mark on the box in town for us. I do not know how much the express was but I'll gladly pay it if you'll let me know. Flora's dress fits me and I kept the little brown dress. I have fixed the belt and nicely darned two or three little holes so it looks very good. I can fix the pink dress for summer. It was very kind of you all to send the things and I wish you would thank everyone for me. I'd do it personally if I could.

I began this last evening but like most letters I have several tries before they are finished. George wants to mail these letters as the mail goes out in the morning and it is a good three miles to the post office. He always walks as he says it is so much warmer than riding and is anxious to get started so this will be a short letter. We finally got moved into the new house and I certainly felt as though we were pioneering in earnest. George had to set up the cook stove and as we didn't have stovepipe enough to put it where I wanted it, we had to put it right in the middle of the floor. I harnessed Kate and took the stone boat and hauled most of the furniture across the farm while George finished up the little things on the house that had to be done. It turned cold – twenty-eight below, but we both worked outside most of the time. I was actually warmer outside than in the house. We mudded the inside of the house after we moved in and it certainly was some job. The ground was frozen so George had to build a big fire and thaw out the hole before he could get out any dirt and then he had to melt ice for water so it took a long time to make the mud. It was cold to put on and the logs were rough and my hands got so sore I couldn't finish my Christmas presents. I began to embroider a bureau scarf for you but couldn't hold a needle, as my fingers were all cracked on the ends.

I didn't send Bessie or Grace a single thing. I intended to make them something but couldn't and it is impossible to buy anything here unless one sends to some mail order house and that takes about three weeks, so I didn't send even a post card. It is hard to pick things out by just looking at a catalogue.

George has been working on the inside of the house ever since we moved in and is gradually getting the cracks stopped up but it was some cold at first. In the morning the top of the bed quilts would be frozen stiff where we had breathed on them and my hair would be just covered with white frost. I never was so hungry in all my life and George said I ate like a young lumberjack. I had sent for our winter supply of groceries and they were at the station in Hafford but George didn't want to make the trip with only one horse. The other three and the colt went away over a month ago and we haven't found them yet. We were nearly out of groceries and for a week we lived on potatoes, bear meat and biscuits made with just soda, as we were out of baking powder and cream of tarter. We had black tea with no sugar or milk but I was so hungry I didn't mind.

Did I write you that we expected to have a fresh cow the last of November but instead we have a dry cow? It is quite a calamity, as we have just the one cow and a year old heifer. I do not want to be without milk all summer, as I'm too fond of cereal and cream for breakfast so I guess we'll have to buy a cow. I've got my groceries from town and we are gradually getting settled so I begin to feel as if we were living once more.

I was ever so pleased with the box Flora and the others sent and I couldn't get all of those things here. I'll write them a letter this week and mail it next Saturday.

My husband is patiently waiting so I'll stop. Hope you had a nice Xmas. I want to hear all about it.

Thank you so much for all you did for us this year. We both send love to you. Please remember me to the members of your big family and tell Flora to expect a letter soon.

Lovingly, Nell

Strongfield, Sask.
Jan. 6, 1923

Dear Reta and Ray,

The little card arrived today and I had to actually read it twice before I could get it through my thick head that I had a new nephew and then I couldn't get over the surprise. In fact, I haven't fully recovered yet. Mother Allen never mentioned it when she wrote lately. You and Carlton can celebrate your birthdays together. I want to make him something but will have to send to Eaton's for some cloth. It will take me about three weeks to get it and then I'll have to make it. How long do you make baby dresses? I haven't the faintest idea how long they should be. We received our Christmas box all right, many thanks. The apron was very pretty. How did you find time to make it? I have such a strenuous life that I hardly find time to mend my husband's socks and overalls to say nothing of doing any fancy work. I suppose if we ever get settled, get fixed financially so I feel I can stop teaching and stay at home, I'll find more time to do fancy work.

School closed November 30th. I planned to play games in the afternoon and let the children out early but the Inspector arrived at noon and spent the afternoon, so I had to have whatever classes he asked for.

We moved the 7th of December and I certainly felt as if I were pioneering in earnest. The house wasn't completed but we thought it could not be much colder than the old shack. George set up the stove. We bought a lot of extra stovepipe but then didn't have enough so George had to set the stove right in the middle of the floor and run the pipe straight up to the roof. He had the door to put in and the lock and knob to put in and that took him sometime, as he didn't have any tools. George got a stone boat and did most of the moving; of course it was only a half-mile across the place. I got all the small things, boxes and trunks moved and then George brought over the bed and chiffonier. Believe me, it was chilly for a few days. George had the outside mudded but the inside walls hadn't been mudded so there were lots of cracks, the logs were green and cold and the upper floor hadn't been laid so it was open way up to the roof – quite a space to heat with one small cook stove. It was so cold some mornings that we sat in front of the oven and put our breakfast on a baseboard, which he held, across our knees. George mixed mud but it was a terrible job. The ground was frozen so hard that he had to build a fire in the hole and thaw it out before he could get any dirt and then chip ice and melt it for water. The mud was cold and the logs were rough and my hands hurt so from mudding the inside walls. Then my fingers cracked on the ends so I couldn't hold a needle. It is never satisfactory to mud when it is so cold, as it freezes before it dries. The walls were wet for over two weeks. They would freeze over night and be nearly all day thawing out and then freeze again and the mud kept dropping off in little places. Next summer we are going to mud the house good both inside and out and then put plaster on the wallboards. They use that here in the west a great deal.

George has laid the upstairs floor and fixed the ends upstairs with tarpaper and building paper and put paper all around the sides so we have a nice room upstairs and it is warm now. We have set up a little stove so it is comfortable in the evening and warm in the morning. I always hated to dress in the cold.

I stayed out of doors a lot when we first moved, as George was working on the house and had the door open a lot bringing in the lumber and the house was cold anyway. One day I went over to the old shack and fixed a place for my hens. We hoped to get a good hen house built before this, but you can't realize how long it takes to get buildings up where you have to cut the logs and haul them and do all the work, besides doing the regular farm work. The old main house had been torn down but there was a big cellar there, also a cellar under the lean to still standing. I just boarded up the front of the cellar under the lean to and covered it with tarpaper. Then I made a door with leather straps for hinges and put in a window. It took me all day but George said I did a very good job. It is as warm as toast and I hope the hens will begin to lay soon. It means a walk of half a mile every morning to feed them but it seems to be the only warm place we had. George has been feeding them this last week, as he had lumber and things from the old shack to bring back but some mornings I go.

Did I write you that a Russian fellow east of us killed a bear about a mile and a half to two miles north of our place? We had quite a big piece of bear meat. I liked it very much. It tasted something like beef. While we were moving I was starved all the time. George said I ate like a young lumberjack.

We had a nice Christmas and Santa was very good to us. We got some things a week before Christmas and have had some parcels every week since so our Christmas has lasted for four weeks. Thank you so much for the stockings and apron. George was pleased with the book. We began it as soon as it came and read it right through. Miss Burns, my first principal in Everett, sent me a book – "The Enchanted Valley". We have just finished that. I had three bath towels and wash clothes, three pairs of woollen stockings, a Bible calendar, a pair of pillow slips with crocheted edge, an aluminium kettle and cover, paring knife, aluminium salt and pepper shaker, coffee holder, (to go in coffee pot), measuring cups and a little pin that looks like two daisies. I think it is made of bone, it is very pretty. Fred and Grace sent it. I had a pair of mittens, three potholders, cook- book, handkerchief, small gift calendar and a box from Flora and Al, Dr. and Miss Pray. It was a square holly box and contained linen thread, both black and white in two sizes, cotton thread, sewing silk, ball twine, several spools red marking cotton, ric-rack braid, tape both black and white, all sizes of white pearl buttons on little cards, common white buttons, a bag of assorted pant and coat buttons, blanket pins, safety pins, common pins, (several papers of each) needles, (plain, darning and tape) an emery, tape measure, thimble and one of those dish cloths to scour pans. I was as tickled with it as a youngster with a toy. It is so hard to get these things here. Louisa sent me an apron and Mabel W. sent me a bunch of waxed flowers. They looked so real that I smelled them.

Did I write you that we expected to have a fresh cow over the last of November but instead have a dry cow? As she is the only cow we own it is quite a calamity. We have been without milk or butter since last September and you know how hard it is to cook without them. I told George I guessed we'd have to buy a cow even if we were very hard up this winter, as I hate to be so long without milk. We have a dandy year old heifer. We saved one of the sows last summer but she disappointed us. I bought two little pigs this fall. They were awfully cunning and doing very well when one suddenly died. We never knew why. The other one got very friendly and would come trotting up to the house for his breakfast. One morning he failed to appear and George found him dead by the barn. We think the cow butted him with her head. We needed meat so killed the big pig just before Christmas so at present we are "pigless".

I have been trying to do some washing. The well gave out before we moved so I couldn't get water enough to wash and then it got so cold and we moved that I had quite an accumulation of dirty clothes. I have had three spells at it so far but don't seem to make much impression on the pile, as it is late when we get up. Then I have to shovel snow and melt it and heat the water before I begin so it is nearly noon before I get ready to wash. I hope to finish it before spring if my courage holds out.

I have a lot of "thank you" letters to write so I mustn't write more now. I wish you would thank Mother Allen for the towel and washcloth. I was using the same towels I used when I began housekeeping in Everett and they were getting pretty worn so I used my Christmas bath towels as soon as they arrived. Tell her I'll write her a letter soon but this will have to do for you both this time.

I wished I could drop in and see you all but I guess I can't for some time. You'll have to come west.

Love to you all from us both, Nell

Lorenzo, Sask.
Feb. 8, 1923

Dear Auntie Marie,

It is almost mail day once more so I guess I had better write you a birthday letter, as I believe you will be having a birthday about the time you receive this.

We have been having two blizzardy days. It hasn't snowed much but the wind blows the snow about so it is disagreeable to be out. We had three dreadfully cold days last Friday, Saturday and Sunday. It was almost impossible to heat the downstairs of our house. The range is small and we really need a heater too but money was scarce this last fall so we thought we would try to do without it this winter. We have a small stove upstairs as I hate to go to bed or get up in the cold so we spend most of our time upstairs on those cold days. My husband is out cutting up his night's wood. It is nice to have plenty of fuel without any expense.

One night a great yapping awakened us. I thought it was a coyote near the buildings but in the morning we found a small, white puppy about three months old. He had long, white, fluffy hair with black patches on him and looked like a ball of cotton-batten. He had a little black tail with a white tip and one eye was dark brown, the other light blue. Jumps did not take at all kindly to him at first. He didn't like this idea of having another dog around. We didn't want to keep him but couldn't seem to find out who owned him so I fed him, as I couldn't drive him away in this cold weather and George wouldn't kill him. We had him over two weeks and then we drove over to the Russian's named Skalezub as George thought he might belong there. He did and they were delighted to have him back.

They asked us in so we went for a little while. The woman could not talk much English nor understand much but she managed to make me understand I could use her sewing machine whenever I wanted to. It is hard to talk to them but they seemed pleased to have you come. The men talk English much better than the women. I suppose they have more chances of getting out and learning English.

I had a letter from Marion last week. She has been hearing from Dana. He has at last got a government job in the Canal Zone and actually sent her a little money. I want to write to him this week. Did Marion ever send you any pictures of Donald? He is a dear little chap.

I was very much surprised to hear of the arrival of Carleton Richner Allen. I ought to make him something but can't get to town in this cold weather.

I started a bureau scarf for you for Xmas but my hands got so sore I put it away. I planned to finish it for your birthday but have been busy mending and making a quilt so it isn't quite done. I'm scalloping the edges now but can't get it done to send tomorrow. I won't be able to mail it until the 17th, so it will be a week late. It is impossible for me to buy anything, as we are so far from stores.

I'm sorry I didn't get it done in time but you know we will both think of you on the 18th and wish we could help you celebrate. I hope you will have a nice birthday and many of them. Give my love to all of your big family and write when you can.

Lots of love to you from both of us.
Nellie and George

Lorenzo, Sask.
Feb. 15, 1923

Dear Reta,

It is nearly mail day once more. If it is warm enough tomorrow I'll try to drive to the Post Office, but if it isn't George will mail it on Saturday when he goes after the mail so then it won't go out for another week. It is two or three weeks since your letter came. Don't worry; it is neither a novel nor a baby. I don't know what I would even do with a baby until we get more settled. Our house is all right in mild weather but it is some chilly when it gets twenty below zero. We have been having a cold spell and some days it was impossible to heat the downstairs. It wasn't at all comfortable so I did what little work as possible and stayed up stairs. We expect to be nice and warm next winter as log houses are very warm when well mudded. We will have to mud it again next summer as it froze this time before the mud dried and keeps cracking and letting in the breezes.

Hope you are feeling quite well by this time. I don't know what one would do in case of an emergency here; in fact, people here are born, live, die and are buried without any Dr. at all. There is a doctor in Hafford now but it takes quite a while to reach him as it is twelve miles to telephone and then it takes the Dr. quite awhile to drive twenty-three miles over country roads.

It is Aunt Marie's birthday the 18th of this month. I have been embroidering a bureau scarf for her but haven't it quite done. I hope to get it finished so I can send it this week as her birthday will be all over anyway before she gets it.

What do you feed your hens and how much? Mine have had wheat all winter and haven't laid a single egg since late in the fall. I have had about ten hens and pullets die this winter. They act kind of dumpy for a day or two and then simply die. I wish they would begin to lay as I'd like some eggs for cooking. We bought a cow this winter, as I hated to be without milk entirely. She isn't a very big milker but was running on the prairie when we bought her so only got straw when the herd came home at night. George has been feeding her grain and she has picked up since we got here and he seems to think she will give more milk after she has her second calf in August. She isn't three until this spring.

I have written several short stories this winter. It seems such a simple thing to do when one reads a story but it is quite different to sit down and write one. Then it takes so long to copy it nicely and get it ready to send. I sent one to the "Modern Priscillas", a story and an article to the "Western Home Monthly" and George thought out one and I wrote it and we sent it to the "Farm and Ranch Review." I have a child's story done which I am going to send to the "Youth's Companion" this week. Maybe they will all come back but Mr. Eisenuein says if you are sure they are the best you can do keep on sending them. I read an article by Bess Strester Aldrick in which she said that she had rejection slips enough to fill a bed tick. She had sold a story on its twenty-third trip out and she was five years hammering at the doors of the "American Magazine" before they accepted a story. So maybe there is hope for me if my courage holds out long enough. I had a letter from Marion recently. Dana wants her to come to Panama and I think she will go this spring or summer. His address is Balboa, Canal Zone, Box 135.

I had a nice letter from Eunice too. She said Han had been in the south on business for some time.

You know that Mother Allen once sent me some pieces for a quilt and I made a patchwork top before I took the flat in Everett but as I had enough bedding I never finished it. I bought some pretty chintz and finished it this winter and we have been glad of it some of these chilly nights. We had our dinner late today but I guess I had better get a little supper now. Give my love to Ray and mother Allen. I'll write to her next time.

Nell

Kleczkowski, Sask.
April 21, 1923

Dear Reta,

    I really don't know whether I owe you or Mother Allen the letter or both-- probably it is both. I can't remember whether I wrote you I was teaching or not. I had a school five and a half miles south east of us offered to me so I didn't take the Lorenzo School this year as they would pay me $120.00 a month here for ten months. Last year I got only a hundred a month and they kept school open only eight months. $120.00 looked good to me so I took this school instead. They have a cute little house right beside the school for the teacher to live in and they furnish the house free and also the fuel besides paying the $120.00. They seem to be a much more energetic bunch in this neighborhood than around Lorenzo. They keep the school building in good repair and it seems as if every week some one comes to fix something. They have cut up five cords of dry wood and piled it up beside my little house for me, cleaned the well, taken the banking from around the house, cleaned the barn and spread the manure around and this week a man plowed and harrowed a great big garden for the school children and one for me. When I look at the size of mine I guess I'll have to plant our potatoes here instead of at home to help fill up the garden. I have been staying here and find it much easier than I did last year travelling between seven and eight miles a day. In the spring I had to walk for over a month and I got pretty tired. I tried to do so much at home that I had to hustle every minute. The teacher's house was all furnished here so I had to bring only a few dishes, my bedding, sheets and quilts, etc. George comes down every Saturday and stays over Sunday with me and several times he has come down Wednesday night and gone home Thursday morning. I have been home just twice since the first of March. I do my cooking here and George takes home a big box of food every time he comes down. I guess he must be out looking for our horses, as he said Monday morning he would come Wednesday if he could and if not come Friday night and get me and take me home but it is now Saturday morning and he hasn't got here yet. He would probably be in by Saturday night and if he didn't get ours George could take his saddle and start out this week and then they wouldn't go over the same ground. As George hasn't come this week I imagine he is riding horseback over the country trying to find the horses. They were always loose on the prairie day times but came home every night. People here let their horses go every winter but George likes to keep them home. Ours were loose for nearly a month last fall and they stayed right around our place. We never dreamed they would suddenly leave until we discovered they had hiked. We will get the place fenced this summer but last year we didn't have the time or the money. It costs quite a lot to fence a hundred and sixty acres and then George had all he could do putting up the house besides his regular farm work.

Did I tell you I had a second hand sewing machine? It is sort of dilapidated in appearance but does very well for plain sewing. There are no attachments to it but I find it a big help to be able to stitch. I have used it a lot and am gradually getting both George's and my clothes fixed up. I had so little time last summer that things got pretty shabby. Auntie Marie sent me a big box of old clothing this winter and in it was a good blue serge of Horace's, and also a little brown jersey dress. I have been wearing them all winter and they make me good school dresses. There was a good pink linen jumper dress that I plan to fix for this summer.

Every year they had a Sports Day in Hafford and all the schools for miles around go in and march in the parade. They have games and races and give prizes, etc. Some schools dress up for the occasion and all the children dress alike, while others just wear anything they have. Last year the girls in this school all wore white dresses made bungalow apron style. They were trimmed around the neck and sleeves with a fancy blue stitch. The people in this neighborhood want the children dressed alike for the parade so I've got to have a bright idea how to dress them. I thought maybe you could think of some costume that would be cute and not too hard to make. Several of the older girls that are through school will help me make them. I thought they would be cute dressed as Mother Goose figures but it is hard to get patterns for such costumes nor the right material here and most of the people are farmers and not any too well off. I think a dress the children can wear afterward would be better. I could send away to get some blue and white checked gingham and make little pinafores and sunbonnets for the girls and the boys could wear overalls and white shirts. Can you think of anything better? If you can't, could you find a pattern of a sunbonnet or have you an old sunbonnet I could cut up for a pattern? Let me know if you can think of anything to help me out.

I must do my Saturday work and I have some washing to do besides. I wish you would tell me how big baby dresses are around the bottom. I want to make Carlton a dress this summer and I haven't the faintest idea how wide it should be around the bottom.

I suppose Ida wrote you that Flora and Al were married on St. Patrick's Day and Auntie has given up the boarding house and is keeping house for a wealthy bachelor. I'm so glad, as the boarding house was too hard for her. I must go to work.

Love to your family and Mother Allen, Nell.

Kleczkowski, Sask.
May 16, 1923

Dear Auntie Marie,

The box of candy came last Wednesday and I got your letter Saturday. Many thanks for the candy. I don't believe I have yet thanked you for George's box. He received it all right but I'm afraid I had more than my share of it. I was awfully candy hungry then, as I hadn't had any chocolate since my birthday last May. We had some hard (Christmas) candy at Christmas time but that isn't ever as satisfying to me as chocolates. George has a tooth that grumbles so I got more than my share of his and they sure tasted good. He was pleased with the handkerchiefs and he always needs them. I wanted to make him a birthday cake but had no butter, eggs or milk and couldn't get any. Also, I have no flavoring so decided it would be a pretty poor cake made of flour, sugar and water so he didn't have any cake. The family forgot when his birthday came and I couldn't get anywhere to buy him anything so if it hadn't been for you he'd have had a pretty slim birthday. We went to an auction sale the end of April and as they sold a pair of sleighs quite cheap and George needed them badly, I bought them. So I told him they would have to be his birthday present and a week later I managed to get enough ingredients to make a cake.

George had not managed to get me anything for my birthday so we went up to the woods and dug up thirty-three spruce trees and transplanted them on the north side of the house. Quite a novel idea, don't you think…in a few years I'll have a nice little spruce grove beside my house. Dad and Mother sent me a pretty lavender cotton dress with a white collar and cuffs and Ida sent an apron and two dishtowels. Ida and Mother sent me an envelope containing twenty birthday cards. I was all out and I can't buy them here. Do you remember the pink linen dress with the things you sent last winter? I have fixed it up and got enough off of the hem to make a belt so it makes me a very good dress.

I guess I wrote you that our horses went away last winter. George rode the country over. He went thirty and forty miles a day for nine days but could get no trace of them. Pushee was gone nearly a week finding his but got them. He looked for ours at the same time but could not find them. George needed horses for plowing and putting in the crop so we bought one last month, a dark brown mare, named Nancy, five years old and this month we bought a horse, dark sorrel, ten years old. He looks enough like Fred, the one that is gone, to be a twin brother. He has long legs and can travel some so I like him. Kate has been home all winter. We turn her loose and if she is a mile or two away and she sees George on the road or he climbs up on the haystack and hollers "Kate", she comes on a gallop. George said that when the crops begin to grow someone would probably run them into the pound. All of the pound keepers have to advertise all horses in the "Saskatchewan Gazette" for forty days. We have sent for the Gazette and I have sent notice to all of the post offices for quite a ways so we probably will get them finally.

I have been planting my garden. They plowed up a big piece of land at school and all of the children planted gardens. I have put in a lot but I guess by the size of the piece they plowed up they thought I wanted to feed a whole regiment. I went home Saturday or rather Friday night. It is only five and a half or six miles but I find it so much easier to stay here as long as they have a good place for me to live in. George had the garden ploughed so I helped him plant Saturday. We got it about half done. He wants to plant carrots and turnips to feed the cattle next winter, so I told him I would come home next week and help him plant horse carrots. The 24th of May is a holiday here, Queen Victoria's birthday, so I have invited the teacher from Lorenzo, the school I had last year, to come down Wednesday night and stay until Friday morning. I haven't met her yet. There is a young man teaching a school four miles from here and he called in for lunch so I invited him down for Wednesday night.

I am so glad Al and Flora are at last married. I want to send them something when I find out what they want. I believe Ida wrote me that Louisa and Bill had gone to Everett. Where are they living? It makes it nice for you to have your family settled and to have them near you. I'm awfully glad you have such a nice place. I used to worry about you and the boarding house because it was so hard for you. I wish I could just drop in and see you and have a good long talk. It is nearly three years since I left Boston. I have certainly roughed it since then but still they have been very happy years. We seem to grow fonder of each other as the years go by and we are happy together. I have never regretted coming so far for I have a very good husband. It is getting dark and I have some schoolwork to do yet.

Give my love to the girls and Fay and the Dr. when you see them. Many thanks for the candy. I ate and ate until it was nearly gone and then I left just a few pieces in the box for George. I left it at home for I knew if I brought it back with me I'd eat those too.

Write as often as you can. Lots of love to you, Nell

Kleczkowski, Sask.
July 11, 1923

Dear Auntie Marie,

Your long letter came about two weeks ago and I know it is a long time since I have written to you but the time seems to go and I don't seem to get many letters written. I hoped my husband would come down to see me tonight but I imagine he is away yet. You know we lost our horses last November and so we have been looking in the Saskatchewan Gazette to see if they were advertised. Every pound keeper has to advertise in two issues of the Gazette before he can sell the horses he has in pound. We thought as soon as the grain began to grow someone would run them into pound. Last Sunday we saw a notice of two horses that answer the description of Fox and Fred so George planned to start early Monday morning but it simply poured. He decided he had better go home first and get a heavy coat, feed for the horses, halters and start with the wagon, as he had only the buggy here. That made twelve miles extra for him, as they were about twenty-five miles from here. It stopped raining at noon so he left for home and thought he could get started about two o'clock but I doubt if he did, so probably he didn't get there until yesterday. There were only two horses advertised so maybe Clyde and Major didn't get run into the pound, unless they got in after this issue was printed. We hope they didn't, as it will probably cost us thirty or forty dollars to get these two out if they are ours. George thought if they were he might find Clyde and Major in that vicinity so it is doubtful if he got back today. I hope he may get them all, as four horses is quite a loss to poor folks.

Many thanks for the pretty apron you sent me. I have worn it lots. It is very serviceable and that is what I need in this country. It is so dark I can hardly see to write and as I'm out of coal oil and there is no way of getting any without making a trip to town I either go to bed before dark or use a candle. I suppose that seems quite primitive to you people but I often have to use one when the oil gives out. I think we are going to have a thundershower, as it is black in the west and keeps lightning and rumbling but there isn't any rain as yet. We had a dreadful hailstorm about three weeks ago. It was on a Saturday night and had been extremely hot all day. I was at home and was glad I wasn't alone. The hail began between eight and nine and we had three storms, one right after the other. The hail was as big as large marbles and they came thick and fast. Fortunately we have no windows on the west, as the hail came from the west but when I came back to school Sunday I found nine panes of glass on the west side of the school broken and they didn't get the hail as bad here as we did farther north. George went out after the last shower, about one, and picked up hailstones as big as hen's eggs. We measured some that were six inches around and they certainly came with some force. The next morning our oats and barley were flat and you couldn't see the garden. We thought we would not get any crop but things started up in a few days and I guess our garden will be all right. The hail thinned things out quite a lot but it has begun to grown again. At present we are having a terrific thundershower. It is pouring in torrents and lightens continually. I went to bed but decided I'd rather be up for a while so got up and dressed.

I put in a big garden here at school and it certainly keeps me busy, as the ground is full of grass roots and by the time I get it hoed I have to begin all over again. I have spent hours hoeing and it is still weedy.

We are gradually getting our house finished. We had a Russian fellow build a brick chimney in the house and then a Russian woman came two weeks ago Saturday and she and her daughter mudded the inside. George cut willows and put on part of them and then I did the rest of the room. They have to nail on the logs like laths. George used a horse to mix the mud and straw and then carried it in for them and they plastered it on with their hands. They make a smooth wall of mud that looks like a plaster wall when finished and dries as hard as a rock. George plans to put in a partition this summer, as it is so hard to keep one room tidy. I would rather have a kitchen and living room than have one big room. When he gets the partition in we plan to kalsomine the walls and then our house won't be at all bad. It surely will be warm and we won't have to put in another cold winter like last.

Last Friday we had a neighborhood picnic. Five schools joined together and we went to Bear Lake, about five miles from this school and ten miles from our farm. George came down Friday morning, as it was nearer. It was a beautiful day and we had lots of people there. There were all kinds of races for the children. They had high jumping, races for the men and woman and even horse racing. They had a booth and sold ice cream cones, orange candy, gum and soft drinks and Mr. Ash took in over eighty dollars. By the way, he came from Massachusetts, someplace near Boston but I don't remember just where. We had a nice day. George and I debated whether to drive home in the morning but we decided to go home. I was pretty weary and glad to tumble into bed.

We had a very dry spring and I guess no rain from last fall until about the first of June. It never rains here in the winter. About the first of June it began to rain and we have had lots of rain ever since.

George got some cement and has been putting a cement foundation under the house. It is quite a job to do it after the house is built, but the logs rot quickly if they are resting on the ground. He dug around one corner to put rocks underneath and that night we had a terrible downpour and it rained all the next day. All the water ran off the roof and into the cellar. There is over two feet of water all over the cellar bottom and I have a box with about eight-dozen eggs carefully wrapped in paper somewhere on the cellar floor. George says they will keep, as the water is cold.

Thursday Night

It has been another hot day and in the south it begins to look like another thundershower. I am busy baking bread. I usually bake it here and then I don't have to bother with it Saturday when I go home. We have to use the dry compressed yeast and that seems to take longer than the other yeast. I usually bake three loaves but somehow I have five loaves tonight.

I got a little card announcing the arrival of Doris Cole and also a card from George's youngest brother's wife in Wells (Maine), announcing the birth of Carleton Campbell. We have two nephews named Carleton now, as that is what Ruth named her last baby. I sent for some cloth to make a baby dress but can't cut one out without a pattern or one to look at. I guess I'll go to Mrs. Agerons one mile from here but I can go part way with one of the children on their buggy and then walk home. I sent for some shoes on the twenty-fifth of May and it is now the twelfth of July and I haven't received them yet. I usually send to Eaton's in Manitoba. It is over four hundred miles but they are a very reliable firm and we get quick service, sometimes in a week or ten days and very seldom over two weeks. I should have sent there as they always send you something. If they don't have what you order, they always send you a higher priced article rather than keep you waiting. I ordered a two-strap slipper from Simpson's as their store is in Regina and I was badly in need of shoes. They sent me an entirely different shoe from the one I ordered, but still I would have kept it if they had written that they took the liberty to substitute and returned the difference in price. I found the shoes they sent in the catalogue and as it was listed for 50 cents less than the ones I ordered, I thought I would have what I ordered or have my money back. So I sent the shoes back and told them to send me what I ordered or please refund the money. I have had a letter and a card from them saying that everything was being done to hasten my order. The last account was that they would be sent on the 26th of June but I haven't any shoes yet and so am wearing high boots with a hole through the sole. It makes me so mad and my husband only laughs and says, "I told you to send to Eaton's." I'm going to write a letter and tell them just what I think of a firm that does business that way and if I don't get something to wear on my feet in the mail on Saturday I shall send the letter. I think I've waited long enough.

It is time for supper and I guess I'll get something to eat while I still have the fire to bake my bread and then I can let it go out, as it is dreadfully warm.

Morton and Bessie sent me a five lb. box of chocolates about two weeks ago. They tasted so good I still have some left but keep nibbling away on them. I can't seem to leave them very long at a time. I seem to owe a lot of letters and don't seem to catch up on my letter writing. I don't think I owe Flora or Louisa one. I intend to send Flora something sometime. We want to go to North Battleford during my vacation and perhaps I can get her something there. The last I heard of Marion she was with her people in Concord, New Hampshire. They own a place there and her father had given up his work in Lowell and they had gone back to Concord. She said Rudolph wrote he would send her transportation the first of June and if he did she and Donald would go to Panama, but I haven't heard since whether she went.

Lots of love to you all and Fay and the Dr.. I haven't heard anything of Miss Edgecombe lately.

Nell

Kleczkowski, Sask.
Aug. 17, 1923

Dear Auntie Marie,

If you will excuse pencil I'll try to write a letter while I'm waiting for the bread to bake. I have a scratchy old pen and just a little ink in the bottom of the bottle so I have to keep tipping it up to get any on the pen, therefore the pencil.

School closes tomorrow for two weeks for which I'm rather glad. It is quite a long term from the 5th of March till now without a week off. We used to look for a week off every eight weeks in the city. George is coming down to school tomorrow night and Saturday noon we plan to drive to Sandy Lake and camp out over Sunday.

We drove up three weeks ago and it is the nicest country you ever saw and such terrible roads. It is nice after you get there but there were hills and valleys and part of the time, especially on the side of the hills, one side of the wagon would be anywhere from a foot to two feet higher than the other side. We came to a stream at the foot of a hill and the horses wouldn't cross for sometime but finally did. Coming home we got into a mud hole and for fifty yards or more the horse went into the mud way to their bellies and it was some scramble for them to get out of it. George thinks the roads have dried up some and that he can find a better trail this time.

I have so many things I want to do this vacation that I probably won't get half of them done. I have an enormous washing to begin with. I could do some washing after school nights but the water here is alkali and so hard that it is impossible to do anything with it so I have to do the washing when I get home on Saturday. Usually all of the dishes in the house are dirty and I have to clean up so it is always late before I begin to wash and things have a way of accumulating. I want to dip that brown jersey dress you sent last winter in some dye, as it seems to be faded in streaks. I wear it a lot and I think I can freshen it up again, also my sweater and George's.

George has begun mudding the outside of the house and I told him I would help as it is a long, tedious job and easier if two are working, as one can carry the mud and the other put it on. We plan to drive to North Battleford the 27th, as we both need our teeth fixed. It is between seventy and eighty miles so will take nearly two days on the road, as we don't have dentists in the country.

Did I write you we found the horses in the pound over thirty miles from here? That is three were in but we could get no trace of Clyde so we think she must have died last winter, as she wouldn't have left the others. Major is a young stallion and there was so much against him that it would not have paid to have taken him out so George left him in the pound to be sold to cover his expenses. We paid the pound bill for Fox and Fred and George brought them home. They had been in pasture all spring and were as fat as could be. On the road coming home George noticed Fox had some trouble with his kidneys so he began to doctor him as soon as he got him home. We sent to town for nitro but the druggist didn't have any. There isn't a vet within forty miles and we couldn't get anything but buck brush tea and saltpetre for him and he lived only week. I think if we could have gotten the right medicine in time he would have been all right. So you see we have just one of the four horses we lost.

I have cut out a baby dress for Bessie's baby and maybe I'll get it finished sometime. Somehow my schoolwork, housework and cooking for George keeps me busy and I don't get any sewing done. I have put up twelve jars of various things so have a small beginning.

My gray kitty that I brought with me from the prairie has four kittens. She disappeared and was gone for nearly ten days, then she came back nights for milk. I watched her but could never find out where the kittens were. Last Sunday she brought them home and put them under the porch. I have her here at school for company. The kittens are big enough to run around and eat. As they have never been handled they are wild. I have caught three of them and they are getting so they don't run under the steps every time I go out. I'm going to keep all of them.

I want to send Flora something for a wedding present; maybe I can get something in North Battleford. It is so hard to shop by mail.

I sent for some shoes on the 25th of May and haven't any yet (Aug. 17) and I needed them badly when I first sent. I guess I wrote you what a time I had about the first ones I sent for. At last Simpson's sent the money back and I sent to Eaton's for some. The shoes they sent were all right except width, as they were double EE they were so wide I could nearly turn my feet around in them and pull them off when they were laced tight. I guess all the Canadians must have wide feet as everything in the catalogue was E or double E so at last I wrote to the "personal shopper" and asked her if she could get me a pair of shoes. I got word Wednesday that they had sent them last week. The mailman left the mail bag for here at Alberton and brought the Alberton bag here so everyone had to wait for papers and bundles until his next trip on Saturday. I have had to wear a pair of high boots all summer that I bought in Boston. I had them nearly a year before I was married so there isn't much left of them but I guess they will hold together a few days longer.

I must stop now but wish we could have a visit together. Give all my love to your big family,

Nellie

Kleczkowski, Sask.
October 23, 1923

Dear Auntie Marie,

I have various things I ought to do such as mend some of George's clothes but I guess I'll write to you instead. The children are busy playing Flinch. I suppose you will wonder why I got a family but I have a girl fourteen staying with me until school closes. She lives nine miles from school and her mother asked me if she could stay with me until school closed and go to school. Nick and Alga came up tonight so I have been playing Flinch with them and now I've left them to their own devices. I guess it is a long time since I have written to you but I've been so busy I seem to owe everyone a letter. I guess I haven't written since we went to North Battleford the last of August. It was a nice trip, about seventy-five miles each way and we drove with the horses going the hundred and fifty miles in three days. We didn't go fast, as the horses are all workhorses and not used to the road. George had a lot of work done on his teeth and spent most of one day and part of another with the dentist but I had only two small fillings. It is only a small place, something like Kennebrink only no streetcars. We went to the movies Saturday night and church on Sunday. The week we got back a woman here celebrated her twenty-fifth wedding anniversary so George and I went to the party. It was midnight before we left. We came back to school, as it was nearer than the farm and school began Monday. We slept late Sunday after our midnight celebration, and Sunday noon Mr. and Mrs. Sande came to dinner. They are Norwegians but rather pleasant.

The middle of September we had our school fair at Hafford. The children made some very pretty things and we got quite a lot of prizes. It came off cold that week and we had the first heavy frost. I thought I ought to get my potatoes in so was busy after school digging potatoes and carrying things in. I got them all in but thirteen rows and a Russian girl wanted to dig them so I gladly let her and helped her carry them in. I had over twenty bushels that I raised all by myself so it was quite a job. I had hoped to take all the things the children made to the fair and as they had to be in as soon after nine in the morning as possible, it meant an early start. Two of the girls at school wanted to go with me so they stayed all night with me. We took one of our horses and one of theirs and borrowed a democrat from one of the school trustees. It is quite a task to get up and harness a team of horses and drive eighteen miles before nine o'clock on a chilly morning. One of the boys went with us so I packed a big lunch and at noon we got a pail of hot coffee at the Chinaman's so had a good lunch.

After dinner it began to rain and by the time we got ready to start for home it was just a steady rain and very cold. Before we got anywhere near home it was pitch dark. We met another one of my boys and it was so muddy he couldn't ride his wheel so we stopped and finally managed to make room for him and the wheel in the democrat. He hadn't had any dinner so we got out the remains of the lunch for him. The roads were so slippery that the horses had to walk for the last ten miles so it was a slow trip. We were so cold and wet that we couldn't un-harness when we got home. I built a hot fire in the heater and made them all a cup of ginger tea. Then I fixed the bed and got Elsie to bed and Nick, Ellodie and I went out to un-harness.

One Saturday I wanted to go to a teacher's meeting in Hafford so George left the horse. I thought the Mill's were going in their car so I drove over to see if I could go along. They had been in the day before but Mrs. Mills said if I would drive in she would go with me, so I stayed there to dinner and then we went to town. I was glad she went with me, as it was nine o'clock before we got back so I stayed at her house all night and came home in the morning. I hate driving over these woody roads after dark. They are nothing but grassy trails and there are so many of them that I'm afraid I'll get the wrong one. Mrs. Mills is a woman of fifty-five and an ex-school marm.

I have been busy mudding these last few weeks when I go home on Saturdays. Our house certainly should be warm this winter, as we have a solid wall about twelve inches thick. It took a lot of mud but we have walls both inside and out that are just like plastered walls. I sent to Eaton's and bought some kalsomine and as soon as I get home from school for good we are going to varnish and kalsomine. I got cream for the ceiling, buff for the sitting room and light blue for the kitchen. I always wanted a blue and white kitchen. I have a light oak varnish stain for the woodwork and floor and some varnish for the furniture. It is all old and dilapidated. I want to give George's armchair a coat of varnish and the old dining table is wobbly on its legs so George is going to cut it smaller and put on new legs for a kitchen table and I have bought Mrs. Sande's round table for the sitting room. They are having a sale this week and going to town for the winter. I'll be so glad to get the house fixed up, as I've camped for so long. You can't realize what slow work it is where one has to do everything himself on the house and run the farm too and there is not much to do it with. George has a partition to put in both upstairs and down and another floor to lay upstairs, but there is so much outside work to be done before it freezes up for good, that he is waiting till it gets too cold to work outside.

I bought a wood heater for the sitting room, a plain oak rocker and a plain kitchen chair. When I get the old furniture touched up I think we'll look just fine.

I haven't done a single thing for Christmas yet. I guess I shall have to send to Eaton's for some cloth and make everyone an apron. I can't buy anything here and I don't seem to get time to do any crocheting or fancy work. I have the cloth for a dress for Bessie's baby but I guess it will never get made. You asked about George's socks. He wears size 10 or 10 ½ and in the winter wears heavy wool socks but lisle or cashmere socks would be very acceptable for summer, as he hasn't any good ones. Common socks are better than any too fine.

I have five cats at present, an old cat and four kittens. She had them in the bushes and never brought them home until they could walk. I went away for two weeks vacation and got one of the children at school to bring them milk every day. The old cat took them away again and  didn't bring them back until I came back from vacation. You never saw such wild cats in your life. The first time I managed to catch one he was like a little tiger and chewed my finger so my whole hand was swollen. The next time I tried to pick one up he landed on the middle of the table nearly on top of the lamp. I grabbed the lamp and he went right up the wall. I couldn't get them into the house until it got cold. I can pick up three of them sometimes but the fourth is still wild.

I had a letter from Marion. She is in Panama with Rudy. I'm glad they are together again. She wrote that he had a good job and was delighted to have them back again. She has a maid and her letter sounds as if she led a lazy sort of life. I can't imagine taking an hour in the morning to primp and then sitting the remainder of the morning in the yard under an orange tree writing letters or reading.

Eunice Hamlin wrote me that Hannibal saved enough money to buy a steam laundry and he and her brother had gone into business in Kentville, N.S. They were living there when she wrote.

Maude and Winfield are at Fort Fairfield, Ohio, near Dayton. She wrote me recently that she bought me a tablecloth while she was in Germany and asked how she should send it. I wrote for her to send it at Xmas time, as it would come through duty free then.

I had a long letter from "Mother Allen". She said Stanley, the younger boy came home from college and helped his father this spring but didn't go back as he was married this summer. She said she was sorry, as she did want him to go through college and be somebody. She was quite pleased when Roy and Reta were married.

I must mend a shirt for George tonight. I expected him down last night, as he always comes to see me Wednesday nights. I guess he must have been threshing, as he didn't come. He could have gone threshing but there was so much to do at home getting the buildings fixed for winter, etc. He didn't go but promised to help Patsy and Pushee when they threshed there. I want to go home tomorrow but don't know whether he can come after me and I hate to walk six miles. Country miles are so long. Well, I must stop and mend George's shirt. I guess it is Faye's army shirt, anyway it is the wool shirt you sent with the things last winter and I kept it. George wore it all winter and now it needs several patches. Write when you find time. I often think of you and just wish I could drop in and visit you. How we would talk. Give my love to all your old family if you see them ever and especially to the Dr.

Lots of love to you, Nell

Lorenzo, Sask.
January 7, 1924

Dear Reta,

I guess it is time I wrote to you. The last time was so long ago that it is quite beyond my memory when it was. Anyway I found a letter which I started last August and never sent. No doubt I had owed you one for sometime or I wouldn't have made an attempt then., so I guess it must be sometime back in the dark ages. It is surely lucky that Christmas comes once a year and then every one takes time to write to everyone else even if it is only to say "Thank You". I want to say "Thank You" but I'll try to do better next time I've owed you a letter so long. School has ended at last for two months. Ten months is quite a stretch with only two weeks off in the middle of the summer. I had forty youngsters and six grades so I kept pretty busy. They had such a nice little house beside the school that I lived there and poor George had to "bach". He came down Wednesday nights to supper and drove home Thursday morning. Then came for me Friday night and I went home for our Sunday, so you see, that way Tuesday was the only day we didn't see each other. I had a nice garden at school and George had a big one at home. I raised about twenty bushels of potatoes all myself - shovelled them in the spring - George did dig them for me but I picked them up and put them into the cellar. George raised about fifty bushels of turnips and we are feeding them to the cows.

In August during my vacation we drove to North Battleford. It is about seventy-five miles from here. We went about fifty miles a day and made the trip up and back in three days on the road. We stayed in North Battleford from Saturday noon until Tuesday noon, as we both had work to be done at the dentists. George hadn't had any work done for nine years so spent one whole day with the dentist and had three teeth pulled the next morning. We went to church on Sunday and the movies Saturday night. We were gone nearly a week and I enjoyed the trip. North Battleford is much like Kennebunk so you see it is small - not even any streetcars yet.

In September we had a school fair and there was a lot of work getting ready for that. The children made some very pretty things and two of the girls at school stayed all night with me and we drove to Hafford early the next morning. It is quite a job to get ready and drive eighteen miles before nine o'clock. We borrowed a democrat and took two horses. In the afternoon it began to rain and by the time we got ready to leave town it was just a cold drizzle. The roads were so sticky the horses couldn't trot. We met one of my boys with a wheel (bicycle) but he couldn't ride through the mud so we put the wheel in the back and took him in. It was so dark before we reached home we could hardly see the horses. We were wet through and nearly frozen. I built a hot fire in the heater and made the youngsters all drink a cup of ginger tea and they were all right the next day.

School closed with a Christmas entertainment, tree and a dance. That seems to be the one big social event of the year. I fairly dreaded it from the account of past times. Nearly all of the people here are Russians and they don't seem to feel that they have had a good time unless they have had plenty of "home brew". So everyone brings a bottle in his jacket and before morning everybody, or rather the male sex is gloriously drunk. It was quite a job getting up the entertainment, as lots of the Russians can't understand English so we had quite a few dialogues with just acting in them. Santa Claus talked in Russian. I sat up until two a.m. on Wednesday morning making a Santa Claus suit. We had the lunch, cake, coffee and sandwiches right after the entertainment and tree, and then George and I went home and left the crowd to dance until morning. I thought the noise was terrible and it was all a perfect bedlam, but everyone said what a nice time they had. The Sande's were here yesterday and they said the crowd was much still than most years. Anyway I was glad when it was over. I was so tired that my brain (what there is of it) just seemed to refuse to work and I seemed to be in sort of a daze.

I packed up the things I had at school and we moved home the next day. Of course the house here was more or less upset, as George has been "baching". I finally found a place to put most of the things and look a little bit respectable but haven't got things to suit me yet. We plan to put a partition in and make two rooms. One big room is so hard to keep clean. We have no ceiling yet, only the rafters and the mud walls are gloomy looking. I have kalsomine, buff for one room, blue for the kitchen and cream for the ceiling. Also, light oak varnish stain for the woodwork and some for my furniture. It is all old and rather shabby and some of it is made of packing boxes so I think a little stain will improve it.

Our house is nice and warm this year, as it is well mudded both inside and out. I suppose you people back east wouldn't believe that the folks here make very good walls of equal parts of manure and sticky mud thoroughly mixed with water. We cut small willows about the size of one of my fingers and nailed them on the logs close together, on a slant. They serve as laths. Then we got a Russian woman one Saturday and I watched her mix the mud. We had a big pile back of the house and then drove one of the horses through it for about half an hour until he had tramped it smooth. The woman picked up great hands full of mud and slapped it onto the willows that were nailed on the wall, and smoothed it down with her hands. It dries smooth and just like a plastered wall only it is mud colored. It will crack at first and you have to go over it again and fill up all the cracks and wash it down with lots of water. After I found out how they did it I used to don a pair of George's trousers and spend my Saturday slapping mud on the outside of the house. It was quite a job but we have a solid wall about twelve inches thick so our house is warm this winter. We nearly froze to death last year.

I must tell you the good news! I wrote a story called "The Postman" and sent it to the "Western Home Monthly" - the only women's magazine in the far west. A few weeks ago they wrote me it had been accepted and would appear in the January issue and upon publication I would hear from their bookkeeping department. I will try to get a Western Home Monthly to send to Mother Allen so you all can read it. It is all true, everything I mentioned I have seen happen at Lorenzo Post Office. I wish I could sell a story occasionally, as it would help out a lot. We want to build another piece on the house so we can use this part for a shed and kitchen and have a living room, bedroom, washroom and pantry in the new part.

I haven't told you anything about Christmas yet. We had a very nice one and Santa Claus was certainly very good to us. We were alone but had a good dinner, - a nice fat goose. We planned to ask a fellow about a mile from here to dinner. He is a college graduate but he did the four years work in a little over two years and it left him sort of odd. He isn't exactly crazy but a little queer. He lives all alone and I thought we ought to ask him up to dinner, but George was busy and couldn't seem to find time to get down to ask him.

Thank you for the book. George began it right away. He had read part of it in the "Pictorial" but he missed the first of it as we didn't happen to get that number but he said it was worth reading again. He likes Lincoln's books. I was very much in need of handkerchiefs. Mine are all in rags and tatters.

Maude sent in a very pretty table cover she bought in Germany, also a blue and white tablecloth (belated wedding gifts) and a pretty handkerchief. Auntie Marie sent me a blue and white tablecloth and half dozen napkins. Louisa sent me percale to make a dress. Flora sent me four linen towels and Auntie Louisa and Bill sent a box of candy. Dad sent me cloth for a dress and mother sent me two pair of stockings. Ida sent cloth for an apron and some bed socks. I was pleased with the warm skirt Mother Allen sent me. Tell her it has been forty-five below since Christmas, - about a week of such weather before it warmed up. You see I'll find the petticoat useful. Emma sent me the "Ladies Home Journal" and three dishtowels and Smithy an outing flannel nightgown. I had a meat chopper, pair of Indian moccasins and a book from George. The children at school gave me a berry dish and half a dozen saucers to match. I also had half a dozen cut glass tumblers. Helen sent me a rubber apron and Mable W. a picture. They sent candy from home and Fred and Grace sent me a box of chocolates. I wish I could do more at Christmas time but there is no store here and I haven't been to town since last September. There isn't anything in town anyway but two stores so I buy everything out of a catalogue and make a few things myself. It is so long since I shopped I don't believe I'd know how any more.

I must write some other letters. Velma has written me three times since I wrote to her. Please let Mother Allen read this and tell her I'll write to her some fine day. I know I have never answered her last letter.

I suppose your babies keep you busy but write when you find time or let Ray do the writing for you.

Love to all, Nell.

Lorenzo, Sask.
January 9, 1924

Dear Auntie and Flora and Louisa,

I guess I'll write a joint letter to the family, as I'm not sure of the girls' addresses.

First of all we want to thank everyone for everything. You may be sure we were pleased with our Christmas boxes. The table cover and napkins are just what I need. George made me a nice kitchen table yesterday out of our old dining table so I expect we will eat our breakfasts in the kitchen. I have some blue kalsomine for the walls as soon as  we get the ceiling in, so my tablecloth will look fine. I was delighted with the cloth for the dress. I am much in need of cotton dresses and as soon as I get some of the mending done, I plan to do a little sewing for myself. Towels are so handy and

Flora was very generous with the towels and they are such nice crush too. George was pleased with his handkerchiefs and socks, something very useful. I have been nibbling candy ever since the box arrived. There were so many different things to try. It is all gone now but three or four of the little penny lozenges and something tells me they are short lived.

We had a nice Christmas and Santa Claus was very good to us. Somehow he seems to bring us lots of things. I wish I could do more at Christmas but we have no stores, so what few things I get I have to send for by mail and it is so hard to get what you want. It isn't like going in a store and seeing so many pretty things. We had a nice fat goose for our dinner and he certainly tasted good.

It is only eight-thirty but I am very sleepy. I have been going to bed anywhere from six-thirty to seven-thirty every night and one or two since school closed and sleeping about twelve hours. I guess I've got the habit.

School closed on December 21st with a concert, Christmas tree and dance. George was a big help to me. He was in several dialogues and dressed up like a darkey and kept things moving. I rather dreaded it, as the Russians don't feel that they have had any kind of a time unless they have some home brew, so all of the men bring a bottle in their pockets and before morning they are all gloriously drunk. I thought they were terribly noisy, but people who have been to other Christmas concerts said they were quieter than other times and nobody got terribly drunk, although most of the men had a little. After the entertainment and tree George and I went home and left the crowd to dance till morning. I was so weary I didn't think I'd want to move for a week, but I got up fairly early and we moved home the next day, as I wanted to be at home for Christmas.

George has gone to a meeting three or four miles from here. The Boy Scouts want to get up an entertainment to earn money for the school and he is acting Scout Master and also Chairman of the School Trustees, so had to go. We expected the Scouts here last Friday but we had a spell of cold weather, --forty-five below zero for about a week, so no one came.

I must tell you the good news. I wrote a story, which I sent to "The Western Home Monthly" and I got a letter saying it had been accepted and would appear in the January issue. Upon publication I would receive a check from their bookkeeping department. So now I'm waiting for my check.

Friday morning

I got so sleepy I went to bed. George is going to the Post Office and if I don't send this along, I can't mail it for another week. Will try to write you more next time but I wanted to thank you all for remembering us so generously. Write soon and tell me all the news.

Love to all from us both. Nell

P.S. The little snap shot on the calendar was taken on the steps of the teacher's residence at Kleczkowski.

Lorenzo, Sask.
January 28, 1924

Dear Reta,

Just a short letter tonight. I believe we are going to drive to Alberton Wednesday. It is a good ten miles from here but there is a post office in a house and the man also carries a small line of groceries. As I'm in need of several things, we'll make the trip and I can mail this letter there. We get our mail at Lorenzo only once a week.

I wasn't as surprised at the news in your letter as I would have been if Ida hadn't written me last week about it. We shall be anxious to know whether it is a girl or boy, - as you said, "Sophie or Jonnie". I hope you won't have a hard time. I'm sorry I didn't send the little dress I had made too, but it looked too small for Carlton and as I had no need for it I sent it to Bessie, as her baby is younger.

I have been busy every minute since I got home from school and I really can't see what I have done either.

There was an entertainment at Bohdan School last Friday. George did a lot toward getting it up. George and I were in a dialogue together and then I was in another dialogue. George gave a recitation and played in Poty's Band. Poty's Band consisted of Jules Poty who played on my oven grate with my flapjack turner, two Russian fellows who each had a tin pan and two silver knives. There were also two combs with tissue paper, a mailing tube that served as a horn and George played the bones. It certainly was a scream. These Russians want something wild and woolly and the wilder the better. It is hard to get up an entertainment, as so few people can understand English.

I am going to teach at Bohdan School next year or rather this year. I would like to go back to Krivoshein this year but it is so far. I have to stay here. Twelve miles a day is too much of a drive and George wants me home. I want to have a nice garden and raise some chickens this summer and I think it would be better for me to take Bohdan, as it is in our district and only two miles from here. They also offered me the Lorenzo School. This will be my last year of teaching, as my certificate runs out in June and I have to go to a Canadian Normal School for the winter term of eighteen weeks in order to get another certificate. The Inspector told me last year to accept a school for the whole year and then write to the department in June and he was very sure they would grant me a permit to finish the year. I think by the end of the year we will have things running so there will be something coming from the farm. I am sending you a few snap shots. We haven't any camera and few people here have. I had a girl fourteen stay with me this fall and winter and go to school and she had a camera so I took ten pictures with her camera.

George has gone to bed. He is great for going to bed as soon as he eats his supper. I have been getting eleven and twelve hours sleep a night since Christmas so am getting all slept out. I have a history lesson to learn tonight, as I'm helping a boy with Canadian History and he comes tomorrow for a lesson. George also has the Boy Scouts here so it will be a busy day.

Write soon or get Ray to write. I'll try to write to Mother Allen soon.

Love to all, Nell

Lorenzo, Sask.
February 15, 1924

Dear Aunty Marie,

I believe Monday is your birthday and I haven't a thing to send you. I planned to make you something but discovered my white thread was all gone. I sent to Eaton's for thread over two weeks ago and it hasn't come yet. Maybe we will get it tomorrow and perhaps not for another week. I hoped to get this letter mailed today but we have been having a heavy snowstorm all day. The roads are drifted, so George hates to harness up the team and drive three and a half miles. Of course we will go tomorrow to get the mail, but if a letter isn't mailed today it won't go out for another week, as the mailman leaves for town early in the morning and doesn't get back with the mail till afternoon.

The winter has fairly flown and I haven't done half I wanted to. I made George two shirts, all but the collars, and then my thread gave out so I had to stop. I sent a dollar to a mill for cotton remnants and got nearly seven yards of nice fine shirting. There were five pieces but as they sent the same kind I could get the shirts out nicely by piecing the tails, so I did and George didn't mind. I felt quite proud to get two shirts and an apron for a dollar.

I washed the blue serge dress Flora sent me and pressed it again so it looks like new. I have taken one of the ruffles off my blue flowered voile I had the summer I was married and made a new waist out of it, as the old one tore out around the sleeves. I've also made two small aprons and a bungalow housedress and an amount of mending, mostly socks. I have twelve pairs of heavy wool socks mended ahead so I guess they will last a little while.

George put in the wall downstairs and we have been mudding it. I want to get the room kalsomined but it takes so long for the mud to dry. The first day we used the washtub and mixed the mud in the house. He got the clay down the cellar. I helped him mud the sitting room side. This week he started on the kitchen side of the wall. We had a lovely warm day Tuesday so he mixed the mud on the ground outside. It turned cold again before noon. I tried to help mud but the mud was just like ice and my hands hurt, so after a little while they made me sick all over. I gave it up. George used up what mud he had mixed, but there is still a big place back of the stove to mud if it ever gets a bit warmer.

I sent to Eaton's for enough linoleum for the bedroom. At present we have only a rough floor with cracks in it and I'm always losing things through the cracks.

I guess George will go to town next week if the weather is good. I shall stay at home as a forty-five mile drive doesn't appeal to me this time of year. I sent to Eaton's for groceries, as one can buy so much cheaper by getting things in large quantities and it is much handier when we are so far from a store. George needs some plaster board for the ceilings and some smooth boards for finishing up a little more inside, so he'll have to make a trip to town.

I am going to send you the story I wrote if it is ever printed. The "Western Home Monthly" wrote me it had been accepted and would appear in the January issue, but it didn't. They wrote that upon publication I would receive a check from their bookkeeping department but neglected to state the amount. George wrote a boy's story which he sent to the "Presbyterian Publication Company" and they wrote right back thanking him and sending him a check for $7.50. It was only a short story too. I was more pleased over it than he was. I guess I'll send you the one I wrote as soon as it is printed, as it is a true account of a visit to the post-office and describes the postmaster to perfection.

I have been anxious to hear from Ruth. She wrote me just before she expected the baby and I haven't heard a word since. She said if it was another boy she was planning to wrap him up and send him by parcel post to us, as she had boys enough already.

Ida wrote me that Dad had been sick. I wrote him a long letter and tried to persuade him and mother to come out and spend the summer with us. Of course we haven't any of the modern conveniences, but our little house is comfortable and we always have plenty to eat even if we are sometimes short of cash.

We'll have three fresh cows this spring so there will be plenty of cream and I use it every meal. The hens are laying now so there will be plenty of fresh eggs soon and we always put in a big garden. It's a lovely country with lots of fresh air and sunshine, and Dad could take one of the horses and our old buggy and jog over the country to his hearts content. He always liked horses and ours are all gentle. I wish he would come out, as I think he would enjoy it.

I'm sending you three little snapshots and will try to send you something for your birthday as soon as I can get something or make something for you. It is hard to shop when one is so far from a store.

We both wish you a very happy birthday and lots of them. I shall want to hear all about your birthday party at Sadic's. We thought of you yesterday. Write whenever you can, as I love to get your letters.

Love to you from us both. Nell

Lorenzo, Sask.
May 14, 1924

Dear Auntie Marie,

Tomorrow is mail day once more so I must write to you or I can't mail it for another week. The package came last Saturday. Many, many thanks. The skirt was just what I needed, as I didn't have a white skirt to my name. George was pleased with his handkerchiefs and he always seems to be in need of them. The thread and finishing braid will be very useful. I know, as it is so hard for me to get such things here.

Spring has come at last but things seem so slow. There aren't any signs of leaves on the trees yet, although the buds are swelling. The 5th of May we had quite a snowstorm. It looked like winter once more and the next day George used the cutter to drive to the post office.

I took a little vacation last week. I don't know whether I had the flu or gripe or what, but I had quite a fever for a couple of days, a dreadful sore throat and a splitting headache. I didn't care about eating anything and stayed in bed. When I got up I was dreadfully weak and wobbly. I'm back at school this week and as near as I can find out, most of the children were sick last week too and some of them are still sick. George has a bad cold now but is out just the same. He is working on the land and yesterday ploughed my garden. I guess I shall have to start planting soon, as it is so big. We had lots of vegetables last year but they are good to have when that is about all we have to eat. We have two little calves so are getting lots of milk. I wish you could have some of the nice thick cream we have every morning in our coffee and on our porridge. The hens are laying so I use all the eggs I want to, as it is a long way to take them to the store and you have to sell them 2 dozen for a quarter. I heard they had gone down since to 3 dozen for a quarter so I'd rather have lots of custards and things made out of eggs.

George has written two more stories since he sold one to the "Presbyterian Publishing Company." I have copied them nicely and we are going to send them to the "Youth's Companion." Of course there's nothing like trying. I think they are both lots better than the first one he wrote.

It is bedtime so I must stop. I'll try to write to the Dr. next week.

I'm sending you a picture that the Nicholson's took one Sunday. We didn't know he was going to take full length and George's pants sadly need pressing. The snow is deep and he tucks his trouser legs into the tops of his socks. He was going to put on his boots but Mr. N. said to come just as we were, so we did. George wanted me to cut it in half and send just the top half of the picture but I think it's rather funny so will send it as is. Tell Flora and Louisa I will write to them sometime. I want to send Louisa something for the baby if I ever can get anything. I sent to Eaton's for something for your birthday and also something for Aunt Ida's birthday but the package hasn't come yet. I hope to get it Saturday. Write whenever you can and give my love to everyone. Many thanks for my birthday presents. Nellie

Lorenzo, Sask.
August 19, 1924

Dear Aunty Marie,

I believe I owe you a letter but am not sure. I have been having my vacation and am back at school once more. The time fairly flew and I didn't get anywhere, in fact, I hardly knew I was having a vacation. George was haying all of the time. We have a big hay meadow and Mr. Pushee wanted to help him put it up on shares, as hay is scarce here this year as it has been so dry. We had to get up at four thirty as usual on account of haying. Then I had two extra men for meals and often one of them stayed over night.

I mudded the partition that George put in, in the winter on both sides. I went over the kitchen and living room walls with a coating of light clay and then kalsomined both rooms. I painted the ceilings a cream color, the living room a buff and the kitchen a light blue. One day I scrubbed all the woodwork and stained it with light oak varnish stain and painted the buggy.

The first Saturday of my vacation I went to town. There were several errands to be done. I wanted George to go but he was busy haying. I got ready and was just about to drive out of the yard when George said he would go with me if I'd wait until he put Kate in the pasture and changed his clothes. I was quite delighted, as forty-six miles is a long drive with no one to talk to and it takes all day to go in and back.

Last Saturday George said we could go to Sandy Lake if we could find anyone to do the chores. We went Sunday noon, although the weather looked threatening. It rained a little before we reached the lake but stopped by the time we got there. George built a big fire and I cooked dinner. It rained in the afternoon but George had the wagon up against a thick spruce thicket and we spread the feather tick and blankets under the wagon so kept nice and dry. I had a nice nap while George read the paper. It stopped raining before it was time to get supper. We had a nice campfire and were not at all uncomfortable. Monday morning was misty but the fog lifted, although it was cloudy all day. We got a boat and went out fishing in the morning. George caught two fish about five pounds each. We fried one for dinner and brought the other one home with us. We got a few blueberries but they are scarce this year. I made blueberry bread for supper and then had enough for a pie.

I believe you asked me about the birds here. There are lots of birds of all kinds. We have quantities of partridges, prairie chickens and ducks. The wild turkeys stay for a while in the spring and fall. There are lots of black birds and the red winged black birds, robins, bluebirds, and yellow birds and lots that I don't know. The birds are very tame, even the partridges roost in the trees all around the house and sometimes come right into the barnyard. I saw a deer one night by the garden and when George was milking the other night, one came into the pasture to feed. He went so near the creamery can that George was afraid he would tip it over and had to stop milking long enough to move the can. Last night he said he threw the box that he sits on over the fence beside a bush and a young deer sprang up. He looked at George a minute and then began feeding. George untied the cows and when he came out of the pasture, the deer ambled off in the bushes. He said he got within ten feet of the deer.

I began this yesterday but like most of my letters it didn't get finished. It is a rainy day today. We have a very dry summer with hardly a drop of rain. The grain was short and began to head out when only a few inches high. This last month we have had lots of showers and the grain is growing tall now when it should be ripening. We have had lots of frosts this year. One of my houseplants froze outside in July and my beans and cucumbers and citron are frozen beyond any hope of recovery. The other garden stuff looks good. I hope next year to have more time to spend on the garden.

My certificate runs out this year so I can't get another one without attending the Normal this winter. They are fussy about granting certificates unless one takes Canadian training and I was fortunate to get a certificate for four years.

Do you people realize I have been married for four years? I'd love to drop in and pay to all a visit but as time goes on the more we seem to get to tie us here. I tell George we are land poor. He took up the homestead north of our place this spring so our farm is a mile long and half a mile wide, three hundred and twenty acres.

We have a dear little colt this spring, two pigs, three calves, four cows and five horses. We are hoping to have three colts early next spring so you see we are getting quite a lot of stock.

I didn't raise any chickens last summer and my flock was reduced to twelve old hens so I had to raise a few this year. My hens won't set but I borrowed two hens and one had nine and the other hatched out all twelve eggs. A hen set herself in the woods and came out with nine. Later George found a nest in the woodpile and as he thought the eggs were old, he took them out and left only one for a nest egg. I shook one and it sounded rotten, so I carried them off in the woods and left them. A few days later a hen came out of the woodpile with one small chick (the egg George left). The hawks are bad and I've lost two of my biggest chickens lately and I just barely saved another the other day. The hawk had him but I rushed out in time to get him away.

I suppose Reta is busy this summer. I haven't heard from her but suppose she doesn't find time to write. I believe I wrote to her while I had the "flu". I'm all right once more but felt miserably for a month this spring. There has been lots of sickness, first the "flu" and then a bad epidemic of the measles.

I took the Bohdan teacher in for two weeks while they were having the measles at her boarding place. She is an English girl but very pleasant. She usually comes to supper once a week anyway. There are so few places here for anyone to visit.

It is time for me to call my children in. Hope you are all well. Give my love to Ruth and her family. Did I send you and Ruth a snapshot of George and me taken this spring (post-card)? If not I will.

Lovingly, Nell

Lorenzo, Sask.
October 2, 1924

Dear Aunty Marie,

I'm afraid this won't be a very long letter but tomorrow is mail day once more and I want to get this mailed on my way home from school tonight. I have written to Flora but Ida wrote me she and Al were moving to New Orleans. Will you please address it and sent it on to her? I have a U.S. stamp but it is at home so I will send you a stamp next time I write to you.

We have had a cold summer with frost every month. Two of my houseplants froze stiff in July. We had no rain last spring or the early part of the summer so the crops are very poor and what did grow, froze.

We have plenty of hay and green feed for the horses but the grain didn't ripen before it froze, so we will have nothing to sell but have to feed it all.

We have had two little snowstorms so far. Just a little snow in the morning, which melts before night. I guess we will have an early winter.

We had enough carrots, beets and turnips for winter but will have to buy potatoes, as we had only 7 bushels and this isn't enough for us. George was going this morning to get 15 bushels and we promised to buy potatoes the children raised at school.

This has been a very busy summer and it seems to have gone so fast. I shall be glad when school closes and I'm home for good. We close the last of November for the winter and then my teaching days are over.

When you write will you please send me Flora's address and also Dr. Emerson's, as I want to write to them? I intended to do so long ago but time flies and I have just put it off.

I must stop now, as it will be late when I get home and the children are harnessing my horse for me. I'll try to write a newsier letter before long.

Love to all, Nell

Lorenzo, Sask.
January 11, 1925

Dear Reta,

The package came yesterday and we were much pleased. I certainly need some new clothes. I haven't had anything but house dresses since I was married and as that was nearly five years ago there doesn't seem to be enough left to make over. The goods are very pretty and will make me a good dress. I sent to Eaton's for some cloth and as soon as it comes I want to make several house dresses, also a gingham for afternoon wear and some underwear. George was pleased with the book. I had read it a long time ago but so long that I enjoyed it too. We have read 196 pages today. We probably would have read more but George retired at 6:30, as he was sleepy. We both woke up at four this morning and at five George decided to get up. I, however, turned over and went to sleep. At eight he called upstairs to see if he had a wife. I wasn't sleepy so decided to study awhile. I'm still plugging along on my short story lessons. Tonight I have five different forms of opening dialogue to write using original plots. Somehow, I can't seem to think of anything brilliant. I have written one and then decided to write some of my "thank you" letters.

George seems to have much more imagination than I have. He can write pretty good boys' stories. He got one in the "East and West" and this winter he has written four. I corrected them, changed the wording in some places and wrote the endings of all of them and then I copied them to send out. One night I copied 4700 words and it surely was some job. I hope he can sell some of these. They all seem better than the first one he wrote. He has two more nearly finished and there is a long one he wrote last winter that I've never had time to fix up for him. I tell him he better be the writer in the family and let me be his secretary.

Many thanks for the photo. Hamlin is a cute youngster and certainly fat. He looks like the Richners but I think he has the Allen look too. We also had a photo from George's brother of their oldest boy, - another Carleton.

I was much surprised to get a letter from Rudy Saturday. I'm sorry I sent their things with yours but I thought they were to be with you and no one wrote me of the change in plans until after I sent the package. It was a dreadfully dirty looking box but boxes and wrapping paper are very scarce, as we seldom go shopping and I was afraid Carlton's Roly Poly would break without a box. I had to send the books for Donald and Hamlin separately, as they were too long to go in. Hope they didn't get lost.

We received Mother Allen's tablecloth but it was all out of the wrapping and there was just barely enough to show where it came from. We had lots of presents, - something every mail day for four weeks. It's nice to have Christmas last so long. I still have quite a few letters to write. I'm ashamed to say I haven't written to Gert Alden yet. If you write tell her I'll get to it soon.

There seemed so much to do after school closed. I taught to the last of November. That gave me just two weeks to do my Christmas presents. As there are no stores here I have to send to Eaton's for what I think I want some time in November. Often you find you need something else at the last minute. Crops were very poor here this year owing to the cold, dry weather so there wasn't much money and I couldn't do as much as I'd have liked.

It was cold all summer and winter began in earnest the first of November. It has been good sleighing ever since. November and December were both cold. It was anywhere from twenty-five to forty-five below all through December. Today it was only twelve below.

Miss. Evans, the Bohdan School teacher, came the last Friday of school and stayed with us until Monday afternoon. I helped her with the candy bags and other things for the Christmas concert.

It was a terrible night, the night of the Christmas tree at school. The going and coming takes all the pleasure away and then these Russians so seldom have any sort of entertainment that when they do they want to make a night of it. After the children got through their dialogues there were a lot of grown up dialogues and plays that they wanted to put on and as lots of the program is always in Russian it isn't awfully interesting. George was Santa Claus. It was one o'clock before the thing was over and then they had lunch and then dancing. George and I left as soon as it was over and Miss. Evans thought we were terrible to leave before lunch but as it was it was nearly three in the morning before we got home and it was cold. The next night I slept thirteen hours to make up. I don't see what fun there is going anywhere at eight in the evening and staying until six the next morning. The night before Christmas two Russian fellows came. The boys like to play Flinch and there are so few places here for boys to go without getting home brew that we are glad to have them come. I always make coffee or cocoa before they go and get a little lunch and they seem to like George.

Christmas we had Jim Watson for the day. He is a bachelor who lives about a mile from us. He went to McGill University and took the four years work in three and then had a nervous break- down and was in the insane asylum for a while. He is perfectly harmless but rather odd. He's terribly dirty but after he's been here a few days helping George he begins to look a bit more respectable. I knew he wouldn't have anywhere to go and I don't see how he ever lives on the messes he cooks, so I told George we ought to invite him. He got interested in a detective story we had from home so I knew he would sit up half the night as he wouldn't leave or do anything until he had finished it. George and I went to bed at bedtime and left him reading and I heard him come upstairs later. He stayed until the next afternoon. It is getting cold so I guess I'll go to bed. I'll return the snap shots you sent me before long but I don't happen to have a big envelope to put them in and I don't want to stop to make one now.

Many, many thanks for our Christmas gifts.
Love to all, Nell.

P.S. Please let Mother Allen read this too as I couldn't write her a very long letter. George was waiting to go down with the mail so I had to cut it short.

Lorenzo, Sask.
January 24, 1925

Dear Aunty Marie,

Your box of good things arrived in time for Christmas. In fact, it came the Saturday before and the temptation was so great I opened it Sunday night and got out the box of candy. I saved everything else until we had our tree Wednesday night and I even managed to save just enough candy for our dinner on Christmas Day. The luncheon set was lovely. It is such a pretty color. Towels are always acceptable and I have been married just long enough to have all my things wear out at once, sheets, pillowslips and towels all seem to be going. Mother sent me a pair of pillowslips and I surely needed them. I had just made a pair out of a couple of flour sacks. George was pleased with his socks. That is something he always needs.

I have been mending his winter socks ever since school closed. He wears three or four pair of wool socks in the winter so it takes a lot to keep him going.

It has been a long cold winter. It started in earnest the first of November. First it blizzards and then turns cold, forty-five below zero then slowly warms up and storms once more and then gets freezing cold again. I don't go very far when it gets so cold. The house and a good wood fire feel good to me.

Santa was very good to us. He always seems to be. I had lots of things and all were useful. Mother sent me an apron and pair of pillowslips and Ida a hot water bottle. Dad sent me a lace collar and cuff set and a ribbon tie. I've got to fix up some of my old clothes to wear it with. The family sent candy and peanuts and George had a book, handkerchiefs, wool socks and a Bible calendar.

I got Louisa's box and was much pleased to see all the nieces and nephews and little second cousins. I wonder if we will ever be rich enough to take a trip east.

I should have to have a whole new outfit of clothes, or people would think I was related to Noah and the Ark. There is no style here and as all of my neighbors are Russian or Galatian they dress much like the Italian women one often sees on the cars coming from the big truck gardens in Arlington. We seldom go anywhere and the silk dresses I had when I was married are all I have to dress up in and I'm afraid they would be sadly out of date. I made two house dresses this last week and have sent for some more cloth but it will be two or three weeks before it arrives. I want to make me a few more house dresses before spring and I sent for some lavender and white check gingham for an afternoon dress. I'd like it rather pretty.

George is writing stories. He sent two last Saturday to the "American Boy." I hope he can sell them. He seems to have much more imagination that I have.

He wrote one for the "Presbyterian Publishing Company", a temperance story. It has been gone quite awhile and he hasn't heard from it yet. He has travelled so much through the north woods that he can make up some interesting yarns. I correct them and copy for him. I tell him he had better be the storywriter in the family and let me be his secretary. I plan to finish my lessons on short story writing this winter and maybe between us we can become an author or authoress.

I must write some more thank you letters, as I haven't written any yet.

I shall want to hear all about your Christmas and what Santa left you. Remember me to all of the old friends. How I'd love to see you all.

Lots of love, Nell

Lorenzo, Sask.
February 4, 1925

Dear Aunty Marie,

I suppose by the time this reaches you it will be your birthday or very nearly so, so I want to wish you a happy birthday and many of them. This is a terrible looking letter but my pen is poor and the ink seems to go everywhere but in the right place.

We have had a lovely warm week. Yesterday it thawed a little around noon, the first thaw for ages. It is warm today but cloudy. George predicts it is the forerunner of another blizzard but I'm not so pessimistic.

I had a long letter from Flora since Christmas. She seems happy in her new home and life. I'm glad she and Al have got interested in church affairs. I only wish we were near a church of some sort. There is never anything here to go to. If we both didn't enjoy reading I don't know what we would do.

We drove six miles east the first of December to call on an English couple we had met and attended the Christmas concert at the school, otherwise we have stayed at home. I drove down for the mail three weeks ago and since then have not been off the place. Last Monday the postmaster and his wife came up to dinner and spent the afternoon. He is French and she Galatian but both speak English fairly well.

I have lots of sewing to do. It seems as if everything has worn out. I've done no sewing since I was married, except on occasional housedresses and heaps of mending. I've got to make some new clothes, as there's nothing left to mend. My union suits are all patches and I mend them all up and they seem to last just about a week and then I have to put on more patches for the next week. I'm hoping I can make them last till spring. I sent to Eaton's for some cloth, got twenty yards of cloth for underwear and have two housedresses finished and two more cut out ready to stitch. I have some pretty lavender and white check gingham and also some blue, white and black check gingham for afternoon dresses and some ratinee Reta sent me for Christmas, so you see I can keep busy.

George is tinkering with the blower that goes on a new forge he has just bought. For some reason the handle refuses to turn. At last count his hands were covered with black grease and there seemed to be a goodly supply of grease on the kitchen floor. I haven't been out recently to see how things are progressing.

I'm sending you a little package. It isn't so hard for me to make gifts for my female relatives, as I can usually find a bit of cloth and manufacture something they can use, but the men... George comes next on my list and I shall have to have some sort of a bright idea before his birthday on April 1st.

You surely are forehanded on your Christmas work. I haven't even finished all of last year's Christmas presents, to say nothing of beginning on this years. I sent for a buffet set for Emma. I got the large piece finished but before I got the two small mats done the brown silk floss and the crochet cotton gave out. I had to send away again so it was three weeks before I could get the materials to finish. I sent the scarf along for Christmas and wrote her the mats would follow later. I must finish them for her.

She is still at the farm and Smithy is working in the mill at South Windham, he goes back and forth morning and night. He was still using the car when Em last wrote but she thought he'd have to use the horse before long.

I'm wondering how Marion's mother is. She wrote a couple of weeks ago that she was very low and they didn't think she could possibly live much longer. I don't suppose you have heard from any of them.

What is Rudy doing for a living? Everyone writes he is working in Boston but I can't seem to find out whether he became a dentist or not. He sent me a big box of candy for Christmas. It was lovely and I still have a tiny bit left but I'm afraid it won't last much longer.

I must stop and get dinner, as the clock has already struck twelve. I wish I could see you. You'll have to come out to visit us, as I guess there's no hope of our coming east right away. Of course we have the farm and quite a lot of stock with prospects of more. There is always the garden, milk and eggs, so we have a good living but what money we have seems to be all tied up in the farm so ready cash is scarce. I'm afraid it will be some time before we can come east.

Write often, as I love to get your letters and we both will think of you on the 18th and wish we could be with you to help you celebrate.

Lovingly, Nell

> George and Nellie Campbell decided to adopt a child.
> They chose a young boy named Emmerson Albin Smith.
> Emmerson was born on August 31, 1922 in Davidson,
> Saskatchewan to Della and John Sydney Smith.
> George and Nellie chose the name of
> Emerson Rudolph for their son.
> *'Blessed with a son we never would have had!'*

Lorenzo, Sask.
November 5, 1925

Dear Aunty Marie,

     I should be sewing for my small son, as his wardrobe is very scanty. It is quiet now as both George and the lad have retired and so I'll seize the opportunity to write to you.

     George went to Moose Jaw (to the orphanage) week before last for the boy  and I kept house while he was away. The weather was very good while he was gone so I didn't mind doing the outside work. He left here Monday morning and got home Friday night. It is only about three hundred miles to Moose Jaw but as he had several changes and long waits at each place it took almost a week to go and come back.

     The lad is a dear. He is very bright and loveable but has a little will all his own. I am going to borrow a camera and take some pictures of my family to send to you.

     I have been busy sewing, as he had hardly any clothes except the ones he wore. George bought him a new overcoat and cap in Regina and I have made two nighties and several pieces of underwear for him. Fortunately I had several old union suits that I could cut up and make into shirts and drawers. Emma sent me a blue serge dress, which fortunately was so long for me that I could cut enough off of the bottom for a pair of knickers and I ripped up an old flannel waist of mine for the top. It made a cute little suit. I have flannel to make him two playsuits if I ever can get a pattern. I sent away before George went for the lad but the pattern hasn't arrived yet. I dyed my old white corduroy skirt two years ago and it came out a lovely blue. As it is quite voluminous (I made it my first year in Everett) I seldom wear it so plan to use it for a dress-up suit. I have flannel for some sleepers but must wait until I can get a pattern, as I haven't the faintest idea how to cut them out without one.

It seems so good just to stay in the house these days and not worry about doing the chores.

We have been having cold weather here. It was four below zero at eight this morning. The general freeze up came unusually early and we have had a miserable fall. It was a scramble to get the garden all in the cellar. In fact, the cold came so early and suddenly that we didn't get some horse carrots and mangels pulled. There seemed to be such quantities of other things that we simply couldn't get to them. I didn't get much canning done. It is so hard to get fruit that it is much cheaper to buy the dried fruit or even the canned fruit, and then do it up yourself.

I spent most of the summer hunting for the cows. It is free range here and no fences so they can roam for miles. I used to walk anywhere from four to seven miles a day hunting for them and often I was gone three hours so you see I had to start out about as soon as I got my dinner dishes cleared away.

The teacher's mother has been with him all this year. They are very much English. As every one here is a foreigner of some sort, I have found it quite nice to have her. She has spent the day with me every week since she came. Usually Wednesdays so I shall miss her when school closes. Miss Evans, last year's teacher, spent a week with me this summer and a bachelor friend of George's came for a few days.

Next Monday, the ninth, is our Thanksgiving. I have invited the Lorenzo teacher and our teacher and his mother, also a man and his wife who lives six miles south of here. I have three young turkeys but as they are the beginning of my flock I shall have to be content with a rooster.

It doesn't seem possible Christmas is so near. I haven't made a thing yet and I doubt if I get to go to town again, as it has got so cold, especially now that Sonny (our boy) is here.

I think wearing apparel is as acceptable as anything you can send. I should be very glad of any kind of cloth, old or new that I could make into clothes for my family. I have a machine and plenty of time this winter and it is so much cheaper to make things than buy them. I can get Sonny a suit out of two or two and a half yards of gingham, galatea, percale or flannel and a shirt for George out of three yards. I would be just as pleased with anything old that I could fix up. If you send anything like that, I think you will find it best to simply roll the things up and stuff them in flour sack. They aren't nearly as heavy as when packed in a box and I had a parcel come that way all right. The bag was securely tied and a tag sewed on. George needs a pair of regular knitted mittens. I have been trying to learn to knit but haven't made a very good success of it so far. I can't seem to think of anything special that I need.

I had a newspaper from home telling of Grandma Rand's ninety-fifth birthday party.

I'd love to come home and see all of you people once more but there always seems to be so many ways for the money that I'm afraid it will be some time before we make the trip. George says when he gets more land ready for crop he might be able to lease the farm for a year and come back east. It seems a long time since I'd seen any of the family but I hope to someday.

I guess I forgot to tell you our boy's name. We call him Sonny for short as his first name is Emerson. He is old enough to know it so we decided not to change it but to call him Emerson Rudolph. I know you will say Rudolph and Campbell don't go together at all but it seems too bad that none of dad's grandsons were named for him so we put on the Rudolph regardless of sound. Write often and I'll try to do better this winter.

Lots of Love, Nell

Judge's Order

IN THE DISTRICT COURT OF THE JUDICIAL DISTRICT OF....BATTLEFORD.......................

His Honour Judge _Buexxx_ ....the

in Chambers ...._15th_ day of ....Oct...A.D. 192_6_.

IN THE MATTER OF The Adoption of Children Act, 1922, being Chapter 64 of the Statutes of Saskatchewan, 1921-22, and in the matter of an application for the adoption of one

....EMMERSON ALBIN SMITH...

an unmarried minor.

UPON READING and upon hearing what was alleged on behalf of the applicants,

Petition Order for Adoption. Affidavit Verifying Petition. Consent

of the Provincial Officer, Consent of the Guardian, Certificate

Payment of Fee and Certificate Waiving Period of Residence.

(Here set out the material filed)

IT IS HEREBY ORDERED that the application of....GEORGE HERBERT CAMPBELL
(Name in full)

of the....POST OFFICE....of....LORENZO...............in the Province of

Saskatchewan....FARMER............and of....NELLIE FLORENCE CAMPBELL
(Occupation) *(Name in full)*

his wife be and the same is hereby granted and the said....EMMERSON ALBIN SMITH
(Name in full)

of the....POST OFFICE....of....LORENZO...............in the Province of

Saskatchewan is hereby declared to be, from and after the date of this Order, the adopted

child of....GEORGE HERBERT CAMPBELL   AND   NELLIE FLORENCE CAMPBELL

Lorenzo, Sask.
Dec. 27, 1925

Dear Auntie Marie,

Your box arrived a whole week before Christmas and it is needless to say we all were delighted. You were so generous that it makes me feel bad to think that I can't do more for you but it is a problem making Christmas presents when one is so far from stores and has little money. I sent to Eaton's a month before Christmas for a few things and made most of everything, but as I was three weeks getting the order it gave me only one week to do all my presents and I didn't get everything made I intended to. There were several people I had to leave out. I guess I'll have to remember birthdays or anniversaries so they won't be all in a bunch until we get into a more civilized country.

Santa was most kind to us. The postmaster says I get more Christmas presents than anybody in this place.

We had a little tree for Emerson and he was delighted. I imagine it was the first time he ever saw one as such things are scarce on the prairie and I know the poor little chap had a very bare living last winter. I guess he thinks he has acquired a lot of nice relatives.

The picture book is ever so cute. Did you make it? He sits and looks at the pictures and talks about them. He had to put the little overall suit right on, in the middle of the tree, and today we were invited out to dinner so I put on some little blue serge pants I made and a gray flannel waist with blue serge collar and cuffs. As soon as he got home he wanted to put on his other "toot" as he called it. I think it is the pockets that he loves. His chicken has turned into a horse. He had a wooden horse for Xmas so he harnesses the chicken and his horse together with yards of string. He sits on a small wooden box, which is his wagon and hitches it along, pushing the chicken and the horse in front of him. He plays with them all day. It's rather hard on the oilcloth.

I was delighted with my dress and the cloth is very pretty. I have been watching the newspaper for some patterns to make it by. I surely can blossom out this spring.

George wore his mitts the other day. They are just what he needs, as woollen mitts don't last long without the leather pullovers. His leather ones were pretty well worn and he had begun to patch them. I saved the little chocolate teddy bear to put in Sonny's stocking and he liked the cracker brownies very much. The chocolates filled a long felt need as we all get candy hungry by Christmas.

I suppose you had a nice day at Louisa's. It is nice that she is so near and you can visit her often. I've actually been homesick this fall but it costs so much to go home. I'm afraid I'll have to get over it. I'm hoping George will sell and buy a farm back east in a few years. At present everything we have is tied up in this place and it is impossible to sell for what it's worth. There is to be a meeting this month to see what can be done to get the government to complete the Hafford Tentleford Branch of the railroad. If they would only finish the line the country would be much better settled and we would be within easy reach of a town. It would make a big difference in selling. George wants to stay until he proves up the homestead but is hoping to come back someday.

Tell Louisa her box came all OK and I will write. I can't write more this time. I'll want to hear all about your Christmas and the nice things Santa brought you. I only hope he was as good to you as he was to me.

Give my love to all, Nell

Lorenzo, Sask.
Feb. 17, 1926

Dear Aunty Marie,

Tomorrow is your birthday and it completely slipped my mind until after George had gone down to the Post Office last week so I'm afraid we're a little late in wishing you many happy returns of the day. I must get out my piece bag tomorrow and see what I can make for you.

We have had the most wonderful winter, very little snow and very warm. Some days it actually melts and I can keep the outside door open a good part of the morning. The twelfth we had the biggest storm we have had all winter and the snow drifted. Since then it has been cold. Ten below when we got up this morning. Most winters are so cold that George doesn't do much outside but the chores. However it has been so nice this winter he has been out everyday and I hardly know I have a husband except at mealtimes. He has been busy cutting brush on the homestead and getting land ready to break next summer. It is slow work clearing land and the winter is a good time to burn the tops of the trees. He has been hauling firewood the last two days and also getting out logs for a barn. He wants to build another one, as ours is small and we are short of room.

The cows are all dry now but one, which keeps us supplied with milk and cream for our porridge.

Emerson is a good lad for milk and some days drinks a quart. He grows like a little weed. I wish you could see him. He is a cute youngster and awfully bright. He seems to be quite musical and sings well. He was only three the last day of

August, still he can sing lots of songs and he can start anyone of them and sing it alone. The other morning he sat up on a chair with my old dust cap on his head and a copy of the game laws in his hand for a book and sang for nearly half an hour. I was busy but watched him out of the corner of my eye and he seems wholly unconscious of anything but his songs. He'd turn a page over and begin a new song. He plays around all day and isn't a bit mischievous. He is very careful of his playthings and hasn't torn his books yet. He sits and looks at the one you sent him but never offers to pull out a picture. The other day a Russian woman came visiting and brought two little tots. One of them grabbed Emerson's rag doll by the leg and he had a great time. "Don't hold Peter that way. Take him by the middle. Mugger don't take me by my legs, she takes me by the middle". He had quite a time till Peter was held, as he should be.

He is just a bit wilful and likes his own way. If I ask him to come to get washed or come to dinner he usually has something to do first. Usually he must tie his horses. I insist on his minding when I speak, so sometimes he has to sit on a chair until he can mind. He's a funny youngster. He'll sit there and never fuss to get down. After awhile if you ask him if he can be good now he'll say, "No me still a naughty boy". Sometimes I'll ask two or three times and then at last he'll say, "Me good boy now. Me can get down". Sometimes he sits there fifteen minutes pondering over his sin, when he might just as well have gotten down at the end of five. He really is a very good little youngster. Most sweet and loveable and he seems quite happy and contented with us. We'd hate to part with him now. I guess you'll think my letter is going to be all about the laddie but it's not.

I had a nice long letter from Flora and I'll try to write to her soon. You might send this to her when you write so she will know that my intentions are good.

George has sold another story. That makes three so far. They really are joint stories. He writes them out roughly so I get the idea then I rewrite them. I use some that he writes and change the wording of other parts so it sounds smooth. Also correct spelling and punctuation and always write the ending. Sometimes there'll be a page or more on the end for me to write. Then I copy them in my best handwriting and we send them forth. It takes me so long fixing up his stories, doing the housework and sewing for the family, that I don't get time to write anything myself. Did I tell you about the best story I have written (5000 words)? I sent it to the "Dominion Magazine" and as I didn't hear anything for a long time, I wrote to them. My letter was returned from the Dead Letter Office marked, "Supposed to be Fraudulent". As long as they have the manuscript and I can't get it back, I don't think I'd have the right to send it elsewhere. I've just finished a story about an old lady that I began ages ago and also an article for a young people's paper, which I intend to send out Saturday. I hope I can sell one of them. I hate to have my husband get ahead of me and he is in the lead at present.

I've been sewing all winter. All of my sheets had to be turned and I also fixed a single blanket the same way. I have Sonny's wardrobe completed. He grows so fast I don't dare make him too many clothes. I've made three work shirts for George and am on the second dress for myself. I got out all my old housedresses and aprons that had faded to a dirty white and dyed them dark blue so at present I'm a "blue" lady.

There was a concert at school a couple of weeks ago. George, Emerson and I blacked up like Negroes and sang two darky songs: "There's One Wide River" and "I'm A Rolling". There are no Negroes in this part of the country so we made quite a hit. Emerson was awfully cute. He wore the little blue overalls you sent him at Christmas and my peanut garden hat. George used stove soot and grease and it was some job washing it off with cold water that was hard. Most of the water in this country is hard. That's why I'm washing up all of the extras while I have snow water. It is a job melting enough snow for a good-sized washing but a lot easier to do all the washing itself.

Hubby went to bed a long time ago and as he wants to get up at six, I'll be sleepy if I stay up much longer. That is one nice part of living on a farm. You are quite independent and if you want to sleep in the morning you can. (That is in the winter). In the summer we're early risers. This winter we've been sleeping until daylight and as it isn't light until eight it gives one a good long night.

I'll surely try to write Flora soon. I wish we might have some kind of windfall so I could visit you next summer while Flora is at home, as I never hope to get as far as New Orleans. We have a good living and plenty to eat with no gas, milk, rent or fuel bills to worry about even if we don't have much cash so I suppose we're no worse off than lots of people in the cities. I like the life and am very happy but I would like to see you all once more.

Write as often as you can, as I love to hear from you.

We all send our love and best wishes for a happy birthday. (You'll have to celebrate it all over again).

Lovingly, Nell

Lorenzo, Sask.
April 25, 1926

Dear Auntie Marie,

It is sometime since George's birthday present came. I'm ashamed to think I haven't written you before. We have had some lovely weather and some that has not been quite so lovely. On the fine days I have been working outside. There are still lots of things to do. I have raked the yard and had various bon fires. One morning I harnessed one of the horses and moved a pile of logs from down by the pigpen up where I plan to have a henhouse. Such a time I had getting started, as George was in the field. The first harness I got on was too short so the whiffle tree hit the horses heels. I had to change harnesses. Then I got an old whiffle tree and when I got the chain nicely fastened around three logs and the horse started, it broke in the middle. I had to make a search of all of the machinery before I could find another one I could get off. The nuts either wouldn't turn or the bolts turned with them so I was sometime getting ready to "start". Then things proceeded fine. I am quite an expert with a saw and hammer so I am going to build the henhouse, but I don't know just about getting the upright pieces "upright" so George is going to put up the corner logs for me. He has been so busy that I can't get him to do it but he promises to help me someday soon. He planted about eight acres of wheat last week and is now ploughing. He ploughed the garden last week but it has been cold nights so I think I'll wait a few days before I put in onions and peas. I want to make a hot bed this week.

My birdies are laying fine. I have only sixteen hens and get fourteen, fifteen and sixteen eggs a day, so you see I haven't many lazy hens. I can't get one to set, however, I have about 150 eggs and not a sitting hen. I have the same trouble every year. They lay all summer and want to set in August or September. I bought an incubator from a woman who is moving away and we have set it up in the living room as that seemed to be the only available place. We are experimenting tonight, trying to get it to stay just at 105 degrees, as I'd hate to cook my little chickens.

Monday morning

This seems to be a pause in my washing. The water got cold and as I can't turn the faucet and get hot water, I have to set the tub on the stove and wait for it to get hot again.

Did I write you that the teacher was boarding with us? He is the possessor of a radio and a camera. We certainly enjoyed the radio. George listens to the news and market reports every noon and we get various church services every Sunday.

I want to take some pictures just as soon as things get green, but just now isn't a very pretty time of year.

I had one of my big turkey gobblers for dinner two weeks ago. He must have dressed 15 pounds. I invited the Lorenzo and Bluebird teachers, as I knew my family wouldn't want to eat turkey all the week and I thought it would be nice for Mr. Doolittle to get acquainted with the other teacher.

Last week the Mill's came over for the day and brought the Alberton teacher with them.

Tuesday noon

I am going to the Post Office this p.m. so will bring this to a close. I don't know as I shall get down again before mail day and if not, it wouldn't go out until a week from next Saturday. You see we are slow here.

Many thanks for George's birthday gifts. The chocolates were something Sonny and I could enjoy too and I'm afraid we had more than our share of them. George dressed up in a "boiled" shirt and put on his new necktie the next day after they arrived.

Tell Louisa I will write her soon. If she has moved will you please send me her new address when you write?

We all send love, Nellie

Lorenzo, Sask.
June 7, 1926

Dear Auntie Marie,

A whole month has passed since my birthday and I'm just writing to thank you for the stockings and candy. The stockings were something I needed and we all enjoy candy.

This has been a busy spring. We had the warmest winter since I have been in Canada and spring came unusually early this year. George had eight acres of wheat planted by the 20th of April.

The garden is up, even the beans and corn and we have had spinach five or six times also lettuce, onions and rhubarb. The radishes will be ready in a few days.

We invested in an incubator and brooder this spring. I had never run one before but got fifty-seven chicks. They were all right the first day I put them in the brooder but the next day I turned the lamp too high and set the brooder afire. I discovered it just in time to run for a pail of water and put out the fire. The chicks were all right, however we had a cold, stormy night and they crowded around the wire frame of the lamp trying to keep warm as the light was too low, that twelve got jammed to death, I have only forty-four left. I set the incubator again and the chicks are hatching today. I have a hen with six little turkeys and the turkey hen has fifteen eggs. They should hatch tomorrow. There is a hen on duck's eggs and another hen on hen's eggs. She had five chicks tonight and more hatching. I joined the egg pool this spring, so that is why I'm going in for chickens.

George went to town today. He asked me to go with him but it is such a long trip, forty-five miles in a bouncy wagon and then I have to start in and separate milk and feed calves and pigs when I get home.

The cows came home early so I got them milked and all the chores done so George wouldn't have anything to do when he got home but tend to his horses.

Mr. Doolittle has been having the mumps and has been miserable for several days but can eat once more and so is feeling a bit more cheerful. I suppose Sonny will have them next. He certainly is a dear little chap and so good. He'll play by himself all day and it takes very little to amuse him. I don't know what I'd ever do without him. I'm listening to a Scotch concert on the radio so my thoughts are rather scattered.

Did you know Marion and Rudy were in Launten? I didn't until I got a letter from Marion last week. She sent some very good snap-shots.

It is now several days later but as I have a chance to send this tomorrow I want to finish it tonight.

I have been mudding the hen house this weekend and it certainly is a messy job. I let the washing go all this week to tend to chickens and so I had to wash today and of course it rained. I only washed what we really needed so have a lot saved for next week.

Sonny used to be such a clean little chap when he played in the house but now he gets as dirty as a little pig and somehow he manages to get dirty in the house too. He is hard on his knees and the seat of his pants. I wanted to get a picture of him in the little overalls you sent him but I'm afraid if I don't hurry there won't be any overalls left. One knee is patched, also the seat and the other knee is sadly in need of a generous patch. I am so sleepy I can't write more tonight.

I had a card from a teacher in Everett saying Hannibal Hamlin was taken suddenly ill and removed to Peter Bent Brigham Hospital where he died. He was unconscious most of the time and then Doctors were undecided as to the cause of his death. Eunice was in Nova Scotia tending to the laundry business he bought a couple of years ago. Have you heard anything about it? I wrote to Eunice and sent it to her sister in Everett, as Helen wrote she was there. Ham was only a little over forty and always seemed so well. I wonder if Louisa got the little package I sent for her birthday. No doubt she has been so busy moving and getting settled that she couldn't find time to write.

Give her my love and we all send love to you.

Nell

Lorenzo, Sask.
July 28, 1926

Dear Auntie Marie,

Sonny is still eating his dinner and George is in town today. I have some washing to do but I'm weary so thought I'd write to you while I was resting.

This has been a lovely summer and crops look well so far. I wish you could see my garden. Probably it is as big as your whole yard. I put two rows of poppies all around the edge and a path through the middle bordered with poppies. They are all in bloom now so it is quite a flower garden. George simply plowed and harrowed and I planted and hoed it since. We had green peas for the first time a week ago. There has been an abundance of swiss chard and spinach, also summer turnips and I have given lots away. We have had new carrots, also beets and of course plenty of lettuce, onions and radishes. My chickens are large enough for broilers so you see we are living high.

You'll be surprised to know we have rented the farm for a year and are coming home in time for Christmas. We can't leave until the crops are in and the grain threshed.

We plan to visit the family, also George's brothers and sister and then George will get some kind of work until harvest time and come back then. I'm really quite crazy about coming and can hardly wait to start.

I have lots of sewing to do to make my family and myself presentable, mostly made over things. Mother sent me some of Connie's things, a very good suit coat and underwear. I feel now I can rip up some of my old things for Emerson. I don't want to do his sewing though until winter, as he grows so fast. The things I made last winter are skintight for him now.

He has been barefooted all summer. I planned to get him canvas shoes for summer but I can't keep a pair on him, so I guess I'll make his old ones do for the little he wears shoes and get some in the fall. He has set his heart on tan boots that "lace like Daddy's". His are button boots.

We drove to town last week, as there has been a dentist there every two weeks this summer. He has a car fitted up as an office and travels from Florida to this cold climate. He certainly is busy when he strikes one of these towns. His wife travels with him and they seem to enjoy life. Someone was telling George that he cleared $30,000 last year. You see he has no office rent and a rushing business everyday and dental work costs.

George has been getting the cows this summer. I did last year but I have to get dinner at night now, as the teacher takes a cold lunch. I like to have dinner between six and six-thirty so I'm usually busy when it's time to hunt them up. I hope they won't be more than a mile away tonight, as I thought I'd try to get them before George got home.

Mr. Doolittle brought home two young crows, which he tried to tame. One died but the other one stays around. He comes home every morning and crows for his breakfast and then he goes hunting for himself. He usually comes back again at night.

There was a concert at the school last Friday evening to get money for playground equipment. It was very good and they took in over sixteen dollars. Emerson gets quite excited. The dialogues are very real to him and he keeps people amused with his questions and comments. He is still talking about it yet.

I must finish the washing and do the dinner dishes.

Emerson's birthday is the 31st of August and he'll be four. He is a cute youngster and I do want you to see him. George says I've been crazy to go home ever since we got him.

I hope Flora and Al will like Atlanta as well as New Orleans. Tell Flora she had better plan to come north while I'm home. As long as the place is rented I may not come back with George in harvest time, but stay until spring. If I'm in the east over a year maybe she'll be home in that time. Give my love to both the girls.

I have a very good snapshot of us which I'll send as they are printed.
Lots of love, Nell

Lorenzo, Sask.
September 9, 1926

Dear Auntie Marie,

How time flies. I could hardly believe my eyes when I looked at the calendar and saw it was the ninth of September. The things for Emerson arrived in time for

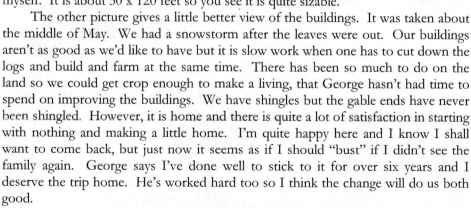

his birthday and he was delighted. The little stick candies pleased him immensely. The overalls are fine. They are a bit long in the legs but he'll grow into them. He looks cute in blue. I wanted to send you a snapshot of him taken in the pair you sent at Christmas but haven't any now. I took one, one morning when he was coming from the barn carrying the milk pails. He looks so cute.

I ran in and got Mr. Doolittle's camera and took a picture of him. I had only one and sent that home but have sent for some more and I'll surely send you one when I get them.

I'm sending you a picture of my garden. George is exhibiting two turnips but we seem to be so far away it isn't very clear. I planted and took all the care of the garden myself. It is about 50 x 120 feet so you see it is quite sizable.

The other picture gives a little better view of the buildings. It was taken about the middle of May. We had a snowstorm after the leaves were out. Our buildings aren't as good as we'd like to have but it is slow work when one has to cut down the logs and build and farm at the same time. There has been so much to do on the land so we could get crop enough to make a living, that George hasn't had time to spend on improving the buildings. We have shingles but the gable ends have never been shingled. However, it is home and there is quite a lot of satisfaction in starting with nothing and making a little home. I'm quite happy here and I know I shall want to come back, but just now it seems as if I should "bust" if I didn't see the family again. George says I've done well to stick to it for over six years and I deserve the trip home. He's worked hard too so I think the change will do us both good.

He has gone threshing about thirty miles from here so I'm running the farm. He went last week and the same night it began to rain and rained steady all the week. He got in a day and a quarter stoking and as things were so wet they couldn't do anything for a week, anyway he walked home over thirty miles. It was twelve o'clock when he got there and pitch black outside. I don't see how he ever found the road. You bet I was glad to see him. He went back this morning so I'm milking cows once more. We're milking four so with the calves, pigs and chickens to feed it keeps me busy. Mr. Doolittle goes for them after school. He rides horseback and as the cows often go two or three miles it is much easier for him than for me. He usually takes George's rifle and sometimes brings home a prairie chicken or a couple of partridges so he doesn't mind going.

I have been trying to do a little mudding. It seems to be a continuous job. There are lots of cracks in a log building. I did the granary as far up as I can reach and have started on the barn.

I'm trying to do a little sewing but don't accomplish much. I have lots of things to make over, as none of my clothes are at all modern. I fixed over an old pongee waist and have made an over blouse of dark green silk poplin. It is done, all but the collar, cuffs and pockets. I guess the sewing will have to wait until I get through working outside but now that George is away I find a lot of things to do to keep me busy.

I enjoyed Pinga's letter and Faye surely is a dear. It seems to me he looks like Louisa but of course it is hard to tell just by a snapshot. Emerson will have the time of his life when he has someone to play with. He amuses himself very well but gets lonesome all by himself. You see neighbors aren't very plentiful and they all live too far away for him to go by himself. I'm busy most of the time and none of my neighbors can speak English so it's no fun calling on them.

I'm so sleepy I really can't keep awake to write more and five o'clock comes very quickly.

Hope Flora is feeling better. I wrote her last week. I hope she can come home while we're still in the east. I'd love to see her.

We plan to go from Montreal right to Portland and see Dad first, and then will make our other visits later. George has brothers and sisters in Wells and North Berwick. I don't know just when we will get to Boston but we surely will see you all before we come back. Thank Louisa for her invitation. We'll surely accept it.

I'll try to write her after the outside work is done. We are getting cold nights and mornings. Heavy frosts the last two nights so I may have to take in some of the garden stuff before George gets back unless it warms up.

I must go to bed, as I'm terribly sleepy. Give my love to Louisa and many thanks for all the good things you sent Sonny.

Lovingly, Nell

97 High St., Berlin, N.H.
June 21, 1927

Dear Auntie Marie,

 No doubt you are wondering just where I am. I seem to be travelling about. My husband decided he could not get along without his family so here we are.

 He came to Portland the night we got home from Louisa's and the next morning we went to North Berwick to see his sister. He saw one of his brothers that afternoon but the other three he missed, as they were all away. He had to leave early Monday morning in order to get back for Tuesday so spent most of the day travelling. I spent a few days with George's brother and his wife in Kitery and the rest of the time with his sister Alice. We had a nice time there. Her children were all grown up but they amused Emerson a lot and Lloyd took him with him when he

George & Nellie on a trip to Maine

went for the cows. He had a nice big place to play and had a good time. George sent a telegram for me to come to Lancaster, N.H. We had a nice trip up through the mountains. It was a clear day and the view was lovely. George met us at the station. He and Mr. Trelman got in Tuesday and had a nice clean boarding place. The food was very good but the family was very rough talking. There was a woman with three girls and a boy in high school. The boy seemed very nice but the girls and their mother squabbled all the time and they weren't at all polite and were very rough talking. I hated to have Emerson hear such talk, as they pick up such things too early.

 The men got through in Lancaster on Saturday and left Monday for Berlin. George took my suitcase to the station and got my ticket and I left about two hours later. The men got here about five and loaded up the truck for morning and then George went to the Y.M.C.A. to see if they knew of a good place. They sent him to the Baptist Ministers. Mrs. Chandler is a very sweet woman with white hair. Her husband was drowned last summer on the last day of his vacation at Old Orchard. She came back and the church asked her to finish his year so she has. Her son just graduated from Wentworth Institute and her daughter from Baten College. In fact, she hadn't returned from graduation when we arrived, but the son took us in.

 She finishes her church work here in the early part of July so is beginning to pack, but said we might stay if we did not mind the upset condition. There is a nice yard for Emerson to play in and it is in a good part of the town. If they leave before we do, she said she probably could find a place for us.

She found a box of building blocks and a steel building set with bolts and nuts for Emerson to play with and he is having a most wonderful time. He has played with it all day.

George's sister gave me lots of pieces of cloth and I cut a lot of squares for my quilt. I haven't cut the pieces you gave me yet. Perhaps I'll get them out so I can make it when I get to Reta's. She is quite disgusted because I haven't been there yet. I believe Marion was going a week ago but I haven't heard for sure.

I made Emerson a cute khaki suit with a red tie while I was at Lancaster and had enough cloth to make an extra pair of pants. I must get something to sew on here to keep me out of mischief.

I have just finished a letter to Grandma Rand and guess I'll venture out to see if I can find the Post Office.

I'm sorry I missed seeing Flora by only a week after I was with Louisa so long. Pinga and Bill were awfully good to us and we had such a good time there. It was a very comfortable place to stay and I did enjoy my visit. This is my last sheet of paper so I must stop. Give my love to all your family. We think we will be here three weeks anyway and if we aren't here I'll leave my address at the Post Office so any mail will be forwarded.

Love to all, Nell

Lorenzo, Sask.
Dec. 8, 1927

Dear Mother,

The box came safely last Saturday. I opened it on Sunday and gave Emerson the Build-A-Toy and he surely was delighted. He had so few things to play with as all his toys were packed in the barrel that George thought he'd enjoy it more to have something now. We're saving the rest for Christmas and plan to have a tree.

I'm afraid I'm not quite so forehanded, as I've just finished doing up my things today. I guess I was slow, as I made everything this year except the presents for the men folks and they seem hard to sew for.

I'm sending some of the snapshots I took and I'll send the other two views as soon as I get some more finished.

It has been so cold that we haven't been to the post office anymore than necessary. This last week has been between thirty and forty below so I don't venture far.

George met with a particular accident one evening. He usually undresses in the living room and leaves his clothes there as he hustles down and builds the fires before Sonny and I get up. The stovepipe runs through our bedroom and the other night after he went up he backed up and hit the stovepipe. It was pretty hot and it sizzled the skin right off in a place most difficult for him to sit on. He planned to haul wood this week but decided it would be rather uncomfortable riding so hasn't done much but the chores.

Tell Grandma not to worry if she doesn't hear from me often. I guess I'll have to send a letter down each Saturday when George goes for the mail, as he hates to go down twice each week. Of course it will stay there a week but he has been walking, as the horses are out and he says it's easier to walk than stop to hunt for them. The snow is deep and it is about seven miles down and back. Unless I send it when he goes for the mail he has to make a special trip down on Friday. I keep thinking we will get down to the office during the week but we never do so Grandma doesn't hear as often as she'd like. I'll try to send them down mail day hereafter, as someone goes for the mail.

Hope this package I'm sending reaches you all right and that you'll all have a very nice Christmas.

I'll thank you all separately when we open the things you sent.

Love to all, Nell

Lorenzo, Sask.
Feb. 10, 1928

Dear Auntie Marie,

I suppose by the time this reaches you, you will be having another birthday so I'll begin by wishing you a very happy one and many of them.

I'm sending a wee remembrance. I can't go shopping so my things have to be homemade. Emerson made the valentine all by himself without any help and he wanted to send it to you.

We are having a most wonderful winter. It was cold during November and December and the snow came early but January and so far this month, have been quite lovely. It is between thirty and forty everyday and today it is fifty-two above.

I have been having a grand time fixing things up. I turned all my sheets, as they were thin in the middle. I think they have done well. You know they weren't new when I got them and I bought them a year before I was married when I kept house in Everett. I've never had any new ones so I think they've done well. I've got part of two patch work quilt tops done but ran out of squares and can't go on until I cut more. I cut big squares out of the biggest pieces and then use what is left for small squares. I thought if I get the tops and backs ready it wouldn't take long to put them together when we had a little money coming in and I could send for cotton. I mended the old quilt you gave me. One side was quite good. As soon as the snow leaves I shall wash it and put on a new back. All of my bedding needs washing. I rather dread washing the quilts as they are so heavy but they have to be done. I made George three work shirts and this week I cut off an old overcoat and made George a mackinaw coat with patch pockets out of the top and a coat for Emerson out of the bottom.

We have a puppy and he gets terribly rough. He grabs Emerson's coat and then both Sonny and the puppy begin to pull. It isn't very good for his clothes. His old coat was nearly eaten up.

We have read quite a lot this winter. I subscribed to the "Free Press", a weekly paper with news and a magazine section and the "Country Gentleman". The druggist in town persuaded George to take the "Saturday Evening Post" for ten weeks, so that comes out from Hafford each week. I like the "Saturday Evening Post".

George has been busy all winter cutting wood. It is a big pile of dry wood for fuel and quite a few building logs. We planned to put a piece on this house but we can't decide just where we want to put it, on the south or west, and this house is low and I'd like a better foundation under it. George wants to fence the homestead next summer so I think that will take most of the money and I think we'll build a new house and do it as slowly as we can. George can get out the logs and dig the cellar and we won't begin until summer after next to build. I think we'd be better satisfied than if we kept tacking pieces on.

I must go feed the birdies. I haven't very many. Nobody seems to have many to sell. George got two from a neighbor today. That swells my flock to seven hens, a rooster and three turkeys.

Write when you can and tell Louisa I'll try to write to her soon. Emerson talks of Faye yet and has named the colt Faye. She should be honored.

Love to you and Pinga and Bill, Nell

Lorenzo, Sask.
April 10, 1928

Dear Auntie Marie,

I guess it is up to me to thank you for the pretty tie you sent George. He was much pleased with it but it is impossible to get him to write a letter. It was the only present he had this year. I made him a birthday cake with little candles on it and Emerson asks every day now when his birthday is coming, as he wants a cake.

I suppose it is quite spring-like around Boston now and you all appeared in new hats for Easter. We had a lovely warm week and we thought spring was right here but it turned cold and the last two weeks have been horrid with snow flurries most everyday. Here it is Wednesday night and I haven't washed so far this week. I planned to today but when we awoke this morning we found we were having a regular blizzard. George brought in a set of harnesses that needed repairing and I have been reading aloud to him out of the "Saturday Evening Post" while he mended them. He is fixing up machinery, etc. so as to be ready to get on the land if it ever gets warm.

I began to clean house and got the upstairs done last week. I planned to do downstairs this week, as I want to set the incubator soon and I don't want to tear things up after I get it going, as I have to set it in the living room. However, one doesn't feel much like house cleaning when it is so cold and the ground is covered with snow. My turkey hen laid an egg yesterday, but the one she laid today froze before I found it so I promised Emerson he could have it for breakfast. I have one birdy ready to set but guess I'll have to give her hens' eggs, as she may get over it before I get enough turkey eggs for a setting.

Thursday

Well, the morning wash is finished and I'm weary so guess I'll finish this while I'm resting. We were invited to the Gammels on Sunday. They are a German family about a mile east of us. The old man and his wife can't talk English but the son and his wife speak very good English. They have two small boys so Emerson has a great time there. They had a nice chicken dinner and a lunch in the afternoon with colored Easter eggs. We were at Louisa's last Easter. It was a cold day here and began to snow just as we started for home.

We have two cows down. A couple of weeks ago they went down to the pond north of the barn. They both slipped on the ice and I don't know how long they were there before George missed them. He came running to the house and I got on my rubber boots and went down with him. Sweeny had broken through the ice and her hind legs were in ice water. It was a job getting her out. George didn't dare go for help as she was so cold we thought the best thing to do was to get her out as soon as possible. George and I both tugged away and finally got her out and dragged her onto the shore. I ran to the house for blankets and got her a hot drink and then we got the black cow onto the shore. She wasn't wet so it didn't take so long. We covered her up and then George went for Mr. Gammel and he and Mr. Diener both came. They got the cows onto the manure sled and got them to the barn. Poor Sweeny was dreadfully sick and I thought she'd pass out before morning. Her hind legs were stiff as sticks. I rubbed them dry and rubbed them with liniment while they were getting the black cow in. George and I have to turn them over every day to change their positions. We hope after they have their calves they will be able to get up. Sweeny eats well now and seems to be improving in general health every day but is helpless. It is so hard to know just what to do for an animal and I don't believe there is a veterinary within fifty miles. I hope they will recover in time, as cattle are high now and we can't afford to lose our two best cows.

I made Emerson a suit out of the black serge skirt you gave me. I trimmed the collar, cuffs and pocket with a double row of bright red braid. I wanted some red buttons to button the pants onto the blouse but can't find any in the catalogue so guess Sonny will have to have black ones instead. I also made a suit out of an old brown and white shirt you gave me. George laughed at it, as he says the cloth is old-fashioned looking but Emerson is quite delighted with it and thinks it is very pretty. I've certainly made good use of the pieces you gave me. Did I tell you I couldn't get the black coat you gave me into my trunk, as it was so full so I sent it to Ruth and she made a winter coat out of it for one of her boys?

I have sent for my garden seeds and will be so glad when I can get out and dig. I'm planning to start some asparagus this year. I'm very fond of it and of course we can't buy such things here. I've also sent for mushroom spawn and am going to have some mushroom. We surely missed not having a garden last summer. We only got potatoes and carrots when we got back and I don't know what we would have done had not the Gammels made a whole barrel of sauerkraut, which they have shared with us. I'm very fond of sauerkraut so have managed without the other vegetables.

It is after four and I must get the clothes in and then think about supper. Thank Louisa for George's birthday card and please send me Flora's address. I'm sorry her second marriage was a failure. I always had a soft spot in my heart for Flora and want to write to her.

Love to all, Nell

Lorenzo, Sask.
May 30, 1928

Dear Auntie Marie,

I did not think of it being a holiday today, until I wrote the date, as we don't observe it here. It was nice to get your letter last Sunday and I do enjoy a little chat with you even if it is a one sided affair.

First I want to thank you for my birthday gift. It must keep you busy remembering all the birthdays. The apron was very pretty and I needed stockings very badly. My old ones had reached the point where I had to darn them every day or two, a regular nuisance in the busy season. I'm glad they were plain cotton ones as silk ones aren't as much use to me here. I've two pair now I've hardly had on since got I got back to this part of the country.

I suppose you want to hear about our cows. Well, George and I turned them over everyday to change their position. A cow isn't very light you know but we did it for a whole month. George thought perhaps after they freshened they might be able to get up, as they seemed well and ate everything in sight. Blackie's calf died and had to be taken. You see we have no veterinary here for miles and no phone but Mr. Diener knew how to do it so George went for him. I stayed in but they needed me too, so I had to go down to help. The calf was dead and Blackie died the next day. She was a good cow and Emerson went down and wept over her.

The next day Sweeny's calf arrived. It was alive but only lived a week and poor Sweeny died that night. So we lost both cows and calves and cream the chicks will be lacking this summer so we won't be able to ship any cream.

I have my garden all planted and it has kept me busy and I put in more than I ever have before. George was working on the west side of the place and as it is quite high the frost seldom hits there. He gave me a patch on the top of his wheat field and I put in a small piece of early potatoes, onions, corn, peas, cucumbers, citron and marrows. They usually freeze in the garden by the house. I started those early. Then George plowed the garden by the house and we put in the upper end to potatoes. I cut them and then when George plowed, I walked behind and dropped them in. It is much quicker that way. The garden here is 165 x 50 feet not counting the potato patch and the piece on the other side of the place is nearly as large, so we should have lots to eat next winter if all goes well.

Emerson has been digging spruce gum off the trees in the back of the house and I have chewed until my jaws ache. He has a great time out of doors and stays out all of the time. He goes back and forth across the place all by himself. He follows George around when he is in the field. He surely is a good youngster and never seems to get into mischief or meddle with things he ought not to. George destroyed a nest of field mice and Sonny rescued two baby mice and brought them home. He kept them in a tin can in the kitchen and tried to feed them cows milk from a wad of cotton on the end of a toothpick. They lived a few days and then passed out, much to my joy.

I have about fifty chickens and eight little turkeys. I hoped to make my everlasting fortune on turkeys this summer but have had poor luck so far. I had twenty-seven eggs but got just eight turkeys. The rest seemed to be rotten. I don't know whether the gobbler is too young to be very good or it was my fault and I chilled the eggs by putting them down in the cellar. Anyway I have a hen sitting on eleven turkey eggs and one of the turkeys is sitting out in the brush pile in the woods on fourteen eggs. My other turkey has begun to lay again, as I miss her everyday but I can't find her nest. I shall have to watch her some morning and follow her but I've been so busy tending to my chickens that she's gone before I know it.

I have washed today. You people ought to be glad you have soft water. In winter I have to melt snow and now there is plenty of water but it is too hard and it is impossible to wash with it, unless you put the wood ashes in a sack and soak them overnight and then pour off the top of the water in the morning. Sometimes I use lye but when I do my hands get so sore I find the ashes are better.

I wish Faye could come out here. There is such a nice place to play and plenty of milk to drink. It is very pretty here now. I wonder if any of my relatives or friends will ever get this far to see me. I hope so. I'm glad we had this trip east especially now that Grandma Rand is gone, as she seemed so pleased to see me and she liked George, so felt much better about having me live so far away. It has kept mother and Ida tied down quite a bit. This is my last sheet of paper so I guess I must stop. Thank you for Flora's address. Tell her I'll write to her soon. Give my love to Louisa when you see her. I often think of you and wonder if you are in Medford.

Lovingly, Nell

P.S. Maude and Winfield have been sent to the Philippines. They were to sail the 20th of May. Maude was busy getting her clothes fixed up. Haven't they seen the country though, since Winfield went into the service? Eunice is running the laundry at Kentville, Nova Scotia and is doing well. She has a house of her own and rents the downstairs.

Love to all, Nell

Lorenzo, Sask.
Dec. 29, 1928

Dear Auntie Marie,

Well! Christmas is over and we surely had a nice one this year. Our last mail before Christmas came on Saturday and both George and Sonny wanted the tree Saturday night. I thought a couple of days didn't make much difference so we had it Saturday. Sonny hung up his stocking on Monday night and I saved several of the small parcels for that and then I cooked the turkey on Tuesday. The tree was very pretty and Santa was more than good to us all. George and Sonny were both delighted with their overalls. I had patched until it was a useless job and I refused to patch anymore for either of them, so I guess I was as delighted, if not more so then they to see new overalls. I just love the silky lavender cloth. It is such a lovely shade and I always had a fondness for lavender. I shall make it for my best dress. The other goods are very pretty and I surely needed housedresses and aprons. Aunt Ida sent me cloth for a dress, also mother and Emma, so I shall have quite a sewing bee when I get started. I put the glass top in Sonny's stocking and he was more than delighted with it. I think he has played with it more than any of his toys except the erector set and his sled. He had so much he hasn't had time to play with all of the things he got. He has been coloring in his drawing book and done splendidly. He likes to do things with his hands but doesn't seem at all anxious to learn to read. He likes to have me read to him but he hates to learn words. Of course he is young yet and he may come to it when he gets to school. I shall start him when school opens in the spring.

I hope you people finally got the box I sent. I'm so sorry it didn't reach you in time for Christmas but I couldn't seem to get it mailed.

I had it done up for a week before I got it off. I wanted to send away to a mail order house for some things and sent a small order the first of November for the men folks. I planned to send again, or soon as George sold a load of wheat but it was so late before he hauled any wheat there wasn't time, so I had to make everything and as the machine decided to take a vacation just then, I had to do everything by hand. Christmas shopping out of my piece bag is certainly a problem. I hope next year I may be able to do more.

We have had a lovely winter for this part of the world. It was cold in October and we had about six inches of snow. I thought winter had come for good but the snow was gone in a week. Since then it has been warm and there is no sleighing yet. That is quite unusual, as we often have sleighing the first of November. We got a little snowstorm the other night and it is snowing again tonight. The wind is blowing and you may be sure the wood fire feels good.

I have had lots of company this fall. George met a man named Smith while he was away threshing. He wanted to look at homesteads in this part of the country, so he and George came home in his car on Saturday and went back to work on Sunday after threshing was over. He brought his wife and baby and a young German chap up for a couple of days while they looked the country over. We are rather hoping they will take land here, as I think they would be good neighbors.

One night six men came. They were on their way to Sandy Lake on a hunting trip and lost their way. It was dark so they stopped here. Fortunately they had lots of meat along with them so it didn't take long for me to get supper for them. I didn't have beds for so many but they said they didn't mind as they had plenty of blankets and they would be sleeping on the ground anyway when they got to the lake. We left them downstairs and they made up their beds to suit themselves. They left after breakfast the next morning.

Mr. and Mrs. Mills, friends of ours who have been in the east for two years came back and they stayed with us for two weeks before going to Vancouver for the winter. Auntie Mills knit Emerson some mittens while she was here and George mittens and two pair of socks. She sent away for a sled for him and also moccasins and rubbers to fit.

I invited one of our bachelor neighbors up to dinner on Christmas, as I knew he'd have no place to go. We had a nice dinner and I ate so much and have kept on stuffing on sweets all the week, so I haven't felt hungry since Wednesday afternoon. Mr. Evans came up in the car and wanted us to go down there to supper. They are an English family who live sixteen miles south of us. George thought that because they came for us we should go. We did the milking before we left and got one of the neighbors to milk in the morning and feed the calf. They had a turkey supper with all the fixings. A bachelor neighbor of theirs was there and he brought up his radio so we had some nice music. We played Pit and had a midnight lunch so it was two a.m. before we retired. Mr. Evans brought us home again the next afternoon. It is bedtime so I won't write more.

Many, many thanks for all the nice things you sent us. I wish I could do more for you but I guess the only thing I can do is to write oftener. I know you all had a nice Christmas at Pinga's. I thought of you and wondered several times through the day just what you were doing. I shall want to hear all about it.

Lots of love and best wishes for a very happy new year! Nellie

Lorenzo, Sask.
Feb. 11, 1929

Dear Auntie Marie,

A letter from Ida says your family is better once more and we surely were glad to hear it. We have spoken of Bill, Pinga and Faye many times and glad to know they are up and around once more.

We have been very fortunate this winter and haven't even had a cold. I suppose where we are so far from the folks and never get into crowds we aren't apt to catch things.

January was a cold month, some days thirty-five to fifty below zero but this month has been warmer. The first part of this winter was lovely so I suppose we must expect some cold weather. George has hauled some wood to town this winter. We are fortunate in having lots of dry wood and the railroad west of us is finished so we have a town only twelve miles away.

I want to clean the house this next week. School opens the 1st of March and we expect to have the teacher board with us this year. The living room is dirty. I think wood fires make a lot of smoke and dust. I want to kalsomine both rooms downstairs and wash all the curtains. I plan to make new curtains for the front of my dish cupboard.

George is going to town today and I want to send this in by him. I can't write more now, as he is nearly ready to start out.

I'm sending you a small package for your birthday. I haven't any pretty card to put in it but nevertheless we all wish you a happy birthday and many of them.

Tell Pinga I'll try to write her soon. Love to all, Nell

Lorenzo, Sask.
March 3, 1929

Dear Auntie Marie,

Ida's card was quite a shock to me, as I didn't know Dad had been sick. I suppose you went to Portland. I looked for a letter on yesterday's mail from some of the family but not a word from anybody however; I suppose you all have been busy and upset. I'm so sorry for you all but glad Dad went quickly without a long, painful sickness. It was so hard for him to keep away from his work. I wish I might have come home but it was over a week before I got Ida's card. I stayed awake most of that night thinking about her. Do you know what she plans to do? I wrote her last week that George and I would love to have her with us. She would be a lot of company for me. Do you think she would be contented so far away from her church work? I really want her to have a few years of enjoyment. I don't want to say anything against mother (stepmother) for I think she had lots of good qualities and was a good wife to Dad in her way but she has such decided views and opinions that she isn't comfortable to live with. It was only this last fall when Dad and mother went on a vacation up in Maine that Ida wrote me what a good time she was having all alone with no one to watch her or criticize everything she did. She was wishing then that she had some place where she could do as she pleased. She surely could here and she would have a grand opportunity to start a Sunday school of her own, as the kiddies have none at all. We would love to have her but I want her to do what would make her happiest. I don't know what Dad did about Ida but one time mother was particularly disagreeable and blamed her for all of our shortcomings for not bringing us up to have more manners. I wrote to Dad about it and he wrote me that I need never worry about Ida being taken care of, as she would have a home as long as he lived and he had left things so she would be taken care of after he died. You know he never talked much about his affairs anyway.

I don't know what mother plans to do now she and Uncle Henry are both alone, but I thought she might go back to live with Uncle Henry and rent the house. If she does stay there, I hope Aunt Ida won't feel it her duty to stay with her because she hates to leave her alone. I wish you would write me about Aunt Ida for I really want to do something for her.

We expected the school to open tomorrow and the teacher is to board here this year. Mr. Gammel went to town to meet him yesterday but he got word the man he was expecting had taken a school elsewhere, so I imagine it will be another week before he can get one. I cleaned house early, as stoves make things so dirty. I put in a strenuous two weeks washing curtains and kalsomining but the house is clean anyway.

I guess Louisa will think I'm never going to pay her the fifty cents I owe her, but I haven't been out of the yard since the day after Christmas. I want to get a couple of paper twenty-five cent pieces that I can put in a letter, as she can't cash a postal note in the states. Although George has been to Altcane several times there is no bank there. Tell her to keep her courage up and she will get it someday.

I'm so glad she and Bill are out once more. There seems to be lots of sickness in the east. Everyone who writes me has either been sick or some of their family have. We have all been well all winter, not even a cold.

I'm so glad spring is coming. It melts a little everyday. Today it is dripping off the eaves.

I must stop and write one or two other letters before it gets dark. Do write me soon.

Lots of love to you all, Nell

RUDOLPH RICHNER -Born in Canton Agau, Switzerland on June 4, 1857 and died on February 16, 1929 in Cape Elizabeth, Maine. Mr. Richner was married twice, his first wife being Miss Florence Hamblin of North Deering and his second wife, Miss Eliza Rand of Cape Elizabeth. Survived by wife Eliza and three children, Rudolph Dana Richner, Hartford, Conn., Mrs. Ruth (Raymond) Allen, Jay, Maine and Mrs. Nellie (George) Campbell, Saskatchewan, Canada; two sisters, Miss Ida Richner and Mrs. Marie Davenport, Watertown, Mass. and six grandchildren.

Rudolph came to Boston at age eleven and two years later learned his trade, that of a manufacturing jeweler. He came to Portland in 1882 and was in business first under the firm name of Richner and Sandborn, and later as Richner and Hunnewell. He was a member of the Woodfords Congregational Church and its Men's Club, and of the Maine Charitable Mechanics' Association.

Lorenzo, Sask.
May 3, 1929

Dear Aunt Marie,

It is a whole month since George received the pretty shirt. I don't know where the time has gone but I haven't seemed to have written any letters. He was much pleased with it and it surely was nice of you to remember him. It was the only present he had. I couldn't get anywhere to buy anything but made him a cake with candles on it.

The 21st of April we all went to Mrs. Mill's for the day. I guess I wrote you the Mill's stayed two weeks with us before going to Vancouver for the winter. Mrs. Mills is over sixty but you know I always like older people anyway. They live about ten miles from us but of course it takes longer for us to travel ten miles than it does you folks, as we have to go with the work horses. George dolled up in his birthday shirt and looked quite fine.

I had a card from Marion last week. Their address was General Delivery, Richmond, Virginia. They liked it so well there that they had decided to stay at least two months and she had sent Donnie to school. She sent me a box just before leaving Hartford and there were two very good-looking hats in it, one a light green sports felt that is quite becoming. There was a good summer coat that just fit Emerson and a frock coat, a real ministerial looking affair that George can wear for chores. There was a light top coat that had a three cornered tear in the back but as the sleeves were long for George I got enough off them to set a piece under and ravelled out enough threads of the goods to make a nice darn, so it hardly shows now. I was quite delighted with a pair of patent leather slippers until I discovered they weren't mates.

George is busy plowing. He got my garden all ready for me before he started on the fields but I neglected to send for seeds. It seemed so cold there didn't seem to be any special hurry but now I could plant quite a few things such as peas and onions and can start the cabbage and cauliflower in the hot bed. I'm hoping they will come tomorrow, as things sometimes come in a week, although it is usually two weeks before we get what we send for.

Emerson has had several starts at school but has had a couple of sick spells. It is a long walk; about four miles over and back and then the roads have been bad. He gets into every puddle he can find, so often he was wet way to his knees when he got home. Of course he had a cold lunch and I think the excitement of having so many children to play with after being alone so much was hard on him, as he plays so hard. The teacher said he wasn't still a minute in school or out and he has been stood in the corner three times already. He just doesn't seem to take school at all seriously and thinks he's there to play. Of course when he is a little older and the novelty wears off he may settle down to business.

Miss Evans, the teacher, is very nice and I was looking forward to a pleasant summer with her here but the people here are complaining because they want a male teacher. Although the trustees want her to stay she says it is most unpleasant teaching in a district where one feels they aren't wanted, so she talks of leaving. She hasn't fully decided yet.

I got through the winter without any cold at all. Emerson woke up on Monday morning with a cold and headache and seemed generally upset so I've kept him home all this week. He is out playing but still coughs a little. A day or two later I felt a cold coming on and yesterday and today my head feels like a "pumpkin". I cough and sneeze and my nose runs all the time and I just feel generally miserable, so that accounts for my writing letters Friday morning instead of doing some of the many things I could be doing. My breakfast dishes aren't quite finished but I wanted to "sit" for a while, so I did.

Tell Louisa her nice long letter was surely worth waiting for. I did enjoy it and have read parts of it over again.

She spoke of thinking that Dad left the estate in a very fair way but I really haven't heard how anything was left. I had a letter from mother last week and she said they sold the jewellery business, as it took so long for the courts to act that they thought the business would all go to pieces. They got very little for it, but of course what they got would go into the estate but she said nothing else so I know nothing about how anything was left.

I set a hen the middle of March and while she was sitting we had the biggest snowstorm of the winter. It was so cold that the poor things didn't hatch out. They were due Wednesday night but by Friday there was no signs of any chickens so I broke an egg to see what was wrong. There was a live chick in it that needed about one day more I should think. I listened to all the eggs and took out four bad ones and left her seven eggs. Then I got the hot water bottle and put under them with her on top and at night I heated flannel clothes to put under the eggs and she got six out of the seven. She would have got the seventh one out only the egg rolled down between the hay and the edge of the box and I didn't find it until it was cold but the chicken was full-grown. I had to keep her in the house a couple of days but the chickens are all right now and are running around as lively as can be. I wish some more hens would set but I guess they think it is too cold. The leaves haven't begun to come out yet and there are still patches of snow in the woods although it is going very fast.

I must go out and finish my dishes and wash the separator.

Louisa wrote Mr. Cummings was sick. I hope he is better by now. Please remember us to him. It will be nice for you to see Flora this summer. Am glad she can make the trip. I wish I could make just a short trip back, but it costs so much to travel about I guess I can't for a while anyway. Write when you can as I do enjoy getting your letters.

Give my love to Louisa and Bill when you see them and keep a good big lot for yourself.

Nell

Lorenzo, Sask.
May 20, 1929

Dear Aunt Marie and Louisa,

I think I'll write a joint letter to thank you both for my birthday gifts. They were just what I needed. My towels are getting poor and it is quite nice to have some new ones now the teacher is with us. They are such a nice size too.

I like the tablecloths immensely. A linen one seems so much easier to launder and they always look nice. It was lovely of you both to remember me so generously. Mother sent me a pretty towel, washcloth and cake of soap and Aunt Ida sent me a bureau scarf. I was pleased with it, as mine were wearing out. In fact, I made a very good looking one this spring out of a flour sack.

I made George a shirt today out of a couple of flour sacks. It really looks quite nice and will look better when I get it dyed.

I have been busy planting my garden and have put in a lot already but still have a lot more to plant. I shall have to wait until George plows up another piece as my garden is full and I haven't got it half done. I dug up half of the rhubarb roots and put them in a nice row up the center of the garden. I think there were twenty odd roots. I left some as I thought I wouldn't have any rhubarb this year if I transplanted all of it. I have set out sixty-six raspberry bushes and about a dozen currant bushes so I hope to have some berries eventually. I've raked the yard and as our yard and garden is as big as the whole of Metcalf Street, you can see I've been busy.

The hens have been late sitting this year. I had one hen that set early but we had a big snowstorm and it was so cold, the eggs didn't hatch. I finally put the hot water bottle under her, as I thought she needed more heat and she got six chickens out. She would have had seven but one egg rolled out and got cold and I spoiled one egg trying to find out why they didn't hatch. The rest were rotten. I have five hens sitting now, each on fifteen eggs. They should do well, as the weather is getting warmer. The leaves are just beginning to come. They aren't out but still the trees at a distance seem to have a faint green tinge.

Emerson is going to school. He likes it but I guess the children interest him more than his lessons. For a bright boy he is positively stupid about learning to read. His mind seems to be elsewhere. He doesn't take school at all seriously and has been stood in the corner three times to my knowledge. Miss Evans is leaving the middle of June. They have always had a man in this district and some of the people did so much fussing that she said it wasn't pleasant to stay where people were always fussing about something, so she gave the trustees her notice that she was leaving. I'm sorry, as she was lots of company for me. Sonny gets pretty tired as he walks about four miles to and from school to say nothing of the trotting around he does at school and after he gets home. He is sleepy every morning. We have been getting up at five or earlier but I let him sleep until a little after seven, as he seems to need the extra sleep.

I had a letter from Eunice Hamlin last week. She is still in Nova Scotia running the laundry and doing well. I guess Eunice had more business ability than Hannibal ever had. She has bought a two family house and lives upstairs and rents the lower part.

George has retired some time ago and five o'clock will be here before I know it so I guess I'd better go too. I certainly enjoyed Pinga's last letter. It was as good as a story and it was so nice to hear all about her doings. I sometimes wish I was where there was something going on once in a while and still I like this life here too. Perhaps, when we get rich, "if we ever do", we will come back east. Many thanks for my gifts. I'm so glad Mr. Cummings is better. Remember me to him.

Love to you all, Bill and Faye included. Nellie

Lorenzo, Sask.
July 14, 1929

Dear Aunt Marie,

I guess I owe you a letter but I am not sure. However, I'll write as it is a peaceful Sunday afternoon and that seems to be the only time I find to write letters.

It is hot today but we have had lots of cool rainy days through June. I think we have the poorest garden we've ever had since we've been here. Things simply don't grow and there are whole rows with great spaces and absolutely nothing in them. The beans and cucumbers froze beyond refrain on June 25th and I set out some cabbage plants where they should have been. The first peas I planted don't seem to be any farther ahead than the last ones. They are just getting blossoms now so maybe we will get some peas by the last of August if they don't freeze first. I spend most of my time hoeing or pulling weeds, which seem to grow faster than anything else. We've had lettuce, radishes, swiss chard, spinach, and beet greens from the garden and I got a few summer turnips the other night. They were small, - just what I thinned out.

Did I write you that the lady teacher they had, left as every one did so much fussing, as they wanted a man. They got the chap they had last year, - a Mr. Taylor. He was in normal from January until the first week in June and came as soon as he finished his exams. He is with us and Emerson thinks he is great. He goes down to the lake after school swimming with the boys and he and Emerson have great times chasing each other around the yard nights. The other evening they were both down on all fours bellowing like bulls and rushing each other. He has taught Emerson to stand on his head so Sonny thinks he is great.

Emerson still is slow about reading but Mr. Taylor says he doesn't think that I need to worry about him, as a boy as bright as he is otherwise, will read when he gets ready. He thinks he has a most remarkable memory for a child of his age. If he tells a story once Sonny can get up and tell it giving all the details and he gets it in the right order. He is very good with doing things with his hands. He simply has so much that is interesting to him that he can't be bothered by learning words. Word drills don't appeal to him.

The other day he said, "Five hundred cents makes five dollars doesn't it?" I said "Good for you." George said, "I guess you can figure out money even if you can't read. You must have a little Jew in you." Emerson said "Naw, that isn't a little Jew, that's just brains." He was perfectly sober when he said it.

He has been busy digging seneca root. He has quite set his heart on a cart. There is one in the Sale Catalogue for $4.75. I told him we couldn't buy it this summer, as money was scarce so he said he guessed he could earn it. He has dug some seneca root and carried books home from school for Miss Evans and does little things for me so I occasionally give him a nickel. He has nearly a dollar saved and is still keeping at it. The school picnic comes the 26th of July and he is hoping to win some of the races as they give money for prizes. He is a regular boy and talks a lot about such things. You'd be surprised to see how he's grown since we were east. But then I suppose Faye grows too.

I have about seventy chickens this year, mostly Plymouth Rocks. I'll be glad when some of them get big enough to fry. George is going to walk but the mosquitoes are too numerous for me and Sonny has a sore toe so I'll stay home. He stubbed his toe last week and complained a little of it. I washed it in disinfectant and it was nearly a week before it pained him. Friday night he fussed all night and I got up ever so many times. I tied it up with salve when he went to bed but it hurt so I took the cloth off and then about one a.m. I built a fire and washed the salve off. In the morning I found a tiny splinter in the end of his toe. I got it out but his foot was hot and sore so at noon George packed his foot in wet clay. As soon as the clay got hot I soaked it in cold water. Saturday night I opened it with a needle and you should have seen the black blood and puss I got out. I put on a bread poultice last night and have kept it on all day. It is through running and Sonny is trotting about with his toe tied up and an old sock on to keep on the bandage. He felt pretty mean yesterday and spent the day on the couch but is playing today so I guess he'll recover. I'm so afraid of blood poisoning or something when we are so far from a doctor. It is a question what to do some times.

George has been digging seneca root lately. Everyone here digs it. He has flour sacks full and has started on the fifth. I some times go out for a couple of hours in the afternoon and dig but the garden, housework and chickens keep me busy most of the time.

It is suppertime once more. I must start a fire and look for something to eat. I sent Louisa a little package yesterday. I've had the things some time but simply didn't get around to sending them. I guess she'll think I'm a lemon taking so long. I did so enjoy her last letter. Write when you can and give my love to Louisa and her family when you see her.

Lovingly, Nell

Lorenzo, Sask.
Sept. 15, 1929

Dear Auntie Marie and Louisa and Flora,

I guess I'll write a family letter this morning. How I'd like to drop in and spend the day with you all.

It is a lovely Sunday morning and I think I'll improve the day by answering some of the many letters I owe, as church is out of the question. Sonny is outdoors making a wigwam. He is the greatest youngster to build himself houses.

Our summer is nearly over and I hate to see winter coming. The summer has been so short. We have had some heavy frosts and it has spit snow twice. We had a cold, wet week the first of September but it is warming up again, so we may get some warm days yet.

I suppose Ida wrote you of Father Allen's death. Reta wrote that the family was quite reconciled to his going as gangrene had set in and he suffered terribly for two weeks. The Doctor said his leg would have to be amputated and also that his mind would never be right again, so it was better that he was taken, as it would have been very hard for Mother Allen.

I don't believe I have written you since we decided to move. I have been living in hopes that we would get some English speaking neighbors, but all of the homesteads around us have been taken and still the foreigners flock in, - Germans and Russians of the peasant type. There is a German woman a mile from us who can talk English and we visit quite often. She is only twenty-four but seems older. My next English-speaking neighbor is a Galatian woman with a French husband, so they both talk English. They are the only ones I visit, except a woman ten miles south and the Evans sisters miles away and as we have to go with a horse and buggy, it takes all day to go and some.

We heard of land in British Columbia that sounded nice so George went out this summer. It is about seven hundred miles from here, - the other side of the Rockies. He said the trip through the mountains was wonderful. The climate is much like that of Maine or Massachusetts. They get snow and cold snaps through the winter, but only for a few days and not six or eight weeks of forty below weather as we get here. It often melts in the middle of the day and is cold nights and mornings. The Rockies shut off the Arctic winds that sweep Saskatchewan, so they get no summer frosts and can raise tomatoes, cucumber, beans, etc., that freeze here and wild fruit grows in abundance. George was fortunate in getting a place right on a graded highway and the people there are working to get the road extended to Stuart. That will make it the direct auto road to Vancouver, as now the traffic has to swing way south of the river. The land George got is right at the end of a lovely lake; seven miles long called Ness Lake. We have six acres on the lake so have a shorefront. There is a log house started on the place and a house about a quarter of a mile around the end of the lake and also a house just across the road. All of the people are English speaking mostly from the states, and there are five ex schoolmarm's who have married and live close by. The trees are gigantic spruce all around the house. The bear and moose are still plentiful. Prince George is a city of 4000 and growing fast and is only eighteen miles from us. There is a hospital, doctor, two dentists and movies, churches and good schools. We are nine miles from town and have good roads, whereas we are thirteen here. The winter is the busy time there, as everyone gets out ties. They can sell all they can cut and there are lots of mills along the Fraser River, so they say there is a big demand for all the foodstuff one can raise and good prices. I shall be so glad to be out of wheat farming. George will do teaming in the winter and we will raise garden stuff in the summer and sell butter and eggs. I'm quite crazy about moving. I still like it here but it will be nice to be in an English community.

I have a lot of sewing to do to get my clothes presentable to travel. I have been sewing for Sonny and just finished a pair of pants. You know the black cape you gave me. I lined his winter coat with it and got two pairs of pants out of it. No doubt Louisa remembers the blue jersey suit she gave me. I wear the coat a lot as a sweater but I hardly ever wore the skirt, so I ripped it up and made Emerson a very good-looking jersey pullover. It looks quite like a store one. I am going to rip up the blue serge dress I had down east, - that one I made from mother's coat and make Sonny a regular suit, - pants and coat. I've got to fix the blue coat Louisa gave me for a winter coat. It is faded across the shoulder and down the sleeves so I got a package of navy blue dye and am going to rip out the lining, dye it and press it good. I think I'll rip up one of my muffs and make a fur collar and cuffs, as I notice all the coats in the catalogue have fur collars. It will be quite a job but I think it will look quite good when I get it done.

At present I've got the hooked rug craze. I'd like painted furniture and some hooked rugs for my log cabin by the lake. I have one rug started and two more stamped on burlap. If Louisa finds it necessary to fill in the cracks in the Christmas package, I wish she would use some of the stockings she had in her bottom desk drawer when we were there instead of newspapers (providing she hasn't mended them all). They work in so good for backgrounds. I have some but not nearly enough. I must skip and take a bath and then it will be time to get dinner. I tell George all I do is cook, eat and wash dishes. I killed two young roosters yesterday and cooked them, so all I'd have to do today was fry them in butter at noontime and I'd get time to sit down awhile. We have a fresh cow. She had a nice heifer calf two weeks ago so we are getting more cream now. It seems a shame to sell them all, as we get quite attached to our animals but it is such a job and costs so much to move them, that we plan to sell everything and will buy what we need when we get there. We probably will have a sale the first part of November but don't plan to leave here until after Christmas.

Write when you find time. Did Tom get work in Boston? It would be nice to have Flora near. I wonder if she will find the winter cold after being in the south. Marion's "back to nature" trip didn't turn out very well, did it? I guess she will wish she'd kept her furniture and continued to do housework. This "back to nature" idea is all very well if you have money, but it costs to travel about the country and stop in auto camps and good jobs don't hang on bushes to be picked off like sugar plums. They thought Rudy would get a job and work awhile in each place as they went along. It might have been all right for a fellow alone but taking a wife and two children along is another thing. I'm sorry for Marion as they had good furniture and were quite well settled and Rudy was doing well. I think Marion was a lot to blame for this change, as she thought she couldn't do so much housework and her idea was to get "back to nature" and the simple life. Perhaps I'm heartless. I don't know where Rudy is, do you? At last accounts he was on his way to Arizona. Marion was at her sister Sid's' and Mabel had the two children, and Ken was to take one of them down to Reta, as Mabel didn't want them both. It's too bad they don't stay settled.

Well, I must really stop. Do write when you can. I don't think I thanked you for Sonny's birthday gift. We thought that because we were moving, a cart would rather be in the way and besides he didn't have enough money for it, so he used your dollar and some from his bank to buy himself a windbreaker. The rest he spent for a magic lantern and slides. It isn't very large so I thought it would pack easier than a cart and perhaps he can get that later.

Love to all your family, Bill and Tom included, Nell

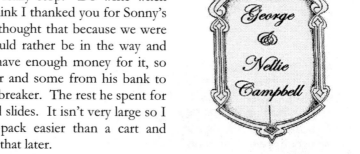

George & Nellie Campbell

First introduced back in 1905, Flinch is now nearly a century old, but still better than ever. Flinch is the seemingly simple but surprisingly difficult card game in which players attempt to discard from their stockpiles of 10 cards by playing them in numerical sequence (when possible).

FLINCH CARD GAME RULES
For 2 to 8 players

1. OBJECT: The object of the game is to be the first player to dispose of the cards dealt to him as a "game pile" by playing them in proper sequence to the center of the table.

2. EQUIPMENT: The equipment consists of a deck of 150 cards made up of ten series, each numbered from 1 through 15, and a plastic card holder.

3. PLAYERS: Any number from 2 to 8 may play. When more than 4 play, players find the game more enjoyable if 2 decks of cards are used.

4. THE LAYOUT: Cards in play are laid out in several different piles. These are referred to in the rules as follows:

a) THE GAME PILES. These consist of the first 10 cards dealt face down to each of the players. Each player places his cards in a pile directly in front of him and turns the top card of the pile face up.

b) THE HANDS are the next five cards dealt to each player. Each player picks up his hand so that he can see the cards but does not expose them to other players.

c) THE STACK is made up of all the cards remaining after the Game Piles and the Hands have been dealt. These are divided into groups of five cards each without being exposed and are placed in the holder in crisscross fashion so that each group lies crosswise on top of the group immediately beneath it.

d) THE RESERVE PILES are formed after play has started. Whenever a player passes or completes his play he must place one card in front of his Game Pile. He places these cards alongside each other until he has started 5 piles. From then on he may play on top of any of the five piles that he chooses. If, during the course of the play, he exhausts one or more of these piles, he must start them again before he can play on top of any of his remaining Reserve Piles.

5. THE DEAL: Select a player to deal. Shuffle the entire deck thoroughly and deal the cards as described above. The Game Piles, the Hands, and the Stack.

6. THE PLAY: The player to the left of the dealer plays first. If he has a 1 card exposed on his Game Pile he plays it to the center of the table and turns up the next card. If that should also be a 1 card he must play it in the center of the table alongside the first card. When the card exposed on his Game Pile is not a 1, he looks in his hand and plays in a similar manner any 1 card that he may be holding. If he has been able to play a 1 card and holds it in his hand, or has exposed on his Game Pile a 2 card, he may play it on top of any 1 card that has already been played. He may continue to play as long as he can build up in sequence on top of the cards that have been played. All 1 cards must be played, but other cards may be held or played as desired.

If during his turn the player exhausts his hand he draws a new hand of five cards from the Stack and continues to play. When he cannot make or does not wish to make any further plays, he selects a card from his hand and places it on the table face up to start a Reserve Pile.

The player to his left plays in a similar manner, and other players follow in turn. If, as frequently happens on the first turn, the first player cannot play, he simply passes and does not play a card to his Reserve Pile.

If, as occasionally happens, no player has a 1 card to start the game, each player lays down all five cards from his hand to start his five Reserve Piles, and each in turn draws a new hand from the stack. If there is still no player able to play a 1 card, players again place their entire hands in their Reserve Piles, but since all five piles have now been started, they may distribute them as they wish. All five cards may go on one pile if a player thinks it is to his advantage to do so. After the first 1 card has been played each player must end his turn by playing a card from his hand to one of his Reserve Piles.

7. THE RESERVE: Once a Reserve Pile has been established, a player may play from it to the center of the table if he has the proper card on top. He may do so at any time during his turn after he has played all of his 1 cards. 1 cards may never be played to a Reserve Pile.

A player is not required to play from his Reserve Pile, but should do so if it will help him to play from his Game Pile, or hinder his opponents from doing so.

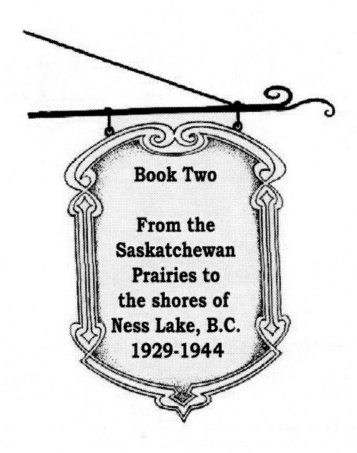

Book Two

From the
Saskatchewan
Prairies to
the shores of
Ness Lake, B.C.
1929-1944

Ness Lake, B.C.
Nov. 29, 1929

Dear Auntie Marie,

I know you have been looking for a letter and I have thought of you often even if I haven't written.

We have had a busy fall - first the harvesting and threshing and then the sale. We had a rotten day so things went cheap and we didn't get as much as we hoped for things. It was a job packing and keeping house for this family at the same time. Mr. Taylor stayed, - in fact we left him there batching. Two of the other teachers came the night before we left and so I had three teachers here to breakfast, and I had to cook it on the heater in the living room, as the kitchen stove was packed. Mr. Doolittle took us to Mrs. Mill's after breakfast and we spent Saturday and Sunday with her. The Evans came to dinner Sunday and took us to their place that night and then to Hafford the next day. We left for Battleford about 3 p.m. and got there in time for supper and saw a movie. We left for Edmonton a little after nine and got there in time for breakfast the next morning. We had all day in Edmonton. I wanted to do a little Christmas shopping but we had so much baggage that I couldn't carry much. There are no 5 and 10-cent stores here but 10 and 15 cent stores instead. I got some books for Ruth's boys and cloth for three aprons, - that's all besides a few cards.

The train didn't go until 11:30 that night but at nine we found that the sleeping car we were in was on a sidetrack, although the train wasn't made up. The berths were made so we could retire if we wished and Sonny was pretty sleepy so I was glad to get him to bed. We were going through the Rockies when we woke up in the morning and we were in the mountains all day. They were very beautiful. We got to Prince George at 7:30.

George got an auto truck the next day to take us out here. We had two trunks, a big packing box, roll of bedding and I bought over $50.00 worth of groceries in town. About half way out we came to a ravine. The road first hugged the hill on one side and dropped off straight down for 50 feet or more on the other. The fellows suggested we walk down and I was glad to do so. It rained the night we got to Prince George and the roads had frozen but thawed, so they were just sticky mud. Emerson's rubbers kept coming off and it was some job getting him to the top of the opposite hill without leaving his rubbers behind. We made it and the car got to the bottom of the hill and about half of the way up the opposite hill, and then stopped. The wheels just spun round and they slid all over the road. I was afraid they would go over the edge into the ravine. They had to take everything off the truck and then they couldn't make it. They decided to go back to town but they couldn't get up the hill they had come down. We found a log house a little beyond the top of the hill and then George and the two fellows began carrying our supplies up the hill. George carried 100 lbs. of sugar, 100 lbs. of flour and 100 lbs. of onions upon his back and in some places it was so steep and slippery, he had to crawl. It began to rain so I covered the sugar and flour up with a blanket and then Emerson and I toted what we could from where the men left it, up to this log house. We got lots of the things in the barn, as the house was locked.

George walked back two and a half miles and got the key to the house and also arranged for a man to come for us in the morning with his wagon. It was dark and raining, so the two chaps with the car started a fire for me and I opened enough of the groceries to get supper. There were two kettles and a fry pan in the house but we found tin covers enough for plates and got along quite nicely. We spent the night there, and in the morning the boys got the car to the top of the hill and we came by wagon.

We are living in the place across the road from our place until we get our house built. There is a very comfortable log house there and we are nicely settled. It seems to be a good English settlement and folks are pleasant and kind. We were invited out to dinner the first Sunday we came and last Saturday evening went to a party to meet some more of the neighbors. We have had two large pieces of moose meat given to us since we arrived. They said the people here do that a lot. If anyone gets a moose they usually divide it with the neighbors. George got a lovely place right at the end of a seven-mile lake (Ness Lake). There are lots of spruce, fir and pine here. At first so many trees seemed rather depressing, but I'm getting over that feeling now. George is working on the house and is going to town in the morning for lumber. I'll be glad when we can get in our own place, as the house is right on the bank of the lake.

We are eight or nine miles from Isle Pierre and as we have no horses yet, have to depend on the neighbors for mail. It is hard to get things mailed, as we don't know when folks are going. I'm making a few Christmas things and have to get things off in time. I've sent to Eaton's for a few things for my "men folks" but it takes so long to get things. I may send the parcels along if I get them ready so they won't be late and send the rest when I get it.

I must go to bed, as George has set the alarm for 5 a.m. so he can get an early start for town.

Are Flora and Tom still in Boston? Has Marion heard anything from Rudy and can you send me her address? Write when you can. Love to Flora, Pinga, Bill, and Faye.

Lovingly, Nell.

Ness Lake, B.C.
Feb. 7, 1930

Dear Auntie Marie,

I have been waiting for writing paper to write you. I sent an order to Winnipeg three weeks ago and the things have just arrived. One of the neighbors brought the freight as far as his place and George found out the things were there yesterday. He opened one of the boxes and got out the writing paper and a few things I wanted, and they will bring the rest of the things later. George sent for the windows for the house, also paint and stove pipes, and I had to buy all new kitchen things and a set of dishes. I waited for the January Sale Catalogue, as things are a lot cheaper then. There were only two small dinner sets in the sale, one plain white and the other green and white. I'm not partial to green dishes and as lots of my table covers are blue and white and I have an oil cloth set with orange and red in it, I decided to get the plain white set. The cups and covered dishes were a pretty shape and I think I'll like it. It was rather fun picking out all the new dishes I wanted. I got an aluminium teakettle, coffee percolator, double boiler, preserving kettle and three small pans. I didn't buy any agate ware this time.

George is working on the house every day. He has the main part up and is putting up the gable ends now. The lean-to that has the kitchen, pantry and shed is up as far as the roof, so I guess next week he can begin on the roof. I think it will be lovely to live beside a nice lake.

We have had a nice winter although everyone here tells me how cold it has been. It is so much warmer than on the prairie, that we don't notice it. January was cold but this month has been lovely so far and we are used to more than a month of cold weather. I washed this morning and hung all the clothes out without mittens and as they were dry, I managed to get them in before dinner. It used to take a week on the prairie to do them at this time of year.

Sonny went to school last week. It seems such a long way for him to go, but he wants to do it and starts off in the morning right after breakfast. He has a mile to go alone - not a house on the way and then he meets a big girl who goes the other three miles with him. He has to leave by half past seven and it is five thirty before he gets home. Eight miles a day is a long hike for a youngster his age. It's lucky he likes school.

There is to be a party tomorrow night at Scott's. They are our nearest neighbors so I think we'll go over. Mrs. Scott spent the day with me last week and the next day we planned to spend the day with Miss Rogers. She is a teacher from Vancouver who has a year's leave of absence and is keeping house for her father here. It snowed so we didn't go to Mrs. Scott's for the day. It snowed all day and the trail across was drifted so I couldn't get over. I guess I'll have to ask Santa to bring me snowshoes next winter for Christmas, as I could go more if I had a pair.

I have been hooking a rug and have it nearly finished and then I think I'll start on a braided one.

Mother started on a silk quilt years ago and I thought this winter I would finish it. The squares are done but only six of them embroidered. I embroidered one square and stamped the others but ran out of embroidery thread, so some embroidery thread would be most acceptable for my birthday since you asked. (About the size of the sample enclosed and any pretty colors.)

I also want a spool of Star Mercerized Cotton Twist, the shade of the lavender dress goods you gave me last Christmas, as I want to make it for summer. I can go out more here so want some pretty clothes. I also need a ten-cent hammer, as George's is always in use when I want one and a paring knife. I think that is the extent of my wants.

I haven't washed my dinner dishes and it is nearly three o'clock. First the water was too hot so I set it back and now it is too cold and the fire has gone out, so I guess I'd better stop writing and tend to the housework.

I had a long letter from Maude at Christmas. Winfield is still in Manila, P.I. Maude had a chance to go to China on one of the transports and the only expense was her food. She was gone a month and had a wonderful trip. Winfield expects to be sent back to the States either in March or June.

Eunice Hamlin is still in Nova Scotia running her laundry. She wrote me at Christmas, too. I was so glad to hear from Flora. It seemed quite like old times to get a long letter from her and I'm glad she hasn't forgotten me. We haven't had any mail for two weeks, but Mrs. Estes thought her son would get the mail Saturday. I hope so, as I'd like to hear from somebody.

Give my love to all your family.

Lots of love to you, Nell.

P.S. I wonder if you will please send me 15 two-cent stamps and 20 one-cent stamps when you write. I'm sending $.50 for them in the little package I'm sending you. I thought perhaps Mr. Cummings would stop at the Post Office for them, some time that he is going down town.

Many thanks, Nell.

Ness Lake, B.C.
April 27, 1930

Dear Auntie Marie,

This month is nearly gone and I guess it is time I wrote and thanked you for our birthday presents. I wasn't expecting the things I wanted until my birthday, but it was nice of you to send them ahead of time and a pleasant surprise to me. Everything was fine and I shall make my dress as soon as we get the garden in and I can get a minute to sew. George was pleased with his shirt and the tie matches so nicely. You always pick out pretty ties.

We have been very busy all spring. George found a clearing on the place, - about three acres. The trees had been cut down and just lay in piles, - such a tangle of dead branches. It had been done a long time ago, as we found a stump with the date May 17, 1922 carved on it. We have been over every day piling up the brush and burning it. Some days we took our dinner so you see I didn't do much housework. It was quite a find, as the land has to be cleared and we didn't expect to put in a crop this year, as we would have no land ready. There is a little more burning to do so we are going over for the day tomorrow and will get it plowed on Wednesday. George got seed oats so we will get a little piece in after all. There is about half an acre that can be plowed so we will have that plowed and put in potatoes. They raise very good potatoes here. George bought ten bushels, of course we will have to save out some to eat, but we will have quite a batch of potatoes. I hope they do well so we will have something to sell in the fall. There was a small piece cleared in front of the house and George has pulled out all the stumps and dug it up by hand. We have peas, carrots, turnips, beets, Swiss chard, onions, spinach and a few cucumbers in, but I'm afraid it is a little early for cucumbers. My cabbages and cauliflower are up in the hot bed and I have some nice tomatoes started in the house. We still have lots more to plant but it takes time to dig up the land. As soon as George gets a little piece ready, I plant it. We set out strawberries and raspberries and a few currant bushes yesterday. It is a beautiful spot here and the lake is lovely. I think we can have a lovely place here in time if we ever get the trash burned up. George has slashed two acres in front of the house and trees are lying every which way, - of course it is green, so fire doesn't burn very good in it. We have fires every evening trying to get rid of part of it.

We have had company today. One of our neighbors had a daughter who was a teacher in Vancouver. She came out last spring to keep house for her father. She

Nellie and her class at the
REID LAKE SCHOOL

had a year's leave of absence but a few weeks ago married a widower who came from Maine. He has been here about fifteen years. She is thirty-seven so I find her quite congenial as she is near my age. Her husband says I'm the first person he has ever seen in the West who can cook Boston baked beans, so they have been here several times to "beans." They came today, so I had beans for his special benefit. There are several new families who came in last week but I haven't met them yet.

I started Emerson in school (Reid Lake School) this spring but since we moved he has five miles to walk, - one mile through the woods and another mile across the meadow before he meets any children. The meadow has been so wet he hasn't been able to cross for three weeks, it is dryer now but the road beyond is muddy. Emerson is the kind that never goes around a puddle but slams through the middle, so although he is eager to go tomorrow, I think I'll keep him home another week. I think ten miles a day is a terrible walk but he will play after he gets home instead of resting.

Are Flora and Tom still with Pinga? I believe Tom was out of work last time you wrote. Has he found anything yet? We don't have much cash but plenty to eat and no rent, or fuel to worry about and I like the sort of a life we live. This seems to be a promising country. At present we are land poor, but Mr. Taylor wrote the charter had been granted for the railroad that was surveyed across our place at Lorenzo. If they put the line through we no doubt will have a better chance to sell the farm there. We have it rented and it will be put in crop this spring.

I'm glad Marion was re-elected as she can feel quite settled for another year. Do you know Rudy's address? I think he has had quite a tough time of it all around. I guess work has been very scarce all over the country from what I hear.

We had a nice Easter even if we couldn't go to church. Cousin Lizzie sent Emerson a large chocolate Easter egg with his name on it in white frosting. It must have weighed a pound or more. Mrs. Taylor, the teacher's mother, sent him a rubber egg with legs and arms that blows up like a balloon. I thought it nice of her to remember him as she had never seen him, and it was last year Mr. Taylor was with us. I dyed some eggs for breakfast using onionskins and bluing. Sonny was quite pleased with the effect and ate three.

I have lots of letters to write, as there are so many people who expect letters and I get awfully behind. I heard from "Mother Allen" last week. She said they were all well in Jay, Maine and she seemed quite comfortably settled. I suppose she finds the village less lonesome than alone on the farm.

Hope you all are well. Remember me to Mr. C and give my love to your family.

Lovingly, Nellie

Ness Lake, B.C.
May 1, 1930

Dear Mother Allen,

We are having a wet morning so I'm taking the time off to answer some of the many letters I owe. It was nice to hear from you and know you are comfortably situated.

As you know we are on our homestead at Ness Lake and we finished the house enough to move into it the 13th of March. It was nice to get into our own house, - "Be it ever so humble, there's no place like home". We have just finished the main part of the house and have one large room downstairs and sleep upstairs. George has one of the ells built but has not put in the windows or laid the floors yet. There seemed to be so many things that needed to be done that seemed more important. Of course, the wall inside is just logs. George put the windows inside, side-by-side making a long window toward the east and a long one toward the west. I dyed flour sacks a very pretty green and put a band of cretonne (a printed fabric used especially for draperies) across the bottom. I made draw curtains for the windows and also for the dish cupboard George built in one corner and for the bookshelf. George made a table of boards with spruce legs and used a packing box crate from Eaton's for an armchair. My other chairs are just boxes. I hope to get legs put on them eventually. There are so many packing box chairs in this country that people are quite accustomed to them. You surely are well supplied with furniture. I suppose the country there has been settled so long things accumulate. While here, second hand furniture cost almost as much as new at the mail order house.

I hope to get things fixed up after awhile but until we get more room I haven't any place to put more. We plan to lay a double floor and I have paint for the floor and wood- work when it is finished around the doors and windows. At present the cracks are chinked with moss but we hope to put in lime this summer.

I took a picture of the house and one of the lake and I'll send them when I get them finished.

You know this is a timber country and all the land has to be cleared. There are stumps but no stones. George found a piece of about three acres that someone slashed in 1922 by the date on one of the stumps. Of course, all the dead stuff had to be piled up and burned and there was a pile of it. Quite a few days we took our lunch and stayed all day. It had been done so long that the stumps were well rotted so not bad to get out. It is all ready to plow so we will have a little patch of oats in after all. There is another place of one half acre that has been plowed and we will put that into potatoes. They say potatoes do very well here and there is quite a good market for them, also carrots and turnips. George has slashed two acres in front of the house and we have fires every evening trying to burn up some of the stuff but it is so - so green it doesn't burn very well. He has dug up a big piece by hand and we have planted peas, spinach, beets, swiss chard, onions, summer turnip and I have lettuce, radishes, cauliflower, and cabbage up in the hot bed. I planted peppers and celery, too, but they are slow coming. The tomatoes are in the house and I have some nice sturdy plants. They say such things will grow here. I hope so as I tried every year on the prairie and the corn, cucumber, beans, squash, etc., always froze. I never got any corn and some years no beans and seldom more than one or two meals before they froze. I hope to have something this year to make pickles of, I do like sour things.

This seems to be a much milder climate than on the prairie. The air is softer and we don't seem to have such extremes here. Folks say it was an unusually cold winter this year but we thought it was lovely. The water is soft and after using hard water for so long it surely is a blessing. All of the people are English speaking and a good class. Several new settlers came in last week but I haven't met them yet.

We saw by the Prince George paper that three men had been to Prince George looking for land. They came from Phillips, Maine and if they took back a favorable report of the country, there were forty families that would come to settle. One of the men's names was Smith but I can't remember the others and we have lent the paper so I can't look them up. Phillips is near Jay, Maine, is it not?

Emerson started to school but he has five miles to walk since we moved. He has one mile through the woods and a mile across the meadow before he meets any children. The meadow has been so wet that he couldn't cross so I've kept him home. He pleaded to go again this week but it is still muddy so I think he'll have to wait until next week. Ten miles a day seems a long walk for him but he will play after he gets home instead of resting. I'm hoping we can get enough children to start a school here.

The ice went out of the lake this week and I hear a loon calling. There are lots of birds here and they start singing when it is hardly light in the morning. Sonny and I have made two birdhouses and stuck them up but I don't think they are tenanted yet.

We haven't our mail this week. One of the neighbors brings it out from town. We had company to dinner Sunday so didn't go for it. We have been so busy getting the land ready to plow that we haven't been for it, but I think I'll walk to Estes this afternoon.

I believe I owe Ruth a letter but no doubt you will let her read this so she will know I'm still living. I have some pretty patterns for hooked rugs. If you or Reta are doing rugs I can send the patterns on, as I shan't use them until next winter and then I think I'll try to draw one on burlap. They are quite simple designs.

Give my love to Ruth and her family.

Lovingly, Nellie

Ness Lake, B.C.
June 3, 1930

Dear Reta,

I have been intending to write for a long time but I seem to lead a busy life and there are so many people who expect letters from me that I get dreadfully behind on my correspondence.

If you never homesteaded you can't realize how many things there are to be done. You know a farm with buildings and some conveniences keeps one busy but George had to clear a space big enough to build the house in.

He has slashed two acres in front of the house but it is a job burning up so much stuff. The laws regarding fires are stricter here than in Saskatchewan for which I'm quite thankful. The fire warden calls the 1st of the month and gives one a permit to burn providing everything is piled and no fires lighted until 5 p.m. You can't clear land by letting a fire run and if one gets away from you the fire warden can call out as many men as he needs and you have to stand the expense. George found 3 acres that had been slashed and he and I spent nearly 3 weeks piling up the dead trees and burning them. It was a job getting the field cleared to plow. He cleared a big bank above the lake and spaded it up by hand and we put in lots of rhubarb and set out red currants, black currants, gooseberries and raspberries and started some apple seeds. I put in a quarter of a lb. of beets, some parsnips, and squash, citron, and marrows and 2 oz. of corn so you see it is a good sized piece. George also put in some parsnip, sage and carrots on the hill. We have cleared a big garden spot and George dug that by hand. It has been a job getting out the roots and burning the trash but it is worked down pretty well and things are growing. People say we can't expect as good a garden the first year on new land but we hope to get something.

I have been canning moose meat and have all my jars full and a piece in brine. We went picnicking last Sunday. We took a lunch and walked as far as Estes and got their boat. George has a dugout canoe that someone lent him for the summer but I thought for three of us I'd rather go in the boat, as it was windy. We ate our lunch on a small island on the lake and then George and Sonny went fishing with a stick. They got over a dozen by just hitting them when they swam in shore. We saw a bear and her cub ambling up the beach, also a loon's nest. The loons make a dreadful noise at night. We saw a porcupine one afternoon in the garden.

We have a very pretty place here and can make it into a lovely spot when we get the stumps dug out of the dooryard and the house finished. It is livable but there is a lot to be done to it before cold weather comes. I am dreadfully short of furniture but there is no need of trying to make any until I get a place to put it. I did make Sonny a very good little bedstead of small spruce poles. It is quite rustic looking and this morning I made a chair and a stool, as I'm tired of sitting on a block of wood with a board on top for a seat.

George took us for a boat ride in his canoe this afternoon but a thundershower came up so we came in and I have been reading aloud to George. We have a bit more planting to do but just finished harrowing the piece this morning and George thought it was so wet it would be better to put it in the morning.

I have two hens setting. I had to wait until all my neighbors got through setting hens before I could get a biddy to sit. I guess I won't have a very big flock this year but it will be a start.

George hasn't built a barn yet, as we've spent all the spring trying to get a little land ready to put into crop. We have picked out the place for the barn and as soon as George gets the trees cut down he wants to put up a small log stable for the present.

There is something fascinating about a new country and George is quite in his element. He certainly likes homesteading. This is his fifth time at it.

I have some sewing I ought to do but don't get at it. I sold my machine before we moved so have to sew by hand. I made Emerson some summer undies and I have cloth for three summer dresses, which I sorely need. I guess I'll have to cut one out and then go visiting for the day with my sewing, as that is the only way I get any sewing done.

I'm hoping we can get some neighbors near us with children so we can get a school nearer. We have neighbors but they are either bachelors or people with grown up families so Emerson is all alone. He went ten miles a day to school for a while but I have been afraid to send him so far alone since the bears came out. He has two miles to go alone before he meets any children. I hear his reading so I guess he won't get too far behind. The government sends out a correspondence course for children who can't go to school and I think I'll send for it in the fall and then he will keep up in all his lessons.

George is making various smudge around the house to drive the mosquitoes away. I'll be glad when bug time is over. I helped George plant potatoes a week ago and some pesky insects stung me on the back of my leg at my knee. I scratched it, of course, and my leg was so swollen and red and painful that George plastered me up with wet mud and I recovered. The bugs always find me.

I wrote to Rudy last week but doubt if he got it. If you ever get his address I wish you would send it on to me before he moves again. If you write him be sure to tell where we are living now. George is going to Estes' for our mail so I must stop. Write when you can.

Love to all, Nell.

Ness Lake, B.C.
June 8, 1930

Dear Auntie Marie,

I guess it is time I thanked you for the book. It came as a pleasant surprise as I thought the odds and ends of thread, etc., you sent were my birthday present. George and I at once started the book aloud and it is now on it's rounds of the neighborhood. A book is something so many people can enjoy and we surely enjoyed that one.

We have most of our planting done for this year. It has been a slow job, as George has had to clear the land and dig lots of it up by hand. We had a man plow three acres and put in half an acre of potatoes and the rest in oats.

We went picnicking one day last week. George has an old dug out canoe that someone lent him for the summer, but I don't like to go in it, so we went as far as Estes in it and got their boat and went to the end of the lake. It is a five-mile row. We had our lunch by the side of the lake, (made coffee and warmed up baked beans) and then called on two families who live at the upper end of the lake. One woman is about my age and was a music teacher until her marriage a year ago. They have just adopted an eighteen-month-old boy. They have a boat so plan to come down this week for the day and bring the baby.

George went fishing the other Sunday with a fellow here and they took a gun along. He came home at night with a quarter of a moose, so I was busy for a couple of days filling my sealers. I must get more sealers, as there seems to be an abundance of wild fruit bushes around. I hope to get some put up this summer if I can get George to go with me, but I don't venture far in the woods alone. Twice we have seen bears when we were in the canoe and two deer came almost to the house the other day. We stood in the open door and watched them and I might have got a wonderful snapshot had I had a film in my camera. They stayed about twenty minutes and one nibbled a bush at the foot of the garden. Yesterday a moose went through the yard when Emerson was out there. They cross the garden and go to the lake for water. We met a porcupine one day and he spent the afternoon in a tree where we were working. There seems to be lots of wild game here and lots of fish in the lake. The country is quite picturesque, - quite different from Maine scenery. I want to take some pictures of the place this summer.

Ida wrote that mother had been to Boston for a vacation. I hope Ida will be able to visit you this summer. She never says how she gets along. She said she had been having a good time while mother was away doing "just as she pleased". That seems to be her idea of a good time. Perhaps it is quite a relief.

Do you know where Rudy is? By the time I get one address from one member of the family someone else sends me another address. I have written to him but doubt if he gets it.

I'm glad Marion got her re-election, as it will give her a settled feeling and she can keep her children with her.

Are Flora and Tom still with Pinga? I haven't heard from Pinga lately but presume she keeps busy.

Sonny is chopping wood, as he wants to pop corn and the fire needs replenishing. He is getting to be quite a lad. I'm hoping we can get near neighbors with lots of children so he will have someone to play with and we can get a school nearer.

Give my love to all of your family and remember me to Mr. S and Mr. C.

Lots of love to you, Nell.

Ness Lake, B.C.
August 1, 1930

Dear Reta,

My husband is busy digging stumps out of our front yard, - his usual after supper job - so I'm going to try to get a letter written. Many thanks for the papers. I enjoy them ever so much. I haven't received the dress yet as no one has been for mail for over a week but I know I shall find use for it, as outdoor work is hard on clothes. I only wish more of my relatives would send me their castoffs. I made over the voile dress Velma gave me three years ago when I was home. It came out very well and I felt quite dressed up in it Sunday.

George has been working on the road. He got in thirteen days. I'm glad I don't mind staying in the woods alone. They plan to do some work on the road about a mile from here. If they do he will be home nights. Have you read anything about the Alaskan Highway? The States wants an auto road to Alaska. A few weeks ago a party of fifty, made up of officials and governors from some of the western states and the Premier of B.C. went over the proposed routes. If the road goes through it probably will go by our door. I'm hoping B.C. will be able to furnish the $5,000,000, their share of the expense of building the highway. It surely will make a big difference to this country. It is lovely here now. We can have a very pretty place in time but there surely is a lot of work to homesteading in a bush country.

Our garden has done well considering it was dug out of the woods this spring. We had green peas for supper and have had beets, carrots, turnips, and lots of greens besides lettuce, radishes and onions. I still have a few jars of moose meat left.

It was quite hot yesterday so the last of the afternoon we went out in the canoe. We saw a deer on the shore and George crossed the lake and went within a hundred yards of him before he even looked at us and then he continued to graze quite unconcerned. We paddled along the shore and he followed the canoe for 1/4 of a mile or more. I have seen quite a few deer this summer and we have three families of bears on our side of the lake. I'm hoping George can get a bear in the fall, as I want the fat.

We went up the lake Saturday afternoon and I got some gooseberries for jam. I have made four 4-pound pails of gooseberry jam. There are lots of raspberries on the island but I can't manage the canoe well enough to go alone. I want to go this week but Mrs. Estes comes tomorrow to spend the day and I go to Mrs. Byers for the day on Friday so the week is gone. It was election here Monday and we had five miles to walk to the school. We started early and when we got to Rodman's they urged us to stop to dinner and ride down with them. When we came back we called on Mrs. Cook and then Mrs. Scott asked us to supper so I had quite a nice visiting day. I don't go much but have quite a bit of company.

I planned to do a lot one week when George was away but had so much company I didn't do half I planned. The English Church have a Sunday School van, in fact they have fourteen vans that travel over Canada stopping at out of the way places and getting the names of children who can't go to Sunday School. They send them Sunday School papers by mail. They called on us in Saskatchewan and stayed to dinner last September. I was quite surprised one afternoon when Miss Body appeared. I remembered her and she knew me as soon as I spoke. She has a Miss Vaughn with her and Mrs. Byers came up so they all stayed to supper with me. One of my bachelor neighbors brought me a big can full of strawberries for supper that night. He paddled across the lake and left them at the landing so I found them when I went down for a pail of water.

Last Sunday the Kalsteads at the end of the lake came in their motorboat. Mrs. K was a music teacher before she married last summer. Her father is a minister and he and his second wife are visiting her. Mr. and Mrs. Byers and Mrs. Byers' father came up so we ate out-of-doors and made a picnic of it. The neighbors seem very friendly and do a lot of visiting.

I suppose you keep busy. I wonder if Margaret and her mother are with you. My! I'd like to see them. I got Margaret's Christmas card eventually and have intended all summer to answer the letters I owe. Perhaps if the Alaskan Highway goes by my door Margaret and her mother might take a trip west some summer instead of east. I'd surely love to have them come.

You asked about my furniture. At first we slept on spruce beds. They are very comfortable if the spruce is changed often. I wanted to get the blankets washed and I couldn't very well as long as we slept on the floor so I found some nice straight spruce poles and proceeded to make a couple of bedsteads. George said I did a very good job. I put a strip of canvas across Sonny's bed for a spring and made him a mattress stuffed with hay and put a thin feather tick on top. It really is very comfortable. I knew the canvas would sag in the middle so wouldn't do for our bed so I put slats across and put the ticks on those. I then made a chair and a stool for the bedroom. For the living room I made a couch out of spruce poles and put sacks across it. I sewed two burlap sacks together and then ran the side poles of the couch through the sacks and nailed the end poles across to make them tight like a stretcher. I put on four nice peeled legs and braced them so it made a very good couch. I made an armchair, a straight-backed chair and two stools and a bookcase. I painted all the furniture pearl gray and put on a stencil in Chinese vermilion which is a vivid red. I also made and painted the washstand to match and painted the frame of the looking glass. Ida sent me some cretonne at Christmas so I made curtains of that and feel the house is quite dolled up.

Most everyone has some home made stuff here and things that seem quite essential back in New England aren't at all essential here. We are quite happy even if our things aren't expensive and I love this sort of a life.

It is getting so dark I can't see.

Do write to me once in awhile and give my love to Margaret and her mother if they are there and also to Mother Allen.

Lovingly, Nell

Ness Lake, B.C.
September 15, 1930

Dear Aunt Marie,

It seemed quite a while since I have written to you. I'm having a lazy day. George is working on the road about three miles from here so takes his lunch and I didn't both much for lunch for Sonny and me as I have to get a hearty meal at night. I thought this would be a good time to get some of my letters answered.

This has been a most delightful summer and I surely have enjoyed it. The climate is so much milder, and corns aren't frozen yet. There is an abundance of wild fruit here and I have made jam galore. At present I am in the midst of pickles. I've canned more this summer than I have any time this summer. There is a teacher at the other end of the lake who was married a little over a year ago. Her father is a minister in Elliot, Illinois and he and his wife were here for a visit this summer. I invited them all down one Sunday, also Mr. Rogers and Mr. And Mrs. Byers, and we had our dinner outside where we could view the lake. Mr. Oppedahl was a fine gentleman, one of the old time ministers. The next week he held a preaching service half way up the lake. We all took our lunch and then spread everything out. We had potato salads, beans, cold meat, all kinds of cakes, cookies, pies, and strawberry shortcake and coffee. The service was splendid and a young chap was baptized. There were thirty-six there. I had a most enjoyable Sunday and then we had a nice ride home in the canoe.

The people here seem quite sociable and I have visited more this summer than I ever have before. Mrs. Scott came over a week ago Sunday and spent the day with us. I went there one day and made a dress on her sewing machine. Another day I took my sewing and went to Mrs. Rodman's for the day. Last Friday Sonny and I spent the day at Mrs. Byers. I take my stockings along and get my mending done. I really do wonders with a bag of old stockings when I go away for the day and it is such a job to sit down and mend them at home. It is nice to have so many places to visit.

School has begun once more but I didn't start Emerson. Last spring he had a big girl of high school age to go with part way but this year she is taking a correspondence course so he has all the distance to go alone. George expects to cut railroad ties this winter. If he does he will be close to Isle Pierre and then Emerson can go to school as we will go to town for the winter. It will be rather nice to be only a mile from the Post Office, as we will get our mail regularly.

Ida wrote me the glad news. I suppose Louisa is quite delighted although maybe uncomfortable. I have meant to write her but I know you pass my letters on to her so she hears from me through you. I guess I owe Flora a letter. I surely was glad to get the one she wrote after Christmas even if I haven't answered it.

Sonny's winter stockings have shrunk so I had to ravel out both pairs the other day and shall have to knit them over. The feet of George's socks are too small and I have about four pair of his to knit on new feet. I don't know much about knitting so I expect it will be quite a job. I got out the piece bag and looked through to see what I could make into Christmas presents so I guess the socks and Christmas things will keep me busy until New Years and then I want to make another hooked rug and finish the braided one I began and make a quilt. I saw a pretty pattern. It was a butterfly cut from print, gingham or percale and appliqued onto a square of unbleached cotton. The alternate square was a plain color throughout the whole quilt. We hope to get the bedrooms downstairs finished next spring and I want a few new quilts. It is my bedding that needs replenishing. My sheets are on their last legs. If sheets have legs. If you have any small pieces of cloth big enough to cut out a butterfly will you send me a wee bundle at Christmas?

You asked for our Christmas wants. George needs a Jackknife as he lost his recently, also work socks. Nothing fine. I guess you'd probably find them at Raymond's. He likes the feet "roomy" and always complains because they shrink. I guess a size eleven would suit him. Emerson would like a book. I think he would enjoy "Grimm's Fairy Tales" or a whole story. Reta sent him "Sonny Boy and the Circus," last Christmas and he thought it was the best book he'd ever had. He'd also like a game, I think. Something like Peter Coddle or some card game that wasn't too difficult. I think it would be an inducement for him to read if he had a card game where he had to read the answers. As for me I have heaps of wants this year so you have a big variety to choose from. All my sofa cushions need covering. George has been using them in the canoe and we take them picnicking so the covers are terrible. I'd like washable stuff such as checked gingham or inexpensive cretonne that I can use without feeling I'll spoil it. Perhaps you could find remnants big enough for a few cushion tops. I need everyday stockings and I'd also be most grateful for some of Flora or Louisa's cast off stockings. I don't imagine they wear them after they are darned much and especially if the legs get runs. They are all right here and I'd have heaps of time this winter to mend them. I need summer under vests and am always glad of cloth for aprons or housedresses. I'd be delighted with anything to doll up my house.

Do write me as soon as you can. Love to all, Nell

Ness Lake, B.C
Oct. 5, 1930

Dear Auntie,

It was so nice of you to remember Emerson's birthday. No one went for the mail and when someone finally went in they went on horseback so brought no bundles up so it was the twenty-fifth of September before he got his things. I made him a cake for his birthday and gave him a Jack-Knife which he promptly traded with an old man here. He got far the best of the bargain as got a cork-screw, leather punch and about a dozen other appliances with the knife he got so was quite fond of his bargaining. He has colored a lot in his color book and the neckties will be nice for him. He had never had a regular boy's suit (just pants and blouses). I plan to rip up the grey suit this winter. Most of the children here wear overalls most of the time even to school but a suit will be nice for dress up occasions.

We have been busy getting in the potatoes. George has finished the cellar and we got our vegetables in yesterday. We didn't have a lot but still I guess there will be enough for winter. We want to go to town and get enough flour, sugar, tea, coffee and coal oil for the winter. Mr. Rodman spoke of going in with the wagon and staying over night and bringing out enough for two families. His wife is ever so nice. She has a house in town and we would stay there over night and all go to the movies.

I'm quite looking forward to it, as I haven't been in a store since I came here last fall.

It is a rainy Sunday. I started to read to George but he promptly dropped to sleep.

Emerson saved up enough to buy himself a small ukulele. He can't play but is having a great time drumming on it and singing "Springtime in the Rockies." I haven't sent him to school this fall as it is so far. The girl who went with him last year isn't going so he has over three miles to walk before he meets any children and nearly ten miles a day is a dreadful hike when one has to go alone most of the way home.

I'm hearing his lessons and George expects to cut ties this winter on Fanshaw's place close to Isle Pierre. He has to get a contract from the railroad and they don't give them out until late. We will go down there for the winter and then we will be only about a mile and a half from the store, post office and school.

The other afternoon I heard someone holler but George thought it was Emerson playing with the cat. Then I heard it again and I knew something was wrong by the voice. The bull moose go on a rampage at this season of the year as it is the breeding season and folks say there is more danger from a bull moose than from a bear. George grabbed an axe and started on the run. We both thought it was a moose. I started but he sent me back with Emerson. I kept hearing these awful shouts and groans so told Emerson to stay in the house and grabbed the grub hoe and started. When I got to the gate I saw George coming in the driveway half carrying the young chap we stayed with last winter. I got the bars down on the fence and then rushed in and got the fire started and the teakettle on. He had gone into the haymow and jumped down onto the pitchfork. Two prongs went way through his leg and the other one broke off. It was high up, - a few more inches and it would have gone through his body. His pant leg was soaked with blood way to his stocking. George got his clothes down so I could bathe it and then went for a neighbor with a car. It had a truck body so we bundled the feather bed in and blankets and they laid him in the back and took him right to Prince George to the hospital. It is only eighteen miles so they got in, in about an hour. We haven't heard how he is getting on.

I sent in the renewal for our weekly paper as I could get a Jack-knife for George for a premium. I guess I put that on our list of wants for Christmas but he will get one before that as I'm expecting it this week.

I've started to knit a pair of stockings for Emerson but I'm awfully slow and haven't one leg done yet. I cut over a wool shirt of George's that was poor and got Emerson a very good undershirt out of the best of it. I had a good fleeced lined union suit that Marion sent me when they moved from Hartford. George won't wear union suits so I got a pair of under drawers for Sonny out of the bottom and another pair out of the top using arms and legs for legs. I have another wool shirt to cut over and then Emerson's underwear is done. I sent for cloth to make George two shirts. I can get two shirts if I make them for what I have to pay for one ready made.

We are expecting some new settlers this fall. I believe four families are coming in south of us nearer the school. I had a letter from a Mrs. Campbell from Indian Head saying they were leaving there the thirteenth of this month. We are hoping they will take land near us, as we are anxious to get a school here. They have two children and we need only seven to get a school.

My family have retired and I have bread to mix so guess I had better be at it.

Do you know where Rudy is? I wrote him in California, but the letter came back. I wonder if Marion has heard lately. Mother was quite "peeved" because she didn't stop on her way home from Reta's. I don't know whether it was because she didn't' call or because mother got meals ready for a whole week and then she didn't come. So she said, "I don't know whether they don't eat when they don't have company or not but I get meals ready anyway."

Write when you can. Nell

Ness Lake, B.C.
Nov. 17, 1930

Dear Reta,

I think you have owed me a letter for some time but trust you are busy. It must be some job to keep the boys clothed. Emerson is in rags once more and I must get busy on some clothes for him. I don't know what I'd do if I had three to sew for. I miss my machine so. We haven't felt we could afford even a second hand one so far so I have to trot to the neighbors when I want to stitch. I went to Mrs. Scotts one day and made George a cotton shirt. I have two flannel shirts cut out for him and must go visiting some day to get them made.

Everyone here cuts railroad ties in the winter. We have lots of ties on our place but we are about ten miles from Isle Pierre. We have no team and it costs so much to get them hauled so far that there isn't much in it. George got a chance to cut the ties on a place about a mile and a half from the station. There was an old log house on it so we moved down there for a couple of months or more while he is cutting. Emerson started school last week. He likes school all right but is a little afraid to walk along through the woods.

The first morning he went George and I went with him, as I wanted to go into Prince George to see the doctor. We met two Bull Moose in the road just after we left the house. They crossed right in front of us and went into the wood on the other side.

I had a miserable cold and thought I was all over it and then my head began to ache and I had the most terrible headache for five days. I just laid in the dark and George kept flannel clothes wrung out of hot water on my head. I was most crazy before I got to Prince George, my head hurt so. I thought I'd have to stay in a day or two, as I didn't want to come back and have the same thing over again so I told George not to meet the train that night. I went in Wednesday and if I didn't come back that night I couldn't come back until Saturday morning. The doctor said my nose was so swollen from my cold that the hole leading into the air passage over my left eye was closed. It should be opened and drained but that was a job for a specialist and all he could do was to give me something for my nose and when the swelling went down it would probably drain itself. If my head ached I was to go to bed and keep the hot clothes on it. He gave me some pills for the pain and stuff to use up my nose and said they couldn't do any more for me if I stayed in the hospital until Saturday so I found a boarding house and went to bed until supper time and then got the eight o'clock train home. It was nine-thirty when I got to Isle Pierre and, of course, George didn't expect me so wasn't at the station. The ferryman had gone to bed and as he was on the other side of the river I couldn't make him hear so I had to stay at the store all night and come home in the morning. My nose is better although my head troubles me some but I hope to recover in time.

I want to make some quilts this winter but can't start until after Christmas. There is a Farm Life Quilt in the paper we take. One block comes every week. The patterns are of some farm scene and are embroidered on a nine-inch square of unbleached cotton. The alternate square is of a plain color and quilted in a very pretty pattern. There is a wide stripe at the top and bottom with a cut out fence. I want to make one and then I have a pattern for a butterfly quilt I'd like to do. I'd be most grateful for a small bundle of quilt pieces if you have any either cotton or wool scraps left from your sewing.

I want to ask you about Dad's will. Did you understand that what was left after Ida got through with what is put away for her, and the real estate when mother gets through with it, comes to the surviving children? In that case if we don't survive longer than mother, our heirs get nothing. Do you just know how it really stands? Uncle Henry wrote me the contents of the will in his own words and also sent me a list of the different stocks and bonds and their value. If you haven't seen one I'll send a copy. As mother is hearty and her mother lived to a ripe old age she may do likewise so there is quite a possibility of one of us passing on first. I'd like to feel I had the right to will my share to George and Sonny. I don't know how you feel about it but if mother outlived you, the way I understand it, all the property left would come to Rudy and me and Ray and your boys would get nothing. It seems to me much fairer if what was left could be divided in three equal parts and if we passed on before mother we would have the right to will our part to our family if we wished. Perhaps you do not feel this way about it and I don't suppose anything could be done unless we all three agreed to it but I'd like to have it that way myself. Please write me what you think about it. Of course we can't change Dad's will but if we agreed to divide the property in three equal parts we could have a paper drawn up to that effect and then our children would benefit from it even if we didn't.

George bought a second hand radio. He got it up and we had fine music for two evenings but there seems to be a loose connection somewhere for we get something then it fades away. I hope he gets it fixed for it will be nice for us this winter to have something to listen to.

I want to do some sewing and the afternoon is most gone. It seems as if mealtime comes pretty often these short days.

Hope all are well. Give my love to Mother Allen when you see her.

Lovingly, Nell

Ness Lake, B.C
November 25, 1930

Dear Reta,

I sent my letter three days before yours arrived so I'll just drop a few lines again as I want to send the picture back before anything happens to it. I guess the newspaperman made a mistake in his date, as it must have been taken in 1894 or 95. Some of them I could have picked out without the names. I was real pleased to get Lulu's letter. I've often thought of her but have never known her name since she was married or her address. Helen and Emma have both mentioned seeing her in their letters and they always say, Lulu Dunn. You might send me her name and address and I'll get around to writing her a Christmas letter. Is Margaret French's address the same as last year?

I wish I had a few of the apples you have going to waste. I paid $2.60 for a box of 150 apples. George planted some apple seeds last spring. We may live long enough to get an orchard. I think they would do well here, as the winters aren't severe if we once got them started. No one here has planted any fruit trees yet. I believe Mr. Roger has a plum and a cherry tree started though.

We went visiting last weekend. Mr. Byers came for us about four on Saturday afternoon and then took us to his place in his car and spent that evening and the next afternoon with them. Mrs. Byers lived in Vancouver until last spring. She came out to keep house for her father and so got a leave of absence for a year. Before her time was up she married one of the many widowers around here. Her father lived near our place so I had her for a neighbor all summer. This fall they all came down onto Mr. Byers place, so they aren't more than three miles from us here.

Did I write you that George bought a radio? It is only a one-tube affair with the earphones but it is nice to have something to listen to when every night is a night at home for us.

I shall be delighted to have your brown silk dress. I've worn the old brown one you gave me ever since I came. There is to be a concert at school at Christmas and I felt I ought to make over something to wear but with Christmas presents and a suit for Emerson and no sewing machine I didn't know where I'd find the time. If you can send it so I can have it in time for the concert I'll be eternally grateful. I'm really quite pleased that you are growing fat. I'm just as skinny as ever.

I must get busy on some sewing. The days are so short now that it gets dark early and I don't accomplish much.

Love to all, Nell

Lovingly yours, Nellie

Ness Lake, B.C.
Dec. 26, 1930

Dear Pinga, Aunt Marie and all,

We surely were delighted with our nice Christmas box. It arrived in lots of time. In fact it was quite a temptation not to open it before Christmas. It is so nice to have an extra pair of headphones. We had only two sets so appreciate Pinga's thoughtfulness in sending them. I love the pillow tops and they represent a lot of work. My housedresses are wearing out so I shall get busy and make me a new one after Christmas. Auntie sent such a generous size pattern I may be able to get out two dresses, - at least a dress and apron. The game was splendid for Emerson. He likes something to do evenings. I haven't had time to read to him, but he likes stories. I had read all the books he has, so will be glad of something new to read. He can read some but still likes to be read to. George was pleased with his knife. I got one for him this fall for a premium with the paper and he lost it in only a week or two, so was quite delighted to get another. He read the book years ago but I have never read it and he says he'd like to read it again, so we will have something to read out loud. The cretonne is just what I need for everyday pillows, as mine get hard usage. I'm saving the pillow tops Pinga sent with my other good things to fix up my living room when the house is finished. All the things in our general room go into the kitchen when we get it built and I want the living room green and buff. The pillows will look well with my room and woe be to anyone who uses them rough. Emerson wore his cap and mitts on Christmas and felt quite dressed up. I made him a suit out of mine and it came out very well. I had never made pants and a coat before and he wanted long pants. He wore one of the neckties Auntie sent him for his birthday. I was quite delighted with the rose curtain drapes, also the pieces to embroider. I can surely use everything like that. George never owned so many good socks in his life. I told him I thought I'd have to borrow some of them this summer and appear in short socks. He wore one pair of his new wool socks on Christmas Day. We were invited out for the day. I made little boxes for the nuts and raisins and hunted up a funny story to go in each box. Emerson made place cards and I wrote a riddle on the back of each one. After dinner we had a Christmas tree and Mrs. Byers made something for everyone. I did the same and we both wrote verses for everything, so we had a lot of fun listening to them. They have a radio so we got quite a lot of enjoyment from that. Emerson and Mr. Rogers played checkers and one of the auto games on the board you sent, so everyone had a good time. We stayed all night and Mr. Rogers brought us home in the sleigh the next day.

Mr. Byers shot an immense moose last week so we brought home a big sack full of moose. It is cool now so it will keep all right outside and I won't have to can it. I have been killing off the roosters and putting them in jars. I have four cans of chicken now and I think there are two more roosters that should be in glass jars.

I didn't include William Jr. in my Christmas box, as I did not know he had arrived when I sent my box. In fact I have heard very little about him and didn't know when he was expected to arrive. I suppose you all are delighted to have a boy in the family. Does he look like Bill? I shall send him something later.

George is cutting railroad ties. It really is quite a job, as the trees have to be sawed down and hewed and peeled and have to be just certain measurements. The railroad company gave settlers orders for only 500 ties this year instead of 1000 as in the past. By the time we pay stumpage, royalty, hauling and cost of loading on cars there is about $150.00 left for us. Of course, I suppose we are lucky to have that much work. So many people are out of work these days. We really are very fortunate, as we have no rent; laundry bills or fuel bills and can shoot our own meat.

Emerson is going to school at Isle Pierre. He has a mile to walk to the river and then the ferryman takes him across the river in a small boat. They took the ferry out when the ice began to come down the river. He has about a mile to go on the other side of the river so has quite a walk every day. He rather hates to go alone, as there are no houses on the way, - only woods. They had an entertainment at school last week and Emerson spoke. He did very well and got a lunch kit with a thermos bottle in it for a present from the school.

I'm going to start piecing quilts now Christmas is over. George hopes to finish the bedrooms this summer and I need more bedding. Mine is old and poor.

Somebody write me about all your Christmas. Were you all at Pinga's this year or what did you do?

I'd surely like to drop in and see you all including William Jr., but goodness knows when we will ever get east again. However, I often think of you all. Do write me soon.

Love to all, Nell.

Ness Lake, B.C.
January 6, 1931

Dear Reta,

Many thanks for our Christmas present. You couldn't have sent us anything we liked better. We took it (Saturday Evening Post) last year but our subscription ran out with the Christmas issue. We sent away this fall for the parts we needed for the radio and that cost about fifteen dollars so we didn't feel we could send for the Saturday Evening Post although we wanted it. George enjoys it, as it has such good articles besides the stories. Emerson was pleased with his money and is sending by mail for an Erector Set. He does not seem to care anything for ready made toys but spends hours modeling machines. He made a moveable runner sled with a steering wheel like an auto. It is wired so he can steer it by the wheel and instead of sliding on his good sled, he pushes this contraption through the deep snow "making roads". He spent all day this week trying to make a weighing machine out of pieces of wood and is quite happy if he can use his hands. He gets excellent at school for handwork. I think he'll like the Erector Set.

We had a very nice Christmas this year. I really enjoyed the day. In fact, our Christmas lasted a week. The school concert and tree was the 20th. Emerson spoke a piece and did very well. All the children got presents from the school. Emerson's was a nice lunch kit with thermos bottle, as he has to take his dinner. Some of the children got skis, others sleds. They all had huge candy bags filled with apples, nuts and candy and they passed oranges, apples and nuts to all the crowd. At midnight they served sandwiches, cake and coffee. Santa backed into a lighted candle and in a moment his whole suit was in flames. The men tore it off somehow and threw it out doors so only the backs of Santa's hands got burned but for a few moments it looked as though he was going up in smoke.

We had our Christmas tree Christmas Eve, as we went to Byers on Christmas day. I wanted them to come here but as we have no chores to do this winter she persuaded us to come there instead. I was quite delighted with the dress you sent, as it arrived in ample time for the concert and fits well. It is very becoming and Lizzie sent me a little brown velvet hat trimmed with chenille just the color of the lace collar, so my costume matches. She also sent a burnt orange silk that belonged to one of the girls. That fit me too without any changing so I feel quite fine with two new gowns.

Mrs. Byers was a teacher in Vancouver and married a widower here last spring. She is about my age. Mr. Byers came from Maine years ago and is very jolly and full of fun. I guess we are the only Maine people here. Mrs. Byers planned the first part of the meal and I did the desert. She had roast venison, mashed potatoes and cranberry sauce. I made a fruit gelatin with whipped cream and small coconut dropped cakes to go with it. I put the nuts and raisins in little three cornered holly boxes and found a really funny story to go in each one. We had lots of laughs over them and most everyone reminded someone of some other funny story they had heard. We had chocolate fudge with nuts, white fudge with coconut and stuffed dates. Emerson made the place cards and I put a riddle on the back of each place card and that kept us busy while Mr. Byers was carving the roast. After dinner we had a tree and Mrs. Byers and I wrote verses for all the things. She gave me a rubber pad to kneel on when I scrub the floor. Maybe you have seen them. She wrote:

"Please don't take this as a hint, for there's not a speck of malice in it,
But when on knees, to scrub, you bend, just slip this under, my slim friend,
To save your floor many a dent and rap, caused by scant covering over each kneecap.
And when you gain flesh to pad your bones, you'll not need this, so give it a new home".

We had lots of fun reading the verses aloud. In the evening we played games and listened to the radio. Mr. Rogers, her father, brought us home in the sleigh the next day. Santa was very good to us and we had a very nice Christmas.

We have been having lots of moose meat, as we had a lot given to us and I got some of the rough meat for the hens. They haven't laid all winter. I had only two old hens that I bought to set and as I couldn't get them until Mrs. Estes got through setting hens it was the first of July before the chickens hatched out. One old hen started laying this fall and after laying eighteen eggs wanted to set again. She hasn't laid since until the last day of December. I guess she thought she'd finish the year well. Both hens are laying but none of the pullets have started and it seems to me it is about time for them to get busy. I have a dreadful time getting my family to eat chicken. George will only eat a piece of the breast the first day it is cooked and Emerson will eat the gizzard. I spend the rest of the week eating the rest of the chicken by myself and by the time I've finished the whole bird I'm so tired of chicken I don't want any more. I have four quarts canned and am waiting for someone to come spend the day so they can help me eat it. I think there are three more roosters that ought to be in glass jars.

Do you remember Blanche Hight? I had a letter from her at Christmas. She lives in California and usually writes once or twice through the year. She thinks it is a most beautiful country. I guess I've written all the news. I washed this morning and as George is cutting about half a mile from home, I take him a hot dinner at noon to save him time, as the days are so short. This noon I took enough for me and sat on a railway tie in the woods and ate moose and potatoes. George built a fire so it wasn't cold even if there is quite a bit of snow. I got Mother Allen's card and will write her soon.

Many thanks for the dress and our Christmas gift. You never have written what you think about dividing what Dad left. Do you know just how the will reads? Have you a list of the bonds, etc.? Uncle Henry sent me one, upon request. I wish you would express your opinion when you write. Do you know where Rudy is?

Lovingly, Nell

Ness Lake, B.C
Feb. 10, 1931

Dear Auntie Marie,

I am going to walk to the Post Office in Isle Pierre tomorrow, so will get a letter written tonight. I believe you will be having a birthday by the time this reaches you. I'm mailing a wee package. It isn't as much as I'd like to send but we don't have stores handy. I have to make things out of what I have in the house and by the time Christmas is over, there aren't many pieces left. However, we all send love and hope you will have a very nice birthday and the little gift may prove useful.

This has been a most delightful winter, - the mildest I ever remember. We have plenty of snow on the ground but the days are warm and sunshiny and the water drips off of the roof.

George is still cutting ties but will be through by the end of the week. Jim Byers has started hauling and has two hundred down to the track now. The teams go by here every day loaded with ties and there are thousands of ties piled up along the railroad track.

It will be nice to get home once more, as there are so many things outside to be done. I really have enjoyed the winter here, as there is so much passing and someone is always stopping in. For two weeks I had company nearly every day. People here usually come in the morning and bring their bag of stockings to darn, or some other work and spend the day. Mrs. Byers has been over twice lately and Mrs. Harkness came last week. We drove down to the Post Office after dinner and got Sonny when he came from school and then she went home. Monday I walked down to the Post Office and one of our neighbors gave me a ride back. Yesterday afternoon I went calling and did some stitching while I was there. Mrs. Boyd sent a note last night by Emerson asking me to come down this afternoon, so I seem to be gadding this week.

The people here are great for giving parties in the winter. A bachelor stopped in yesterday and invited us to a party at his place on Saturday night. The young folks dance and the older ones play games, but the worst of it is, they stay all night. It was four a.m. before we got home from the school concert and then we came away early. We don't go to many because we don't feel good the next day if we stay up all night, but this chap said he was coming down with the sleighs Saturday afternoon to get folks, so I guess we'll go.

I have to knit one pair of stockings for Emerson this winter and am on the second pair. I never did any knitting before so am quite proud of myself. Last week I made two dresses all by hand out of the cloth Aunt Ida sent me at Christmas. I want to make up the cloth you sent me, but Mrs. Fanshaw said she had a pattern I could use, so am waiting until I get it, as I'd like to make a dress for afternoons out of it.

It is nice Flora and Tom have found a place. I suppose Flora will be busy fixing it up. Tell her I'm still looking for the letter she said she was going to write. She had better write me a long one. I know Louisa is busy with the baby. They surely can keep one on the trot but of course she wouldn't want to part with him even if he does. I'd love dearly to see him. I guess I wrote you there was a music teacher who lived at the other end of the lake from us. She was about thirty-eight and married only a year ago last spring. They had a nice log house fixed up very prettily inside. Last spring she adopted a baby eighteen months old and almost as soon as she got him, she found she was to have one of her own. Her father is a minister. I guess I wrote you he was here last summer and we had a church service by the lake. He insisted that she come to Illinois for the event, so she took Gordon, the adopted baby and went in November. Two weeks ago her husband got a telegram she died, and they were taking her to Minneapolis for burial. Her husband left here on the first train. His brother was here last night and he had a short letter from him saying she left a ten-pound boy. He surely is going to have his hands full with two babies. He wrote he intended to bring them both back with him. I would think it would be a task for a man to take a tiny baby for a four or five day trip on the train all alone.

I had a letter from Emma lately. She is well. Smithy's brother's wife had a shock (stroke) this winter. They had no money and he was out of work and she was wholly paralyzed. They came to Emma's and Em wrote that Bertha could sit up a little and use one side now, but she didn't think she would ever walk again.

I'm still making quilts in my spare time. I have three partly done. One is a wool quilt. I had never made one out of wool pieces before.

Emerson has been busy making valentines. They don't have such things at the store here and I should have sent away over two weeks ago to buy any. I had saved a lot of fancy linings to envelopes and I had several fancy red wrapping papers from Christmas, so he has pasted the last two evenings. He has five made, all different and has three more to do, as there are just eight children at school. He loves to do anything with his hands.

I hope your cold is better and you are able to get out once more. Give my love to all of your family.

Many happy returns of the day on February 18th.

Lots of love, Nell

Ness Lake, B.C.
May 3, 1931

Dear Aunt Marie,

Here it is a whole month since George's birthday and I haven't thanked you yet for the pretty shirt you sent him. Blue is such a good color for him and it was a very neat pattern. He was quite pleased with it.

We are having a rainy day today. The sun is almost out and yet it rains just enough to be disagreeable to work outside. We have been busy on the garden. It was either fence the chickens or fence the house lot, garden and all. One of our neighbors has goats and some days some cows stroll in so it is safer to have the garden fenced. George set the posts and they cut small birches about six inches through and we weave them in and out of the posts like a basket. The top branches filled in and made the fence close so the chickens can't get through and it really is quite an artistic fence and goes well with the setting. It was a lot of work, as we had to carry all the birches and some were quite heavy and you'd be surprised how many it took. I have planted sumac bushes by each gate and sunflowers and poppies along the inside of the fence by the chicken house. I have a few flower seeds and want to have a flower garden all along the path. We set some strawberries last spring and last week transplanted the runners. There were such a lot of them that it seems as if we should have strawberries this summer. We had rhubarb last year from seed and it has done fine. We had rhubarb sauce for supper last night. I hope there will be some to can this summer, as my family is very fond of it.

George has been kind of under the weather for a few days. He didn't want anything to eat but potato soup. He ate some mushrooms and he thought it was them, but Mr. Rogers came in yesterday morning on horseback and he was sick to his stomach. He is quite old and has been staying with his daughter about five miles from here all winter. His place is close to us and he wants to put in the garden there, so comes over for two or three days and then goes back to his daughters. He said he felt so sick that he thought two or three times he'd have to get off the horse and lie down. He decided to stop in and ask for a cup of tea, but when he got here he said he felt better so would go on home and get his dinner. I offered to go in and make tea but he wouldn't stop. He rode in again about suppertime and lay on the couch awhile and ate a good supper. After supper he said he'd go home and if he did feel better today, he'd come back. His daughter worries about him when he goes away for a few days, because he is old and has dizzy spells. There seems to be a stomach flu around so perhaps that is what George had.

We are all out of groceries. It is such a nuisance to be so far away from a store. We usually lay in a big supply of things. I get 400 or 500 lbs. of flour and 100 lbs. of sugar, several lbs. of tea, coffee and cocoa and ten or fifteen lbs. of raisins. We can buy cheaper in Prince George than in Isle Pierre, but the roads have been poor. They have been working on a bridge across the canyon, so we haven't been able to go to town. It is such a job trying to cook without anything. George expects to go in soon now and I'll surely be glad, as we are down to eggs, bread and potatoes. I try to vary them as much as possible. Our peas, spinach, radishes and lettuce are up so we will be having green things soon.

I was so glad to hear from Flora and will try to write her soon. I'm glad she has a home at last and hope she is feeling quite well. I suppose young William keeps Pinga busy these days. How I'd like to drop in and visit you all.

I haven't heard from Marion for ages. I think she must be peeved with me for I have written her several times and she hasn't answered. She writes to the rest of the family.

George has retired and I guess I will, as I have to work tomorrow. I don't have any regular washday but wash whenever I feel like it.

Give my love to all of your family and write as often as you can, as I like to hear what you and the girls are doing.

Lovingly, Nell

Ness Lake, B.C.
May 23, 1931

Dear Aunt Marie,

We are having a rainy Saturday. George is out planting beans but I decided it was too moist outside for me, so came in. Emerson has been down to the lake bailing out the water from the canoe, as we thought we might go up the lake picnicking tomorrow. We haven't used the canoe this spring and the rain got in it.

I was ever so pleased with my pretty dress. I wore it one day to go up to Mrs. Estes', but will save it for a Sunday dress, as it is such pretty goods. I wish I had yards and yards of stuff just like it to cover a shirtwaist dress box for my bedroom and make curtains for a dressing table and some cushions. I have been looking in the catalogue for just those colors. I could find plenty of blue and white stuff but nothing with a touch of yellow in it. Perhaps by the time I get ready to use it, there will be something with blue and white and yellow in the new catalogue. I'm so anxious for George to get working on the house, but we have to get the garden all in first. We had about an acre plowed. We put in half an acre of potatoes and a big piece of turnips and carrots and then a patch of wheat and barley so the chickens would have feed. George has spaded up over half an acre by hand and we have that planted. Things are coming up fast and the peas, spinach, lettuce and radishes are growing like everything. I guess everything is up, except beans, cucumbers, pumpkins and corn that have just been put in.

My biddies continue to lay and not one of them will set. I want to go to Estes' in the canoe tomorrow to see if she has a setting hen I can get, as it is getting so late. The summer will be over before mine get around to setting.

I suppose Louisa and Flora are busy these days. How I wish I could drop in and visit you all some day, but I guess it won't be this summer. Both Helen Peabody and Mabel Widell talk of taking a trip to B.C. Mabel talked of coming this summer but has to take a course at Columbia University either this summer or next. She thought she better take the course this year, as her mother is with her, and they have an apartment on Long Island.

It is beautiful here. I hope to take some pictures this summer when things are at their best.

I have baked beans cooking. I guess I'm the only one around here that has beans on Saturday night. It seems to be a New England custom but George feels terribly cheated if he doesn't get his beans.

I must patch up Emerson's pants for tomorrow. His clothes are all fit for the ragbag. Just as soon as everything is planted, I shall have to take a few days off and make him some clothes. I have been helping George outside so haven't done anything inside but get meals. I ripped up that blue serge dress I made out of the coat mother gave me when I was back east, washed it and cut him out a suit, coat and pants. I want to make that and I have enough flour sacks to make his summer underwear.

I guess George and Sonny will both be good and wet, as they are still out and it continues to rain as hard as ever.

I mean to write to Flora soon but I know she hears from me through you. Hope you are all well. It was nice of you to remember my birthday and I like the dress a lot. Do write as often as you can, as I love to hear what you all are doing. You all seem quite like my own family.

Love to all, Nell.

Ness Lake, B.C.
Sept. 30, 1931

Dear Aunt Marie,

I guess it is about time I thanked you for the nice things you sent Emerson for his birthday. He did enjoy the book so much. In fact, I read it aloud to the whole family. He can read, but not fast enough to enjoy the book by himself. He got quite excited over the adventures of the youngsters on the island. He likes the game. He is playing with it tonight. There are so few toys he cares much about, but he likes to make things. We all enjoyed the candy. Emerson is very generous when he has sweets and it is queer because he has so few of them.

We have been busy getting in the garden. George started to finish up the house. He had to make the shingles by hand, got the roof of the lean-to finished and the windows toward the lake cut out, and then it turned cold so he dug the cellar bigger. We had only a small one, but we had so much garden he had to dig a hole under the back of the house and make the cellar bigger. You wouldn't think there would be so much dirt in a big hole in the ground. I helped him some and we finally got a nice deep cellar under the whole house. He put in nice bins for everything. We all went over and dug the potatoes. We had two tons of potatoes and about two and a half tons of turnips. It was quite a job digging the "taters" and picking them up and pulling the turnips and cutting off the tops. It is too bad there is no sale for turnips at present. I sold some green tomatoes and some onions and we are taking a pig in exchange to help us eat the turnips. There may be a sale for garden stuff in the spring but everybody who had a place big enough to put in anything, planted something this year. We will have enough to eat even if there isn't much cash at present.

Perhaps you have heard me speak of a teacher from Vancouver who married a widower last year. He is a Maine man and always joking like B. Fay. They live only 5 ½ miles from here but the road hasn't been cut out yet. One can get through with a horse, but not with a car. They have to come about twelve miles around to get here with their Ford. She sent over word last week for me to get my sewing ready, as she had borrowed a sewing machine. They would be over the middle of this week to get me for a week's visit and I could get all my stitching done while I'm there. I'm leaving my men folks to bach. Emerson has written you a little letter, which I am sending along. I have to get dinner and go get some grain in the field for the chickens so won't write more this time.

I often think of you and wish I might drop in to see you all. Remember me to Pinga and Flora. I suppose the babies are doing fine. I'd surely like to see them. Don't do much for us this Christmas, as I'm afraid my Christmas presents won't be much. I can't get anywhere to buy anything and my piece bag is getting low.

We are all well and hope you people keep so.

Love to all, Nell

Ness Lake, B.C.
Jan. 1, 1932

Dear Aunt Marie,

You see I am starting the New Year right anyway. The package you sent reached us safely and we all were delighted with its contents. Santa was very good to us in spite of the hard times. We had our tree on Wednesday night. I planned to have it Thursday evening but we got all the packages we would get before Christmas on Wednesday, and Sonny just couldn't wait any longer for his things. So he trimmed the tree after supper Wednesday while I washed the supper dishes, and he had a grand time opening things. The stockings and gloves you sent help out a lot and I'm ever so pleased with my dress goods. I shall make me a housedress and an apron. Mother sent me some dark goods for aprons and I was glad to get it, as I work outside so much it won't show the dirt so easily. We had five books this year and have read two already and we are on the third. I know we will enjoy the book you sent, as we can't get library books here. While I think of it, do any of you happen to take "Woman's Home Companion?" We are reading "Captain Archer's Daughter" but Mrs. Estes' subscription runs out and she can't afford to renew it so we won't get the last installment. I thought if any of you folks happened to have the December issue you might be willing to pass it on.

Premier Bennett has put a tax on all magazines from the States, so that brings the Saturday Evening Post from $3.00 to $4.50 this year so we will have to give that up. I don't think much of Bennett!

To go back to Christmas we had a very nice day. Mr. and Mrs. Byers and Mrs. B's father, Mr. Rogers, came to dinner. I roasted a couple of young roosters and opened a jar of string beans, had mashed potatoes and turnips, small cucumber pickles, parsley jelly and new whole wheat bread, gelatin pudding with whipped cream, Christmas cake (Mrs. Byers brought a bit of hers so we had both light and dark fruit cake) and the usual nuts, salted peanuts, stuffed dates, figs and home made candy.

Emerson did justice to everything and at night complained of not feeling well. I asked him if his stomach ached and he said, " No, but it just felt awfully full."

I sent the package to Louisa, as I thought you probably would spend Christmas there. Hope it reached you all right and in ample time. Tell Louisa and Flora that I didn't forget Little William and Sally Marie, but I saw in the "Home Loving Hearts" page that some lady would send a pattern for a stuffed dog called "Spare Ribs" to anyone sending her a stamped addressed envelope so I sent for it. It was so late before I got the pattern that the other gifts would be late if I stopped to make them, so I sent the other things. George and Emerson needed mittens so I knit them each a pair before Christmas. I knew both babies would be so well remembered that they wouldn't mind if their "doggies" didn't get there until later. I have made them and they are ever so cute but rather bulky. I will get them mailed as soon as I can, but it is a long way to the Post Office and walking is poor. The last time George went in he had ten packages of various shapes and sizes beside the stack of letters to carry on his back, and they grow heavy before you have walked eleven miles through the snow. He had about thirty-five or forty pounds to bring back so had a load for the whole twenty-two miles. Mr. Walker walked down this week and brought us some letters but said he couldn't bring along the packages, as there were too many, so we will be having another Christmas when we can get the rest of the bundles.

George is trapping this winter. He wanted to cut ties but the railroad isn't buying any. An old trapper here asked George to run the north end of his trap line for him this winter. George wanted to slash and get out logs for a barn and put up a shop, but he thought it would bring in a little and we would need money in the spring for another supply of groceries, so he spends his days tramping the woods. Some times he stays over night and makes a two-day trip, as he has quite a distance to cover. So far he hasn't got anything but squirrels and weasels and one very nice mink. He hopes to make more in the spring when he can trap muskrats and beavers, but the law forbids them until March.

I'm glad your knee is better. Ida wrote me you had trouble with it. Hope it will be all right again, as it is hard not to be able to get around.

I shall want to hear all about your Christmas. I have lots and lots of letters to write. I had a letter from Maude and also one from Eunice. I guess I never wrote you, but Winfield became infatuated with some young lady in her twenties and wanted Maude to get a divorce. She said he had been having these affairs on the side for the past six years and she just couldn't stand it any longer, as they were terrible while they lasted. She has been staying with her sister Carolyn, who is a widow in Los Angeles. She wrote me she got an interlocutory decree in September, but the final decree wouldn't be issued until October. She has been terribly upset over it as she didn't want the divorce, but Winfield said he would get one if she didn't. She didn't have the means to follow him about and oppose it, so she said it seemed to be all she could do. I'm afraid Winfield will some day regret it, for Maude is a fine woman. I'm afraid some men don't make very good husbands. Eunice is still running the laundry and doing well. I had a letter from Johnny Hamlin, Leander's son. Cousin Lizzie wrote me she heard from him occasionally and he asked where I was. She sent him my address as he said he'd like to write, but he never did. So this Christmas I wrote him all about the place and sent some snaps and asked Lizzie to forward it, as I didn't know his address. He wrote me a long letter and seemed awfully pleased that I wrote. He said he sometimes felt awfully alone in the world, as Lizzie usually sent him a card at Christmas and rarely a letter and she was the only one of his relatives that ever wrote to him. He begged me to write again and soon. I guess he is the only one of the Hamlin's that ever stuck to anything and he has worked in a shoe factory all his life. He is foreman of the cutting room and his son works in his room.

We got the radio fixed this fall so that is nice in the evenings. It gets dark so early we have long evenings.

I must write some more letters. I guess if they are all as long as this one my paper will give out before I get my thank you letters done.

It was nice of you to remember us all so generously and we were pleased with all of our gifts. I wish I could do more for you folks but you may be sure I think of you all often and I hope someday our purse may be fat enough to stand another trip east. Please pass this on to Flora and Louisa. I guess I never thanked you for the snap of Flora and Sally Marie. I'd like to see them and I'd also like a snap of Tom if he has one. I think it is about time I saw my new cousin.

Love to all, Nell

Ness Lake, B.C.
April 4, 1932

Dear Aunt Marie,

I had a letter from Marion's sister this week saying that Marion was very sick. Her operation last summer, teaching, and the radium treatments she took this winter were too much for her, and she simply went all to pieces. She was taken sick early in January and her sister Sid, the nurse, took her to her home as soon as they realized she would be sick for a long while. They gave up the apartment, stored the furniture and her sister Enid took the two children. Jane wrote that Marion could not even sit up in bed yet and it bothered her to try to talk to anyone. Sid and her husband had taken her back to the hospital the day June wrote and they had decided it was best to leave her there until she showed some improvement. If you want to write her, send it to her at 10 Berkley St., Lawrence, Mass., care of Dr. Carl Mockel.

Marion heard from a friend in Panama last January and she said they were glad to see Rudy (Dana) when he was there. (Marion always called him Dana.) Of course she wrote right back and asked about it and Jane sent the reply she got back to me. Mr. Lewis wrote that Rudy had been working for the Club Aluminium Co. in Honolulu on a commission basis, but business was so poor he couldn't make his expenses. He had accepted an offer to work his way back to the States on some ship going to someplace on the east coast, - he thought Philadelphia. He told Mr. Lewis he was pretty sure he could get work on the Munson Line out of Seattle. He left Panama on the 10th of July, last. Jane wanted me to see if I couldn't find him and induce him to help a little with the support of the children, even if it was only a very little. She said Enid's husband was on part time and they had two children of their own and Don and Dorothy would soon be needing more clothes, so if I could find Dana and get him to help even a little, it would mean a lot to them. She thought perhaps I could write to the Munson Line in Seattle. I don't see why some of them didn't long ago. I decided that if he was working his way back to the States he was out of funds (as usual) and Seattle is a long way from Philadelphia. He would naturally try to get some sort of work when he landed, so I have written to the Chief of Police in Philadelphia to find out if he got work on any boat out of Philadelphia and if so where bound. George has quite a bit of faith in the American Legion, as it is a big organization and supposed to help war veterans and their families. He thinks they have a thousand chances to my one, so I asked them to try to find him. I have written Mr. Lewis to tell Dana of Marion's condition should he pass through the Canal again. If he gets work on any steamship line he may be in Panama sooner or later. I don't know what else I can do for the present.

I thought that perhaps Louisa might have a few things that Faye had outgrown that would help out on Dorothy's clothes. I know Faye grew awfully fast and as Louisa always bought her nice things, I thought she might have outgrown some of them. Jane is quite handy about sewing so no doubt could fix them up if Louisa happened to have anything she thought they could use. I know it would help out. Faye seems to be the only one her size and things too big are easier to fix over than things too little. I'm sending a snap shot of Don and Dorothy that Jane sent.

We have a lot of snow here yet and the lake is still frozen solid. I'll be glad when I can work outside. I have started the tomatoes and celery in the house. George is still trapping. He wouldn't have done so bad this winter if fur prices hadn't been way down. He got $6.75 for a mink that usually brought $15.00 to $18.00. Weasels that have brought $1.00 to $1.25 have brought $.30 - $.40. He got two beavers so we have had quite a lot of beaver to eat. It is rather good, - greasy meat and tastes somewhat like pork and somewhat like duck, if you can imagine the combination. He shot a deer but we gave half of that away, as we had a quarter of moose and I didn't want too much meat when warm weather came. I'd like George to get another deer and I'd can a bit more for summer.

I set a hen today. Every year the hens won't set until late, and since we came here I haven't been able to get any chicks hatched until July and then they won't lay before the next spring. I was quite delighted when this hen showed signs of setting.

I hope the two babies are both fine. Tell them they will get their Christmas doggies some day.

The ferry is out now so anyone going down has to cross the river in a boat and walk over a mile to the Post Office. They have to leave the horses on this side. I hate to ask the neighbors to carry a lot of things, as they usually have butter or eggs of their own to carry. When George gets through trapping he may go down but we have no horse so it means a walk of 22 miles for him. The dogs are as big as good-sized Teddy bears so rather bulky to carry. I'll get them off one of these days.

It is going on to five so time I fed the chickens and got the fire going. George has been up the lake all day, so wants a hot supper when he gets home.

Thanks for the Easter cards. I invited some new neighbors to dinner Easter on Sunday so we had a nice day.

Give my love to all your family.

Lots of love, Nell

Ness Lake, B.C.
May 30, 1932

Dear Auntie Marie,

I must thank you for the nice slip. It is something that I needed very much and hankies are always useful. I'm waiting for George to come to dinner. We have been out all morning planting potatoes. George digs the holes, Sonny drops them in and I cover them up. George suggested that we take the net and go fishing this afternoon. Some people came yesterday (Sunday) and George and Emerson went up the lake fishing with them. They got over seventy fish in a short time, but George only took one for dinner today as we can go fishing any day. I came back from the potato field and got the potatoes and fish going and popped a rhubarb pie in the oven to take with us this afternoon, as George said we'd have supper at the lake.

Later

We are home once more and Emerson has gone to bed. One of our neighbors came this afternoon and said that he was going to town tomorrow (21 miles) so George decided to go in with him and get some groceries, as we are all out of everything. Emerson is going with him and is quite excited, as he has never been to Prince George since we landed there 2 ½ years ago.

We have been busy this spring. George trapped until March so that left a lot of garden for me to put in. I planted green onion seed all by hand and it was slow to start. The peas are up and we have had radishes a couple of times. There is lots of rhubarb and we eat it morning, noon and night.

I guess I did not thank you for George's birthday presents. He was pleased, as it was the only remembrance he had. I made him a birthday cake but could not get him anything. He likes useful things and socks are always acceptable in this family. The tie was very pretty.

Sonny is getting along well with his lessons. He is half through Grade III and gets very good rank although he hates terribly to study. I have let up on him the last two weeks, as I've been so busy outside I haven't had time to teach him, but he has done one lesson and it is ready to send. I guess I had better send it tomorrow or they will wonder what has become of him. Had a letter from Emma. Smithy's brother's wife had a shock (stroke) a year or more ago and they were with Emma all last summer. He got work last fall and they went to Portland, Maine, but he is out of work again so is back once more. Her brother has been out of work too so they have been helping him. I guess people on farms are as well off as any one in these hard times. We have lots of fuel and plenty to eat even if cash isn't plentiful.

Later

It is past bedtime and I still have some stockings to darn for Emerson. Walkers have been having a terrible fire all around their place. The smoke got so thick Saturday that we went over and we all carried water from the lake until 7:30 trying to save their buildings. It was pretty hot and smoky but the buildings didn't go, even if the logs on the garage and toilet were smoking. She came running over tonight saying that the fire had started again so we went over and just got back. There's another big forest fire four or five miles from here but across the lake. The sky is all red tonight. I can't write more now but I wanted to thank you for your gifts to both me and George and I don't know if I'll have another chance to get a letter off.

Lovingly, Nell

P.S. I wrote to the "American Legion" and asked them to try to find Rudy and they wrote they would be glad to advertise for him and it would be published in 4000 publications, both here and abroad.

Ness Lake, B.C.
Oct. 1, 1932

Dear Aunt Marie,

I guess you people will be looking for a letter. I have meant to write and thank you for Emerson's birthday gifts. It surely is nice of you to remember him when you have so many folks both big and little to remember. One of the neighbors brought the package. Two old men, - both seventy-eight, invited us to go to a barbecue at Nukko Lake with them. We were just driving and then we met a chap on horse back with the mail. Emerson opened his package on the road and got the birthday cards mixed up, so I didn't know what you sent or what came from Aunt Ida, but he surely was pleased with everything. I didn't get any peace until I had read the book aloud. He thinks I ought to read aloud every evening to the family. George usually drops to sleep while I'm reading. I guess Sonny would do more reading if I'd read less for he is crazy for stories. He enjoyed the marshmallows; in fact we all did as we seldom see store candy. The blouse and stockings were useful. He has worn both. He keeps his blouses for dress up occasions as all the children here wear overalls, even to school. It is quite a saving on the washing. I make Emerson coveralls of blue denim, as I can make them cheaper than I can buy them. I sent this week and got some bloomers for winter and have two sleeping garments cut for Emerson. It is slow sewing by hand. I sewed last evening, but something stung me yesterday while I was over in the field picking up potatoes, and my one eye is all puffed up. Today I helped him gather the oats into bundles and something bit my finger under my wedding ring and now my left hand is all puffed up. I told George I wouldn't be bad looking if I could swell up even all over, but swelling in bunches, as I do, isn't awfully becoming.

We thought we were going to have Dot with us. Sid's letter in early July gave no hope for Marion. She had written a friend of mine to see if she could visit me and bring Dot.

Of course we got busy on the house, as I needed another bedroom. George brought clay mud from the lake and I put the willows on the walls in two rooms in

the lean-to for him to mud. It was quite a job but we finally got both rooms mudded. We tinted the kitchen walls pale yellow and George built a chimney of homemade bricks. He made the bricks and dried them in the sun. When we got the two rooms done we needed more furniture. As there was no money to buy the many things we needed, we bought some plain lumber. I set to work making furniture, as George doesn't care much for fussy jobs. I made a kitchen cupboard, - sort of cabinet affair with shelves for my dishes, a kitchen table with a drawer in it for knives and forks, and a washstand with a shelf underneath for my flat-irons, clothes pins, etc. For the living room I made a table with two leaves, which I can put in if we have company to a meal, a bookcase and a couch. I made

two single cots for upstairs so if Emerson has one of the boys for overnight he can
have them upstairs in his room. The room looks well with a cot on each end. It
makes a cute room for him. You know you sent me some cretonne a year ago for
cushions. I used it to upholster one of the living room chairs. Another chair made
from a crate my crocks came in, I covered with cretonne Ida sent me several years
ago. I had used it for curtains but it looked as good as new when washed and
ironed. It made quite a classy chair. We painted the furniture in the living room
jade green and the walls are a light spruce green color. I made white voile cross
stitch curtains for the windows and the kitchen really is quite cheerful and homelike.
The bedroom walls are pale pink and the bedstand and chair are ivory enamel. I
think the bed was really quite my masterpiece. I got heavy canvas and turned a wide
hem on both sides and then ran poles through the hems. George bored holes in the
sidepieces and end pieces and we bolted the corners of the spring. The canvas
could be stretched awfully tight this way and the bolts hold it. It makes a very good
spring and sags very little. I made the bedstead of plain lumber and shaped the head
and footboards like this.

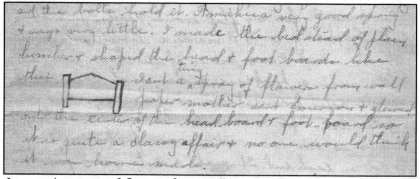

I cut a tiny spray of flowers from wallpaper mother sent Emerson and glued
this onto the center of the head-board and foot-board, so it is quite a classy affair
and no one would think it was home made.

The homestead inspector was here after we got all "dolled up" and he said,
"You people certainly deserve a lot of credit for all you've done in the time you've
been here." It has been a lot of work and a lot of fun too. I'm really quite proud of
my house when I think even the doors, shingles and bricks are homemade and all
our furniture too.

I had a letter from Marion last week. I do hope she is going to get better. She
had heard from Rudy and I was quite happy she wants him back and wants to start
all over again. She certainly has had a hard time. It makes it hard to accept help
from ones relatives especially when it is given grudgingly, and Marion wrote that her
sister did not let a day go by without her reminding her that she had spoiled her
whole summer for her. She was so anxious to get better and get her family together

again. She has a lot of courage and I wish I could help her financially. Isn't it dreadful to be poor when there are so many things you'd like to do?

A moose came into the yard the other day and stood and looked at the house. Emerson wanted George to shoot it, but I had just taken care of a quarter of a moose we had given us and canned thirteen hens and chickens and we have a big pig to kill as soon as it is a bit colder. I can't see any sense in killing an animal when you don't need it for food. I was sorry I didn't have a film in the camera, for it seems a shame not to take a picture when a moose comes into your yard and poses five minutes for you, before he ambles off in the woods.

My family has retired and I guess it is time for me to do likewise. Give my love to the girls. It is nice of Louisa and Bill to take care of Dot. I know she will have a very happy time with them. I shall always remember how good Pinga was to us when we were there. She is a comfortable person to live with.

Do write when you have time. Many thanks for remembering Sonny so generously.

Love to all, Nellie.

Ness Lake, B.C.
Dec. 12, 1932

Dear Aunt Marie,

It is almost Christmas once more and I want to wish you all a Merry Christmas, for that is about all I'm doing this year, is wishing folks Merry Christmases. I have just a wee package for you. It isn't much but all I could do this year.

Of course, there is no work of any kind here and in a new and underdeveloped country one cannot raise big crops until the land can be brought into cultivation. It all takes time and so far we use all we raise so have nothing to sell. However, with a cellar full and plenty of meat, fuel and no rent we really don't feel the lack of money as city folks do. We are warm and comfortable so have lots to be thankful for.

Donnie wrote me asking me to copy some letters of application for an undertaking job for Rudy. He is still out of work and has no money to buy paper, envelopes or stamps so Marion wanted me to write and send out as many as I had the time and could afford. She was asking for help from Ruth and one of her sisters. I knew all of you folks would be well remembered and would never miss the little I could do for you, so I am using the money on postage, hoping it might help Marion. She wants so much to have Rudy come back and get her family together again. I hope he may get a job back in New England. I wonder if Mr. Shorey would know of any openings. If he did, would he get in touch with Rudy at 245 North Delaware St., Indianapolis, Indiana? I'll enclose one of the letters of application Marion sent me so he can tell what experience Rudy's had in case he knew of any place. Do you know how Marion is really getting on? She writes quite cheerful letters, but Donnie said in his letter he was writing, his mother was too nervous to write.

I'm still fixing up the house. The curtains are all dirty and I want to wash them before Christmas. We have lots of snow this year. It came the last week in October but has not been cold until this last week and then it sure has been snappy, - between 30 and 40 below. There is one good thing about it, - it warms up in a few days here and doesn't stay that way for months at a time, as in Saskatchewan. I spend my time filling the heater with dry wood and we keep comfortable. George has gone to look at his traps today. So far he hasn't caught anything but squirrels and weasels and not many of them. I'm trying to bake bread but it seems to be slow rising.

Ida wrote they did well at the church fair. We haven't felt we could afford the radio this winter so we have been reading aloud evenings. George got eight books from the Prince George Library and we can keep them six weeks. A trip of forty-two miles is quite a trip though, especially when one is apt to have to walk all the way. Last time he got a ride part way. He plans to go in on Monday, as the books are due.

I suppose you will all be at Louisa's this year as usual. Wish I could drop in and see you all. We plan to have a tree for Emerson and I think I'll ask the people north of us down to dinner. Cousin Lizzie sent Emerson a nice winter overcoat and a pretty bathrobe. I let him wear them, as he really needed them in this cold weather. I also had a letter from John Hamlin. (Leander's son)

I hope you all will have a very nice Christmas and that Santa will be as good to you as he usually is. I shall be wanting to hear all about your Christmas celebration. Give my love to the girls. I'm sorry I can't remember you all year. I'll get George to send the package to you when he mails this.

Merry Christmas to all – Nell

Ness Lake, B.C.
Jan. 13, 1933

Dear Aunt Marie,

I know you will be looking for a letter. I wrote Louisa so no doubt you have heard all about the nice Christmas we had. Louisa's mother's package arrived in time for the tree and then no one went for the mail for a week and we got eight more packages, so had a second Christmas a day or two after New Years. I think we enjoyed it all the more having things come that way. I just love the goods you sent me. It is just what I needed for a good dress. It isn't too light and yet the bright spots give it color. Mother sent me two pairs of black silk stockings speckled with white that will go well with it. I have been looking through the catalogue to see if I can find a pattern to make it by. Cousin Lizzie sent me some green and white muslin for a dress and Helen C sent me percale so I'm going to start fixing up my clothes right away.

George's shirt was very nice. I like the color and Emerson's sweater was just what he needed. We all enjoyed the candy. Fred and Grace sent me a big box from S.S. Pierces, - nuts, candy, dates, raisons, figs, and fancy crackers. Such things surely taste good when we so seldom have them. I'm sorry I couldn't do more this year but hope the Campbell family will be more prosperous another year.

I have been making quilts this week. I made single cots for Emerson's room, - one across each end of the room. The bed quilts are all too wide for them and besides I haven't any too much of it. Last year I made a patchwork top of cotton pieces and one of wool, but never got them put together. I've made them up and then pieced another wool comforter. I save all the scraps, as I can use them for either rugs or quilts. Do you remember the quilt you gave me when I was home? I covered one side of it several years ago, as the patches were so worn. The cover was dirty so I took it off and washed it and dyed it old blue and dyed some other cloth old rose and have it all ready to cover. Then I think I'll start fixing up the family clothes when that is done.

I was so pleased with the spread Louisa sent me. I wish you could see my bedroom. It is very pretty even if it is all "homemade."

My biddies laid four eggs in December and stopped. I got another one today so hope they are going to start in earnest. George is trapping but has got nothing but weasels so far, so isn't getting rich. He keeps busy all the time. We smoked our pig last week so have two big hams, two shoulders and lots of bacon. One of the neighbors drove in yesterday and left about 100 lbs. of moose meat. We certainly have all the meat we can use.

I have been expecting Mrs. Byers this week. Her husband said he was planning to bring her over this week when he came for a load of hay and she planned to stay seven days but she has not come yet.

I had a letter from Maude at Christmas. She got her divorce in September and Winfield was married right away. Maude and her sister have an apartment in Los Angeles.

Rudy sent me a card but did not say whether he had work or not. I haven't heard anything from or about Marion for some time. Do you know how she really is getting on? Is this improvement permanent? It is nice for Louisa to do so much for Dot. I know three children must keep her busy. I wish we lived nearer so she could visit me. She could eat and sleep to her hearts content. There are days at a time when no one passes and sometimes I see no one but my family for a week or more. The last time I went to Mrs. Estes I waded through snow to my knees. Now it has turned warm, so there is eight or nine inches of slush all over the lake under the snow, so I shall have to stay home until the walking gets better.

Many thanks for our nice Christmas box.

Lovingly, Nell

Ness Lake, B.C.
March 2, 1933

Dear Aunt Marie,

I guess you will think I am a good one but I forgot all about your birthday until the 26th of February. You see we only have a weekly paper and sometimes we don't get the mail for a couple of weeks. I don't notice the date particularly unless I happened to look at the calendar for something, and the 26th arrived before I was aware of it. Since then there has been no chance to send mail, but George is talking of going down soon, as his insurance is done and he is anxious to get that paid, so I thought I'd have a letter ready to send to you.

Mother sent Louisa's letter on to me and it was nice to hear from her once more. I am glad you all had such a nice Christmas.

We have lots of snow here. It came the last week in October and has snowed every two or three days since. It hasn't been extremely cold but stays just cold enough so the snow doesn't melt even in the middle of the day. There have been no thaws as there usually is, so the snow has just piled up until it is three and four feet deep on a level. It is impossible to go anywhere without skis or snowshoes. I guess there will be lots of water if it gets warm suddenly and it seems as if it should get warm soon. We had two cold snaps, one 34 below and one 42 below, but thank goodness they lasted only a couple of days and not a month at a time as in Saskatchewan. The climate here is really quite nice and the summers are lovely with a very even temperature.

Emerson is busy doing lessons. He is now in the fourth grade. I think I'll try to send him to school next year. Of course ten miles a day is quite a hike, but he will be older and he needs the association of other children. If he can't stand the trip everyday in cold weather he may be able to go three days a week and do his lessons at home the other two.

I cut out the goods you sent me for Christmas. I'll send a picture of the pattern I sent for. I'm awfully pleased with it, as it will make me a "best dress" and that was what I needed.

I must see a dentist as soon as I can. My teeth ache and some days the lower front ones all seem to be "on edge."

I ripped up my coat, as it was rather antiquated. Mrs. Walker thinks it is going to be a job putting it together, as the sleeves are so big. She doesn't think I can cut it over but I've sent for a pattern and have got to do it somehow or go coatless. I'm far more cheerful about the prospects of getting something modern out of it than she is. I sent for some good looking shoes out of the sales catalogue and although they were size four, the same as the canvas shoes I got last summer, I couldn't even get them on. They were awfully good looking and I hated to send them back but had to. So I ordered five's. It surely is a job buying shoes by mail. I don't mind other things but the shoes never seem to fit. I want to get my coat and dress finished so if there ever is a chance for me to go to Prince George, I'll have some respectable clothes to wear.

I had a letter from Marion yesterday. She said she was still gaining, - had got to 110 lbs. She was still in the Memorial Hospital in Concord. George and I were talking a few weeks ago about her, and George thought it would be nice if some of her friends would do something for Marion personally. I thought there must be so many little things that she really needed such as nighties, boudoir caps, writing paper, money for stamps and endless little things she hated to ask her sisters for. They aren't any too willing to help her, so it would be nice if some of her friends remembered her with some little gift just for her own personal use. I wrote Mrs. Lewis in Panama, and several of her friends in Everett and elsewhere, suggesting they remember her in some way on Easter, if only with a cheerful letter. It must be hard to be sick and wholly dependent on others when they do it unwillingly. George told me to send her a dollar in my last letter, and I did, and she wrote right back that she was "tickled pink" when she got it. She had a dime Donnie gave her and she had hung on to it for a month. She said she was going to buy a couple of oranges and an apple right away. I really am awfully sorry for her and wish I could do a lot more for her. Isn't it terrible to be poor when you'd like money to help other people?

She wrote that Rudy was in the Veterans Hospital in Indianapolis. He was operated on February 6th for a hernia. He expected to have to stay there three weeks, as that was the usual time for such an operation. He got two favorable replies to letters of application that I wrote for him before Christmas. Marion said he was awfully pleased and excited and had answered the one from Boothbay Harbor. She didn't think he was in any condition to "hitch hike," as she called it, but he said he was going just as soon as he got out of the hospital.

I do hope he can get the job and get there and perhaps he may be able to get his family together again. I think they both would be far better off if they could be together. Rudy is much like a ship without a rudder and will continue to drift if he doesn't have Marion to steer him.

I haven't made my bed this morning and I guess I'd better stop writing and finish my work.

George has been trapping this winter but has made only enough to pay for his licenses so far. The snow is so deep the smaller animals aren't running and the snow covers the traps and then they freeze. The season on beaver and muskrat opened yesterday and George is hoping for a little better luck. I hope so, as he surely works hard enough.

Emerson got the Valentine from Faye. I guess he'll write her some day soon. It is hard to get boys to write letters. Have you had a nice birthday? Give my love to the girls. Is your knee all right now?

Lovingly, Nell

P.S. Did I write you that Maude got her divorce in September and Winfield was married again almost immediately? She is still with her sister in Los Angeles. Cousin Lizzie sent us a big roll of the Magazine Sections out of the Sunday paper. Each contains a complete novel so we have had a grand time reading. That is all we have to do evenings, as we never can go anywhere. I pass our reading matter on and Mrs. Estes lends us their papers.

Ness Lake, B.C.
May 15, 1933

Dear Aunt Marie,

     The rain seems to have called a halt on my gardening so I'm seizing the opportunity to write a few of the many letters I owe. I haven't thanked you yet for George's birthday gift. We all enjoyed the book and I read it aloud. How do you think it ended? Did Richard Hardy die? George and Mrs. Estes think he did but I don't think so. The dollar we used to buy a pair of overalls. I was pleased with my bath towels, as I needed them. This spring I "turned" four bath towels, as the edges seemed good but the middles were awfully thin. I've done sheets that way before but never towels but it seemed the only way to get a bit more wear out of them so you see new ones were very acceptable. The hankie is very pretty and we all had a taste of the candy.

     George has been trapping all winter but has got very little, as the snow has been so deep that the traps were buried half the time. The animals stayed denned up, as it was so hard for them to get around. He finishes up today, as the season closes. The ice didn't go out of the lake until a week ago, so he hasn't had much chance at the muskrats, as he couldn't get out in the boat. He got an animal in a muskrat trap on Saturday that he thought was a mink, but it didn't look like the mink he got last winter to me, so I got out a trapping book he had and I think it looks like a fisher. I hope it is, as they are worth a lot more than a mink. Fur is so cheap there isn't much in trapping so one good fur would help out a whole lot.

     I have been trying to get the garden in so George could trap to the 15th, but it is quite a job. George plowed it last fall but it had to be harrowed. We have a hand cultivator so I went over it with that and then used the rake. As soon as I got a good-sized piece done, I planted it. I have put in lots of flowers this summer. I had lots last year but I wanted some Old Fashioned Pinks, some Asters, African Daisies, Oriental Poppies, Dianthus and a few others I didn't have. There was a corner of the yard that didn't seem in use and it has a fine view of the lake and is always cool and breezy. I thought it would make a fine out door "sitting room" so I planted Delphinium, Bachelor Buttons, Poppies, and yellow Daisies on three sides of it. I think I can make a couch hammock for one end and if we have a table there will be lots of times we can eat out of doors, as it is close to the kitchen door, so will be handy.

I have a hen with twelve lively chicks. I can't seem to get any more to set. I guess I'll have to go to the neighbors and see if I can get a setting hen or two.

I have been planning for some time to go to Prince George to the dentist. It is quite a trip, as it is twenty-one miles. We have no horse or car so George walks when he goes, but forty-two miles is quite a hike. I can walk eleven miles to Miworth and go in on the train but the train goes at 5 a.m. one day and comes back at 11 p.m. the next day. It will be four years next November since we came here. I guess you don't wonder why I don't go more often. I made up the goods you sent me for Christmas for a good dress and fixed my over coat. I ripped it up and washed it, cut over the sleeves and collar and made a belt and bound the buttonholes and it really looks quite modern, I sent away for shoes. That is the only thing I have trouble getting by mail. I wish Flora lived nearer so I could collect some of her discarded shoes (perhaps she doesn't discard them as she used to). Her shoes used to fit me. I sent back three pairs that I couldn't wear.

It takes ten days or so to send and another ten days or more to get the order back, so I decided I better keep the fourth pair. I can wear them but they are cut high on the sides, and the right one hits my anklebone when I walk, so I don't know how I'll ever get to town if I have to walk. I guess I'll have to carry my shoes and put them on when I get to town, as they used to when they went to church in older days.

Alice McCausland and a Miss Fay who had the room next to mine sent me a year's subscription to "The Woman's Home Companion" for an Easter Gift. I was much pleased to be remembered thus.

I haven't heard from Marion for some time. I made her a pretty pink and white muslin dress for Easter. I had to make it all by hand, as the snow was so deep I couldn't get anywhere to stitch it. I made four dresses and a windbreaker for Emerson by hand this spring. I hope Marion gets better. It is a shame Rudy doesn't settle down to something and support his family. I wrote him as soon as Marion wrote me he was sick but never heard from him. She thought he was going to get a job when he got out of the hospital. Did you ever hear if he got work? It is too bad he isn't a Canadian. I rather hated to leave the good old U.S.A., but I don't know of a country that does more for her people than Canada. They have an old age pension and when one has been in Canada twenty-five years and reaches sixty-five, if they need it, the Government gives them twenty dollars a month. That gives a man and his wife $40.00 a month to live on and they can stay in their own home. If they have property they are supposed to leave it to the Government and when it is sold and the Government takes out what it has spent, the remainder goes to the heirs. If a man has no property the Government never collects a cent. They also have a pension for widows and deserted wives. They get thirty-five dollars a month for themselves and seven a month for each child until the child reaches sixteen.

There is a young woman here whose husband left her with a small child. She has her pension each month and has bought five acres and put up a log house and has a horse, cow, and some chickens and puts in a good garden every summer. She was up one day last week to dinner.

You see if there was something like that, Marion could get herself a small place in the country and have plenty to take care of her and the children, as soon as she got stronger. I wish I could do something for them.

The rain is over for a while so I must go out and drop in a few more seeds.

George will be home tomorrow for good. Emerson has a great time camping. They have a cabin up the lake and go one morning and come back the next night. I'm glad I don't mind staying alone nights.

Many thanks for remembering us so generously. It always makes me wish I could do more for other folks when they are so good to me.

Give my love to the girls.

Lovingly, Nell

Ness Lake, B.C.
Sept. 4, 1933

Dear Aunt Ida,

I suppose you people have been celebrating Labor Day today. It has been quite an uneventful day here. School starts tomorrow and I started Emerson on his lessons this morning. He didn't do much on them in June, as they stopped sending them to him. They wrote they had over 800 lessons on hand to correct so he got through a month sooner than the children at school did. There is talk of discontinuing the Correspondence School to cut down expenses, - in fact they have dropped some of them, but Emerson still gets his lessons. There is to be an election in October and if the Liberals get in they may not feel so "poor" as the Conservatives. I hope they will continue the Correspondence School anyway, as it will be a long walk for Sonny if they don't.

He celebrated his birthday a week ago. I went over to Mrs. Taylor's to do some stitching the day before his birthday and Emerson went to Scott's for Herbert. The boys came home with me and went for a swim while I was getting supper. After supper I plucked two chickens, made a birthday cake and some candy, and then I fried the chickens while I was getting breakfast. George took the boat and went for a load of clay and kept on to the cabin he uses when he is trapping. I packed a lunch and the boys and I walked as far as Estes and George met us there with the boat and took us up to the cabin. We had dinner and then the boys spent most of the afternoon in the water while George and I mudded the cracks of the cabin. It will be a lot warmer next winter. The boys had a glorious time. We got back in time for supper and then I read aloud to them after supper. They were both glad to go to bed.

We had a fair at the school the 23rd of August. It is the first one ever held here. People turned out well and brought vegetables and embroidery and cooking. They didn't charge any entry fee so we had no money for prizes, however some of the merchants in town donated things and we got 100 lbs. of fertilizer for a prize. The ladies all brought lunch. While the judging was going on, they had a ball game and races for the youngsters, and then everyone had supper and after supper there was a minstrel show. It was very good but late when we got home.

I made me two outing flannel nighties, stitched three towels (I make them out of flour sacks) and made a shirt of denim for Emerson. I got denim pants to match nearly finished. I thought I did quite a bit for one day. I get things cut out and then go visiting and stitch.

I have two shirts cut out for George and I wanted to make him a pair of pants. I sent for a tweed pant length but am rather disappointed in it, as it is cotton stuff and he needs wool pants for winter. Clothes are quite a problem.

I got my teeth all fixed. I had to have one of my front teeth out but it doesn't look bad as it hardly shows when I talk. It will cost fifteen dollars to have one put in, so I guess I'll have to go without for a while.

George left right after breakfast to borrow a scythe from a fellow six miles from here and hasn't got home yet. Perhaps he couldn't get it and went elsewhere. It is bedtime so I'm going to retire.

We have a small black kitten. She certainly is lively and races all over the house.

We have had a very cool summer, - only about two weeks of really hot weather. I suppose we will have to expect a frost soon. Last year the killing frost came the 15th of September.

Have you heard anything from Marion lately? Is Rudy still in Indianapolis?

We haven't had any mail for two weeks now, as no one has been to the Post Office. I guess I owe most everybody a letter. I seem to keep busy most of the time and don't find time to write many letters.

Sept. 22, 1933.

It is some time since I started this and tonight seems a good time to finish it. The package came some time ago. George said it looked as if we all had had a birthday. He was delighted with his pants. They just fit him and will be nice and warm, as they are such good wool material. Aren't they dad's wedding pants? It seems I remember seeing them years ago in a trunk in the attic. The coat fits me and I am a little undecided whether to keep it myself for a chores coat or make pants and a windbreaker out of it for Emerson. I'm still wearing the old dark coat of Connie's and it's just splitting all over so I really need it.

Emerson was pleased with his things and as soon as I can get him some pants made, he'll have everything he needs to dress up. He has put his belt and tie away for special occasions. People seldom wear neckties here, so one lasts quite a long time for the few special occasions they are used. I'll have him write to you and mother soon.

A fellow six miles from us came up last Sunday. He wanted George to go to his place to do his chores for him. He has been called on the jury and didn't know just how long he would be gone. He has been awfully good to us since we came here so George hated to refuse him, even if there was a lot to do at home. He got the potatoes in before he left. He had the wheat cut and stooked and then a neighbor's cow discovered it. The field is back off the road a half-mile but she hikes through the woods until she gets there. I chase her out and she comes right back again, so I spend my time walking between the wheat field and the road. Yesterday Mr. Cook went to Walkers to plow and as he had to pass our field I went over and asked him if he wouldn't haul the grain over when he went home. He brought over one good load and came in to supper and after supper I pitched it off and he stacked it. We went back for another load, but it was so dark when we got back that he left the load by the stack and went home. Emerson and I had it nearly unloaded when he got here this morning so he didn't have to wait long for his rack. Soon after we got it stacked it began to rain and has rained all day, so I'm glad we went back last night for the last load instead of waiting until he came home tonight as he suggested. I saw the man across from us driving his cow home tonight, but as there are only a few piles of scatterings Emerson and I raked up left, she won't get much and perhaps we can get those in before she eats all of them. I've had nice day mending. I hope it clears off, as I have beets and carrots to pull. I'll be glad when all the outside chores are done and I can settle down to getting the sewing done for winter.

Emerson has just finished taking a bath. I've got to wash tomorrow even if it is Saturday and thought I'd have him change his clothes tonight.

I rather look for George home to dinner Sunday. He can come up after he does the milking in the morning and get back in time to milk at night.

I had a letter from John Hamlin last week.

I guess I had better retire or I won't want to get up early tomorrow.

Many thanks for the things. The pants and coat were a big help. Emerson will write soon to thank you for his birthday things. I haven't heard from Aunt Marie for some time but rather think I owe her a letter. You might send this one on, as I shall be busy for some time until I get the rest of the garden things in and then I have pickles and sauerkraut to make. I know she likes to hear from me. I owe so many letters I'll have to take a day off soon just to write letters.

Love to all, Nell

Ness Lake, B.C.
Nov. 11, 1933

Dear Auntie Marie,

Your letter came a week ago. Thank you so much for the money, but I feel you shouldn't do so much for us. Sonny bought a box of 22 shells for his rifle and put the rest away for snowshoes. I told him I couldn't give him but a dollar for his Christmas present, so he said instead of buying anything for him, he'd like the money for snowshoes. He has saved the rest and I gave him some out of what you sent so he has enough. He is a queer youngster. Just as soon as he got enough for his snowshoes, he started saving for a new 22. He shoots every squirrel he sees and skins it and he has snares out for rabbits and hopes to earn $5.00 with rabbit and squirrel skins. I made out a small order for little things. I wanted to find a good use for the money but I think you are too generous, you have so many ways to use your money. I wish I were wealthy so I could do more for people. This has been a busy fall, - in fact, we were busy all summer.

They held a fair at the school in August. It was our first fair. People turned out well and brought a lot of garden stuff. We entered all of ours in the Household Collection and got 2nd prize, - a hundred lbs. of fertilizer, - so we are planning on a fine garden next year. George got a little more land cleared this summer. I got out and helped on some of the stumps and kept the fires burning. It takes so long to burn up so many trees, as they all have to be cut, piled and burned and then the stumps dug out and burned. It seemed as if we had fires every evening.

We've had lots of company this summer. In July there was a picnic here. It was to have been a surprise, but one of my neighbors sent me word, for which I was very thankful. There were about a hundred here. We spread the lunch out under the trees and I made tea in the wash boiler. We made a four-gallon crock full of lemonade for the youngsters. All the boats on the lake were here and the young fellas had a fine time in the water and on it. I had eleven here to supper that night.

People are great for visiting here. They come in the morning and stay all day. George has started trapping. He has got five coyotes so far. Last year the trapping was poor, as the snow was so deep. He didn't make hardly anything. He has a little cabin up the lake and often stays there over night. This week he was gone a couple of nights. I'm glad I'm not afraid to stay alone.

We killed the pig last Tuesday. I always go up to help Mrs. Estes on Wednesday. They have been awfully good neighbors to us and this last year she has been poorly and can't do her washing. They haven't any money to hire anyone and you couldn't hire anyone here if you had money, so I trot up every Wednesday and do her washing and wash her floors for her. I figure it doesn't hurt me any and they do a lot for us in other ways. Last week I got through early, so decided to come home before dinner, as I wanted to take care of the pig we butchered. I got part way home when Mrs. Byers overtook me with the team. She was bringing a man from Peace River over to look at land near us and they were coming here to dinner. It was lucky I came home or I should have missed them. George brought home a deer yesterday so I had that to can. We gave away half of it but I ground some up to go with the pork for sausage. I saved out some to fry, but we are having such warm weather I was afraid it would not keep, so fried most of it and put it in sealers. It keeps well that way. I've made hogs-head cheese today and have a big kettle of bones on cooking for soup. It is so handy to have meat canned. George wants to get another deer before they go to the river.

I take it from your letter Dot is back with Louisa. The last I heard she was at Sid's having her tonsils out and being vaccinated. It is nice she can go to school. I wish I might have had her, - she would have been so much company for Emerson. He is alone so much and needs the association of other children. He still does his lessons by mail, as it is too far to go to school. There is a play at the school (local talent) Friday night. I want to go but they always have a dance afterward and lunch at midnight and it is two or three a.m. before people go home. Six miles is too far to walk alone through the woods at that hour, so I'm going to ask Gladys Scott if I can go down with them and come back there and sleep until daylight. I know I can, as she wanted me to come over to a political meeting and a dance two weeks ago. George is so busy he hates to go and Sonny has got to an age where he likes to go to things.

Don't try to do a lot for us Christmas. We'll call the money you sent a Christmas gift. I really haven't many wants this year but 10 cent ones. I do want a couple of aluminium pans or sauce pans like you get at the Ten Cent Store, also a paring knife and a blank book with a stiff cover to paste in recipes and clippings I have saved. George needs a match safe he can carry in his pocket, a knife or suspenders, and Sonny I think would like a propelling pencil or a knife. Please don't try to do a lot for us for you have so many folks to remember. Give my love to the girls. I ought to write to them. I often think of you all and wish I could drop in and see you.

Lots of love, Nellie

Ness Lake, B.C.
Jan. 21, 1934

Dear Aunt Marie,

I guess it is about time I got busy and wrote my "thank you letters." This was a queer Christmas for we were "snowed in" and couldn't get our mail or groceries for nearly three weeks. I ordered a few extra things for Christmas, but the day Gail Estes went down with the team they were taking the ferry out and he couldn't get across the river. We had the longest cold spell we've had since we came here. I think 46 below was the coldest but it lasted nearly three weeks. The snow was waist deep and no roads broken so you could hardly blame anyone for not going to town (a twenty-two mile trip) in such weather. We got most of our bundles and our Christmas groceries the last of the week after Christmas so had our tree then.

Thank you ever so much for my nice kitchen things. The saucepans are such a nice size and I needed them so badly. I like the paring knives and am glad they had green handles for they match the kitchen stool George gave me. Emerson was pleased with his tie and pencil. George finds his match safe very handy. He put his suspenders right on. I like to get useful things. It is needless to say we all enjoyed the candy.

Santa was so good to us. It makes me feel I have a very nice family to remember me so generously every year when I can do so little in return.

We are having nice weather now after our cold spell but the snow is deep. It is impossible to get anywhere without skis or snowshoes. We gave Emerson snowshoes for Christmas. I put the money you sent for his birthday with it to get them.

They started a Ladies Aid here and meet every two weeks. They are making a quilt to be raffled off this spring and the money used towards a Community Hall. At present everything is held in the school and it is so far away we can't get to things. It was built before a lot of the settlers came in and they want the Community Hall more in the center of the district. I hope they will get it nearer this way so we can get to things once in awhile. We read every evening or rather I read aloud to the family.

Cousin Lizzie saves the magazine sections out of the Sunday papers and sends them to us. There are some quite interesting stories in them.

I am making a quilt out of old wool pieces. As soon as things get beyond wearing I cut out what is good and wash the pieces. I washed some gunnysacks to sew them to and have a partly worn blanket that I can use for the back.

A young chap and the girl he is engaged to are coming Saturday to supper and stay Saturday and Sunday nights, so I want to get it done, as I need it. George took bedding up to the cabin, as he is trapping and often stays there over night so it leaves me short of bedding here. I have lots of sewing to do but it is slow work by hand.

I have Emerson's lessons every morning and when George is out all day tending traps I plan on a hearty meal at night so don't seem to get much time to do more than the mending. It is bedtime. Emerson has gone to bed and is reading "Little Men." He likes to read awhile after he goes to bed. I have bread to mix tonight. I'm a long way from a bakery so I have to do all my cooking, as I can't drop into a store and buy such things.

I suppose you went to Pinga's for Christmas. My! How I'd like to drop in and see you all. I shall want to hear all about your Christmas and what Santa gave you. Give my love to the girls and keep a big lot for yourself. Tell Pinga I'll try to write her this week too.

Lovingly, Nell

Ness Lake, B.C.
Jan. 24, 1934

My Dear Louisa,

I seem to be dreadfully slow getting at my "thank you letters" this year. We had a very nice Christmas even if it was a bit late this year. It made it all the nicer to have it last so long. My only regret was that we couldn't send any mail for nearly three weeks because of cold and storms. With the thermometer at 46 below and snow waist deep and no roads broken, you could hardly blame anyone for not making a twenty-two mile trip for mail and groceries. I was just about out of everything but there was no way of getting anything from the store, so we managed quite a nice Christmas dinner without the "fixings."

I was awfully sorry not to send Bill anything in the package. I planned to send him a calendar with a view of the lake on it but sent it to a place in Wisconsin for them. As we didn't get any mail for nearly a week after Christmas I didn't hear they were held up at the Custom's Office in Prince George until then, so I have just got them and now they aren't at all what I expected. That is the trouble with shopping by mail. It isn't much, but Bill will know we haven't forgotten him.

Santa was very good to us this year. We had so many useful things and I always like to get things of that sort, as we have so little use for "pretty things" here. The gloves you sent are just fine. I've worn them several times. I like the writing folio and writing paper is always handy. I guess I'll use it before I get the stack of letters ahead of me answered. I heard from so many people this year, even a chap who taught at Lorenzo ten years ago is now teaching in Los Angeles. I had no idea where he was.

Emerson goes to bed and reads his books. He had read Tom Sawyer or rather I had read it to him about two years ago. He was reading Huckleberry Finn at Christmas so read Tom Sawyer over again and I guess he enjoyed it more than when I read it to him. The girl you invited out to supper when I was with you sent him

"Little Men" and he has just gone to bed with his book and an apple. I needed aprons badly so was glad of the cloth. It is pretty good and I want to get it made up right away but have been trying to get a wool quilt pieced.

A young chap (Chris) who lives about three miles from us is coming up on Saturday with the girl he is engaged to. They plan to be here Saturday and Sunday and Monday Chris is going up the lake with George. He shot a deer before Christmas and brought half of it home, the rest he cached in a tree. George promised Chris one of the front quarters so they plan to go after it Monday and bring it home. I'm out of meat again, only a bit of ham left, so a quarter of deer will be acceptable.

I must get my quilt finished, as I need it before they come. I have two cots in Emerson's room and a couch in the living room. George took a supply of bedding to the cabin at the other end of the lake, as he often stays there over night when he is trapping, so it leaves me short of bedding here. I hoped to make a hooked rug for the fair next summer but I've had so much patching and mending to do and Santa brought me goods for three summer dresses, so I want to get them made and it takes time to do them by hand. I made four dresses last winter all by hand. I want to get all the clothes fixed up for the family before spring comes, as there is so much outside work to be done then. George traps till the fifteenth of May so that leaves the garden for me to get in. We have about an acre plowed around the house now so it is quite a task. I got everything in last year but the potatoes and we did that after George got through with trapping.

Sonny and I went to a play at the school one night. We went to Scott's to supper and rode down with them, and as there was a dance afterwards, it was 2 a.m. when we got back to Scott's. We stayed all night and came home in the morning. Another night we went to a wedding shower and dance with the Scott's. It was 5 a.m. when we got back. Gladys wanted me to stay and go to bed but George was at the cabin. I thought all the fires would be out and it would be cold and my biddies hungry, so after we had some coffee and got warm, Sonny and I walked home. It was still moonlight so we could see the path through the woods. We planned to go to the Christmas Concert but it was so cold and stormy we gave it up. They are talking of building a Community Hall. A lot of the country has been settled since the school was built so it is a long way from the center of the district. They want the hall as near the center of the district as possible. It will be a lot nicer for us, as we can go to things occasionally.

George was pleased with the gloves and will find them useful. The socks are a nice weight and something he needed. We all enjoyed the candy.

You spoke of sending a wool dress later. I'd love to have it but I hate to have you do so much for us. I know you have lots of expenses, especially with Dot to care for besides your own family, so if you send me a package I'll gladly return the amount of postage on it. If Flora happens to have a pair of discarded shoes I wish you'd tuck them in. I have such a time buying shoes by mail. The last time I sent back three pairs. It cost me nearly a dollar on postage and took nearly two months and I vowed I'd keep the next ones. They are miserable things, - most uncomfortable. I have to wear a felt insole and an extra pair of socks to fill them up and then they hurt for all they are big. Flora's shoes used to fit me and I don't care even if they are worn, as George can fix them, but I get so discouraged trying to get shoes to fit. They just aren't the right shape for my feet. I can also use discarded underwear, if any of your men folk happen to have any. I think it will come better rolled up in as tight a bundle as possible and cost less than if packed in a box. I'll be glad to pay the postage.

I'm enclosing a few pictures of the place. I'll be glad to hear all about your Christmas. I know you had a fine time. How I'd like to drop in and spend a Christmas with you!

I know your family keeps you busy, but I'd love to hear from you.

Many, many thanks for our nice Christmas box.

Lots of love to you all, Nell

Ness Lake, B.C.
Feb. 18, 1934

Dear Aunt Marie,

Today is your birthday and I want to wish you a very happy one and many of them. I meant to write last week and send you a small remembrance, but the calendar I sent for didn't arrive until today. We get the mail only once a week and frequently not that often, so the package from Eaton's did not arrive as soon as I hoped. I wish it were more for I'd love to do a lot more for my relatives than I can do, as they all are so good to me.

We are having lovely weather and have had a mild winter with the exception of three cold and stormy weeks just at Christmas time. I guess our winter has been much warmer than yours even if we are quite a bit farther north. George has worked a lot bare handed. He has been trapping and now is cutting ties. The Institute got 10,000 railway ties to cut. That gives them a Manufacture's License and if they have that, they can then buy groceries at wholesale. The whole community plans to club together and get groceries by wholesale, just as soon as they can get the Community Hall built. It will have a basement with a storeroom for groceries, also a kitchen and supper room with the hall above.

Did I write you that they formed a Ladies Sewing Circle the first of the year and meet at the different houses? The first two meetings were four and a half miles away and the walking isn't very good, so I didn't feel like walking the nine miles down and back. The last two meetings have been nearer so I could go. They open with a hymn and have scripture reading and the Lord's Prayer. We have made a quilt and meet this coming week to quilt it. It is to be raffled off and the money used to buy dishes for the Community Hall. They hold a social evening once a month. The last one was a Valentine Party last night. George was out looking at traps so had supper at a bachelor friends near where the party was held and came over in the evening. Emerson and I walked one and a quarter miles to Scott's in the afternoon and stayed to supper and went down with them. We walked back to Scott's this morning and got there at 4 a.m. and retired and then came home after breakfast. People are very cordial here and invite you to spend the night often. A young lady came home from the Sewing Circle with me last week and her young man came to supper and they stayed over night and Sunday another neighbor and her boy about Emerson's age came just as I was getting dinner. I like company and people are very neighborly.

We plan to hook a rug at the Sewing Circle and raffle it off at the fair this summer. As it is to be made of discarded silk underwear and stockings, I'm afraid I can't donate much toward it, as I own just one pair of silk bloomers that I wear on state occasions and only have one pair of silk stockings. I'll have to work on it instead.

I must drop Emma a line tonight. I had a letter from her today. She wrote me her husband had heart trouble and had been poorly. The Doctor said he could not work for a year. Today she said he got pneumonia and it turned to something with a long name. She had a trained nurse 11 days and then they had to take him to the hospital and drew off three quarts of puss from his lungs. He got a little better and they put him in a ward, but he grew worse and had to go back in a private room with special nurse. She said he didn't know anyone and the Doctors said the poison had gone all through his system but it seemed to be draining well. I hope he gets over this.

I could write a lot more, but must drop her a line and have to get up early tomorrow, as George is going to town.

I hope you had a very nice birthday for it will be over when you get this. I thought of you even if I'm a bit late as usual. I'm wondering if Eunice Hamlin, Han's widow, wouldn't take Dorothy for a while. She is in Kentville, Nova Scotia. She wrote me at Christmas that she got very lonely and wished she had adopted a girl long ago. She said she might do it even yet.

I must stop but will try to write more soon.

Lovingly, Nell

October 30, 1934

Dear Aunt Marie,

Thank you very much for the belt and necktie.

I am wearing the belt now and saving the necktie until some occasion to wear it.

We had a party at school today in which we ducked for apples. There was a dish filled with beans at one end of the room and two pans at the other. The object was to see who could carry the most beans to a pan in a certain length of time.

Thanks again for the gifts.

Lovingly yours, Emerson Campbell

Dear Aunt Marie,

Emerson's letter seems to be short and sweet so I'll write a bit on the end of it. It has been a peaceful Sunday. Miss Sherk went to Prince George yesterday to a Teacher's Convention and as it was Halloween, Emerson went to spend the evening with one of the boys and stayed all night. It was noon today before he got home. I spent the day knitting, as we can't get batteries for the radio until we sell the fur and the minks won't be ready to pelt until later. I am knitting Emerson a pair of socks.

George shot a moose on Friday. I hope it will be cold enough to keep without canning it, as most of my jars are full at present. George got a neighbor to help him bring the animal in so he gave him half.

George is building a rabbit house. Bessie had ten little rabbits. They are awfully cute and she is expecting more any day now.

I had a letter from Cousin Lizzie today. One of her girls is married and has a baby and the other is nursing in N.Y. and her boy is in college. How these children grow up. Emerson is a couple of inches taller than I am. I'm going to make him a windbreaker out of an old coat of mine. He got lots of good out of the one you and Pinga sent him, - in fact he is still wearing it but it has holes in various places and as it is quite snappy in the mornings I guess I had better get busy and make one. It is time for me to feed the rabbits and then start a fire to get supper.

Wish I could drop in some day and see you all but I guess it will be some time before I get that far. Was glad Ida could get to Boston. She said she hadn't been well. How do you think she really is? I feel better than I did but get tired easily. The club meets with me on Armistice Day and they plan to come to dinner. I want to wash the curtains and windows this week, as they are some dirty! Please, excuse the paper, as this is all I had.

Lovingly, Nellie

Ness Lake, B.C.
Nov. 1, 1934

Dear Mother,

I'm sending you a very belated birthday package with best wishes for many happy birthdays. It isn't much, - just what I could make, as I can't get to town.

I hoped to get to Prince George before winter to see the dentist, but when George went in last week there was eight inches of snow on the ground, and the truck that goes every Saturday was so late it didn't get to town until afternoon. The time before that George went in, something happened to the lights so they had to come twenty-one miles in the dark. It is dark with woods on both sides of the road. The fellows had to get off and go ahead with torches made by soaking rags in gasoline and light the truck down some of the hills, so it was ten p.m. before George got home. As we have a mile and a half to go after we leave the truck and our nearest neighbor, - a bachelor, went in that day and got gloriously drunk, I was glad it was George walking home at 10 p.m. instead of me.

We had our first snowstorm the 19th of October and I was afraid it had come to stay, but we have had several rains so most of it is gone. I had my first sleigh ride last Saturday. The Home Makers Club met with Mrs. Rodman. Gale Estes took his mother in the cutter and called for Mrs. Walker and me. She came over and had lunch with me. We went over a bump and I went out headfirst into a snowdrift. It didn't hurt me any. Mrs. Byers came home with me for a couple of days so we sat down in the bottom, as we thought it was safer.

George has started trapping. He took food and bedding to the cabin and stayed two nights, as it takes some time to get his traps out. He came home tonight with a skunk, a weasel, a muskrat and also a rabbit. I'm saving the rabbit skins. Marjorie Roberts saved them last winter and sewed them on something and used them for the lining of a quilt. I think I'll make a quilt that way.

Our minks arrived Saturday. We got five, two males and three females. One of the males caught cold on the road and died of pneumonia. He was sick when we opened the crate. We brought him in the house but we couldn't save him. Of course the man we got them from may send us another, but if he doesn't it isn't a dead loss, as we will get about what we paid for him for his pelt. George gave me one for my very own. They are getting used to us and I hope I can get them tame enough to handle. I tried to rub one of them on the nose yesterday and she bit my finger. I hope we have success with them. George has worked so hard since we came here. It is slow making a start in a new country and there seems to be no local market for farm produce and freight rates are so high there is nothing left if one does sell. We have three and a half tons of potatoes and at present potatoes are 50 cents per 100 lbs. and it costs 25 cents per hundred to get them hauled to town and ten cents for a sack, so there isn't much left for the farmer.

Our cellar is full so we have lots to eat and lots of fuel and no rent to pay, so we can get along with little cash.

I'm afraid I can't do much for Christmas unless George can sell some furs before that, as it took every cent we could make to buy our minks. I felt we had to make a start in something, as I don't want George to work out all the time. I don't like staying alone so much and I'd like to have something that will bring us in something.

Aunt Ida wanted to know what we wanted for Christmas as she wanted to shop early. Clothes are our biggest need. I'd be glad of anything I could make over for George or Emerson. They both need warm clothing. I've mended George's underwear until it is just about all patches and it would be hard to find the original garment. Any discarded underwear that I could fix over or any old sweater or scarf that I could ravel out and knit into mittens would be most acceptable. My clothes are all fairly good. Tell Ida not to do much, as we can do so little in return.

Emerson went to school all of September and October and I am now starting him on the Correspondence Lessons. The teacher wrote me that she was very sorry to lose him, as she had found him a "delightful character" and a very conscientious student. She hoped we would have an early spring and I would send him again just as soon as possible.

It is bedtime and I have to get up early.

Hope the package reaches you safely and I'm sorry it was so late. George was away three weeks cutting ties and only got home last Saturday and then has been gone two nights this week so I haven't had many chances to get mail away.

Hope you had a nice birthday and we'd like to hear how you celebrated.

Lovingly, Nellie

Ness Lake, B.C.
Jan. 19, 1935

Dear Aunt Marie and Louisa,

Well, I guess it is about time that I started my thank you letters. We received the package you sent and were delighted with everything. The dress just fits me and is very pretty. I put it on last Sunday. I needed stockings so was more than pleased with those. George's socks were nice, also Sonny's. I do like to get useful things and socks and mittens are things my men folk always need. We got the radio going once more after being packed away for three years. We get some good programs even if it is a small one with earphones. George certainly enjoys it. We got the school finished. Everyone turned out and worked on it. The men give their time. We gave them a little supper and played games when it was finished and New Years evening they held a dance at the school and invited the Reid Lake and Sylvan Glade Districts. School opened the 8th of January. The teacher came from Victoria and she is staying with us. There was only one other family that could take her and she decided they were too far from the school. I moved our bed upstairs and put a bed couch and heater in our downstairs bedroom. It is very comfortable. I sent for some cheap paint and made curtains for the closet door and washstand, and covered a stool. It is old blue with yellow so it is clean and comfortable and I also made a braided rug with quite a bit of blue and yellow in it. I had to fix up the room so that is why I didn't get to writing letters sooner.

Santa was very good to us all. I don't see why my family keeps on remembering me when I do nothing in return. I had so many nice things. Cousin Lizzie sent me a most wonderful box with thread, buttons, tape, machine needles, other needles, bobbins, a bell for the machine, dress buckles and so many odds and ends one needs and it is hard to get here. She also sent me goods for a dress and a rubber rain cape. Mother sent me dress goods and a collar to go with it and Aunt Ida sent me a nightie for which I was most grateful, as I fell through mine before Christmas and was wearing a pair of George's pajamas. Ruth sent me a lovely bag. We had a quiet day at home. Fred and Grace sent us a box of good things from S.S. Pierce's. Usually they send nuts, candy, dates, etc. but this year the box had olives, sardines, sandwich spread, fruitcake, pickles, jelly and so many things that have been a wonderful help in putting up Miss Whyte's lunch for school. Emerson comes home at noon as the school is close but three of the children have to take their lunch so Miss Whyte stays. She is ever so nice and seems so appreciative of what I try to do for her.

Aunt Ida wrote the ground at Portland was bare. We have snow enough that the mailman had to go to Prince George with sleighs last Friday, although the snowplow has been out several times this winter. Emerson said he heard it again today but they turn a mile and a half from here and go south, so I'm glad of snowshoes.

One of the neighbors got a moose last week so we got a quarter of it. I roasted some for dinner today. It was very nice. Some moose are much nicer flavor than others.

We have had a lovely winter so far, - about the mildest since we came to B.C.

I expected the Reid Lake teacher up this weekend, as I wanted her to meet Miss Whyte but she has been sick and in the Prince George Hospital. She just got back in the middle of the week and didn't feel quite equal to walking four miles but hopes to come up next week. She often comes to see me and I like her ever so much.

My biddies are laying once more and it helps to have eggs to cook with.

I suppose you had a nice Christmas and Santa remembered you as generously as usual. I'd love to see Pinga's new house. I can't seem to picture just where it is, although we travelled quite a bit around Medford. I'm so glad she and Bill have a home of their own. I hope Flora may be very happy this time and that she is getting a good husband. Give her my love and best wishes and when you write, please send me her new name and address, as I'd like to write to her.

I must try to write some more letters tonight or I'm afraid my family will begin to think I didn't appreciate all the nice things they sent me this Christmas.

Many, many thanks for our Christmas presents. We all like everything. Do write me a letter soon.

Lots of love, Nellie

Ness Lake, B.C.

Ness Lake, B.C.
Feb. 7, 1935

Dear Aunt Marie,

I guess by the time this reaches you you'll be having a birthday. I hope it will be a very nice one and there will be a lot more of them and I wish I might drop in to help you celebrate.

I was glad to get your letter. Santa surely was good to you. I thought you had a lot of letters and cards, but a letter from Mrs. Lewis in Panama, that I just received, states she had 300 letters and cards this Christmas. I wonder how she ever will get that many answered.

George is still away cutting ties. I'll be so glad when he gets home for good. We had a few cold days, 40 below weather, just at Christmas and then it went to 28 and 30 above. Three weeks ago we had another cold snap for over a week. It took a lot of wood for the heater. Emerson and I went out every afternoon and sawed wood for a couple of hours. It was pretty chilly some days, but we kept at it. George got worried for fear I'd be out of wood so came walking home one day. I was certainly glad to see him. He stayed home three days and sawed wood, so left me quite a pile. It was while he was home that one of the minks died. I had been worrying about him for over two weeks, as I thought he was growing thin but he had a tremendous appetite and ate about twice as much as the others. George didn't think any animal that would eat as he did was sick but I didn't think it was natural for him to be so ravenous. We certainly were sorry to lose him, as that leaves us without a male and breeding season is pretty close. George is trying to get in touch with a man at Cluculz Lake who has mink. I don't know whether they are Quebec Mink or not.

The snow has been pretty deep and it has been hard to get anywhere. I went to the Sewing Circle on the 12th of January at Mrs. Chamberlain's. As there was a card party that evening most people wanted to get home early so we went to dinner. It was terrible walking. As I'm the only one from this way I had to wade through snow over my knees for over a mile. I should have worn snowshoes. A week ago Tuesday I wore them up to Estes, but it was hard going even with them. It thawed for several days last week and felt just like spring, so lots of the snow went and the walking isn't too bad just at present.

I have been making a quilt out of wool pieces. I washed some gunnysacks and ripped them up and used them to sew the wool patches to. I featherstitched all around the patches and then used an old blanket that was getting thin for the back. It makes a nice warm quilt. I think I have enough wool scraps to do another one. I have some sheep's wool that I'm picking at present. I wanted to card it but everyone who owns cards seem to be using them so I thought I'd start picking it by hand.

The moose have been very thick around here. One day I was coming from Estes and I met one on the road. Emerson came to meet me and he saw two standing in the road when he turned a corner. He stopped and began to whistle and they went off into the woods. There was one down by the spring a little over a week ago, and Emerson was quite disgusted because I wouldn't let him take the shotgun and try to shoot it. I did need meat but wanted George home to skin and cut it up. I thought it was too big a job to tackle in cold weather.

One of the neighbors brought me some moose ribs the other day, so I have all the meat I can use at present.

George met a fellow (Bob Rigler) twenty years ago on a threshing outfit and they took quite a liking to each other and went north together trapping and camped together all one winter somewhere in the north. In the spring they separated and never saw each other again until three years ago they happened to meet in Prince George. He lives there and has seven children. His wife died two years ago and he got a housekeeper with one boy so they have quite a family. He has taken a homestead near us and plans to come out soon to put up some buildings and the family will come this spring. Two of the boys were here three weeks last summer and they had a wonderful time.

I was so glad to get a letter from Flora. I didn't know her address before but will try to write to her before long.

Emerson is doing his lessons at home this winter, as the roads are drifted so he couldn't possibly walk the nine miles a day. As soon as the days get longer and the walking better, he plans to try going again.

Do you ever use Crisco? I see there is a Crisco contest advertised in the last "Woman's Home Companion." I'd like to enter but need a wrapper off a 3 lb. Crisco tin. I could get Crisco if I could get to Prince George, but have never seen it at our little country store. Most people have a pig to kill so have their own lard. If you have a label off a Crisco can, I'd love to have it but if you haven't it is all right, as I probably wouldn't win a prize anyway. I never did. I thought if I could get a wrapper before March 1st I'd send in a name for the pie.

I have a lot of sewing to do. Emerson needs blouses. I have material in the house but hate to do them by hand. I think I'll cut out lots of things and then go to Mrs. Chamberlain's early some morning and see how much stitching I can do. I think the goods Pinga sent me will make a very neat dress and I want to get that made. There is so little time for sewing when spring comes. The summers are so short that I like to work outside most of the time then.

I have some stockings to darn this evening so I guess I had better get at it, as I'm sleepy already.

Hope you will have a very happy birthday and many of them.

I'm looking for George to come home this weekend and I know he would send his best wishes too, if he were here.

Lots of love to all, Nell

Isle Pierre, B.C.
Feb. 8, 1933

Dear Aunt Marie & Aunt Louisa,

I am slow in thanking you for my
windbreaker. It is a very nice one and I like the
color. The school teacher liked it very much.
I recieved another just like it but blue from
Cousin Lizzie. We have lost another mink he died
of what we think was anemia. He died two weeks
ago. I caught a rabbit in my trap this morning
They say that the ling are biting I must get some
fish lines out.

Daddy is coming home tomorow. Mother is baking
beans for daddy when he gets home. I am doing
my lessons at home now. Last Saturday I went
to Harry Ralphs and played all day He came
home with me. It was dark when we got home He
played with me all the next day. I hope Aunt
Marie has a happy birth day.

youre lovingly
Emerson.

Ness Lake, B.C.
June 2, 1935

Dear Aunt Marie,

I guess you will think I'm a good one not to have written to you before this. It isn't because I haven't thought of you, for I have. George was pleased with the dollar you sent him and it bought our garden seeds. They are in and some of them up. I got enough spinach leaves to add to a raw carrot salad today and we had our third feed of asparagus. It takes quite awhile to get a bed started, but ours is progressing. It was nice of you to remember me so generously. The hankie is very pretty and the satchel is a nice Christmas idea. I think I'll try to make a few for friends I like to send a wee remembrance to. The dollar went for stockings. The hankie I sent you on your birthday looks rather small when you do so much for my family. I wish I could do more for everybody.

George trapped until the 15th of May, but it was a very late, cold spring and the ice did not go out of the lake until just a day or two before he stopped, so he could only trap along the north shore. He didn't get as many muskrats as last year.

I tried to get some of the garden in but it wasn't plowed so I took the grub hoe and went at it. I'd grub a little piece and then plant it and do the same the next day and so I got quite a bit planted. We got it ploughed as soon as George got home and he planted potatoes and turnips and I got the rest in. Everything is done but transplanting the tomatoes and celery and putting in a few pickling onions. If I plant them too early they get too big before I get ready to use them.

I have a sewing machine at last and I'm quite pleased. George took my hooked rugs to town last fall and the Furniture Man said he'd try to sell them for me. He had them all winter so I wrote to Mrs. Hunter, the wife of the Forest Ranger. She has lived in Prince George over twenty years and is about the only one in town I know. I thought she might know someone who would swap a machine for my rugs. As it wasn't as much as the Machine Man wanted, she finally made the machine dealer come down to what I could get for the rugs. I got the machine just the other day and expect to have a grand time stitching. I have so many old clothes to fix up. The machine is a New England Queen. It has rounding drawers and a drop top, - not a bad looking machine and does very good plain sewing. There are no attachments but I probably would not use them if I had them.

We are going to have two new settlers. George had a friend (Bob Rigler) that he worked with twenty-one years ago. They went north one winter and camped together all winter. They parted in the spring and never saw each other again until three years ago. He had been to the war and married a nurse and had a big family. His wife died two years ago and he has just married another nurse. He has taken land close to us and they are moving out on his homestead just as soon as he can get up a house to live in. George let him have one of the fields to put in garden stuff as of course he has no land cleared, and it takes a lot to feed eight children. The other man has four children all of school age so there is a good prospect of our getting a school this summer.

We have filled in the names of the children in the district and sent it to Victoria and the Inspector said he would be out soon to look things over. If there are ten children the Government has to put in a school. They furnish the lumber, doors, windows, and school furniture and pay the teacher. The men in the district have to cut the logs and put up the building. They give their work free. I'm hoping we can get a school by fall.

We had three families of little minks. The day after Countess' family arrived we had a late snowstorm, - May 5th. It snowed all day. Countess was out playing in the snow and having a grand time. We think she got her babies wet and they died and she ate them. Anyway they utterly vanished. The other two minks have young. We can hear them in the nests but we can't even peek until they are four weeks old. I hope nothing happens to these. If the mother mink gets frightened she will kill her young. I have been trying to get them tame. The male mink is a perfect gentleman. He never bites but the females snap when you put your hands in. I got so I could put my hand in Queenie's pen. She would grab my hand but did not bite down hard. I was showing George how tame I had her. He hadn't been near them for over a week and I think he was strange to her. It was the day before her family was born and she might have been cranky, - anyway she grabbed my hand and she didn't let go as usual. She just about chewed my thumb up. I had to take my other hand and grab her head to make her let go. George says he thinks they are treacherous like a weasel. I bet I can get the young ones tame even if George thinks the old ones are too old to tame.

It is time to go to bed. Five a.m. comes pretty soon. Like most of my letters, I started this some days ago and it didn't get finished.

Bob Rigler has been here about a week planting and left this morning for Prince George. He plans to bring out a tent and go onto his own place now that his crop is in. He wants to get started on his house.

I washed this morning and did quite a few extras. Martha Hamlin sent me a very pretty summer coat last fall. It is thin with no lining. The wrapper was torn to shreds and Mr. Estes brought the parcel up in the wagon that they had taken meat to town in and nearly everything was streaked with blood. I was afraid I couldn't get the spots out of the coat but I washed it and it all came out. It was a bit large and shrunk just enough to be a good fit. I've fixed over two summer dresses she sent since I got the machine.

This week she sent a package with the loveliest suit in it for George. She said Clyde simply couldn't wear it, as he'd grown too stout and she hoped it would fit George, as it was such a nice one. It looks just like new and couldn't fit George better if it had been made for him. There are two pairs of pants with it. She sent me two silk dresses she couldn't wear and lovely-embroidered voile she bought in

Honolulu. They were all too short for her now but are plenty long for me. It surely is nice to be little.

The School Inspector arrived this afternoon and asked George to show him around the country. He has to look the ground over and see the families in the new proposed district before they come to lay out the boundaries. They were gone all afternoon and appeared at suppertime and went out again this evening. Emerson said he told George he didn't intend to go back to town tonight, so I presume he intends to stay here so I made up the couch clean. We are rather crowded yet, as the lean-to roof leaked, so I moved my bed upstairs last fall and the kitchen furniture into the living room. George has to put a new roof on the lean-to and hopes to get it done this month. As soon as it is finished I want to kalsomine the whole house and it will be nice to have a bedroom and kitchen once more.

I had a letter last week from Margaret French. She is the girl Reta chummed with in High School and roomed with in college. She teaches at the University of Illinois. She and her mother plan to visit me this summer. They have a car and take a trip somewhere every summer. This year they are thinking of British Columbia, as they never have taken a trip west.

Mrs. Byers invited me to drive down to Isle Pierre on Saturday morning with her. I haven't been to the store for about a year now. I think I'll go if I can get my family up and my work done and walk to her place by 7 a.m. Many, many thanks for our birthday gift.

Love to all, Nell

Ness Lake, B.C.
Feb. 12, 1936

Dear Aunt Marie,

I should have gotten your package off last week, as we have only one mail a week and I'm afraid your birthday will be over before your apron arrives. We all wish you a very nice birthday and many of them.

The days seem to fly and I don't get much done.

School opened the 8th of Jan. and the teacher is very nice. They showed her the available boarding places and she decided to live with us.

We have had a lovely winter with very little cold until last week and my! Wasn't it cold then? It kept me busy keeping the three fires going. Archie Estes said for a few hours one day it was 50 below zero at his place. I walked to Byers one noon on snowshoes and it was 24 below zero when I started home and it was dropping then. The fire felt good after a three-mile jaunt. It has been cold today, probably quite a bit below zero, but not as bad as last week. I suppose we can't complain when the rest of the winter has been nice. The snow is awfully deep.

Emerson shot an owl on Sunday. He had been watching the minks for several days. When he went out to pick him up, he waded in snow way to his waist. He could hardly pull his legs out it was so deep.

I have made a gingham dress since Christmas and have another one cut out but can't seem to get at it. I have been picking wool and carding it for quilts. All of my bedding needs fixing up. I made some patchwork one day on the machine. I had lots of small pieces and no money to buy cloth so I thought a couple of patchwork tops would help out.

Emerson is busy tonight making valentines. The teacher plans to have a valentine party at school. Emerson is getting quite a "kick" out of school, as he has never been, so has missed all these things. I'm going to make a cake and frost it, also heart shaped cookies and stick them together with frosting. The teacher has made cute little red and white baskets for candy and plans to make candy tomorrow night. They will have hot cocoa so probably will have quite a nice time. There are only ten children. Miss Whyte has bought jack knives for the boys and balls for the two little girls instead of valentines but they have a valentine box.

I hope Flora will be very happy this time. Where is she living? How is Pinga? I know she keeps busy. I'd love to drop in and see you all and see Pinga's new house. I'm sure they will enjoy owning their home. It is getting late and I have to get up early these days. I'm usually up at 5:30 and it comes before I know it.

The minks are fine. I hope they all have big families this spring so we will have something coming in next winter. This has been our hardest year getting started with the minks but they are bought and paid for, and now I'll have the teacher's board money coming in and that should feed the whole family. We sent four mink skins to the Small Breeders Association and I am hoping they will bring enough to pay our grocery bill so we can start straight. We thought we'd hear last week, as they were sold on the 20th of January at the New York Auction but we didn't. Minks are high now so that helps out. Don't try to do much for us, as you have so many birthdays to remember. My chief need is stockings, cotton ones for everyday. I get them for 15 cents a pair. George wants a mouth organ. He had a 50 cent one but has blown it for several years and it is getting wheezy.

I shan't wake up in the morning if I don't go to bed. Tell Pinga I'd love to hear from her, all about her new house and I'd also like to know what Flora's husband does for a living and where they live. Hope you will have a very nice birthday. I'd love to see you but as that is out of the question you may be sure I'll think of you.

Lots of love, Nell.

Ness Lake, B.C.
May 21, 1936

Dear Aunt Marie,

 Your letter and parcel came yesterday. I was awfully pleased with the apron and the kit. Louisa sent us a kit like it several years ago and we had used up just about everything in it, so I'm sure it will prove very handy, as we have to doctor ourselves if anything goes wrong. The handkerchief is very pretty. I have some red and white voile that I want to make up and my hanky will match my dress.

 It was good to hear from you. I wrote you a long letter just before your birthday and sent a package with an apron I had made for you and a scarf and cold meat fork for Flora. The scarf wasn't strictly new as I had washed it once but we were snowed under and I couldn't get anywhere to get anything and had no money to send away for anything but thought she could use it in her new home. I haven't heard from either of you until yesterday so wonder if the package ever reached you.

 We had a terribly cold February, a whole month of weather from 20 to 40 below. I believe for two days it was 52 below zero. The snow was deep. The snowplow doesn't come out this far so the snow just piled up in the road, so one had to wear snowshoes to get anywhere. I had to walk three miles every other day for milk, so managed to get plenty of fresh air and exercise. We hope to get a cow this summer but raising feed is the problem here, as there is so much heavy timber to clear away and burn. We are planting oats for green feed this spring so will have enough to feed a cow or two, but it has been slow work grubbing out the stumps by hand to get a field.

 The minks are fine. I like them a lot and wish we had started raising them when we first came here. Of course there is the question of feed for them, but we have the lake and only have to pay $1.00 a year for a permit to fish with a net. George brought up 90 suckers this morning. He put part of them back in the lake, as it was more than we needed. We have seven females and three males. Five of the females have families already and another one will soon we are sure, but the seventh we are a bit doubtful about. She is so fat she waddles but has gone a long time over time and seems to be fat all over, so I guess it is just fat. Anyway, we will be pleased with six mink families. They have four or five as an average, although they may have anywhere from two to ten. Last year the two with families had five each. If we get twenty-five or thirty young this year it will keep us busy building new pens, as they have to be separated as they fight.

 It has been hard work making the start, but things look as if we'd soon have an income. It has been a big help to have a teacher's board money. Teachers around here pay $20.00 a month so that is all I asked her, but after the first month she insisted on paying $25.00. I told her I had agreed to take her for $20.00 and I didn't feel like taking more but she said that made no difference, - from then on she was paying $25.00. She is Scotch too. People don't usually insist on paying more board than they have to.

George has been trapping. The season closed on May 15th. He was anxious to get as many muskrats as possible, as they are a good price this spring. I wanted to get the garden in or at least some of it, so we would be getting green stuff. The garden wasn't plowed so I grubbed up a piece everyday with the grub hoe and planted it. I got a lot planted and things are coming fine. Last Friday I had a big washing. We are sixty-five feet above the lake and the hill is steep. It is a chore carrying water. George was gone so I helped Emerson get up the wash water and then I scrubbed the floors after washing. Saturday morning I walked three miles for milk for our breakfast and Miss Whyte's, and then to the school and Mrs. Chamberlain and I scrubbed the school floor. You see we have no janitor and the larger boys each have one day to build the fire and sweep after school. We women have to take turns scrubbing the floor.

The lake is very pretty now. I wish you could see the view from our west windows. I don't care anything about going in the lake but I do like to look at it.

I'm so glad Flora has a nice husband and I hope she will be very happy. Louisa must be very busy with so many things to attend to. I wish I could just drop in and see you all.

The women here have a club that meet around at the different homes every two weeks and I enjoy going and I am Secretary this year. We usually sing O Canada or The Maple Leaf and one or two hymns and have the Lord's Prayer. After the business is over some member has charge of the meeting and we have a program of some sort. At one meeting we had a guessing contest. Mrs. Nelson had a lot of tiny sacks with brown sugar, coffee, tea, cocoa, cinnamon, allspice, ginger, yeast, etc. in them. Each one was numbered and we were given paper and had to write down what was in each sack by the smell. It was fun and the winner got two boxes of spices for a prize. We had a musical program one week and are meeting on gardening. The last one was on handicraft and Mrs. Scott took up hooked rugs but it was held about seven miles from here. I could get a ride by walking four and a half miles, but there was no team going from here and nine miles is quite a walk when you have supper and a lot of other things to see to when you get back. We had little minks and the mother will sometimes kill the young if she gets badly frightened. I thought I'd better stay at home and tend to things, as George was away trapping. I hope I can go to the next meeting.

I must write to Mother and Ida tonight, as I want to mail my letters in the morning. They won't go out for a week if I don't.

I'm enclosing a letter from Reta that I thought you and the girls might like to read. You might send it on to Ida when you are done with it, as she may not have written home. Give my love to the girls and keep a big lot for yourself.

Lovingly, Nell

Ness Lake, B.C.
Oct. 17, 1936

Dear Aunt Marie,

I'm rather slow in thanking you for remembering Emerson's birthday. I made him some candy and a birthday cake and that is all he had until your gift arrived. He was much pleased with the belt and is wearing it everyday. People here only wear neckties on dress up occasions, so there has been no opportunity for him to wear his ties and I doubt if he'll "dress up" before the Christmas Concert. I was going to have him write but have been out of writing paper and just ran across a few blank pages in the back of an old notebook. I'm writing small to make it go as far as possible.

We have had a wet summer and fall. It rains all the time although today happens to be nice. Emerson took his lunch to school, also the shovel, as some of the boys planned to bank up the school at recess and noontime. They take turns building the fire and carry water. Tuesday is Emerson's day to be janitor so he has to stay after school to sweep. The government pays the teacher but the people have to put up the building and tend to the chores free, as there is no money for such. We have a new teacher this year. Miss Whyte came back on a Friday and school opened the following Tuesday. She taught one day and after school the Inspector called and wanted her to take another school the other side of Prince George. She hated to leave but felt it was for her own advantage to do so. He brought the new teacher the next morning in time for breakfast.

I've had rather a hectic summer, - seemed to have one thing the matter right after another. I was sick most of July but kept going as George was away haying, so I had all the chores to do. We bought a cow and the man who owned her wanted us to take her before she freshened. I thought George would be at home but he was away and one night another neighbor brought the cow and her calf after eight. She was a heifer and had never been milked and of course everything was strange to her. Between butting and kicking I didn't get more than half of the milk. It was dark and Emerson said, "If you get hurt, mother, you're simply asking for it." I got up early and strapped her hind feet together and then went at it properly. George took over the milking when he got home and I went to bed for a couple of days. The next month I was in bed nearly a week. I guess it is my age. Mrs. Rigler said I should keep off my feet as much as possible each month. I hadn't done any outside work this fall. Emerson had to miss several afternoons to help get in the potatoes. We have two and a half tons of them in the cellar so I guess we won't starve. There seems to be no market for them at present. George killed the calf this week. It is too warm yet for meat to keep so had to can part of it. I have it on this morning cooking in the sealers.

I'm trying to knit Emerson some stockings. I unravelled an old knit scarf and am using the yarn double. I have the worst time trying to keep my family in socks. I sat up late the other evening patching socks for Sonny. Some of them have two or three big patches, as the holes are just too big to darn. I have lots of clothes that need a little fixing. I don't seem to wear out things, - they just get out of style. I want to get at them but Emerson and George keep me busy patching. I made Emerson a shirt out of sugar and oatmeal sacks and dyed it dark blue. It looked large but he is bigger than I am, - was fourteen his last birthday. His feet and hands aren't so large as he only wears a five shoe, I guess he could wear a four and a half but he seems to be growing tall and broadening out. I've got to patch the front of George's pant legs so better get busy. I will try to write a larger letter when I get some paper.

Give my love to the girls. I'd love to see you all. Had a letter from Emma last week.

Lots of love, Nell

Ness Lake, B.C.
Jan. 6, 1937

Dear Aunt Marie, Flora, and Louisa,

This is a family letter but I want to write to you all, so as you often see each other I know you can pass it on.

We had a very nice Christmas and we all want to thank you folks for helping to make it such a nice one. You always send us such nice things and such useful ones. I find my little sweater so nice to wear about the house. It is nice in the evening when I listen to the radio. I needed the nightgowns very much. I don't like summer ones in the winter and that was all I owned, so I started wearing them right away. George needed socks very much. You should have seen the ones I had been mending. He wears heavy socks in the winter but often wears a thin pair underneath, as some of the wool is so itchy. He was pleased with the shirt and is wearing it. I'm afraid I'll have to send Emerson's shirt back, as it is too small for him. He is quite a big boy now and wears a 14 and a half. I wonder if Louisa could exchange it. I hate to bother her but it is too small for him. He is such a big boy now. How these children grow up.

The teacher we have this year lives on Vancouver Island. It is a long trip but she is young and had never been away from home on Christmas, so went for her holidays. The teacher we had last year is teaching five miles the other side of Prince George, so spent the vacation with us. We had a wee tree. I opened the packages the day before Christmas but we each saved something to put under our tree. With what I made for the family we had four or five presents apiece. I wrote verses for all of them. Miss Whyte dressed up as Santa and passed out the presents. Afterwards we had a sing. I took the week off too. I have to get up early all the year, so as Miss Whyte wanted to sleep in the morning, we decided we all would. We had breakfast about 9:30 and dinner between 3 and 4 and then I got something to eat before we went to bed, - usually something I could get on the heater. We read a lot and just enjoyed life. It really was a nice vacation for me. The Reid Lake teacher came up and spent one night with us. I was glad to have her come.

I had a lovely pair of embroidered pillowcases from Winfield and his new wife. He is now a Major and is stationed in Texas. Maude lives with her sister who is a widow, in Los Angeles. They go in for lots of Club work and Civic work. I had a long letter from Maude. I believe Winfield pays her $150.00 month alimony.

I suppose you spent the day at Pinga's and had a tree and all the fixings and Santa was as good to you all as usual.

I'm trying to get rested up this winter as much as possible. My sick spells last summer seemed to take a lot out of me and we both have worked so hard without any vacation, summer or winter that I was tired out. I am feeling better and some days have quite a bit of pep. I want to get rested up this winter so that I can do a lot when spring comes.

I had a letter from Marion. She said she thought she was back to 75% of her old efficiency. She hadn't been able to work, as she couldn't let Don run wild as he did when she worked, so she said she scrimped along as best she could. She certainly has had a hard time of it.

I went to Prince George one Saturday and got a tooth pulled and the next week one on the other side started aching. I have a toothache nearly everyday or sometimes in the night and it is most painful to eat, as it aches if anything hot or cold hits it. I'd like to go to town but dread the trip. The mailman goes in every Saturday, but carries the Chief Lake mail as well as the Reid Lake mail, so he has to go to Chief Lake before he comes home so it makes a trip of seventy-five miles. He told George he couldn't take the truck this week because the roads are drifted and he will go with sleighs. That is a long ride when it is twenty or more below zero. I think I'd rather have a toothache. I had lots of Christmas cards and letters this year. It looks as if I'd be busy sometime answering them all.

I'm trying to fix up some of my clothes. I haven't been anywhere, so sometimes it seems rather foolish to spend time making over things when I stay at home for weeks at a time. I ripped up the red dress Louisa sent me two years ago and cut it over. I have it nearly done but want to send for a bit of velvet for the collar and buttons down the front. I have a rug that I started nearly a year ago to finish. I hope to get some of these things done.

It is only 7:30 but I did big washing today and scrubbed my floors, so I am taking a magazine and retiring. Mabel Windell sent me "The Readers Digest" for another year. This is the third year she has sent it. I do enjoy it a lot. Do you ever see it? It has such good articles in it.

This isn't a very interesting letter I know.

We all thank you all for remembering us so generously. I shall want to hear all about your Christmas. I'll try to get Emerson's shirt off to Louisa by this same mail. Am sorry to trouble her with it but he takes 14 and a half now. Do write me one of your nice long letters.

Love to all, Nellie.

Ness Lake, B.C.
Feb. 14, 1937

Dear Aunt Marie,

I'm afraid I'm a bit late in wishing you a happy birthday and many of them. It has been hard getting letters mailed this winter. It is five and a half miles to the post office, which means a walk of eleven miles, and the walking hasn't been very good. The mailman carries the Chief Lake mail this year so it makes a round trip of seventy -five miles for him. It wasn't so bad as long as he could use the truck, but since the roads are drifted and he goes with horses, one never knows when he will return. Sometimes he leaves Friday morning and it is one or two a.m. Sunday morning before he returns. Thorsness' came to dinner two weeks ago Sunday and tried to get our mail, as they live near the Post Office. It was ten a.m. when they were at the Post Office and he had not yet returned. The mail is supposed to come on Saturday but it is useless to go for it then, as he is seldom back and he won't give out the mail on Sunday. As Emerson goes to school all the week, it has been rather hard this winter to get our mail or get anything mailed.

I had a nice long letter from Louisa. She doesn't write often but when she does she surely makes up for lost time. Tell her I got her nice long letter some time last spring so her efforts were not wasted, as she feared. I saved it, as it described her house and the color scheme in each room. I hope some day to make her a hooked rug for her house, - that is - if we both live long enough. I have a rug started now, - began it last spring but I was so busy as well and miserable most of the time, that I didn't get a thing done on it. George spent so much time last summer hunting and fishing for the minks that he could not do the other work. This year he plans to buy more feed and spend more time on farm work, which has to be done. The mink ate a whole horse from the last of November to the last of January, and Saturday George and Chris Roberts butchered a big bull. We have half of it for the mink. Today a young chap brought a horse, which he wanted to sell for mink feed. We didn't intend to get any more now, but George bought him, as it is cold now and he will keep. If all goes well we should have between forty and fifty young minks this spring and they are ravenous when they are growing. We have fifteen old ones this winter.

They have had a new teacher at Reid Lake School since Christmas. He is a young chap, musical with lots of pep. There was a Valentine Party at the Reid Lake School last night. The Ladies Club put on a party every year, but he sent a note to the last meeting saying he would like to put on a program up to the lunchtime. I planned to go down, but George was at Robert's butchering and wouldn't get home until late so Miss Sherk and Emerson left about two. They went on skis. Mrs. Cook invited us to stay there over night, as six miles is too far to walk home at midnight and in the dark. I couldn't leave early and didn't feel like walking that far alone when George got home. Emerson stayed at Cook's all night and came home this morning. He said the entertainment was awfully funny. Miss Sherk has not come home yet and it is nearly time for me to get supper. Emerson thought she went home with the Byers, but was not sure.

We had a cold January, - in fact it started the last week in December and was from 10 below to 30 or more below all of the month. It has warmed up once more so is quite livable once more. I've minded the cold more than usual this winter, - perhaps because I go out so little I feel it more when I do. I went to the Club meeting two weeks ago. It was two miles from here so I wasn't too bad either. This week they meet at Mrs. Ralph's. It is only a little over a mile straight across but no road so it makes a walk of two and a half miles each way for me, as the snow is too deep to cut across the meadow.

I have quite a few things in the line of clothes that I'd like to fix up for spring, but I don't seem to accomplish much. It seems to take me all of my time to do the work without doing extras. I'm getting slow in my old age, I guess. It is time for me to get the fire started and think about supper for my family.

We begin to notice quite a difference in the length of the days now.

Tell Louisa I'll try to write to her before long.

Best wishes from us all for a very nice birthday and many more of them.

Lovingly, Nellie

P.S. The picture on the bookmark is the Bowl in California where the Easter Services are held. Sorry that I haven't more to send you but thought you might like this to use in your Bible.

Ness Lake, B.C.
March 25, 1937

Dear Aunt Marie,

It was so nice to get your letter. We always like to hear what you all are doing. I don't know how Aunt Ida happened to send me paper with Portland, Maine on it, but however, I'm very glad to have it as I'm out of paper. It is hard to keep supplied when I have so many folks to write to.

I hear you have had quite a mild winter. We haven't had as much snow as usual, but then we have had quite enough. There is no snowplow, it just piles up all winter and as there is so much heavy bush, it stays with us a long time. There are a few bare spots showing up but the garden is still white. I'm trying to hurry things up a bit, - I have tomatoes and celery started in the house and also a Hyacinth in bloom and another budded.

I have been terribly lazy this winter. Usually I get a quilt or rug or something made but this winter I've poked around and accomplished very little. Having the teacher here makes extra work, as I have to have a hearty meal at night. I like my dinner at noontime much better. She is a very nice girl but requires more waiting on than the one we had last year.

George is busy with the mink, as March is the breeding season. It takes a lot of time and patience, as they are such scrappy little animals and fight so much. We think we have them all bred but one of them fights terribly.

George has retired and wants me to come up to read aloud. His eyes have bothered him in the evening this last year. I guess our lights are poor and that makes it harder to read at night. I'll finish this later.

<u>Friday evening</u>.

We had a weekly paper that has the news, cooking and household articles and two continued stories in it each week. There is one now by Robert Chambers that is quite interesting.

I have been having quite a birthday time. Mrs. Byers, one of my neighbors, had one on the 16th of February, so I had her up to dinner and made her a birthday cake. Early in March a little girl who lives five miles from here walked up one Saturday. She told me it was her birthday and she was ten that day. I sent Emerson out sliding with her in the afternoon and made her a cake with pink candles on it. She was quite delighted. Last Tuesday was Miss Sherk's birthday so I told her to invite a girl friend for the weekend and Sunday we made ice cream. I had a young couple and two young chaps she likes up to dinner and then we had the ice cream and her birthday cake in the afternoon. She has a banjo, Emerson has a violin, and Jack had his guitar. Emerson can play a little, enough so you can tell what he is attempting but he plays just by ear and has had to pick it up all by himself. He does very well on the mouth organ.

Today is the beginning of the Easter vacation. The teacher has gone to Reid Lake. The Reid Lake teacher boards at Thorsness' and he was up to dinner today so she got a ride down. It is about five miles and the walking isn't any too good at present.

<u>Saturday night.</u>

We have just been listening to the National Barn dance. Do you ever get it? They have such good music. I usually have some mending to do and tonight it was Emerson's pants. I get sleepy unless I have something to do when I listen.

This seems to be written in pieces, as it is now Sunday afternoon.

I'm expecting the teacher back sometime soon, as she plans to go to Prince George for a few days and the mailman goes in tomorrow. He is our only means of travel.

There was a dance at Reid Lake School on Saturday night. They had one on Valentines and the teacher (he is new since Christmas) put on a very funny entertainment before the dance. We didn't go down, as we don't dance. Two weeks ago they tried to have a St. Patrick's entertainment and the men had just got their tie money and some of them had been to town and brought out booze and some from out of the district came drunk. From all accounts they spoiled the evening, as they made so much noise they couldn't hear the Irish jokes and the songs planned for the evening and when they started to dance one of the men ran into the stove and spilled all the coffee on the floor. I think it is quite disgusting. The people here don't even seem to care about anything but dance and card parties. I wish we had some sort of church service but we get a good service on the radio. It comes in from Los Angeles about 6:30 and there is a lot of good music on the program.

It is Ida's birthday on the twelfth and I must write to her, so I guess I had better stop as it is getting on toward suppertime.

I decided not to bother Louisa with the blouse, as she has so many things to do. I'll have to get Emerson some every day shirts soon and I think maybe I can swap the one Pinga sent, in town for a larger one, - anyway I'll see.

I'm going to try to write, as I try to keep in touch with all my relatives and I have so many letters to write.

I must feed the biddies and also my family. Love to see you all. Had a letter from Emma last week.

Lots of love, Nell

Ness Lake, B.C.
June 20, 1937

Dear Auntie Marie,

Isn't it disgraceful that I haven't written before this to thank you for the stockings you sent me? They were just what I needed and I was delighted with the darning cotton, as I had just one needleful left. It is little things like that that I appreciate, as it takes a week to send and a week for things to come back.

I am so glad it is spring or rather summer and I'm feeling quite energetic once more. Just at the moment my feet have been bothering me. I guess I've been on my feet too much. My day starts at 5:30 and stops about 9:30 or sometimes 10:00 at night.

George trapped this spring as usual but there weren't as many muskrats. We're hoping prices will be good. We send them to the Auction Sales in Montreal and won't get the money until about the middle of July.

We got the garden plowed early this year, so I got quite a bit planted before the trapping was over. I like to get it in so we get early vegetables. We have radishes, asparagus and spinach, also winter onions and I have quantities of rhubarb, which helps for dessert. My sand cherries will bear this year for the first time and the blackberry bushes have blossoms. I think I can pick gooseberries soon and it looks as if we have lots of strawberries. We have red and black currants, too, and tame raspberries as well as lots of wild raspberries all over the place. The only thing that troubles me is when I'll ever get time to pick and can it all this summer.

The little minks have arrived. We had ten families but one mink lost her whole litter. She went a long time over her time and I think they were born dead. From the nine minks we got the 48 young. They are beginning to run around now and have to be fed three times a day so it keeps me busy as I do the feeding. I have to cook porridge and grind up meat and fish for them so it takes quite a lot of time getting their food ready. We have about eight rabbits and it takes more time to feed them, as we have to keep them shut up. We want to get a field fenced and then just let them run, as they would be a lot less work and it is impossible to let them out or we'd have no garden. It means pulling grass and weeds for them to eat.

I started this over a week ago. School is nearly ended - next Wednesday is the last day. The teacher is giving a Box Social and dance at the school tomorrow night. A young girl was here to supper and she made me a box this evening. I told Miss Sherk I'd fill it but we'd find some young girl who hadn't a box and put her name in. Anyway it will give her one more box to sell. I do not think she will come back next year as she dislikes one of the parents immensely (in fact everyone does), so she has asked to be transferred to another district.

I owe everyone a letter but just don't get to write these days. My house is very dirty, the walls get so smoky with three wood fires and I was so miserable all last summer I didn't get it kalsomined. As soon as Miss Sherk leaves I'm going to get

Emerson to help me and get the walls done over. It will be cleaner anyway. The club meets with me in three weeks. I'm planning to have the District Agriculturist and his wife out to dinner some Sunday soon. They are going to bring the Librarian from Prince George with them. She is ever so pleasant. Do you remember Blanche Hight that lived in Somerville? I visited her one summer when I was in high school and she came out to see you one Sunday. She was a little plump girl full of fun. She married the same year I did and has been living in California. Her husband died just before Christmas. I got a card from her at Christmas but did not know he had died until she wrote me about a month ago.

It is nearly ten o'clock and I've been up since five-thirty. I have extra baking tomorrow. I made bread today, as Miss Sherk wanted two loaves for extra lunches and I promised to make her a cake, too, to take to school. I must put beans to soak and shut up the biddies, as coyotes sometimes go in the hen house if the door is left open and kill the chickens.

I'd like to see you all and have a chat but guess it won't be right away.

I'm enclosing some stamps for Faye. Give my love to Pinga and Flora. Perhaps they'd like to read this even if it isn't very interesting.

Write when you can.

Lovingly, Nellie

Reid Lake, B.C.

<u>MINUTES OF THE MEETING:</u>

Owing to the lapse of time and the fact that most of us have made one or more moves since the last meeting of the Homemakers Club, the minutes of that last meeting seem to have utterly disappeared. So in writing up these minutes for our present meeting, I have tried to think of the things that might have happened at that meeting and been set down in the lost record book.

It could have been that Taddy Roberts had saved enough wee bits of cloth to make herself another quilt of one inch blocks (or were they 1 1/2 inch squares), 5000 of them I believe, and then she invited us all to a quilting bee. Of course we appointed members early to put the quilt in the frames the day before, so all would be in readiness when we arrived. It really was fun but I doubt very much if on these days Tad saves such small bits for a quilt.

It might have been that we planned a baby shower for one of our members as we held one for Lena Nelson. How surprised Lena was when she opened the door! She simply sat down and said, "Well, you take over." Then we all had the surprise of our lives when Wilson informed Vernon that Lena had presented him with twins. As Vernon did not deny it, we talked of giving her another shower after she came home, but it was not necessary, as that was the time Connie was born. So, of course none of us Homemakers believed that Lena had twins when she actually went ahead and did it.

We might have discussed ways and means of earning enough money to buy a copper boiler or more cups and saucers for either the Reid Lake or Ness Lake schools. That usually led to carding wool and another quilting bee. Our rug making was not so successful, as so few could work on a hooked rug at one time and the quilting bees were really fun.

If our last meeting was in the summer, it was in all probability, spent in discussing the Fall Fair and I'm sure Mary McCabe was put in charge of building booths, as she was the year we attempted to convert the old Rodman place into a Community Hall. She was always so good at wielding a saw and hammer and I well remember one day that she kept us all busy doing carpenter work in preparation for the Fair that was held that year, in our newly acquired Community Hall.

We might have discussed making a baby quilt for some member and each taking a block home to embroider, had we not voted at a previous meeting to give a dollar to each new-comer instead. It had seemed such a wonderful idea at first, but after presenting Marjorie Roberts with four baby quilts we decided it would be much simpler to just give a dollar to each wee baby.

Possibly, someone brought a box of material from the Salvation Army and we spent the afternoon deciding who would make boys shirts or small girls dresses from the remnants or do a bit of knitting instead. In those days we always seemed to have ample time to do those things.

We could have decided to do something just for ourselves at that meeting. There was a time when we voted to make a crazy patchwork quilt. We donated flour sacks for the back and someone dyed them a lovely rose color. It chanced that Mrs. Ralph had some pink outing flannel with gay little nursery figures all over it. She felt it was most inappropriate for her, and the pink flour sacks would be more serviceable, so after due discussion we exchanged material and used the outing flannel for the back of the quilt. That quilting bee was held at Mrs. Ralph's down on the old Rodman place.

How do I remember so much about this particular quilt? Well, we each put in a quarter and our names were drawn from a box at a social at the Ness Lake School and I still have that quilt.

I well remember a meeting held one cold winter day at Agnes Scott's. Betty Rigler Clements had offered me a ride down. Unfortunately the small box sleigh had no pole so the horses galloped madly down each slight incline to keep the sleigh from hitting their heels. Betty hung onto the lines while I hung onto the baby and baby carriage in the back. It was a wild ride as we raced down the narrow bush trail missing the tree trunks by a fraction of an inch. It was at the top of Harper Hill that we finally ended up in the ditch, - horses, sleigh, baby buggy and all. Fortunately, Mrs. Scott and Thelma were not too far ahead of us so Mrs. Scott waited patiently in her old cutter while Thelma raced back up the hill and helped Betty get the horses and sleigh back on the road while I took charge of the babies. Somehow, we always managed to arrive at our meetings in one piece, even if we did have difficulties at times and have to borrow a bit of haywire, as we did that day to get home

Well, those days are gone and our minute book is gone too. I believe it was Mrs. Emma Roberts that first suggested that we meet together once in a while for a social afternoon, so we owe much to her. I believe those little get-to-gethers did much for all of us in those early days of homesteading in Reid Lake. I know you can all look back on many pleasant times we had together and I'm sure I'll always have fond memories of those homesteading days.

It is rather hard to write minutes for a meeting one can't remember but with such a wide range of activities as we had in our Homemakers Club any of the things I've mentioned could have happened at that meeting.

Knowing the honesty and integrity of all of us Homemakers I feel that we all can be rest assured that wherever the lost minutes are, - they are absolutely correct, - how could they be otherwise?

So, I would like to suggest that the members approve the minutes of our last meeting, - wherever they may chance to be and whoever wrote them.

Submitted by N.R. Campbell, Sec. Pro-Tem.

Ness Lake, B.C.
October 23, 1938.

Dear Aunt Marie, Louisa and all,

I owe every one of you a letter so this will be a family one.

First, I must thank Aunt Marie for remembering Emerson's birthday. He was delighted and took the money with the $2.00 that Aunt Ida sent and went to town. A truck runs in every Saturday, - you see the country is progressing. A school chum of his went along and they had a grand time seeing the sights and shopping. His principle purchase was a flashlight and also shells for his gun, - emery paper and such things, -not a cent for candy or ice cream. He is such a funny youngster. Louisa's letter came and I want to thank you both for the subscription. "My Country Gentlemen" runs until 1943, so I used the money and $2.00 that Emma sent to get the "Saturday Evening Post" for four years. We like it a lot and it comes every week so it keeps us in good reading. I think some of the stories are grand. We surely thank you for our Christmas present. I'm sure there is nothing that we would like better.

This has been a beautiful summer, hot and dry. The past few years have been wet and cold so we enjoyed this last summer. Usually we get a killing frost somewhere between the 1st and 15th of September, but it was way in October this year. The frost hit early in some places but not here. The berries simply dropped on the ground because I couldn't find time to pick them. I canned gooseberries, strawberries, rhubarb, raspberries, huckleberries, blueberries and some combinations of each with rhubarb and have made marrow preserves with lemon and ginger. I canned sand cherries and made cherry jam, currant jelly, high bush cranberry jelly, strawberry and rhubarb jam and plain rhubarb jam. I have pickles, greens, string beans and asparagus, -in fact my cellar shelves are full. The vegetables are in and we had a quarter of a moose given to us yesterday so I don't care now how early I get "snowed in".

I've trotted around from 5 a.m. until 9 p.m. or after every night and I tell George I'm going to be lazy this winter but he laughs at me.

We have such strenuous summers that we need to let up a bit in the winter.

The mink are lovely, - the best we have raised yet. It takes time to learn about them and the feed they get makes a lot of difference in their fur. They are a lot of work. We had sixty this summer and they kept me busy. They had to be fed three times a day and it takes some time to grind up their food, - 65% meat or fish, 30% mink meal and 5% fresh vegetables.

George worked on the road for five weeks and left before seven every morning, as he had four miles to walk to work and the same back at night. The rest of the time he spent pulling his fishnets, as we fed the mink fish nearly all summer. When we couldn't get enough in this lake he changed his nets to Saxon Lake and walked nine miles to the lake every morning, pulled his nets, cleaned the fish and packed between forty and fifty pounds on his back the nine miles home. It was a hard days work but the mink require a lot of food while they are growing. It looks as if there would be some profit in it this year.

It has been hard starting on nothing and then when we could pelt a few; the money has had to go for lumber, wire and more fishnets. I can see we have gone ahead a lot this last year so it is encouraging. I don't mind working when I can see I'm getting somewhere.

Did I mention Miss Room? I met her three years ago. She came to Prince George to open the Pentecostal Mission. She has been out to see me once or twice every summer. Last year she and her assistant, Miss Turnbull, brought two B.C. Shanty men ministers out one afternoon. This year she drove out one afternoon and brought a young minister from Oregon, with her. Miss Turnbull brought her piano accordion and one of the neighbors dropped in during the evening with her whole family, so we had a grand sing. Miss Room asked if we'd like a meeting in the school so we put up notices and they came out on Friday evening. There was a good crowd and she came out every Friday for 8 weeks. There were over thirty out to some of the meetings. I surely enjoyed them. Emerson took his guitar and helped with the music, which was very good.

Did I tell you Emerson made himself a guitar? He is quite musical. He can play the violin, guitar and a mouth organ. He plays by ear but seems able to play anything he hears. Mr. Shick, his teacher, says he has "an ear for music and an eye for color". He is very clever with his hands but doesn't care for school, although he gets good rank.

We are going to sell our cow to the butcher, as she jumps fences, kicks and won't ever come home so one has to hunt miles for her. She has held up her milk all summer so has about dried up and as we have to buy hay we don't feel like paying $45.00 to feed a dry cow this winter. I'm alone so much that I'd like a cow I could milk without putting cow kickers on every time I milked. We'll use canned milk this winter and try for a gentle creature in the spring.

I'm so glad Bill is improving and hope the adhesions have cleared up. I suppose such things take time. I really had not thought much about the power of prayer in healing, but Miss Room is a firm believer in prayer and claims she was cured of neuritis when the doctors couldn't do anything for her. George says he feels if God can create he surely can heal as well. I told Miss Room about Bill and asked her to pray for him and she said she would. I'll also add Bill to my prayers. I'm glad he is feeling so fine these days.

It is getting time to start my fire for supper and I hear the cowbell so I better put her in the barn before she wanders beyond reach.

I'm so glad Auntie Marie can be with you; it is nice for you both.

Do write me all your doings. I love the description of your home and the little diagrams. I love to picture folks in their surroundings and your descriptions help a lot.

Lots of Love, Nellie

Ness Lake, B.C.
Dec.22, 1938

Dear Reta,

I'm afraid I'm a bit late in wishing you a Merry Christmas but we all send wishes and a Happy New Year.

The time seems to fly and I don't get half of the things done that I want to do. We had such a busy summer. George trapped as usual until May 15th. I got in as much of the garden as I could and he and Emerson planted potatoes and the winter carrots and turnips after the trapping season was over.

The little mink began to arrive the 1st of May and by the 17th all of the families had arrived. They begin to eat solid food when they are four weeks old and then it keeps us busy. This year we had sixty mink. George spent a lot of time fishing. It takes time to pull the nets every day. We dried over 2000 fish in the spring and they were a big help during the summer. The little mink grow so fast that they have to have three meals a day and as all of their food has to be ground or cut fine, it takes time. George got work on the road for five weeks. Part of the time he was about four miles from home so had to walk morning and night but got dinner at the road camp. They finished the strip of road connecting the road past here with the Reid Lake road so now we have a truck service past our door twice each month. The mail man goes in every week so we can get to town if necessary by walking 1 1/2 miles to the Reid Lake corner and then riding part way to Chief Lake both going and coming as he has to pick up the mail there. It is a long cold ride in the winter on the back of a truck. About 65 miles round trip. It is nice to be able to get groceries delivered at our door.

We had church services every Friday evening for eight weeks in the school this summer.

Miss Room and Miss Turnbull have charge of the Pentecostal Mission in Prince George. They usually visit me once or twice during the summer. This summer they brought out a young minister from Oregon for a visit. They brought out some hymnbooks and Miss Turnbull brought her accordion. After supper we had a grand "sing". One of the neighbors came over with his whole family. Miss Room said she would be glad to hold a service if we thought people would be interested. There were over thirty at the first one and so they came for eight weeks. We had over thirty people out some evenings.

Emerson took his guitar and helped Miss Turnbull with the music. He made a guitar and can play both Spanish and Hawaiian. He can play some on a violin and does well on a mouth organ. He never has had any lessons, but seems to play just by ear. He suddenly decided that he didn't want to go to school any longer. He loves music and is quite keen on making things. He seems to have a mechanical mind, but got neither music nor any hard work at school. French and algebra did not appeal to him. I'm sorry that he didn't want to go longer. He wants to get a job so started out on his wheel (bicycle) for Vanderhoof - 63 miles from here. He got there in one day and that night landed a job on a truck freighting to Fort St. James, 43 miles beyond Vanderhoof. Work is slack this time of year. He was in the garage part of the time but there wasn't enough work to keep a helper so Emerson was gone only 3 weeks. The fellow in the garage told him to keep in touch with him and if he needed a helper in the spring he would send for him. He wants to go, as he liked the work.

The government has been holding Industrial Schools for Youth Training and there was one in Woodpecker 60 miles from here. Emerson went down for a couple of weeks and took Agriculture. He had a grand time and thought it was well worth going to.

We are getting a new teacher after Christmas. I hear it is to be a woman this time.

Do you ever use my book on short story writing? One of my neighbors is interested and is trying to write. She wanted to take it. She has a typewriter so I got her to type an article that I wrote on Mink. I haven't sent out anything for a long time but sent this article to "Women's Wear" in New York. It hasn't come back yet, - so I'm hoping! If you're not using the book will you send it back sometime?

I wanted to send you something for Christmas but the Mink Sale at Montreal isn't until January 4th, this year. It was a warm fall and the mink didn't prime up as early as some years so we couldn't pelt as early. We won't get the returns until about the 22nd of January. The muskrats we sent last June aren't sold yet. There was a Fur Worker's Strike on in New York so prices dropped and we asked them to hold the muskrats over until the September Sale. There was a misunderstanding and they weren't put on that Sale so they will be sold in this January sale. It has made us short of money for Christmas. I've sent a few things and will try to remember you later. Do you have to pay duty on things? I never have to pay duty on anything here and I've had lots of things sent me.

I'm enclosing a snap shot of my family. Hope you all have a nice Christmas. Give my love to Mother Allen.

Lovingly, Nellie

Ness Lake, B.C.
Jan. 10, 1939

My Dear Louisa and all the rest of the family,

I think it is time I thanked you for such a nice Christmas parcel. I thought my subscriptions that you sent this fall were my Christmas presents so it was a most pleasant surprise to be remembered a second time. I'm quite pleased with the couch cover and as I'm planning to paint my furniture soon, the colors will fit in nicely with the colors I had in mind.

The Lewis family have sold their house and business in Panama, - bought a trailer and are touring the States. They are due to visit me this spring. I'm really quite thrilled to have someone I've never seen come to visit me. They are friends of Marion's and I got in touch with her about five years ago when I was trying to locate Rudy. Since then we have written quite regularly - hence the visit.

I want to doll up my house a bit before they arrive but will wait until it is a bit more spring like.

The snow came early, although it has been extremely cold - only a few snappy days right at Christmas, - 42 below zero for two days after Christmas. It has warmed up again and the roof has been dripping today. The snow keeps coming and we have over 30 inches now on the level and it is deeper where it is drifted.

The teacher left at Christmas. The one hired did not come so school was a week late in opening - no doubt the youngsters were glad of a longer holiday.

I did not put in a bid for the teacher this year, as it means extra work and I find quite enough to keep me busy especially when spring comes and there is the garden and the baby mink. The new teacher is boarding two miles from school and the road isn't plowed. He came in yesterday on his way to school. He had never seen so much snow. I may have to take pity on him yet. He may stick it out if the walking doesn't get worse. I used snowshoes the last time I went to Mrs. Estes, but it is to wet today and Emerson said I'd find it too heavy for snowshoes.

Our days are short and I don't seem to get much done. I want to get all my clothes fixed up before spring. Yesterday I ripped up a silk dress to make over.

There is a Box Social at the school on the 21st. A young couple here have a baby that was injured at birth. There was a pressure on its head that paralyzed the muscles that control movement. The baby is going on three but can't even sit up yet. The Women's Institute in Prince George will be sending the child to Victoria for treatment. Our Club is having the Box Social to try to earn enough money to pay for the mother's fare so that she can take the baby down herself and see the Doctor there.

Aunt Ida wrote me she had been up to visit you folks. So glad she could get to see you. I wish I could drop in some time but I guess that is out of the question.

I suppose you all had a nice Christmas with lots of presents as usual.

Santa was very good to us all. I don't see why my friends do so much for me when I do so little.

My package to you was late in starting but we have only one mail a week. I started to the Post Office one morning, - it is 4 1/2 miles. I'd gone a little over a mile when I met a man coming up to see George. He wanted George to go in with him in buying mink pens and wire from someone selling out and as I happened to have the family purse with me I thought I'd better walk back with Chris, as George might want the money.

I got up at five and started Emerson to the Post Office right after breakfast, as the mailman leaves at eight. He got there but some of my packages were just marked "Christmas Gifts" and Agnes said she had to know what was in each package to make out the Declaration.

Emerson didn't know so they had to wait at the office a week and Emerson had to make another trip down to fix them up. I walk down once in a while but find it a long walk when roads are bad. Emerson doesn't seem to mind walking but 9 miles is plenty for me.

We sent our mink to the Auction Sale in Montreal but haven't got the returns yet. It would be nice if we could get our money before Christmas but we have to wait for the fur to grow and they aren't ready to pelt until December and the Sales come in January. George didn't sell the muskrats last June, as prices were low so we asked them to hold them until the September Sale. There was a misunderstanding and they weren't sold so they will be sold at this sale with the mink. Our money comes in bunches with a long time between the bunches.

The mink are doing fine. We keep a few more each year. We now have three mink houses up, - about 68 pens. If all goes well we should have 100 mink next summer. I was busy this last summer feeding 60 mink three times a day. It is lucky that we get a lull in the winter. George takes over the feeding until he starts the spring trapping and then I tend to the mink, as he is away so much.

I washed clothes this morning but it is slow work as I have to melt snow for water and it seems as if I spend half of my time running out for a pail of snow. It takes a lot of pails of snow to make a pail of water. It is a lot of work carrying in snow and then carrying out all the water you use to empty it. We hope someday to build a new house and I want a sink.

How is Flora? I got her Christmas card. Imma wrote that she is busy as usual. I had 38 cards and letters so I shall be busy for some time answering them.

I hope Bill is feeling fine once more. He surely looked fine in the picture - the same cheerful grin. You look the same only older. Fay is a big girl - does she remember me? I'm awfully pleased with the picture. I want to put it up but am waiting until I clean my house and then will put it in a frame, as they get so dirty if not covered from the fire in our stove.

Maude Hamlin writes me every Christmas. She lives in Los Angeles with her sister. You know Winfield married again and is now a Major and is stationed at Rantoul, Ill. I had a card from Alice McCausland and she is teaching in Everett.

What is the trouble with Morton & Bessie? I wrote Morton last Christmas but have never heard from him. I got an announcement of Ester Cole's wedding but do not know her address. If you know will you send it to me? I'd also like Florence Bremmer's address. I haven't that either. Fred Coles always sends me a box of lovely edibles from S.S. Pierce's in Boston - pickles, olives, jam, fancy crackers, dates, candy - sweet chocolate, sardines, sandwich spread and saltines (soda crackers). He has every year for six or seven years. I never have a letter or a card but just the box at Christmas.

It is bedtime. I'm not nearly as sleepy at night as I am in the morning but I have to get up early, as I have some reports to fill in. We have to fill in one every year about the mink - how many sold for breeding purposes, how many pelted - how many kept - how many died - what they died of - how much we got for the pelts, value of the mink houses, etc., etc., etc. George wants to get it away and I'm expecting company to dinner so I'll have to get up early.

I'm glad Aunt Marie can be with you. It is nice for you both.

I shall be looking for one of your nice newsy letters.

Lovingly, Nellie

Ness Lake, B.C.
Jan. 27, 1939

My Dear Reta,

I think it is about time that I thanked you for our Christmas gifts. Santa was so very good to us that it has taken me a long time to get all of my letters written.

We have lots of snow, - forty inches or more on a level and deeper where it is drifted. Our mink pens are just about buried.

It is 4 1/2 miles to the Post Office and that means a 9-mile walk. Emerson usually goes down on Wednesday morning, as the mailman leaves on Monday for Prince George. If the mailman can get through with his truck he gets back Monday night, but if he has to use the sleigh it is Tuesday night before he gets back, as it is an eighty-mile trip. As we don't know whether he went with the truck or not it is safer to go on Wednesday. I usually send my letters down then but they have to stay at the office until the following Monday, as we have only one mail a week.

I have been trying all of this week to get up to see Mrs. Estes. She can't get out so I like to go to see her, as she doesn't have any callers. One day this week a young married lady (married this last November) came to spend the day. Her husband was trying to break a road to his brother's place. He lives just north of us off of the main road so crosses our place to get to his farm. Ella Barrett came in the morning before I had my dishes done and spent the day. The next day an old man over seventy came and spent the day so I couldn't get out and today Emerson took both pair of snowshoes. He met two moose on the road and Mr. Slater wanted to get one so Emerson came in for the gun and two pairs of snowshoes. The moose circled around and came in back of the mink pens but the men missed them so came in to dinner and then went out again. Douglas and Margaret came over about four to say their father and Emerson had returned without even seeing the moose again and Emerson was staying there to supper. The fellow north of us came in to say he had just shot a moose and for George to come up in the morning for a piece of meat. We butchered our cow last fall but I really like moose meat better than I do beef. I want to can some now for summer.

I am expecting friends of Marion's and Rudy to visit me this spring. They have sold their home and business in Panama, bought a trailer and are touring the U.S.A. They visited Marion, and a card from Mrs. Lewis at Christmas said that they were starting west. They hope to get here in the spring.

Many thanks for our Christmas gifts. I like the table cover a lot. It is quite different from anything I ever owned. It just fits my table. This spring I want to kalsomine the whole house and paint all of the furniture again. I'm saving the table cover and couch cover from Louisa until I get my house "dolled up". I did use the table cover the other afternoon when the teacher came.

I'm sorry my box is so late but we have to wait for the mink to grow their winter coats and then the Auction Sales come in January. Our money comes in bunches and the bunches are far apart. I did do a little but didn't get your box or Marion's things away.

We are so far from stores that I have to do all of my shopping by mail.

I'm taking life easy this winter. There is so much snow that one can do little outside so George is fixing up his nets. He strings them up across the living room and I read aloud while he works on them. Today he was re-lacing his snowshoes. I have been fixing up some of my clothes. I made a silk dress this last week out of one Martha sent me and made a silk slip and a silk waist from another silk dress.

My bedding needs fixing up too. I don't seem to find time to do any sewing in the summer.

I had a letter from Maude and also Johnnie Hamlin and Eunice. Clyde and Martha are in Middleton, Pa., - they were transferred late in the fall. Lizzie has given up working in the store but went back for the Christmas trade. She sent Emerson the "Popular Mechanics" magazine for Christmas. It is a shame he couldn't go to some sort of a trade school. His head is full of "inventions". He wants to go back to Fort St. James next summer to work in the garage. The fellow he worked with wrote him last week. The garage is closed now, as there isn't any work in the winter.

Do you remember Blanche Hight? She lives in Los Angeles and writes me quite often. Her husband died a couple of years ago. I don't know just what is wrong with Blanche but she has to have a woman with her all of the time as she wrote me, "It was so hard for her to get around". That is all she ever said. Esther Cole was married shortly before Christmas. Louisa wrote that she thought Morton and Bessie would separate. I know Bessie has been in Florida a lot and Morton has been around Boston.

It is getting to be my bedtime. I will try to get your box away soon.

We all send wishes for a very happy 1939.

Lovingly, Nellie

Ness Lake, B.C.
Feb. 6, 1939

Dear Reta,

I think it is about time I got busy and thanked you for my nice table cover. I like it a lot. It is just right for the living room table, which is also our dining table. I'm ashamed to think I haven't got your box away yet but we are simply "snowed under". We have about four feet of snow on a level and more than that where it has drifted. The snowplow tries to keep the road from Prince George to the Post Office in Reid Lake open - a distance of 24 miles. Each time they plow the space grows narrower and the drifts on each side are higher, so there is just room for a truck. Fortunately there is little travel, as it would be impossible to pass. I heard they weren't going to plow again, as there is no place to put the snow so the mailman will have to use a sleigh from now on. George went in last week on Monday and came out on Tuesday. He walked about 15 miles before he got a ride, but got a ride out. The road by here isn't plowed so we use snowshoes when we go out. The Club meeting was only 1 1/2 miles from here last week so I managed to get there. The next one is 3 1/2 miles away but I think I can get there on snowshoes.

I was much pleased to hear from mother Allan and delighted with my mittens. I always wear mittens here. It was nice of her to make them.

Aunt Ida wrote that you were teaching again. Your family is grown so you aren't tied down any more. I think it is rather nice. What grades have you or is it High School work?

Marion wrote me she was teaching in Manchester, N.H. - this year. A friend of hers from Panama visited her around Christmas and I am expecting her, her husband and son to arrive here in the spring. They bought a trailer and are touring the U.S.A. I got in touch with her over five years ago when Marion was so sick in an effort to locate Rudy and we have written ever since. It is quite thrilling to have company you have never seen.

I had lots of letters at Christmas. I heard from Maude, Eunice, Winfield, Clyde, Martha, John Hamlin, Lizzie, Fred and Grace Cole, Flora, Minnie and Daisy Bailey. Besides all the folks that always send presents, Blanche Hight also wrote to me.

I tell George I really need a private secretary.

I have written a short, short story - also an article on mink and have another story nearly finished. Taddy Robert is taking a course in writing and we have grand times discussing things. She has a typewriter. I'm hoping I can get one by fall. I get a lot of fun out of writing even if I don't make much money. Some time will you send my book on Short Story Writing? I've promised it to Taddy.

I have a few things ready to send you and hoped to get something for the boys but as we are snowed under it will have to wait a bit yet.

Give my love to all the family,
Lovingly, Nellie

Ness Lake, B.C.
March 27, 1939

Dear Reta,

I'm finally mailing a small package marked "Easter Gifts". I hope you don't have to pay any duty on it. We never have to pay any duty on anything here.

We have just been snowed in all winter. I have never seen so much snow since we came here. We got our first thaw last week and the snow dropped about two feet but there is still two feet or more left to go. George has shoveled out the mink houses so many times it makes him think of a warm climate. I'll be glad when I can get out and dig in the garden. I have tomatoes and celery started in the house so I'm looking for spring eventually.

The last two Club meetings have been at Reid Lake so it has meant a long hike for me. I use snowshoes about two miles until I reach the Reid Lake Road. That has been plowed on account of the mail. When I go to the Club meeting, as I usually am invited somewhere on the way to dinner, I make a day of it.

Emerson is working in a mill at Quesnel. It is too bad he wouldn't go to school longer. He seems to be crazy for an engine and for music. He's an awfully good youngster but just isn't interested in farming or mink. He wanted to get a job so George told him he could try. We had no idea he would get anything but he started to Prince George with the mailman two weeks ago and last week I got a letter saying he had a good job in a mill in Quesnel, 105 miles from here. He wanted me to send him a blanket and some new rubbers I had bought for him just before he went and they hadn't arrived yet when he left. It seems quiet here without him and I have quite a time trying to cook right amounts. He is our big eater and I can't seem to get meals now without a lot left over.

How is school and what grades have you or is it High School? I haven't heard from Marion in some time. We are hoping that her friends the Lewis' will write soon.

My friend is taking a course in journalism so we have some great times together. She came up two weeks ago and brought her little boy and stayed a couple of days.

It is time for me to get supper once more. I have to make some biscuits for supper. I've got bread started and must bake tomorrow if I go to Club meeting on Wednesday.

George and I walked up the lake a couple of days ago (it is glare ice now). We met a fox and a moose on the ice, or rather, saw them cross ahead of us. We walked about six miles that morning. Game has been plentiful this winter. Emerson shot a moose and a deer. I have enough meat canned for all summer.

Hope the package will reach you. I'll mail it on Wednesday when I go to the Club meeting.

Lovingly, Nellie C.

Ness Lake, B.C.
Feb. 23, 1941

Dear Ruth and Mother Allen,

Mother Allen's letter came on this last mail and reminded me that I ought to write to both of you so here is a family letter.

I got the mail when I went to the Club meeting last Wednesday and was glad to hear from Mother Allen. Mr. Dixon, the welfare man asked me to take a young girl and her baby who were absolutely on their own and needed a home. I had hoped for a quiet winter, as we had two young men from Dr. Kenyon's "Church of the Air" from the middle of June until the 1st of September, besides two B.C Mission girls from Vancouver for a week in June. They were here for a week last summer and George said to Miss Fraser, one morning, "I should think you would find it hard going into new districts where you don't know anyone and don't even know where you can stay". She said, "The Lord has been very good in going ahead and opening up the way for us". I said, "He sends all of you missionary ladies to me". There seems to be so little we can do to help spread the Gospel and we always have plenty to eat even if we don't have much cash so we never mind two or three extra.

Clara and the baby came the last of December. The baby is a cute little thing - nineteen months old and into everything. I don't get anything done as I spend most of my time playing with the baby. I planned to sew and kalsomine the whole house and none of it is done yet. Last month Mrs. Rigler went to town and Clara went in the same day, so they both left their babies for me to take care of. One was nine months old, the other nineteen months. They were very good and I got along fine with them.

We have had a wonderful winter, very little cold or snow. Cars have run by our place all winter. Two years ago we had over six feet of snow on a level. It has been nice and sunny, not as much grey weather as usual.

I have my new teeth and am trying to get used to them. It takes me longer to eat but no doubt I'll learn how to manage them in time.

Emerson came home for Christmas. He has been working in a sawmill for over a year. As it is about sixty or seventy miles from here he had no way of coming except on his wheel. He rode his wheel home at Christmas so you see we haven't much snow. When he got back to work he came down with the flu and was pretty sick for four days. A camp isn't a very good place to be sick in so he came home as soon as he was well enough to get up. He was home about five weeks and then went to work for the fellow who hauls the lumber from the mill. He thought he would be on the truck. He boards at the same mill but was working for the truck driver. He brought him out Sunday for his clothes and blankets and Emerson said he worked for a week for Swanky and then the boss asked Swanky if he could spare Emerson Friday afternoon and asked him to go into the mill. He did and they asked for him Saturday again, and then they asked him to work this week in the mill so Emerson said, "I don't know whether I'm back in the mill or working for Swanky." He has been very lucky in getting a job whenever he wants one and has been at the same mill now for over a year. He is interested in engines and trucks but books don't seem to appeal to him.

Clyde and Martha have gone to Stockton, California. Clyde retired in September. I wrote Martha in October, but sent it to Pa. and got a card from her the same week giving her new address as Sacramento. I wrote her at Christmas and again last week but have never heard a word from her since she sent her address last October. Vivian and Winfield both sent a letter this week and they said Clyde and Martha were in Stockton.

Lizzie Kierstead wrote me last week. She had a bad heart attack last spring and was in bed for twelve weeks so she said she is taking life easy. Her family is grown up. Irma is married, Elva is still working in the hospital and Vernon is in the Duport Plant. Maude Hamlin wrote me at Christmas. She still lives with her sister in Los Angeles. Do you remember Blanche Hight who boarded at Sarah Holms's? She lives in Glendale, California. Her husband died several years ago. She writes to me often and I hear from both Minnie and Daisy Baily every Christmas. Minnie sent me a years subscription to 'The Upper Room".

Thank you for the "Saturday Evening Post." I have a four-year subscription to the "Post" so I wrote and asked them to change it to "The Ladies Home Journal." I trust that was all right. "My Country Gentleman" runs until 1948 so I didn't want to extend that. Winfield sent me "Good Housekeeping" and Margaret French sends "The American" each month. George seems to find more time for reading than I do. He doesn't care much for the stories but likes articles. I think the radio takes up a lot of one's time. I know we don't read as much as we did before we got it. I guess it is easier to just sit and listen and besides I can't see as well as I could once. It has to be a good print for me to read at night.

I have been a long time this year answering my Christmas mail. Santa is always so good to us and I have so many cards and letters I tell George I think I need a private secretary to take care of my correspondence.

Aunt Marie wrote that she has taken sick on Christmas night and was in bed for three weeks but was up and out once more.

Aunt Ida or Mother have never mentioned Aunt Ida's not feeling well but I suppose she is getting old, - I don't remember her age but I think she is seventy or seventy-one and Aunt Marie is older.

I want to go down to the Club meeting next week. It is way at the other end of the district next time so that means a good twelve miles walk round trip but I don't mind walking. Most of us go in the morning and stay to dinner. I go to the Post Office and get the mail and make a day of it. We are starting a crazy quilt at the next meeting and the meeting after that is to be a baby shower for one of our members. She was a schoolteacher in Peace River and came here only last July.

Winfield and Vivian spoke of coming to visit us next summer. I'm hoping some of my relatives will come sometime.

Did I tell you that we took the flat roof off of the lean-to and put on a pointed roof? It gives more room and the house looks a lot better. I'm going to kalsomine inside soon. I have paint and everything I need but I think I'll wait until Clara and the baby leave me, as it is hard to paint while the baby is around. Clara has a very nice young man and they plan to be married soon. He came out to see her this afternoon. He walked twenty miles from town so will probably stay a day or two, as he has to walk back.

It is time for me to cut up meat for the mink's supper. George usually feeds them in the winter and I take over in the spring but this year I've fed them all winter. Trapping will soon commence so then I'll be busy.

George is making muskrat boards today so that he will be ready for pelting. We divided the downstairs bedroom and made a small shop or workroom for George, and a pantry or storeroom. We find it most convenient. I'm sending two snap shots taken last June. George says I haven't changed any. I suppose because my hair hasn't changed I look about the same. I don't think I have any grey hairs.

I think I've rambled on enough and I'll go and get the mink feed ready.

Thanks a lot for our Christmas magazine.

Lovingly, Nellie

Rogers, Arkansas
April 20, 1941

My Dear Nellie,

It is about time I answered your letter that came last month. It was forwarded from Texas. I left down there on the 18th. I am staying with an old lady of 75 that I have known for 28 years. She lives alone, although she has children. A daughter lives a block away, another daughter 15 or 20 miles from here, the others, 3 boys, are scattered.

The youngest boy is 43 and single, he has been home all winter, he left last week for the southern part of the state to inspect fruit. I suppose he will be away all summer.

I pay Mrs. Gipple $10.00 a month and help with the work and I buy my milk when I want it. She owns her own home.

My oldest brother lives 5 1/2 miles north of here.

I decided this would be the best place for me until I get back to normal, if that is possible. I feel it is going to take a long time, although I am much better than I was. I have days when I feel quite cheerful, and others that are so depressing and blue, that the future look's very uninteresting.

Thank you for the pamphlet, Mrs. Wipple and I both read them. They are interesting. I believe in prayer and pray everyday to be helped in my trouble and heartache.

I went to church all my young life, too, but in later years felt the churches were, - as you say, - more social gatherings, to show new clothes, etc., and not used for the purpose intended.

I am so glad you were cured of your intestinal trouble by prayer.

Thank you, Nellie. I guess there isn't anything you can do to make things easier for me. Just say a little prayer for me occasionally.

I have wished so many times you didn't live so far away. I would love to see you. Bruce used to get enthused when one of your letters would come, and say that we would go up to see you some time, but he has a very changeable disposition, and couldn't seem to make up his mind what to do and stick to it. He is impulsive; too, that is why I am afraid his marriage to a young woman will not be the right thing for him. I feel so sorry for him, I think he misses so much enjoyment in life.

If such a thing should ever be, that I was able to come to see you, you needn't let a little thing like home made furniture and a log house bother you, for I'm like you, it isn't material things that count in this world. I found that out long ago.

I hope always to keep in touch with you, for I have enjoyed your letters so much and I have felt you were my cousin, as well as Bruce's, and I am glad to find you feel the same about me. I am fond of all of Bruce's relatives, I have always done all the writing you see, and they still write to me.

I had a letter from Elizabeth Keirstead, also one from John and Blanche Hamlin. Elizabeth has heart trouble and has to take things easy. She hasn't worked for some time.

Blanch has high blood pressure. The doctor brought the count down some, and she lost 12 lbs. so was feeling weak.

My fingers are cold, so my pen is hard to hold. We had a week of heavy rains, causing a lot of damage. Then yesterday the sun came out. The wind began to blow, and it turned real chilly. Everyone is hoping it won't get cold enough to damage the apples and peaches.

Everything is so green now. Lots of flowers are in bloom; lilacs are just getting out to their best. Bruce is fond of lilacs.

Elizabeth didn't write to me at Sacramento, that is, I didn't get the letter if she did, but Bruce got all the mail and sent me what he wanted me to have, so I don't know how many letters I missed. He isn't writing to any of his relatives, except Winfield. He always seemed to enjoy hearing from all of them, so I know he misses hearing from them. Of course, I feel I did all I could for Bruce as a wife, and yet, sometimes I think perhaps I failed somewhere. Several of our friends, his aunt, and cousin in Dayton, all have told me I spoiled him, but I don't know. He was cross so much of the time; I humored him so much to keep peace. That may have been a mistake, but how is one to know. I just did the best I could to get along with him peaceably. If his marriage should fail with this woman, I feel I ought to be ready to go to him if he needs me.

I am glad you have had nice winter weather; it is easier to get around.

Is Emerson still working at the sawmill? I guess you miss him being away all the time. But you have had a busy winter. After all, I imagine you are the kind of person that can always find plenty to do.

I am wondering if Clair was able to get married to her young man, because of her age. I hope they can manage it. Although, May is almost here, and they won't have to wait long. I hope they are very happy.

I didn't know until now that you had chickens. Do you have enough eggs to do you? I guess goat's milk is very healthy, especially for the baby, but I never did like the taste of it. Did you ever get your dental plate after you had your teeth out? They will be hard to get used to. I have two partial plates.

How are your minks getting along, fine I hope. How many do you have now? How did you come out on what you pelted last winter?

I hope you enjoyed the baby shower you were to go to, but I know you did.

I went to one last fall for one of my nieces and I enjoyed it. There were 25 there, and several who couldn't come sent gifts, so she never had to buy many things. She had a little girl February 22nd. She has two other children, 12 and 14. They are all so proud of the baby.

Thank you for the snap shot of you and George. Bruce didn't send the other one to me. He had opened the letter, but sent the pretty hankie.

Aunt Lydia and Uncle Lee have reminded me in every letter that I am very welcome at their house, and they would be glad to have me, which makes me feel comforted in a way. Aunt Lydia is real cross with Bruce and thinks he has done wrong.

If nothing else comes up in the meantime, I may go up to spend the winter. I haven't decided yet, as I feel I am not mentally capable of making decisions any time ahead. I just let the days go by, doing the best I cannot to give way entirely.

Mrs. Gipple is a cheerful, congenial soul, keeps up to date on every thing, and it's a help to be around her. It may be that I will be recovered enough when summer is over to go to work.

I really like California better than any place, although the spring months here are grand. But I expect to be here all summer, and if there is any change I'll surely let you know for I feel you are my cousin too.

I cut and made Mrs. Gipple a print dress and altered one that was a little tight. I also, embroidered a pair of pillowcases for myself. I bought them a year ago. My brother's wife will crochet some lace on them for me, as I have finished embroidering a refreshment set for her of one of my large and 4 small doilies.

The sun is out today, but it is windy and cool.

I have been having some trouble with my stomach, (gas pains) so I went to a doctor yesterday and got a prescription which helps me. I have too much acid.

I have some cousins a block from here. I see them every day or two and I walk up to the Post Office or stores every few days. It is at least a mile. Rogers is only a small town of less than 4,000.

I think I have written everything of interest I can think of. I hope this finds you all well and not working too hard.

Please, write when you can. I enjoy hearing from you.

Lots of love, from Martha

Ness Lake, B.C.
June 17, 1941

Dear Reta,

I went for the mail the night your letter came telling of Aunt Ida's death. I thought if I rode back part way with the mailman I'd save quite a walk. But as it happened the cab door flew open as he swung around the corner and I fell out on a very hard spot, so I haven't been doing much walking since as I hurt my back.

Eddy wanted to take me to Prince George to the hospital but I finally persuaded him to bring me home instead. I'm up again but my back aches a lot. One of my neighbors stayed a week with me while I was in bed. I would have liked to have her longer but her daughter came to take her to Giscombe so she left. I've been doing a little and then lying down awhile. I'm getting better but it seems awfully slow and there are so many things I can't do.

I didn't feel much like writing at first and waiting as you said you would write me the details so I looked in every mail for another letter but trust you have been busy, as school is closing and that is a busy time. I wrote to mother while I was in bed but have not heard from her. Aunt Marie wrote me this week and that was the first letter from anyone since you wrote me. I'm glad she and the girls could get down to the funeral and I'm very glad that Aunt Ida was not sick a long time. She wrote me just the week before and sent me a dollar and a very pretty handkerchief for my birthday.

Mother wrote me but didn't mention Ida's not being well and Aunt Ida wrote just a short note with the birthday card and said she had been having bowel trouble but didn't speak as though it was anything serious.

Mr. Clark, the minister, wrote me a nice letter. Aunt Marie said auntie was buried from the Funeral Home on Congress St., but did not say whether she was buried at the Cape where Dad was or at Evergreen where mother and grandmother Richner were. Aunt Marie said she had written to mother twice but hadn't heard from her. She said mother said she planned to live alone. She must be over seventy now. Does she seem well and strong? Of course I haven't seen her for about 13 or 14 years. She has neighbors close and a telephone but I don't think much of living alone. Does anyone know where Rudy is? I suppose he will have to be located if such is possible.

How is Marion? I haven't heard from her for some time. I suppose Don is quite grown up. He was older than Emerson and Emerson will be nineteen the 31st of August. I hope he will not have to get into this war. At present he is working on the C.N.R Dragline on the stone crusher. He was in a sawmill for over a year but the mill closed down for several weeks while they moved it to a new location. He still had his job but while he was waiting for the mill to open he got this job so he didn't go back to the mill. I had a letter from him the night I got hurt and another last week. He was to be at Newlands until July 1st and then I don't know where they move until he writes me again.

George is hoeing. We are having lots of rain and the weeds grow faster than the vegetables. I have four little mink in the house. Their mother died so I have them to take care of.

Write me when you can find the time.

Lovingly, Nellie

Ness Lake, B.C.
Aug. 1, 1941

Dear Reta,

I was glad to get your nice long letter. You sounded as if you didn't get my letter. You spoke of reading my letter about getting hurt, at mothers. I wrote you after I got up. I was in bed for four days - a long time for me. The doctor told me to stay there, as I'd be back in bed if I got up and it would be worse than at first but I prayed about it and George did too. Then one morning George turned on the radio to Dorothy Goodman who preaches on "Everyman's Chapel". She was talking on, "I can do all things through Christ who strengthens me". I quite believe in divine healing - (not Christian Science) - I simply felt I could get up and I did. I couldn't do much at first. George carried the feed to the mink pens for me and I fed the mink. I was rather slow for a while but I kept at it and now I'm almost as good as ever.

I walked to Reid Lake last Wednesday, ten miles round trip from where we live on Ness Lake, so that's not so bad for an old lady.

I have been expecting to hear from Uncle Henry about Dad's estate but have not heard from him yet. At the time Dad died he sent me a copy of the will and also a list of the different stocks in which the money was invested. According to the Will the 2/3's that was set aside for Aunt Ida's support was to be divided amongst us three as soon as all expenses for her burial and all bills were paid. The real estate was to be divided when mother was through with that. I wrote him this week and asked him for a statement of monies spent for Aunt Ida's support. Dad's will was probated so there doesn't seem as if there should be any court delays. Aunt Marie said that Aunt Ida left $800.00 in the bank. She seemed to think that would be divided but George thinks Auntie Marie was her nearest heir and it would go to her.

We have had some unusually hot weather. Two weeks ago we had a hot week. Bushes were simply burned by the sun. I don't know how the garden stood it but it did. We were late getting things in this year. I picked a most inconvenient time to get hurt. The ground was warm when things finally got planted so they came fast. It is nice to have green peas and new carrots to eat. We just about live out of our garden.

The fall fair is on the 27th of this month. It doesn't seem possible that summer is so near gone. I want to enter some things in the fair. I ripped up my summer coat and am trying to make it over for the Thrift Entry and I have goods for a dress if I can get it made.

The mink have kept me busy. We have seventy this summer and until just lately I have fed them three times a day. Now I've cut the feeding to two meals a day. I have to grind the feed and there are so many pens to clean I spend a lot of time outside. I've got them all changed to new pens so there are only six pens now with two in them. They fight so they have to be separated.

Maude's address is 1237 North Ogden Drive, Los Angeles, Cal. Blanche Hight lives in Glendale, Cal. That is a suburb of Los Angeles and about ten minutes from the city. Her address is Mrs. George Thiessen, 1135 Irving Street, Glendale, Cal. Her brother Harold has an automobile and he operates a Service Station at the corner of Melrose and Robertson, Hollywood, Cal. He sends me a calendar every year. I met him once years ago. He has grown up children. I know the girl just started to work a year or so ago. I'll try to write Maude. It would be nice for Hamlin to meet her.

Martha didn't say much when she wrote me. She is quite upset at the whole affair and doesn't seem to be able to adjust herself to the change. I think she would be glad to hear from you. Martha is one of these people who doesn't write again if you don't answer her letter. She often asks about you but wrote me a long time ago that she hadn't heard from you for a long time, - that you didn't answer her last letter. She seems very lonely. At present she is in Rogers, Arkansas. I think I can find her last letter. I'll send it on if I can. If you drop Maude a line giving her Hamlin's address, she no doubt will look him up or invite him out, as she always was so good about entertaining Rudy and his friends in the Navy.

I think we are very close to the end of this age and the Second Coming of the Lord. George and I studied the Revelation quite a bit last winter. The World Events seem to be following pretty close in the lines of Bible Prophecy.

It is six o'clock and George has gone up the lake for fish and will be home to supper any minute so I had better finish things up.

Emerson is in Prince Rupert working on the C.N.R Dragline. He writes he doesn't care much for the coast.

Write me again soon. Love, Nellie

P.S. I haven't received the box you spoke of. I trust it is on its way.

LETTER FROM MARTHA
Batovia, Ohio.
Aug. 30, 1941

My Dear Nellie,

I thought that I would begin answering some letters tonight so as to have them ready to mail Tuesday. Monday is "Labour Day", so no mail.

Your letter was dated August 31st, but it must have been July 31st.

I was glad to get your second letter, and am sure you must have my answer long before now.

I am upstairs trying to write. They have the radio on quite loud, so it sort of distracts my thoughts.

Uncle Lee likes the Barn Dance programs, and that's what they have on. It is quite hot up here, the second night in over a week when it has been uncomfortable up here after the sun down.

Aunt Lydia says some time September is as hot as August. I don't like hot weather.

Well, I am surprised that Ruth's boy Hamblin is going way out to Los Angeles to an airplane school. It seems there should be one closer than that. We thought those three boys were fine. I would like to see them now.

I suppose we did have the hot wave you did, for it is usually hot all during July and August, although we have had quite a lot of cool nights this month, and sometimes it is cool all day.

If you received my other letter you know I am with Aunt Lydia and Uncle Lee, but am going to leave 9th. I can't please Aunt Lydia at all. No matter how closely I follow her instructions, there is some thing wrong with just about every thing I cook.

She is sarcastic. I am reminded of Bruce every day, they are so much alike. So I am going up to my youngest brother's in White Plains, New York.

I haven't worked so hard in twenty years as I have since I came here. I have put up 79 quarts and 40 pints of vegetables and fruit. Also, about 8 pints of jam, and 83 glasses of jelly, so they will have plenty for the winter.

My nerves got so bad they affected my stomach, so when Uncle Lee had the doctor for Aunt Lydia, I had him check me over and give me some medicine, which has helped me, and I sleep better.

I have been here for seven weeks.

I know it is nice to have green things out of your garden. July seems so late to me, but seasons vary in different places. It has been much too dry here, so the garden has burnt up. We only had a few messes of corn. I canned 17 quarts of beans, and 19 1/2 quarts tomatoes. There are still some tomatoes in the garden.

There has been lots of apples. While they are faulty, they make nice sauce and pies. I canned 25 quarts, and also a lot of grapes after they were seeded.

I would like to see your mink. I know it is a lot of work, but one has to do something to earn money, and I suppose they aren't any more work than some other things.

Are you allowed to kill any of those deer you see? I like venison, but it has been many years since I had a taste of it.

I think your hens do fine. It is seldom that all of the flock laid, even a small flock. Uncle Lee did sell a few eggs to the neighbors, but he is only getting 3 and 4 a day now from 12 hens.   I too wish I could come to see you, but you are so very far away. If you were in Eastern Canada I would try to come.

Yes, Bruce did retire, but he is working in Defense Training, as an instructor.

I don't know why they didn't add Mississippi to Biloxi as the place where Winfield and Vivian were transferred. I think I told you in my other letter about it.

Biloxi is on the very southern edge of Mississippi, right on the Gulf. Winfield likes fishing very much so he enjoys that.

I hope you had no trouble with the made over coat you wanted to enter at the Fair. Also, I hope you received a prize for it and the organdy dress, too.

It is getting hot up here. I mean too uncomfortable, so I will go down and read a while. I have two new magazines, "McCalls" and "Ladies Home Journal."

Sunday Afternoon

I just looked this over, and corrected it in several places. I hope you will pardon the messy look.

When I get to White Plains, I want to have some pictures taken. I may send you one. I've been taking the doctor's medicine since Friday morning, and have had three nights of good sleep and two naps, yesterday and today. I feel rested and my nerves aren't quivering like they were. The doctor told me, right in the room with Aunt Lydia, it was my work here making me nervous. He says, "While you may not have so much to do, it is always a strain taking care of old folks". As for, "Not much to do", he should be here some times when there is canning going on, or a big washing. Oh well, my conscience is clear. I have done my very best, so I'm not going to let that bother me. Other things hurt my feelings.

The dinner you describe sounds very tempting. I'm sure it was very good. I wish I had been there.

My brother, the youngest one in New York, is my favorite and we are very congenial. I am fond of his wife too, she is a grand person. Their only son is married and lives next door. They have a little girl, born last January, and my brother, - having no girls, thinks she is the only child there is. Of course, they are both fond of her. My other brother there, has a daughter living across the street from my youngest brother, she has two children 5 and 8. So, I have plenty of relatives to visit before I take other work. I also have some friends on Long Island.

I am feeling much better mentally, lately. I am getting a different view of things in general, and I believe I will come out all right.

I have stopped grieving for Bruce and am looking forward to making a life for myself, as Maude had to do after Winfield pushed her out. They were married longer than Bruce and I.

I can understand better so many things about both of them since I came here, as Aunt Lydia has given me quite a history of their background and the things the little boys saw and heard when just a little more than babies. It is really pitiful.

Aunt Lydia, as you know, is their mother's sister. Uncle Lee knew all these things, too, as they were married and living in Missouri at the time.

I just wonder if I should ever get near enough, if Ruth would like to have me come spend the day. It is only a 70-mile drive from Portland, about 2 hours drive. She never writes. Of course, she may feel I am not a relative and she only saw me the one time. We haven't kept up a correspondence like you and I.

Oh yes, I wanted to tell you, we have some of the most beautiful butterflies around the garden, I ever saw. So large and so many colors. But not many birds. I don't know why.

I must stop and get dressed. I usually undress to take my rest in the afternoon. I seem to feel better afterward.

I must get my hair washed next week, somehow. I wanted to yesterday but it was cloudy.

When you write, address it to my brothers, 108 Lincoln Ave., East White Plains, New York.

I hope this finds you both well.

Lovingly, Martha

LETTER FROM COUSIN JOHN
Wolfeboro, New Hampshire
Sept. 7, 1941

Dear Cousin Nellie,

I received your nice letter a long time ago. I was very glad to hear from you.

I intended answering long before this but I am getting old and slow.

We have had a very dry summer here; lots of places are short of water. The crops are not as good as usual. The war is having its effect on us down here. Everything is taxed heavily and food prices are going up all the time.

In the shops where they make war material there is plenty of work and good wages but in the other lines they have slowed down owing to scarcity of material. Where I work on women's shoes, it is hard to get leather as they are taking the best of it for army shoes. I work about half time and ride 50 miles a day back and forth to my work.

We go down through Alton Bay each day. It is 10 miles from here.

They had two weeks of camp meeting in August. We were down on Sunday. Yes, we are advents; we belong to the church here. We do not take the "World's Crisis", but I wrote to them and asked them to send you a copy. I hope they did. It sure looks like the last days were approaching just as it tells in Revelations.

I sent the pictures and letter from Clyde and Birdie to Lizzie, as you requested. I have had a letter saying she received them O.K.

She also told me of your Aunt Ida's death. I was sorry to hear about it. I remember her well and that she was always kind to me when I visited your house as a small boy.

How the years have flown. Now I am 64, about the age of my father when you last saw him.

I hope you folks have had a good summer and the minks have done well.

I owe Martha Hamlin a letter. She wrote to us in April, she was in Rogers, Ark. at that time. I hope she is getting reconciled. It was a very hard blow for her. Blanche and I felt very sorry for her. She and Clyde visited us twice and we both liked her. She is a good woman.

The grandchildren are growing. Betty has just started her third grade work in school. She will be eight in December. Robert was five in June and John will be four in October. The boys are the same height, only Bob is heavier.

They stick pretty close to me when I am home and if I am working in the garden they always want to help.

Now please excuse me for not writing sooner. I get home at night and have supper and sit down to read my paper and I fall asleep. Then the children come over to see me before they go to bed and after that I am sleepy and have to go to bed myself.

Blanche has high blood pressure and has to take Doctor's medicine all the time and be careful what she eats.

I hope this letter finds you and your family all well and happy.

Best wishes from us both. Cousin John

Ness Lake, B.C.
Oct. 2, 1941

Dear Reta,

It was nice to hear from you. No doubt you have received my letter saying that I received the package and thanking you for it. I wrote soon after I received it but the letter stayed on the shelf two weeks before I mailed it.

I think it is a grand idea for you, Gert and Louise to come out and see me. I think Gert is right and you should set the date now and let nothing prevent.

I heard from Martha recently and she has gone to her brothers. I will enclose her letter, also one from cousin John.

I am still waiting to hear from Uncle Henry. I sent him a registered letter a week ago, as he did not answer the other one I sent him. It is nearly five months now since Aunt Ida died and he has never written me a thing about how things stand. According to Dad's will, what remained of the amount set aside for her support, was to be divided among us three children or our heirs after Aunt Ida's funeral expenses were paid and Uncle Henry had taken out a reasonable amount for his services. As Dad's will was probated at the time of his death it does not seem as if there should be court delays now.

I hope Hamlin will like California. Has he joined the Army or just studying aviation on his own?

I wish you had a little of our rain. It has rained every day or some part of it for over a month. A lot of hay and grain has rotted in the field. We are not keeping any stock this winter so we won't miss it as much as some.

We are going to sell all of the mink, as I do not feel able to do so much outside work. We both feel we have earned a vacation so plan to spend our time on the garden and if we have no stock we can go away for a day or two if we wish. You better plan to come out next summer. I wish you would send me Geri's address and I will write to her.

Emerson started this letter for me on the typewriter. He would rather take the typewriter apart than write but as long as he can get it together again, with no parts left over, I do not mind.

Write often and I will try to do better.

Lovingly, Nellie

LETTER FROM MARION
Manchester, New Hampshire
April 10, 1942

Dear Nellie,

I am aghast at the idea of not having answered your Christmas letter and thanking you for your present to the children and me. Now perhaps I have done so, - but I can't recall doing so despite the many times I have started to do so and have been sidetracked in the process.

You sent me two dishcloths, which I use as tray clothes under Dot's plate at the table, as she is still careless. Dot received dress material and has cut and basted a spring dress for herself, but forgotten to finish. As it is getting warmer she will soon want to wear it and will finish it and wear with pride. So I thank you for each of us, even if late. It is at least cordial and sincere.

Now about Rudy! I visited with Aunt Marie on Easter Day. Jean Fraser (Dons' girlfriend) took Don, Dot and me to spend a few hours at Aunt Louisa's. Aunt Marie has failed a lot but can still get up and down stairs. Her bedroom is very nice; the most home like room in the house.

Now I tried to get in touch with Rudy, although I did not believe he was alive. I wrote to the Veteran's Bureau in Washington, D.C. to see if he had registered in the Draft on Feb. 16. I enclosed a nice gentle letter attempting reconciliation and told him also about his father's money waiting for him. Now he apparently received my letter as soon after he wrote to Uncle Henry (or someone wrote) and demanded his share. Then Uncle Henry wrote him and asked him to come east to get the money and talk over with Marion what was best to do with the money. But Rudolph had a lawyer write and demand the money saying he could not do so. As yet he has not received the money according to a letter Mother Richner wrote to me yesterday.

Now Rudy has not answered my letter and it is six weeks since he received it. It looks as if he did not care to thank me but what his mind is thinking I cannot guess. I do not think I should run out to California and see him, I would if I had the money but I have none.

Lovingly, Marion

P.S. I am enclosing one of the last letters I received from Rudy years ago. Please return - you see he does like us yet.

Ness Lake, B.C.
April 11, 1942

Dear Reta,

How time flies. I could hardly believe April was so far gone. I guess I wrote you that they couldn't get a teacher at Reid Lake and it looked as though the school would have to close so I went down in January. I agreed to take it until they could get a teacher. Since they have been moving the Japanese from the coast there are lots of teachers without jobs. As many of the schools have been closed, I won't go back. I taught up until the Easter vacation. I had first, second, fourth, fifth and seventh grades. I had never had general science, nor read any of their Prose and Verse, nor Health, so it kept me busy keeping one jump ahead of them. I'm glad I am at home again. I boarded there during the week and walked home after school Friday. It was five and a half miles, too far to walk morning and night.

George is building a new chimney. We nearly burned the house down this winter. The logs caught fire behind the mud on the wall from the heater. We woke up to find the house full of smoke and then had to chip the plaster off the wall to get at the fire. We decided to put in a furnace in the cellar, as I can't keep the kitchen fire all night and the kitchen is cold if I let it out after suppertime. Our chimney didn't seem to be in the right place for a furnace and besides it didn't go down into the cellar. It is just made out of sundried bricks and was cracking and we decided to put a good chimney in. George has put in new floors but couldn't kalsomine and clean up much until he got the chimney built, as it will make so much dirt tearing out the old chimney. He couldn't start the new one until he could open up the back of the house and it was too cold to do that. He made a start on it yesterday and now I'll be glad when it is finished. All the letters I have been getting from Maine and Mass. have been opened and examined. They are sealed with a bit of paper tape giving the number of the censor. Are my letters opened before you receive them?

I planted tomatoes today in the house. I got the seeds out about three weeks ago when I was home Sunday, but George never got around to getting the dirt.

We got a new radio last fall and I'm so glad now we did, as radios will be hard to get. We really get a lot of enjoyment out of ours, as we never go any place. There is an old man who lives across the cove from us. He has been coming over every Sunday since last fall to listen to the "Old Fashioned Revival Hour" on Sunday night. He drank, swore and smoked and has led a pretty rough life, but was converted and has given up his drink and tobacco at seventy-five. He lives alone and seems to enjoy coming over every Sunday. He gets talking when we run out of church services and asks a lot about things he doesn't understand in the Bible and

never goes before twelve and has stayed until 2 a.m., so I'm usually sleepy Monday. I have been having Sunday School here all winter for the children. George and I both got a bicycle. We thought we'd like to get out a little this summer and it seems useless to buy a car these days with gas and tires uncertain. We feel we are very close to the end of this age.

Emerson was home a few weeks ago. He is working at a sawmill at Willow River, about 50 miles from here. His boss brought him home in his car. He and his wife came out and stayed to supper. We had met them before and they are both Christian workers. Emerson is a pretty good youngster. He has been around a rough crowd in mills and lumber camps for the past three years, but he doesn't smoke, drink or use bad language. I made him nice wool comfortable (quilt), as he said his bedding was getting worn out. I mailed it to him a couple of weeks ago. I made it like a sleeping bag so that he would have wool under him as well as on top.

I'm hoping he won't have to get into this war.

You sound as if Hamlin led a busy life. I'll try to get time to drop him a line.

It is a beautiful Sunday morning. I'm expecting a German lady and her husband up to dinner. She adopted an eight-month-old baby when she was sixty-three years old. The mother wasn't able to keep it, and it would have died if Mrs. Ellas hadn't discovered it and persuaded the mother to give it to her. It is a cute youngster two years old now. I've asked Mr. Swanston, the old man across the lake, over to dinner as he and Mrs. Ellas are both "old timers" in this country and they have grand times reminiscing. The youngsters usually come to Sunday school at 2 p.m., so Sunday is a busy day for me.

Sorry that Mother Allen has been sick. Now I'm home again maybe I can write a few of the many letters I should write. Emma sent me a letter that Orville had received from a lawyer in Concord. He was representing Rudy's children and wanted to know what proof Orville would require as to Rudy's death. I understood from the letter that Uncle Henry had or was going to turn the money due to Rudy over to the States as unclaimed. I hope Marion will be able to get it. I have other letters to write and my dress to change.

Lovingly, Nellie

P.S. Give my love to mother Allen and tell her I'll try to write her soon.

LETTER FROM MARTHA
East White Plains, New York
April 20, 1942

My Dear Nellie,

Your welcome letter reached me March 31st. I am always glad to hear from you.

I guess you are back home by now and busy as can be with your housework and teaching school. Any other kind of work away from home is all right if one can go home nights and don't get too tired trying to work and keep up a home, too.

I'm reading your letter over, you said you had sent Vivian and Winfield's Christmas remembrance to Bruce, but had not heard anything from them. It seems that the least they could do, would be to let you know they received it and I feel sure Bruce sent it on. I just heard in a round about way that Vivian and Winfield were in West Virginia, but it came through Aunt Lydia and Uncle Lee or a neighbor of theirs, so it may not have been repeated correctly. Vivian hasn't written to me since long before Christmas and she used to write quite often. I don't know why. I understand she is working so perhaps doesn't have much time to write. She doesn't write to Aunt Lydia as often as she used to, so Aunt Lydia told the neighbor.

You have probably had that promised letter from Birdie May by now and she has told you all the news about where Vivian and Winfield are.

It is to bad the candlesticks were broken. They must not have packed them properly, or the package was handled to rough.

I imagine it is still too cold up there to open your house and put up the new chimney, and by the time it gets warm enough for that you will be making the garden.

We had quite a freakish streak of weather the week after Easter, on Thursday and Friday it snowed. I imagine there would have been 10 - 12 inches, if it hadn't been so wet and melted so fast. It looked so pretty, even if it was disagreeable and there was rain with it. By Monday it was all gone. We had some nicer weather after that, but the past two days have been rain and cold, it is cloudy today, more like fall. It's too cold for comfort. I had quite a bad throat last week and felt pretty bad all over, aching and tired, but the swelling has disappeared from my throat, leaving a little cough and I feel better. I want to go back to work this week.

I left the place I had ten days ago. On Sunday, April 12, my nephew's wife was taken to the hospital where 1 1/2 hours later a little boy was born. They have a little girl 15 months old. My sister-in-law has to take care of her and keep up the housework, cook for her son (baby's father), and do a hundred other things. So I feel I ought to stay and help her by doing the work here, also staying with the baby some, too. The mother will be home Wednesday, but Lena, my sister-in-law will still have to help a lot.

The son lives in a bungalow in front of the lot and my brother lives in the garage apartment in back. It belongs to my brother. The double garage was made into a modern apartment several years ago. There isn't much room, not half enough, as they have lots of company, but it's better than paying rent, and part of the year my brother is out of work, so his expense isn't so much while living here.

Well, I made two aprons and would like to make a couple of housedresses, but I guess I will just keep the material until later on. I can get along on what I already have.

I don't know whether I will get to visit Eunice and Ruth or not. I was just turning the thought over in my mind and hoping I would be able to. Ruth is so slow to answer my letters, but I guess she is busy with her house and teaching, so doesn't have much time.

You said you were having a small book sent to me right from the publisher, but it hasn't arrived yet. Thanks for thinking of me.

Yes, your letters always reach me. Even if I do move around, they are forwarded and you won't lose track of me.

I am sitting upstairs writing right at the top of the stairs, and my sister-in-law is talking all the time to Linda, the baby, and it bothers me. I like to write when it is quiet, but don't often have the chance, so please excuse the mistakes.

Let me know if you hear from Winfield or Bruce. How they are, etc., and tell me where Winfield is if you hear, and I will do the same by you.

I hear from John Hamlin every once in a while. He writes nice letters. I am glad Blanche is feeling better.

I hope this finds you all well, and don't work too hard. Write when you can. I am always glad to hear from you.

How many mink have you now, and did you get a good price for the pelts you sold last winter?

With Love from Martha

Ness Lake, B.C.
May 8, 1942

Dear Reta,

I don't owe you a letter but will write a few lines, as I wanted to send on Mother's last letter to you. I hope she will be able to visit you this summer. I'd love to have her come here but I seem so far from everyone I can't persuade anyone to come and see me.

Emma wrote me that she saw in the paper this winter, the death of Helen Cushing's father. I wrote to Helen, but haven't heard from her for a long time. I miss Aunt Ida's letters for she always told me the Woodfords news. I do not think Helen has many relatives left.

It is nice to be home again. Moving the Japanese from the B.C. coast closed lots of schools there so there are plenty of teachers. I was glad to come home, as I do love to grub in the garden. I have been house cleaning and gardening ever since I got home. I've canned three quarts of dandelion greens and two of rhubarb, so have made a start for winter. The asparagus is up so will be eating asparagus this week.

Vernon Kierstead wrote me last week. He is stationed at Fort Bragg, N.C. His address is: Private V.H Kierstead, F104, F.A.R.C. Fort Bragg, N.C.

I have just written to him. No doubt he is lonesome, as he asked me to write.

I suppose you are busy with schoolwork. Won't you be glad when vacation comes? I shan't look for a letter until then, but try to write to Martha.

It is time to get dinner as the children come to Sunday school at two.

Love to all, Nellie

P.S. I had a letter from Marion. She located Rudy. I'll send her letter on to you.

Ness Lake, B.C.
October 25, 1942

Dear Reta,

I'm sending on Martha's last letter. She is still worrying because you haven't written to her.

We all took a trip south. There were a couple of camp meetings at Langley Prairie, twenty-eight miles from Vancouver. We took a tent and all went. I was so glad Emerson could go with us. He met a girl at the camp from Victoria so decided he would rather work in Victoria than in Prince George. She seemed like a very fine Christian girl. They were both badly smitten, so only time will tell whether it is a passing fancy or something deeper. There were quite a few young folks from Victoria at the camp, so Emerson has gotten in with a Christian group and he is a good lad himself so I don't worry about him. We had a nice time, grand services and we met some fine folks, but I was rather glad to come home again.

Hope you will write to Martha, as I think she'd like to visit you while she is in Portland. Did I write you that I had a letter from Maude? Rudy had been to see her. His address is: R.D. Richner, General Petroleum Corp., Box A Terminal Island, California.

You asked about our wants for Christmas. It seems early, but I suppose Christmas will be here before we know it. I need a common white petticoat with a hamburg ruffle, - nothing elaborate or expensive. There will probably be sales in Jordan's basement before winter. A colored tablecloth is most useful. I don't care whether it is red or blue check, - a yard and a half is plenty big. Common crash towels, - not too fine, or pillowslips would be acceptable. George needs a comb or shaving supplies, handkerchiefs, - common ones - not too good, - or heavy socks. He has quite a supply of ties at present. As he seldom wears one, his ties are all pretty good. It is hard for me to get cloth here as I never can pick out what I want so three or four yards of gingham, percale or print will make me a bungalow apron or house dress. I have a machine now so I want to do some sewing this winter. The box Flora sent last winter has been so nice to have and a few yards of narrow ribbon, lace or hamburg trimming, such as one can get quite cheap at the 5 & 10 Cent Store in Boston, are the things it is hard to get here.

I haven't done anything for Christmas yet, but I suppose I ought to, as I have to teach until the 21st of December and get up a Christmas Concert and tree for the children, so I'll probably be busier than I am now.

Give my love to all of your family, and write often.

Lots of love to you, Nell

P.S. I am enclosing a letter from Martha.

LETTER FROM MARTHA
Sunday afternoon,
June 21, 1942

Dear Cousin Nellie,

I see by the date on your letter, I have let too much time go by without writing. Just the next day after your letter came, I went to the country to work for a month and didn't have much time to write, as I was pretty tired nights when I finished my work - they had lots of company.

I finished on the 19th of this month and I am now getting my belongings ready to go to Maine next week. I have quite a few things to get finished up, so I will be quite busy for the rest of the time here.

My brother and family are on a picnic today with some of the other relatives, so I am alone this afternoon, and thought I would get my letters answered. I will write three this morning.

I was glad to hear from you again. I had a letter Friday from John Hamlin. He said he was working in Wolfsboro now, for the summer. Not much money, but close to home and he can raise a garden. They want me to come over and see them, but I don't know yet whether I will get to, I would love to see them both. I'll see after I get to Portland.

I suppose you have your new chimney built by now, and will be busy doing your Kalsomining and other work.

Even if you are in the country you seem to have plenty of company. Isn't the schoolteacher afraid to stay by herself?

I hope George got his new teeth before the dentist left. Did you get yours?

I just had a new lower partial made and three teeth extracted, so I hope now, I can get along without a dentist for some time to come. They used the new material called "lucitone" in the two plates I've had made this year. It is pink and transparent.

Did Emerson come home? Is he old enough to be drafted?

I know what a job it is, to put new ticking on pillows and feather beds. I have done the pillows and watched my mother fix the feather bed. One seldom sees a feather bed any more. My brother-in-law has one that was my mother's; also, my oldest brother has one.

You have surely been busy with your quilts and bedding. I'm sure the old man appreciated the wool comforter you made for him.

I don't know whether Bruce is still in San Antonio, or not. He sent me a check May 4th from there, but this month I haven't received any check, or heard a word from him. I'm going to write to Vivian today to see if she knows where he is, if he has moved. I haven't heard from her either, but I have their address in Mississippi, so will send it there. I don't think Bruce has been transferred. He may have had a chance to sell. He wrote me last summer the heat hurt him so much he wasn't going to stay there another summer. If I hear anything from Vivian I will let you know. Or if I find out where Bruce is.

John Hamlin said he hadn't heard from any of the cousins, except me, since Christmas. I thought you write them. Ruth never answered my letter I wrote last winter in Dayton.

I was amused that you listen to the program, "Lum and Abner", way out there. My brother Chris always listens to them, unless someone comes in and he forgets to tune in. He hates to miss them. We all like them, don't you?

I know your new dresses will be pretty. They sound like something I usually pick out, - the blue polka dots, especially. Your idea about cutting off your suit jacket is good.

I haven't any thing new in ready-made things except a straw hat. I bought material for a house dress a couple of months ago. I already had four dress lengths of different materials, so I thought if I got one sort of dressy ready made, I could get along until I got the others made up. I haven't any dresses suitable to wear out for the evening, although I never wear a real evening dress. I prefer tailored things.

I have an appointment tomorrow for a permanent. I haven't had one since 1936. My hair get so stringy in the summer, the curls won't stay in, as my hair is fine and straight. I heard of a good operator who gives nice permanents.

I intended to see a friend of mine, this afternoon, but the weather looked quite threatening. I had quite a way to walk from the bus, so I thought I had better stay home and write letters. It is 10 minutes of 4 and the sun is out, so it doesn't look like rain anymore.

I think I have written all I can think of that would be of interest to you. My address is General Delivery, Portland, Maine. As soon as I get settled I will send my new address.

I hope this finds you all fine, and your garden will be in and growing.

Lovingly, Martha

Ness Lake, B.C.
Dec. 13, 1942

Dear Reta,

I am sending you a small package by tomorrow's mail. Hope it will reach you all right. We read a book recently that we enjoyed very much. I thought you and Ray might enjoy reading it together as we did, so have ordered one sent direct to you from the New York Publishing Co. If you don't receive it let me know so I can look it up.

It is a Bible study but we found it interesting and there seems to be such a need for Bible study today. There seems to be so much time for social affairs in the church today and so very little time for Bible study and prayer. We hope the book will prove a blessing to you both.

We have been busy since we got home fixing up the house. George did most of the work himself. The house is very comfortable now. He put a furnace in the cellar so the kitchen is warm even when the kitchen fire is out. He also built on an entry, pantry and porch on the north side of the house. When we get a winters supply of groceries in the fall, I've always wanted a pantry. It has been such a problem to know where to put sacks of flour, etc.

It was lucky we took our trip when we did, as now we can travel only fifty miles by bus. We enjoyed the trip. I always wanted to see Vancouver and the Pacific Ocean. Vancouver was just like any other city, - crowds, noise and bustle. Some folks thought if we went south we wouldn't want to come back here, but home looked good to us.

Emerson decided to stay down, and went on to Victoria and in September joined the Navy. He writes that he likes it and had gained eight pounds in the first five weeks. He said he was still gaining. I hoped he could get home for Christmas but he can't come home before March. Where are your boys? Aunt Marie wrote me that Hamlin was in Squantum. Morton Cole lives there and she said she was writing him to hunt Hamlin up. It will be nice for him to know someone.

I have several others to write to. I walked to the Post Office in Reid Lake yesterday. It is an eight-mile round trip if we cross the bog. George went with me and we had to break trail for over a mile. The snow is quite deep already. Last week I walked down twice. I hope to go down again Friday to the concert at the school.

Hope you will have a nice Christmas. Let me know if the book does not arrive.

Lovingly, Nellie

Ness Lake, B.C.
May 26, 1943

Dear Reta,

It is some time since your card came. I am so sorry that you have been sick. No doubt you are back at school teaching at this time.

Spring was a long time coming this year. The ice didn't go out of the lake until the 7th of May, - almost two weeks later than last year.

We started planting early, but there were heavy frosts every night so we stopped for a week. It is warm now and we have finished planting everything, except transplanting the celery and tomatoes outside. It is a little early for that.

We put in eight hundred pounds of potatoes, so should have some spuds in the fall. There has been a good market for potatoes and firewood this past year.

George cut quite a lot of wood last winter.

I'm canning dandelion greens, (leaves from young dandelions, - tastes like spinach when cooked). I was out in the garden all afternoon so they didn't get cooked and they are boiling now.

Emerson came home for a few days in April. He was en-route to Halifax. He writes that he doesn't think much of the place. I imagine he finds it damp. I know I noticed the dampness when we went to the pacific coast last summer. We are 2,600 feet above sea level and the air is clear and dry. Victoria is supposed to have a delightful climate, but Sonny said he was cold all winter. A damp cold is much worse than dry cold. He never felt cold here, even when it dropped to forty below.

The night before last a moose came into the yard. He simply stepped over the fence and stood for some time by the end of the woodpile close to the house. Finally he stepped back over the fence and ambled away into the woods. I saw a moose and her calf standing on the potato patch about six weeks ago and have seen two deer in the road lately.

I've needed glasses for some time. An optometrist has just come to Prince George. George and I went into town two weeks ago and had our eyes tested. We got our glasses this week. George needed them only to read, but I needed bifocals. It is rather hard to get used to them. I'm always looking out of the wrong part.

Last year I met a lady who had had a shock (stroke). One side was paralyzed. She lived in a miserable place in town, - just two rooms. One room had windows on the north, the other had no window at all but got only what light came over the partition. The front opened onto the street and the back on a narrow dark alley. I invited her out and Brother Persing brought her here in his car. She was here six weeks and she gained so much weight. She got so she could walk holding on to me. I massaged her legs and back every day and she got fresh air and sunshine. She went outside every day. I'm sure if she had stayed she would have walked alone.

I went to see her when I was in town and she nearly cried, she wanted badly to come back. She was in bed that day but gets up some. I went to see the doctor and asked him to check up on her heart, lungs and kidneys - (she has only one) before she came out. They are poor and she doesn't get much care there. Her husband is very kind but sort of a helpless kind of a man. He doesn't seem to know what she needs and she is the most patient thing and never asks for anything.

I expect she will be out soon. I'm glad I can have her here.

Our radio has been punk all winter. Sometimes we get something and sometimes we don't. George has been laying it to the winter but I don't believe we have poor radio weather quite all the time so we're going to take it to town.

How is mother Allen? I don't know whether I owe her a letter or not. I write to so many people, I don't always remember. You might pass this on to her.

Don't bother about our Christmas presents. You know the longer I live the surer I am, that Christmas as we celebrate it is a heathenish custom. The date of Christ's birth is unknown. At first Christmas was observed only by the Catholics. The day chosen was the anniversary of an old pagan festival.

The present way of celebrating it, is giving gifts to people who really don't need them and eating more than is good for you. I can't see where it is at all honoring to Christ.

I rather think that next year I shall use the money I usually spend, for the furtherance of the gospel. It seems as if the observance of Christ's birthday should not be so commercialized.

We both feel that we are very close to the end of this age (the Church Age) and the coming of Christ for the true Church, his bride, and the short reign of the anti-Christ here on earth - II Thess. 2.

I feel that I should do what I can for the spreading of the Gospel in these last days and I'd rather others would do the same, than spend the money on me. Maybe you think I'm queer but that is the way I feel.

I suppose you will be glad when school closes. I know I always was.

It is getting dark. Give my love to all of your family.

Lovingly, Nellie

Ness Lake, B.C.
July 30, 1943

Dear Reta,

The parcel arrived safely a couple of weeks ago but our strawberries are ripe so I haven't been writing many letters.

I was much pleased with the dress goods. It is just my idea of pretty cloth. I hope to make it up right away. I need some summer dresses but I don't seem to get around to sewing.

Mrs. Manzinoja, the lady who was with me last summer is here again. She can't walk without help so I keep busy moving her around. One of my neighbors (she lived six miles from me but has been in town since last January) came out a week ago to spend her vacation with me. She goes back tomorrow.

Emerson is on the east coast. He is stationed at Halifax or rather that is his address. He is in submarine detection and is on the ocean somewhere. He had been to Sidney and to New York. He said his neck was stiff for a week from gazing at the skyscrapers.

I was surprised to have come papers from Mattie Young. I haven't heard from her for a long time.

I had a letter from Hazel Cadis Pearson recently. She is married and has two children, a girl sixteen and a boy twelve. She still is with the "Woman's Home Companion".

Marion wrote a week ago. Rudy had been to see them again. He had been around the world in the past six months and just landed in New York. He was signing up for another six months so Marion was teaching another year. She had planned to join him in California after school closed but thought it foolish to go to California if he was to be gone so decided to stay where she had friends.

We had a late spring and it hasn't been very warm all summer. The garden was slow in starting but looks nice now. We certainly enjoy the green things in it. I have been trying to can but sugar is a problem. Each person is allowed ten lbs. for canning so I have twenty lbs. to put up fruit. I'm not making it very sweet, as I have so much fruit. I don't think I'll pick the gooseberries. They are such sour things. Mrs. Mann was telling me today that someone told her you could let them get ripe and then dry them and roll them in a little sugar and use them for raisins. I may try a few to see what they are like.

Thanks for the pictures of the boys. They don't look much alike. Where are Hamlin and Carleton now? I suppose Richard will soon be in the war too.

Do you plan to teach next year? You and Ray will be sort of alone with all of your family gone.

George and I were alone last winter. Our school is closed for lack of pupils and all of the young folks gone. I rather enjoy the winters and don't mind being snowed in.

It is nearly eleven p.m. Mrs. Mann is pounding away on my typewriter. Mrs. Manzinoja is snoring lustily and George has retired. We have been sitting up after the others have gone to bed and usually have a midnight lunch before we retire.

Mrs. Manzinoja enjoyed the book but we have been too busy to do much reading yet.

Thanks for the things. I love my dress goods.

Give my love to Mother Allen.

Love to all, Nell

Ness Lake, B.C.
Sept. 27, 1943

Dear Reta,

I guess our last letter crossed, as I heard from you just after I wrote thanking you for the dress goods. I do like it a lot. It is prettier than any I could buy here. I do most of my shopping by mail and these days they never send half of one's orders and lots of things are substituted. George has just finished digging potatoes. We got three and a quarter tons of good potatoes, No. 1's, and plenty of seconds for our own use. George kept track up to 1500 lbs. and then stopped. There is a big bin full.

It has been a cool, wet summer and some folks have had frost every month but we are high above the lake and seem to escape frosts. This is one of the last places to freeze every year. We didn't get a killing frost until the 17th of September, but the spring was late. The blackberries, sand cherries and corn didn't ripen and there were very few cucumbers. They seem to need warm nights.

Mrs. Manzinoja has been with me since the 18th of June. She had a stroke two and a half years ago. Her left side has been paralyzed. I met her over a year ago. Her husband is a musician, - very clever, - a sort of genius, but he lives in the clouds somewhere and although kind to her, doesn't seem to see that she needs care. He keeps six cats in two rooms and as they live in town, the cats are never allowed out of doors as one is blind, one is lame and one is mangy. They jump up on everything and drink out of the water pail. Poor woman, I don't see how she ever stood it. I invited her out last summer and she gained a lot in the two months she was here. She went home for the winter and I didn't get in to see her until spring. She spent a lot of time in bed to keep warm and had a bad cough and was thin and pale. I went to see the doctor, asked him to go to see her and check up on her heart, lungs, kidneys, and blood pressure, and then I got a taxi to bring her out to our place at Ness Lake. She went back in for a week the last of August.

As I hadn't been anywhere all summer, George and I thought we'd like to do a little gadding together. He was busy building a woodshed and I had beans to can. Then the Sylvan Glade teacher, the one they had last year, dropped in one evening unexpectantly, and stayed until the next afternoon so it was Thursday before we went anywhere. There is a lake about nine miles from here that I had never seen so we set off in the morning on our wheels with a lunch. We built a fire on the shore of the lake and made coffee. After dinner we followed another trail back in the bush for three or four miles and picked a ten-pound pail of blueberries. It was 8:30 p.m. before we got home. We feel we went twenty-five miles that day. The last five miles we came in a pouring rain.

Sunday morning we rode twenty-one miles into Prince George and got there in time for church. Brother Persing used to hold services here in the school, but a year ago he built a church in town and doesn't come out any more. We went home with the Persings, and then back to church in the evening. George went home on Monday morning but I stayed at Persings as it was Labor Day and I couldn't do any shopping. Tuesday morning I did the errands and then got a taxi to bring Mrs. Manzinoja back with me. She was sitting at the table in her nightgown and her husband insisted that I have a cup of coffee. It smelled so catty that I didn't know if I could possibly drink it. Four times a cat landed on the table so all she had was a cup of coffee. Someone came in for a lesson on a horn so while weird sounds came from the front room I helped her into her clothes and packed her bag and before the lesson was over the taxi arrived. She said she felt miserably all the time she was home and couldn't eat, as she had no appetite. She hadn't been dressed all the week but had sat on the edge of the bed in her nightgown. He locks her in and goes out to play for a dance until three or four in the morning - such a life for a sick person! She said three cats slept in the bed and three on the floor. She loves to be clean and have clean clothes. She is a lot stronger and sits on the porch every morning and George helps me get her down on the ground in the afternoon. She can walk by holding onto me. I think it would be foolish to send her back this winter to lose what she has gained. I think she'll stay with us until spring. You see we have no house rent or fuel to buy and we raise so much that our food doesn't cost much, so we never miss what an extra person eats.

Brother Persing came out last week and brought my bicycle with him. He and George went hunting. They hoped to get a moose or deer, but met a bear instead, so we have been eating bear meat. I canned some for winter.

Game is plentiful. Three times this summer we have watched a moose step over the garden fence and stand close to the cabin. George met one on the road the other morning but didn't have a gun. There has been a doe around all summer. Every few days we have seen fresh moose and deer tracks across the potato patch. I met a deer the other morning on the road and she stood quietly just off the road while I passed her. Last night one came into the yard. George grabbed the gun, but by that time she had crawled through the fence into the potato patch. We saw she had no horns, so we stood on the porch watching her. She stayed in the yard about ten minutes before she ambled on. Brother Persing is coming out again but George wanted to get potatoes dug before he went hunting again.

Emerson is somewhere on the Atlantic coast. His address is Halifax, Nova Scotia, but he has been to New York and last week a card came postmarked from Boston. He wrote he had been out for a month so got four letters from me when he got into port. Of course he can't say where he is, but he is in submarine detection and on a convoy on the East Coast.

This is a rainy day. I seem to get so far behind on my letter writing. I guess I write to too many folks.

Emma wrote not long ago and I still hear from Helen. She lives all alone. I'd like to have her come out here for a visit but she says she can't until after the war.

I also heard from Hazel Cades Peason not long ago. She states she is with "The Companion" and has two children, a girl sixteen and a boy thirteen.

I suppose you are teaching by now. Don't you miss the boys? Emerson was never a noisy lad but it seems so quiet when he was gone. He loves his life on the sea so it is nice for him. It is so much easier if they like what they are doing.

I must write some more letters, as I won't get any until I answer a few. Give my love to Mother Allen and Ray.

Love, Nellie

Lovingly yours, Nellie

Ness Lake, B.C.
May 14, 1944

Dear Reta,

I believe I owe you a letter but somehow my letter writing seems to have been sadly neglected of late.

Mrs. Manzinoja was with me all winter. She suddenly lost her eyesight so I brought her in to see the doctor. I expected her to come right back but it was some time before she got fitted to glasses and meanwhile Emerson came home and on his brief stay decided to get married. Jeannie is a little French girl from Montreal. She is dark and vivacious. They were married at the Pentecostal Tabernacle in Prince

George, - on April 17th. Emerson had to return to Halifax on the 20th, so Jeannie is with us until Emerson knows where he is to be. The corvette he was on is out for a general overhauling so he didn't know whether he would be sent out on another corvette or stay on shore and study for six months. Jeannie finds it rather quiet with us as she is used to city life and not much interested in a farm.

We had a bit of excitement on the 6th. The Reid Lake folks all came to dinner. It was quite a surprise party for my birthday. I hadn't the faintest idea that they were coming until they landed on the porch. I heard the cars too, but thought it was the truck with a sack of seed oats George was expecting and never bothered to look out. There were eighteen to dinner. They brought a kettle of chicken, jello, cream, canned strawberries, bread, butter and even tea, so with what I had prepared for dinner there was plenty. Everyone gave me a present and Jeannie cards with money, so she got $7.00 in silver.

You will get a wedding announcement eventually but we couldn't send for any until after the wedding and then we had to send to Winnipeg for them.

We had part of the garden in and the early peas, turnips, lettuce and radishes are up. I don't know how the poor things grow with frost every morning but they do.

We are expecting a Christian Worker to stay with us this summer. The Christian Missionary Alliance is sending one to take over Brother Persings church, as he wants to go out in Evangelistic Work. They wrote us a man would arrive by May 14th to stay with us and work in the country districts around us.

Jeannie and I came into town yesterday. It made an early start as they are repairing the Nechako Bridge so no cars can pass between 8:00 a.m. and 5:00 p.m. They tear up a small section in the morning and have it done by night so you simply stay on one side of the river or the other during the day. We came in because Rev. Gaglardi is holding an evangelistic Campaign in town. We met him when we went to Langley Prairie, near Vancouver, summer before last. He has a beautiful tenor voice and at one time sang on the radio.

Last night I went down to the Salvation Army meeting. I know several of the women who attend. The soldiers conducted the meeting and afterwards we were invited into the Captain's house at the back of the hall for tea and tarts. I do enjoy the Christian Fellowship. If our missionary did not arrive yesterday, George planned to ride in on his bicycle this morning.

I'm sorry I can't have Mrs. Manzanoja back but with Jeannie and the preacher there I have no room and I like to get out a little. I can't go anywhere when she is there, as I can't leave her alone.

Say hello to Matty when you see her. I had a letter from Marion not long ago. She sent a snap shot of the house she had bought. She said Rudy was chief steward in some military hospital in California. He did all of the buying and hiring of help.

I had a newspaper clipping this winter from Helen Letlig of Warren Stout's death in Italy. Speaking of Rudy made me think of it, as they played a lot together.

We will be going home on the mail truck tomorrow. I'd hate to live in the city.

I think it is about time that I woke Jeannie up and we went out to get us some breakfast if we plan to go to church today.

Give my love to Ray and Mother Allen. Tell her that I think of her even if I don't get around to writing.

Lovingly, Nellie

Marie Blanche Eugenie Tent
of Montreal, Quebec
And
Emerson Rudolph Campbell, R.C.N.V.R.
of Reid Lake, British Columbia
Announce their marriage
On Monday, April seventeenth
Nineteen hundred and forty-four
At Pentecostal Tabernacle
Prince George, British Columbia
Canada

Ness Lake, B.C.
June 13, 1944

Dear Reta,

 I want to thank you for the box of ribbons and bias tape. I do appreciate having them, as it is so hard to get such things these days. Usually when I send away an order half of the money comes back. I think I sent four times before I got a pair of flannelette sheets and then only one pair. Jean has been making pillowslips and dishtowels and tablecloths out of flour sacks. They aren't bad when bleached and embroidered. Today she tried to make a sheet but has quite a time stitching as she can't seem to hold the goods even, no doubt she will learn.

 We are having a very dry spring. There was very little snow last winter and we had spring rains, only an occasional shower that barely wet the surface. We surely need a good soaking rain.

 We are eating lettuce, radishes and spinach. It helps out to have a little green stuff. We raised a pig last winter so have bacon and ham for summer. I got six hens, as I feel lost without something to take care of.

 I suppose you got the wedding announcement. I didn't suppose Emerson would get ahead of Hamlin. He rather surprised us all. Jeannie is small and dark, part French and part Spanish. He was home only three days after the wedding and then had to rush back to Halifax. As it was he was eight hours late so he lost three days pay and three shore leaves and wrote he was scrubbing decks. It seemed best for Jean to stay with us until Emerson knew what he was to do. He no sooner got back to Halifax than they sent him to Vancouver. He seems to be between Victoria and Vancouver judging from his letters but it is hard to say how long he will be there.

 We have a Christian worker staying with us this summer. He is a young lad from Bible School and has to go back in the fall. There seems to be so little we can do for the Lord that we offered a home to anyone who could or would come to this district. There seems to be such an indifference to the Word of God in these days. The worker is holding meetings in the Sylvan Glade School five miles from us and also in the Chief Lake School about eight miles away in another direction. Jeannie rode my bicycle over to Sylvan Glade Sunday and George and I walked. He and Clem rode the bicycles home, as they were going on to Chief Lake and Jean and I rode home with a man who was bringing a couple of beaver over to the corner to ship in on the mail truck on Monday morning. I wish you could have seen Jean's face when she saw what we were to ride on. There was absolutely no place to sit but on top of the butchered animals. The hides were still on and their ribs made quite a springy seat, not bad at all. It was the last straw when Jeannie's purse slid inside one of the creatures and she had to fish it out.

 Did I tell you that I wrote my experiences homesteading in the west? I sent it to Doubleday, Doran Co., in New York and I had a very nice letter from the editor.

He said he found that it had both basic appeal and charm but it had some faults. He told me what they were and how to correct them. He said I should leave out some of the extraneous detail and show more of my reactions, as the reader was interested in me and my husband as people. He said I had a wealth of exciting material and my script was off to a good start and had the making of a fine book.

I thought it was nice of him to write me a personal criticism so I spent the winter writing it. I sent it out again this time to a Canadian Publishing House. It came back today with a nice letter. They said that they got many manuscripts of a similar type but none that have been more successful in holding the interest of the reader. They said that at the present time publishing conditions were so unsatisfactory that they had to curtail their publishing lists very drastically so they were returning it. At least I've had a personal letter from both editors instead of the usual rejection slip.

A book on writing says it is often necessary to send a book to twelve or fifteen different publishers before it is accepted. I'm sure my friends would enjoy reading it; maybe they wouldn't be quite as critical as the editors.

How is Mother Allen? I often think of her. I seem to have rather neglected the letter writing. I write to so many people that I guess I need a private secretary. I had a letter today from a missionary in Nigeria, Africa and a Miss Le Rhine in Toronto writes me, also a Mary Zimmerman from Lancaster, Penn. - so many people that I've never seen. I do enjoy their letters though.

Well, I guess I've rambled on quite long enough.

Is Barbara a Jay, Maine girl? What is her other name?

I shall be glad when this war is over. It is hard on war brides to have no home and no husband.

Myself, I don't see how there can ever be peace again until Christ comes to rule in righteousness. Man has failed all along the line and will fail without God. I believe that God will soon pound out his wrath upon the wicked nations and the "Time of Jacob's Trouble" is not far off.

Well, I better not start on that. Thanks for the bias tape. I had a surprise birthday party. My Reid Lake neighbors came to dinner, eighteen in all. Everyone brought me a present and brought Jeannie cards of congratulations and money so she got $7.00. It was a surprise to both us.

I suppose your school will soon close and you will be home again.

I'll be looking for a letter then.

Lovingly, Nellie

Ness Lake, B.C.
August 8, 1944

Dear Reta,

I'm enclosing a letter Jean sent on to me to send you. I'm sure I sent her your address but she must have overlooked it. I've had the letter a couple of weeks or more, so I'm the tardy one, not Jean.

She was hoping she could see Emerson if she got to Montreal but I don't know whether she did or not. She wrote me last week that Emerson made arrangements for her to come to New York but she was sick and the doctor told her to stay in bed a week so she didn't go.

Emerson wrote on the 24th and I just got it today saying the last mail was closing and he was going on a long trip, - not to worry if I didn't hear anything for two or three months. It is rather hard on these war brides without a home or a husband either.

We got Barbara and Hamlin's wedding invitation. I'd loved to come to the wedding but we were too far away. I am going to write Barbara right away.

We have had the driest summer since we came to B.C. It seems to rain in some places but has a way of passing us by. However, our garden isn't too bad and we seem to get quite a bit out of it.

I've had quite a lot of company. This seems to be "Open House" and I never know when anyone is coming. We have had a fine young Christian lad with us since the first of June. There is so little we can do for the Lord that we undertook to support a worker for the summer. It has been nice to have services in the school but he has to go home now to help with the harvest and then back to Bible School another year. We shall miss him.

Last weekend two girls who were holding Vacation Bible School in Reid Lake came up to spend the weekend with us. One day last week I had thirteen to dinner and today four came just before I peeled potatoes. Mr. Persing brought his engine and put it on our boat and the men have gone up the lake looking for a bear. There seem to be a lot around this summer.

I want to write a few lines to Jean and send my mail off when they go back to town.

I'll try to do better next time and write sooner.

I heard from Blanche Hight and Emma today.

Love to all, Nellie

The following is an excerpt from a letter of Nellie's sister, Ruth, dated May 13, 1977.

As to what I know about our ancestors...

Our grandfather, Jacob Richner, was Swiss and came from Ruppersye, Switzerland that is a small town between Basil and Zurich. His wife Anna was German. I believe her parents objected to her marrying Jacob because they were well off and he wasn't. However, she married him just the same. After their four children were born he decided to come to America. He wanted to go alone and find a job and place to live before the family went over, but she said she had heard of men going to America and never being heard of after – so where he went she was going. They settled in Rosendale, Massachusetts where there were other German speaking families. He died at the age of forty-three leaving my father, Rudolph, to look after his mother. Rudolph, my father, learned the manufacturing jewelers trade and, in 1882 he moved to Portland and established his own business. His two older sisters married and his mother and his younger sister, Ida, came to Portland and lived with our family until they died. I don't remember much about my

Rudolph & Florence Richner

grandmother Richner as I was very young when she died. I remember her as a large, comfortable person with a nice lap to sit on. The only thing my cousins about my own age remember about her is that she scraped her apple to eat it instead of cutting it. Sometimes I wonder what one of my peculiarities my grandchildren will remember about me.

As for the Hamblin family (on my mother's side) Gideon had a farm in North Deering very near Portland. He and my grandmother, Vienna had, I think, twelve children. After my grandfather died my grandmother came to live with us. She spent her time reading and making quilts. She made a quilt for each of her grandchildren and I still have mine and my brother Rudolph's, although they are the worse for wear by now. I think Nellie was the most like Grandma Hamblin in her looks. I think in her younger days she must have been an active person as Nell was.

May They Rest In Peace

*George & Nellie
in their later years*

*George Herbert Campbell - was born in Wells, Maine on April 1, 1882
and died on June 30, 1972 at the age of 90.*

*Nellie Florence Campbell - was born in Portland, Maine on May 6, 1890
and died on October 1, 1961 at the age of 71,
They are buried in the Prince George Cemetery*

CEMETERY

CAMPBELL

GEORGE
APRIL 1, 1882
JUNE 30, 1972

NELLIE
MAY 6, 1890
OCTOBER 1, 1961

© Mended Memories

Book Three

Published
Articles
Written by
Nellie & George
Campbell

I NEVER GET LONESOME

By Nellie R. Campbell

I read Mary Smith's article "Prairie Farm Women Are Lonesome," with deep interest for I, too, came to the prairies as a bride but that was thirty years ago. Had it not been for a most terrifying incident that took place in the early part of my married life I might have become another Mary Smith.

Bert and I were married in a little prairie town so like hundreds of prairie towns that the name doesn't really matter. His shack was in no way different from the other bachelor's shacks that dotted the prairie 30 years ago. It was small, grey and weather beaten and stood alone on a never-ending prairie. The first two weeks of my married life were busy ones transforming the bare little room into one of beauty; however, kalsomine, dainty muslin and yards of gay cretonne did the trick. With my house all set in order there was very little for me to do. Then came a sudden "let down".

It was July. The days were hot and I missed the trees and my friends. At suppertime Shorty appeared. He wanted Bert to come to look at a sick animal. I watched them drive away in the wagon. I looked at the clock, then settled down to read. Bert should be home by nine. The shack was so still and empty I could not keep my mind on the story, so I picked up my mending. Nine o'clock came and went, nine-thirty, then ten, ten-thirty. I grew madder and madder. Bert simply couldn't do this to me—leave me all alone. The stillness was unbearable. The clock struck eleven and my anger died as suddenly as it had been born. Bert had been hurt. Why hadn't I thought of it before? The horses had run away. Bert was somewhere out on the vast prairie with a broken leg—he might even be dead. The clock ticked on while I sat and conjured up all sorts of dire catastrophies. With the stroke of twelve I realized I must do something, but what? There was no telephone so I would have to go out and search.

THE COYOTES HOWL

The sky was overcast and the prairie stretched out black before me. I was glad I had left the light in the window. The prairie was uneven and I went slowly, and suddenly I stopped frozen with fear. From out of the darkness far ahead came the howl of a coyote. When the last wailing note had died away, I turned and ran for the small light shining in the window. Once inside the shack I bolted the door and then threw myself across the bed and sobbed. It was sometime after one that I heard the rumble of wagon wheels and then Bert's cheery whistle.

Long after Bert was asleep I lay awake doing some very serious thinking. He and Shorty had been cutting hay in a big slough close to Shorty's place. While he was in the vicinity of this slough, Bert had decided to throw on a load. It would save him a trip down in the morning. He had thought that I might like to ride into town with him on the load and while he was delivering the hay at the livery barn I could do a bit of shopping. Of course it had been the logical thing to do and had never once occurred to him that I would worry. I had not known that in those early days men often worked early and late and because of my loneliness and fear of the prairies I had made myself most miserable making mountains out of molehills. After all, would not my life here on the prairie, be exactly what I made of it? I had left my friends and my old way of life back in New England but I could make new friends and find other interests here on the prairie. I would have chickens and there was the garden Bert had planted and never had time to tend. Could I not find real happiness in my home and in those little commonplace incidents that from now on will be a part of my new life? I felt sure that I could, and before I finally went to sleep I knew that never again would I let the loneliness or the vastness of the prairie get me down.

CLOTHES TO MEND

It was fall. I felt I must get out and walk away my restlessness, so I started off across the prairies. That was how I discovered the badger holes. It was a deep hole slanting into the ground. I was sure some animal had made it. Could he, by any chance be lurking inside? I stooped down to see. There was something inside but it wasn't an animal—it was cloth. I reached in and pulled out a perfectly good shirt of fine khaki flannel, that is, it was good except for the lower part of the sleeves which needed patching. At the next hole I retrieved a pair of overalls and two pair of wool socks. The overalls were still wearable with a bit of mending. I could knit new feet in the socks. My loneliness was entirely forgotten as I searched for more badger holes in the vicinity of our shack.

When Bert came home in to supper he stopped and stared and then that slow grin spread over his face. In our one and only chair was a heavy brown mackinaw, shirts, overalls, underwear and socks which I had gotten out of the badger holes. It seemed that Bert had had the mistaken idea that because I had always lived in a city that I wouldn't want to begin my married life by mending a lot of old clothes. He had discarded his old cook stove and bought an oil stove just before my arrival. One couldn't possibly burn up old clothing in an oil stove and in July the prairie was too dry to think of starting a bon-fire. What better place than the badger holes?

ROOSTER TROUBLE

It was one day in September that Nick, my German neighbor, brought me a hen with seven downy little chickens. He had found them in his haymow. I was delighted with my little flock but Bert was most sceptical. "It's too late to think of raising chicks," Bert averred. However, I could visualize a flock of Plymouth Rocks of which anyone might well be proud. "All right," Bert said, "but you'll have to take care of them."

Several weeks later friends gave us a young Plymouth Rock rooster for our Thanksgiving dinner. There was still a couple of weeks before Thanksgiving so Theobold (we named him for the family that gave him to us) strutted proudly about the barnyard. By the time Thanksgiving actually arrived I had persuaded Bert that it was a crime to kill such a lovely bird and that he should be willing to forgo his

Thanksgiving roast in order that Theobold might become the father of the flock I was about to raise.

In the spring a neighbor lent me several setting hens. By the following spring my flock had increased in such proportions that I felt that I should buy another rooster. He was a heavy Barred Rock that we called Turner. Poor Turner—he had hardly time to survey his new surroundings when Theobold strutted around the corner of the barn. Hostilities began at once. "There's nothing you can do about it," Bert declared. "They will keep it up until one or the other is boss." Then one evening Bert found Turner sitting dejectedly beside the well. His head was bloody and both eyes were shut. He carried him to the henhouse and placed him on the roost. The next day Theobold strutted about the yard calling and chortling to his many wives who came running at his beck and call. At last supremacy had been established or had it?

The following day Theobold was far less perky and then I noticed that he was no longer eating. After he had gone to roost we went to the henhouse to examine him. We thought that his jaw was broken but it was too dark to be sure so we carried him to the house. "With a broken jaw he will never be able to eat," Bert said, "so the only thing to do is kill him." As the axe was at the barn and it was already dark, Bert suggested leaving him in the box at the end of the shack until morning.

"Well, if he must die at dawn, the poor bird's not going to bed hungry if I can help it," I replied. Seated on the floor beside him I offered him bits of bread soaked in milk. He gulped them down greedily from a silver teaspoon. He did so well the next morning on bits of porridge and fried potatoes that execution was stayed. He seemed quite content to remain in the box by the shack which was some distance from the barn and to be fed from a spoon. He became very tame during the weeks of his convalescence but the day came when his jaw was completely healed and he no longer needed to be fed. It seemed useless to return him to the barnyard, as hostilities would only start afresh and besides I had grown very fond of him.

"Well, you know we missed out on Thanksgiving dinner," Bert hinted rather broadly. "All right, we'll have a roast bird for dinner tomorrow," I replied, "but let's eat Turner."

THRESHING

I remember how excited I had been that day the threshing rig came up the road and made the stand in the field across the road. I could hardly wait until supper was over and Bert would go over with me so that I could watch the machine in operation. It was the first threshing machine that I had ever seen. Then there was that first threshing crew to feed.

I saw Martha, our one and only close woman neighbor, coming across the stubble one morning, her faint blue apron flapping in the prairie breeze. She suggested that the machine make its stand between the two places and that we feed the crew at her house. She brushed back a wisp of greying hair with a capable hand.

"You know I'm getting old and it would be so nice to have a little help this year," when all the time I was the one who needed the help. Martha taught me the two essentials in cooking for a threshing crew ---good food and plenty of it and meals on time. She always sent me to the field with the afternoon lunch. There was time to watch the empty racks go bumping across the field and the racks piled high with bundles pull into the machine. The steady stream of yellow grain pouring out always fascinated me and I watched the straw stack grow bigger and bigger. After the last dish was washed and the table set for morning I would trudge back across the stubble with Bert to our own shack. It would be the same tomorrow and the next day and the next but I loved it all.

We seemed to live such a strenuous life on the prairie from early spring to late fall that I actually found myself looking forward to winter. When the threshing was finally over and the last load of grain hauled to the elevator we could relax. I enjoyed the luxury of staying in bed until it was actually light –something I had never done in my teaching days. Then there were our leisurely breakfasts each morning. We could sit and talk as we sipped a second cup of coffee. There was no need for haste. There was time to read and Bert and I read many worthwhile books during those winter months. Sometimes Bert would read aloud while I knit or sewed or I would read while he mended a set of harnesses or did some other repair job that he could bring into the house. One winter I took a correspondence course – one that I had wanted to take for some time. The winter passed and it would be spring again almost before we knew it.

Webster defined *'lonesome'* as secluded from society, depressed. Bert and I have certainly been secluded from society the greater part of our married life but we have not been 'depressed'. I wonder if after all, loneliness is not more a matter of the heart. If one has real peace and contentment within I doubt if he ever could be lonely.

Published Jan. 25, 1950
Family Herald and Weekly Star
Sold--$17.13

WE BUILT A LOG CABIN
By Nellie R. Campbell

It was that small pamphlet on "How to Pre-empt Land in British Columbia," that started the whole affair. By the time that Bert, my husband, had finished reading it he was quite sure that there was nothing for us but the simple life. His soul yearned for the lakes and forests and for those wide open spaces far from the maddening crowd and yes - a bit of land he could call his own.

However, I was still a bit skeptical. A hundred and sixty acres of land for only a two dollar entry fee sounded too good to be true. Bert had skipped a bit too lightly over that five year residence clause and also that one about making improvements to the value of fifteen hundred dollars. "Naturally one would want to make improvements and as for staying, why, you just couldn't pry me off the land," Bert argued. Who was I to object in the face of such optimism?

That was how we found ourselves, one day in late autumn, cutting down trees to build ourselves a log cabin on the shore of lovely Ness Lake, just north of fifty-four. As soon as we saw it, we both knew that we had found the ideal spot for our log cabin. The ground was fairly level at this point and lay at the top of a bank that sloped gently down to the lake below. Bert began at once to clear away the underbrush and level the ground for building. The fact that we had had no experience in building and that we had less than three hundred dollars to buy the necessary lumber and our food for how 'long' could not dim his cheerful optimism.

If this was to be our permanent home, we knew that there should be a good foundation but we also knew that over twenty miles of rough trail lay between us and the nearest town.

Already ice was beginning to form on the edge of the cove and we realized that it was too late to think of any cement work, so Bert decided to cut heavy blocks of Douglas Fir for corner posts on which to rest the bottom logs to prevent them from rotting. He could replace them later with cement posts.

We soon gave up the idea of building a spacious cabin of nicely peeled spruce logs, as we discovered that the smaller logs of Jack Pine and Douglas Fir that grew close to our building site were all that we could handle when cut in fourteen foot lengths. Slowly day by day the walls went up. Bert bored holes in each log to pin it to the log below with heavy wooden pins. He had been told that this would make a straighter wall and prevent it from buckling.

The question of obtaining lumber in this wilderness for roof boards and flooring loomed ever before us. This problem was solved in a most unexpected way. A trapper, who owned a small cabin farther up the lake, had bought a quantity of mill ends and had them shipped to a railroad siding fourteen miles away. Could we use some of this lumber as he found he had more than he actually needed? It mattered little to Bert that the lumber proved to be of varying lengths, widths, and thickness for with careful planning he could use most of it.

There was a decided nip in the air both morning and evening and we were learning that camping out in the north in November is not the pleasure that it can be in June. One morning we awoke to find that winter had actually come. Our tent roof sagged under it's weight of snow. Our cook stove wore a white shroud and the branches of the birches glistened in the morning sun. That day we moved into our cabin even if it was not finished. We were brought to a realization that there were two important factors that we had utterly failed to take into consideration, the length of time it would take us to cut and peel the logs and put up the cabin and the shortness of the summer north of fifty-four. We were to learn that the snow often comes late in October and remains until sometime in May.

To be sure we had four walls, a floor and a roof, but one who has never built a log cabin can have no idea of the many, many cracks that must be filled. The temperature was dropping steadily and the wind whistled in between the logs. Filling these cracks with mud plaster was no easy task in zero weather. Even after mixing our mud with boiling water, it froze as soon as it was forced between the ice cold logs.

The ground was white and the quiet cold that had settled over this northland still seeped into our cabin. Bert decided that the only thing to do was to mud the cracks on the inside of the cabin as well. Sure that it would keep out the cold, he made a small trap door in the floor and started digging. The small pit he dug was an ideal place to keep our few vegetables which had hitherto been wrapped in blankets

that were sorely needed. All day we forced wet mud between those icy logs. By night our hands were red and sore, but our cabin would be warm and comfortable and that feeling of accomplishment quite offset all of our physical discomfort.

Even Bert's cheerful optimism

George is building his log cabin

was somewhat dimmed the following morning when he viewed our walls. There had not been sufficient heat from the cook stove (we had no heater) to even begin to dry the mud, and it had frozen. Already white hoar frost had begun to appear along each crack. It widened and the frost grew thicker day by day. We donned our winter coats, for instead of a snug log cabin we had built ourselves a Frigidaire.

THOSE STOVE PIPES

With no upstairs floor, what heat we had promptly rose to the peak of our new home and left us shivering far below. To make matters worse, our long length of stove pipe without sufficient support had a tendency to part company at the most inconvenient moments. There was only one thing to be done. One of us must climb up on a chair on top of the table and struggle valiantly with hot stove pipes until they were once more in place. I could wear sufficient clothing to keep warm but I never could become accustomed to those rifle like reports that woke me in the dead of night. Even after I knew that they were caused by the expansion of frozen logs in our walls, I would lay awake for hours. The moisture from my breath had formed hoar frost on my eyebrows and hair and this same moisture released in a sub-zero temperature soon congealed on the edges of our blankets. How could one sleep with icicles under one's chin?

I soon made no pretense of setting the table in the morning and our breakfasts became most intimate affairs. Bundled up in our winter coats with the breadboard across our knees, we sat huddled close beside the open oven door. The coffee pot, fry pan and porridge dish remained on the stove within easy reach and we simply helped ourselves. If the side closest to the fire became too warm while the shivers raced up and down the other side there was only one thing to do - change places.

REAL PIONEERING

The steady cold continued. The sharp, tangy air gave us ravenous appetites and daily we watched our supplies dwindling until there was nothing left except a few small potatoes and a little bear meat. One night our lamp flickered and then went out. There was no more oil. We soon discarded the saucer filled with bear grease with a rag for a wick. Eskimos may like their blubber lamps but ours certainly could not be called a success. Besides smoking badly it gave off a most offensive odour.

It was nearly the end of January before the terrible cold abated and our nearest neighbor made the forty-two mile trip into town and back, his sleighs loaded with the groceries that we had ordered over two months before from a mail order house. A juicy bear steak sounds most appetizing but a steady diet of bear meat can grow rather monotonous as Bert and I found out that winter.

With the coming of the warm spring days the mud with which we had so laboriously plastered our cabin, began to thaw, crumble, and then drop off. This sad experience taught us that mud plastering is really one of the fine arts. Fortunately there was a Ukrainian family living only a few miles away and as mud for construction had been employed in Russia for many hundreds of years, surely anyone having lived in White Russia would know this art.

We found Mrs. Linenko a kindly sympathetic soul. It seemed that we had done everything wrong. Our soil had been far too light and sandy, as the plaster required a sticky clay. This mud plaster must dry without freezing so mudding must be done in the summer months. She advised us to clean out every bit of the old plaster between the logs and then to cut small willow or poplar withes to be used as lathes to hold the plaster. These must be nailed onto the walls diagonally about one inch apart giving the walls a ribbed effect. Bert could find real gooey clay at the west end of the island. She assured us that by the time we had followed her instructions she and her daughter would come to take a hand in the actual mudding.

PLASTERING AN ART

It was a warm, sunny morning when they rode in on horseback. At once they set to work carefully raking the ground directly in front of our cabin door. The top soil was loosened with a hoe for the depth of six inches or more in this cleared space and then the clay which Bert and I had brought down the lake in an old dug-out canoe loaned to us by a trapper, was heaped in the center.

The Ukrainians use manure, chaft, or chopped slough grass to give fibre to the plaster but lacking these materials we used a fern like moss that we found beneath the trees in shady places.

After the whole area had been saturated with water, the young girl sprang nimbly into the saddle and the mixing began. Back and forth and round and round she drove the horse in this small area. At first the moss kept the horse's feet fairly clean but as it was tramped into the clay and silt below, great gobs of mud clung to his hooves. More water was added and the sticky mixture pulled back into the center with the hoe. The tramping and mixing went on until there was a sucking sound each time the animal raised a foot and when his hooves came out clean from the stiffening clay, the plaster was ready for use.

Bert was kept busy filling pails with plaster for the women. It seems that when one is accustomed to it, this sort of work goes very quickly. They began at the bottom and worked upward. A large handful of mud was literally thrown at the wall from a distance of three feet or more. This was done to fill up all the chinks and force the mud around the willow withes making a solid wall. As soon as a small area had been covered, it was smoothed with the wet palm of the hand. When one wall had been finished a smooth, wet board was used to even the wall and take out the imperfections. Starting from the top they worked downward, keeping the board wet so that it would slide easily over the plastered surface. By later afternoon the logs had been completely hidden behind solid mud walls.

Before our kindly neighbors left they gave us final instructions if the door and windows were left open, the circulation of air would hasten the drying. We were not to be at all alarmed when small hair-like cracks appeared, as the plaster dried. These must be filled in when the wall was dry by wetting a piece of sacking and gently rubbing the surface. The sacking must be kept wet to resurface the wall. Then when it was thoroughly dry it was ready for a coat of lime or kalsomine.

Many of the Ukrainians mud plaster both the inside and outside of their houses. The inside resembles lime plastered walls while the outside has the appearance of stucco. We decided that we much preferred our log cabin here in our wilderness so we set about mudding the cracks between the logs on the outside — this time with plaster that we were sure would stick. Today all of our rooms have mud plastered walls, kalsomined in light shades. If it had not been for that first chilly winter, we no doubt would have not learned the fine art of mud plastering.

Each year as time and money would permit, Bert has improved our cabin home. One summer he built the addition on the south side giving us two more rooms downstairs and a bedroom above. Then there was the summer that he built the storage room in the basement for the vegetables and preserves. The next year he built a brick chimney on the outside of the cabin and installed a hot air furnace.

In this country where it is necessary for us to get in the bulk of our winter's supply before the end of October, a storeroom is most essential. A few years ago we built on a pantry and a screened and glassed in porch overlooking the lake.

The original shakes, made by splitting thin slabs from blocks of fir have long since been replaced by cedar shingles. I am quite sure that moving in and then building the house around one as Bert and I did, is not the approved method of building. Had we sufficient capital and a good set of blueprints we might have avoided many of the mistakes that we made but would we have had the fun of saving, planning and working together with our own hands to build a home in virgin forests?

The little pamphlet was partly right – rivers, lakes, forests, wild game – they are all here but there was one thing that it failed to mention –that peace and contentment could be found in a small log cabin on the shore of one of its lovely lakes. It was Bert who discovered that.

Published February 14, 1952
Family Herald and Weekly Star
Sold $28.00

IT WAS A GIFT!
By Nellie R. Campbell

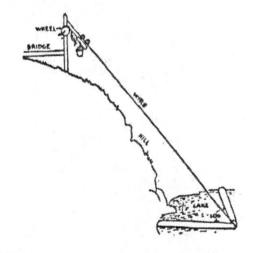

Perhaps, had we not stopped that day to buy a Bible in the Czechoslovakian language, we might never have had any water works. It was our first trip to Vancouver. For a long time I had known that our Czech neighbors had wanted a Bible in their own language. At the British and Foreign Bible Society we found one. It was the very last one in stock and as these were war days it would be impossible to get any more. We had it carefully wrapped and mailed to our neighbor.

A few days after our return our Czech friend came to see us. He was delighted with his Bible and wanted to pay us. "But George," I protested, "that was a gift. One never pays for a gift." He pondered my words for a while and then left rather abruptly. Had I offended him in some way, I wondered?

A few days later he was back. This time it was Eaton's Catalogue that he wanted. He sat at the kitchen table turning its pages. His face lighted up - he had found what he had been looking for. He pointed to a cotton clothes line, a clothes line pulley and some heavy wire. "You buy rope, wire, and pulleys and Steve and I make water works for you." His tone was decisive.

Bert and I had never felt that we could afford to buy an engine to pump the water from the lake that lay sixty-five feet below us. For years we had packed all the water that we used up this steep hill. It certainly was very little to buy and everything could be purchased at our local hardware store the next time we went into town. It was a sunny morning a little over a week later that George and Steve appeared ready for work. They first cleared all the underbrush away making a straight path from the bank of the house down to the lake. This done, they cut two tall Douglas Firs on the lakeshore. They were cut into twenty-five foot logs and peeled. The butt ends of the logs were then securely anchored to the shore about fifteen or eighteen feet apart and the two logs drawn in to meet in a point out in the deep water. They were bolted together at the point.

Nobody Ever Pays . . .

Then work on the bridge began. A wooden platform was built from the roadway back of the house for twenty-five feet out over the brow of the hill. One of the outer corner posts extended all of seven feet above the bridge. A hole was bored through this post a few inches down from the top and one end of the wire passed through the hole and attached to a windlass fashioned from a four inch birch pole which had been attached to the back of the post. The wire was then taken down the hill to the lake and the other end fastened securely at the point where the two logs in the lake met. By means of the small windlass on the back of the post the wire could be kept taut at all times as it could be tightened or loosened as the water in the lake rose or fell.

The two clothes line pulleys were attached to the top of a short piece of 2 x 4 at either end and a snap was fastened at the bottom of the 2 x 4 in the center. The clothes line pulleys were slipped onto the wire just before it was passed through the hole in the post and attached to the windlass.

They next constructed a wooden wheel 22 inches in diameter with wide flanges, using three layers of smooth boards. This wheel was set in a wooden frame work fastened to the inside of the tall corner post and was turned by a wooden handle attached to the axle. One end of the clothes line was nailed to the rim of the wheel and the rope wound around the wheel. The flanges on either side prevented the rope from slipping off. The other end of the rope was fastened to the end of the 2 x 4 on the wire with a heavy staple. As the rope on the wheel is unwound the pulleys on the wire carry the empty pail snapped to the bottom of the 2 x 4 to the lake sixty-five feet below. The pail hits the water on a slant and fills instantly.

Thirty-five turns on the wooden wheel brings a brimming pail of water back to the bridge.

Bert wanted to pay our good neighbors for the two days it had taken them to install a water system that would mean so much to us, but George slowly shook his head. A slow smile spread over his face. "That is a - what you call him - a geeft. Nobody ever pays for a geeft."

Published July 27, 1950
Family Herald and Weekly Star

THE THANKSGIVING WE FORGOT!
By Nellie R. Campbell

Bert had just finished skinning the big buck deer he had shot the day before and was cutting it into pieces that I could handle for canning. One soon learns to depend largely on game when he lives in this north country over twenty miles from a town.

Sonny was struggling valiantly with an arithmetic problem, his pencil clutched grimly between stubby fingers, a deep pucker between his brows. The nearest school was six miles away, much too far for even his strong legs to travel twice a day over bushy trails in this unsettled country.

I had just taken a peep at the chunk of venison roasting in the oven and sending forth such appealing odors, when we heard the chug, chug of a motor. In those days cars were not common north of fifty-four and one actually stopping in front of your own cabin door was an event. Our guests proved to be the district

Forest Ranger and his wife. Perhaps it was because of his great love for these giant forests and the wild life that surrounded us, that Bert found in this tall, gaunt ranger, a kindred spirit.

Martha took off her hat and looked at Sonny still struggling with his problem. "Surely your mother doesn't make you do your lessons on Thanksgiving day," she asked, with sympathy in her voice.

Thanksgiving day, surely this beautiful October day couldn't be Thanksgiving. My mind went back to other Thanksgiving days in old New England. They were always near the end of November. The ground was frozen and the chill winds had stripped the leaves from the trees leaving them standing gaunt and bare.

'TWAS A GOOD DINNER

There had been days of preparation. The entire house had to be put in apple pie order. The silver must be clean and polished until it fairly shone. All day the day before Thanksgiving, the house was filled with the most delectable odors. There were mince and pumpkin pies browning in the oven, fresh bread and cinnamon buns, spice cookies and sugar coated doughnuts cooling on the kitchen table. Then, of course, there was the plump turkey that must be cleaned and stuffed the evening before and the huge roaster set away in a cool place to await the exciting moment when the bird would be placed in the oven to roast. With everything in readiness there was ample time to attend the Thanksgiving service in the church. It was just as the vegetables were beginning to bubble merrily in the pot and the turkey was turning a delightful, crunchy brown that our guests would arrive.

Here were my guests, but where, oh where was my Thanksgiving dinner? I had forgotten that in the land of my adoption Thanksgiving came in October. Bert and Alex were already planning a trip up to the lake in our old dugout to look at a bit of timber. "Want to come, Sonny?" Bert asked.

I watched the sturdy little legs go racing down the hill to the lake, far ahead of the men. Arithmetic problems were forgotten.

"We'll be back in about an hour and a half," Alex called. I looked at the clock. Just eleven. "I'll have dinner at one," I promised. Just two hours to prepare a traditional Thanksgiving dinner.

Martha and I made a trip to the root house and came back with our arms laden. Martha had even stopped to pick a cluster of Oregon grapes that she had spied growing just off the trail. "These beautiful glossy leaves will add a festive touch to the table," she confided.

"If you'll prepare the vegetables, I'll get a couple of pies into the oven in short order and then make a pan of baking powder biscuits. I'm sure the roast is brown enough so that we can finish cooking it slowly on the back of the stove."

It was nearly one when we saw the canoe gliding silently into the cove, but our Thanksgiving dinner was ready. I turned from the wide windows that looked out upon the blue, blue water of the lake, now still as glass. My home was only a log cabin on its shore. Most of our furniture was homemade, yet as I glanced about our living room that Thanksgiving day, at the shelves filled with books, the pictures on the walls, the old couch with it's many cushions, yes, even the cluster of Oregon grapes that Martha had placed on the table, I knew that it had that homey, lived in look.

The men were unanimous in declaring that roast venison was a very good substitute for the traditional turkey. The size of the helpings proved it. I looked at the big glass bowl, piled high with mashed potatoes, tiny rivulets of golden butter trickling down the sides of the creamy mound. It was the first of July when Bert had discovered that the seed potato, so carefully planted that spring, was being eaten up by yellow wireworms. It had been a slow and tedious task to dig up each bit of seed in the entire patch and pick out the worms from the seed and each hill as well, replanting the bit of honeycombed seed, but we had done it – and such a yield.

The carrots were coming my way. There might not have been any carrots at all, if Bert had not curbed my activities just in the nick of time. I had offered to hoe the garden but in my zeal to get all the weeds, I had overlooked the fact that young carrots are such very tiny little plants. Half of one row had entirely disappeared when Bert came to their rescue.

THANKFUL MEMORIES

Canning peas had looked such a formidable job to me until Bert suggested that we all take a hand at it. He and Sonny would pick peas while I washed and sterilized the jars, then we would have a shelling bee to see which one could shell the most peas. It was agreed that the losers would have to get supper that night. My - how the peas had popped out of those pods. Sonny, with the optimism of youth, had been sure that he would win but I had beaten him. There had been much whispering between the losers and then a raid on my pantry and supper turned out to be a picnic lunch served on the lakeshore after the last jar of peas had been lifted from the boiler. There had been a story and a swim and then back to the cabin and bed. It had been fun after all.

We had discovered the cranberries quite by accident. They grew on the bog that jutted out into the lake. Had it not been for an otter that slid off an old log that evening just as we were gliding silently by in the dug-out (canoe), Bert might never had explored the bog. He was sure that otters had a home there. That was when he found the cranberries.

Bert cut a generous piece of blueberry pie and topped it with whipped cream. I remember the day we had climbed the mountain - or was it only a high hill? Anyway, the biggest, juiciest berries grew near the very top. We had come down just at dusk, our pails that had been filled with lunch, now overflowing with luscious blueberries.

We stood in the doorway watching a small car chug it's way out the lane that led to the main road. Somehow the Thanksgiving we forgot had turned out to be one that we would always remember. The pleasant memories of those long summer days when we had been gathering fruits and vegetables for those long winter months that we knew lay ahead, had been woven into this Thanksgiving day. We had had a most bountiful feast and what was still better, congenial friends to enjoy it with us. I knew that here in the land of my adoption I had many, many things for which to give thanks to my Heavenly Father and I resolved that in the years ahead, each day would be one of real heartfelt thanks giving.

Published October 4, 1951
Family Herald and Weekly Star
Sold – $12.98

WHERE WOOD ABOUNDS
By Nellie R. Campbell

I watched the trucks loaded with wood, emerge from the woods trail, cross the clearing and come to a stop beside the woodhouse close to our log cabin. As I continued the preparations for dinner, I could hear the constant heavy thud of cordwood as it was added to the ever growing pile.

Bert came in, stamping the loose snow from his feet and settled himself in the big, red rocker in the kitchen. He pulled off his heavy boots and reached for his slippers. "Well, that's that for this year," he said, making for the washbasin. "Twelve cords of good, dry birch, - that should keep us warm. If it doesn't there's as much more piled in the bush."

Nellie standing beside their woodpile

As we sat down to eat, I noticed that Bert was in one of his reminiscent moods. "Remember that time way back on the prairie years ago when the tracks were drifted, so that no train got through from Regina to Saskatoon for six whole weeks, and there was no coal in any of the prairie towns."

I thought of the folks who had actually cut blocks off the bottoms of the telephone poles and let them drop back into the deep snow. It was only the wires that held them upright as every second or third pole grew shorter day by day. "That was the winter of 1907 and she was a tough one on the open prairies," Bert remarked.

It was a year or two later that our nearest neighbour had set out for the Sand Hills over thirty miles away. At that time small poplars could be found growing in pockets between low, sandy hills. He had left soon after daybreak, planning to stop at a homesteader's shack about six miles this side of the hills. With an early start the following morning, he could get his load and be well on his way back before dark.

When he reached the small poplar growth, he worked quickly, making every blow count. By the time the wood was cut and loaded, his heavy undershirt was wet with sweat. He pulled on his heavy mackinaw (coat) and headed the team toward the trail.

It was not until he had left the sheltering hills that he first noticed the high wind and the fine, sifting snow. By the time he struck the open prairie, the blizzard was on him. The wind shrieked and the biting particles of ice stung his face as they whirled about him. Scotty, his small terrier, crowded closer to him on the seat. The world had been changed into a smother of whirling white. At times he could not even see the horses that plodded on. The cruel wind penetrated his coat and chilled him to the bone, yet he dared not leave the sleigh to run behind. The horses lurched on through the blinding snow. Then his heart sank. He felt one runner sinking into the snow beside the trail. He quickly slid to the other side of the seat and pulled on the lines, but he was too late. He could not get back on the trail. The runner sunk deeper and the load tipped over.

He knew that it was impossible to right it in that raging blizzard. Already his fingers were numb with cold. There was only one thing that he could do – pull the pin from the eveners and leave the load where it was. With his numbed fingers it was no easy task to free the horses, but he knew they all must find shelter. He snatched Scotty up under one arm and drove on, but the dog refused to be carried and he found that he needed both hands to hold the team.

THE HANDY CABIN

The blizzard seemed to be increasing in fury and he had lost all sense of direction when the horses suddenly stopped. He urged them on, but they stood motionless in that swirling mass of white. Somehow he stumbled to their heads and found that their breasts were against the only barbed wire fence in the country at that time. He turned them and they followed that tiny strand of wire until they found an open gate. If he could only find a barn, he thought. He stood peering in all directions. For just a moment he thought he could see a dim outline and then it was blotted out as the snow whirled about him. He drove on and the horses once more stopped. This time they stopped before a barn door.

It was after the team was safely inside, that he missed little Scotty. He called and called, but the wind seemed to be laughing in derision, as it hurled his voice back at him. He waited but there was no joyous response. He clung to the corral fence. The house could not be far off. His entire body was growing numb with the intense cold. It was when he bumped into a woodpile that he found the house beside it. There was no response to his shouts but the door was unlocked.

It was the custom in the early days on the prairie to leave doors unlocked, because of the prairie blizzards. He found wood piled neatly beside the stove and food in the cupboard. He supposed that the owner had driven into town and the same blizzard that had kept him marooned in the cabin for two days and nights had prevented his return.

The sun shone brightly on the morning of the third day but it was close to noon before he had located his overturned load, righted the sleigh and once more – loaded on his wood. It was late that night before he finally reached home from a trip that had cost the life of little Scotty, and had it not been for a barbed wire fence, might have taken toll of his own life as well.

We had finished our dinner and Bert stood looking out of the window at the long pile of dry wood, but I knew that he was thinking of those far off days when so many of the prairie farmers had burned straw for fuel. Big oil drums were converted into heaters. They were packed solid with dry straw that burned slowly upward letting the fresh straw that burned slowly drop down into the fire, much in the same way that our modern sawdust burners do today. The only inconvenience was that when the straw in one drum had burned out, the drum had to be disconnected from the stovepipe, rolled outside to cool and be refilled and a new drum put back in its place.

He turned from the window. A wood fire was crackling in the big kitchen range. There was a good fire in our homemade furnace in the basement and waves of heat were pouring from the registers in both the kitchen and living room. The house was warm and comfortable in spite of the cold and snow outside. Although we had lived in British Columbia for many years, I knew that Bert had never wholly lost his love for the open prairies. He smiled as he again pulled on his heavy felts. "For real honest to goodness farming," he remarked, "the prairies are hard to beat, but for good, all round comfortable living, - well, I guess British Columbia is a little bit ahead of the prairie."

I heard the door close and I knew that Bert was on his way to the bush to cut more wood.

Published March 13, 1952
Family Herald and Weekly Star
Sold--$11.70

TIE HACKING IN BRITISH COLUMBIA
By Nellie R. Campbell

How well I remember the day that Bert told me that he had just signed a contract to cut five hundred ties. Ties, - at that time the work meant absolutely nothing to me, for those heavy timbers to which the rails were securely spiked, had always been called railroad sleepers, back in New England.

It was in 1930 and we had been in British Columbia just long enough to build a log cabin on our newly acquired homestead and to raise a small vegetable garden on the bit of clearing by our door. In all new countries, and this portion of British Columbia was very sparsely settled at that time, there seems to be some way in which the homesteader can make a living until his land becomes productive. The solution to our financial problems, like that of many of the settlers, was tie hacking.

It was in November that we locked our cabin door and moved onto the tie limit Bert had taken up at the top of the long hill that led down to the Nechako River. The trail curved in and out through a deep coulee with high rock cliffs on either side. It was a treacherous trail, not wide enough at any point for two tie sleighs to pass. On the upward trip each driver paused as he rounded a bend and gave a lusty shout. Often there would be an answer from somewhere along the trail above. The driver of the empty sleigh would promptly make for one of the few places cut into the bank and wait for the loaded sleigh to pass.

Late one afternoon, as I was returning from the Post Office across the river, I gratefully accepted a ride up the long Coulee Hill on one of the empty tie sleighs. At the first bend in the trail, the driver shouted, only to be answered by a shout dangerously near. A heavily loaded tie sleigh was just coming around the bend ahead. The long rawhide whip landed on the backs of the team and they sprang forward. Madly they raced up the hill toward the fast approaching load of ties. Fearfully I watched the distance narrow. The driver of the loaded sleigh was straining every muscle to hold his team back, while we were frantically urging the horses on. The two teams not more than a rod apart when the horses plunged into the opening at the side of the trail and stopped with a jolt, their sides heaving. The loaded sleigh slid past, the edge of the ties just scraping the end of our sleighs.

A DIFFICULT JOB

"Well, that was a pretty close one," the burly driver remarked as he drew out a big bandanna and mopped his face.

Tie hacking is not an easy job, especially for one not accustomed to swinging a heavy broad axe. Tall, straight Jack pine and Douglas fir are used mostly for ties. The trees must be cut down during the winter and early spring months before the sap begins to flow. After the limbs have been trimmed off, the tree is scraped with a single or double bitted axe, then the tie hacker stands upon the fallen tree trunk and hews both sides of the log with quick, even strokes of the broad axe, an axe with a wide twelve inch blade and weighing eight pounds or more.

All ties must be hewn to meet certain railway specifications. If the ties cut from the butt of the tree are too large, they are squared to the exact measurements. As the lot narrows, it is hewn on two sides only and the two rounded sides are peeled with a spud or draw knife. The log is then sawn into ties eight feet in length.

To facilitate the work of the tie loader in keeping tally of ties shipped by each individual, the tie maker has his own marker made of raised numbers and letters on a heavy hammer head. A single blow of the hammer on the end of a finished tie, cuts his number deep into the wood. Some tie makers mark their ties with a coloured crayon, but there is far less danger of loss if a marking hammer is used.

As soon as winter snows begin to deepen, trails are cut into the bush and tie hauling commences. In the winter of 1930, the drivers were experiencing great difficulty in getting the heavy loads of ties across the Nechako River to the C.N.R. tracks on the other side of the river.

I still marvel at the ingenuity of some of those early settlers. It would seem almost impossible to build a floating bridge of ice across the raging water of the Nechako River, but as soon as slush and chunks of broken ice came rushing down the river, the ferry had to be taken out and only a row boat attached to a heavy cable crossed the river until a bridge of ice was constructed.

The current along the north shore and in the centre of the river is so swift that water does not freeze solid even in our severest weather. For this reason, two fin-booms were thrown out into the water from the north bank extending well beyond the centre of the stream. A cable attached to the outer end of the boom was brought back and anchored securely to the shore holding the boom at a sharp angle to the bank. This boom shot the swiftly moving water toward the opposite bank and created a pocket of still water on its lower side, which soon froze solid. Logs were then cut on the south bank of the river and rolled to its edge, where they lay parallel with its bank. One end of a heavy cable was attached to the log lying farthest down stream and the other end fastened to a "dead man" (a log sunk into the ground, back from the waters edge).

Two men in a small boat, then dragged the other end of the log into the turbulent river and the swiftly moving current carried the log, and the boat, as well, across to the other end of the boom where it was fastened with a cable. Four heavy logs were carried across in this manner and fastened to the boom. Next small poles were thrown across these timbers and brush placed on top. The water, slush and broken ice, pouring constantly over this wooden framework, soon froze into a solid mass of ice which, extended all the way from the north bank to the south bank of the river, and day after day the loaded tie sleighs crossed to the C.N.R. tracks.

In 1930, slush and broken ice came rushing down the river, so the ferry was taken out and only a small rowboat attached to a cable carried passengers across the river. Day after day, the tie haulers hoped for a spell of sub-zero weather, so that the ice bridge could be put in, but the days remained fairly mild. There was no way of getting the ties across the river to the railroad siding a mile away.

As the days lengthened, there was less and less prospect of constructing the ice bridge and ties began to pile up on this side of the river. The tie men requested that the ferry be put into the river again, for green ties are heavy and they knew that all of those ties must be re-loaded and taken across the river to the railroad siding.

Both the tie haulers and the tie makers fretted as the days passed and there was no response to their request. It was on a Sunday morning that several of the tie haulers appeared at our cabin in an angry mood. They had decided to take matters into their own hands and shove the ferry in, in spite of strong protest from the ferryman. They needed Bert's help. It was some time before he had persuaded them that such, high-handed methods seldom paid and a day or two longer wouldn't make much difference. Rocky Clifford immediately set out on horseback for Prince George, over thirty miles away to see what could be done. In two days he was back with orders to begin the ferry service at once. A telegram had been sent to Victoria. Tie hauling now began in earnest and load after load of ties were ferried across the river.

The snow was beginning to melt and a few bare spots were showing on the Coulee Hill. A long strip of gravel marked the approach to the ferry. It was about a week after the ferry began to operate that Fred Ellas came down the Coulee Hill with a big load of ties. He had not been using the customary brakes on the back of his sleigh, but simply rough locks on the runner. As he neared the last steep pitch down to the ferry, he felt it would be a waste of time to stop to adjust the rough locks for the strip of gravel would surely slow up the team of horses sufficiently. As the horses rushed down the last pitch of the hill to the ferry, the ring at the end of one of the hames on the harness snapped, - letting the pole drop. No brakes, - no rough locks, - no pole, - nothing to help hold back nearly five tons of green ties sliding onto their heels. They raced across the strip of gravel, onto the ferry and plunged to their death in the icy waters of the Nechako River. As the load slid over the edge of the ferry, the driver jumped and caught the rail of the ferry. That night, each tie man was very glad that the ferry had not been put in without the consent of the Government.

THE CHANGING SCENE

The cutting still goes on in the forests of British Columbia. Many ties are still cut and hewed by hand as in those early days. In three districts alone in the Prince George area, eighty-three thousand ties were made by hand, this last year. But unlike those early years, many ties are now sawn out in the mills around Prince George, Vanderhoof and Fort Fraser. It is almost impossible to get an accurate estimate of the number of sawn ties produced in 1952 at the many mills, as they are no longer counted as ties, but as board feet.

Today, a railroad tie is worth far more than it was in 1930. A No.1 brings $1.70, No.2 - $1.50, and No.3 - $.90. Nearly all of the ties cut in this area are purchased by the C.N.R. for repair and construction work on its lines across Canada.

   As the years pass methods change. No longer does one see heavily loaded sleighs making their way down the Coulee Hill to the river, for trucks have taken their place. No ice bridge has been built across the Nechako River at Isle Pierre for many years now. Huge "cats" clear the roads into the bush for the tie loaders. Even the Nechako River has changed, for the completion of the Kenny Dam has changed the flow of the mighty river from east to west, so that the once turbulent Nechako has been reduced to a small stream. No doubt time has wrought many changes, but as long as trains run on tracks there will be a demand for ties, and so the hacking will go on in the forests of British Columbia.

Published May 14, 1953
Family Herald and Weekly Star
Sold--$20.00

SHE WAS JUST PLAIN ORNERY
By Nellie R. Campbell

Molly was just an ordinary cow, - that is, we thought she was that night we brought her home, but it was not long before Bert declared that there was nothing ordinary about her, - she was just plain ornery, - that is, she was at times.

Ever since our marriage, Bert had tried to convince me that the average prairie farmer, especially if he was a bachelor, had no time to fool around with a cow, pigs, chickens, or a garden either. But all this was changed. He was no longer a bachelor and I simply couldn't picture a farm without animals. That was the reason that I used the first money I earned, teaching at our district school, to buy Molly. I already had acquired a few chickens and felt confident that by fall I could persuade Bert that we really needed a pig.

I think it was sometime the first week that we had Molly, that Bert came running in late one afternoon and shouted, "Come on out and take a look at Molly."

"Just come and see for yourself," he answered, picking up the milk pail and vanishing through the door.

I followed meekly, picturing all sorts of dire catastrophes that might befall a cow. However, Molly was standing placidly in the field where she was tethered.

"What's wrong with her," I asked. Bert merely caught her by the head and pried her mouth open. "Well, take a look," he demanded. "She hasn't any front upper teeth. How do you expect a cow to eat these oats and give a full pail of milk without any upper teeth?"

Bert was right. Her front uppers were all missing. I felt ire rising. "The old skin-flint," I burst out, "charging me a hundred dollars for an old cow with no teeth. I bet Grenwood knew it all the time."

"I bet he did, to," Bert agreed.

A DIRTY DEAL!

I was far too angry to note the sly twinkle in his eye as I marched back to our prairie shack to prepare supper.

"What are you going to do about it?" he demanded, when he came in with the milk.

"Do with it? – Why I'm going to tell Grenwood exactly what I think of anyone who would pull off a dirty deal like that." I was still mad.

"Oh, I don't think I'd say anything about it," Bert said, placidly, - "you see, the good Lord saw fit to give all cows no upper teeth in front and they seem to do very nicely without them."

Bert thought that this was a huge joke. I might have a theoretical knowledge of cows, but I certainly didn't possess a working knowledge of the creatures, as I was to find out that fall.

If it wasn't for Molly he could work the team with a threshing outfit ten miles away. "But I can milk Molly," I assured him. From the glowing accounts of the summers I had spent on farms in New England where there were cows, one would gather that I had become quite adept in the art of milking. Not for worlds would I admit that I had never actually milked. It looked so simple that I was sure there was nothing to it.

Bert was milking Molly only once a day now. Molly seemed a bit puzzled over the whole performance, but stood patiently until I finally got the hang of it. My wrists ached before the five-pound pail was full, but I kept doggedly at it. Molly seemed quite relieved when the ordeal was over. She really wasn't half as ornery as Bert made out. It was all in the way you handled her.

A ONE TRACK MIND

By the next night Molly had come to the conclusion that she wanted no more of my milking while I decided that it was far easier on Molly to walk to the well, than it was for me to carry six pails of water to the oat field as I had done the night before. That was my first mistake. No sooner had I untied the chain from the stake, than she kicked up her heels and bolted, - her objective, - the wheat field. It was then that I learned that Molly had a one-track mind, coupled with determination. What was ninety pounds on the end of a fifty foot chain, - yet I hung on tenaciously. If Molly once escaped, how would I ever catch her again? My hat flew off. My hairpins dropped out one by one, as we charged across the oat patch and into the field of stooked wheat. The chain was slipping. I could not stand the pace. At last Molly stopped beside a stook at the far end of the field and began to eat the ripened grain, keeping a wary eye on me as I slowly and cautiously approached. When within ten feet of her, she snatched a final mouthful of wheat and once more bolted, but I grabbed for the chain that

Nellie and Emerson milking Molly

was racing past me and falling over the stook I clung to both stook and chain. Little by little, I pulled Molly back to the stook and got hold of her halter.

I would lead her to the well. That was my second mistake. Bert told me later that she had never been taught to lead. One walked behind her with a willow switch. She simply braced all four feet and refused to budge. I pulled and yanked until, with a sudden burst of speed, she literally lifted me off my feet and carried me twenty or thirty feet, stopping with a decided jolt and bracing her feet once more. She repeated these tactics time after time, but I stayed with her and each burst of speed seemed to bring us closer to the well. After she had had a drink, we used the same method to get back to the oat patch. It was not until the chain was once more securely tied to the stake, that I breathed a sigh of relief, and went for the pail and milking stool.

This is where I made my third mistake. How was I to know that she should have been tied up short for milking? No sooner had I begun, and the milk was actually coming, than she calmly walked away and left me. I followed. A bit more milk and she was gone. Time after time, I meekly followed her. My pail was nearly full when she once more walked away. I picked up the stool to follow when she suddenly turned and charged with lowered head. The chain caught me directly across the knees. I lay where I had fallen, too hurt to move. Milk was running down my neck and then I thought of Molly, with lowered head. This was no place to be, so I hastily sat up. Molly was standing only a few feet away, still with lowered head, surveying the havoc she had wrought. Every bone in my body seemed to ache and my right arm hung limp from the shoulder. Molly appeared quite indifferent to my misery and presently began to graze, so I felt that it was perfectly safe for me to sit there in the oats and weep awhile. At last I remembered that Bert had said that I must strip her at each milking. Well, I still had one good arm, so I wearily picked up the stool to finish my job. This time Molly stood perfectly still. As I carried a little dribble of milk back to the shack, I knew why Bert said Molly was just plain ornery and I heartily agreed.

It was early the following March that we traded her three month old bull calf for a small black heifer about the same age. It made little difference to Molly as her calf had been in a pen by itself and fed from a pail from the day it was born.

The feel of spring was in the air and bare spots were beginning to appear on the prairie roads, so we made haste to move to our new home before spring break-up. Spring might be coming to the prairies, but one of the worst snowstorms of the entire winter was raging that morning. The freight train car containing all of our worldly possessions was shunted onto the siding one hundred and fifty miles northwest, in northern Saskatchewan. With roads drifted as they were, it was possible to take only the most essential things on that twenty-three mile trip north to our newly acquired farm. Molly and the calf would have to be left in the livery barn. It was then that Molly adopted the little black heifer, as her own.

The country was sparsely settled, and there was little travel, so snow still lay deep on the road when Bert returned to town for more of our possessions and Molly. With the sleigh loaded and the calf tied securely in the back, Molly was turned loose to follow. Bert figured that it would be easier for her and the team, too, if she could set her own pace. At noon he stopped at a log farm home to milk and give her a brief rest, and then the journey was resumed. If she lagged too far behind, a frantic bawling from the rear of the sleigh seemed to lend speed to her tired legs. Twenty-three miles she came that day, through the snow all for the sake of a small black calf that was not even her own. What if she was ornery at times?

MOLLY'S DEPARTURE

It was an ideal cattle country to which we had come and with the purchase of two more cows, we watched our herd increase. I do not know whether it was because of her age or because of her at times, cantankerous disposition, that she became boss of the herd. They roamed the miles of free range to the east and north of us, growing fat on the lush pea vine.

At last the day came when we realized that Molly must be sold. She was sleek and smooth that morning Bert unloaded her in the corral beside the tracks and went up town to buy much needed groceries. When he returned, she was still peacefully munching the hay he had thrown to her, but as he untied the team her head went into the air and she emitted an angry snort. She was ready to go too. As Bert drove away, she raced madly around her narrow confines, searching for some way of escape and bellowing loudly.

"You know, Bert," I said, "I never felt so sorry for an animal in all my life. You expect a horse and a dog to show intelligence and affection, but a cow, - her to care in the least. If I hadn't already spent the money for the groceries, I think I would have brought her home again."

It was most fortunate that I didn't go to town with Bert that day, for if I had, I am sure I would have returned the groceries and brought Molly home.

Published September 13, 1951
Family Herald and Weekly Star
Sold--$14.82

THIS MOTHER CAT FEEDS MINK

Ever hear that a cat will adopt mink? Mr. G.H Campbell of Ness Lake, B.C, has a cat, which adopted seventeen mink. A female mink gave birth to a litter, but the mother did not have sufficient milk to feed them. The kits were hungry; they would cry by the hour and crawl out of their nest box.

Mrs. Campbell (Nellie), who assists her husband with his fur farm, would find them in this condition every morning, crying and lying chilled outside of their nest box. One morning she brought two chilled mink into the house to warm them in the oven, as this was the only way they could be warmed, satisfactorily. Fanny, the cat, came over to see them. She had two kittens in the box and promptly tried to take the young mink out of the oven. Mrs. Campbell drove her away, thinking she might harm the kits, but Fanny persisted several times and finally reached in the oven and took the young mink in her mouth and put it in the box with her kittens.

As the young were born on the mink ranch, every day there were two or three more to be added to her family, until Fanny had seventeen mink and two kittens. She did her best, but there were too many to feed and Mrs. Campbell had to assist

Fanny in her great task, arising in the night and feeding warm milk from an eyedropper. Fanny was good to the mink; she kept them clean and dry. Then, one day, four kits died and it was hard to determine the cause, but something was wrong. Mrs. Campbell discovered that she did not realize that the kits were ready for a meat diet, as well as milk, so all the mink were taken away from Fanny, but three. The others were put in two boxes and were large enough, by this time, to be attended to by Mrs. Campbell, without the aid of Fanny. But Fanny did not forget her adopted family. She would leave her family of two kittens and three kits to eat with the others. She always tried to take several back to her box.

The weather was getting warmer and it was time for the young mink to be put in the mink house. Fanny had done a good job and I am wondering if it would not pay mink ranchers to keep a number of female cats for such emergencies as this one; however, it might cost too much for upkeep and they

Fanny the cat is feeding the orphaned mink.

might not be docile like Fanny. Some cats might consider the young kits as nothing more than rats or mice. Fanny, nevertheless, raised about a dozen mink which, otherwise, would have had no mother. She is one cat, which has a very prominent place in the rounds of mink ranch life. Who knows, she may have introduced a new era in mink ranching. A rancher, however, might travel a long way to find a cat with a heart as big as Fanny's. What do you think?

Published April 5, 1950
Family Herald and Weekly Star

THESE KITTENS ARE KILLERS

I have a treatise before me that states that the cougar, when full grown, will perhaps measure seven feet in length from tip of tail to nose, certainly no more. On Feb. 12th and 13th of 1940, George Dyer of Red Rock, B.C. shot a cougar that measured eight feet eight inches in length. In 1938 he shot one that measured nine feet eight inches from tip to tip. V.C. Flick, of Woodpecker, B.C. shot a cougar that measured nine feet eight inches. Here are three authentic records, gathered from my files, which prove that cougar measure far more than the seven-foot measure, but in other parts of the continent they measure nine feet and more from tip of nose to tip of tail.

Although we are writing concerning the cougar of North America—panther, puma, painter or mountain lion –this animal ranges as far south as Patagonia, South America. The color is usually of a yellowish brown on the sides, a trifle darker on the back, and white on the throat and underparts. They are deadly where deer are concerned but will sometimes prey on wild sheep, goats, and moose as well as domestic stock. There are, however, no enemies, including man, more deadly to deer. Cougars know no closed season and kill both bucks and does.

Cougars will wait above a game trail and, as the unwary deer pass below, will drop upon their backs. In this manner they kill many deer during a lifetime. At times they creep toward unsuspecting prey, a short rush and pounce and the big cats have a meal of tender fawn or deer. Watch your cat or the neighbor's cat creep up to unsuspecting prey and pounce, and you will have a good idea concerning the big cats under similar circumstances stalking larger prey.

The cougar is reported to be polygamist in habit, a number of females have been seen in company with a tom. This may have been coincidence and not authentic proof, however. But the cat family is not inclined to be monogamist in habit, and the cougar is of the cat family. Its habits seem much the same as the household pussy, even to cleanliness.

Not always will cougar run from dogs. One party, on a fishing trip, with his fox terrier for company, was fishing a stream for trout when his dog let out a howl. He saw his pet terrier disappear into the forest, held in a cougar's jaws. I have been told that cougar's appreciate dog meat and more than one small dog has made a meal for the big cats. But I am inclined to think that cougar pounce upon stray dogs and at times attack man without provocation when they are old and their teeth are well worn. The cougar's cousin, the Bengal tiger, becomes a man-eater for this reason. There may be other contributing factors, but the one outstanding need always in the animal kingdom is that of food.

I read about a panther that had attacked a man. Eventually, the man killed the cougar with an axe. This big cat had worn claws and teeth; it was an old one and not able to kill its wild prey. Thus, I believe that dogs are killed by cougars and eaten when the big cats have no alternative; they are hungry and small dogs make easy pickings. Again, they may have a yen for dog meat. Tastes once acquired are not easily broken – even in the animal kingdom.

Rubin Hagen, twenty-three year old logger of our district, here in central B.C., wrestled on the hard packed snow of a logging trail for several minutes. He was not having a friendly bout with a companion of the logging camp; a 200-pound cougar had attacked him. The cougar attacked and sank teeth and claws into Rubin Hagen's right leg, piercing through rubber boots, pants, under pants and then into the flesh of the logger, spilling blood into the boot.

Feeling a terrible pain in his leg, Rubin Hagen fell on top of the cougar, grasping a hind leg. He twisted the leg, but the animal kept clawing at his arms and thighs. Finally, it rolled out from beneath him and sank its teeth into his thigh. He shouted as hard as he could for someone to come to his rescue, but it was several minutes before the cougar decided to make off into the bush.

Here, again, are contributing factors. The deep snow in the locality and the age of the animal prevented the big cat from obtaining its normal prey. Hunger caused the animal to attack man. But as a general rule, the cougar does not attack man, except when cornered.

Published May 17, 1951
Family Herald and Toronto Weekly Star

ALONG THE TRAPLINE
By Nellie R. Campbell

> *Deep in the backwoods many odd and interesting incidents occur to our pioneer folk. Some of them will be featured under this title each month.*

Nan had remarked several times that a baked ling would be a most welcome change from our steady diet of moose and bear meat. From the look in her eye this morning, I knew she meant it.

The lake was frozen over and we had discovered that ling caught through the ice had a nicer flavour than at any other time of the year. With a dip net, I managed to catch a few small suckers to use for bait and that afternoon put out about a dozen set lines.

Quite early the following morning I started up the lake. Surely there was nothing on the first one but the bait was gone. I cut the ice at the second hole. The line jerked as I pulled it up. Suddenly, two large ling came to the surface. I stared, -- two ling on one line, - I could hardly believe it. Yet there they lay on the ice before me, two beauties each weighing eight or nine pounds. Then I noticed that the line passed through the gill of the fish and it was the other one that swallowed the bait.

I took the fish, still on the line, back to the cabin to show Nan, puzzling all the while, how one ling ever got strung up on the line. It was not until we cleaned the other one that the mystery was solved. Inside we found a small ling not more than twelve inches long. It was this fish that had swallowed the original bait. It was then that the large ling had come along. Most folk are well aware that a ling possesses a huge head and jaws and a cannibalistic nature, sucking down its prey. The small ling, however, had proved more than a match for its adversary, and in some way had forced its way through the large gill pulling the line through with him. It was after he had made his escape, but was still on the line, that the second ling had come along and succeeded in sucking him down. So you see, I actually caught three fish on one hook.

Nan just looked over my shoulder. "Surely, you're not going to send in that story, are you? Of course it's true, but folks will think it's a fish story." "It is a fish story," I replied, "and a mighty good one, too, if you ask me."

Published November 1951
Caribou Digest
Sold--$2.08

ALONG THE TRAPLINE
By Nellie R. Campbell

Deep in the backwoods many odd and interesting incidents occur to our pioneer folk. Some of them will be featured under this title each month.

It was during those early days of the depression that Nan and I moved onto our newly acquired homestead just north of fifty-four. With miles of unsettled country all around us, trapping seemed to be the only means of livelihood. Not that I knew a great deal about trapping but I was willing to try.

I remember how elated we both were over the first mink that I brought home. Being a mere novice in the art of trapping I left the pelt on the drying board until it had become dry and hard. I experienced some difficulty in getting the hide off the board but it was not until I attempted to turn the thing that my troubles really began. After struggling valiantly with it for some time, I managed to turn it all but the head, which simply defied all human ingenuity.

"Here, Nan, you take it, "I said, maybe you can turn the thing."

Nan was sitting on the cabin doorstep working patiently on the recalcitrant mink head when an old Indian, who trapped just east of me, stopped as he passed our cabin. He eased his pack to the ground and without a word, stood intently watching Nan.

"Say, how do you ever turn those things," I asked. He paused.

"Squaw, she chew head. Head soft, turn easy."

He gave Nan a withering look as he shouldered his pack. "White women make poor squaw," he muttered as he started down the trail.

Published December 1951
Caribou Digest
Sold--$1.29

ALONG THE TRAPLINE
By Nellie R. Campbell

*Deep in the backwoods many odd and interesting incidents occur to our pioneer folk.
Some of them will be featured under this title each month.*

It was one of those clear, fresh mornings in early spring when it was good to be alive. I was on my way to a small lake that lay just beyond the big meadow. Suddenly a big hawk seemed to swoop down from nowhere. He struck the meadow not more than fifty yards away from me and when he rose swiftly into the air there was a small brown animal dangling from his claws. Presumably it was a mink.

As I watched the little creature suddenly disappear, he was no longer dangling from those cruel talons yet I had not seen him fall. The hawk flew higher but suddenly his flight seemed to have checked. He hovered for a moment in the air and then the huge wings began to flap crazily as he began to drop back to earth.

He struck the meadow only a few rods from where he had risen. I rushed to the spot. The big bird was gasping and struggling feebly but there was no sign of that tiny animal that had been clutched in his talons only a moment before. All I could find was a wee hole in the neck of the hawk. He must have caught the mink by its hind legs and it had been able to swing itself up sufficiently to reach the jugular vein. He had held on tenaciously and ridden safely back to earth. There was no doubt that the small creature had brought swift death to his foe and made good his escape.

*Published January 1952
Caribou Digest
Sold--$1.29*

ALONG THE TRAPLINE
By Nellie R. Campbell

*Deep in the backwoods many odd and interesting incidents occur to our pioneer folk.
Some of them will be featured under this title each month.*

Nan had asked me to put out a few ling lines. After all it wouldn't be a great deal of trouble to take a look at them each afternoon when I came back down the lake from re-setting my traps.

I had cut out the ice from the first and second holes but there were no fish on either hook. At the third hole I carefully chipped the ice away with the ice chisel. As I opened up the hole I could see the line jerk. It was when I attempted to flip out a piece of the cracked ice with the blade of the chisel that the thing slipped from my hand and disappeared. I quickly pulled up my fish line. I had caught a beauty, - all of eight pounds. After I had taken him off the hook I took a look down the hole to see if the chisel was anywhere in sight. It had gone straight down and the blade had imbedded itself in the mud at the bottom of the lake while the handle stood upright but it was down too far for me to reach it.

As I opened up our cabin door, I called to Nan. "I got you a fish, but I lost my only ice chisel. It just slipped out of my hand and went straight down to the bottom, --too far for me to reach."

"But what will we ever do without the ice chisel?" Nan exclaimed. "It will be a long time before you can get another one."

"Oh, but I got it," I replied. "You see, I just sent the fish down after it and he brought it up."

"Don't be silly," Nan said, giving me a disgusted look. "Surely you don't expect me to believe that yarn."

"But that's exactly what happened," I replied. "You see, while I was looking down at the chisel, the ling gave a big flipflop that landed him close to the water hole. Quick as a wink, I grabbed him, tied the end of the fish line tightly around his tail and then eased him gently back into the water. He went straight down and it wasn't very long before he had the line twisted round and round the handle of the chisel, then I pulled him up again and he brought the ice chisel up with him."

Nan stared at the fish for a moment in silence. "And then you propose to eat him after he has done you a favor like that," she remarked.

"You'll have to admit that the favor was wholly unintentional on his part, --and after all a baked ling is a baked ling."

"Well, no doubt you are right," she finally admitted and as the fish was the cause of loosing the ice chisel in the first place, it was rather clever of you to send him back down to get it." She knew perfectly well that that was what I had been waiting for her to say.

Published February 1952
Caribou Digest
Sold--$2.65

ALONG THE TRAPLINE
By Nellie R. Campbell

> *Deep in the backwoods many odd and interesting incidents occur to our pioneer folk. Some of them will be featured under this title each month.*

I was quite proud of that underwater beaver set that I had just made. There seemed to be every sign that beaver had been at work there recently. I returned to the cabin with a feeling of elation for I was quite confident that there would be a beaver in that trap by morning.

I got an early start. The lake was quiet. As I neared the beaver dam I saw no signs of wild life save for a lone drake which was swimming around in circles close to my beaver set. Then I saw it. A beaver's nose stuck just above the water, -or was it a beaver? Although the drake seemed to become more excited at my approach, he did not fly but swam about in wider circles watching that bit of brown showing above the surface of the water.

I had reached the set and peered down. There in the trap, held firmly by her bill was Mrs. Duck. She had no doubt, mistaken the V on the pan for some choice morsel and dived, striking the pan. The jaws of the pan had held her, head down, with just the tip of her tail feathers above the surface. No wonder Mr. Drake had become worried when Mrs. Duck had suddenly defied all laws of nature and failed to return to the surface.

~~~~~~~~~~~~~~~~~~~

Although I had been told that there were no grizzlies in this part of British Columbia, I did not doubt for a moment that Joe, the Indian, whose trap line joined mine on the east, had actually encountered a grizzly that morning. It was barely daylight when he reached the small ravine, a heavy pack on his back. He had taken only his .22. It was not until he neared the bottom of the ravine that he glimpsed the huge animal standing partly concealed by a willow clump close to the trail. He noted the light, powdery snow that had been falling intermittingly, still clung to the animal's back and head.

Grizzly Bear near Prince George, B.C.

"Bull Moose," Joe thought, as he continued fearlessly on his way. He was almost abreast of the animal before he realized it was no bull moose. The creature suddenly rose on its hind legs and emitting a roar that fairly froze the blood in old Joe's veins, started for him.

A grizzly, --Joe knew it would take more than a .22 bullet to stop him. His one thought was to divest himself of his cumbersome pack and get out of that ravine. It was not until he had nearly reached the top of the trail that he even glanced back. The grizzly had paused to investigate the packsack.

Joe covered the four miles to my cabin in record time. "Gun," he panted, resting his worthless .22 against the wall. "Him plenty big bear."

We started for the ravine, Joe armed with a .401 while I carried my 30-30. We found Joe's pack, --or what was left of it. The grizzly had ripped the canvas bag into ribbons and devoured Joe's food supply. His extra traps were scattered in the snow. We followed those huge imprints in the snow for perhaps a mile. It was now snowing harder and we knew that before long those tracks would be obliterated. We decided to give up on the chase. It probably was a male bear who had been crossing to the mountain ridges farther east.

Back in the ravine, Joe picked up his tattered packsack and retrieved his traps. "This show he no moose, --him big grizzly bear." He followed me back to the cabin for hot coffee. It had taken a grizzly to break down old Joe's reserve.

Published February 1952
Caribou Digest
Sold--$1.13

ALONG THE TRAPLINE
By Nellie R. Campbell

> *Deep in the backwoods many odd and interesting incidents occur to our pioneer folk.*
> *Some of them will be featured under this title each month.*

It had been a very poor day. I had walked miles and my traps had yielded almost nothing – two measly squirrels and a weasel that was still brown and quite worthless. As I neared the narrow lake that lies about a mile north of our cabin, I saw two ducks swimming lazily about, not far from the shore. At least here was something that we could eat.

As I encountered the small clearing near our cabin home, I saw Nan swinging vicious blows at a block of wood. As they seemed to be having very little effect, I stood my gun against the doorstep and went over and took the axe from Nan's hands.

As we each picked up an armful of wood I told her about the plump duck I had shot. At the cabin steps Nan stopped. "I thought you said you left it on the door step," she said.

"I did," I replied.

"But it's not there, "she cried, "it's gone."

Nan was right. The bird that I had laid on the doorstep not more than three minutes before had completely vanished. Quick as a flash Nan dropped her armful of wood and rushed around the corner of the cabin. I reached the corner of the house just in time to see a large owl rise from beneath the lilac bush with the duck clutched in its claws. Before I could get the gun, Nan was away in hot pursuit.

The duck was fairly heavy and the owl seemed to be having some difficulty in gaining altitude. He was flying about on a level with Nan's head, straight for the heavy timber that grew on the other side of the clearing. Nan was only a few feet behind, waving her apron and shouting imprecations as she went. As long as Nan and the owl were so close it was impossible to shoot.

The owl had nearly reached the shelter of the big spruce when it happened. He lost his grip on the duck which came tumbling down at Nan's feet. It was intact; all but the head which lay on the ground by the lilac bush. Nan picked up the duck and came back across the clearing.

"I might have shot that owl," I remarked, "if you hadn't been in the way."

"But I didn't want that owl," Nan protested. "All I wanted was to get back our Sunday dinner, and I did," she said triumphantly.

Published February 1952
Caribou Digest
Sold--$2.10

ALONG THE TRAPLINE
By Nellie R. Campbell

> *Deep in the backwoods many odd and interesting incidents occur to our pioneer folk. Some of them will be featured under this title each month.*

It was a question of who really owned the coyote. It all happened like this. Nan was returning home from a visit with her nearest neighbor a mile and a half to the west when she met the neighbor living east of us, driving along the grassy trail. She stopped just for a friendly chat.

"Look," Charlie exclaimed. There coming down the trail was a large coyote. Had the team been moving, he might have dashed into the bush, but all was quiet so he promptly sat down in the middle of the trail apparently to take a better look. He was a large coyote and the frosty autumn nights had made his hair stand out thick and dark while the black forepaws shaded into a lighter grey tinged with yellow on the under part of his body.

"Isn't he pretty?" Nan breathed.

"Pretty ---he's a perfect shot if ever there was one," Charlie replied.

"I'd take a shot at him too, if I wasn't afraid the horses would run away."

Thinking of her few plump chickens at home, Nan had volunteered to hold the horses for him. As she climbed into the democrat, Charlie slid out of the other side, gun in hand. The coyote still sat in the trail, head slightly to one side watching the proceedings. Charlie went cautiously a few paces closer to the coyote and then a shot rang out. With a howl the coyote leaped into the air and was gone.

"Must have fired a bit too low," Charlie muttered, when he returned. "I could see where the bullet hit the ground just where he had been sitting but there are no signs of blood. I must have missed him but I don't see how I could have.

About a week later I caught a large coyote in a trap not far from our cabin. When I skinned him, I found a fresh bullet wound well up on the fleshy part of one hind leg. The bullet had gone completely through leaving a clean wound that was just beginning to heal. No doubt the soreness in that leg had made it difficult for the coyote to procure food and he had become less wary than usual.

"By good rights, the coyote belongs to me," Charlie remarked one day, "because I shot him."

"Maybe you did," I retorted, "but just remember that possession is always nine points of the law and I've got him."

Published February 1952
Caribou Digest
Sold--$2.10

COYOTE TRAILS
By Nellie R. Campbell

Each night the discordant howls of the coyotes seemed to come closer and closer to our cabin home, yet it was over a year before I actually saw one. After having read that small pamphlet on "How To Pre-empt Land in British Columbia", Bert had been convinced that there was nothing for us but the "simple life." That was how we found ourselves in a snug log cabin that we had built on the shore of one of B.C.'s lovely lakes. (Ness Lake)

In this wilderness, trapping seemed to be the only way of making a living and although Bert was a novice in this art, he tackled it with the same cheerful optimism with which he had undertaken the building of our cabin home.

It was on the trap-line that he had caught Necheko, a beautiful female mink. She, with a bred female we had purchased from a Quebec Mink Ranch, were the nucleus of our small ranch. It was one morning when Bert was cleaning the mink pens, that the coyote came boldly into the small clearing that surrounded our cabin. For a moment she stood clearly etched against a background of small willows. Keeping a wary eye on Bert, she suddenly snatched a bone, which the mink had discarded, and vanished in the bushes.

"What a shot – if I'd only had the gun. It's too late now. She won't be back." But Bert was wrong. In less than a half hour she was back, snatched another bone and silently vanished. It seems that the mother coyote is very devoted to her young and often will take desperate chances in order to procure food for them.

It was then that Bert decided that the bone pile, which he had intended to burn, might prove valuable after all. He went to bed that night confident that he would have that coyote by morning, for in that pile of old bones was a cleverly concealed trap. It was fastened securely to a heavy log, which no animal could pull far without becoming tangled in the heavy underbrush.

It was sometime after midnight that Bert sprang out of bed and groped for his trousers. Howls that shattered the habitual stillness, and died away in an agonized wail, had brought us both into instant action. Grabbing his gun and thrusting the lighted lantern into my hand, Bert opened the cabin door. Now, a death like stillness lay over the clearing. We stood beside that small pile of old bones staring at each other. There was no coyote, -- no trap – even the heavy log had vanished. We searched the ground for signs but it was frozen and there were no marks. We even followed a narrow trail that led into the forest, pausing often to listen, but only the distant hooting of an owl broke the stillness of the night.

At last we returned to the cabin, but there was no more sleep that night. At the first faint signs of dawn, we started out once more. Behind a thick clump of willows, not even ten feet from the pile, we found the log and crouched beneath overhanging branches was a black and tan dog. Bert returned to the cabin for a short piece of rope for a muzzle, as the sudden pressure on an animal's foot often causes intense pain and he is apt to snap at his captor.

It was about two the following morning that the stillness about our cabin was shattered by deep-throated howls. As we drew near to the old bone pile we could make out the form of some large animal standing just at the edge of the clearing.

"It's a timber wolf," Bert exclaimed exultantly, but at the sound of his voice a short, joyous bark told us it was Sheba, a large sleigh dog belonging to a neighbour who lived over three miles away. She was a temperamental creature, a cross between a wolf and a hound. More than one claimed that she was an ugly brute. She may have had her likes and dislikes, but she had slept more than once in our living room when Mary, her young mistress, had spent the night at our cabin, so I had no fear of her. She stood quietly while Bert opened the jaws of the trap and released her foot.

The following morning Bert burned the bone pile. We had learned that the cunning, inquiring disposition of the coyote is often more than a match for man's ingenuity in the matter of traps. An old trapper told Bert that he had found that most coyotes were trap-wise and he had always had the best success with poisoned bait, but of course there was always the possibility of losing the coyote as he became thirsty and invariably went in search of water. If one lived in open country, a coyote crossing a marsh or meadow made a good target.

We thought of a Ukrainian neighbour in Saskatchewan, who spent each winter hunting coyotes. He rode a powerful, jet-black stallion, which had been trained to jump any barbed wire fence, as there is no time to open and close gates when in pursuit of a coyote. If he could drive the animal out of some sheltering bluff, it was as good as his, for no coyote can travel far or fast through deep snow and it would not be long before horse and rider could overtake him. One morning as we were eating breakfast, something flashed past our kitchen window. We were just in time to see the stallion clear our garden-fence. A single shot sounded from the other side of the bluff behind our house. We knew Jack Serienko had got his coyote.

However, we were now in a country that was heavily wooded, so Bert continued to set his traps, confident that some day he would be able to outwit the wary coyote.

Although the coyote is ever alert to danger, let one suddenly cross your path and often he will show the coolest effrontery. It was in the late fall that I was going along the trail that led to my nearest neighbours, a mile and a half away, when I met another neighbour coming along the same trail. "Turn around quick", he said. Not more than fifty yards away was a large coyote. At the sound of a voice, he stopped abruptly and after eyeing us coolly for a moment, sat down in the middle of the trail. He was a pretty creature. The dark grey hair stood out on his back and shoulders, while the dark paws and fore-legs contrasted sharply with the yellowish tinge showing through the lighter grey of the under body.

"I'd take a shot at that fellow," Charlie exclaimed, "if I wasn't afraid the horse would run away."

"I'll hold the horse," I offered, picking up the lines as I climbed into the buggy. Gun in hand, Charlie slid out the other side and took a few cautious steps toward the waiting coyote. As the shot rang out, the coyote leaped into the air and was gone. There was no sign of blood, only a mark where the bullet had plowed into the road, just where the coyote had been sitting.

"Must have fired too low," Charlie muttered, as he climbed into the buggy. It was less than a week later that Bert caught a coyote in a trap. There was a fresh bullet hole through the upper part of one hind leg close to the thigh. No doubt the wound had proved painful and hunting rabbits in the marsh had not been easy, so hunger had caused the animal to disregard his usual cautiousness.

The coyote usually hunts at night, sometimes alone, but often in packs. They disperse at daybreak and in the more settled places, each finds some secluded spot among rocks or thick brush in which to sleep away the day. However, in this northland, it is not usual to meet one at any time on some forest trail. The coyote's one objective in life seems to be to satisfy an insatiable appetite and his unusual sagacity is devoted wholly to this end. Bert found that a coyote would follow a wolf track for miles on the mere chance of picking up a few morsels left from some kill. More than once he has found the remains of a deer that had been pulled down on glare ice by the pack. Coyotes know that on land the deer is too fleet, but on ice it is impossible for a deer to get footing.

The young resemble puppies. There are five or six at a birth, which occurs in May or June. They romp, bark and bite, just as young puppies do while the mother forages for food for her ever-hungry offspring.

It was near Fort Graham that a lad out with the survey gang for the Alaskan Railroad, saw five pups romping on the point of a narrow strip of land that jutted out into the Findlay River. Pointing them out to an Indian at the camp, he took off in the light plane. Terrified by the noise as the plane roared back and forth over the entrance to this narrow neck, the young coyotes clung to the point and were easy marks for the Indian as he crept toward them.

Our northern winter was nearly over. Bert had done well on the trap line and was more then elated over the fifteen coyotes he had trapped. Then something happened. One morning as he made his rounds, there was another coyote, but this time it was different. The cruel jaws of the trap had completely shattered the bone in the left front leg. In the long hours of its captivity, the animal had turned and twisted in its futile effort to escape. Bits of splintered bone protruded through the torn and blood encrusted flesh. Only a tough shred of hide still held the animal in the trap. Suffering and misery were written on the coyote's face.

"Maybe he was only a coyote," Bert said, but I'm through trapping,"

He read the unspoken question in my face. "How will we ever live in this wilderness without the trap line?"

"This will never be cattle country – the wealth lies in its timber. Some day there will be settlers and there will be good roads." I looked across the clearing. Tall Douglas firs, giant spruce and graceful white birch, -- they extended for miles. Bert was right. The wealth of the country lay in its forests.

"We have a small start in mink now," I heard Bert saying, "and we'll make out somehow." I knew Bert would.

A short, sharp bark followed by several more in rapid succession, awoke me. The barks grew faster and the pitch higher until the sound all ran together in a long drawn out howl in the highest possible key. This strain was taken up time after time, by different members of the pack. The discordant howling grew louder and louder. I turned restlessly. Bert laid a soothing hand on mine. "Its only the coyotes," he murmured sleepily, "they're running again in the meadow."

Published February 1952
 Rod and Gun
Sold--$20.00

THE THREE BEARS
By Nellie R. Campbell

This is a story of three bears. Not the big father bear, the middle sized mother bear and the wee, wee baby bear that Goldilocks found living in a neat little cottage in the woods, but an old mother bear and her two cubs who lived somewhere in the dense forests that surrounded Ness Lake, in the northern interior of British Columbia.

The warm spring sun had melted all but a few patches of snow here and there in shady places and water was trickling in tiny rivulets down hill sides, when she emerged from her den, weak gaunt and hungry from her long fast. She made her way slowly to a big jack pine and with teeth and claws, slashed at the bark at its base on the sunny side of the tree. The sap would be running there. Ripping the bark upward, she ate the succulent bittersweet inner bark. It acted as a spring tonic to her emaciated body. She lay basking for a time in the warm sunshine as she gathered strength and then ambled slowly away in search of food, her two cubs following her.

Underneath fallen and rotting logs lived thousands of insects, so the old bear and her cubs spent days roaming through the woods, overturning rotten logs and greedily lapping up the ants and grubs they found underneath. The days were getting warmer. The suckers were spawning. Sometimes we would see her pacing slowly along the lakeshore. Then she would stand perfectly motionless with the water lapping gently about her feet as she watched the flopping, wriggling fish in the shallow water about her. They were depositing their eggs on the warm, pebbly bottom. A sudden sweep of one huge paw would send a half dozen or more of the unsuspecting fish into the air. The cubs would rush forward and gobble them up before they had hardly hit the ground. She lived along the lakeshore until the spawning season was over, then went back again into the heavy timber. The cubs were growing like weeds and she was no longer gaunt and hungry. There was plenty of small game in the bush and soon the berries would be ripe. That was the year that a late frost hit the berry blossoms and there were very few berries. At first the old bear was not too much worried, but as the days went on she again became hungry.

A little over a mile from the lake a homesteader lived in a neat log cabin. He had a small fenced-in clearing and in the corner along the road, two healthy young pigs rooted in the grass and low brush. Len Barrett was quite sure that the electric fence would keep his young porkers in, but when the mother bear and the fast growing cubs, began walking boldly down the highway that led to Prince George, he wondered if the fence would keep a hungry bear out. Then some days the flock of young turkeys ventured a bit too far out on the clearing and several times one had been missing when they returned to the barnyard.

Then one morning the mother bear emerged from the heavy bush in front of the cabin just as Ralph, the three year old, ran into the road. He raced back to the house screaming, "Bear, get me, bear get me." His mother grabbed the gun and ran to the road but the bear was going back into the bush and although she is a good shot, she decided not to tackle a mother bear when she was alone.

A day or two later, Cliff Wing was riding along the highway just at dusk. About a quarter of a mile this side of the Barrett homestead, he saw the old bear nosing about in the road. He slowed down a bit, but long before he reached the spot she had disappeared. A sudden crashing in the bushes and the big bear landed in the road directly in front of his bicycle. There was nothing to do but jam on the brakes and jump. The cubs were nowhere to be seen, but it was quite evident that their mother was in an angry mood. Her lips curled back in a snarl showing strong, white teeth and an ominous growl came from her throat.

"I never was so scared in all my life," Cliff said afterward. "I knew that I must keep the wheel between us. She rammed her nose into the spokes of the front wheel trying to reach me and that didn't improve her disposition any. We zigzagged back and forth across the road, she on one side growling and snarling, and I on the other side frantically gripping the handle bar. If she had stood up on her hind legs she could have reached me easily, but she didn't seem to think of that, and you can bet I didn't mention it to her. She just kept ramming her nose into one wheel and then the other, getting more ugly all the time. At last she gave it up and turned toward the bush. I was so relieved to see her go that I thought I'd just speed her on her way a bit. I swung the bike around and rammed the front wheel into her rear end as I let out the most terrific war whoop you ever heard."

He sighed. "Guess I must have offended her dignity or something, because she turned around and came back at me and we started zigzagging back and forth across the road all over again. At last she turned and started for the bush again and believe me, I didn't help her this time."

"How long was she there?" I asked. Cliff grinned. "It seemed to me like a good long half hour, but I guess if anyone had actually timed it, it would have been between five and ten minutes, counting both times. But that was plenty long for a guy like me." He raised his good arm and mopped his forehead. You see his other sleeve hangs empty.

After this incident, Len decided that it was no longer safe to have the old bear around. The next time she appeared in the road just below his homestead, he took down his gun and went after her.

"I hope you got all three of them," his wife said when he returned. A sheepish grin spread over his face as he hung the gun in its accustomed place. "Got the mother through the heart. She never knew what hit her. Guess I could have got the cubs but they are such cute little devils and they aren't mean yet," he said as he went out the door.

All summer the two young bears stayed close to the highway. One Sunday morning Bert and I had been to a neighbour and were riding home on our bicycles when a light delivery truck overtook us. They were friends from town on their way to our place to dinner. As I was the cook, it was decided best for me to go along with them and Bert could follow at a slower pace on his wheel.

"We'll go ahead and scare the bears out of the road," one of them called back. A few moments later we swung around a bend in the road and there was one of the young bears. His front and hind legs seemed all mixed up as he raced along the highway in front of the car. At last he ducked into the bush.

It was hunting season. Daily hunters were coming in from the south and from the coast in search of moose. One day toward evening we heard a single shot. It sounded very close. The following morning a young chap crossed our homestead. He was off for a day's hunting but stopped a few moments to chat with Bert.

"Got a young bear last night just across from your roadway. I cleaned it and hung in up in those old buildings close by. Tried to give it to Len Barrett, but he said he'd had all the bear meat he wanted. Maybe you'd like it," he offered hopefully.

Bert brought the little bear home. The hair was thick, soft and silky and a glossy black. The hide would make a wonderful rug. And the meat – a friend from town remarked – "That's the nicest meat I've ever tasted," – and it really was.

It was really getting cold and we knew that it would not be long before winter settled over this northland. Bert was coming across the homestead near our north line. He happened to glance across a small knoll. He had discovered an old bear den there one day in the summer. There on the side of the slope was a young black bear. He was digging furiously at the entrance of the old den. Bert watched him for a moment and then turned quietly away. "I could have shot him," Bert said, "but the little fellow's had a rather rough time this summer. Maybe next summer will be a happier one for him."

Now that the snow lies waist deep over this north country, I sometimes think of a cub bear curled up in an old bear den on the north side of our homestead sleeping the long winter away and I sometimes wonder if he is dreaming of happier times.

Published January 1953
Rod and Gun
Sold--$20.0

BEWARE OF THE GAY MARAUDER
By Nellie R. Campbell

As I passed that August morning to listen to the sweet twitterings that came from the silver birches just back of our cabin, I little realized the trouble these gay little songsters were to bring us. A large flock of small grey or brown birds, conspicuously streaked with the same colours, had suddenly dropped down from the blue above. At first we thought that they were some sort of a sparrow and paid little heed to them as they darted joyously to and fro. Their sweet chirpings filled the air morning, noon and night.

Each day as I made my way to the edge of the garden, the air suddenly would be filled with small brown birds. It was only as they flew that one noted a flash of yellow. Their sweet melody would drift down from the birches, then one by one they would dart down toward the raspberry patch and me, swerve suddenly and vanish beneath the heavy foliage in the garden. At least our garden should be entirely free from insects, I thought, with a whole flock of birds to take care of it.

It was not for several days that we discovered that insects held no attraction for our little visitors. It was the outer leaves of the cabbages, already in head, upon which they were feasting. Already many of them lay in shreds, -- just the stiff midrib with a few strings attached, was all that remained. They surely believed in doing a thorough job.

"Maybe a scarecrow would keep them away," I suggested hopefully, but Bert didn't agree. That afternoon I stood motionless in the midst of the cabbage patch with the hot August sun pouring down upon my defenceless head. Not that I particularly resemble a scarecrow, but I simply wanted to prove my point. However, I did not have long to wait. There was a flash of yellow and a small brown bird settled down almost at my feet, then another and another. They were not the least bit interested in me, but in the cabbage leaves.

Bert went to the wood shed and brought back the old fish net that we had used in our days of mink ranching. We carefully draped it over the entire cabbage patch. "If we can catch just a few in the net, it will probably frighten the others away." But Bert didn't know his bird.

It was no trouble at all for them to walk through the two and a half inch mesh and continue their depredations. It was only when I started for the cabbage patch, shooing and clapping my hands together loudly, that they encountered any difficulty. If they spread their wings too soon they became tangled in the net but the majority soon learned to go in and out with ease. We caught thirteen, but soon learned that our gay little songsters were a most heartless bunch. They could light right beside a dead comrade and feast upon a juicy cabbage leaf without the slightest qualm.

Our bird book told us that we were entertaining the Pine Siskin, a close relative of the Gold Finch. Its middle and greater wing coverts were tipped with white. The basal portion of wing and tail feathers were pale yellow and almost concealed, showing only when in flight. The bill was small, conical and acute.

It was not long before I discovered that I must pick my gooseberries if I were to have any of them. It was not the fleshy part of the berry, but the seeds that attracted them. The ground beneath the bushes was strewn with large, plump, hollow gooseberries. One day as I was picking, a siskin lit on the branch close to my hand. The bird book had said that they often were seen hanging head downward from ends of branches as they fed upon buds or seeds and when thus occupied, were very approachable.

When not actually picking gooseberries, most of my time was spent in racing madly between the cabbages and the gooseberries and hoping they would not decide to add something else to their diet. It mattered little if my voice was hoarse from shoo-ing and my hands sore from constant clapping. From the top of the birches came sweet melody until my back was turned. A cessation of sound was a sure sign our feathered guests were in mischief once more.

However, as the days passed, I noticed that the flock was growing smaller and smaller. The children reported seeing a lot of them feeding along the roadside about a mile away. There were none seen by my nearest neighbour a mile and a half east. It seems that this bird is most uncertain in its abode. One year, so our book states, they may be seen in large numbers about one group of mountain peaks or valleys. The next, not a single siskin will be seen in that entire district.

One morning I noticed a fluttering in the net. A small siskin was caught by one leg. Carefully I untangled the bit of twine that held him fast. His bright eyes looked up at me and he gave a joyous little chirp. I looked at our graceful birches back of our cabin. There were only a few of these greyish brown birds to be seen. The greater portion of the flock had moved on. Slowly I opened my hand and watched the small bird fly away.

Although the Pine Siskin is such an attractive little bird, with its sweet song and its flash of yellow, as it darts quickly about, we are hoping that he won't return to pay us a visit next summer. Don't ever let this small, debonair bird with its sweet song ever fool you for you will find that after all, he is nothing but a gay marauder.

Published September 4, 1952
Family Herald and Weekly Star
Sold--$7.65

AND WHAT YOU CAN'T EAT – CAN'
By Nellie R. Campbell

With ever increasing threats of famine in all parts of Europe it behooves us, who live in rural districts where nature has provided such vast stores of food just for the gathering, to utilize to the fullest her great abundance. Every ounce that we can store for our future use leaves just that much more to alleviate the present suffering of humanity.

In some localities mushrooms are plentiful and lend themselves readily to canning, however it is most essential that one know his mushrooms.

A neighbor who came from Czechoslovakia, gathers quantities of mushrooms each summer and dries them in the sun. They are soaked in just enough water to cover them and then the liquid and mushrooms are added to meat gravy or soup. Often they are simply fried in fat and served as a vegetable.

In most of the provinces of Canada there is wild fruit. Most people living in rural districts and many town dwellers have a few rhubarb roots growing in their back yards. It is best to can rhubarb as early as possible while the stalks are tender as they are far less acid and require less sugar, an item to be taken into consideration these days. Rhubarb combines very well with other fruits.

The serviceberry, or saskatoon as it is called in the west, is often allowed to go to waste. The Indians in British Columbia dry large quantities of these berries each year. If one likes its slightly almond flavor they will find it an ideal berry for canning, as it requires very little sugar. It is a fruit that combines well with rhubarb.

Equal parts of rhubarb and saskatoons with chopped oranges and lemons make a wonderful conserve.

The high bush cranberry is very plentiful in many parts of our Dominion, yet it is a berry that requires a great deal of sugar. Last year I solved this problem by using just enough sugar to sweeten the fruit juice and boiling it down to the consistency of syrup instead of the usual jell. This fruit syrup used on hotcakes in the morning made an appetizing change from ordinary syrup.

My neighbors from Czechoslovakia gather quantities of rose hips, those bright red berries found on the wild rose bushes late every fall. These are washed and boiled in very little water until soft and then the pulp is pressed though a sieve. A small amount of sugar, a bit of grated lemon rind and the juice of a lemon with a pinch of ginger is added and the fruit pulp allowed to simmer until thick, then bottled hot. This makes an excellent spread for bread and will be a change in the lunch box.

We who live in a part of Canada where there are various kinds of greens, quantities of wild fruit and an abundance of game, have very little excuse for not having well stocked shelves long before the snow flies. Remember, what you are able to can this summer leaves just that much more for someone who is less fortunate. Now is the time to start canning.

Published June 12, 1946
Family Herald and Weekly Star
Sold-- $2.34

DAD BUILDS A SMOKE-HOUSE
By Nellie R. Campbell

A SMOKE-HOUSE is something that every farm home should possess, yet few of the farms in our country, especially in the homesteading areas, can boast of one. Perhaps it is because a smoke-house is needed only at butchering time, which usually comes each spring and fall, that the man of the house fails to build one. That was the way it was at our house.

Mom is a mild sort of person and usually left the outside affairs strictly to Dad and the boys, but once in a while she puts her foot down, and when she does both Dad and the boys know she means it.

It was last spring and the pork had been in the brine for about four weeks when Mom suddenly announced, "I'm not going to eat any more salt pork."

Dad looked at the boys and the boys looked at Dad. They all knew that there must be a smoke-house. "You boys finish up the work in the back field," he said, as they went out. "I'll be busy this morning."

They say the Yankees are noted for their ingenuity and Dad certainly had his share. We all knew that Dad was immensely pleased with himself when he came in to dinner. We were not surprised when he invited us to come to inspect his new smoke-house.

We all followed him around the end of the woodshed to a small log building built into the side of a hill. Dad had put it up the first year we came onto the home-stead. Its uses had been varied but for some years it had not been used and Dad had threatened periodically to pull it down.

The heater from Dad's workshop stood in front of it and a long length of stovepipe disappeared through an oblong of tin nailed over what had been the window. We peered in. The stovepipe ended in an elbow headed down toward the dirt floor.

"What is the idea of the elbow on the end?" I ventured. Dad gave me a scathing look.

"Remember the smoke-house Bill Jones built when we lived in Saskatchewan?" he asked.

We all did. Bill had built a model smoke-house and the entire family had boasted that they were going to have ham and eggs on Easter morning. Bill hung the meat in his smoke-house and went to bed with rosy dreams of a breakfast fit for a king. In the morning, when he looked out, there was no smoke-house there.

"You see, this one is perfectly safe." Dad said. "No spark can set this low roof on fire if the elbow points down, and the smoke is cooler before it hits the meat."

Dad had done a wonderful job at cleaning

George and Nellie in front of their new mink pens & smokehouse.

the little house up. In the rafters were even rows of spikes on which to hang the heavier pieces of meat. Across the end nearest the stovepipe was a neat rack about fifteen inches down from the ceiling on which to hang the smaller cuts.

"Hard wood makes the best smoke for curing meat." Dad told the boys. "Back in the States, we always used oak or hickory. I used to save all the broken eveners and any bits of hard wood back on the prairie, just for smoking. I guess we'll have to use those green birch chips over in the wood lot for this meat."

We left the smoking of the meat to Dad and the boys. Judging by the results we made a wise decision. Some time later we enjoyed the first sample.

"That's mighty good ham, Dad," Mom said, as she took a second piece. She had been just a bit disappointed when she had viewed our ramshackle job, but as Dad said, ours did have certain advantages. Furthermore the results backed it up.

There was no danger of fire. The smoke was cool when it reached the meat, so the hams were tender and juicy, and not dried out by a hot smoke. Then too, there was no need of opening the smoke-house door to replenish the fire, thus losing precious smoke, nor did one have to work in a smoky atmosphere when tending the fire. It took only a few minutes to set up the stove and adjust the pipes whenever they were needed.

Dad was so pleased with his achievement that he even offered to smoke some fish last fall. We split them down the backbone after removing the head. If split down the back they will lie flat. We cleaned and washed them and then spread them on the rack in the smoke-house, flesh side down, to drain over night.

In the morning we took them from the rack and rubbed both sides with a small amount of salt. A bit of brown sugar added to the salt gives them a browner tint when smoked. They were put back on the rack and turned a couple of times during the smoking process. They proved to be much better than any of the smoked fish we get at the market.

"After all, looks don't count so much when you're homesteading. Dad's smoke-house turns out good products and the proof is in the eating!" said Mom.

A smoke-house need not be a thing of beauty, but it should do a good job of smoking meat. On this basis the author of this account says that Dad's fills the bill!

Published November 13, 1946
Family Herald and Weekly Star
Sold-$5.59

SUGAR CURED HAM AND BACON
By Nellie R. Campbell

All over Canada the little pig that so contentedly rooted about in our orchards in the early spring is finding his way into the pork barrel. Two inquiries regarding the curing of meat have recently come to my desk, therefore this article.

There are two methods commonly used for curing meat, -- the dry cure or the brine cure. From our own experience we have found the brine cure the more satisfactory one as both salt and saltpetre used as preservatives are astringent and if used too freely the meat becomes hard and dry. For this reason the brine cure gives a milder cure and the meat is less stringy and salty.

The animal to be butchered should not be fed for 24 hours before killing. Plenty of water may be given as it helps to keep down the temperature of the animal. After butchering, the meat should be cooled as quickly as possible in order for it to become firm. Do not allow it to freeze. If it is not thoroughly cooled before it is put into the brine, gasses are retained that give off an offensive odour. It is well to let the meat stand for twenty-four hours before curing.

The best containers are hard wood barrels or crocks, but crocks are expensive. Whatever container you use be sure that it is thoroughly washed and scalded. Select the pieces to be cured. Salt, sugar, molasses and saltpetre are the preservatives used. Never use prepared chemical preservatives.

The following are tried recipes for making brine:

For 50 pounds of meat allow three quarts of coarse salt, 2 ounces of saltpetre, one quart of good molasses and 2 pounds of brown sugar. Add enough water to cover the hams. Ordinary sized hams should be kept in this pickle for five weeks, larger ones six weeks. They should be taken out once a week and those which were on the top, laid in first and the lower ones last.

Another good recipe for sugar-cured hams and bacon is as follows:

Rub each piece with salt and drain overnight. Pack in barrel. For 100 pounds of meat use 8 pounds of salt, 2 pounds of brown sugar and 2 ounces of saltpetre dissolved in 4 gallons of boiling water or sufficient to cover the meat. Be sure that the brine is cold before pouring over the meat. Turn pieces every week. If the brine becomes ropy it should be poured off the meat and boiled and scum which rises to the surface skimmed off. Cool and pour back over meat or make a new brine. It is necessary to keep a weight on the meat and see that all pieces are covered with the brine.

DRY CURE:

For each 100 pounds of meat use 8 pounds of salt, 2 pounds of brown sugar and 3 ounces of saltpetre. Wash the meat well in cold water, as this will cause the salt to stick better. Using half of the above mixture rub the skin, flesh side and edges with this salt taking care to rub it in well around all bones. Large hams are better if the dry cure is used. Spoilage occurs usually around the bone. Leave the meat on a table in a cool room but do not let it freeze.

At the end of 7 or 8 days repeat this process using the remainder of the salt. Leave the pieces in a cool, dry place until curing has been completed. Allow from 3 to 4 days for each pound of weight in each piece.

SMOKING:

When the meat has been cured the required length of time, remove from the brine and soak the pieces in lukewarm water for an hour. Wash each piece thoroughly in cold water using a brush to remove all film accumulated during the curing. Hang the pieces in the smoke-house and allow them to drain thoroughly before starting the smoke.

Be sure the meat is hung well above the fire and the smoke is cool, as hot smoke dries out the meat. Hard wood makes the best smoke. Hickory, maple or oak, are good. In some parts of the east, corn cobs are used for smoking meat. As we had none of these we always use green birch chips. No matter what you use, remember that a slow, gentle smoking produces the best, cured meat.

Thirty–six to 40 hours is usually allowed for smoking. Some people prefer to smoke the meat for 2 to 3 hours a day, over a period of two weeks.

STORING:

To some, the storing of the meat presents a problem. One of our neighbors wraps each piece carefully in waxed paper and packs it in a barrel of oats. She puts a layer of meat, no pieces overlapping, on about 2 inches of oats in the bottom of the barrel, a layer of oats and one of meat, until all is stored. She covers the top layer well with oats.

Each piece may be put in a clean cotton sack and the sack given a coat of lime whitewash to which a little liquid glue has been added. These sacks should be hung in an airy place.

A year ago last spring, we were late in butchering and warm weather was upon us by the time the hams were smoked. What to do with them was the problem. When I read that hams and bacon could be kept for two years by storing in wood ashes, I was most sceptical about it, yet I was willing to give it a try. We were careful to follow the directions given.   Use a box large enough to hold the meat. Put an inch of wood ashes in the bottom, then a layer of meat, more ashes, another layer of meat and so on, finishing with 2 inches of ashes on top. This method of storing meat is both fly and mouse proof. It keeps the meat dry in a moist atmosphere and prevents it from becoming dry in a dry one. Ham will improve in flavor if properly cured and dried before put in. Whenever you wish to use a piece, brush off the ashes, then wash in lukewarm water and wipe dry.

Did this method work? It did, and we enjoyed juicy ham and crisp bacon all that summer.

Published January 8, 1947
Family Herald and Weekly Star

Note:

In May, 1947, a Family Herald and Weekly Star subscriber in British Columbia, writes to the newspaper to say that the story on "Home Curing Pork" by Nellie Campbell has been very useful to her, and goes on to say:

My husband and I invested in two baby pigs last August. Carefully fed, they grew and grew. But as the day of their doom drew nearer, so did our dismay increase. Nowhere could we find directions as to how to cure the pork! And then, just in the nick of time, we received our Family Herald and Weekly Star newspaper with Nellie Campbell's useful article, "Sugar Cured Ham and Bacon."

SPRING COMES WITH A RUSH

By Nellie R. Campbell

Here in the interior of British Columbia, just north of fifty-four, spring often comes with a rush. So it was last year.

One week we looked out across fields still buried beneath a blanket of white, trees bending under the weight of a late snow. We heard the lake groaning and moaning and sending out long rumblings that told us that the ice was going – spring was coming -- and suddenly it was actually here.

Bare spots showed up on the northern slopes and about the buildings, the rhubarb poked through two inches of loose snow, a warm breeze blew from the Pacific. It was time to get out the garden seeds and start planting.

Bert got out the grub hoe and soon our early garden was ready to plant. We knew that by the time the peas, radishes, lettuce, onions and summer turnips had thrust their heads above ground, the snow would be gone and there would be little danger of a killing frost. The nights were still chilly, and we often wondered how the tender little shoots survived – but they did.

When the main garden plot had been plowed and worked down ready for seeding, we brought the seed potatoes from the root house, gave them a formaldehyde bath and Bert spread them on the floor of the spare bedroom to sprout.

By the time the winter root crops were in, the seed potatoes had developed sturdy green sprouts and it was time to plant them. Within a week they were showing through the ground.

Towards the end of May the days are longer and the night air is less chilly, so we plant the cucumbers, squash, marrows, pumpkins, bush and pole beans and set out the tomato plants started earlier in the house. I am sure that the lake often saves us from late spring frosts and also from the first fall frosts, but it also pays in this north land to start the garden just as soon as the land can be worked.

We have always been able to raise all of these things in quantities sufficient for our own needs but we have never tried to raise them on a commercial scale. Occasionally, the cucumber crop fails, so there are no cucumber pickles that fall, or frost may hit the corn when we are just beginning to enjoy it and we wonder why it couldn't have remained warm just a little longer until all of the corn had ripened.

By September the tomato vines are loaded with large, smooth tomatoes but they are still green. Since we installed a furnace in the basement this does not trouble us for we pull all of the vines with the fruit attached, at the first sign of a killing frost. Each vine is hung on a nail driven into the cellar wall. From September until early December we pick ripe tomatoes each day from the vines hanging on the walls of the furnace room. Even the small tomatoes ripen and none rot as they often do when picked and packed in a box to ripen.

By the time all of the snow of our long northern winter has melted it is usually near the end of April, and some years the first week in May. The ground has had very little, or no frost in it as the snow usually comes long before the severe weather sets in. Potatoes left in the ground in the fall will usually grow the following spring. One year we had enough volunteer potatoes to supply our needs and the needs of a neighbor for the summer.

We have learned, during our sixteen years on the homestead at Ness Lake, that one can raise corn, beans and cucumbers as far north as fifty-four with just a little care and forethought. It is necessary to start the garden just as soon as the land can be worked, even if it does mean grubbing up a large portion of it by hand just as fast as the snow melts.

Published May 7, 1947
Family Herald and Weekly Star
Sold-- $13.79

SURE CURE FOR WIREWORMS
By Nellie R. Campbell

In the Family Herald and Weekly Star recently under the heading "Horticulture," a question was asked regarding the control of wireworms in a field. Worm traps were recommended for small garden plots. The method consisted of sinking tubers beneath the surface and carefully marking the spot so that they could be dug up when they had lured the worms. This system works, and who should know better than I? Here is the story.

It all happened when we came to British Columbia, to homestead on the shores of Ness Lake, in 1929. We needed potatoes that first year to keep us going so we carefully spent our last ten dollars for seed potatoes.

The field was plowed, disked and harrowed and the precious seed planted with the utmost of care. Days passed but nothing happened. We made periodic trips to our potato patch but it still remained black – not a green shoot anywhere. June ended. It was the first Sunday in July, and I was getting supper when Bert returned from a walk to the field. For a while he sat in the big armchair that we had made out of a packing crate, completely lost in thought.

"I know why the potatoes aren't growing," he suddenly announced.

"Why?" I asked. I had been quick to condemn the soil in this new country.

"Wireworms," Bert stated laconically. "They're eating up the seed potatoes."

Our last ten dollars, -- there would be no potatoes to sell in the fall, worse still there would not be any to eat.

"But Bert, what can we do?" I asked in despair.

"We can dig up the seed and pick out the worms," he replied, just as if picking worms was nothing unusual.

"A whole half acre?" I protested.

"We planted them, didn't we? What's to hinder us digging them up?"

I had lived with Bert long enough to know he meant what he said. The next morning we went out armed with a jam tin and a crochet hook. The crochet hook was my idea. Sonny was only eight at the time but he had to do his bit.

Bert found the first row, -- the plowed field looked all the same to me. We dug with our hands in the loose soil until we found the bit of seed potato just bristling with yellow wireworms. The crochet hook proved ideal for hooking the little pests out of the potatoes and dropping them in the cans. The next potato should be about eighteen inches away in a straight line. Sonny went ahead searching for potato seed and picking up any loose worms he found in the holes while I hooked them into my can. Each bit of seed yielded from eight to eighteen stiff yellow worms. There was nothing left but a piece of honeycombed seed potato but we put it back and carefully covered it. Bert had started on the next row and managed to keep up with us.

Each noon when we returned to the cabin our jam tins were over three-quarters full of wriggling wireworms. It was the same at night. What to do with them was a question. I looked doubtfully at my dozen hens. If I threw them to the chickens some were sure to escape and crawl back into the garden by the cabin. Then there would be no lettuce, radishes and green peas. It seemed heartless, but boiling water seemed the only thing to do before feeding them to the chickens. For a week my biddies feasted on parboiled wireworms, for it took us just one week to dig up that half acre of potatoes, pick out all of the worms and replant the seed.

Did it pay? At the time it seemed to me a most tragic experience but that fall when we dug two tons of sound, marketable potatoes from our half acre field, we could laugh at the backaches and those days of kneeling on a plowed field in a hot July sun picking wireworms.

Yes, the method mentioned in the Family Herald and Weekly Star works, -- it is a sure cure for wireworms.

Published June 4, 1947
Family Herald and Weekly Star
Sold--$4.00.

HOW TO CAN MOOSE AND DEER MEAT

This article deals with the actual processing of deer and moose meat. Taken for granted that the meat has been properly butchered and prepared for preserving, the first step is cleanliness. A damp cloth may be used to wipe off pine or spruce needles or dirt of any kind. Portions of meat may need to be trimmed with a sharp knife. But, if at all possible, do not wash the meat with warm or cold water, but cleanse it in the manner described. The meat is then cut into small chunks or slices, not too large, and not too small. Your processing jars will help you judge accordingly, as the meat should be cut up proportionately to pack into the jars.

Be sure that the body heat is completely out of the meat. If you let the meat hang for a day or two, away from flies or other pests, it will be that much better for keeping. Two hunters of my acquaintance shot a moose and processed it almost immediately after killing the animal, as it was shot near their home. The body heat was still in the meat. Unfortunately, scores of quart jars of meat had to be thrown out. Remember, before preserving be sure that the body heat is completely out of the meat. This is of the utmost importance or all your efforts and meat will be wasted.

Now for the actual preserving. Some people cut up their game and put the raw meat in the preserving jars, adding a teaspoonful of salt to each quart jar, sealing and processing for about three hours. But better results can be obtained, with richer flavor, if the meat is first partly fried before placing in the sealers. Using a frying pan, the meat should be fried on both sides until it is browned richly, over a hot fire. Then the meat is placed in the sealers, packed in as tight as possible, and sealed. The processing time is about two hours. But be sure to use new sealer rings. A lot of moose or deer meat can go into a quart jar, and it is better to be safe than sorry, and one should use good jars and sealer rings to avoid spoiling the meat. Jars should be stored in a cool, dark place. Moose and deer meat tastes very good.

Published June 8, 1949
Family Herald and Weekly Star

CUTTING SEED POTATOES
By Nellie R. Campbell

"Why do women always do things the hard way?" Bert asked. I had volunteered to cut the seed potatoes for him. To be sure, it was a bit awkward to stoop down for the potato and then bend again to put it into the box but at least I had a comfortable chair to sit on.

"Here, let me show you." Bert was sharpening one of my wide bladed kitchen knives, which he drove into the end of a three foot board. Placing the board along the top of the box into which I had been dropping the cut seed potatoes, he sat astride the box. The sharp knife blade was directly in front of him. He pushed a potato against the knife blade, then turned it and cut the other way, dropping all four pieces in the box at the same time. It had taken less than half the time and there had been no bending.

"If you do it this way, you're not nearly as apt to injure the sprouts," he remarked.

Here, north of fifty-four, our growing season is short. Of course, the long days help, but there is always danger of a summer frost in late July or August. For three or four weeks before it is time to plant potatoes, my guest room is occupied. Bert uses it for his sprouting room.

If the seed is not absolutely clean and free from scab, he gives it a Formalin treatment. The potatoes are immersed for two hours in a solution of one pint of commercial Formalin to thirty gallons of water. This bath may be used several times in succession but if left overnight, a new solution should be prepared. The potatoes are taken out of the water and spread out on the floor with the seed end up. In a room with light and an average temperature, the potatoes will grow heavy, dark green sprouts which will appear above ground in about a week after being planted. Use dormant or only slightly sprouted whole tubers when treating; sprouted or cut tubers may be damaged by seed treatment. The treatment should be given at least fifteen days before planting and seed should be planted the same day as cut.

Bert has found that here in the interior of British Columbia, where the growing season is short, sprouting the potatoes in the house pays big dividends.

Published March 8, 1951
Family Herald and Weekly Star
Sold-- $4.52

CHRISTMAS FOR THE SHUT-IN
By Nellie R. Campbell

Quite often we have an invalid or a shut-in on our Christmas list that seems to present a real problem. So many other gifts that are suitable for mother or for sister Sue are neither appropriate nor of any use to one confined to his room.

This is how I solved the problem of the shut-in on my list last year. I made a laundry bag out of bright flowered cretonne (flowered drapery fabric). On the outside was fastened a pretty Christmas card with this verse written on the back:

I wish you a Merry Christmas
The merriest you've ever had
With a lot of lovely presents
To make you happy and glad.

This bag is full of good things,
One for each day in the week;
So every morning look inside,
And there a present seek.

They bring you Christmas Greetings,
And hopes for much good cheer;
Besides enough friendly wishes
To last throughout the year.

The bag contained just what the verses said, - a present for every day in the week following Christmas, the last one to be opened on New Years Day. The gifts were not expensive, but every one was something that a sick person could use. Each present was wrapped carefully in red, green or white tissue and bore a card with the date on which that particular package was to be opened. Inside the wrapping was an original verse with each gift.

The package dated December 26th contained three face cloths with this verse:

I know you'll find these useful
When 'ere you wash your face;
So don't forget to hang them
In some convenient place.

It isn't very much to give
To a friend so kind and true;
But they bring the best of wishes
To you the whole year through.

For December 27th there was a cover for a hot water bottle. It was made from a double thickness of outing flannel and cut the exact shape of the hot water bottle. The back was cut long enough to fold over the top of the bottle and fasten with a snap on the front. An opening was left at the top for the neck of the bottle and one the bottom of the tape. These were bound with bias tape. Pinned to the cover was this little verse:

A water bottle is a thing
That you are sure to need,
If you are cold or have a pain
It brings relief, with speed,
But oft, you find it is too hot,
Heat, more than you can bear;
And that's the very time, my friend,
This cover it should wear.

For December 28th there was a green package tied with white ribbon – a pad of writing paper, envelopes and a pencil. Inside was this verse:

I know you need writing paper
Whenever you write to a friend,
Or jot down those things you'd remember,
Or have a message to send.

This packages is filled with good wishes,
There are wishes one, two and three,
Health, happiness and God's blessing,
Are the things I'm wishing for thee.

A bright red package bore the date December 29th. It was a box of nicely scented toilet soap and inside was this verse:

I hope you'll like this toilet soap
And use it every day –
Just rub it in, - then rinse real well,
That is the "beauty" way.

When a person is sick, especially if meals must be served in bed, the top of the quilt is very apt to become soiled. A quilt protector seemed to be the remedy. It was made from a strip of cloth 54 inches wide. It was neatly hemmed. I used rose broadcloth and embroidered a simple design in the centre of the front edge. This strip could easily be basted over the top of the quilt allowing about 12 inches on the front where it was needed and 5 or 6 on the back. It is much easier to launder a quilt protector than a heavy comforter. The gift was wrapped in holly paper and dated December 30th. Inside was this verse:

A heavy quilt is hard to wash,
And so are blankets, too.
I find their edges sure to soil,
No matter what you do.

So I have made this little gift,
To keep your bed quilt clean,
Just baste it over the top edge,
You'll see just how I mean.

A white package with a sprig of holly tucked under the red bow had this verse wrapped around a jar of homemade jam.

Everyone likes a bit of jam,
To spread upon their bread;
It's made of juicy berries,
So ripe and sweet and red.

It brings a cheery greeting
To carry on its way;
It brings both joy and gladness,
Not just for Christmas, but for every day.

The package dated January 1st contained a book. It was a story that I had read and had enjoyed immensely. This little verse went with it:

Here is the last of the bundles,
Perhaps you'll think it the best;
At least, I hope that you'll like it,
As well as you have the rest.

It's just an interesting story,
To brighten up your day;
But it brings the hope that gladness
May go with you along life's way.

There are a number of gifts that would be acceptable to an invalid besides the ones I have mentioned. A box of talcum powder, bedroom slippers or crocheted bed socks, a bed jacket or kimono, a box of paper hankies or a few cotton handkerchiefs, a metal cover to keep food hot or an extra cushion – all these would surely be appreciated by anyone confined to her room. If original verses seem to be an utter impossibility for the giver, a cheery message quotation or a Scripture text could be added to the gift.

Often it is not the present itself that brings the most pleasure to the shut-in but the thoughtfulness back of the gift. That is what really counts.

Published November 20, 1946
Family Herald and Weekly Star
Sold--$4.58

TRUTH IN ANCIENT GUISE
By Nellie R. Campbell

It all came about by a chance remark, "Well, I've been all round Robin Hood's barn this morning," I said as I sank into my favourite rocker.

Marjorie, aged twelve, looked up from her book. "How funny—Robin Hood's barn," she repeated. "Where did you hear that one," she asked, "on the radio?"

"Radio, nothing," I replied, "why, that is as old as the hills."

"Old as the hills," she said. "Where do you get those expressions? I never heard them."

For a moment I sat and looked at her. She was slim, attractive, and yet I felt that perhaps the child's education had been sadly neglected. She probably never had heard any of the sayings that had been a part of my up bringing.

"I don't suppose you ever heard this one then," I said. "Everyone to his own taste, as the old woman said when she kissed the cow."

"But that's just plain nonsense," she said giving me one of those pitying looks that one sometimes sees on the faces of the very young.

I sat and mused. What had become of these old sayings that had held so many of the fundamental truths? They were old. Nobody knew how old. They had been handed down from generation to generation and yet they were no longer in common use.

"Put tire to tire and at it again," I could see my grandmother sitting beside a pile of wool. The big box by her side was overflowing with fluffy, white batts. The carding had been a long and tedious task. Put tire to tire and at it again. Involuntarily her stooped shoulders would straighten and she would attack the diminishing pile of wool with renewed energy.

Then, there had been that one about the Lamplighter. "He went like a Lamplighter." Of course the days of the Lamplighter were a thing of the past when I was young but the picture of the Lamplighter in our old third reader always fascinated me. I can still see him hastening down the village street, the lamp on the post behind him burning brightly. It was a race with time.

LITTLE PITCHERS

There were times when our elders discussed things that were supposed to be of no concern whatsoever to us children. My uncle Earl was one of these topics. He had become a doctor and then instead of settling down in good old New England, as any promising young man should have done, he had completely upset the entire family by taking his young bride and sailing away to South America. I always had a secret admiration for Uncle Earl, but Grandma was wont to say, "A rolling stone gathers no moss." If we showed too great an interest in this exciting episode we were sure to hear about little pitchers having big ears.

At the tender age of seventeen my father had found himself left alone in a big city with his mother and a crippled sister to support. He did it and did it well. Perhaps that was the reason that we were never allowed to forget that. A penny saved is a penny earned. He was never mean or miserly, simply careful. This oft repeated truth did far more in teaching us economy than a scolding for some of our ill advised spending ever would have done.

Another saying along this same line was beautifully carved around the edge of our breadboard. It was a round board of smooth, hard wood. The edge had been turned with a lathe and in raised Old English letters were four short words, - Waste not – Want not. More than once mother patiently reminded me that I was supposed to be cutting the bread for supper instead of standing there idly tracing those beautiful letters with a small finger. Perhaps I was not wasting time after all because those four little words somehow became a part of me.

HOMELY TRUTHS

Nor were these maxims confined entirely to our home life. They even followed us to school. Our teacher was a tall man with piercing blue eyes behind gold rimmed spectacles. In spite of his stern manner we all loved him. He had two sayings that still stand clearly in my memory. A place for everything and everything in its place. I have often been most thankful that he saw that this rule was ridgedly adhered to. Then there were times when lessons were hard and work became difficult. You know, "Where there's a will there's a way," he would say, not unkindly. There always seemed to be something so reassuring about these old sayings that they gave one courage to keep on trying. The life of a homesteader is not always an easy one and many times I have felt deep gratitude toward a grey haired man who taught me many things not found in books.

It was my first school. I guess most girls are unduly elated when their training is ended and then finally begin to teach. I know that I was. Mother and Grandmother listened quietly to my graphic account of my first week and to the drastic changes I had made. "A new broom always sweeps clean," mother remarked. Grandma stopped her knitting and looked at me over the rims of her spectacles, "but it's the old broom that gets the corners best," she finished quietly and resumed her knitting. The bubble of my pride and self-esteem had suddenly been pricked.

No matter where you live or who you are, there are times when troubles come. Sometimes we feel that we are getting a bit more than our share. It is then that we know that it is a long lane that has no turning and that it is always darkest just before the dawn. There is a lasting, enduring quality about these old sayings that give us strength and courage to look ahead. It is then that we often glimpse that silver lining that is behind every cloud.

My mind went back to Marjorie and to the hundreds of children like her who had never heard these old sayings. Some of them may have been crude but each expressed in a homely sort of way some fundamental truth. It was upon these simple truths that we, our mothers and our grandmothers, had built our lives. With the passing of these wise old maxims it seems that the Marjories of today have missed a great, great deal. What do you think?

Published April 12, 1950
Family Herald and Weekly Star
Sold--$8.88

WATCH OUT FOR THE COLD GERM
By Nellie R. Campbell

Most of us are susceptible to colds and at this season of the year the cold germ seems to be most active in both city and rural communities. In most diseases "an ounce of prevention is worth a pound of cure," and this old axiom surely can be applied to a cold.

But how can we prevent a cold? Perhaps the simplest way is to look back to some of its causes. Sitting or leaning on a cold object or sitting in a draft, going from an overheated room in to cold atmosphere without sufficient clothing, allowing the body to become chilled or run down by insufficient rest or food, all make one more susceptible to a cold.

There are a few simple rules that it is well to follow, --

1. Do not go to work or school without a warm breakfast.
2. Wear sufficient clothing to be comfortable in severe weather.
3. Form the habit of breathing through the nose, keeping the mouth shut. This allows the air to become warm before reaching the lungs.
4. Do not go to bed with cold or damp feet. Keep your feet warm at all times.

If you do catch a cold there are many simple home remedies that are effective. Whether it is a head cold or a chest cold, rest is important. Keep warm, avoid drafts, drink plenty of liquid and keep the bowels open.

Always use paper hankerchiefs and burn them.

One of the best remedies for a cold and one not at all unpleasant to take is hot lemonade. The patient should drink 2/3 to a pint as hot as possible upon retiring and keep well covered.

AN OLD STANDBY

If one has a dry, hacking cough, 2 or 3 tablespoons of flaxseed may be added to the juice of 2 large lemons, 2 tablespoons of sugar and 1 quart of boiling water. Put in covered dish on the back of the stove to steep until the mucilage has been drawn out of the flaxseed. Take a tablespoon every hour or oftener if needed to relieve the dryness in the throat.

I do not know where my grandmother got this recipe but it was handed down and onion syrup became a standby in our New England home. Slice a few mild onions and sprinkle sugar over them. Set in an open oven to heat just enough for the sugar to bring out the juice forming a thick syrup. We children were given a teaspoonful or less, according to age, four or five times a day. This is a simple yet safe remedy for even the smallest child. It is claimed that onions have a high food value and that the nourishing property of the onion more than doubles that of the potato. The onion also possesses a soothing quality.

A pinch of salt will often loosen phlegm and used as a gargle it is both healing and antiseptic.

Steam has proven most efficacious in relieving congestion and in opening closed nasal passages. If the patient is confined to bed, a simple inhalation tent may be made by placing an umbrella draped with blankets over him. A kettle of water on an electric stove, a coil-oil heater or sterno placed on a chair or table close to the edge of the bed will provide sufficient steam. A funnel made from heavy wrapping paper should be placed over the nose of the kettle to carry the steam under the edge of the blanket.

We all know that a bad cold is a disagreeable experience for the grown-up but doctors say that it is even harder for the baby or very small child. For this reason we should all take precautions to prevent colds. Don't take the baby into crowded places and do not let people having colds go near the baby. If you yourself develop a cold and have to take care of the baby, use a mask. A piece of folded gauze 4 by 6 is a good size. Be careful to wash your hands before handling the baby. Do not give him a tub bath if he has a cold but sponge him, keeping him covered during the process. Put him to bed but not out of doors to sleep in his carriage. If the baby is old enough to toddle about, see that he wears slippers and that his feet are warm. Never urge a baby to eat more that he wants when he is sick. Orange juice is good and the child should have plenty of liquid.

These are just a few simple rules that the busy housewife can follow when a cold invades the home. An old recipe book printed over sixty years ago gave this bit of advice regarding colds, -- *"keep your feet warm, your head cool, and your mouth shut and you will seldom catch cold"*. Maybe this is good advise for the modern generation.

Published March 16, 1949
Family Herald and Weekly Star
Sold - $7.05

YOU DON'T NEED TO LEAVE HOME
By Nellie R. Campbell

Should farm women have an annual vacation? Last week I had a short note from one of my neighbors. It was a cheery little note. Her husband was taking his annual vacation. "Of course I'll have the chores to do while he is gone, but it shouldn't be too hard. Come on down and see me some day," she wrote.

We were chatting as I helped her clear away the dinner dishes. "Too bad you couldn't have a vacation, too," I said.

She looked surprised. "But this is my vacation," she replied. "You see I always take my vacation at home while Jim is away."

How could anyone take a vacation at home with five small children and seven cows to milk morning and night, I wondered. She smiled at my puzzled look. "Yesterday we packed a lunch and the children and I went down to the creek for the day. You should have seen Bess paddling in the water. I even took off my shoes and stockings and went paddling, too. Dale caught enough fish for our supper.

Mom has promised to take care of the baby tomorrow and we are going berry picking down on the old burn. The children love these picnics. We've planned something different for every day Jim is gone. I don't find the chores too hard, as Dale is such a help now. She smiled fondly at her ten year-old son.

Jim does so enjoy his trip to the city every summer and we couldn't both leave the farm and take the children. I'd worry every minute if I left them at home. Everything works out just fine this way. It's a nice change for both of us and even if the garden is neglected while Jim is away we catch up on things when he gets home."

As I walked home that night I thought of how a young woman alone on a large farm with five small children and the added burden of chores, had turned the two weeks, that to many of us would have been a real hardship, into a holiday for herself. I knew that she was right. She was actually finding more pleasure at home with her lively, little brood than she could ever find alone in the finest summer resort the country afforded.

I believe that many farm women could have an annual vacation – one that they would really enjoy, without ever leaving home.

Published July 16, 1947
Family Herald and Weekly Star
Sold--$1.70

WHY NOT HAVE A GUEST BOX
By Nellie R. Campbell

"What a charming bedroom," I exclaimed, as Nancy showed me into the room I was to occupy. The sun poured through the south window giving the room such a cheery aspect. There was a big armchair covered with the prettiest green and white cross bar material imaginable. It looked so cool and inviting that I could not resist the temptation to settle myself comfortable in it while I looked about me.

The bed was a plain wooden one, - I had seen hundreds of them stored away in old attics in the east, - and yet Nancy had contrived to make it look as if it had been made especially for that room. It had been painted a soft grey-green and had a wonderful spray of flowers in the centre of the foot and the headboard. The straight backed chair in front of the desk was painted the same soft shade of green only the spray on the wooden back was much smaller. I learned afterward that the sprays of flowers were Decalcomanias and could be applied quite easily after the painting was finished.

The floor was of plain boards stained a pleasing brown. Two lovely hooked rugs, - one by the bed, the other in front of the door we entered, took away any bareness that there might have been.

Beneath the east window, which was long and narrow, stood a writing desk. It was such a jolly little affair painted green like the bed and chair that one would never have dreamed that it had been made from two packing boxes set well apart with a smooth, wide board across for a table top. Joe had fitted a long narrow drawer under the top in the space between the boxes and Nancy had made the same dainty green and white curtains for the side boxes to hide the shelves beneath.

The ink bottle and quaint pen on the large green blotter reminded me of all the letters that I intended to write while on my vacation. Yes, Nancy had even placed a writing pad close at hand for my convenience.

Beneath the south window was a cozy window seat piled high with pillows – just the sort of place I had loved to curl up upon when a girl and read.

'But, Nancy," I expostulated, "how did you ever do it? Here I come west to visit you, expecting no conveniences whatever in the log house you've written about and I find a charming little room as comfortable as any I've ever seen."

Nancy's eyes twinkled and that gay, happy laugh that I remembered when we were together at school rang out.

"It's my secret, Madge, but I'll tell you. It's my guest box."

THE CONTENTS

"Your guest box?" I queried, looking about. Nancy pointed to the long, low window seat covered with the same dainty green and white material as the chair. "It really is my guest box," she confided.

"You see, Madge, when Joe and I were married we had just two rooms, - this bedroom and a general room, - a living room and a kitchen combined. You know that I have always loved to have company but honestly, Madge, before that first year was over I actually dreaded to see anyone coming to stop overnight. Of course, Joe had to build fires and do chores and I had to get breakfast, so it was impossible to put guests in our one general room. It meant that I must give them this room. I can still see myself rushing about with my arms full of bedclothes, changing beds, hunting for clean pillowcases, a nice towel and a fresh cake of soap. We had very little money, so I knew that to build on another room for a guest room was quite out of the question. It was then that I thought of a guest box.

Joe built my window seat box, and I began at once to fix up my guest room. I tried to make the old furniture as comfortable and as pleasing to the eye as possible for my own pleasure as well as my quests, and I was careful to choose material for all the curtains and chair coverings that would look both cool and dainty and yet launder easily. Then I began to fill my guest-box. Of course, it took me quite a while for I didn't have the money to buy the things I wanted. Some of the things I have made, a few I have bought and the rest are Christmas and birthday gifts. It really is the things in my guest box that "dress up" the room and make it a pleasure to have people stop overnight for it is no longer any trouble to me. I keep a pretty quilt, blankets, clean sheets, - both cotton and flannelette ones and a nice pair of pillowslips, - everything I need for the bed, - inside my box. Then there is always a fresh cover for the dresser and the washstand, clean towels, brush, comb and a new bar of toilet soap. I even have a nightie, one I found far too fine for everyday use, stored away just in case someone isn't prepared to stay.

I can just slip into the bedroom and "presto" everything is ready in a few minutes for I'm always sure that everything I need is in my box. And the best part of it is that when my box is empty, my guests can use it for their clothes. See, it is divided into four sections, similar to drawers and so it is not necessary for me to empty the bureau drawers each time company arrives. With so little space I don't know how I'd manage without my guest box.

"Nancy, you're a genius," I exclaimed.

"No, Madge," she replied, "I'm just one of hundreds of women living in two or three rooms and trying to make them comfortable and homelike."

Published November 17, 1948
Family Herald and Weekly Star
Sold--$8.10

HOW EFFICIENT ARE YOU?
By Nellie R. Campbell

Just how efficient was I as a housekeeper? That was the question I asked myself after reading an article in a recent magazine written by an Efficiency Expert. It seems that any woman should be able to get a hot breakfast, hustle the children away to school on time, clean and with a lunch pail of nourishing food, attend to the numerous needs of a small infant, dispatch the family wash, prepare dinner and supper and keep the house tidy without being all fagged out at the end of the day, - that is, if she is an efficient housekeeper. In other words, - if she lets her head save her heals.

I looked about my kitchen. To all outward appearances it was a very pleasant kitchen with ample cupboard space but did it really let my head save my heels. There was the matter of washday for instance. The bags of Blue were in the bottom drawer, the washing soda was in one cupboard while the soap was in the cupboard across the room and the bottle of bleach was under the sink. My clothespins were in a pail in the pantry, - thirty-four steps to collect these things, when they all might just as well have been on a shelf by themselves at the top of the broom closet. There was ample space for a shelf there and the closet was in a convenient place. Fifty-two wash days in a year, - 1768 needless steps.

How much wasted time gathering the things needed for breakfast? Having spent all of my married life over twenty miles from a town and stores we have always bought in quantities and kept staple supplies ahead. My pantry shelves have always been more or less a matter of pride to me, however, how much more sensible it would be to keep the cereals in the cupboard near the stove. I had been taught to stack all pots and pans neatly in one cupboard yet the double-boiler and a cup on the shelf with the breakfast cereal would save countless steps in the course of a year. It was the same with coffee and tea. The coffee can with a measuring spoon inside belonged beside the coffee pot in the cupboard near the stove. That too, was the place for the teapot and tea canister. Of course salt, so indispensable in all cooking, should be close to the stove.

COMFORT IN THE KITCHEN

I found that I had been guilty of wasting time in washing dishes. With a pan of piping hot water beside my dishpan I could dip each dish as I stacked it in the drying rack and then go merrily on my way to some more important task and let them dry themselves. There would be no more dishtowels to wear out or wash. The whole process would not only save time but would be far more sanitary.

The author of this article on efficiency (by the way he happened to be a man) believed that every kitchen should be equipped with a high kitchen stool and a good old fashioned rocker. There was a time when my kitchen could have boasted both of these pieces of furniture but in trying to achieve the "modern look" both had been crowded out. However, they are coming back. I'm sure that I peeled vegetables and shelled peas just as efficiently sitting comfortably in that old rocking chair as I ever did standing straight beside the kitchen sink. My kitchen stool is also coming into use. There are countless jobs, - ironing for one, - that I can do just as well sitting down, thus relieving both the feet and the back.

With a rack under my dish pan to make it the right height to work without bending, the stove raised an inch and my ironing board lowered, my cupboards re-arranged so that needed articles are immediately at hand, I am well on the way to becoming an efficient housekeeper. There is only one thing that is troubling me now. Will I loose precious time and energy searching for the countless things that have vanished from their long accustomed places or will I become such an efficient housekeeper that ere long I will find time hanging heavily on my hands? I guess only time will tell.

Published November 16, 1949
Family Herald and Weekly Star

THREE NECESSITIES
By Nellie R. Campbell

It was a lovely pair of slippers! Just the kind I had dreamed about for the dance. To be sure, they were a bit narrow, but I could squeeze my foot into them and what was a little discomfort, - they would stretch with wearing as all shoes did. They would have been mine, had not Grandma gone shopping with me that day.

She took the golden slipper from my hand and carefully laid it back in its box. I knew then that those dream slippers would never belong to me.

That was many years ago, but I have never forgotten the things Grandma told me that day. According to Grandma there are three things that are quite essential to every woman's happiness and well being. The first is good shoes. By that, I do not mean a shoe of the latest style, but a shoe of soft pliable leather – one that conforms to the shape of the foot. Most people have the idea that feet are – well, just feet, pretty much the same except for size, but experts tell us that feet are by no means standardized and are as individual as faces! They have family and racial characteristics just as faces have.

A good foot should be both flexible and muscular. The muscles in our feet play a most important part in our every day life so in choosing foot wear one should look for a shoe that does not interfere with the natural mobility of the more than twenty moving parts of the foot. In a well fitting shoe the heel-casing or counter is the only part that should be snug fitting. The forepart should allow free movement of every joint including those of the toes. Most of us at some time, either from vanity, ignorance or economic necessity, have subjected our feet to unnecessary strain and sooner or later we will be called upon to pay for our indiscretions.

SECOND ESSENTIAL

The second essential is a good light. Just as we subject our feet to undue strain, some of us are guilty of subjecting our eyes to constant strain because of the poor lighting in our homes. There were times in those early days of homesteading when many of us had to be content with a small coal oil lamp that left the greater part of the room in deep gloom, but those days are past. With the coming of electricity into many farm homes, the problem of providing sufficient light for each room should not be too difficult. Perhaps the most important room in the house is the kitchen as this is the room in which the housewife spends the greater part of her time, yet it is often poorly lighted. The kitchen should be arranged that there is good light by the stove and the worktable, both day and night.

Even we, who live where electricity is not available, can discard our old coal oil lamps in favor of gas lamps and lanterns. With proper shades, one can have sufficient light for ordinary work, reading or mending without that glare that is so hard on the eyes.

THIRD ESSENTIAL

The third essential is a good bed. Having homesteaded both in Saskatchewan and in British Columbia in the early days when homesteading was homesteading, I have slept on the ground, in a horse stall, on top of a haystack, on a spruce bed and on a tick filled with the fluff from cat-o-nine tails. However, as I grow older, I am more and more convinced that every woman is entitled to a good bed. If the housewife can appear each morning refreshed and cheerful from a night of real rest, the day is off to a good start. Did you ever notice how mother's morning attitude affects the entire family? So after all, what is more essential than a good bed?

We have only one pair of feet, one pair of eyes and one back to last us an entire life time, so it behooves each one of us to treat then with the respect that is their proper due.

Yes, Grandma was right – good shoes, good light and a good bed are all essential to every woman's happiness and well being.

Published October 12, 1950
Family Herald and Weekly Star
Sold--$5.61

STUNT PARTIES ARE FUN
By Nellie R. Campbell

Winter is the time of year that everyone enjoys a good party so I want to tell you about a stunt party that really is fun. By using seasonal decorations it can be a holiday party at any season or it can just be a party that is fun for all ages.

You will need as many small tables (card tables or small household tables) as events you plan to have. Each guest draws a name from a bowl to select his partner. The partners line up and each is given a scorecard. These cards give the hostess great scope for ingenuity as they may be in the shape of hearts, rabbits, egg shaped, bells or just plain oblong cards according to the season of the year in which you are giving the party. Ten events are a good number for an evening's fun but you may have more or less. The events should be numbered and printed in a vertical row on each scorecard. Each table is numbered 1 to 10. On each table has been placed the material needed for the stunt corresponding to the same number on the scorecard. The hostess starts each event by the tap of a bell. Three minutes is long enough for each stunt. When the hostess gives the signal to stop, each contestant must stop immediately. Each one counts the score that he has made and then proceeds to put the things back in order for the next contestants. The table must be left just as it was found. The hostess moves quickly from one table to the next punching the scorecards. The winner at table 1 will move to table 2, while the winner at table 9 will move to table 1, but the loser must remain behind and do that stunt all over again. This makes it more interesting as partners are constantly changing. If your party is a large one, then four may be seated at a table and the two having the highest scores would move on.

NO DULL MOMENTS
Now for the stunts and the fun.

No. 1. Peas – A bowl of round peas in centre of the table. Each contestant has a small dish and a silver knife. Object: To transfer the most peas from the bowl to the small dish using the blade of the knife only (no fingers) and trying to avoid spilling them as every pea must be picked up when the stunt is finished.

No. 2. International – Each contestant is given a slip of paper at the top of which has been written the word International. Object: To make the most short words using only those letters found in the longer word, as – rat, ten, etc.

No. 3. Peanuts – A tin dish full of peanuts in the shell in centre of table. Each contestant has a steel knitting needle. Object: To spear the most peanuts. (No fingers allowed).

No. 4. Needles – Pin-cushion in centre of table filled with needles of various sizes. Each contestant has a spool of thread. Object: He must break off a piece of thread, tie a knot and then thread on as many needles as possible in the allotted time.

No. 5. Nails – Each contestant has a hammer, a can of shingles or lath nails and a small piece of board. Object: To pound the most nails into the board. It is advisable not to pound them in too far as contestant must remove them when stunt is finished.

No. 6. Buttons – A box or dish of assorted buttons in centre of table. Each contestant has needle and thread and small square of heavy cloth. Object: To sew the most buttons on the cloth. One thread is sufficient providing it will hold the button.

No. 7. Rhymes – Each contestant has a paper and pencil. On the top of paper is list of simple words as cat, mouse, bee, etc. Object: To make short rhymes using the words given, as:

She had a cat
Which was very fat
The cat caught a mouse
As big as a house

No. 8. Words – Each contestant has a box of cut up letters such as children use in school. Object: To make short rhymes using the letters.

No. 9. Alphabet – Each contestant has a piece of brown paper and a pair of scissors. Object: Starting with A cut as many letters as possible free hand.

No. 10. Feather – A large sheet is spread out and everyone stands around it with both hands holding the edge of the sheet. The hostess tosses the feather into the air. It is the object of each player to prevent the feather from touching him. If it does he must sit down. Of course the last one standing wins. Players should keep the sheet taut at all times.

While the feather game is being played, the hostess sees that all stunt material is removed from the tables and each spread with a cloth or paper doilies. By the time the game has ended the guests will be quite ready to return to their tables for refreshments.

If a party is to be a success there must never be dull moments and I can assure you that there will be few dull moments if you decide to give a Stunt Party.

Published March 8, 1950
Family Herald and Weekly Star
Sold--$8.31

PRETTY PACKAGES
By Nellie R. Campbell

Girlish laughter rang out. Busy fingers reached for bits of gold or silver paper salvaged from chocolate bars, or snipped small pieces from the gaily colored Christmas cards that lay on the table. What were we doing? You never would guess, - we were covering discarded egg boxes. With Easter just around the corner, what better container could one wish for those Easter Eggs than an honest-to-goodness egg box, providing of course, that it had an outward appearance appropriate for the occasion.

Sometimes a tiny picture of an angel, bird or flower was carefully cut from a card and fitted into the mosaic-like covering of the box. When each box had been completely covered with tiny bits of bright colored paper and the paste had dried, it was given a coat of clear shellac.

We had just as good a time filling our boxes as we had had making them for there was the opportunity to sample the goodies that went inside. Each small compartment with its colored straw made an ideal nest for the small eggs or the larger chocolate coated ones.

Then, when each box had been wrapped in cellophane and tied with yellow, green or lavender ribbon there were the trips to the Orphanage and the Hospital. I believe that this was the most fun of all for each of us came away with the memory of a childish face aglow with the happiness because of a simple gift.

Published March 22, 1951
Family Herald and Weekly Star
Sold--$2.00

GRANDMA AND HER MAGIC BAG
By Nellie R. Campbell

It was in those good old horse and buggy days that Grandma came to live with us. I still remember the awe with which I viewed her plump feather bed atop its tick filled with fresh corn husks – no modern bed for Grandma. Then there was her high backed rocking chair. Long since, the cotton padding beneath its gay chintz cover had conformed, from constant use, to Grandma's ample curves. Her desk, the grain of the beautiful oak wood, hidden beneath several coats of bright red paint – Grandma had an eye for color – stood across one corner of her room.

As a small child I am not sure which really fascinated me more, her fragile blue and white plate and cup and saucer, which we children must handle with the greatest of care, or her bag of herbs. Possibly it was the herb bag for out of it was sure to come a cure for no matter what ill befell any member of the family.

Grandma knew a sight about herbs. She knew that plantain leaves mashed to a pulp, took the pain out of cuts and bruises and open wounds, that sassaparilla, yellow root and black alder bark were good tonics, that dandelion root and hoarhound herb toned up the liver and that pennyroyal, yarrow and sage leaves produced perspiration, if taken hot, and were useful in breaking up a cold.

GATHERING HERBS

Grandma's family had consisted of a baker's dozen and no doubt, it was because she often had been forced to rely upon her own resources in case of sickness that she had become a connoisseur in the art of gathering herbs. She knew that to obtain the full medicinal value of each herb that it should be gathered in the morning in clear, dry weather after the dew was gone. They were best when the plant was in bloom. The leaves of biennials were always best in their second year of growth. They should be spread out thinly on a clean paper on the floor and stirred occasionally. Well dried leaves, should retain their natural green color and never be packaged until thoroughly dry. Dampness will turn them black.

Sometimes Grandma used the entire herb as medicine. She stripped off the flowers, small leaves and very small stems discarding the woody ones. These she dried in the same manner as the leaves. Often the flowers have more medicinal value than the leaves and they are always at their best as soon as they open. They should be dried the same as the leaves and should retain much of the natural color.

If seeds are to be used medicinally, they should be gathered as soon as they ripen. Only the plump, fully developed seeds are of value and Grandma winnowed out the rest.

Bark may be gathered in either spring or fall. The rough outer bark of wild cherry and other rough barks must first be scraped off and then the inner bark peeled, for it is the inner bark that is used for medicine. Most barks may be dried in sunlight but wild cherry is best dried in the shade.

Bulbs should be gathered as soon as the leaves of the plant have dried. The outer covering of the bulb should be taken off and then the bulb dried by artificial heat – below 100 degrees Fahrenheit.

Dirt should be removed from all roots either by shaking or rinsing. The roots should then be spread out on clean racks and dried in the sunlight. Grandma always brought them in each night to avoid the dampness of the night air.

With the coming of Grandma to live with us, our Sunday afternoon drives often took us away from the seashore into the back country. With old Kit, our sorrel mare, hitched to the democrat, we would jog along little used country roads for Grandma remembered where we would be sure to find checkerberries or maybe it was tansy that she wanted. It was in early spring that the balm of Gilead buds must be gathered. A peculiar, agreeable, balsamic odor would fill our kitchen as Grandma boiled the buds in lard or pure olive oil and strained the liquid through fine muslin into jars and small bottles to cool.

It was in the late fall that Grandma made her hop salve by boiling in lard two parts of stramonium leaves with one of hop flowers. This was an excellent application for skin irritation and itching.

RED FLANNEL

In my young days, colds were probably the most common ailment in our family and Grandma's magic bag contained remedies that would put to rout the most persistent cough or cold. I was the only member of our family who suffered from an attack of mucous croup each winter. At the first raucous whoop out came the large bottle of goose grease that Grandma had brought with her from the old farm and my chest was well rubbed with its oily contents. It was Grandma that insisted that I wear red flannel shirts all winter. I have never been able to discover the special merits of red flannel but Grandma maintained that it was far superior to white and not even mother would have thought of contradicting her. In spite of vehement protests on my part, each winter I donned my red flannel shirts for I lived in an age when children were taught to obey. The day that I had to try on my new dress, made especially for the Christmas Concert and I stood before the dressmaker, arrayed in my red flannel shirt and smelling of goose grease, deep humiliation filled my soul. Tears were of no avail for red flannel, goose grease and quantities of hot pennyroyal or sage tea were Grandma's remedy for croup.

She always said that the best way to get rid of a nasty cold was to "sweat it out." There were various herbs in her big bag that caused increased perspiration. These were made into tea and taken hot in large quantities at bedtime. Pennyroyal, yarrow, hoarhound, sage and tangy were favourites for tea whenever the cold germ struck.

Pennyroyal – the whole herb is used. It grows in barren and dry fields flowering from June to September. It may be recognized by its small light blue flowers and fragrant odor - which, it is claimed, is obnoxious to insects. It is a gentle stimulant and causes the evacuation of waste material through the sweat glands. It also dispels flatulency of the stomach. We rather liked its pleasing flavour, especially when allowed to add cream and sugar to our tea. Grandma used a teaspoon full of the herb to each cup of boiling water.

COMMON HERBS

Yarrow – may be found growing in pastures and along the roadside. Its white or faintly pinkish flowers grow in a knot or cluster at the top of a leafy stalk. It has a sharp, astringent taste due to tannic acid. The whole herb is used and one teaspoon of the herb cut very fine and steeped in a cup of boiling water and taken a mouthful at a time throughout the day affects the sweat glands and acts as a tonic.

Hoarhound – This herb may be distinguished by its white, hoary appearance and the whole herb should be gathered before it blossoms. It has rather an agreeable odor and a bitter and persistent taste. It is a stimulant tonic, aids excretion of mucous and increases the flow of urine. The dose consisted of one teaspoon full of the herb steeped in a cup of boiling water and taken cold during the day. We children never objected to molasses candy flavoured with hoarhound which Grandma insisted was good for growing youngsters.

Sage – Most New England gardens had one or two sage bushes so Grandma never had to go far a-field for sage. If taken hot before retiring, it causes perspiration but one or two cups full taken cold during the day are mildly tonic. One teaspoon full of the dried herb to a cup full of boiling water is sufficient.

Tansy – This herb is called Bitter-buttons and in olden days was supposed to be a cure for most ills. Many years ago *Gerards* wrote, "In the spring time, are made with the leaves hereof newly sprung up, and with eggs, cakes or Tansies which be pleasant in taste and goode for the Stomache." A magazine published in 1656 assures maidens that tansy leaves laid to soak in buttermilk for nine days, "Maketh the complexion very fair." It was no wonder that Grandma planted tansy in her flower garden. It is claimed that drying destroys much of the activity of the herb but even then it should be diluted in making tea, as one teaspoon of the herb to a pint of boiling water is sufficient.

Mullein and hops were herbs that Grandma used for various ailments.

Mullein – Both flowers and leaves are used. Even Grandma gathered mullein. We children loved to stroke the large, thick, plush leaves, – elephant's ears, we called them. The yellow flowers growing on a tall, stiff spike and opening only a few at a time, are not at all beautiful and yet in spite of this, I always protest when Bert suggests uprooting the mullein in my garden here at Ness Lake, B.C. Is it because of those early days – and Grandma?

A hot infusion was good for coughs and diarrhea. Grandma sometimes boiled mullein in milk and sweetened it to make it a bit more palatable. A fomentation of the leaves in hot vinegar was used as a local application for external irritations as itching piles. Grandma sometimes put a handful of mullein leaves in a teapot and covered them with boiling water. The steam inhaled from the spout of the teapot was good for nasal congestion or catarrh and relieved throat irritation.

SPRING MEDICINE

It was in late winter or early spring that Grandma always brought forth her tonics, for what person's system does not need a little "toning up" come spring. Perhaps her favourite was dandelion root. One teaspoon full of the root cut very fine and steeped for half an hour in one cup of boiling water made a very bitter drink, most unpleasant to take, but very good for you Grandma averred.

Yellow Root and Gold Thread – These are both members of the Crowfoot family and are powerful tonic. With yellow root it was just the root that Grandma used but she used both the root and the plant of the gold thread. One teaspoonful of the root to a cup of boiling water and steeped for half an hour made a pure bitter tonic. It was taken a tablespoon full at a time, three to six times a day.

It was when we had canker that we came running to Grandma for she had learned that gold thread root makes an excellent gargle.

Published June 11, 1953
Family Herald and Weekly Star
Sold--$15.39

MENDING TIME AND EVERYTHING'S HANDY
By Nellie R. Campbell

Now's the time to attack that huge pile of mending accumulated or to do a bit of new sewing or work on makeover garments.

A wonderful time saver is a small piece of wood 4 by 12 inches with two rows of finishing nails 1 ¾ inches long driven into it about 1 ¾ inches apart. With two small picture nails hang this strip of wood over the sewing machine within easy reach. On it hang your spools of thread and basting cotton, scissors, emery bag, thimble and a small cushion well filled with pins and extra needles. There will be no delay in searching for these necessary things.

Perhaps you have had trouble with the children's underwaists tearing out at the hem from their garter pins. This can be avoided if a narrow strip of cloth folded double for strength is stitched from the shoulder seam down the center of each front of the waist. The strip should end in a short tab about one inch below the hem of the waist. If the garter pin is pinned to this tab there is no strain on the waist and no danger of tearing.

Published March 5, 1947
Free Press Prairie Farmer
Sold -- $1.70

SPINNING – A LOST ART
By Nellie R. Campbell

Did you ever go adventuring? It really is a lot of fun. My husband and I had ridden a long way that morning on our bicycles. The woodsy trail that turned off abruptly to our left looked cool and inviting. Of course, it might be only a bush road leading to some homesteader cutting mine props in the forest, or, -- well, who could tell just where that woodsy trail would lead?

We turned off the dusty highway. The large clusters of deep purple saskatoons invited us to stop and eat. It was at the top of a small rise that we caught the first glimpse of a shake roof and then the log walls of the cabin came into view. The land sloped away in front to a broad meadow dotted with grazing sheep, --70, at rough count.

A man and a woman were standing in the doorway as we approached. They were central Europeans, -- both had been born in Bulgaria and had come to Canada many years ago. Mr. George had worked on construction jobs so could speak good English, but Mrs. George could only smile her welcome. The men talked together of many things. When at last the conversation turned to gardening, they went outside to look at the neat garden just west of the building. For a while we sat in silence as neither one of us could speak the other's language.

SHARED INTERESTS

I had often carded wool but had never before seen wool carded in large round batts such as these in a large pile near the bed. I pointed to the heap of snowy white wool. Without knowing it, I had hit upon the one subject most dear to her heart. She rose and picking up a fluffy batt, reached for a stick about 27 inches long. It had been carved by hand, but was worn smooth by much handling. She thrust the batt over one end of the stick and fastened it securely by winding a narrow fold of cloth around it just a little above the base of the batt. She seated herself in a low chair and thrust the other end of the stick down the binding of her skirt under her left arm.

I watched her fingers as she pulled a thin strand of wool from the base of the batt with the thumb and forefinger of her left hand. It increased in length – 18, 20, 30 inches. The end was then fastened around the middle of a slender spindle held in her right hand, then brought up to the top of the spindle and two half hitches made. As she pulled the wool out in a thin thread with her left hand, the fingers of her right deftly twirled the spindle twisting the wool into yarn. A quick twist of the wrist loosed the half hitches at the top of the spindle and she wound the yarn around the middle of the spindle, and then quickly made two more half hitches to prevent her steadily growing ball of yarn from unwinding as she twirled the spindle to twist more yarn. She spun rapidly, absorbed in her work.

I watched intently, marvelling at the speed and ease with which her fingers moved. At last she looked up. She smiled, and then she passed the batt and spindle to me. I thrust the stick into my belt and held the spindle at my side, but the wool refused to flow in a thin, even thread. It was bunchy – thick in some places and thin to the breaking point in others. The spindle refused to twirl in quick, even rotations. The half hitches slipped off and the ball of yarn began to unwind.

Her black eyes twinkled as she noted my fingers that seemed to be all thumbs. She laughed and shook her head when she saw my awkwardness. Then she placed a firm hand over mine and pulled upon the wool, -- again it flowed from the batt in an even thread.

A steady hand over mine twirled the spindle and I saw the thread grow into twisted yarn. She stood back watching me. I had caught the motion of the wrist. We had both become so engrossed in the spinning lesson, that we gave no heed to the men when they returned. Her husband spoke to her and she answered him in her native tongue. "She says in two or three days you will make good yarn," he vouched.

We did not need to talk as she showed me the blankets she had made from virgin wool, -- blankets large enough for an ordinary bed. She had washed, carded and spun the wool, then knit the blankets entirely by hand. There were heavy socks, such as lumbermen wear in these northern woods, and warm mittens all made from pure wool. Her days were happy days spent in spinning and knitting.

She brought a plate of sugar cookies from the other room, then strong black coffee. She offered me cream and sugar, but drank hers straight. I glanced back as we rode out that woodsy trail that led to the highway. She was waving to me from the doorway of her cabin.

This winter, when the snow lies deep in this part of northern British Columbia, I shall often think of a little Bulgarian woman living in a log cabin at the end of a woodland trail, busily spinning and knitting. I shall remember her pleasure at our unexpected visit and her warm hospitality. I shall never think of her as being lonely for I know that she is quite content with her humble way of life.

Yes, it really is fun to go adventuring.

Published January 8, 1947
Family Herald and Weekly Star

RUGS FROM OVERALLS AND STOCKINGS

By Nellie R. Campbell

Rug making becomes a fascinating pastime during the long winter evenings. There are two kinds of rugs that are very easy to make and both utilize those odds and ends of clothing that are past mending and are of no use to anyone.

Old stockings make the best material for the crocheted rug, while a less stretchy material such as overall, wool or cotton fabrics make a firmer braided mat.

Perhaps the crocheted rug is the simplest for the beginner. Sort the stockings according to colour. Dye the lighter ones different shades that will carry out the colour scheme of the room in which it is to be used. Brown, beige, rose and green make a good combination or brown, red, beige and blue make a brighter rug. In dyeing the stockings, remember that as your rug increases in size, you need one third more material for each change of colour, -- that is, if you use 18 yards of red, you need 24 yards of beige and 32 yards of blue to keep the same width in each colour. Cut off the toe of the stocking and start cutting a strip about 1 ½ inches wide. In this way you can cut one continuous strip round and round the stocking. Most stockings have a double hem. Rip this out to give added material. Cut a wider strip from a very thin stocking than you do from a heavier one in order to keep your rug yarn uniform in size. One stocking will yield about six yards of yarn for your mat. As it is cut on the bias, if you pull gently, the rough edges will roll in and you will have a yarn very similar to that sold on the market for crocheted or hooked rugs. Sew the end of your yarn to the next stocking and roll the yarn into firm balls as you go. Even if the stockings are frayed or worn, by cutting a little wider strip at that point, the hole will disappear as the edges roll in with pulling.

You can buy a rug hook or one is easily made by driving a three inch nail into a wooden handle. File off the head and then file a crochet hook in its place.

When your yarn is all ready, the first step is to find a good book or story and initiate some member of the family in the art of reading aloud while you work. I am one of those fortunate women whose husband really enjoys reading aloud.

Now you are ready.

Directions:

For an oval mat, crochet a chain of 45 stitches, then make a single crochet in each stitch up both sides of the chain. Continue crocheting around, increasing three stitches at both ends of all rows to keep the rug flat. Every three or four rows change colour.

If you prefer a round rug, chain two, work two single crochet in each stitch on both sides, continue crocheting around increasing occasionally if the edges begin to curl.

A square or oblong rug may be made by crocheting 12 inch squares of different colours, then using coloured twine, crochet the squares together as you would an afghan. One plain colour and one variegated square crocheted together, alternating, make a pleasing combination for this type of rug.

Perhaps the oldest rug – the one made most frequently by our grandmothers and great grandmothers, is the braided rug. Old overalls and pant cloth, worn bed blankets or discarded clothing make good material. If you have too much of one colour, dye part of it.

In cutting your material into strips, the width of the strip will depend somewhat on the weight of the material used. An inch and a half is a good width for pant or overall cloth, while stockings or flannelette should be cut about two and a half inches in order to keep your braid even. I like to use one plain colour for the centre of the rug.

Fasten securely with a large pin or tack, three strands of material to some steady object, then braid, turning in the rough edges as you go. Be careful not to make a loose braid, but keep it firm and even. If you plan to make an oval rug, braid 36 inches and then fold your braid in the middle, sewing edges together with a herring-bone stitch, -- that is, a stitch in one braid and then across in the other. Always use heavy linen thread for sewing rugs. In sewing, hold the outer braid a little loose, so that the rug will lie flat. I find it much easier to make three or four feet of braid and then sew it. In this way you can change your colours every three or four rows, keeping the different colours in even strips. A black centre and several rows of black for a border, with the brighter colours in between make a very attractive rag rug.

Published January 15, 1947
Family Herald and Weekly Star
Sold--$4.02

A GIFT SO GAY – FOR VALENTINES DAY
By Nellie R. Campbell

The custom of giving Valentines dates back to the early Roman days, however, the lacy creations of a century ago are no longer in vogue, but the useful Valentine is becoming more and more popular.

For one with nimble fingers, the making of Valentines is fun. In making a gift, however small, there is the opportunity for the giver to express his own personality and these homemade gifts always bring happiness to the recipient.

Last year a friend sent me a small heart-shaped sachet. It was made from a scrap of lace net with a bit of peach coloured silk beneath. The heart was edged with narrow lace and filled with lavender grown in my friend's garden. Such a small gift, yet all the year it has sent out its fragrance reminding me of the thoughtfulness of this friend.

Another gift, quite simple to make for some book-loving friend, is a bookmark. This can be made from a piece of ribbon with three small hearts cut from red cartridge or drawing paper, pasted on it. Hearts with scalloped edges and a very small flower decoration are very pretty for this. One can buy a box of gummed flower seals, or small flowers painted with watercolours, or cut from a seed catalogue to make fine Valentine decorations.

Two heart shaped potholders in a heart shaped holder make an ideal gift for mother. Made from unbleached cotton and bound with red bias tape, they are not only attractive but also easy to launder. A face embroidered on each gives them a gay, holiday air.

Did you ever try making a plaque of Plaster of Paris? It is quite simple to make, yet most inexpensive. Plaques may be made by using a small oval platter, an oblong or square cake tin or even a saucer for a mold. Pour a little water in the bottom of the mold, then lay the picture you have chosen, face down in the centre. When the picture is thoroughly wet, pour off the water remaining and with a tiny bit of Vaseline or cold cream on the tips of the fingers,  grease very lightly the rest of the mold, taking care that no grease touches the edges of your picture in the centre.

Mix several spoonfuls of Plaster of Paris with cold water, stirring it into a smooth paste. It should be just thin enough to spread itself out evenly when poured into the mold. The amount of Plaster of Paris used will depend entirely on the size of the mold. Three rounding tablespoons is enough for a saucer plaque. Take care that your picture is in the exact centre and does not get pushed to one side as you pour in the Plaster of Paris. It is a good idea, before pouring in the Plaster of Paris to make a small mark at the exact centre top of the mold so that your picture will hang evenly. Make a small loop of heavy twine or ribbon, and push it into the wet plaster allowing it to dry in the plaque. To remove from the mold, use a small knife to loosen it from the edges of the dish.

Who wouldn't like a box filled with heart shaped cookies for a Valentine? Using any good sugar cookie recipe, several kinds can be made from the one batch of dough. Cut some medium sized hearts and decorate with red icing. Make some small heart cookies and stick two together with red and white icing. Add a bit of red colouring to the remainder of the cookie dough and make a few pink heart cookies. If you do not happen to have a heart shaped box to hold your cookies, any box can be trimmed with red paper hearts.

Although many of the lacy Valentines of a century ago were lovely, I am sure that we, of this generation, like a Valentine gay done in the modern way.

Published February 5, 1947
Family Herald and Weekly Star
Sold--$4.21

USEFUL VALENTINES
By Nellie R. Campbell

Soon the shop windows will be filled with gay Valentines – wonderful creations of dazzling bits of paper. Of course, it would not be a true Valentine, were that little verse declaring one's undying love, to be omitted. From childhood on, we look forward to Saint Valentine's Day. We eagerly open each dainty missive, read its sentiment, then, - very shortly lay it carefully away to be forgotten.

Perhaps it is because we are living in such a very materialistic age that the practical Valentine is coming more and more into favour. For the invalid or an old person, what could be more delightful than a pretty box decorated with small red hearts and containing an assortment of crunchy, homemade cookies cut in heart shape. To add variety, decorate the larger cookies with red icing and two of the wee hearts could be put together with icing between. One will find great scope for ingenuity in decorating Valentine cookies.

Most any girl will treasure a dainty tea apron made of sheer white muslin with red heart motif.

Gay holiday wrappings will turn that lovely picture, - either framed or unframed, into a Valentine gift that will be treasured long after the day itself is forgotten.

Heart shaped potholders made of unbleached cotton and edged with bright red bias tape make a gift that mother will find most useful. A bit of embroidery makes them even more attractive.

A potted plant makes another good Valentine gift for it will bring pleasure to the recipient for many months to come. If you have a flare for writing poetry, original verses to accompany your gifts bring added pleasure.

Practical Valentines cost very little more than the expensive creations of paper, lace and ribbon that we see in the shops, yet they bring far more pleasure for they are constant reminders of the ones who were thoughtful enough to remember us on this day. They are something tangible and lasting, - not merely a Valentine for the day.

Published February 14, 1952
Family Herald and Weekly Star
Sold--$2.92

MAKE 1952 A HOBBY YEAR
By Nellie R. Campbell

Nearly everyone has some pet hobby. Some people have several. You can have a hobby for every month in the year, -- that is, you can if you are Scrapbook minded. All you need is sharp scissors, paper, cardboard, paste and desire.

This is a good recipe for paste that will keep indefinitely.
½ pint sifted flour,
1 pint cold water,
2 ½ ounce powdered alum,
1 ½ ounce glycerine,
1 dram wintergreen oil,
1 quart boiling water.
Mix flour with cold water and stir until smooth, add boiling water and cook until it thickens, stirring constantly. Let cool and then add the alum and glycerine slowly. Stir in the oil of wintergreen and put in jars and seal.

January is such a good month to start a picture scrapbook. A good quality of building paper, or manila drawing paper, makes good leaves (pages). If you use building paper, cut it 20 x 28 inches, folding it in the centre. Your book will then be 10 x 14 inches. Your stiff cardboard covers should be cut just a little larger. You can make the front and back covers most attractive by covering them neatly with some of your lovely Christmas wrappings. An inch and a half strip of firm cotton cloth in some contrasting colour, pasted down the back edges of your covers, will prevent them from tearing out when your book is laced together with a bit of left over Christmas cord.

FUN AND FACTS

There is such an abundance of attractive pictures that it should not be difficult to find pictures that will appeal to either young or old. If it is a scrapbook of beautiful scenery you might be able to add something of interest about each scene. Pictures of children or animals are always appealing to a small child. Your Christmas cards will also furnish material for your picture scrapbook.

Your February scrapbook might well be a cookbook. It should not be too large, -- just a convenient size to handle. Cover your cardboard covers with bright oilcloth. Divide your scrapbook into sections, as Bread – Cake – Meat – Fish – Salads – Dessert. Make your title pages attractive by printing the headings either in colour or in India ink. Perhaps mother has a collection of recipes that she would be only too glad to see pasted into a neat book. It is fun to collect recipes for unusual dishes from friends.

March is usually a cold, blustery month, -- a time to think about indoor games. You'll be surprised how many games you can think of. List your games alphabetically and write down the rules for playing. Search the magazines for new games and ideas for parties. Your scrapbook of games and party fun is one you will use many times and come to treasure.

In April we see the first signs of spring, so your scrapbook should have a spring-like cover, possibly a budding tree or some early spring flowers. You will find it fun to make it in the form of a diary, -- the date the ice went out of the pond, -- the day you saw the first robin. Record all the little signs of spring and add your own personal comments and reactions. If you are clever at drawing, little pen or pencil sketches will brighten up its pages.

The May scrapbook might well become a bird book describing the habits of the different birds about your home. Often you can find interesting articles or stories about our feathered friends.

June is the time to think about outdoor games. List them as you did the indoor games. Exchange games rules with friends in other parts of the country. You'll be surprised to learn how rules for playing well-known games may vary in different localities. You might search for outdoor games that are played by children in foreign lands.

Many of the wild flowers are in bloom in July, so that is a good time to make a flower scrapbook. A few years ago a friend in Maine asked me what wild flowers grew in British Columbia. That was how I came to start a flower collection. Pressed and neatly mounted on heavy paper with the common name and the Latin name printed beneath each flower, and a description of the place found and the date, they made an ideal Christmas gift for my friend, when the sheets were placed inside a flower bedecked cover.

August is the time to collect those snapshots that you've always intended to paste inside an album but never have. Use dark grey paper for the leaves of your album and cover the cardboard covers with birch bark. It can be sewn onto the cardboard by using bright yarn in a blanket stitch.

THE SCRAPBOOK HABIT

September is the month to collect poems. They, too, will make a nice Christmas present for some poetry-lover, if attractively arranged in a scrapbook with a pleasing cover.

A fall scene on the covers of your October scrapbook will give it a really autumn look. Written in diary form with illustrations done in crayon or India ink, it will make a companion book for your Spring Scrapbook.

November is the time to search for all those little helpful hints on making Christmas gifts and ideas for Christmas decorations. My Christmas scrapbook has games and riddles for the holiday season and also recipes for popcorn balls and Christmas candy. When Christmas rolls around, my Christmas scrapbook suddenly becomes the most useful book in the whole house.

You probably will be too busy to make a scrapbook in December for I am sure that you will find odd clippings to be pasted in some of your books, -- a bit of colouring to be finished or a page that needs to be decorated – so that all of your scrapbooks will be finished before Christmas.

Here are just a few simple rules to follow. Make your covers attractive. Cardboard covered with bright paper, birch bark, oilcloth or pretty print, makes most attractive covers. If your scrapbooks are laced together with cord, it is easy to add additional pages. Gummed reinforcements will prevent the pages from tearing out as they are used. All cutting should be exact and even. Care should be taken in the arrangement of your material. Neatness should be your watchword.

You may cherish all of your scrapbooks or you may find that some of them will make much appreciated Christmas gifts. At least you have had a year of fun making them and you probably have acquired the scrapbook habit.

Published January 3, 1952
Family Herald and Weekly Star
Sold--$9.66

USEFUL HINTS
By Nellie R. Campbell

When driving a nail into the wall use a piece of corrugated cardboard as a bumper. If the hammer slips you will not dent nor scar your wall.

Perhaps you own an inexpensive paintbrush that does poor work. Dip the brush in liquid glue and let harden. Shape the edge with sandpaper and then wash out the glue.

Printed July 2, 1947
Family Herald and Weekly Star
Sold --$2.00

USEFUL HINTS
By Nellie R. Campbell

An ordinary pants hanger is excellent for holding together small pieces to be glued. It is also convenient for holding those bits of lace, baby booties and all articles too small to pin to the line on washday.

To start a screw in some unhandy place or one that will not start easily, put a small piece of adhesive tape over the end of the screwdriver and wedge it tightly into the slot of the screw. This prevents the screwdriver from slipping.

Printed July 9, 1947
Family Herald and Weekly Star
Sold--$2.00

HINTS FOR THE MAN OF THE HOUSE
By Nellie R. Campbell

If you have to move a ladder for some distance just place one end of it on the wheel-barrow. Strap the sides of the ladder securely to the handles of the wheel-barrow. This extends the handles of the wheel-barrow and the ladder can be pushed along much easier than it can be carried.

When doing a job of painting that requires more than one color, you can keep your brushes from drying out overnight by inserting the bristles in paper bags. When this is done all of your brushes can be inserted in one can of linseed oil without danger of the different colors running together. When using a plumb bob on a windy day it can be steadied by letting it hang suspended in a glass jar of light oil. The clearest cylinder oil possible should be used so that you can see the bob for marking.

A strip of inner tube tacked to the lid of a toolbox makes a good holder for small tools such as augers, bits, screwdrivers and punches. The stretch of the rubber makes it easy to insert a tool, yet the rubber will hold it firmly in place when toolbox is moved.

You can protect both yourself and the blade of your scythe when moving it in a car or wagon by slitting a rubber hose the length of the blade and, slipping it over your blade.

Published February 22, 1950
Family Herald and Weekly Star
Sold--$2.25

DO IT YOURSELF
By Nellie R. Campbell

This is such a lovely picture. "Someday, when my ship comes in, I'm going to have it framed." I know that most of us have said that more than once. But why not frame it yourself? You can, you know, at very little expense and it is not difficult to do.

All you need is a good smooth surface to work on, a bit of glass the right size, two thickness of smooth cardboard for the back, a picture hanger and a roll of Passe Partout for picture binding. Passe Partout comes in a variety of colours – red, green, brown, black, gold and silver, and can be found in all art stores and in many department stores.

Your picture may be one that does not need a mat, but if you decide that one will set off the picture and enhance its beauty, choose cream or some soft shade of construction paper that will bring out the colours in your picture. Place your picture on the mounting paper measuring carefully to see that it is equivalent from the top and two sides, but a little wider margin at the bottom. A little paste on the two upper corners will hold your picture. Do not cover the back of the picture with paste, as it will cause it to wrinkle. You may want to add a narrow border to your picture before mounting it. Use Passe Partout binding for this, allowing only a narrow edge to show.

You may prefer the window type of mat. Mount your picture on a plain piece of paper. Using the placement of the picture as your guide, rule very lightly an opening ¼ inch smaller than the picture on all sides. Cutting this window is easy if you use a sharp razor blade on the corners and then finish with scissors. If your hand is steady you can do a neat job with just the razor blade. You can make oval or round windows, also, it you desire.

With your picture mounted you are now ready for the glass. This you can buy at any art store, but you will find it cheaper to get clear glass at the hardware store and have it cut the size of your mounted picture. You may have bits of glass around the house that can be cut to the correct size. Wash the glass and polish both sides so that there will be no finger marks.

FINISHING TOUCHES

For the back you will need two thickness of smooth cardboard. The backs of writing tablets are ideal for this purpose. Do not use corrugated cardboard. Cut them the exact size of your glass. You will need picture hangers. These are small brass rings having two prongs attached, which can be pushed through the cardboard back and the prongs pressed open. Measure very carefully so the hanger will be in the exact centre of the back 1 ½ to 2 inches down from the top. With a sharp point make a small hole and push the prongs through and bend them back.

Lay the glass on the table and place the picture face down upon it, next to a piece of cardboard. This extra piece will protect your picture from the prongs of the picture hanger inserted in the back. When all are in place, to prevent slipping, fasten with tiny strips of transparent tape or I prefer to tie them with a string wound several times around the picture. Cut two pieces of picture binding just the length of the sides and crease lengthwise through the centre. This will prevent your frame from being wider on one end than it is on the other. Moisten the gummed surface and press it firmly along the edge of the glass bringing it over the edge and pressing firmly down on the cardboard back. Rub gently with soft cloth until both edges are stuck. Then do the other end. You will no longer need the string, as the ends will hold the picture in place. In the same way, put binding on the top and bottom taking care to cut the ends of strips at an angle to get the effect of mitered corners on your frame.

You will find this method of framing pictures inexpensive. It can become a hobby, and what is still better, it can even become a paying hobby.

Published May 4, 1950
Family Herald and Weekly Star
Sold--$5.88

A PORTABLE SAW-HORSE
By Nellie R. Campbell

It is often easier to carry your saw-horse to a fallen log than to carry your log down to your saw-horse. If you have ever used a portable saw-horse I am sure that you never would be without one. It is a simple little contrivance, inexpensive, light and easy to carry in the bush.

All you need is a smooth pole five feet long and two 27 inch posts. Cross the posts at nine inches down from the top. Cut a groove in one so that the other one fits snugly to give it strength. Then with a two-inch auger bore a hole through centre of posts at point of crossing and insert pole. Be sure that it fits tightly.

It is quite easy to saw a log with one end resting on the saw-horse and the other on the ground or if the logs are large and there is fallen timber at hand, a notch may be made in a down log to hold the log to be sawed and the portable saw-horse placed at the most convenient angle for sawing.

Published July 23, 1948
Family Herald and Weekly Star
Sold--$3.53

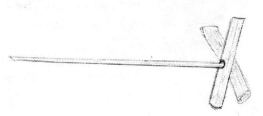

Family Recipes

A REALLY NEW PIE.

Dear Housewife,—I would like to ask my Canadian sisters, especially those of the Prairie Provinces, if they have ever wondered what they could use to make a pie. Here is something new. Friend husband thought of it so all the credit goes to him.

Turnip Pie.

One and one-half cups of boiled and sifted turnip, one cup of milk, one-half cup of sugar, one-half teaspoon salt, one-half teaspoon cinnamon, one egg beaten lightly.

Mix in order given. Line a plate with pie crust, put on rim and fill with above mixture. Bake with one crust.

It tastes much like squash pie. Try it. If we can't raise fruit for pies I'm sure we all can raise Ruta Bagas.—N. R. C., Sask.

> Nellie Campbell loved to cook for her family and friends and was always creative with new recipes.

ADDITIONAL RECIPES

Green Tomato Conserve

4 lbs green tomatoes
4 lemons
½ lb crystalized ginger
1 lb seeded raisins
4 lbs sugar (light brown)

Slice tomatoes scald + chop fine. Slice lemons cover with cold water + simmer until tender.
Chop raisins + lemon fine Cut ginger. Mix all together. Add sugar + stick of cinnamon. Let stand over night. Then simmer until quite thick. Remove stick cinnamon before canning.

CAMP COOKERY THAT SATISFIES
By Nellie R. Campbell

Camping on the shore of some inland lake may be an ideal way to spend one's holidays – that is, if the camp cook knows his job. As an old woodsman once said, "Roughin' it's swell, -- so long as roughin' it don't interfere with the quality of your grub."

Having married a man who is always ready to pack up for a camping trip at a moments notice, I soon discovered this to be true. Bert had left me by the campfire to watch the coffee "perculating" in a shiny, new jam tin. It stands to reason that water always boils quicker in a kettle with the lid on. With some difficulty, I adjusted the lid and then sat down beside our campfire to await results. The coffee would be piping hot when Bert returned from the lake.

Family Herald and Weekly Star, July 7, 1948

The lid shot high in the air and a shower of boiling-hot drops trickled down my neck.

I had not long to wait. Bang! – The lid shot high in the air and a shower of boiling hot drops trickled down my neck while my face was plastered with coffee grounds. I snatched the pail from the fire, but it was empty. All that day I nursed a grouch and a large white blister on the lobe of my right ear. It might have passed for a pearl earring, had there been a matching one on my left ear, but who was there on the shore of that lonely northern lake to admire pearl earrings anyway. It was right then that I decided that if I was to spend a lifetime with Bert, I had better learn something about camp cooking.

Flapjacks make a most satisfying camp breakfast, especially if one can serve a bit of crisp bacon or pork sausages with them. With so many canned meats on the market, this is easy to do and flapjacks are not too difficult to make over a campfire.

Flapjacks

One cup flour, 1 tbsp. sugar, 3 tbsp. powdered milk, 1 tbsp. shortening, 2 tsp. baking powder, ¼ tsp. salt, 2/3 cup water.

Mix dry ingredients and sift. Add water gradually and stir until smooth. Add melted shortening and beat batter well. Drop by spoonfuls into hot, well greased pan and cook over medium fire turning cakes once.

Frying Pan Biscuits

Two cups flour, 1 cup powdered milk, 2/3 cup water, 4 tsp. baking powder, ½ tsp. salt, 2 tbsp. shortening.

Measure and mix dry ingredients and sift. Cut in shortening. Add water gradually and drop from spoon into a well-greased frying pan. Cover and cook over a medium fire until brown and then turn and brown the other side. This makes 12 biscuits.

Bannock

One cup flour, 1 tbsp. powdered milk, ½ tbsp. lard or bacon fat, 1 tsp. baking powder, 1/4 tsp. salt.

Mix dry ingredients and work in shortening. Then add enough water to make a firm dough. Put in a well-greased pan and bake slowly until a straw inserted in the middle comes out clean. A little sugar and some raisins may be added to make a sweet bannock.

Soups and chowders make a most filling outdoor meal and are easily made over a campfire.

Bean Soup

One pint dry beans (red or brown), 6 potatoes, ½ lb. salt pork, salt and pepper to taste, ½ tsp. soda, 4 or 5 small onions, ½ lb. lean beef, celery salt (if desired).

Soak beans overnight. Drain and add fresh water and bring to a boil for a couple of minutes. Add soda and boil a couple of minutes longer to soften them and then drain and rinse and add 6 or more cups of fresh water and the salt pork and beef diced. Let boil for about an hour and then add the potatoes and onions cut fine. Add seasoning and boil until all the ingredients are tender.

Fish Chowder

One-half lb. dressed (cleaned) fish, 1 qt. boiling water, 1 small onion, salt and pepper to taste. 1 potato (large), 1 inch square of salt pork, ½ cup powdered milk, 2 or 3 broken pilot crackers.

Cut fish in small cubes. Cut potatoes small and cover fish and potatoes with boiling water. Add salt. While these are cooking, fry the salt pork and onions, being careful to cook the onion without browning it. Add onion and pork to fish and potatoes. Mix powdered milk with water and stir until smooth. Add to chowder and heat. Season to taste, and when hot, add broken pilot crackers before serving.

Pot Roast

Cut of meat or game, flour, ½ tsp. salt, 1 onion, 1 cup canned tomatoes.

Place meat in a well greased kettle over a moderate fire and brown the outside of meat, turning it until all sides are well browned. Add enough boiling water to partially cover the meat. Add salt and onion and simmer over a slow fire until the meat is tender. About ½ hour before taking from the fire, add the cup of tomatoes and a few bay leaves, if they are available. Thicken the gravy with flour just before serving.

Scrambled Eggs

Two-thirds cup of milk, 6 eggs, 3 tbsp. butter, ½ tsp. salt.

Put milk and butter in frying pan and heat. Beat eggs slightly, add salt and pour into hot milk. Stir constantly, until eggs are set. Chopped ham, or chopped cooked bacon or cheese, may be added to the beaten eggs before cooking.

To save space in packing needed supplies of eggs, they may be wiped with a dry cloth, then packed in flour, salt or cereal in a tin can.

Save your bacon fat and keep it in a covered tin. You'll find it mighty handy.

Don't forget to carry extra matches in a waterproof container and keep it with you always. You never know when you will need a fire.

Always build your campfire on rock, sand or cleared earth. Humus and dry roots will smoulder for days underground and then suddenly burst into flame. Wet everything thoroughly and be sure your fire is out when breaking camp.

On short camping trips, two pieces of small iron pipe about thirty inches long will take the place of a stove. Rest them on two flat stones and build a small fire between the stones. They can be wrapped in paper and strapped to your fishing rods when travelling.

But be sure that your bed is comfortable. An uncomfortable bed can spoil your whole outing. When making a bed on the ground, always remember that as much cold comes from the ground as from the air, so have protection beneath as well as on top. If the ground is cold, heat several large flat rocks in your campfire and place them on the ground where you intend to sleep. As soon as the ground is warm, remove them and make your bed at once. If you spread out your blankets in a warm afternoon sun and then roll them up tightly while they are still warm, you will have warm blankets at night.

If your canoe upsets, stick to it unless you are a good swimmer, and are sure that you can reach land. An overturned canoe will hold up several people if they rest lightly on it and keep low in the water.

If you are looking forward to an ideal holiday spent in the great out of doors, don't let an uncomfortable camp and poorly cooked food spoil your outing. It is quite true that the discomforts of camp life often outweigh the enjoyment. But this need not be so, if one will give a little time to the arrangement of their camp and some thought in planning the meals.

"Roughin' its just swell, so long as it don't interfere with your comfort."

Published July 7, 1948
Family Herald and Weekly Star

NOW IT'S PICKLLING TIME
By Nellie R. Campbell

Ever since I can remember I have been overly fond of pickles so I always look forward to pickling time. To me no smell is as tantalizing as that of good apple vinegar blended with brown sugar and spices simmering gently on the back of my kitchen range. When Bert sees me rushing about the garden in search of button onions, wee cucumbers or large heads of snowy white cauliflower he invariably remarks, "What, --pickling time again?" Unfortunately he is not as fond of pickles as I am.

There is such a variety to choose from. They range from those small crisp cucumber pickles that seem to belong with delicious baked beans and steamed raisin brown bread to the relishes and chutneys that add so much to a dinner of meat or fish hash. One of our favorites is Olive Pickles.

OLIVE PICKLES
Pare and slice one peck of cucumbers, sprinkle them with 1 cup of salt, let them set over night. In the morning drain well and chop 1 quart of onions. Add 1 tbsp. mustard seed, 2 tbsp. celery seed and 1 cup olive oil, (salad oil may be substituted) and one quart of vinegar. Mix well and seal. This will keep for years if you have good vinegar.

Perhaps you are one who likes a crisp cucumber pickle. This is a good recipe and needs no cooking.

CUCUMBER PICKLES
Wash and wipe dry, small cucumbers and pack in sterilized jars. 1 gal. cider vinegar, 1 cup salt, 1 cup dry mustard, 3 cups brown sugar.

Mix the dry ingredients with a little of the vinegar to a smooth paste, then add the rest of the vinegar. Stir well and pour cold over cucumbers seeing that cucumbers are completely covered. Seal.

Have you ever tried Rhubarb Chutney? I'm sure you'll like it.

RHUBARB CHUTNEY
One qt. rhubarb – cut, 1 qt. onions – sliced, 4 cups brown sugar, 2 cups vinegar, 1 tsp. cloves, 1 tsp. cinnamon, 1 tbsp. salt, ½ tsp. pepper.

Boil ingredients together until tender then bottle hot and seal in sterilized jars.

Then there are those times that one wants a relish to service with roast meat. Spiced apples and spiced raisins are both good. Spiced apples are especially nice with roast pork.

SPICED APPLES
Four qts. crab apples, 1 oz. whole cinnamon, 1 oz. whole cloves. Cover the apples with equal parts of water and vinegar. Add spices and cook until apples crack. Pack apples in jars and strain liquid. Add 1 lb. sugar to each pt. of juice and boil for 20 minutes. Pour hot syrup over apples and seal in sterilized jars.

SPICED RAISINS

One package seeded raisins, ½ cup water, 1 cup cider vinegar, ½ cup sugar.

Stick cinnamon and whole cloves to suit taste. Bring vinegar, water, sugar and spices to a boil. Boil 3 minutes and pour over raisins. Allow raisins to cool and absorb syrup and it is ready to serve as a relish.

KETCHUP

One gal. ripe tomatoes, ½ tsp. cayenne pepper, 1 lb. sugar, 2 tbsp. cinnamon, 2 tbsp. salt, 1 and ½ pts. vinegar,

Pour ripe tomatoes through chopper. Pour into jelly bag and squeeze out juice and pulp. Add other ingredients and boil until as thick as desired. Bottle hot in sterilized jars.

SWEET PICKLES

Twelve ripe cucumbers, 4 cups vinegar, 2 tbsp. allspice, 1 tbsp. ginger root, 2 tbsp. chopped red peppers, 2 cups sugar, 2 tbsp. cloves, 1 tbsp. mace, 1 stick cinnamon, ½ cup salt.

Pare cucumbers, remove seeds and cut remainder in strips, sprinkle with salt and let stand two hours. Rinse and drain. Put spices in bag and boil in vinegar for five minutes. Remove spices and add sliced cucumber rind and simmer 30 minutes. Bottle hot in sterilized jars.

Did you ever try corn relish? If you have ever lived in New England I am sure you have, as this is a New England recipe.

CORN RELISH

Ten cups corn, 10 cups cabbage, 6 red peppers, ¼ tbsp. mustard, 3 lbs. sugar (less if you do not like it sweet), 2 tbsp. salt, 2 qts. vinegar.

Chop cabbage and peppers fine, add corn cut from cob. Add other ingredients and bring to boil. Let it boil for 15 minutes and seal hot in sterilized jars.

I never feel that my pickling is finished until there are several jars of mustard pickles on my cellar shelves.

MUSTARD PICKLES

One qt. small whole cucumbers, 1 qt. large cucumbers sliced, 1 qt. green tomatoes sliced, 3 green peppers cut fine, 1 qt. small button onions, 1 large cauliflower divided into sections.

Make a brine of 4 qts. water and 1 pt. salt. Pour it over the mixture and let stand overnight. In the morning heat just enough to scald. Drain well.

Mix 1 cup flour, 6 tbsp. ground mustard, 1 tbsp. tumeric with enough cold vinegar to make a smooth paste, add 1 cup sugar and sufficient vinegar to make 2 qts. in all. Boil until this thickens and is smooth, stirring constantly. Then add the vegetables and cook until heated through. Seal while hot in sterilized jars.

Published Aug. 24, 1949
Family Herald and Weekly Star
Sold -- $7.02

THE BOTTOM OF THE BARREL
By Nellie R. Campbell

An apple a day keeps the doctor away, so the old saying goes, but one, two, three, four or even more is an equally good rule. Apples are so good even when they have been stored all winter in the fragrant apple barrel.

I always remember, too, that delightful smell of apples cooking and still hold fond memories of the wonderful dishes mother could concoct from a few apples and a bit of spice. Of course there was mincemeat, and here are two New England recipes. Perhaps you can use those last few apples you have stored in the barrel, in some of these recipes.

APPLE TAPIOCA

One third cup fine tapioca, 1/3 tsp. salt, 3 cups milk, 6 small apples, ¾ cup brown sugar, ¼ tsp. cloves.

Cook tapioca, salt, ½ of the sugar in the milk in top of double boiler. Pare and core the apples and arrange in buttered baking dish. Add cloves to remaining sugar and fill cavities in apples. Pour cooked tapioca over the apples and bake in moderate oven until apples are tender. Serve with cream.

SPECIAL MINCEMEAT

Five lbs. cooked meat, 1 ¾ lbs. suet, 5 lbs. raisins, 1 1/2 lbs. currants, 5 lbs. brown sugar, 2 tbsp. cassia, 2 tbsp. allspice, 1 ½ lbs. citron, chopped, ½ bushel apples. 2 qts. molasses, 1 ½ qts. sweet cider, 3 qts. water used to boil meat, 1 tbsp. cloves, 3 tbsp. salt.

Pare and core apples and put apples, cooked meat, suet and raisins through the food chopper. Add liquids, sugar and spice. Mix well and let stand over night. In the morning heat to the boiling point and seal hot in jars.

Here is a recipe for a small amount of mincemeat.

MINCEMEAT

One cup chopped cooked meat, 2 cups chopped apples, 1 lemon, ½ cup chopped raisins, 1 cup jelly, ½ cup sugar, ½ tsp. cinnamon, ½ tsp. allspice, ½ tsp. nutmeg. Mix in order and make as large recipe.

An apple coffee cake is something a bit different and just the thing to serve when friends drop in for an afternoon cup of tea.

APPLE COFFEE CAKE

One cup sugar, 2 tbsp. butter, 1 egg, 2 cups flour, 2 tsp. baking powder, 1 tsp. salt, ½ tsp. nutmeg, ¾ cup milk.

Cream the butter and sugar and well beaten egg and add dry ingredients alternately with the milk. Pour into buttered cake tin. Slice apples in thin even sections. Arrange apples on top completely covering the batter. Sprinkle top with sugar and dot with butter. Bake in a moderate oven 35 to 40 minutes. When cake is half-baked pour ½ cup of cream over the apples.

APPLE CRISP

Six medium apples, ¼ cup granulated sugar, cinnamon, ¼ cup butter, ½ cup flour, ¾ cup brown sugar.

Peel and slice apples into buttered baking dish. Sprinkle them with the granulated sugar and cinnamon. Combine the butter, brown sugar and flour and sprinkle this dry mixture on top of apples. Bake about 30 minutes or until apples are soft and top a golden brown. Serve with cream.

Applesauce is always good served with roast pork, sausages, duck or goose. If there is just a bit of that roast goose or duck left but not enough for a meal try Duck-In-Apples.

DUCK-IN-APPLES

Cut every scrap of meat from the bones. Add to it any of the dressing that remains or lacking this add a few breadcrumbs and a bit of poultry seasoning. Peel and remove the cores from tart apples. Stuff each apple with the meat mixture. Place in covered baking dish with just enough water to keep apples from burning and bake in moderate oven about 45 minutes. Serve each apple on a slice of fried bread or strips of fried corn meal mush.

APPLE ICE CREAM

Two cups grated apples, ½ cup fine granulated sugar, ½ pint whipped cream.

Grate the unpeeled apples. After a small amount is grated, measure and sprinkle with a part of sugar to prevent discoloration. Continue grating till you have 2 cups of apple pulp. Whip cream and fold into apple mixture, then freeze.

The next time you make a loaf of gingerbread, cut in squares for serving, split each square and put a spoonful of applesauce on bottom half. Replace top and cover with whipped cream with a bit of pink applesauce as a topping.

CHEESE APPLE PIE

Line pie plate with pastry. Cover with thinly sliced apples. Allow 2 tbsp. sugar to each apple used. Add a little cinnamon or nutmeg to sugar and sprinkle over apples, dot with butter then add more apples, sugar and butter until pie plate is well filled. Roll ½ cup of grated cheese into pastry for upper crust. Cover pie with cheese crust and bake in hot oven for 15 minutes, then reduce heat and bake slowly until apples are done.

APPLE CUSTARD

One and a half cups milk, 3 eggs, beaten, 1/3 cup of sugar, 1 tbsp. grated orange rind, 2 tbsp. orange juice, ¼ tsp. salt, 1 cup strained sweetened applesauce, ¼ tsp. nutmeg.

Add the milk to the beaten eggs, orange rind, orange juice, salt, applesauce and nutmeg. Add to the milk and eggs and stir until all the ingredients are well blended. Pour the custard mixture into six well greased glass custard cups. Place the custard cups in a pan filled with hot water to a depth of about one inch. Bake in a moderate oven, 350 degrees F., about 30 minutes or until the custards are firm.

Published April 5, 1951
Family Herald and Weekly Star
Sold -- $8.42

TRADITIONS AND CRANBERRIES

By Nellie R. Campbell

Tradition seems to play an important roll in our diet. We may eat delicately browned chicken a dozen or more times throughout the year and never once think of cranberry sauce as an accompaniment, but just mention roast chicken or perhaps a delicious roast turkey for our Christmas dinner and we know at once that we must have a bowl of rich, red sauce or jelly. Dinner would not be complete without it – why? – tradition.

It was the mere mention of Christmas that caused Bert to remark, "I wonder if there are any cranberries on the old bog this year." You may be sure that I was quite ready to find out. The moss was soft and springy and decidedly wet. The water oozed through our canvas shoes at every step but did not matter in the least, for all through that soft, wet moss were tiny hair-like vines covered with crisp, red berries. I immediately thought of the many things that one could make with cranberries. They have a delicious flavor quite unlike any other berry and the best part of gathering cranberries is that they do not have to be cooked at once but will keep indefinitely if stored in a cool, dry place.

As we paddled our dug-out canoe back across the cove, our pails overflowing with firm red berries, Bert asked, "How about a cranberry pie?" There are two kinds of cranberry pie that are quite popular in our household — one made of just cranberries and the other a combination of cranberries and raisins.

CRANBERRY PIE

Two cups cranberries, 1 large cup sugar, ¼ tsp. cloves, pastry for 9 inch pie tin. Line pie tin with pastry, fill with cranberries which have been washed and well drained. Mix cloves with sugar and sprinkle over berries. Cover with crust and bake until berries are soft and juicy.

MOCK CHERRY PIE

One cup cranberries cut in half, 1 cup raisins (chopped), 1 heaping tsp. flour, 1 cup sugar, 1 cup boiling water, pastry for 9 inch pie tin.

Boil ingredients together until slightly thickened. Pour into pastry lined pie tin and top with pastry cut in strips to form lattice work. Bake until crust is a golden brown.

Then there is that cranberry pie for special occasions when one wants something just a bit out of the ordinary.

SUGARLESS CRANBERRY MERINQUE PIE

Two cups orange marmalade, 2 medium apples, 3 cups cranberries, 2 tbsp. cornstarch, 2 tbsp. water, 2 egg whites, 3 tbsp. corn syrup, 1 deep baked pie shell.

Pare and cut apples fine and add to heated marmalade. Cook for 3 minutes then add cranberries and cook until cranberry skins pop open. Make a smooth paste of cornstarch and water and add to cranberry mixture. Cook, stirring constantly, until mixture is slightly thickened and fruit is transparent. Cool and pour into baked pie shell. Beat egg whites stiff and add corn syrup while beating. Pile meringue in peaks around edge of pie. Bake in a slow oven for 15 minutes or until meringue is a golden brown.

Perhaps you are one of those persons who prefer a pudding to a pie.

CRANBERRY PUDDING

Two cups flour, 4 ½ tsp. baking powder, 1 cup sugar, 1 cup milk or water, butter, 4 tbsp. shortening, ¼ tsp. salt, 1 cup cranberries (cut), ½ cup raisins (cut), 1 tsp. cinnamon.

Mix flour, salt, baking powder and ¼ cup sugar and sift. Cut in shortening and add milk. Knead lightly and roll out ¼ inch thick. Spread dough with softened butter, sprinkle with ¼ cup water to which spice has been added. Chop cranberries and raisins fine and spread over dough, and then sprinkle them with ¼ cup of sugar and spice. Roll up the dough to form a loaf, pinching in the ends, and then brush top of loaf with melted butter and sprinkle with the remaining ¼ cup of sugar and spice and bake in a hot oven 12 to15 minutes. Cut in slices and serve with sauce or whipped cream.

HOT PUDDING SAUCE

Half cup sugar, 2 tbsp. flour, 1 cup boiling water, 1 tsp. to 1 tbsp. butter, 1 tsp. vanilla, few grains salt.

Mix flour and sugar and stir in water slowly. Cook until smoothly thickened. Brown sugar may be used in place of white. Flavor with 1 ½ tsp. lemon juice, ½ tsp. grated lemon rind and a few gratings of nutmeg.

CRANBERRY SHORTCAKE

Two cups pastry flour, ½ tsp. salt, 4 tsp. baking powder, 4 tbsp. shortening, 1 scant cup of milk (enough to make soft dough).

Turn out on floured board and knead lightly with fingertips. Divide in two parts. Pat one piece to fit into a greased pan, brush with soft butter, place second layer of dough over it and bake 20 to 30 minutes in hot oven. Split warm shortcake, spread with butter and put together with cranberry sauce to which broken walnut meats or chopped almonds have been added. Top with more cranberries and nuts and sweetened whipped cream.

CRANBERRY SAUCE

Pick over, wash and drain 4 cups of cranberries. Make syrup of 2 cups of sugar and 2 cups of boiling water. Bring syrup to boil and boil gently for 5 minutes, add cranberries and cook until berries are tender and transparent. Chill before serving.

CRANBERRY JELLY

Wash and drain 8 cups of cranberries, add three cups of water and boil, stirring occasionally until berries are very tender. Strain juice through two layers of cheese cloth. To each two cups of cranberry juice allow 1 cup of warmed sugar. Bring cranberry juice to a boil and then add warmed sugar and stir until dissolved. Simmer for 5 minutes. Remove from heat and let stand a few minutes, skim and pour into sterilized jars and seal.

Here is a salad that is different.

JELLIED CRANBERRY ORANGE SALAD

One and a half cups hot water. 1 pkg. lemon jelly powder, 1 orange, 2 cups raw cranberries, 1 tsp. grated orange rind, ¼ orange rind cut small.

Add water to jelly powder and cook until as thick as honey. Wash, dry and put through food chopper, 2 cups raw cranberries. Add to partly thickened jelly. Add 1 tsp. grated orange rind, ¼ of orange rind cut in small slivers and the pulp of an orange. Turn into individual moistened molds and chill. Unmold on crisp lettuce leaves or finely shredded cabbage. This may be served with salad dressing as a dinner salad or with a whipped cream dressing as a salad dessert.

Perhaps you are one of these people who like a hot drink before going to bed. Hot cranberry punch is tops and it is just as nice served ice cold.

CRANBERRY PUNCH

One lb. cranberries, 1 qt. water, 6 to 8 cloves, 1 to 1 ½ cups sugar, ½ cup orange juice, 2 tbsp. lemon juice.

Pick over and wash cranberries. Cook with cloves in water until berries are soft. Press through sieve, add sugar, orange and lemon juice and heat to boiling. Dilute with 1 to 2 cups of hot water and serve hot.

This punch may be bottled for future use. Bring to boiling point and fill hot sterilized bottles to the top. Seal while hot with corks or screw caps which have been dipped in parawax. When the bottles are slightly cooled, dip tops in wax several times to be sure you have a perfect seal.

Published Oct. 12, 1949
Family Herald and Weekly Star
Sold - $11.61

YOU CAN EAT 'EM LATER
By Nellie R. Campbell

Half the fun of Christmas is in the preparation. If you are fortunate enough to belong to a large family, you will all, from the tiny-tots to the teen-agers, love a Christmas tree with decorations that you can eat. After all, why shouldn't the branches of a Christmas tree be loaded with good things to eat?

There was a time when yards of glistening tinsel were quite unheard of and we never even thought of tinsel as a necessity for our tree. More than one evening was spent in popping corn, and stringing it in long white chains to drape over the dark green branches. All you need is a pan of popped corn, a dish of bright red cranberries, a long string, a darning needle and a pair of willing hands. You'll find it fun to string the crisp white kernels of corn with a red berry between every ten or twelve kernels. There is sure to be a race to see who can string the fastest and popcorn and cranberries make very good eating.

Then who wouldn't be delighted to pick gold and silver walnuts off of their Christmas tree? They glisten in the candle light like the gold and silver ornaments one buys, but hold a deeper fascination for the children for, ere long they will be picking golden walnuts from their tree. Just tie a bit of linen or coarse cotton thread around each nut lengthwise. The deep crease in the nut helps to hold the thread. Gild [paint – usually with gold or silver] the nut and the thread and as soon as dry they are ready for the tree.

Gingerbread Men

Every one likes the cookie decorations and there are such a variety of shapes, - Stars, diamonds, wreaths, shamrocks, small Christmas trees and Gingerbread boys and girls. Here is where the teen-agers can vie with one another in decorating the many fancy shaped cookies. There is ample scope for imagination and the teen-agers delight in displaying their artistry.

Using your favourite molasses cookie recipe, with a sharp knife cut out Gingerbread boys and girls. After they are baked they should have hair, eyes, nose, mouth of coloured frosting and just a touch of frosting to represent clothes.

Use a good sugar cookie recipe for the wee Christmas trees. These too, will have to be cut with a sharp knife so will vary somewhat in size and shape. They may be thinly covered with green icing or just the edges iced. Tiny dots of red and green give them a gay touch. Small candles used for decorating birthday cakes or gumdrops cut in tiny pieces are good for that needed bit of colour.

Cut some cookies round and place well apart on the greased cookie tin, then flatten with the floured fancy base of a water glass. You will be delighted with the design. Several designs may be printed on the cookies by using different glasses. Place a raisin in the centre of some or sprinkle with coloured sugar before baking. A bit of bright red cherry adds colour to plain cookies.

The Christmas wreath cookies are cut out with a doughnut cutter. They truly look like tiny wreaths when frosted with green to imitate leaves. A bit of red for a bow and a dash of red for berries make them most realistic.

Edible Varieties

To hang your cookies on your tree you must have loops. Cut pieces of string 6 inches long. Fold each one double and tie ends together in a knot. Drop loops into a cup of water and soak until wet through. When the cookies are in the pan, before baking, press the knot in the loop into the top of a cookie about ½ inch in from the edge. If you have a moderated oven, your cookies will be done before the string burns. If you prefer you can drill a hole through each baked cookie by using a large sized darning needle. A smaller needle should be used to draw a bit of fine yarn through to form a loop for hanging. The hole should not be made too close to the edge or the cookie is apt to crumble.

There is such a variety of shapes and so much that one can do with a bit of coloured frosting and wee candles that your decorations should be not only good to eat but pleasing to the eye as well.

Published December 13, 1951
Family Herald and Weekly Star
Sold--$7.08

GIFTS FROM YOUR OWN KITCHEN
By Nellie R. Campbell

Candy Bags have always held a special appeal for children and I'm sure a fat little boy full of candy will delight most boys and girls.

Cut a pattern the desired size. (11 inches long by 5 1/2 at the widest point is a good size). Using the pattern, cut bags from red and green linen. Sew the two pieces together with colored yarn using a blanket stitch. Leave head open. Peppermint sticks or hard candy pulled and cut the right length are ideal to fill the arms and legs. The body is filled with hard candies, raisins and popcorn. A crisp cookie with eyes, nose, mouth and hair of frosting is just right for the head and don't forget to put on a generous sized loop at the top if the candy bag is to be hung on the tree.

WHITE CANDY
Two cups sugar, ½ cup cold water, 1/6 cup vinegar, 1 tbsp. glycerine, butter size of egg, ½ tsp. cream of tarter, 1 tsp. vanilla.

Mix sugar, water, vinegar and glycerine and boil without stirring until crisp when dropped into cold water. Add butter, cream of tarter, and vanilla and pour in pan. Just as soon as it is cool enough to handle, pull until white and hard. Cut in sticks or small pieces. A pair of scissors is ideal for cutting pulled candy.

**For the invalid—
Several small jars of jam or conserve are always appreciated by a shut-in.

CRABAPPLE OR APPLE BUTTER
Six cups sieved apple or crabapple pulp, 2 cups sugar, juice and grate rind 1 orange, spices if desired; ½ tsp. cinnamon, ¼ tsp. cloves, ¼ tsp. nutmeg.

Quarter and cook unpeeled apples until tender, then press through coarse sieve. Add orange juice and grate rind to apple pulp and cook for 5 minutes. Add sugar and spice if desired and cook until thick and clear. Turn flame low and stir constantly to prevent burning.

RAISIN JAM
One qt. cranberries, 1 cup boiling water, 1 lb. raisins, 1 ½ cups sugar, 1 cup light corn syrup, ½ cup broken walnut meats.

Cook cranberries until soft then add raisins, sugar and corn syrup. Cook 15 minutes. Add nuts a few minutes before taking from fire.

**For the woman who entertains—
A box of assorted cookies is always appreciated by one who is socially minded.

RUBY RED JAM
Four cups finely shredded beets, 2 cups finely shredded carrots, 2 cups boiling water, 3 lemons; juice and grated rind, 4 oranges; juice and grated rind, 5 cups sugar, ½ tsp. cloves, ½ tsp. cinnamon, ¼ tsp. ginger, ¼ tsp. allspice.

Peel beets and carrots and shred very fine. Boil vegetables in 2 cups of water for 20 minutes. Add the other ingredients and simmer until sugar is dissolved, stirring frequently, then cook rapidly until desired consistency. (About 45 minutes).

POINSETTA COOKIES

Three-quarters cup mild flavoured fat, ½ cup sugar, 2 eggs, 2 cups pastry flour, 1 tsp. baking powder, ½ tsp. salt, 1 tsp. vanilla.

Cream fat and sugar well. Add beaten egg. Add vanilla and blend in flour mixed with baking powder and salt. Roll to about ¼ inch thickness on floured board and cut with 3 inch cookie cutter. Make four cuts at equal distances from outer edge toward the center and fold points to the center as a pinwheel. Place a piece of candied cherry in the center. Bake in a moderately slow oven until cookies are lightly browned, about 15 minutes.

MINCEMEAT BARS

Three-quarters cup shortening, ½ cup brown sugar, 1 egg, ½ cup honey, 1 ½ cup sifted flour, 1 tsp. salt, ½ tsp. soda, 1 ½ cups rolled oats.

Cream shortening and sugar. Mix in honey, egg, flour, salt, soda and rolled oats. Combine well. Spread ½ of mixture on bottom of cookie sheet, cover with mincemeat. Spread rest of mixture over the top. Bake in a slow oven 35 minutes. Cut into bars.

PEPPERMINT BROWNIES

Half cup of shortening, ½ cup sugar, ½ cup of light corn syrup, 2 eggs, 1 tsp. vanilla, 2 squares melted chocolate, 2/3 cup sifted flour, 1 tsp. baking powder, ¼ tsp. salt, ½ cup walnut meats.

Cream shortening and sugar, blend in corn syrup. Beat in eggs and add the melted chocolate. Mix baking powder and salt with flour and stir in. Add vanilla and broken walnut meats. Pour onto greased cookie tin and bake in slow oven for 30 minutes. Spread with peppermint frosting and cut in squares while still warm.

**For the business woman—

Any woman who spends long hours in store or office work and does her house work in the morning and in the evening will be pleased with these handy mixes.

MUFFIN MIX

Six cups sifted flour, 2 tsp. salt, 8 tsp. baking powder, ¾ cup sugar, ½ cup shortening.

Sift these ingredients two or three times to be sure they are well blended. Work in the shortening with fingertips. Put in a covered jar.

Write the following directions neatly on a small card to be placed in the top of the jar. To 2 cups of lightly packed mix add 1 egg and 2/3 cup of milk beaten together. Bake in greased muffin tins in a hot oven for about 10 minutes. Keep jar covered and in a cool place when not in use.

**For the bachelor—

To any man who gets his own meals a Christmas Pudding or Fruit Cake is a most acceptable gift.

MINCEMEAT FRUIT CAKE

Three-quarters cup brown sugar, ½ cup shortening, 1 large egg, 1 cup mincemeat, 2 cups sifted flour, 3 tsp. baking powder, ¼ tsp. salt, ½ tsp. cinnamon, ¼ tsp. cloves, ¼ cup candied fruit, ½ cup chopped nuts, 1/3 cup milk.

Cream shortening and sugar, add mincemeat and beat well. Sift dry ingredients and add alternately with milk. Fold in fruit and nuts. Bake slowly in a greased, paper lined tin for 1½ hours.

ECONOMY FRUIT CAKE

Half cup shortening, 1 cup brown sugar, 1 pkg. raisins, 1 tsp. cinnamon, ½ tsp. nutmeg, ½ tsp. allspice, ½ tsp. cloves, 1 cup hot water, 2 cups sifted flour, 1 tsp. soda, 1 tsp. baking powder, 1 tsp. salt, 1 cup chopped nuts, 1 tsp. vanilla, 1 tsp. lemon extract.

Cook shortening, sugar, raisins, spices and water together for 6 minutes, then cool. Sift dry ingredients together and combine with cooked mixture. Add nuts and flavoring . Pour into a paper-lined greased loaf tin and bake in a slow oven for 45 minutes.

ICE-BOX PLUM PUDDING

Two envelopes plain gelatin, ½ cup cold water, 2 cups hot water, 1 cup sweetened fruit juice, (apple, grape, prune or peach) 2 tbsp. lemon juice, 1 cup chopped walnut meats, ½ cup sugar, ½ tsp. salt, 1 cup grape nuts, 1 cup chopped dates, 1 cup seedless raisins, 1 tsp. almond extract.

Soften gelatin in cold water, then add hot water, fruit juice, sugar and salt. When gelatin is partly set, fold in the other ingredients. Pour into mould and chill in ice-box until firm.

Published December 14, 1949
Family Herald and Weekly Star
Sold $7.78

HULLED CORN

By Nellie R. Campbell

So many of the dishes that were quite common in grandmother's day are no longer in every day use. Hulled corn seems to be one of them. Perhaps, it is because the modern housewife has become so accustomed to buying foods already prepared for her, such as the canned, baked and frozen foods on the markets, that many of these dishes that require time and labor in preparing are no longer served.

Here is a recipe for Hulled Corn for those who still enjoy the old time dishes.

Shell dry corn and cook in a large kettle or boiler until the corn swells. To ½ boiler of cooked corn add 2 tbsp. of lye dissolved in 3 gal. of water. The water should come well up over the corn and should be just strong enough to loosen the hulls easily. Remove from the fire and stir with a wooden stick until the hulls become loose, then pour off the lye water. Add clear water and rub corn with hands loosening hulls which will float to the surface. Wash the corn in five or six waters to be sure that no lye remains. Then add sufficient water to cover the corn and cook for three hours. Drain and pour corn in shallow pans set outside to freeze. It may be kept frozen all winter and a little brought in at a time as needed or it may be packed in sealers and sterilized in boiling water for three hours.

To serve add the corn to cream sauce or brown gravy or it may be eaten with cream and sugar.

Published October 30, 1946
Family Herald and Weekly Star
Sold -- $1.13

ASPARAGUS TIPS
By Nellie R. Campbell

An Asparagus Bed will pay rich dividends. Long before the lettuce and radishes have grown to table size, the asparagus tips are pushing through the ground. What delicious dishes one can prepare with a bit of tender asparagus! Here are a few asparagus "tips."

ASPARAGUS LUNCHEON PLATE

Asparagus Luncheon Plate — 6 shredded wheat biscuits, asparagus for 6, 1 pimiento, cut in strips.

THIN WHITE SAUCE

2 tbsp. butter, 1 cup milk, 1 ½ tbsp. flour, ½ tsp. salt.

Cut off hard portions of asparagus and boil in small amount of water until tender. Arrange Shredded Wheat, split in half, on plate and moisten lightly with the water that the asparagus was cooked in, dot with bits of butter and set in oven for a few moments until butter melts, then pour over the White Sauce and arrange the asparagus over the biscuits. Garnish with the strips of pimiento.

ASPARAGUS OMELET

1 ½ cups soft bread crumbs, 6 eggs separated, 1 ½ cups milk, salt and pepper, 1 ½ cups of cooked asparagus cut in small pieces.

Mix crumbs and milk and let soak, then beat until smooth. Beat egg yolks, add salt and pepper and combine with bread mixture. Add the asparagus which has been cooked in salted water and well drained. Fold in the stiffly beaten whites and pour into a hot, greased pan and cook slowly until firm. Cook in a slow oven for the last 10 minutes to brown the top. If one prefers, this same mixture may be cooked as scrambled eggs.

CREAM OF ASPARAGUS SOUP

1 small bunch of asparagus, 2½ tbsp. flour, 1 cup of boiling water, salted, 1 cup evaporated milk, 1 tbsp. minced onions, 2 ½ cups sweet milk, 2 tbsp. finely chopped celery, 1 bouillion cube (chicken flavor), 4 tbsp. butter, 1 tsp. salt, 1/8 tsp. pepper.

Cut asparagus in small pieces and cook until tender in cup of boiling water. Drain, reserving stock. Saute onion and celery in butter in top of double boiler, add flour, stirring until smooth. Place over water in bottom of boiler and add evaporated milk, sweet milk, asparagus stock and bouillion cube and cook until thickened, stirring constantly. Add asparagus, salt and pepper. Whole milk may be substituted for the evaporate milk.

If your asparagus bed yields more than you can use, now is a good time to can the surplus for asparagus dishes during the winter months.

Wash, scale, cutting off hard portions, tie in uniform bundles, stand upright in 2 inches of boiling water. Boil for 4 minutes. Pack hot, tips up, except for 3 down in the centre of the jar. Add ½ tsp. salt to a pint sealer. Cover with boiling water and process. A pint jar requires 30 minutes at 10 pounds pressure or 2 hours in boiling water bath.

When using pressure cooker, --for each 1,000 feet above sea level, increase the pressure by half a pound. When using boiling water bath, --for each 1,000 feet above 1,500 feet, increase processing time by one-fifth.

Published April 10, 1947
Family Herald and Weekly Star
Sold -- $4.62

DRESSING UP THE 'SPUD'
By Nellie R. Campbell

Have you ever seen Junior view his half eaten potato with disgust and then demand, "Have I got to eat it?"

Upon being told that he must, he downs it with the air of a young martyr.

There are doubtless more different ways of cooking potatoes than of any other of our winter vegetables yet, in how many homes are they served the same way, -- usually boiled, --day after day. I really believe that most men like their potatoes boiled, baked or fried. These three ways of serving potatoes quite satisfy them, but there are other members of the family like Junior, who would welcome a change.

Potatoes are especially good food as they contain vitamin C—that vitamin found in many of the fruits and vegetables that it is hard for so many housewives to procure at this season of the year. It not only contains vitamin C but vitamins A and B and also iron.

"But potatoes are fattening, I have to watch my calories." I hear someone say. It isn't the potato, the experts say, but the 'fixings', the butter and the rich gravies that add those pounds. A fair-sized potato contains the same number of calories as a large orange or apple, four average sized prunes or a thick slice of bread.

There are many ways of cooking potatoes but to get the best food value they should always be cooked in their jackets. Peeling them early in the morning and leaving them covered with cold water until time to cook, gives one the least food value. The skin holds in the soluble nutrients, thus the iron and vitamin C do not dissolve in the cooking water. Statistics show that a potato cooked in it's skin contains the same amount of iron as a raw potato but one peeled before cooking has lost 10 percent of its iron. For this reason baked potatoes are especially good, and who doesn't like to eat a baked potato? However, there are a few rules to observe in baking potatoes.

1. They should be medium sized and also uniform in size.
2. They should be well scrubbed with a vegetable brush.
3. They should be baked from 40 to 60 minutes in a moderately hot oven. If the oven is too hot, the outer skin becomes hard and burned. This crust prevents the heat from penetrating into the potato thus slowing up cooking and the skin is no longer palatable. Some like the skin of the potato rubbed with bacon fat or drippings before baking. This makes a soft, greasy skin with a pleasant flavor.

If you like baked potatoes you are sure to like Baked Stuffed Potatoes.

BAKED STUFFED POTATOES

Select large potatoes and scrub, then bake 60 minutes. Slice off the broadside of the potato and scrape potato out of the shell, taking care not to break the skin. Mash adding salt, pepper and a little butter and hot milk. Beat until fluffy then add 1 tbsp. grated cheese for each potato. Refill the shell and sprinkle grated cheese on the top of each. Place potatoes in a pan and return to the oven until the cheese is melted and slightly browned.

I have used this same recipe using canned salmon instead of the cheese. It is necessary to drain the salmon well and flake it before adding to the potato. Add the liquid poured off the salmon in a milk gravy. Left over ground beef or ham make a good filling for Stuffed Potatoes.

If you are having mashed potatoes for dinner add a little hot milk and beat until fluffy. There are so many things that can be done with a bit of left over mashed potatoes.

PIGS IN BLANKET

Wrap up cooked sausage in left over mashed potato. Roll them in flour. Put in enough bacon fat or lard to cover the bottom of the frying pan and fry until brown.

POTATO CROQUETTES

Two cups hot riced potatoes, 2 tbsp. butter, ½ tsp. salt, ¼ tsp. celery salt, 1 small onion grated, 1 egg, 1 tsp. chopped parsley.

Mix ingredients in order given and beat. Shape, then dip in crumbs and beaten egg, then crumbs again and fry quickly in hot deep fat, drain on brown paper. If you can not get fat for deep frying, they can be shaped in flat cakes and fried until brown.

A good way to use up leftovers is a meat pie with a potato crust.

MEAT PIE WITH POTATO CRUST

Two cups of diced meat, 1 small finely chopped onion, salt and pepper, sufficient gravy to cover well, 1 cup sifted flour, 1 ½ tsp. baking powder, ¼ tsp. salt, ½ cup cold mashed potatoes, ¼ cup shortening, ½ cup milk.

Put meat, onion and gravy in casserole. Sift flour, baking powder and salt, add potato and blend. Cut in the shortening and add the milk. Stir lighly and turn on floured board. Roll out ½ of an inch thick and place crust on top of casserole pressing down the edges. Bake in hot oven until crust is brown. Be sure that the meat and gravy are close to the boiling point before putting on the crust.

DUTCH POTATO PANCAKES

Three pounds uncooked potatoes (8 or 9), 3 eggs separated, 1 ¼ cups pastry flour sifted, ½ tsp. salt, 1 large tart apple grated.

Peel potatoes and chill for an hour then grate them and drain through colander. Add the egg yolks, flour, salt and grated apple. Fold in the stiffly beaten egg whites. Have your griddle hot and lightly greased. Pour out a small amount of batter at a time as it spreads. Brown on both sides turning only once and serve hot with butter and syrup.

CHOCOLATE POTATO CAKES

One-half cup hot riced potato, 2 squares unsweetened chocolate, 1 cup brown sugar, 2 eggs separated, 1 cup sifted flour, ½ cup milk, 3 tsps. baking powder, ½ tsp. cinnamon, 1/4 tsp. cloves, 1/2 tsp. nutmeg, ½ cup chopped nuts.

Boil 1 large potato and put through ricer. Add the grated chocolate and stir until it is melted. Cream the brown sugar and shortening, add the well beaten egg yolks and potato mixture, then the dry ingredients alternately with the milk. Add the nuts and fold in the stiffly beaten whites of the eggs. Bake in an 8 by 12 pan in a moderate oven.

Potatoes and kraut make an excellent supper dish.

POTATOES AND KRAUT

Put 2 tsp. bacon fat or drippings in frying pan. When hot add 6 medium sized potatoes sliced raw and 1 cup of drained sauerkraut. Season with salt and pepper and add just enough water to barely cover the potatoes. Cover pan lightly and cook slowly until potatoes are soft and moist. If the water boils away add just enough to keep the potatoes from sticking to the pan.

Served with cold, sliced meat and hot baking powder biscuits. I am sure that the men folk will forget that they ever believed that boiling, frying or baking were the only ways to cook a potato.

CREAMED STEAMED POTATOES

Six potatoes, melted fat, 2 tsp. salt, 1 cup water, 1 ½ cup medium white sauce, parsley.

Wash and pare uniform-sized potatoes. Brush with oil, place in baking dish and sprinkle with salt. Add water, cover closely and steam two hours. Place in serving dish, cover with hot white sauce and garnish with parsley. Serves 6.

Printed Feb. 4, 1948
Family Herald and Weekly Star
Sold - $10.53

EVERYONE LIKES BLUEBERRIES
By Nellie R. Campbell

It was berry picking time. Each evening the berry pickers would come down the long, grassy hillside, hot, tired and dishevelled—their pails overflowing with large juicy blueberries. Sometimes there would be one lone berry picker but more often they came in groups of two, three or four, the children laughing and chatting as they hurried to their homes in the village that lay far below the hill. I knew that in many of these homes there would arise that delicious aroma of fresh blueberry pie.

I remembered our blueberry patch at home when I was a very small girl. As far as I know nothing ever grew on it but blueberries but they were such big, luscious berries and mother,--well, she knew just what to do with blueberries. There were blueberry biscuits that weren't biscuits at all for the dough was always baked in a large sheet. They were never cut lest the cold steel knife spoil some of the lightness but broken in pieces of eatable size. I loved to watch the golden butter melting into their purple and white lightness.

Of course there were always blueberry pies with just a bit of lemon juice added to give them that piquant flavor. Sometimes the blueberry kuchen was served cold with tall glasses of milk for us children and iced tea for the grown-ups—sometimes warm with whipped cream. We all loved mother's blueberry crumb dessert but her steamed blueberry pudding was our favorite. Turned out upon a deep plate with hot blueberry sauce running in purple rivulets through its topping of hard sauce and trickling down its sides, it was a pudding fit for a king.

BLUEBERRY BISCUITS

2 cups sifted flour, 4 ½ tsp. baking powder, ½ tsp. salt, 2 tbsp. sugar, 4 tbsp. shortening, 1 cup milk, 1 ½ cups blueberries. Sift together flour, baking powder and salt, add sugar and cut in shortening with dough blender or cookie cutter then add the blueberries. Make a well in the center of mixture and pour in the milk all at once. Stir lightly until mixed and spread in greased biscuit pan. Bake 12 to 15 minutes in hot oven. Do not cut but break. Serve with butter.

BLUEBERRY CRUMB PUDDING

½ cup sugar, ½ cup butter, 1 cup flour, ¼ tsp. cinnamon, 1 1/2 cups blueberries, ½ cup brown sugar. Put blueberries in casserole. Add cinnamon to sugar and sprinkle over them. Work butter and brown sugar into flour until mixture is crumbly and then sprinkle mixture over the berries. Bake until berries are cooked and top slightly browned. Serve with cream.

Did you ever try adding a bit of lemon juice to that blueberry pie?

BLUEBERRY PIE

Pastry for 9 inch pie plate, 2-3 cups sugar, 2 tbsp. flour, 3 cups blueberries, juice of half a lemon, 2 tbsp. water, 2-3 tbsp. butter.

Line pie tin with half of pastry. Blend sugar and flour and add to the blueberries, mix well, then turn into pie shell. Mix lemon juice and water and sprinkle over berries. Dot with butter. Put on top crust and bake in hot oven for 40 to 45 minutes, reducing heat after the first ten minutes.

BLUEBERRY KUCHEN

1 ½ cups sifted flour, 2 ½ tsp. baking powder, ½ cup of sugar, ½ tsp. salt, 1 egg, ¼ cup milk, ¼ cup melted butter, 2 cups blueberries, 1/3 cups powdered sugar.

Sift flour, baking powder and salt together. Beat egg until light, gradually beat in the ½ cup of sugar, add milk and melted butter. Add the dry ingredients and mix well. Turn into a greased 8 inch square pan. Spread the blueberries over the dough and sprinkle the 1/3 cup of powdered sugar over them. Bake in a moderate oven until done. Serve either cold or warm with whipped cream.

STEAMED BLUEBERRY LOAF

2 cups sifted flour, 3 ½ tsp. baking powder, ½ tsp. salt, 3 tbsp. sugar, 2 cups blueberries, 1 egg, well beaten, 1 cup milk, 3 tbsp. melted shortening, 1 tsp. grated lemon rind.

Sift dry ingredients together and add blueberries. Combine egg, milk and melted shortening and add to the dry ingredients stirring lightly only until mixed. Turn in top of greased double boiler, cover and steam for 2 hours. Turn out on a deep plate and heap with hard sauce or hot blueberry sauce. The hard sauce is made by combining butter with icing sugar and beating until light and fluffy. The blueberry sauce should not be too sweet but boiled until slightly thickened and rich in flavor and color.

Published Aug. 13, 1947
Family Herald and Weekly Star
Sold--$10.23

TIME TO MAKE COTTAGE CHEESE
By Nellie R. Campbell

Cottage Cheese, tart and refreshing, is a popular food this time of the year, when there is surplus milk on hand. It's especially popular with the cook too, for it can be prepared in a variety of ways, to add zest to spring and summer meals. One half cup of cottage cheese contains as much high-grade protein as one serving of meat, so it can serve as a meat substitute, too, to ease the strain on the budget.

If you are making your own cottage cheese, milk that has soured quickly and sweet milk are good, but milk that has soured slowly or is stale, should not be used as it is apt to impart a bitter flavor to the cheese. The method is simple:

COTTAGE CHEESE
Four quarts of milk, 1 to 2 tsp. salt, ½ to 2/3 cup cream.

Warm milk to 75 degrees F., in a pan over hot water, stirring constantly. Let milk stand at warm room temperature, about 75 degrees F. until well clabbered, for 24 to 30 hours. At this time a curd will form which should separate into chunks when cut with a knife. Cut it criss-cross, into about 1-inch squares. Add 4 quarts water, which has been heated to 150 degrees F., stir in to mix thoroughly, and let stand for 1 ½ hours at room temperature. This cooks the curd. Drain through a clean cloth bag or a cloth-lined strainer. Save the whey for use in cooking. Wash the curd if desired with twice its measure of cold water and drain. Add salt to taste and sufficient cream to give desired consistency.

A refreshing drink can be made from the whey.

LEMON WHEY
Add the juice of one lemon to the whey which drains off from curd when making cottage cheese from one quart of milk. Sweeten to taste, strain and chill.

COTTAGE CHEESE DRESSING
Beat 1 cup of sour cream until stiff. Flavor with lemon juice and then fold into this ½ cup of cottage cheese. This makes an excellent salad dressing for fruit and vegetable salads.

BAKED CHEESE LOAF

Two cups of cottage cheese, 1 cup left-over cereal, 1 cup breadcrumbs dried in oven, ¼ cup peanut butter, 1 tsp. onion juice, pinch sage, ¼ tsp. soda, salt, pepper, paprika to taste.

Mix and form into loaf. Bake in greased pan for 20 to 25 minutes. Serve hot.

COTTAGE CHEESE PIE

One cup cottage cheese, 2/3 cup sugar, 2/3 cup milk, 2 egg yolks, 1 tbsp. butter, salt, ¼ tsp. vanilla. Mix the cheese, sugar and milk. Add melted butter, salt and vanilla to well-beaten egg yolks. Combine the two mixtures. Bake in one crust and use the stiffly beaten egg whites for meringue.

CHERRY CHEESE CAKE

One and a quarter cups fine graham crackers or gingersnap crumbs, 1 cup sugar, 1/3 cup softened butter, 3 eggs, well beaten, 5 tbsp. flour, ½ tsp. salt, 2 cups cottage cheese, 1/3 cup heavy cream, ½ cup whole cherry preserves.

Mix together crumbs, 2 tbsp. of sugar and butter. Press on bottom and sides of a buttered, shallow baking pan. Mix together the eggs, cheese, flour, salt, cream, and remainder of sugar. When well blended, pour this mixture into cracker lined pan and bake for 1 hour in slow oven (300 degrees F.). When cool spread the top with cherry preserves.

COTTAGE CHEESE TURNOVERS

Two cups sifted flour, ½ cup shortening, 6 tbsp. sugar, ½ tsp. nutmeg, ¼ tsp. salt, 1 cup cottage cheese. Cream shortening, add sugar, nutmeg and cottage cheese. Stir in the sifted flour and salt. Wrap in waxed paper and chill until firm enough to handle easily. Turn out on floured board and roll ½ inch thick. Cut into 3-inch squares. Place 1 tsp. of jam or jelly on one half and fold over into a triangle. Press the edges together. Place on a baking sheet and bake in hot oven (425 degrees F.) for 15 minutes or until lightly browned and puffed. Then cool, sprinkle with icing sugar.

Published May 31, 1951
Family Herald and Weekly Star
Sold --$5.97

TURNIP PUMPKIN PIE

By Nellie R. Campbell

It all started with Bill's hankering for a piece of pumpkin pie, the kind his mother use to make, or perhaps it started long before that —say, late last July when Jack Frost paid an unexpected visit to our garden and ruined the pumpkin vines. Anyway, Bill had a yearning for pumpkin pie and there simply weren't any pumpkins.

It was then that I remembered a thin, grey-haired teacher in a country school in New England. "Where there's a will there's a way." How often I had heard those words in my school days!

I made a trip to the cellar and returned with a yellow turnip—just an ordinary Rutabaga. At least the yellow cubes of cooked turnips somewhat resembled pumpkin. I got out my nicest recipe for pumpkin pie.

Turnip Pumpkin Pie

1 ½ cups cooked pumpkin—in this case turnip)—2-3 cups brown sugar, 1 cup milk, 2 eggs, 1 tbsp. cornstarch, ¼ tsp. each of cinnamon, cloves, nutmeg, ¼ tsp. salt, 1 cup cream.

Mix sugar, cornstarch and spices, add to turnips, add well beaten eggs and cream. Cook in top of double boiler until thick. Pour into a baked pie shell and pile high with whipped cream. Dust top with a bit of cinnamon.

Bill pushed back his chair. "That's as good a pumpkin pie as my mother ever made," he said. Then his eyes fell on the snow-shoe trail that led from our cabin on the shore of a northern lake. There was four feet of snow on the level and 12 miles to a country grocery store. Bill scratched his head.

"Say, where did you get that pumpkin, anyway?" he asked. "Where there's a will, there's a way," I quoted glibly. Bill still maintains that that was as good a pumpkin pie as any his mother ever made and he is still wondering where I got the pumpkin—but that is my secret.

Published April 7, 1946
Family Herald and Weekly Star
Paid - $1.55

PAINT YOUR CAKE

By Nellie R. Campbell

Sally set her cake down on the end of the table and carefully removed its wrappings.

"How lovely!" I exclaimed. Through the lattice–work of green that criss-crossed the smooth white icing, peeped gay yellow blossoms with deep burnt orange centers.

"But how did you ever do it?" I asked, still admiring her handiwork.

"It's really quite simple," she replied. "Just paint your design on with a paint brush."

"But what did you use for paint?" I asked.

"Oh, just a bit of artificial food coloring." She answered, sweeping the wrapping paper into the wastebasket.

As I stood admiring the lovely yellow blossoms peeping through the green lattice-work, I knew that there would be no more fussing with tubes and different colored icing the next time I decorated a cake! Why, --I could simply brush on flaming red hearts, bright green shamrocks, cute little Easter bunnies and all sorts of gay summer flowers with only a paint brush and a bit of food coloring.

Published Oct 1952
Family Herald and Weekly Star
Sold --$1.47

HANDY QUANTITY MIXES
By Nellie R. Campbell

Hot biscuits for dinner! "When did you ever find time to mix them?" I asked, remembering the unusually large wash on the line.

"Two weeks ago," my hostess laughed as she set the plate of piping hot powder biscuits on the table.

It seemed that my hostess was one of those busy farm women whose outdoor chores increase as the summer advanced. There were chickens and gardens and berry picking besides all those innumerable household tasks that fill the lives of all housewives.

"It saves time to mix things in quantities and then they are ready to use at a moments notice," she explained. "I always keep Biscuit Mix, Muffin Mix and Pancake Mix on my pantry shelf so it's no trick at all to make a batch of baking powder biscuits on washday or whisk up hotcakes for breakfast. Perhaps you'd like my recipes?"

QUANTITY TEA BISCUITS

8 cups sifted all purpose flour or 9 cups sifted pastry flour, 6 tbsp. baking powder, 1 ½ tbsp. salt, 1 cup of lard or mild flavoured fat. Sift dry ingredients together 3 times. Cut in fat with two knives until the mixture resembles breadcrumbs. Store in a covered jar in a cool place. Use 1/3 cup of milk for each cup of biscuit mix. Mix lightly and cut on floured board. Bake in a hot oven 12 or 15 minutes at 400 degrees or 20 minutes at 350 degrees.

DRY MUFFIN MIX

12 cups sifted flour, 4 tsp. salt, 16 tsp. baking powder, 1 ½ cups sugar, 1 cup shortening. Makes about 7 dozen 2 inch muffins. Sift dry ingredients together 3 times, work in shortening with fingertips until the mixture is mealy. Keep in a covered jar in the refrigerator or cool place. To 2 cups of muffin mix add 1 egg and 2/3 cup of milk which have been beaten together. Stir only until flour is moistened. Bake in greased muffin tins in hot oven—425 degrees for 10 minutes.

PANCAKE MIX

1 box of cornstarch, 5 cups cornmeal, 15 cups white flour, 2 cups powdered milk (optional), 1 cup white sugar, 1/3 cup salt, 1 cup baking powder. If you have milk to mix your pancakes leave out the powdered milk. Sift all the dry ingredients together three times and then store in flour sack or in cartons.

Published August 6, 1947
Family Herald and Weekly Star
Sold ---$2.77

THOSE SUCCULENT SPRING GREENS
By Nellie R. Campbell

Each spring there seems to be such a long interval of waiting between the time the seed that we so painstakingly selected from the gaily colored seed catalogue, are planted and the succulent green onions, tender lettuce leaves and spicy radishes are ready for the salad bowl. It is during this time that the greens growing along the edges of our garden patch may prove to be a real blessing – the tonic that we know we need. Carrots, turnips and beets that have been stored all winter have lost all of their appeal and were it not for those humble greens, that push themselves through the ground at the very first signs of spring, there would be that danger of our meals becoming drab.

MARCH MARIGOLDS

When we see flashes of red in the treetops and we hear the clear, sweet call of the robin, we know that it is time to put on our high boots and go in search of March marigolds. They may be found on springy ground, low meadows, swamps, riverbanks and even ditches. You will know them by their beautiful broad, heart shaped, glossy leaves and their bright, shining yellow flowers.

Some people claim that it is nothing short of sacrilege to consign their crisp, glossy leaves to the cooking pot, while others smack their lips and maintain these greens are every bit as good as spinach. The tender buds are often used in white sauce as a substitute for capers.

SORREL

Children love this lowly little sorrel plant because of its sour tasting leaves. While still young and tender it makes delicious greens and a few leaves added to soup or salad will give them that different taste that adds interest to an otherwise ordinary dish.

BRAKE GREENS

Brake Greens is really one of our most common ferns. Perhaps it is better known as fiddlehead as the young fronds are curled at the tips into a tight knot or fiddlehead. When the fronds are young and still tightly curled, they make excellent greens. I remember a shady nook on my grandfather's farm where the brake grew thick each spring. Long after the farm had passed into other hands and grandma had come to the city to live with us, she got that hankering each spring for "jest one mess of brake greens," and some member of the family had to make a trip back to the old farm for brakes to satisfy grandma's appetite.

LAMB'S QUARTERS

I'm sure that grandma always called lamb's quarters plain pigweed greens. No doubt this cousin of spinach is one of our most common garden weeds. The underside of the pale green leaves is covered with a silvery pinkish substance that gives the leaf a delicate frosted appearance. If the plant is nipped off three or four inches from the top it will branch out and these new shoots may also be used for greens.

Like spinach it cooks very quickly and may be used in a variety of ways. It makes a quick and delicious luncheon dish if drained well, combined with scrambled eggs and served on slices of buttered toast. A few jars of canned green on your pantry shelf can do something to that meal that might otherwise be unappetizing.

DANDELION GREENS

The bright sunny blossoms of the dandelion are surely a harbinger of spring and what can be more tempting than that pleasing bitterness of tender dandelion greens. Of course they must be dug while still young and the blossoms is still tiny and furry. If the plants are cut off just beneath the surface, all trace of root and dark, dry skin removed and grass and dirt shaken out, the washing is not difficult.

They should be washed thoroughly in several waters. Grandma always added a small piece of salt fat pork to the greens while cooking but we like strips of nicely browned bacon laid across the drained greens and the bacon fat poured over them. If you like hardboiled eggs with spinach, you will like them just as well with dandelions. Some people serve a slice of lemon with the greens to suit individual tastes. You may like the flavor of a bit of raw dandelion cut fine and added to that salad bowl.

I am sure that if you look, you will find other wild greens growing in your neighborhood that are well worth serving on your table. Curley dock, milkweed, chickory, nettles, cowslip – all, if prepared when young and tender, make appetizing greens. They are prepared as other greens. It is at this time of the year that we feel the need of spring tonic that is hidden away in the leaves and stems of many of our common plants. How fortunate we are that we live in a country where we can roam about in the warm sunshine and gather our tonic in a basket!

Published March 26, 1951
Family Herald and Weekly Star
Sold--$7.00

IF YOU HAVE A SWEET TOOTH
By Nellie R. Campbell

Our kitchen was always such a delightful place just before Christmas. We all felt that half of the fun was in the getting ready for that wonderful day. Those delicious odors of boiling molasses, corn a popping and the smell of butter and vinegar as it was dropped into the kettle of bubbling sugar candy, made us all eager to help.

With the extra holiday baking that requires sugar, making candy may seem to be an utter impossibility unless those recipes are used that require a minimum of sugar or no sugar at all. Yes, -- there are a few kinds that will delight the grown-ups as well as the children and yet they are neither hard on the sugar rations nor the pocket-book.

GUESS WHAT?

1 cup nut meats, 1 cup dates or prunes, 1 cup raisins, 1 cup puffed wheat or puffed rice.

If prunes are used instead of dates, soak them for several hours then drain and dry thoroughly with a towel and remove stones. After putting the ingredients through the food chopper, press mixture into a shallow pan and place a weight upon it. In 24 hours cut in squares and drop each piece in melted, sweetened chocolate.

MOLASSES BUTTER-SCOTCH

3 tbsp. molasses, 2 tbsp. water, 2 cups sugar, 1 tbsp. butter, 1 tsp. vanilla.

Boil molasses, water and sugar together until brittle when dropped in cold water. Be sure that it is brittle. Add butter and vanilla and then drop with a teaspoon in small round wafers onto a buttered tin. Set in cool place to harden.

If you are one of those people who are fortunate enough to live in that section of our country where sugar maples grow and you can obtain maple sugar, a most delicious candy can be made from it.

MAPLE SUGAR FUDGE

Boil together 2 cups of maple sugar, 1 cup of sweet cream and a piece of butter the size of a walnut, until it forms a ball when dropped in cold water. Remove from fire and add 1 cup of chopped nut meats, if desired, then beat until it begins to sugar and pour into buttered pan. Cut in squares.

MOLASSES CANDY

2 cups molasses, 2 cups of white sugar, butter the size of a walnut, 2 tbsp. vinegar, pinch of soda.

Boil all ingredients except soda until it forms a hard ball in water, remove from fire and add the pinch of soda, stirring vigorously. Pour into buttered plate and when nearly cold, pull until very white. Cut into small pieces with scissors. These may be wrapped in small squares of waxed paper and used to help fill the candy bags or the children's stockings.

STUFFED PRUNES

Select the largest and nicest prunes. Soak for two or three hours, then drain and wipe dry with towel. Remove the stones and fill the cavities with one of the following mixtures.

-Walnut meats.

-White of 1 egg, beaten stiff with enough powdered sugar stirred in to make a stiff mixture—flavor with vanilla or maple.

-Chop nuts and combine mixture 1 and 2.

Roll prune in granulated sugar.

Popped corn is something that finds favor with both young and old. No matter how much candy we had, Christmas was never complete without a large platter full of corn-balls and what fun we had making them!

CORN BALLS

1 cup molasses, 1 cup sugar.

Boil together until it forms a hard ball when dropped in cold water. Add 1 tsp. vanilla and a small piece of butter, then set the kettle in a pan of hot water on the back of the stove so that the molasses will pour easily.

Have a large pan of popped corn ready. Put about a quart of corn in a smaller pan and pour over it, in a thin stream, just enough of the boiled molasses to stick the corn together. With buttered hands press the corn into firm, round balls. Add more corn and then pour over more of the boiled molasses. It is much easier to work with a small quantity at a time as the molasses is apt to harden too quickly if all poured in at once.

PINK POPCORN BALL

1 cup honey or ½ cup syrup and ½ cup sugar, 1 ½ quarts popped corn.

Boil the honey to the hard boil stage. Add pink coloring a little at a time until syrup is lightly tinted. Add popcorn and mix well. When cool enough to handle, grease hands with butter and shape into balls or press hard into pan and cut with sharp knife into squares.

Published Nov. 9, 1949
Family Herald and Weekly Star

FROM OLD WORLD KITCHENS
By Nellie R. Campbell

Canada is fast becoming the melting pot of foreign cookery, for each war bride coming to our shores, brings her favorite recipes with her. Even the war brides of an earlier generation still serve many of those delectable dishes made in their homeland. Is it any wonder that with women of every nationality in our vast Dominion there are dishes that appeal to the most epicurean tastes? It is now no longer possible to tell just where Canadian cookery ends and Old World cookery begins as so many of these foreign recipes are finding their way into Canadian homes. Such new and tantalizing odors of fresh, crusty dark breads from out-of-door ovens, stews simmering gently to bring out their rich goodness, and that delightful aroma of spicy fruit, greeted us as we visited in the homes of some of our Old Country friends recently.

It was a little French war bride who showed me how to make Ragout. Her large, dark eyes sparkled with pleasure when she found I had never even heard of the dish and that she could teach me something.

RAGOUT
Two pig's feet. 1 pound of hamburger, 1 onion, 6 medium sized potatoes, salt and pepper to taste, brown gravy.

Cut the pig's feet in small pieces and add one onion cut small. Cover with water and boil until nearly tender. Peel the potatoes and put in the kettle about ½ hour before serving. Form the hamburger into balls and fry well. About 20 minutes before serving add the hamburger balls to the pig's feet and potatoes. Make a gravy by browning 2 tbps. flour in the pan in which the balls were fried. When brown add sufficient cold water for gravy. Bring to a boil, stirring constantly; let boil a minute or two and then add it to the kettle. Push the kettle to the back of the stove to simmer gently for about 20 minutes.

It was in a Ukrainian home that we first ate Holubchi, but one does not have to be Ukrainian to find that Holubchi is good eating.

HOLUBCHI
One lb. hamburger or hamburger and sausage meat mixed, ½ cup of uncooked rice, 2 medium sized potatoes, cut small, 1 small onion chopped, salt and pepper to taste. If you have any bacon, cut it up into small pieces and add. 1 small cabbage and 1 can of tomatoes.

Remove the core of the cabbage and place the head in a kettle of boiling water. Set it on the back of the stove until the leaves have wilted.

Mix the hamburger, rice, onion and potatoes well and shape into rolls the right size for a single serving. Pick off the wilted cabbage leaves and wrap each meatball in a leaf, turning in the edges. Place the rolls in a greased baking pan or roaster.

Over this pour 1 can of tomatoes or tomato juice. Add sufficient water to cover. Bake for 2 ½ hours, tightly covered.

The Mennonites still use many of the recipes they brought with them from the Old Country. It was a spotless, whitewashed kitchen that we found a busy housewife preparing Chicken Noodle soup for a haying crew. She smiled her pleasure at my interest in dinner preparations.

CHICKEN NOODLE SOUP

Clean a young chicken and cut in pieces. Boil until tender, adding a little salt and parsley to the water. To make Noodles:

One cup of milk, 3 eggs, flour and salt. Add milk and salt to well beaten eggs and work in flour to form a very stiff dough. Knead well and roll out very thin. Let this rolled out dough dry for several hours in a warm room, then fold and cut in ¾ inch strips.

Cook the noodles in salted water and add them to the chicken broth shortly before serving.

In the home of a woman of Russian and German extraction we were served Strudle. It is an ideal supper dish to serve on one of our cold Canadian nights when the children come home from school with ravenous appetites.

STRUDLE

On a day when you are baking bread roll out a piece of well risen bread dough and spread with melted lard, leave it to rise for 10 minutes and then stretch it. Sprinkle flour over the table to prevent sticking and roll and stretch until it is as thin as paper. Cut off about ¼ of this and roll up in a long, thin roll. Continue making rolls until all dough is used.

Peel enough potatoes for supper and cut them into small squares. Put sufficient lard or bacon fat in the bottom of the roaster, add the diced potatoes, sprinkle with salt and just enough water to cover them. Coil the long, thin rolls of bread dough over the top of the potatoes and cover tightly. Put the roaster on the middle or back cover where it will cook slowly. Let it cook until the water has all boiled away and the potatoes begin to fry. Do not remove the cover before it is done or the bread dough will fall.

This recipe comes from a Spanish war bride. Her husband, a young Canadian lad, agrees with her that Tortillia should be in every Canadian cookbook.

TORTILLIA

Six medium sized potatoes, 3 or more eggs, 3 or more tbsp. of undiluted canned milk.

Peel and slice the potatoes then fry them in bacon fat or drippings. When nearly done beat 3 eggs or more, adding 1 tbsp. of undiluted canned milk for each egg used. Add salt and pepper and beat well. Pour the eggs over the potatoes and bake in the oven until the eggs are set.

Published Feb. 19, 1947
Family Herald and Weekly Star
Sold - $4.65

USEFUL CHRISTMAS GIFTS
By Nellie R. Campbell

    This is to be a "Bottle Christmas" at our house. Being one of those individuals who just can't seem to throw away anything that might some day be used, it was not surprising how many small jars and odd shaped bottles had accumulated on the top pantry shelf. After I discovered how easy it was to frost glass I decided to turn my collection of jars and bottles into useful Christmas gifts.

    A tall six-sided jar made a lovely vase when frosted a pale yellow with a feathery design. Use one part boiled linseed oil, one half part turpentine, one fifth part clear varnish and mix well. Add powdered whiting to this mixture until mixture is very white. By moistening a bit of red or yellow ochre or any dry colour with just enough linseed oil to make a smooth paste, you can have coloured glass. Apply the mixture to the glass with a brush. By making a cheesecloth pad and tapping the glass lightly or twisting it you can make different designs.

    A couple of small, low jars exactly alike and tinted a deep rose, made an attractive set for a dressing table. One was filled with vanishing cream, the other with powder.

Hand Lotion
    Use equal parts of glycerine and lemon juice. Add a few drops of alcohol and a little rose water to give it a slight perfume.   Another good lotion is made by using one part of aqua ammonia to two parts glycerine. Add enough rose water for a slight perfume.

    The squat, wide mouthed jars, when filled with pickles, jam or sweets, need no decoration other than gay wrappings. If the enamel top has been scratched or bears the name of the product it once contained, as many tops do, a coat of quick drying enamel, either red or green or a bit of silver or gold paint, will give it a Christmas air.

    Equal parts of clear lacquer and lacquer thinner form an exceptional vehicle for metal powders such as gold, silver or bronze used in gilding. Mix a small quantity of the powder with the lacquer to form the desired consistency and apply with brush. This covers well and dries quickly.

Cranberry Conserve
    1 quart of cranberries, 1 cup raisins, 2 oranges, ¼ cup nut meats – (the kernel of a nut), 3 cups sugar.

Wash cranberries and cook in water to just cover until tender. Press through coarse sieve, add chopped raisins, chopped pulp and grated peel of oranges. Cook slowly for 10 minutes and then add sugar and simmer gently until thick. Chop nut meats and add a few minutes before cooking is complete. Pour into hot, sterilized jars.

Dixie Relish

1 quart chopped cabbage, 1 pint chopped onions, 2 tbsp. salt, ¼ cup mustard seed, 1 quart vinegar, 1 cup brown sugar.

Chop cabbage and onion, add salt and mix well, set overnight. In the morning drain in bag and then add vinegar, sugar and spice. Bring to a boil, and seal hot in hot sterilized jars.

Guess What?

1 cup nut meats, 1 cup dates, 1 cup raisins, 1 cup puffed rice cereal.

Put ingredients through meat chopper, and then press mixture into shallow pan and place weight upon it. In twenty-four hours cut in squares and drop each piece into melted sweet chocolate.

Yes, this is surely going to be a "Bottle Christmas", for my empty jars and bottles are being turned into useful, as well as ornamental gifts.

Published December 11, 1952
Family Herald and Weekly Star
Sold--$3.76

BIRD FEEDERS
By Nellie R. Campbell

One lb. suet, ½ cup peanut butter, birdseed, 2 cups popped corn, 1 cup rolled oats, corn flakes, or other coarse cereal.

Melt suet and peanut butter. Add dry ingredients and mix well. Use cups for molds. Stand a 4 inch nail head down in centre of cup. Pack the suet mixture tightly around the nail and set in cool place until suet is hard. To un-mold set cup in warm water for a few minutes and pull bird feeder out by the nail. These bird feeders can quickly be driven into the porch rail or window ledge and are a great attraction for the winter birds all about us. Often the recipient receives as much pleasure from watching the birds as her feathered friends do from her bounty.

Published December 11, 1952
Family Herald and Weekly Star
Sold--$2.00

GAY CHRISTMAS CARDS
By Nellie R. Campbell

An inexpensive Christmas card can be made to look like a more costly one with just a little work and a bit of care. You are sure to find pretty but expensive cards at your local Five and Ten-Cent Store. Choose cards with snow scenes, Christmas trees or Christmas bells.

With a package of mica and a bottle of library paste you are ready to begin dressing up your cards. Sift the snow so that you get only the fine particles (the rest can be used around your tree). With the paste outline lightly the roofs of houses, trees, etc., on your card, then sprinkle artificial snow over it. Let the card dry and then shake off the surplus snow. Place your cards face down on a hard surface and weight down with books to prevent them from curling. They really are pretty and easy on the budget at Christmas time.

Published December 11, 1952
Family Herald and Weekly Star
Sold--$1.50

THOSE THREE CHRISTMAS CARDS
By Nellie R. Campbell

Who doesn't look forward to opening his Christmas mail with a feeling of pleasure, yet there were three Christmas cards in my mail last year that failed to bring me the joy and happiness that I am sure their senders anticipated.

I slipped a dainty card from its tinted envelope and eagerly read the Christmas greeting written in a neat hand. It was signed simply, "Grace." Now I happen to know four persons with that name. I turned to the envelope for a clue, but it bore only a postmark, -- Vancouver, British Columbia. None of the four lived in Vancouver, yet any one of them might have spent her Christmas holidays there. Suddenly I remembered that the parents of one of the "Graces" actually did live in Vancouver. No doubt Grace had spent Christmas with them. Promptly a little card of thanks went on its way with all good wishes for the coming year. It was not until later that I learned that Grace had spent Christmas in her own hometown in a small village many miles from Vancouver. A year later I am still wondering which of the remaining "Graces" sent me the lovely card with the cheery message.

One could tell at a glance that it was an expensive card. The greeting within was written in small, even, precise letters but I failed to recognize the handwriting. There was no signature, -- just a few words of greeting. The envelope bore the postmark Prince Rupert, British Columbia. During the two years we had spent at the coast (teaching the Indian children at Kitkatla), we had met quite a few people.

Which one had sent us this beautiful Christmas card? The year has passed and still we do not know.

The Hawley's had owned a large house in town. It was in the early spring that they had sold their home and left for the coast. "I want less house, and a bit more land," Mrs. Hawley had explained. They hoped to find what they wanted somewhere on Vancouver Island, but would stay with their married daughter in Vancouver while they looked around a bit.

The cluster of pinecones on the front of the card reminded one of our northern woods, -- maybe that was why she had sent it. Inside I read, "Greetings from the Hawley Family. Do write soon and tell us all the Prince George news."

I looked over the postmark, - Vancouver, -- no other address and somehow I felt I had lost a friend. Three lovely cards, - that have never been acknowledged, because of the lack of name or address.

Published December 3, 1953
Family Herald and Weekly Star
Sold--$2.89

CHRISTMAS IN AN INDIAN VILLAGE
By Nellie R. Campbell

It was Christmas and we were hundreds of miles from home. Since the first of September, Bert and I had been comfortably settled in the teacherage that was built on a point of land jutting out into the Pacific Ocean at Kitkatla, British Columbia. It was my duty to teach forty-six small Indian boys and girls reading, writing and arithmetic each day, while Bert dispensed the medicines that the Canadian Government gives to all Indians living on Reserves in isolated places. There were also minor cuts and bruises to be bandaged and the mail to give out whenever some Indian boat chanced to make the forty mile trip into Prince Rupert and bring back a sack containing mail that often proved to be two or three weeks old.

For generations this tribe of Tsimshean Indians have made their home on Dolphin Island, southwest of Prince Rupert, British Columbia. It is off the route of travel so no boats call except packers and fishing boats during the fishing season, the Police Boat on its regular run through northern waters, and occasional Mission Boat and the Kasskeena, used by the Indian Superintendent and his assistant in visiting the tribes under their supervision.

The Indians live in fairly modern homes built along the one narrow street that runs for half a mile along one side of the island. There are no motor vehicles, no modern machinery, no animals except dogs and cats, on the island. The natives make their living by fishing, hunting and trapping. They are keen on sports and after the fishing season is over the long winter evenings are spent in playing basketball. There is keen competition between the teams on the island and sometimes boys from other villages along the coast come for several days of sport.

Anticipation

What would Christmas be like on this small island cut off from the rest of the world? Had these Indians adopted our Christmas customs as they had so many of the white man's ways or did they celebrate it according to their own traditions, we wondered?

As I look back it is hard to tell just when Christmas actually began or when it ended. Even on that last day of school the children who usually appeared so unemotional, had an expectant air. Could it be the box in my closet filled with bags of homemade candies and small tissue wrapped gifts, or the concert to be held on Christmas Eve that made lessons quite impossible? We sang our Christmas songs and some of the choruses they had learned in Sunday School and loved. The story of the birth of Christ and of the shepherds watching their flocks by night while angel voices sang "Glory to God in the Highest", became more real to them as these scenes were depicted on the flannel-board.

I had given them the candy and small gifts. Amid the laughter and crackling of tissues as they unwrapped their gifts, Norma, usually so shy, suddenly spoke, "We haven't said our prayer yet."

Quite unintentionally the prayer had been omitted from our opening exercises. "Well, we can say it now." The voice came from the other side of the room. It was Jerry, a six year old with black eyes and still blacker hair. Instantly the room was quiet, hands were folded and small heads bowed. "Our Father who art in heaven," – they repeated it with me in unison and then I dismissed them. Their good-byes were still ringing in my ears as I watched them troop up the wet path that led to the road, each clutching his bag of candy and his Christmas gift. It was little moments like this that made me love these dark-skinned boys and girls.

It was a beautiful day. The sun shone and the air was warm. There was not the slightest hint of snow even if Christmas was only three days off. It was like a spring morning. A native boat was going into town. We stood on the beach and watched as they took on our empty oil drums. I almost regretted our decision to spend Christmas in Kitkatla. We had not been off the island since we came in September and there might not be another opportunity before spring.

However, I was glad of our decision to remain, for the next day the waves were pounding on the rocky shore and rain was coming down in torrents. It was one of those storms that come up almost without warning and may last for days.

In spite of the rain there was unusual activity about the village. Several of the women came to the house to help tag the gifts that had been sent by St. Mary's Church in Kerrysdale, for the children. The rehearsals for the concert continued in spite of the weather. The whole village took on that air of expectancy.

It was early Christmas Eve when the native boat returned bringing the Rev. Charles Lomas, a travelling missionary for the Diocese of Caledonia, to spend Christmas in their village. As Bert and I were the only white people in the village, we were expected to entertain him.

It had been nearly eighty years since Christianity had come to their island and strange as it may seem, it was not the white man who brought the Gospel to them, but other natives from Metlakatla. In 1889 Chief Shaker made a trip to Victoria and brought back a stone monument, which was erected on the main street of the village. At a solemn ceremony in the presence of other tribes from neighboring villages, the Indians of Kitkatla pledged to forsake their old customs and "take the ways of Queen Victoria." In memory of this occasion they sent the Queen a beautiful sea otter skin worth hundreds of dollars. In return she sent them a life-sized portrait of herself in a heavy gilt frame.

Ever since Christianity came to their island, the service in their church has been an important part of their Christmas celebration.

The Chief is Host

The concert in the Church Army Hall on Christmas Eve was quite unlike the concerts held in schoolhouses all over the prairies. There were no plays or humorous skits, no references to Santa Claus, no refreshments, nor dancing. The concert opened with a hymn and prayer in their native tongue. The children, always shy in public, took their places before the microphone for their soft voices would not carry across the hall. They spelled the word "Christmas" with Bible verses. They quoted scripture, fifty verses from memory. The recitations and dialogues were all based on "The Christmas story". The older people sang the well-known Christmas hymns.

The closing tableau was really, very lovely. It was done by the teen-age girls of the village. They were dressed in long white satin gowns with gauze edged with tinsel fastened at the back of the neck and down the back of the sleeves to give the appearance of wings whenever the arms were extended or raised. The girls stood at spaced intervals on the platform that was built in tiers. The lights were lowered and a spot light turned on the stage. One of the younger married women stood at the right front of the platform. The girls took a single step forward or backward raising or extending their arms as they sang "Nearer My God to Thee." Slowly and clearly her voice sounded through the hall as she sang. Before the last stanza was finished there was audible weeping, then the entire audience rose and came down the aisle and knelt in front of the hall before the altar.

Christmas Morning

It was ten o'clock. There came a knock on our door. The Chief Councillor, who had been the acting Chief since the death of the former Chief, entered. "You are to eat dinner at my house."

The statement was simple and direct. We had heard that there was to be a feast held in the Chief's home but until that moment we had not known that we were to be guests. As we lived among these people we learned that an invitation to any affair was never given until the event was about to take place. By the time I had removed our own Christmas dinner from the fire and changed my dress, the church bell was ringing for the Christmas service. It is one of their customs to hold Communion at the close of the Christmas Service so it was after one o'clock by the time we reached the Chief's house.

Had I not known that this was the home of an Indian Chief, I would have thought it any well-ordered Canadian home for that is what it really is. A young man, a relative of the Chief, took our coats and then escorted us to our table. There were two tables at the end of the large living room, each seating eight guests and a long table at one side of the room accommodating sixteen. There is still class distinction among these Indians. They say the British have Royalty, so even in this small village there are the high and the low families. As white guests we were accorded the place of honor at the head table.

The room was beautifully decorated with streamers of red and green placed criss-cross across the ceiling. The lights on the Christmas tree by the stairway twinkled among the branches draped with tinsel. The tables were set with fine linen cloths, shining silver and lovely glassware. Each knife, fork and spoon was in its proper place. The oil burner gave a pleasant warmth to the room.

The Chief, a big man in his early sixties, entered. His greying hair seemed to set off his rugged features and his kindly eyes. He was dressed in a neat, brown, well fitting business suit. He scanned the room. All the guests were in their places. He welcomed them in the Tsimshean language although he speaks English. His stepson interpreted his speech. He was most honoured that we had accepted his humble invitation. The feast was given to show his good will toward us, and all his people. This Chief then called upon Rev. Charles Lomas to ask God's blessing upon this feast. At the close he quietly left the room. Neither he, nor his wife ate with their guests. It was then that I discovered that I was the only woman to have been invited to this Christmas feast. All the leading men in the village were present but their wives were absent.

There was chicken noodle soup, followed by delicious roast turkey, cranberry sauce, mashed potatoes, peas and carrots, buns, pies, Christmas cake and Christmas pudding. There were oranges, apples, raisins, nuts and candy. When everyone had eaten all they possibly could and the tables were still heaped with good things, the Chief again entered and asked the minister to give thanks to our Heavenly Father for his abundant provision.

After Dinner Speakers

One by one, the guests arose and spoke in their native tongue. I listened to the flow of words, which I could not understand, and wondered just how much of what I told my boys and girls each day, they really understood.

Solomon Brown was speaking. Occasionally I caught the word MYAN, which means Lord or Master. Suddenly his voice rose in song. It was a hymn of praise.

We all joined in. These Indians are very musical and many of the men, and women, too, have fine voices.

The Chief was the last to speak. Several times we heard our names but had absolutely no idea of what was being said about us until a young man interpreted the Chiefs remarks for our special benefit. He had thanked us for what we had done for their children and for their old people since coming to their village. It was time for Bert to thank them for their kindness and hospitality toward us.

The feast was over, - but no, - Solomon Brown was passing me the oranges. I politely refused. A look of surprise passed over his face. "Take one," he said. I did. "Now, take another. They are all ours."

I glanced across at the other tables. No one any longer wore his gay paper hat. He held it in his hand and was filling it with nuts, raisins, candy, fancy cookies and Christmas cake. Their pockets bulged with apples and oranges. I had almost committed a social blunder. The Chief had provided this feast for us and to have left anything on the table would have been most discourteous. This is one of their ancient customs that they have not given up and it seems to me to be a very nice custom.

It was growing dark when we went down the narrow road toward home but the children were still playing along the street, some with new toys. There was no snow, not even frost on the ground but the air had a sharp tang that made one think of late autumn. Several of the Indians stopped in at the teacherage to wish us well. I did not feel that I should ever want to eat again, but Bert suggested a good pot of tea. I prepared a light meal and the Indians who had called, stayed to enjoy it with us. By the time we had finished supper, the bell was ringing for the evening service. This time it was held in the Church Army Hall and was attended by nearly the entire village.

It is a Christmas that I will always remember. It had been a day of quiet, and of reverence. Each year at this time, I will remember the two years that I spent in this Indian village. To me these Tsimshean Indians, who have had the light of the Gospel for less than a hundred years, will always be a loveable and an amazing people.

Published December 21, 1949
Family Herald and Weekly Star

CLAMS FOR THE MARKET
By Nellie R. Campbell

Time and tide wait for no man. That was why the whole village was astir even if day was just breaking. There are only a few hours each day at low water when one can capture the elusive clam buried in the mud along these western shores. This is the clamming season.

Kitkatla is an Indian Reserve situated on Dolphin Island, 40 miles southwest of Prince Rupert. There is half a mile of dirt road leading around one end of this small island and ending at the narrow boardwalk that leads to the float, which had become the centre of activity these days.

For generations, this tribe of Tsimsheans have made their living from the sea. Their very existence depends on the ocean, - their lives governed by its tides.

There is a brief respite after the halibut and salmon season is over, and then clam digging begins. Snow was still on the ground this year in February when the season opened and often a bitter wind was sweeping in from the ocean when the younger men and women hurried toward the float carrying pails and long handled clam forks. Presently the boats were leaving. The rhythmic hum of a high powered Diesel, or the steady put-put of the motor on some smaller boat, drifted across the water as the natives left for some inlet or sheltered cove where they knew that clams were plentiful. Often a couple of girls or women would start off alone in a small skiff or dugout for some island close by. It is doubtful if there is a woman on the island who cannot handle a boat well. They, too, are as much at home on the sea as on the land.

As the tide rises, the clam digging ceases and one by one the boats return to the float with their cargoes. It is essential that the clams be kept alive and in good condition, so the sacks are cached in salt water near the float to be ready when the packer arrives.

Unceasing Labour

Darkness never interrupts clam digging. At the turn of the evening tide, once more the boats put out. Sometimes a large gas boat will stop to pick up a couple of girls rowing in semi-darkness. They scramble aboard the larger craft with pails, sacks and lantern, for a light is an absolute necessity in night digging. Some of the Indians carry gaslights while others still use the old-fashioned coal oil lantern. Quite often the older women and the school age children, who have been at home throughout the day, will dig along the beach close to their homes at night.

A tap at my door and I look into a shy, dark face and large black eyes. "Please, teacher, coal oil." A lantern with a smoky globe is held out. With lantern filled, the chimney (glass globe) cleaned and the wick, which is stationary and must be pulled up with a pair of scissors, properly adjusted, the child runs lightly down the path that leads to the beach where her mother is waiting for her.

Rain is another factor that one might think would put an end to clam digging but the Indians seem to be immune to weather. No, clam digging goes on day after day, regardless of the weather.

It is when the packer arrives, towing a large barge, that the float becomes a beehive of activity. The sacks of clams that have been dug for several days but kept in cold salt water to keep them fresh are brought to the float. The barge is large and roomy and a most convenient place to work. Boats pull in and anchor to the barge while the sacks of clams, weighing from 100 to 150 pounds, are unloaded.

The west coast Indians are large and well muscled. One or two Indians swing the sacks onto the scales where four or five sacks are weighed at one time. As the pile of sacks on the barge increases, the scales are pushed to a new position to make room for more clams. From the barge, the clams are loaded onto the packers, which ply continually between Kitkatla and Prince Rupert. The native receives one and a half cents a pound for his clams, but four pounds is deducted from the weight of each sack to allow for the weight of sack and sand, as the clams are not washed until they reach the cannery.

Mr. Barnes, who does the weighing for the Francis Millerd Canning Company of Prince Rupert, has a speedboat named "Scripps", which is kept anchored to the end of the barge. Its cabin serves as an office and it is here that he makes out the sale's slip and pays each Indian in cash, while more clams are being unloaded for weighing from another gas boat that has just pulled in or being lifted from a dugout that has come along side of the barge.

The Francis Millerd Company, situated at Sea Cove, Prince Rupert, is one of the smaller canneries on the west coast, yet they are kept busy canning clams and later in the season, salmon. Already this season one hundred and seventy tons of clams have left this small village which is made up of only thirty-three dwellings and less than one hundred and fifty adults. The cannery has asked for another hundred tons of clams.

The Clam Digger

"Will the Indians be able to dig that many more?" I asked. "Yes, and even more," he replied.

I talked with an Indian who was packing for the Millerd Company. He was a genial fellow, well past middle age, and had spent the greater part of his life on the sea. He said that he picked up very few clams from Porcher, Dundas and Stevens Islands, and that, - comparatively, few clams were dug by the whites. The bulk of the clams, bought by the Millerd Company, were dug by natives of Kitkatla. He told me that several hundred miles south of here an American Company was buying clams at Alert Bay.

The clams dug in this vicinity are called butter clams and are in good demand as they are especially good for canning. A larger clam, known as the razor clam, comes from the Queen Charlotte Islands. The Company pays five cents a pound for these clams, and two cents a pound for packing. At Prince Rupert they are frozen and shipped to Seattle where they bring seventeen cents a pound.   Mr. Barnes verified this statement. "Did he tell you what they do with them in Seattle?" he asked. "Use them for crab bait."   It would appear that Seattle crabs possess epicurean tastes.

Where do these clams go? They go to overseas and to eastern markets. Two hundred and seventy-three tons of clams are a lot of clams, - and, most of the digging has been done by the women and teen-age girls of the village. This season most of the men have been busy completing a large recreation hall and working on the water system, which the Government has been putting into their village. Nor will the clam digging be entirely over when the last of the two hundred and seventy-three tons have left the float for Prince Rupert, for the natives are very fond of sea food which comprises a large part of their diet. They must prepare clams for their own use while they are still good. The clams begin to deteriorate about the first of May and then is no longer marketable.

Although the canned meats and vegetables found on the shelves of the general store have proved quite popular with the younger generation, the older people still like their native food, - rice with dried sea weed, dried or fresh fish eggs, smoked salmon and smoked clams. Just as soon as the commercial clam digging comes to an end, smoke will be rising from the smoke houses along the beach and clams shucked and strung on short sticks twelve to fifteen inches long, will be spread on racks over a slow fire to dry and smoke. Some of the native women possess modern canning machines and not only can clams, but salmon and halibut as well. The nicest canned salmon I have ever eaten, - was canned here in this Indian village by a native woman.

Although these Indians have adopted many of the white man's ways, some just cling to a few of the old customs and traditions. They all have a deep love for the sea. The name, Kitkatla, means People of the Sea, -- and that is what they are. Clamming, halibut and salmon fishing, -- it is their living. Generations ago they learned that time and tide wait for no man. They love the ocean yet they know their lives are governed by its tides.

Published July 13, 1949
Family Herald and Weekly Star
Sold--$24.00

COMMUNITY CO-OPERATION
By Nellie R. Campbell

Co-operation – one needs only to spend a little time in this Indian Village to understand the full meaning of that word. Kitkatla is situated on Dolphin Island, forty miles southwest of Prince Rupert. Perhaps its very isolation has taught these natives co-operation, for what is of interest to one in this small village, is of interest to all, or it may be the fact that in this machine age, when in so many of our rural settlements husking bees have become things of the past, these people perform all the tasks connected with their village life by man power alone, for there is no car, truck or tractor, not even a horse on this small island.

When their lovely church building caught fire from an overheated furnace, the loud insistent jangling of the bell called the entire village to duty. Two lines were quickly formed from the burning building to the water hole in the muskeg – women in one line, men in the other. Quickly the women passed the empty pails and kettles from hand to hand and just as quickly they came back along the opposite line brimming full. There was no running and rushing madly about, or crowding and pushing at the water hole, but a steady stream of water was poured on the blaze and the people were able to save their beautiful church building because of their co-operation.

Last year the old tower that housed the Prince Rupert fire bell was deemed unsafe and the structure was torn down. As the big bell was replaced, by a modern siren, it was offered as a gift to the natives of Kitkatla. A huge bell weighing two and a half tons, forty water miles from their home might have presented an insurmountable barrier to some, - but not to the Kitkatlas. With teamwork it was loaded on one of the larger native fishing boats and brought to the island. It was late December. The entire village deemed it fitting and proper that the new bell should ring in the New Year. The bell on the Recreation Hall called the men to work and the huge bell, resting on heavy timbers, was dragged along the village street the half-mile from the float to the church. There it was raised sufficiently to ring on New Year's Day. The top of the steep cliff at the right front of the church was chosen as the ideal spot for their new bell. This spring a strong frame of heavy timbers was erected. It was no easy task to drag a two and a half ton bell up the steep cliff and raise it to the top of the tower. Yet, - it was accomplished by these natives working in perfect unison. This year its clear tones rang out from the top of the tower, calling people to the Easter Service. Again it rang a few days later calling the village to the inauguration of their new Chief. Each night ten slow strokes of the big bell warn the children that they must leave their play. It is bedtime.

Their large recreation hall has been another of their community efforts. Although the building has been in use for several years, war shortages have retarded its completion and they still dream of the day when the interior is finished. Last year a beautiful hardwood floor was laid all by volunteer labour. This year the purchase of a furnace made a brick chimney a necessity. Twenty-five hundred bricks were purchased in Prince Rupert and brought to Kitkatla on a native boat. As the motor died and the boat edged in toward the rocky shore, the bell on the hall called all the men in the village. Quickly they formed a single line from the hall to the water's edge. One by one, the bricks were passed from hand to hand along this human conveyor belt. In considerably less than one half the time it had taken to load these bricks in Prince Rupert, the twenty-five hundred bricks were unloaded and neatly piled beneath the hall. With the storing away of the last brick, the line dispersed.

Down through the ages these Indians have never depended on machines. They have done heavy work with their own strength and their own hands. They know that to perform any task with a minimum of labour they must have co-operation.

Published August 17, 1949
Family Herald and Weekly Star (Eastern Edition)
Sold--$10.02

THE MAKING OF A CHIEF
By Nellie R. Campbell

They called him Chief Hale. Chief Russell Gamble, Chief of the Kitkatlas. It was Easter Week, and we recall that Easter in this Indian Village was a time of great rejoicing for had we not attended the special Easter services and festivities throughout the week we may have missed understanding what was to follow. This year, however, it would be different, for the usual Easter festivities would end with the installation of their new Chief.

As the time drew nearer, the entire village was eagerly making the necessary preparations for these special events. Even though the Recreation Hall had been in use for several years, there were still finishing touches to be added to the interior. The water system bringing clear water from a lake hidden in the woods, to taps along the village street, must be completed before the guests arrived. Even the children felt the need of picking up the old tin cans and bits of broken glass that caused so little concern at other times. We could even feel the air of expectancy that pervaded the entire village as we watched the boats arrive from other Indian villages along the coast. They came from Aiyansh, Bella Bella, Port Simpson, Hartly Bay and the Nass River. Each day we encountered new faces along the village street, for this was a gala occasion. Kitkatla has always been a Church loving village and most of the two hundred guest arrived in time for the Easter Service, which began on Good Friday. There were pictures on Saturday night showing the crucifixion and resurrection of our Lord.

The beat of a drum brought me back to the land of reality very early on Sunday morning. The women were singing Easter hymns as they marched along the village street. I reached the Army Hall just in time for the Sunrise Gospel Services. There were services throughout the day.

Installation Ceremony

It was on Monday morning that the sports began. An old Indian quoted to me a Scripture that had greatly impressed him. "Let us run with patience, the race that is set before us." He had evidently taken the verse literally and there was no time then to explain its true meaning to him, as the races were already beginning. Baseball, basketball and races of every description, both for the young and old, filled the next three days. In all these sports there was a keen competition between the Kitkatlas and the visiting teams.

It had been three years since the old Chief had died. His people had missed his guidance and wise council, still they had been in no hurry to choose a new leader for just as in the olden days, a Chief must prove himself. Would the young son of the old Chief carry out the Gamble traditions?

The village watched and waited. His people were well pleased when he married a sweet girl from Hartly Bay, a girl of sterling character. He brought her to his mother's home where she would learn the many things needful for her to know as the wife of an Indian Chief. It was a happy home and as one entered it he would never dream but that he had entered into any well ordered modern Canadian home, were it not that the centre beam in the ceiling rested on the tops of two beautifully carved Totem poles which had been set into either wall of the spacious living room. Like family trees, these Totem poles depicted the story of the tribe.

At last the village was assured that the son of their old Chief would serve his people faithfully and that the Gamble tradition for integrity would be carried on. It was then that a Council Meeting had been called and the name of Russell Howard Gamble had been presented to the Indian Superintendent, F. Earl Anfield, who forwarded the name together with his recommendations to the Dominion Government and leaders of the Kitkatla Council. As they moved toward the boardwalk that led to the church the people of the village, with their guests, fell in line and marched to the music.

The service was simple yet most impressive. The people remained standing while the Band played "O Canada." At the close, the Chief Councillor took the right hand of the Chief Elect and said in a clear voice, "Sirs, I present to you, Russell Howard Gamble to be made Chief."

The Archdeacon then prayed for God's blessing upon this ceremony. The scripture reading was taken from the ninth chapter of 1 Samuel, the anointing of Saul as king by the prophet Samuel. It was re-read in Tsimshean for those who did not understand English. After the singing of the beautiful hymn, "Breathe on me, breath of God," by all of the people, the Indian Superintendent read the document of appointment of Russell Howard Gamble as Chief of the Kitkatlas.

This was followed by his challenge to the new Chief. "You have been called by your people and you cannot deny that call. Are you willing, God helping you, to take on this office and carry it on the best of your ability?" The new Chief's voice was low but distinct as he answered, "I am." He then knelt before the altar and the four leaders of the village each placed a hand upon his head. The Archdeacon then placed his hand on top of theirs while he prayed for God's blessing.

The Indian Superintendent then received from the hand of Lady Gamble, the Chief's mother, the Medal of the Order of the British Empire that had been bestowed upon the young Chief's father by the late King George for the services that he had rendered to his people. He presented it to the new Chief, to be kept by him in trust in Kitkatla forever.

Then came the charge to the people of Kitkatla. "They too, had a duty, -- to follow where he leads." The Kitkatlas stood and repeated in unison, "We accept you. We will follow you. God bless you."

At the close of the hymn, "O God Our Help In Ages Past," the Band formed outside the church. The Chief, escorted by the police, Village Council, Archdeacon, Indian Superintendent and visiting Chiefs passed down the centre aisle and the people of the village followed row by row. First, one from the right, -then one from the left. The Band led the way to the Recreation Hall where tables were set for all of the guests and the people of the village. The Port Simpson Band played throughout the feast that followed. At the close Chief Hale spoke briefly to his people. There were other speeches. Mr. Anfield mentioned the life-sized portrait of Queen Victoria that hung above the stage. It had been a gift of the Royal Family of England to the Royal Family of Kitkatla, by the Queen herself.

The Indians love a joke and applauded the Archdeacon when he spoke of his first view of Kitkatla, as the Nasskeena drew near to Dolphin Island. The British flag was flying from the top of the flagpole. He felt something must be wrong for he remembered someone had said that the flag should always be flown at half mast when an Archdeacon arrived, because he was only half a Bishop, so he felt most gratified when he reached Kitkatla to find they had flown the flag from the very top of the mast for him.

Unlike our people, the wife of the Chief did not sit at the head table and share the honour bestowed upon the husband. Dressed simply in a rose coloured dress with a dainty lace apron, she, with the other women of the village waited upon the tables. When the representatives of the Canadian Fisheries and the B.C. Packers presented her with beautiful cut flowers and a silver tea service, she came slowly from the rear of the hall where she had been sitting, bowed graciously as she accepted the gifts, then returned to her place among those who had served.

The visiting Chiefs all spoke in their native tongue with the exception of the Chief from Aiyansh, who spoke in broken English. He referred to Christ, as our Good Shepard and presented the new Chief with a beautifully carved wooden staff as an emblem of love and peace.

The toasts to the New Chief were drunk with Coca Cola for the Village Council allows no liquor to be brought to their island. It was Joseph Innes, Chief Councellor of Kitkatla, who summed up the feeling of the village in very few words. He spoke of their great love for their late Chief and how keenly the people had felt his loss. "We were a people with hands and feet, going about our daily tasks, but we had no head. We are still a people with hands and feet, but," bowing to the Chief, he concluded, "we once more have our head."

Yes, Kitkatla once more has a Chief. Chief Hale, Chief Russell Gamble, Chief of the Kitkatlas.

Published April 3, 1952
Family Herald and Weekly Star
Sold--$19.98

WHEN TELKWA WAS YOUNG
By Nellie R. Campbell

No matter where one goes he will still find a few of those men who possessed the spirit of adventure and were in the country long before steel was laid. This is the story of one of those pioneer settlers and ... Telkwa.

Perhaps had we not gone to see our nearest neighbor before leaving Prince George for our summer holidays, we would never have heard of Jack McNeil and those early days in the Bulkley Valley.

Telkwa ... the name brought back to him memories of those days when he had taken a pack train over the Telegraph-Yukon Trail from Old Hazelton to Aldermere, the small settlement that had sprung up on the hill not far from the present site of Telkwa.

It was early one night and darkness was fast falling over the few log buildings that made up the town. At that time Jack McNeil and his partner Lem Broughton had a small store in part of the shack they occupied. Jack Dorsey, who had walked across the country from the Nass, was staying with them. On his way he had captured two wolf cubs. Fortunately one of them had died, but the other one had grown into a huge, shaggy animal, most devoted to his master but equally antagonistic toward strangers.

As George Swanston dismounted from his horse before their cabin door, the wolf leaped at him --- hair bristling, lips curled back showing cruel fangs. Well, a wolf is a wolf, and there are times when discretion is the better part of valor. Although Swanston was a powerful man, strong and well built, he knew instinctively that this was one of those times. One jump and he was back in the saddle and his horse's hooves were thundering down the trail. That night he made camp at Tyee Lake and, after the weary pack animals had been unloaded and turned out to graze, he returned to his friend's cabin making sure that the wolf was securely chained before dismounting a second time.

The story goes that Dorsey later took his wolf west and won considerable money by pitting him against fighting dogs all up and down the coast. However, his money soon went for at one time finances were at such a low ebb that he was forced to pawn the wolf to get money to return home. It was Guy Farrow that later loaned him enough to return to Seattle for his wolf.

At one time Dorsey went on a short trip leaving the wolf chained at home. After three days and nights there seemed little possibility of the wolf following his master so he was turned loose. Immediately the animal took up the scent and was away. It was toward dusk that the wolf reached an Indian's cabin where Dorsey had put up for the night. At the sight of the huge wolf racing toward his cabin, the Indian fired. It was a good shot. Dorsey's wolf was dead.

Deeply interested, we listened to the tales of those days long before the steel was laid (railway) and goods must be brought in by pack train from the wharf at Old Hazelton to Aldermere.

"When you folks get to Telkwa, be sure to see Jack McNeil." We had promised our neighbor that we would.

Our tents were pitched on the bank of the Bulkley River about two miles from the town of Telkwa. Just as soon as our summer camp had been made ship-shape, we started out to find Jack McNeil --- but Jack McNeil was dead. The funeral was to be held that afternoon.

Jack McNeil had been born in the state of Maine but his father had moved to Washington and from there gone into the Yukon. McNeil was about thirty years of age in 1905 when he made his way from the north into Aldermere. Always shrewd and sharp at driving a bargain, he and his partner had prospered from the very first. At that time their store was small. All necessary supplies were brought up the coast from Vancouver to the Skeena River and then up the Skeena to Old Hazelton. From there pack trains transported the goods across country over narrow trails.

The news reached Aldermere that the Grand Trunk Pacific was extending its railroad to the west coast. Construction was to begin at both ends --- the western crew starting at Prince Rupert would work east and the eastern crew starting at Tete Jaune Cache would work west. The golden spike would be driven where the crews met.

Railroad construction was not easy in those days. There was no modern earth-moving machinery. The country was rough. There were mountains to tunnel through and rivers to span. With the prospect of train service to Aldermere, McNeil and Broughton put up a large log store, a new hotel, and a fine livery barn. The pack trail was widened so that heavy freight wagons could bring in the goods piled up on the wharf at Old Hazelton to the new store at Aldermere. It was George Swanston and Ed McBeth that were hired to drive these heavily loaded wagons through that sparsely settled country.

Great excitement reigned in the town when an automobile arrived one day in 1910. It had reached the west well in advance of the steel. Its driver was carrying a letter from the Mayor of Seattle to the Mayor of Hazelton. What did it matter if Hazelton could not boast of a Mayor at that time? --- the townspeople would do just as well.

Up the old Caribou road it had come to the Stony Creek trail, then west. Things went well until the town of Stella was reached, but there the trail dwindled to a bare three feet in width. The driver had started for Hazelton --- still many miles to the west. There was a letter to be delivered, and such a little thing as a trail far too narrow could never stop the "Pathfinder" (Ford automobile). The folding top was quickly removed, then nuts unscrewed until the car lay in pieces that could be packed on horses. She was going through. At Burns Lake the trail widened so the car was reassembled and went merrily on its way.

To the people of Aldermere, the arrival of the "Pathfinder" was an important event. The town turned out en masse and the visitors were given a royal welcome. The banquet that followed is still talked about by the old-timers. Over the rough road that led ever west went the Ford on its way to Hazelton. Later it returned over the same route bringing a letter from the folks of Hazelton to the Mayor of Seattle.

One might think that after such a jaunt, the usefulness of that early car would be at an end but not so. In 1930, twenty years later, the "Pathfinder" again made the trip from Seattle to Hazelton. The old Ford led a caravan of cars up the Caribou road to Prince George and then west to Hazelton on a tour of Good Will.

Mail service proved to be quite a problem in those early days. Like all other supplies the mail must be brought from Hazelton. In 1908 Gabriel Lecrouix, an Indian who had settled in the fertile valley near Round Lake, undertook to bring the mail on pack-horses once each month.

Mail day became quite an event as the settlers from as far as thirty miles east as well as from the west, came into Aldermere for supplies as well as for mail. Then one day the two pack horses arrived, one dragging a battered oil can and the other a sack of His Majesties Mail, but Gab was not with them. A search was made for him and he was found at the end of the lake peacefully sleeping off the effects of too much liquor.

Something must be done so Gabriel was obliged to sub-let his contract to another Indian. All might have been well had it not been for a bear. One mail day the settlers arrived from the east and west but there was no mail. The hours slipped by until someone from the west said that the mailbags were hanging in a tree at Canyon Creek. It was here that the mail carrier and a friend had encountered a bear on the trail. Who ever heard of going on a bear hunt with two heavy sacks of mail? The only logical thing to do was to hang them up in a tree while he and his friend pursued the bear. The animal proved to be much larger than they had anticipated. It was much too difficult to pack the meat out to the trail so there was only one thing to do – camp beside the carcass until they had their fill of bear meat.

The next mail carrier was a white man. Jack Seely carried the mail east from Hazelton and as far as it is known he never once was lured from the path of duty either by bears or strong drink.

Before steel was laid there were very few cattle in the country. It was impossible to bring meat in from the west so McNeil and his partner solved the problem of supplying fresh meat to their customers by bringing in cattle from the country around Williams Lake. Each year Lem Broughton started east on his big saddle horse named Chief, accompanied by his faithful collie dog named Cap. They followed the Caribou road south to the cattle country. There Lem bought cattle which he drove back over the trail. A wave of his hand would send Cap racing ahead to some side trail. If the dog became leg weary he seemed to know that he was at liberty to ride and a sudden leap would take him into the saddle in front of his master, but after a few miles in the saddle he was always willing to herd cattle once more. It is said that Lem Broughton never lost a steer on the long journey from the Chilcotin to Aldermere. If Cap sometimes chanced to round up a few extra head on these long trips – well, he, Lem could hardly be blamed could he? The steers were kept on McNeil's home ranch a few miles from Aldermere and butchered when needed so there was always fresh meat at Broughton and McNeil's.

It was 1913 before the first train came over the newly made road. The railroad had followed the flats along the river banks so the point where the milky-white waters of the Telkwa River came tumbling into the swiftly moving Bulkley was chosen as the new town-site. Gradually the town moved from Aldermere on the hill to Telkwa by the river. That same year McNeil bought out his partner's share of the business but retained the old firm name of Broughton and McNeil. In the spring of 1915 he built a large corrugated iron store building and warehouse on the main street of the new town. McNeil's activities were not confined wholly in the management of his store. He seems to have been one of those men who are ready to embark on any venture as long as there is a prospect of a good profit. While the railroad was under construction, thousands of railroad ties were needed and McNeil contracted to supply them. For a while he operated a coal mine a few miles out of town.

When he sold his stock in his store at the beginning of the depression, he invested in horses and cattle and moved onto his home ranch. The last of his life was spent between his ranch and the home he owned close to Smithers.

Jack McNeil had made money in the Bulkly Valley – but he left it in the valley – to the woman who had cooked for him each haying season – to the lad who lived with him and went to High School – to the hospital in Smithers.

The summer was over. We had rolled up our tent and broken camp. We were leaving Telkwa. "When you get to Telkwa be sure to go to see Jack McNeil." What tales he might have told of Aldermere and those days when the country was still young. With the passing of each of these settlers many stories are lost forever. They are gone – never to be written

We were just too late to meet Jack McNeil, but we did meet several of the early settlers who had come into the country several years ahead of the steel and had played their part in the building of the town.

We will always remember the beauty of that western town built on the bank of the Bulkley river. We will often picture the foaming white water of the Telkwa tumbling down the mountainside from the melting glacier above and churning over jagged rocks as it spills into the Bulkley. We will see again and again the snow-capped mountain peaks that rise so majestically in the distance and that never failed to thrill us each day. We will see in memory the fertile farms on the slopes of those green hills that surround the town. Nor will we forget the sweet smell of the new-mown hay as we rode along its country roads. And its people – how can we ever forget their kindness?

Jack McNeil is gone and so is Aldermere, but Telkwa still remains. It is a place one will not soon forget.

Published May 1, 1949
Caribou Digest
Sold–$12.00

VACATIONING IN THE BULKLEY VALLEY
By Nellie R. Campbell

A camping trip is an ideal way to spend one's vacation, - that is, if you are fortunate to have a congenial companion, a love for those wide open spaces and do not object too strenuously to a few mosquitoes. It is doubtful if anyone ever started out on a camping trip knowing as little about the place to which they were going as Bert and I that morning we started for Telkwa, British Columbia. From the train window we had caught just a fleeting glimpse of the town the previous summer as we had been travelling east from Prince Rupert.

The town had been built at the junction of the Telkwa and Bulkley Rivers. The foaming white water of the Telkwa tumbling down the mountainside from the melting glacier above and churning over jagged rocks, spilled into the Bulkley. The heavily wooded hills just back of the town, which lay on the opposite bank of the river, levelled out into fruitful hay meadows with snow-capped mountains in the distance. It was a picture that still lingers in our memories, so it seemed quite natural the following summer when we decided to spend our holidays camping that we both thought of Telkwa.

It was late afternoon. Bert checked over our luggage, tent, bedroll, folding cots, cooking utensils, duffel bag and suitcase. We were in Telkwa, but now the question was, just where were we to pitch our tent? We knew that the pleasure of a camping trip depended on the choice of the campsite, but I am sure that neither Bert nor I would ever have thought of searching for it in an oat field, yet there it was on the bank of the Bulkley River.

We had just returned from an inspection of Tyee Lake, which lay over the ridge behind the town. It proved to be an ideal spot for a day's outing,- picnic tables, float and springboard, but not just what we had pictured as our camping spot. Was it our dejected air or just his desire to be helpful that caused the taxi man, whom we had seen earlier at the station, to stop? Soon we were speeding along the highway that led to Smithers. Two miles west he turned the car into a grassy trail that led to a hay field. Here the road ended so we walked across the field to the

Nellie on a camping trip

riverbank. At the left edge of the field was a grove of young poplar and tall saskatoons. A narrow footpath led down to the water's edge and then meandered away through the trees. This side of the bluff was lower than the field and the river had backed in forming a quiet pool in which trout lurked.

The rushing waters of the river, at flood tide the previous spring, had failed to make the sharp bend at the west end of the field and had cut deeply into the rich soil washing it away and in its stead had left two huge piles of drift wood, now high and dry. There was ample wood not only for all our cooking purposes, but also, for the fire each evening in front of our tent, - a fire when night steals quietly over field and forest, and seems such an indispensable part of camp life.

In a pleasant farm kitchen, a mile nearer town, we found the owner who assured us that it was quite alright for us to camp anywhere along the river bank on his property, that we wished. It would also, be quite all right for us to drive across the field with our camping equipment. As it was now far too late to think of setting up camp, we drove back to the hotel, tired but happy. We had not only found an ideal spot to camp, but had discovered a Scotsman who would accept no remuneration for camping privileges and a taxi driver who had just refused a fare.

For a few days it was nice just to enjoy the relaxation of life in the open. The piles of driftwood proved a veritable treasure trove. A small door fitted nicely between two poplars and provided a shady table. The bottom of a battered washtub made an ideal top for our camp stove made of rocks. We salvaged enough boards of varying lengths for a washstand and a couple of benches.

With good roads for bicycling it was not long before we had that urge to explore the country around us. Our first ride took us along the old road to Smithers, which ran along the top of the ridge behind the town. The present highway has been built along the flat by the river. I doubt that there is a place in British Columbia that can surpass the Bulkley Valley for natural beauty. From the roadway high on a ridge, the land sloped to the north, its farms light patches of green set in the darker blue. It was the Bulkley River winding its way to the sea. A little gem of blue in a setting of velvet green, - that was Tyee Lake.

A tall man in working clothes came out of a wooded lane just ahead of us. The hill ahead was steep so we decided to walk. He waited for us.

Hospitable People

"Strangers?" he asked laconically. When he learned that we were camping out by the river he urged us to turn back and follow the wooded lane that led to his farm home. He assured us that his wife would love to make us a cup of tea. Were all the people in Telkwa this hospitable, I wondered. Although we did not accept his invitation, we then promised to avail ourselves of his hospitality at a later date. We did and received a warm welcome from his wife and a cup of tea.

Perhaps we might never have seen them had not Bert suddenly glanced upward that day. The Indian Fingers the townspeople called them. There they stood at the top of the wooded slope on the right of the highway, huge fingers carved out of clay and rock by hundreds of years of erosion. We promptly left our bicycles by the side of the road and followed a cow path that appeared to lead upward as we wanted a closer view of this strange formation. Alas, it was not long before the path veered away from the cliff and turned downward. However, Bert and I continued to climb until we reached the base of the cliff. There in the clay, softened by a recent shower, was a fresh bear track. The huge animal appeared to have had no difficulty in scaling the cliff, but we decided that it would be sheer folly to attempt to follow in his footsteps, so we rather reluctantly returned to the road.

The following morning we again attempted to reach the Indian Fingers, this time armed with a camera and a long length of rope. Bert soon discovered an old wagon road, now overgrown with grass and weeds that apparently led to the hay meadows on the top of the cliff. He argued that it would be far easier to make our way down the almost perpendicular bank, than it had been to climb up. At last we saw the Indian Fingers just below us. Bert doubled up the rope around the base of a young poplar growing at the top of the clay bank and made his way down clinging to the rope with one hand and clutching the camera with the other. It was not difficult for me to follow. Even then, we were still above these odd rock imbedded clay formations, so pulling the rope down after us, we again looped it around another tree and continued downward. Once on a level with the "Fingers," it did not take long to get a good picture. With the help of the rope we were able to work our way around the face of the cliff and take a picture from a different angle.

We could see the cow path just below us, so decided that it would be easier to continue downward than to try to retrace our steps. The bear prints were still there, but the hot morning sun had dried the clay so that they were now hard, and our heels fitted neatly into those imprints as we made our way to the path below. Back at camp, we spoke of the hundreds of years of the beating rains and driving winds it must have taken to carve the Indian Fingers out of that hard rock imbedded clay.

An Unwelcome Visitor

It had rained all day, but it had been rather nice to lie in our tent and read. The sound of the rain on our canvas walls had lulled me to sleep, more than once. It was nearly seven when the rain finally ceased and Bert went outside to light our campfire. A warning gesture brought me to the door. There directly in front of the tent, in midstream, was a big black bear. He would land at the foot of the path. The thought of the strip of bacon we had just bought, made Bert think it was policy to turn him back lest, he raid our larder after dark. A stick of dry firewood landed in the water with a sudden splash, not far from his head. He wheeled and, with powerful strokes, set out for the opposite shore and quickly disappeared in the forest. That was the only bear we saw.

It was in the Post Office that we met him, - one of those early settlers who had come in just after the turn of the century. He had built a log cabin not far from Round Lake, ten miles east of Telkwa. Years later, he had put up a comfortable frame house a short distance from it. He still owned the original homestead. Before leaving the Post Office with his mail, he had persuaded us to ride out to his farm on the following Monday and have dinner with him. We knew that he had stories of those early days that he was eager to tell, - stories that we were just as eager to hear.

It was a beautiful sunny morning and the air was filled with the sweet smell of new mown hay. We rode slowly along the highway. Bicycling was a pleasure on the smooth road for we never knew what beauty of nature we would discover just around the next bend or over the hill beyond. Having been born in conservative New England, (USA) I still marvel at the hospitality of the west. His wife greeted us warmly and made us feel we were really welcome. It was not long before our host came in from the fields and, over a most abundant meal, he talked of those days when the country was young. At last my curiosity got the best of me, and I could not refrain from asking about the large, greyish white stone we had noticed along the highway just before turning into the long lane that led to his farm home. It appeared to be a monument of some kind, yet there was no inscription on it.

It seems that many, many years ago, no one knew just how many, the Nass Indians had come overland. Trouble had arisen between them and the interior tribe. In the battle that followed, two young braves had been killed. It was when peace had been made between the coast and interior tribe that the stone had been set up by the Indians in memory of their peace pact.

We learned that there was a sequel to this story. In the construction of the present highway, one of the workmen had injured his foot. As a joke, his fellow workmen had written his epitaph. There it stood the following morning on the face of the old rock in bold, black letters for all to read. To my hostess, to deface this old Indian monument in this manner, was nothing short of sacrilege, so that evening she had taken a pail of warm, soapy water, a bit of steel wool and a cloth and scrub brush, and set to work on the old stone. It had required quite a bit of elbow grease to remove the black marks but before she went home the old stone gleamed greyish white in the moonlight, just as it had for so many, many nights since the Indians had put it there.

It was late August and time for us to be thinking about breaking camp and returning to the Indian Village where I had been teaching. We both knew that we would always remember the rare beauty of this small country town on the bank of the Bulkley River.

Published August 2, 1951
Family Herald and Weekly Star
Sold--$37.00

DEATH OF A RIVER
By Nellie R. Campbell

Do Rivers ever really die? I wondered as I read these words emblazoned on the front page of the Prince George Citizen dated October 9, 1952. "The mighty Nechako River officially died at twenty-seven minutes after ten o'clock yesterday morning. Shrouded with secrecy, a crew of workmen at the Kenny Dam sealed off the cavernous tunnel through which the river has been diverted during construction period. Officially, the Nechako River flows no more."

Of course, we who have lived for many years in the interior of British Columbia have had a keen interest in the area around Tweedsmuir Park and in the development of the Aluminium Company of Canada, - a company who spent over a million dollars in preliminary surveys relative to the construction of their $500,000,000 plant. We realize that the rapidly increasing population of British Columbia required, an ever increasing, expansion of industry and the vast power of the province must be utilized to carry on this expansion. Yet, many of us had failed to realize that the Kenny Dam would mean the death of a grand, old river.

There were no newspapermen at the scene, for the date of the sealing of the tunnel had been kept a deep secret. Norman Kerr, editor of the Vanderhoof local paper, The Nechako Chronicle, and Rich Hobson, the author of the best seller, Grass Beyond The Mountains, were the first to realize that something of great importance was about to happen. By the time they had reached a spot fifteen miles down stream from the dam and had climbed down the steep banks to the channel, the great river was already receding from its shores and young trout were struggling helplessly in the tiny pools left by the receding river. Between the dam and the Nautly River, the once mighty Nechako will be reduced by 95%, while the flow of water in the lower reaches of the river, still fed by the Nautly, Stewart and Mud Rivers, will be greatly reduced.

It is a beautiful country through which the Nechako has flowed. There are deep, narrow gorges that no man has ever been able to explore. There are farm homes lying on the low lands along the river. The C.N.R. winds its way along the river bench with steep rock cliffs on one side, while the river winds its way on and on for many miles to mingle with the swiftly flowing waters of the Fraser at Prince George.

It was a morning in late June that Bert and I left the train at Burns Lake and started south with pup tent and blankets strapped to our bicycles. The large sign near the station had read, "Entrance To Tweedsmuir Park." That first night we pitched our tent on the shores of Francois Lake, fifteen miles south. For several days we revelled in the beauty of the country about us, then one morning we rolled up our blankets and crossed the lake on the Government ferry to South Bank.

We laboriously pushed our bicycles up the long hill that led to a higher and more level country and on to Grassy Plains, - a country of grass, pea vine and fat cattle. But Tweedsmuir Park still lay ahead of us. The park is in a country still in its natural state where game may roam at will.

Quite a few of the people there were old timers. Some had come in over the trail from Bella Coola on the west coast bringing supplies and their few possessions in on packhorse.

A Bicycle Trip

We were only too glad to abandon our tent one wet and windy night and, accept the hospitality of one of these early settlers who had erected a large log dwelling in those early days, which was still used as a stopping place. His brother owned a farm close by and one afternoon we climbed to the top of the high, rocky cliff at the back of his pasture to an old look out which had been built on the highest peak. It commanded a wonderful view of lovely Ootsa Lake and Tweedsmuir Park.

One day we followed the highway that sometimes led us close to the lakeshore and then took us farther inland through farming country or stands of timber. It was nearly noon when we came to a dividing of the trail. The left hand road brought us back to the lake and a farm house built on its shore. We had reached the end of the road. Leaning our wheels against the board fence we opened a gate and walked toward the house. A pleasant faced woman met us.

"But how did you ever get here?" she asked.

"We came on our bicycles," I replied, "but we left them out by the road."

She looked at me for a moment and then expostulated, "Are you the woman who sometimes writes things in the Family Herald and Weekly Star and rides around the country on a bicycle?" I had to admit that I was.

"Well, do come in," she said. She dismissed our inquiries about the road with a shrug. "My son will be in to dinner in just a few minutes and he can show you a short cut so that you won't have to go back to the turn. Of course you are going to have dinner with us. I wouldn't think of letting you go without dinner."

Landmarks Disappear

The kindly hospitality of the early days still remained. Last winter I had a letter from one of the women I had met on this trip. She had built her home on the shores of Ootsa Lake many years ago. She wrote, "It doesn't seem possible that by next fall my home will be completely under water." With the completion of the dam which checks the flow of the Nechako River, thousands of acres of timber and farming land are slowly but inexorably being inundated by the rising water, and Ootsa Lake is destined to become a great inland sea. The homes of those early settlers, the farmlands of later comers, the store and cabins built for tourist trade, will disappear beneath its surface.

And what of Tweedsmuir Park? Lady Tweedsmuir recently wrote to a friend, "I have never seen anything so lovely as Tweedsmuir Park and it is heartbreaking to think of its being spoiled."

In order to save the park, the foreshores must be cleared ahead of the slowly rising water. Will this be done, or will the beauty of the shores along the great lake which man has created, be marred by dead and uprooted trees and the rubble of inundated homes?

The younger generation will see only the immense power created by this huge Alcan project for the development of British Columbia. They will see the rich deposits of tungsten and other minerals at Whitesail Lake. They will look ahead to the development of the vast resources of the province made possible by the construction of the Kenny Dam.

We, who have known the Nechako River in her many moods, will always remember a great river. We will remember those trips in the dead of winter when no ferry could live in her wicked waters, and the tie teams crossed on a swaying bridge of ice while the river boiled beneath on its way to meet the Fraser. Sometimes we will recall the constant roar of the rapids at Isle Pierre. Often we will think of her in her pleasanter moods. Of the nights we camped upon her banks and were lulled to sleep by the gentle lapping of the water on her shore.

The Nechako Chronicle, named for the river, carried an obituary on its front page. It was for the beautiful Nechako River which had flowed for thousands of years from Fort Fraser to Prince George, - a river which died in the year 1952 at the hand of man.

Do rivers ever really die? I knew the answer for the mighty Nechako, whose upper reaches have become a mere trickle of water and whose lower reaches have been reduced to a small river fed by still smaller streams, will live on in the memory of those who knew her long ago.

Published December 4, 1952
Family Herald and Weekly Star
Sold--$18.00

WHEN THE STEEL CAME TO PRINCE GEORGE
By Nellie R. Campbell

Prince George was not always the thriving town one sees today. It seems that every new country has it forerunners. In the north and west the Hudson's Bay Company has always been the advance runner of civilization and its posts extended to the far corners of the North American Continent and far into the Artic Circle wherever fur was to be found.

As early as 1804 Simon Fraser had founded a Hudson's Bay Post at the junction of the Nechako and Fraser Rivers and had given it the name of Fort George, in honor of George the Third, the then reigning monarch. At that time the trade was wholly with the Indians.

The trapper and the prospector were always sure to follow in the wake of the Hudson's Bay explorers and it was not long before the white trapper had established himself within trading distance of some Post and the Indian found that he must compete with the white hunter.

Next followed the surveyors in search of a favourable route for a railroad. With the coming of steel, small towns sprang up along the route of travel and settlements were formed. In every new country there are always a few hardy pioneers that come well in advance of the steel.

So it was with the founding of Fort George. The government had surveyed a large tract of land just north of the Hudson's Bay Post, at the junction of the rivers, for an Indian Reserve. The early white settlers founded the town of Fort George just south of the "Bay" on the banks of the Fraser.

With the news that the continuation of the Grand Trunk Pacific to Prince Rupert would pass through this territory, a new townsite was immediately laid out northwest of the original town of Fort George, on the banks of the Nechako. This, too, was given the name of Fort George. The original town soon became known as South Fort George, or, as it is more often called today, simply South Town.

Many of those settlers believed that on account of its location at the junction of two navigable rivers, the vast resources of the surrounding country as yet undeveloped, and the miles of unsettled country to the north and west with no outlet except its rivers, Fort George was destined to become one of the leading cities of Canada.

City lots were surveyed for ten miles north of the Nechako, country that was still a wilderness—the home of moose, deer and bears. Flaming posters extolled the benefits to be derived by getting in on the "ground floor." They depicted large modern school buildings, new stone office blocks and cars rolling over smooth macadamized [paved] roads. Land speculators began to arrive in Fort George. It was not long before the flaming posters were bringing results and Eastern and American capital was pouring in, in an effort to pick up some of this choice land before it was too late.

The land boom was on. Almost overnight Fort George became a lively town. It became one of those towns one sometimes reads about but seldom sees. No other town on the North American continent could boast of a bar sixty-five feet long. Twelve bartenders dispensed drinks to the crowds that lined the bar, sometimes two and three deep, from six o'clock each morning till eleven or twelve at night. If some were carried into the "snake room" adjoining the bar, to sleep off the ill-effects of drink, it in no way dimmed the hilarity in the saloon. The town was wide open. There was once during the three years that Fort George was in the grip of the boom that the law took a hand and closed the bar for three whole days until an unusual burst of rioting had subsided. It is claimed that the owner made a hundred and sixty thousand dollars in three months.

The land companies, too, were doing a thriving business. It made little difference to them if some "choice lot" sold to an Eastern buyer chanced to lie at an angle of forty or even sixty degrees on the banks of the Nechako, or even if the flat along the river where the breaking ice backed up each spring and the swiftly running river over-flowed its banks. They were all "choice" house lots. City lots ten miles out, in heavy timber, sold for two and three thousand dollars, sight unseen.

Recently one of the oldtimers told me of driving a man out to inspect his newly acquired possessions. He had purchased city lots north of the Nechako to the amount of thirty thousand dollars. They crossed over the river on a ferry and drove for ten miles over little used trails. At last he reached his corner post. The driver obligingly offered to follow up his lines for him through the dense forest, but the buyer had seen enough. His "city lots" no longer interested him, so he returned cast, sadly disillusioned.

Not all, however, took their losses so philosophically. One man, on finding that his land lay beneath the icy waters of the Nechako, which was on a rampage and had just overflown his banks, calmly filled his pockets with stones and then walked out into his inundated property.

Fort George was growing daily. New business enterprises were springing up. Steamers and scows plied up and down the rivers, bringing in the passengers and supplies. Ashcroft, on the main line of the Canadian Pacific, lay three hundred and twenty miles to the south. There were automobile service from Ashcroft to Soda

Creek, but the remaining distance must be traversed by boat. The trip required four days. Passengers were allowed only forty pounds of baggage. Excess baggage was charged for at twelve and a half cents per pound.

The Grand Trunk Pacific operated a regular freight and passenger service from Edmonton to the end of the steel. Settlers were urged to club together and build their own scows at the end of the rails for freighting their goods the remaining distance into Fort George. Large quantities of supplies could be handled in this way and competent guides could be secured to bring them safely down the swiftly flowing river.

With the rapid growth of the town came the appointment of town officials. Everyone seemed eager to hold some office in this growing metropolis—even a half-witted Swede who spent much time hanging around the bar. One day, much to the amusement of the crowd gathered in the saloon, the proprietor appointed him Chicken Inspector at sixty dollars per month. There was much hilarity over this appointment, but it was no joke to Olie, who took the job quite seriously. It also was no joke to some of the citizens, who at last strongly objected to Olie's entering their chicken-houses to inspect their fowl whenever he pleased. So Olie was arrested. The story came out in the court and the perpetrator of the joke not only paid court costs but Olie's salary as well.

In those days, Charles Miller of Toronto, the instigator of the famous stork Derby, was the managing director of the British Columbia Express Company, which operated a stage line from Fort George to Ashcroft. Although it was a distance of three hundred and twenty miles and the road ran through rough and rocky country, the stages were run on schedule time and were seldom late, as the stage horses were changed every fifteen miles along the entire route. The company had its own carriage makers, its own blacksmiths that saw that the horses were always well shod, and the animals used were kept in first-class condition.

Miller became greatly interested in the rapidly growing town and purchased a thousand acres of land for speculation. This section of the town is still known as the Miller Addition.

When the Grand Trunk Pacific suddenly purchased the Indian Reserve from the Government for its townsite, all building in Fort George ceased. One by one the businesses moved to the new townsite, which the railroad officials had named Prince George. Controversy was rife among the settlers for many maintained that Fort George, the name of the old Hudson's Bay Post, a name known throughout the West for over a hundred years, should be retained. But in spite of protests the new town became Prince George.

It was not until the end of January 1914, that the steel actually reached Prince George. For a time it was doubtful just where the golden spike that marked the completion of the road would be driven, as the laying of the steel was proceeding from both ends of construction. Each day saw the gap between the ends of the steel lessen as the crews from the east and the west worked feverishly. Soon it became known that the track gangs were going to leave a trial mile in the center of the gap and then race for it. The golden spike was driven about a quarter of a mile from Fort Fraser on the banks of the Nechako, the western crew winning just by a few lengths of steel.

Extract from the Fort George Weekly Tribune, Saturday, January 31, 1914:

"January 27 is a date that should in later years be marked in red on the calendar of Fort George. On that date in the year 1914 the railroad arrived.

For some days the tracklayer had been at work on a temporary bridge across the Fraser River, and the date of its arrival on the west bank of the river was difficult to foretell. Monday evening, however, the Pioneer reached terra firma on this side and word went out that next day the arrival of the steel was to be celebrated by the people of the district.

Tuesday morning dodgers were hastily struck off in the printing office and over every telephone the news was flashed that at two o'clock that afternoon the public would attend to see the Pioneer lay the rails of the Grand Trunk Pacific into the terminal.

Short notice was enough. By two o'clock every road and trail leading to the railway tracks was thronged and at the hour set for the celebration there must have been between fifteen hundred and two thousand people assembled on the grade from George Street east toward the bridge.

The Pioneer had crossed the river the previous evening and laid steel to a point half way between the end of the bridge and George Street. It was now waiting for the necessary material for further advance.

It was one of the coldest days of the season. The temperature, hovering about eight below zero at two, gradually sank lower until by early evening the thermometer registered seventeen degrees below. However, the chill did not keep people from assembling and waiting for hours to see the tracklayer work.

There were Indians there, gazing curiously at the big, black machine that had brought the railroad to their one-time primitive haunts. Surveyors, in the garb of the trail, were there with their implements, and even a dog team. Hudson's Bay trappers, with toques and sash, mingled in the crowd. In sharp contrast to these pioneers were the men of the modern era, garbed as civilization expects.

It had been arranged that there should be a parade illustrating the various stages of development in the district. Owing, however, to the very cold weather and the unexpected wait for the steel train, it was impossible to carry the program out to the letter. The various elements of the parade were there, mingling with the crowd of spectators, and the general effect was almost as picturesque as the parade would have been.

A brass band of ten pieces from Fort George was on hand and braved the icy air to play a series of tunes, standing about a fire of sticks the while to keep from freezing their whistles.

After a long and weary wait in the cold, a whistle from the bridge announced that the steel train was on its way. All was expectancy, but hope was deferred when it was announced that the tie conveyors on the side had been damaged by striking a pile of lumber at the end of the bridge. While this damage was being repaired there was another wait.

At last the train moved up behind the Pioneer, the couplings were made, and while the crowd in front of the big machine crowded curiously the ties began to pass forward along the rollers of the conveyors; the tie buckers sprang into their places, and the railroad began to add to its mileage.

The Pioneer began to move at a brisk pace. An endless stream of ties began to pass forward, each tie as it reached the end of the conveyors was seized by a tie bucker and carried forward to be flung hastily in place along the grade. There was a steady stream of these workers labouring like huge ants in the procession. Along the conveyors on the other side of the Pioneer came the steel rails. As each rail came to the end of the rollers, it was seized and swung out by means of a derrick until waiting hands could guide it to its place on the fish-plates. Two bolts were then hurriedly screwed into place and over its own steel the Pioneer moved forward to lay another length of steel. The spiking was left to be done at leisure. So rapidly did the Pioneer work that the crowd in front was kept on the constant move to keep out of the way of the buckers."

Thus was the coming of the railroad to Prince George. The men of that day marked the coming of the railroad as the end of pioneer days. They envisioned the wooded country for miles around laid out in productive farms. They saw in their mind's eye the rapid development of the country's vast resources. They pictured Prince George as the leading metropolis of the Northwest.

If January 1914 brought the railroad to Prince George, August of that same year ushered in the First World War. Building operations ceased. Vast sums of money had already been spent on the railroad from the south to connect with the Grand Trunk Pacific at Prince George. The road was never finished. Plans for the building of the B.C. and Alaska Railway were forgotten in those days of strife. Prince George, that had started out to become one of the principle cities of the West, was at a complete standstill.

When we came to British Columbia at the very beginning of the great depression that followed the financial crash of 1929, Prince George was still a small town situated at the junction of the Fraser and Nechako Rivers. Only a little used grass trail led north through the country that had once been surveyed in town lots. Moose, bear and deer roamed through the forests that were to have been the thriving city of the Northwest. One might occasionally pass a deserted cabin, but settlers were few and the thick branches of spruce and fir formed an arch over the narrow trail.

The dream that someday Prince George would be the principle city of this great Northwest seemed to have ended and yet with the outbreak of World War Two new industries sprang up and vast building projects were undertaken. Its location makes it not only an important link with Alaska but a centre toward which all lines of travel converge. With 250,000 acres (by government survey) of good farm land available to the new settler, forest resources estimated at 32 billion board feet, with last year's cut of 129 million feet valued at more that $6,000,000 and the fur taken from the traplines scattered over the portion of British Columbia that lies north of the city amounting to $1,000,000 in a single year, there is little doubt that the dream of those early pioneers is rapidly coming true and that Prince George will some day become a great commercial centre.

Published Caribou Digest
May 27, 1947
Sold - $10.00

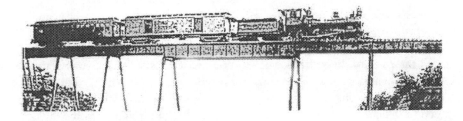

ADVENTURES OF A FERRYMAN
As told to Nellie R. Campbell
  By H. Fanshaw

The old ferryman stood beside me on the bank of the Nechako River at Isle Pierre, a ferry crossing, about 35 miles west of Prince George.

I knew that he had spent many years on the river and had seen her in her varied moods. Perhaps he would tell me about the days when he first came to British Columbia, and about the life of a ferryman, the men who operated the cable ferries still found on the Fraser, Nechako, Quesnel and other interior rivers.

"It was in 1922 that I took over the first ferry, --that is if you could call her a ferry. She was an old scow, --that's what she was. Been used on the Stuart River and some Indians brought her down the Nechako to Isle Pierre. In due time the cable and towers were erected and then I took over.

She worked like the present ferry, --ran on a cable. By swinging the bow downstream at an angle the current pushed her across. That old scow wasn't too bad to handle and she got folks across the river but she could be contrary at times. At first we had trouble making the landing on the other side of the river. You couldn't blame the passengers for not wanting to wade ashore so I always had to take to the water and haul her in. It was some time and many arguments later that we decided she'd work a sight better if the cable was set square with the current. It took some complaining, I'm telling you, before we got that cable moved down the river on the east side and then she ran fine.

To load a team, --there weren't many cars crossing the river in those days, --this scow had to be turned broadside to the current which ran about eight miles an hour. It was one day in June when the river was unusually high from the melting snows up in the mountains that she tipped and caught the full force of the river.

She went on a real rampage that day, --overthrew one of the towers, tore the rigging out and then went racing wildly down stream toward the rapids with me still aboard her. I grabbed a rope and scanned the shoreline for something to snub her to but by that time we were travelling so fast I doubted if I could hold her even if I was lucky enough to get the line around something. The falls were getting too close for comfort. Fortunately the small boat was still tied to the scow and I lost no time in getting into it and cutting her loose. The old scow crashed over the falls and went to pieces on the rocks below. I guess she'd served her purpose anyway and I can't say I was sorry to see her go.

Each winter more settlers were cutting ties and they simply had to get them across the river to the railroad siding. You know most of those early settlers were ingenuous chaps. They didn't expect too much in a new country but went ahead and made use of what was at hand. They built two twenty-four foot pontoons and rigged up a deck between, tackle and steering wheel and then lined the outside with logs for protection from the broken cakes of ice constantly swirling down the river, crashing and grinding against the pontoons.

There was only one thing the matter with this homemade contraption, --she just couldn't seem to support the load and the team at the same time. Those ties had to be taken across so between us all we got a bright idea. It was to drive the loaded sleigh to the very edge of that last steep pitch that led down to the ferry, unhook the team and lead them aside, then hook a chain behind the load and fasten it to a snubbing post on the bank. The chain had to be just the right length to stop the load in the center of the ferry. As ferryman it was my job to grab hold of the sleigh pole and as soon as some of the men started the load down hill, race onto the ferry with the load of ties at my heels. Of course I relied on the chain to stop her at the right place.

It was a good idea and it worked fine for a while but one day the chain slipped off of the snubbing post. The boys were all so busy watching me sprint onto the ferry with a load of ties that not one of them noticed there was no anchor. I reached the middle of the ferry but the ties kept right on coming so I let go of the pole and sought shelter on the deck railing. Those ties took to water just like a duck and went bobbing away down the river and over the falls. The sleighs sank but we managed to get a hitch on them and pull them out with the help of the teams.

This ferry was sunk twice and finally another fellow and I took her through the rapids to a drilling outfit camped below the falls. They were testing the bottom for a projected pulp dam, which you know, never materialized. I rather enjoyed that trip. We rigged big steering sweeps fore and aft and let her drift. Then I skulled into a backwater at the camp. I took the bow sweep and if we'd ever hit a rock, --well, I guess I wouldn't have been here to tell you about it.

"Most years you had to take the ferry out when the ice came down the river, didn't you?" I asked. I remembered that the first winter we spent in B.C. there had been an ice bridge across the Nechako.

"Oh, yes," he said. "The ice got pretty bad at times and no ferry could stand the constant pounding and grinding of ice against her sides. We just hauled her up on shore and waited for a good cold spell. You know the kind of weather I mean, -- when it gets to forty-five or fifty below, --then the settlers would put in the ice bridge so that they could drive the tie teams right across.

The current along the north shore and in the center ran so swift that water would not freeze solid even in the coldest weather so the tie men threw out two fin-booms from the north bank extending well beyond the center of the stream. A cable attached to the outer end of the boom at a sharp angle to the bank. This boom shot the rushing ice-filled water toward the opposite bank and created a pocket of still water on its lower side which soon froze solid in the sub zero weather. They then cut logs on the south bank and rolled them to the water's edge where they lay parallel with the river bank. One end of a heavy cable was fastened to the log lying farthest down stream and the other end attached to a 'dead-man' --a log sunk deep into the ground, --back from the water's edge.

Two men in a small boat then dragged the other end of the log into the swiftly moving current which carried the log and the boat as well, across to the end of the boom where the log was fastened to a cable. Four long, heavy logs were carried across in this manner and secured to the boom. The men then threw small poles and brush on top and the icy water and chunks of ice pouring constantly over this wooden frame work, soon froze in a solid mass of ice that extended all the way from the north to the south bank of the river. The tie teams had no difficulty at all in crossing on this bridge of ice."

"Do you remember the winter we came to B.C. and lived in your old cabin at the top of the hill while Bert cut ties?" I asked.

"I surely do," he replied. "Seems to me that was the winter that was so mild we couldn't get the ice bridge in. I remember how the tie men grumbled and cursed because there was no way to get the ties across to the railroad siding. Green ties are heavy and you can't blame 'em much for not wanting to load and unload 'em twice. This side of the river was full of ties waiting to go across. Let's see, wasn't that the year that Fred Ellas's team plunged off the end of the ferry and his horses were drowned?"

How well I remembered that day. The ferry had been out for a long while and the only way of crossing the river was in a small boat attached to the cable. All of the settlers had asked that the ferry be put in even if large cakes of ice were still coming down the river. While the Government delayed the tie hackers grew madder and madder. At last a few decided to shove the ferry back in without the consent of the Government.

"Of course I didn't much blame 'em," the ferryman said, "but I couldn't tell 'em to go ahead. A few of the cooler headed ones persuaded them to ask once more before taking matters into their own hands. I remember that Rocky Clifford covered the thirty-five miles into town on horseback, sent a telegram to Victoria and was back before anyone expected him. The ferry was to go in the next day. As it turned out, it sure was lucky that he got permission to shove her in, for it was only three or four days later that Fred Ellas came down that hill with a big load of ties. His brakes weren't working and he had no rough locks on but he thought a bit of gravel at the approach to the ferry should slow the team up enough. It might have, too, if the ring at the end of one of the hames hadn't snapped just as the horses were racing down that last steep pitch, letting the pole drop. There were no brakes, no rough locks, no pole, --nothing to help the horses hold back nearly five tons of green ties sliding onto their heels. They raced across the ferry and plunged to their death in the icy water of the river. Ellas jumped and caught the rail just as the sleighs went over."

For some time the ferry man stood silently watching the mighty river that had been changed into a slowly moving stream by the Kenny Dam upstream.

"Well, I guess those days are a thing of the past," he mused. "I've spent a good many hours on this old river and I've had some pretty close calls." He chuckled. "Did I ever tell you about the time I fell in when it was fifty below?

The ferry was out and we were crossing in the rowboat but when it's that cold the ice would freeze on her sides and she was apt to be frozen in the ice in the morning. One night I sawed out a little bay to get in closer to shore leaving the boat snubbed in the swift current overnight to keep her from getting frozen in. Next morning I loosened the rope to go across for some passengers and forgetting all about the bay, - the ice all looked the same with fresh snow on it, - I hurried out on the thin ice only to go through and completely out of sight. There was water above me and below me. I clung to the rope in my hand so as not to be carried in under the ice and somehow I managed to come up the rope and with the help of the boat I managed to crawl out. We weren't living by the river then but in the little cabin at the top of the hill. In no time my cloths were frozen solid. You should have seen me rattling up that hill, my pant legs as stiff as stovepipes. I covered that mile in record time. Got into warm, dry clothes and raced back down the hill to make the trip across for the passengers shivering on the other side.

You know, in spite of the hardships, those were good old days and I often wonder if this present generation isn't missing a lot of the real fun we early settlers had."

I thought of the neighborliness, the little "get-togethers' on long winter evenings, the real desire to help each other out, and I knew deep down in my heart that the ferryman was right.

Published Northwest Digest
Mar/April 1956
Sold $10.00

MADE IN B.C.
CHRISTMAS TREE TRADE GROWS EACH YEAR
By Nellie R. Campbell

JACQUES GIBELLEAU was his name but to his friends he was always "Frenchy."

"I come to cut Christmas trees in the swamp!" An expressive hand gestured in the general direction of that hitherto apparently worthless bit of land.

"Maybe I stay at your cabin, --Yes?" he flashed his winning smile. It was quite plain that "Frenchy" would get on in this world.

Each morning he would shoulder his axe and disappear down the trail that led to the old swamp. Each night he would reappear.

"Good day today, --I make 13, maybe 15 dollars." His white teeth would flash as his voice rose in some old French chanson.

Yes, the pay is good while it lasts, but the Christmas tree season is short. Each year men like Frenchy begin to drift into B.C.'s northern woods sometime in October. About the middle of November shipping commences and all trees must be out of the bush and baled for shipment. The first of December is the deadline. It was in the late 1920's that the Christmas tree industry had its beginning in British Columbia. In less than 20 years it has developed into one of vast economic importance in certain sections of the province.

Some of the trees are not marketable. The Christmas tree trade demands certain qualifications, and any tree that does not meet these specifications is promptly cast aside as a cull. The farmer, or woodsman, must know his tree.

In the vicinity of Prince George, a swamp spruce is cut almost exclusively. Its needles are a dark, rich, glossy green and although the color may vary slightly in different localities, it is generally known as the swamp or black spruce. The trees grow straight and tall, terminating in a cylindrical point bearing innumerable deep brown cones.

Only the very tip of these trees is marketable as a Christmas tree; a 25 or 30-foot tall trees must be cut to obtain a Christmas tree from two to six feet in height.

The Prince George district is the only place where these trees are cut and they have been given the name of "Hofert Specials."

Because the Christmas tree trade demands high quality trees, the British Columbia Forest Service is encouraging the actual farming of Christmas trees.

There is a section of British Columbia that might well be called Christmas Tree Valley. On its east rise the majestic peaks of the Rockies, on its west flows the Columbia from Sinclair Canyon near the famous Radium Hot Springs to the town of Luxor.

In this vast area many a farmer has come to realize the importance of the Christmas tree crop as it adds dollars to his income, and Christmas tree farming is now being carried on throughout the entire year.

The limbs on the north and west side of the stump have a tendency, due to the pull of the sun, to assume a vertical position more rapidly and it is these branches that are encouraged to grow as their development greatly reduces the time required to produce a uniformly shaped tree.

One can readily see the advantage of propagation by means of a "limb tree" since many of the six-foot trees on the market are obtained from trees that are 24 to 36 years old. A good Christmas tree may be produced from a "limb tree" in from eight to twelve years.

Then too, the Christmas tree farmer has learned that pruning is most beneficial. Added growth and thickness can be forced into the upper branches by cutting away the lower ones. This method of forcing the growth to produce a thick, bushy tree has one disadvantage as it conflicts with "limb tree" propagation.

In order to overcome this difficulty, many of the tree farmers are leaving several of the lower branches as potential Christmas trees and pruning away the limbs just above them.

Farmers are reporting favourable on this method of pruning as the growth is forced into the upper branches where it is needed and they still are able to retain their "limb tree."

It has been found that the trimming of "wolf trees" so as to product "limb trees" provide many young trees for future cutting. In certain areas of British Columbia there is scrub fir which has little value except as cordwood. The logging of some of this old growth fir greatly benefits both the growth and quality of the Christmas trees being produced in these areas.

In November trucks plow through the newly fallen snow in the Caribou to load the thousands of trees piled along the country roads. These have been hauled out of swamps and forests on sleighs or drag sleds.

It is not only the farmer and transient woodcutters like Frenchy, who are busy in November days, for the trees must all be graded, tagged and bailed for shipment at some railway siding often 20 or 30 miles away.

All day men work at the bailers, --wooden racks made to hold the trees while they are pressed down and tied securely with bailing cord into neat bundles. The wee little trees, only 12 to 18 inches tall, are called "Aces" and there are just 10 to a bale which bears a white tag.

The trees two to three feet in height, are tied eight in a bale and display a bright red tag.

There are only six trees three to four feet in height, in the bales marked with the blue tags.

The larger trees, five to six feet tall, are bailed four to a bale and labeled with a gay pink tag.

In normal times boxcars are used for shipment of these trees to the United States. From four to six thousand trees are loaded into each car. A few cars are booked for the prairie provinces but most of the trees cut in British Columbia go to the mid-western and southern United States.

It is very doubtful if the woodsman who cut the fragrant little swamp spruce with its thick clusters of rich brown cones, would ever recognize it when once it has fallen into the hands of the Christmas tree vendors, for then the little tree undergoes a veritable "facelifting".

As soon as the bailing cords are cut, it is steamed to remove all flatness and to restore its graceful lines. Its soft brown cones are colored by spraying and then waxed. Often the whole tree is dyed a blue aluminium or some pastel shade. Of course one must pay more for a Christmas tree that matches the living room drapes!

Published December 24, 1948
Vancouver Daily Province

An excerpt from Nellie's letter to Reta dated January 7, 1924

I must tell you the good news! I wrote a story called "The Postman" and sent it to the "Western Home Monthly" - the only women's magazine in the far west. A few weeks ago they wrote me it had been accepted and would appear in the January issue and upon publication I would hear from their bookkeeping department. I will try to get a Western Home Monthly to send to Mother Allen so you all can read it. It is all true, everything I mentioned I have seen happen at Lorenzo Post Office. I wish I could sell a story occasionally, as it would help out a lot.

THE POSTMASTER
By Nellie R. Campbell

Marjorie Appleton pushed back her chair from the table and looked earnestly at her husband. "Joe," she said finally, "do you realize that we haven't had any mail since we moved here. Two whole weeks without any mail, not even a newspaper," she continued: "Today is mail day and I'm going to hustle through my work and drive down to the post office this afternoon. I hope I'll get enough mail today to last me another two weeks," she laughed, as she began to clear away the dinner dishes.

Joe rose slowly from his chair and reached for his hat, which hung on a nail by the door. "Well Marj," he said, "two weeks isn't so long to wait after all. You know we're a long way from town. And we're lucky to have the mail brought out as often as that."

"I suppose we are," Marjorie assented as she began to wash the dishes.

Marjorie Appleton's ideas in regard to life were undergoing a rapid change. Her father had been a very prosperous businessman in a large eastern city, and Marjorie had always enjoyed all the advantages a large city could offer her. Then Joe had come into her life. He had come east on business and she had met him at the home of a friend. After his return to the west Marjorie had tried to settle down to the social life to which she had been accustomed, but theatre parties and dances no longer held their former interest for her, and afternoon teas simply bored her. She began to look forward to Joe's letters, and then one day she suddenly realized that Joe Appleton had come into her life to stay. Then Joe had asked her to come to him and she had left her home in the city to share the life of a farmer in Saskatchewan. Joe had met her at the station of a small Western town and they had been married at the minister's home and then driven endless miles through sparsely settled country to the quarter section Joe had bought on the edge of the small timber lands.

Marjorie emptied the dishwater into a pail by the door, hung the dish towel to dry, and then donning her prettiest gown - a soft flowered voile with ruffled skirt and dainty organdie collar and vest and a long coat of peacock blue, she started for the post office three miles away.

The day was clear and sunshiny, one of those bright, sparkling days in early spring when everything has a 'Springy smell," and one begins to look forward to warmer days, although a little chill still lingers in the air to remind one that winter is not yet far past. The horse ambled slowly over the winding trail that ran through a long coulee, and Marjorie looked at the stretches of rolling prairie beyond, dotted here and there by bluffs of poplar and balm of gilead with a few tall spruce trees showing dark against the blue sky. "What a glorious day, and what a beautiful country," Marjorie murmured to herself, contentedly.

As she neared the post office she noticed vehicles of every sort and description in the yard and several saddle ponies were tethered to the corral fence. "Well, I guess I'm not the only one anxious for the mail," she said to herself as she drove to the corner of the fence, and after tying the halter-rope around a post, made her way to the house. The low kitchen with a slanting shed roof and mud walls seemed dark after leaving the dazzling sunshine, and Marjorie paused for a moment in the doorway. She was aware of five or six women seated about the room, and a small thin woman standing by the stove with a large mixing spoon in one hand and a tin cover in the other. At her appearance, the hum of conversation ceased abruptly, and she felt five or six pairs of curious eyes travelling from her little flower-covered toque to her small patent leather slippers. She felt a warm red suffuse her neck and face as the curious eyes continued to stare. "I came for my mail," she finally faltered.

The woman standing by the stove jerked her spoon in the direction of a small room just beyond the kitchen, from whence issued the sound of masculine voices. Holding her head very erect, Marjorie hurried through the dirty kitchen to the small room adjoining. There were several men sitting about on upturned boxes of various shapes and sizes. Across the further end of the room was a rough wooden counter, which was piled high with papers, magazines and parcels. A large pleasant-looking individual with a much be-whiskered face and a genial smile, stood behind the counter chatting amiably with a tall, lean man, whose legs seemed much too long for him. Suddenly, the conversation ceased for a moment and the stout man began to search through the papers on the counter before him. He passed one to the man and then the conversation was resumed. Three times, the conversation stopped and the search among the papers began, only to end again before its completion. The talk of the men seated about the room stopped for an instant when Marjorie entered, but was hastily resumed. She noticed inquiring glances cast occasionally in her direction, but they were not like the curious stares of the women in the kitchen. As the conversation between the long, lean man, and the stout, genial faced one was once more begun, Marjorie sank upon the one remaining empty box. Almost wishing she had remained in the kitchen, but dreading to face the curious stares should she return, she sat upon the box hoping that the lean man would soon pick up his mail and leave. After a fourth, and this time fruitless search among the papers, the lean man gradually unwound himself from the counter over which he had been sprawled and started for the door.

"Jim, say Jim!" called the postmaster, "I got a couple bags of flour for you in town. You'll find 'em in the back of the democrat. Sorry I didn't have room to bring more but that will last you awhile. Need any help?" he called, coming from behind the counter and gazing after the retreating Jim.

Marjorie arose quickly from the empty cracker-box upon which she had been sitting, but an alert little man with beady black eyes and a small moustache was already standing before the counter. The postmaster returned to his post, and once more began his search among the papers and parcels on the counter.

"I expect a parcel today," said the little man in a brisk voice. "Yes, I know," drawled the soft, pleasant voice of the postmaster, "but you won't get it till next mail day. You know its funny about that there parcel," he continued, "Member the day you come in for a money order to send away, I didn't happen to have any so I told you I'd fix it up when I got to town. Well sir, I laid that letter right there," ---he indicated a pigeon-hole in the wall behind him. "Yes sir, I put that letter right there, so's I'd be sure to take it with me and when I got to town that letter was still there in that pigeon hole where I put it the day you gave it to me. I took the money all right. There that money was right there in my pocket when I got to town but the letter was here. If I'd-a known what you wanted to send for, I'd-a made out a new order and sent it, but I didn't, so I couldn't send it till today. You bet I took the money and the letter today." He chuckled, "so you ought to get the parcel in a couple of weeks."

"Two weeks longer to wait," thought Marjorie; when the poor man has waited two weeks already. She expected a tirade to burst from the lips of the little man, but he merely nodded and picked up his papers. "Any letters?" he asked crisply. The postmaster took a bunch of letters from a pigeon-hole behind him and began to look at the address upon each one. Suddenly he laid the bunch upon the counter before him. "Why, here's a letter for me!" he exclaimed. "Funny I didn't see it before. I've been over that bunch twice already." He continued. "Guess it must-a stuck on to the one right on top o' it." He tore it open and turning to the end, read the signature. "Well, what do you know!" he exclaimed, "this here letter is from Sim Corbett. You all 'member Sim." He leaned back and settled his broad shoulders comfortably against the wall and began to read. "Boys," he exclaimed, "Sim's sold his old place -- sold it to some city folks round Prince Albert way --got a good price too, he says." There was a pause for a few moments. "Wants I should go over and get a mower and a set o' harness he left there and sell 'em for him if I can. Any of you want to buy 'em?" he asked, glancing about the room.

"Don't know as I do," responded a man sitting in a far corner, "but I'll take a look at 'em next time I come for the mail."

The postmaster folded the letter and slipped it back into the envelope, which he thrust into his hip pocket and then began once more to look over the pile of letters. "No letters today," he said as he reached the last one, and collecting them into a pile he shoved them back into the pigeon-hole behind him. The little man uttered a few commonplace remarks, and, picking up his paper, departed.

Marjorie sprang up as quickly as possible, determined to get her mail and leave.

"I guess you must be the new missus that's just moved onto the old Jake Smith place," he said. "How d'you like this part of the country!" he enquired, without even waiting for Marjorie's affirmation to his first statement. "I think we shall like it very much," Marjorie replied, "as soon as we get a little more settled. Have I any mail?" she asked quickly as the postmaster had settled himself comfortably against the wall for a long chat. He shifted his position and reached for the pile of letters he had so recently thrust into the pigeon-hole and began once more to scan the address on each letter. One by one he took the top letter and laid it on the counter before him. "Found things in pretty bad shape, didn't you," he asked, pausing in his work and looking over the top of his spectacles at Marjorie. "Used to be a pretty fair house on that place," he went on, "but land's sakes, no one lived on it for going nigh on six years now. Old Jake Smith took up that homestead and after he proved it up just went away. That was when folks first began to settle here, 'bout nine years ago. Pretty lonely country then. I heard someone tore the house down and stole the logs. I ain't been up that way myself for most three years now. Was a good barn there once too, but that burned down in a forest fire 'most five years ago --or was it only four? Say Joe" he asked, turning to a man seated near the window, "was it four or five years ago old Jake Smith's barn burned down?"

"Summer after old Jake left, wasn't it?" responded the man. "That would be five years this coming summer."

Marjorie made a little movement of impatience, but the postmaster paid no heed. "You know it's funny whatever became of old Jake Smith," he continued. "He just left his homestead and went off, no one seemed to know where, either. Didn't leave no address with me and his mail came here for over a year and I had to send it all back to the senders or the dead letter office."

There seemed to be a second's pause and Marjorie's voice broke in coldly: "Is there any mail for me?"

"Oh yes," replied the postmaster, smiling genially and beginning once more his task of looking over the letters he still held in his hand. Marjorie picked up the letters he had thrown upon the counter. The postmaster thrust the bunch of remaining letters once more into the pigeon-hole and leaned back comfortably against the wall.

"There should be several papers and magazines too." Marjorie volunteered, glancing along the counter. He slowly withdrew his hands from his pockets and once more began to search among the papers.

A man rose from one of the boxes and started out the door. The search for the papers stopped abruptly, and without a word the genial-faced postmaster hurried from behind the counter in pursuit of the fast-disappearing form. He stopped in the outside door and Marjorie heard him call to the man, who had just untied his horse from the corral fence.

"Say, Sandy, I saw the doctor while I was in town, so I told him about your baby, and he said to keep her wrapped up warm and if you had any camphorated oil to rub it on her chest and then put on a flannel rag. Didn't know as you'd have any oil, so I bought a bottle as I won't go to town again for two weeks."

"Thanks," replied the man, returning to the kitchen. He paid the postmaster, took the bottle and left.

"Let's see," said the postmaster, upon his return, "I was looking for papers, wasn't I?" Once more he looked over the pile of papers on the counter, and as he handed her the last magazine that she was expecting, Marjorie breathed a sigh of relief. She quickly drew a couple of letters from her coat pocket. "I'd like to mail these now, as I shan't be down again before the mail goes out," she said. "A couple of three-cent stamps please." He picked them up and gazed at the address. "Um-hum," he said, "going to the States. Did you come from the States?" he asked, glancing up at Marjorie.

"Yes," she assented, "may I have some stamps, please," she asked hastily, before he could make further inquiries.

"Well, I don't know," he said slowly, scratching his head, "but it seems to me it takes a four-cent stamp for a letter to the States. You see," he said, almost apologetically, "I don't send many letters to the States. Most the folks hereabouts are Russians and Galatians; some French too, so send a heap o' letters across the water, but I don't know when I've sent a letter to the States." He turned around and began rummaging in various pigeon-holes in the wall. "There ought to be a book here somewhere that tells," he murmured. "I don't use it very often, but it ought to be here somewhere."

At last he drew forth a paper covered volume which had been crammed into one of the pigeon-holes with a pile of old papers and began slowly to thumb its pages,

"Here it is!" he cried, stopping at a page and running his forefinger down its length.

"United States --three cents," he read, "Now ain't that funny, I thought it was four." He replaced the book, and taking down a large manila envelope, much the worse for wear, from a shelf above the row of pigeon-holes, he extracted two three-cent stamps.

Marjorie breathed a sigh of relief --at last she was through, and could leave-- then an expression of surprise slowly spread over her face. She turned the stamps to the light to be sure.

"I can't use these stamps!" she cried, "there isn't any mucilage [glue] on them!"

"We can fix that in just a minute," replied the postmaster, pleasantly. He reached across the counter, and from the corner of the window-sill took a bottle of mucilage, which he handed to Marjorie. She quickly unscrewed the little metal cap; but a fresh surprise awaited her--the mucilage was frozen.

"It is frozen," she said, passing the bottle back to the still smiling postmaster.

"Now I didn't suppose that would be frozen," he said, "but there," he added, "I never keep a fire in here through the week and I only built it up since I got home from town. Must ha' been frozen pretty hard and ain't had time to thaw out yet. Today's real nice, but we've had some pretty cold days this last week." He passed the bottle back to Marjorie. "Just take it out in the kitchen and ask my wife to melt it," he said, once more settling his broad shoulders against the wall and thrusting his hands into his pockets. An angry flush spread over Marjorie's face, and for a moment she hesitated, then took the bottle and turned toward the kitchen. The buzz of conversation again ceased suddenly. Somehow her presence seemed to put a damper on the talk of the women who still eyed her curiously, so after passing the bottle to the thin woman who still stood by the stove and punctuated her remarks with a flourish of the spoon she held, Marjorie returned to the other room and stood by the wooden counter, restless and ill at ease.

"You know the pesky flies ate all the mucilage off the stamps last summer," volunteered the postmaster. "Had a whole envelope of stamps, too, and not a bit of mucilage left on 'em. Flies are awful bad here," he continued, looking at Marjorie. "You ain't been here yet in fly-time. I always keep my stamps in that envelope," he said, pointing to the much-dilapidated envelope lying on the counter. "You wouldn't think the flies would get in them, now would you? But they seem to like glue."

At last the woman entered and set the bottle upon the counter. "Ain't thawed much," she said, "but guess you can get enough for a stamp."

"Have you a brush?" asked Marjorie, politely.

"Did have," responded the woman, "but the baby lost it. You can use your finger," said the woman, leaving the room.

For a moment Marjorie looked extremely doubtful, then plunging her little finger into the sticky mess she quickly put the stamps upon her letters, and wiping her finger as best she could on the corner of her handkerchief, picked up her mail and hastened to the door.

"These letters won't go out for a couple o' weeks," called a cheery voice after her.

Marjorie paused only a moment to respond, and then fled into the yard.

The sun was low in the sky as she urged the horse over the grassy trail toward home. As she drove into the yard she saw Joe standing in the doorway.

"Well Marj," he said, beginning to unharness, "what kept you so long? I was beginning to think I should have to resort to bachelor pancakes for supper."

"Kept me!" expostulated Marjorie angrily, "why that postmaster kept me the whole afternoon giving me four letters, a couple of newspapers, a week old, and three magazines. Of all the ways to run a post office! I was thoroughly exasperated before I got my mail." She hurried into the house to get supper. "I wonder how long people in the city would put up with such service," fumed Marjorie as they ate their belated supper. "I have been used to having my mail delivered regularly three times a day, and I tell you in a city a postmaster has to be punctual and know his business. To hold such a position there, one has to be very efficient, and if we had an efficient postmaster here, it wouldn't take half a day to get a little mail."

Joe laughed good-naturedly. "Wait Marj, till you've lived in the West a little longer and things won't seem quite so long to you," he said.

"The length of time I live here won't alter the fact that a postmaster should be efficient," she retorted.

It was a day in early summer a little over two years later that Marjorie drove into the yard as the sun was nearing the western horizon. Joe appeared in the doorway with one of her aprons tied about his waist. "I thought sure it was pancakes for supper tonight," he laughed. Marjorie sprang lightly from the buggy and hurried into the house.

"Seven o'clock!" she exclaimed, looking at the little nickel clock that stood upon a rough board shelf, "why I hadn't the faintest idea it was so late!" She quickly untied the apron from Joe's waist and tied it about her own. "I'll have supper ready in no time," she said, gayly. "As soon as you get the horse unharnessed, come in, dear; I've had such a nice afternoon I want to tell you all about it."

Once more they sat down to a belated supper, but Marjorie's face glowed with happiness. "It's been such a nice afternoon, dear," she said eagerly. "You know I always love that drive down through the long coulee--it's so pretty there. I let Kate walk all the way today and just enjoyed the view. When I got to the post office there were lots of people there. You know the last time I went to the office I lent Mrs. Skalazub a pattern for a coat. Well, she couldn't understand how to set in the pockets. It was easy enough, but you see, dear, she can't read English, so she couldn't read the directions on the pattern. It didn't take but a few minutes, so I cut the slits and basted the pockets in for her. Old Mrs. Prestupa was there and she told me how to make those molasses cookies she had that day we drove over to her place. You know I liked them so much. I wrote down the recipe, and it's in my coat pocket."

"Oh Joe! You know that young Serhienko boy--the good-looking one? He got badly burned on their gasoline engine. I don't know just how it happened, but at first they thought they'd have to take him to the city to a hospital, but the doctor came out from town, and he says he can come out every few days. It's a long trip, but the roads are good now and it doesn't take so long with an auto. As soon as he can eat something, I must make him something good."

"Mrs. Kiwas' baby has been sick the last few days. She told me just how she was taken and I knew at once it must be measles. My doctor's book happened to be down at the post office. I took it down one day last spring when little Josephine was sick, and it's been there ever since. I looked up measles to be sure and told the poor woman what to do."

"Oh, I almost forgot! We're going to have some new neighbors. Maybe they are there already. The postmaster said someone had taken up that quarter north-east of us. I hope it isn't another bachelor. They didn't seem to know at the office, but the name is Johnson, so it looks as if we'd have some English neighbors at last."

"Did I tell you that Mrs. Rogoza promised to show me how to make sauerkraut this fall? I'm so glad we planted a lot of cabbages this year."

Joe pushed his plate away and leaned back in his chair.

"Good gracious!" exclaimed Marjorie, "are you through with your supper so quick? Why I've hardly begun, and I was ravenously hungry too. I shan't tell you another bit of news until after supper."

As she began to eat her supper, which was nearly cold, she saw Joe's eyes begin to twinkle and a little smile play about the corners of his mouth. He shook his head slowly.

"Such a way to run a post office," he said mockingly. "Now if we had an efficient postmaster it wouldn't take half a day to get a little mail. In the city----"

Marjorie suddenly laughed. "Joe, dear, that was two long years ago," she said, "and since then I've changed my mind. Don't you think that any man who can discourse on any subject from the care of sick horses to the latest politics, hand out all the latest news and the mail at the same time, to say nothing of doing all the errands for the whole community, and never appear the least bit excited or flustered, nor lose that genial smile, isn't efficient? Why, Joe, I've decided that man is an efficiency expert!"

Published February 1924
The Western Home Monthly

IT'S VACATION BIBLE SCHOOL TIME IN CANADA
By Nellie R. Campbell

She was a pretty girl of fifteen or sixteen years. A wisp of golden hair had escaped from the flowered kerchief tied over her head. Her big eyes lighted up in recognition as we rode along that country road. We had met her the year before, picking saskatoons by the side of the lonely road, and had stopped to chat with her and give her a few Sunday School papers.

"Where are you going?" she asked, as we got off our bicycles.

"We are holding a Vacation Bible School in the old log school house about six miles from here," I replied.

Her smile disappeared and a wistful expression crossed her face. "I wish we could have a Vacation Bible School here," she said. "You know we have never had one and we'd all come."

It was two weeks later, at the close of the Bible School in Mapes that we returned to make arrangements for a Vacation Bible School in that Mennonite Settlement. There was no school building, for all the children in the district did their lessons by Correspondence. The only place available was a one-room shack standing in a pasture. What did it matter if the single window had no glass, that we had only a long table with rude benches on either side, made from a few rough boards that we had found in the shack, and our black-board was a large cardboard box opened out and tacked to the wall? At least we had a group of bright-faced boys and girls eager to learn the songs and choruses and memorize Bible verses.

It was in fall of 1926 that Lloyd Hunter left his work of Evangelism in Minnesota and came by train to contact John Bellingham of Ellm Chapel, who, like himself, felt the great need of reaching boys and girls in rural areas with the Gospel. As a result of that meeting with John Bellingham and several of Winnipeg's Christian businessmen, the Canadian Sunday School Mission came into being in April 1927.

Memory Tests

Lloyd Hunter firmly believed that a knowledge of the scripture was the key to Christian experience and memorizing scripture was an important factor in the spiritual growth of our youth, so a province wide Scripture Memorizing Contest was launched. It was no easy task to contact the 145,000 school children of the Province, but 1800 letters went out to the rural schools, containing a poster that explained the rules of the contest and asking for the co-operation of the teacher. There were prizes offered for just learning Bible verses. Ten Bible verses learned brought a book-mark, twenty-five, a New Testament, while forty entitled one to a book and there was another book for each forty thereafter. But, the best prize of all, was eight wonderful days at Bible Camp, absolutely free for memorizing five hundred Bible verses. Is it any wonder that in a short time the boys and girls of rural Manitoba had become Scripture minded?

Other provinces saw the results of this work begun in Manitoba, and at the end of seventeen years the Canadian Sunday School Mission was reaching boys and girls in Manitoba, Saskatchewan, Alberta and Northern Ontario with Gospel teaching. Besides the hundreds of Vacation Bible Schools held, Sunday School Lessons were sent to these children by mail each week.

Miss Margaret Fraser, a Vancouver stenographer, hearing of the wonderful work the C.S.S.M was doing among the children in rural areas, started a similar work for the youth of British Columbia. She was backed by a group of Christian business men and women and successfully carried on the work in the isolated districts of British Columbia until 1944, when she suggested that the B.C organization be taken over entirely by the Canadian Sunday School Mission.

A call came from the Maritimes and once more the work of the Canadian Sunday School Mission was extended. A year later the Mission was established in Quebec and now every province, from British Columbia on our west coast to Newfoundland, our newest province in the east, is served by the Canadian Sunday School Mission.

It is at the close of the school year that a small army of Christian workers go into the isolated parts of our great Dominion to carry the Gospel to children who, all through the year have no opportunity to attend Sunday School. Nor is the Canadian Sunday School Mission the only organization that is carrying on this work of Evangelism in rural areas. The West Coast Children's Mission established by Mennonite Bretheren, with headquarters at Yarrow, British Columbia, and the Pacific Coast Children's Mission, both carry on a similar work among boys and girls. The Pacific Coast Mission meets the needs of children living in small settlements in bays and inlets along the west coast that can be reached only by boat.

Many of these Christian workers are young men and women from various Bible Schools and no spot seems too remote or too difficult for them to reach. They travel by car, bicycle, canoe, and often on foot, to reach the boys and girls in these out of the way places. A few, who are interested in work among the children, go out independently and meet their own expenses without the support from any organization.

Having lived for many years in a district which is miles from stores, churches and even a telephone, we have seen the need of Gospel teaching and felt a deep interest in this work among the children. Each summer we have gone into districts where there are no services of any kind. One day as we were following a wooded trail that we hoped would prove to be a short cut back to the main road, we came, most unexpectedly, upon a low log house. The father was Serbian, the mother

Russian. The four children, ranging in age from six to twelve, were most eager to come to Bible School, which was to start the following day. The father was not opposed to Gospel teaching, but had a contract to cut log mine props. The children attended day school until the end of June, so the summer months were the only time that he could get help from them, so they must work. The girl of nine could peel the props with a raw knife. Even little lads of six and seven were big enough to pile the waste brush and peelings for burning. In spite of their pleading, he remained adamant, - the children must work.

It was the girl of twelve who overcame the difficulty in a most unexpected way. "If we have to work every day," she said, her dark eyes lighting up, "we can all come to Bible School every evening." She gave me a winsome smile as she tossed a heavy, black braid back over her shoulder.

As we rode along the wooded trail back to the main road, we knew that if these children were willing to come to Bible School after walking three miles each day to and from the bush and peeling mine props and piling brush all day, we could repeat the lessons for them each evening. We found it was necessary to have the flannel-graph story and handwork first, while it was still light, so we could sit outside on the school steps and learn our scripture verses and sing choruses long after the evening shadows fell. It was nearly dark each night when we walked through the wooded trail with these children, for one night they had seen a bear. It was the same family who, when we returned the following year and found the teacherage occupied, invited us to stay in their home for the two weeks of Bible School. It proved to be a happy time, for the work was so arranged that the children could attend Bible classes, and an enduring friendship was formed.

Nor are the children, contacted during the summer months, forgotten when the snow lies deep over a large part of our Dominion, making travel in these far away places almost impossible. The different Sunday School Missions carry on Gospel teaching by mail and many a small boy and girl watch eagerly for the weekly or bi-monthly mail, for they know that there will be Sunday School papers and lessons for them.

Father Reads a Story

We have tried to keep in touch with boys and girls by personal letters and by sending good Christian reading into the homes each month. In one home that we visited, where there was no radio, nor even a weekly newspaper, the mother told me that whenever a roll of paper arrived it was almost impossible to get her family to bed. They all gathered around the big kitchen table and looked at the papers and each picked out a story for the father to read aloud. At the mention of bedtime it was always, "just one more story."

Summer time usually means that school is over, but not so for the Children's Missions. With them, school is just beginning. It is July and August that the children in rural areas where there are no Sunday Schools and no religious teaching, must be reached with the Gospel. J. Edger Hoover, head of United States Federal

Bureau of Investigation, declared, "Today's un-churched child is tomorrows criminal." It is because this statement is only too true, that the Christian workers, who realize the great need of reaching our boys and girls, go into these isolated districts in our Dominion. One need not go very far back from the railroad to find them.

And what of the boys and girls in these districts? Some are very shy, some are more or less indifferent while others are eager to come and a few come out of curiosity, - but they come. They soon find out that Bible School is a most interesting place. They love the bright action choruses, many with a real message. They vie with one another in Memory Work. The Bible lessons depicted on the flannel board, become very real even to the smallest child. The Hand Work always appeals to all ages and is a lasting memento of two happy, busy, weeks spent in Bible School.

Two weeks seems such a very short time and yet during this brief period much has been accomplished. A desire for a better way of life has been planted in young hearts and young lives are often changed. Many boys and girls continue the Bible study by mail, and all look forward to another Bible School or even a week at Bible Camp, next summer.

Published July 3, 1952
Family Herald and Weekly Star
Sold--$27.68

THE MIRACLE BIBLE CAMP AT NESS LAKE
By Nellie R. Campbell

Do you believe in modern miracles? This is a story of one but I really do not know just where it should begin. Should it be at Ness Lake, on the first day of May in 1953 or should the story start way back in the Pacific Garden Mission in the year 1913?

It was the first day of May 1953, that Henry Unrau, Superintendent of the Canadian Sunday School Mission in British Columbia, made his way over a narrow trapper's trail that hugged the shores of Ness Lake, twenty one miles northwest of Prince George, British Columbia. He skirted small patches of wet snow, climbed over huge tree trunks, which had fallen across the path, and stood watching the rotten ice crumbling and sinking beneath the surface of the lake. Small patches of blue water were showing beneath the blue sky above. The wind stirred the branches of the tall spruce and Douglas fir trees on the shore behind him and he knew that in a few days the lacy branches of the silver birches would be showing delicate green.

Surely the gift of seven acres for a Children's Bible Camp, on the shores of beautiful Ness Lake, had been a direct answer to prayer. He walked along the four hundred and seventy-three foot frontage and noted the low bank and sandy shore. He knew that there was much to be done before the happy girls and boys would be hiking over wooded trails or swimming in the clear water of the lake, or they could gather on the beach around a camp fire during the long summer evenings and sing and listen to the Word of God.

Land must be cleared, buildings erected, camp equipment acquired, and he also knew that the Mission had only fifty dollars for the building of this camp. Would it be possible to hold a Bible Camp for rural boys and girls for the month of August? Only if God undertook.

In spite of the fact that the Canadian Sunday School Mission could pay its workers only $15 a month, providing there was that much in the treasury at the end of the month, five young men, all students at the Prairie Bible Institute at

Three Hills in Alberta, willingly spent their summer cutting brush, piling and burning it, erecting cabins and tents, building tables and benches. Several evenings each week, as well as on Sundays, they did visitation work or held services in the rural schools round about so the parents had the opportunity of hearing the Gospel as well as the children.

As soon as work was actually started on the camp, Christian friends for many miles around rallied to the support of the Canadian Sunday School Mission to supply the needs. For a lack of a road, all building material and supplies had to be taken two miles up the lake in a barge which the boys built from lumber donated by a kindly mill man for that purpose. As if by magic, two camp ranges, heaters, tents, cots and mattresses, kitchen cupboards, sinks and dishes appeared. 19,000 feet of board lumber was given with the use of trucks to haul it from Prince George to the shores of Ness Lake where it could be loaded onto the barge. One mill man even loaned his planing mill evenings and Saturday afternoons when the men were not working, to plane the lumber.

The summer days surely were busy ones. Stan and Jack, both from the West Coast, - we called him Peace River Jim, to distinguish him from Kansas City Jim – and Ken, a lad from Texas, worked early and late. Until buildings could be erected on the campsite, our log cabin on the east end of the lake became general headquarters and home to the workers.

There was the sound of axes as they felled tall spruce and jack pine on the bank behind our cabin to wall up the big root cellar they were building at the camp to keep the food supplies fresh. There were shouts and laughter as the heavy logs were rolled down the steep bank to be rafted two miles up the lake. There was music in the evening as the boys played on violin or trumpet in preparation for the Sunday services.

Often on Saturday afternoons groups of young people came out from town to supper. As twilight fell the sound of young voices came clearly across the tranquil water as they sang their favourite choruses. Then the busy day ended with a time of Christian fellowship.

I do not remember which of the lads tacked this Bible verse on the cabin wall: "Do all things without murmurings and disputings. Philippians 2:14." No matter how disagreeable the task might be – and there were unpleasant tasks – they were done cheerfully.

On August 3rd, the first eight-day camp opened for boys and girls between the ages of 9 and 15. Very little advertising had been done, as at times it was doubtful if all would be in readiness by that date. However, on the morning of the 3rd, the barge carried happy boys and girls for eight wonderful days of camp life. 46 children attended the first camp. There were 99 boys and girls at camp during the month. With the opening of this camp in British Columbia, the Canadian Sunday School Mission now have a children's Bible Camp in every province of the Dominion.

Published July 1954
Family Herald and Weekly Star

I'M FINE – THANK YOU
From Nellie Campbell (1961)

There is nothing the matter with me,
I have arthritis in both my knees
And when I talk, I talk with a wheeze
My pulse is weak and my blood is thin
But I'm awfully well for the shape I'm in.

Arch supports I have on my feet,
Or I wouldn't be able to be on the street
Sleep is denied me night after night
But every morning I find I'm all right.
My memory is failing, my head's in a spin
But I'm awfully well for the shape I'm in.

The moral in this as this tale I unfold
That for you & me who are growing old
It's better to say "I'm fine" with a grin
Than to let folks know the shape I'm in.

How do I know my youth is all spent?
Well, my "get up & go" has got up and went.
But I really don't mind when I think with a grin
Of all the grand places my "get up" has been.

Old age is golden I've heard it said
But sometimes I wonder as I get into bed
With my ears in a drawer, my teeth in a cup,
My eyes on the table until I wake up.
E're sleep come o're me I say to myself
"Is there anything else I should lay on the shelf?"

When I was young, my slippers were red
I would kick my heels right over my head.
When I grew older my slippers were blue
But still I could dance the whole night through.
Now, when I'm old my slippers are black

I walk to the store and puff my way back.

I get up each morning and dust off my wits
Pick up the paper and read the "obits"
If my name is still missing, I know I'm not dead
I get a good breakfast and go back to bed.

PUBLISHERS THAT GEORGE AND NELLIE CAMPBELL SUBMITTED ARTICLES TO

The Family Herald and Weekly Star, Toronto Star Weekly, Vancouver Daily Province, Field & Stream, Western Producer, Hearth and Home (USA), Farm and Ranch Review, Free Press Prairie Farmer, Western Family, Rod & Gun in Canada, Your Health, The Country Guide, Women's Day, Women's Wear (NewYork), Readers Digest, Saturday Evening Post, Caribou Digest, Saskatoon Digest, Zane Grey Western Magazine, David Cook Publishing, Canadian Home & Garden, Canadian Home Journal, American Home, National Home Weekly, Montreal Standard, New Liberty, This Week, Mother's Home Life, Household, Wilson's Ladies Journal (London, UK), Chatelaine, Junior World, Junior Boys and Girls (USA), Our Little Friend (USA), The Sentinel (USA), Onward, The Friend, Northern Messenger, Magazine Digest, Tower House (London, UK), Giant Western (USA), Outdoor Life, American National Fur and Market Journal, Evangelical Publishers, Sunday School Times, Family Circle, Northwest Digest, Every Women's Magazine, Michigan Farmer (USA), The Furrow Deere & CO. (USA), Atlantic Monthly, Country Guide, Author & Journalist, The Canadian Author & Bookman, B.C. Anthology, Widon's Ladies Journal (UK), Dominion Publishing, and The Western Home Monthly.

BRITISH COLUMBIA

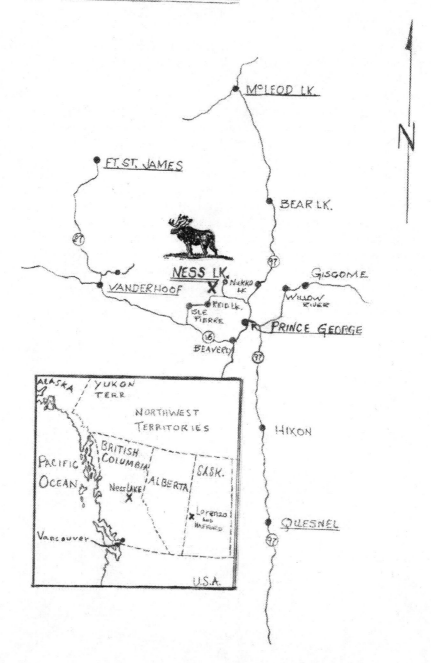

INDEX

ISBN 1-41204371-9